Modern Mathematical Methods
for Economics and Business

SERIES IN QUANTITATIVE METHODS FOR
DECISION-MAKING

ROBERT L. WINKLER, Advisory Editor

INTERNATIONAL SERIES IN DECISION PROCESSES

INGRAM OLKIN, Consulting Editor

A Basic Course in Statistics with Sociological Applications, 2d ed., T. R. Anderson and M. Zelditch, Jr.
Introduction to Statistics, R. A. Hultquist
Applied Probability, W. A. Thompson, Jr.
Elementary Statistical Methods, 3d ed., H. M. Walker and J. Lev
Reliability Handbook, B. A. Kozlov and I. A. Ushakov (edited by J. T. Rosenblatt and L. H. Koopmans)
Fundamental Research Statistics for the Behavioral Sciences, J. T. Roscoe
Statistics: Probability, Inference, and Decision, Volumes I and II, W. L. Hays and R. L. Winkler
Statistics for Decision Making, Y. Chou
Statistics: Probability, Inference, and Decision, Combined ed., W. L. Hays and R. L. Winkler
An Introduction to Probability, Decision, and Inference, I. H. LaValle
Elements of Probability and Statistics, S. A. Lippman
Modern Mathematical Methods for Economics and Business, R. E. Miller
Decision Making and the Theory of the Firm, I. Horowitz
Linear Optimization, W. A. Spivey and R. M. Thrall

FORTHCOMING TITLES
Probability Theory and Elements of Measure Theory, H. Bauer
Elementary Probability, C. Derman, L. Gleser, and I. Olkin
Probability Theory, Y. S. Chow and H. Teicher
Statistical Inference, 2d ed., H. M. Walker, J. Lev, and J. Elashoff
Statistics for Psychologists, 2d ed., W. L. Hays
Decision Theory for Business, D. Feldman and E. Seiden
Statistics Handbook, C. Derman, L. Gleser, G. H. Golub, G. J. Lieberman, I. Olkin, A. Madansky, and M. Sobel
An Introduction to Statistics and Probability for Engineers, C. Derman and P. Kolesar
Statistics for Scientists, M. Zelen
Mathematics Models in Experimental Design, M. Zelen
Time Series, D. R. Brillinger
Applied Multivariate Analysis, S. J. Press
An Introduction to Bayesian Inference and Decision, R. L. Winkler
Multivariate Linear Model, J. Finn
A First Course in the Methods of Multivariate Analysis, D. Jensen and C. Y. Kramer

Modern Mathematical Methods
for Economics and Business

Ronald E. Miller
Wharton School of Finance and Commerce,
University of Pennsylvania

HOLT, RINEHART AND WINSTON, INC.

New York · Chicago · San Francisco · Atlanta
Dallas · Toronto · Montreal · London · Sydney

PREFACE

This book introduces some important mathematical techniques that are being used with increasing frequency on a wide variety of problems, especially in business and economics, but also in other social sciences as well. It contains material that has been used over a number of years at the University of Pennsylvania (1) for mathematical analysis and quantitative methods courses in the Master of Business Administration curriculum of the Wharton School and (2) for courses in the Graduate School of Arts and Sciences, attended primarily by students from regional science, economics and city planning. In both types of curricula in recent years there has been a marked increase in the amount and also the level of quantitative analysis considered desirable—a trend that shows little sign of reversing. Although the present book has been written primarily with this audience in mind, the selection of material, and the level at which it is presented, should also be useful in some cases to an undergraduate program.

In view of the diverse backgrounds of business and social science students, it has seemed appropriate to begin on a rather elementary basis. Thus, the reader who is familiar with matrix algebra will probably find much of Chapter 1, or at least the initial sections, unnecessary, or at most a review to be considered very quickly. On the other hand, he may not have been exposed to the use of matrix algebra concepts for an analysis of types of solutions to linear equation systems, which is the subject matter of Chapter 2. Similarly, this same student (or others) may recall quite well the essentials from differential calculus that are used in identification of maximum and minimum points for functions of only one or two independent variables; for him, Chapter 3 will constitute a brief refresher. However, he may never have been exposed to (or else recall less clearly) maximization and minimization techniques for functions of many variables, possibly with side conditions in the form of either equations or inequalities; these topics are covered in Chapter 4. The first four chapters, therefore, are really a review and extension of mathematical fundamentals.

Chapter 5 utilizes simple optimization criteria in the context of inventory and waiting line problems. The major aim of this chapter is not to discuss exhaustively these two models from the operations research field but rather to indicate the underlying logic and fundamental relations in each and to illustrate how, ultimately, optimization methods are required. The final four chapters deal with the newer optimization techniques of linear and nonlinear programming.

This book emphasizes mathematics more than applications. As the fundamentals are mastered, the instructor can provide detailed examples tailored to the interests and needs of a specific class. Set theory, probability, and statistics have been omitted, because these topics do not seem as essential to the general development presented here as do matrix algebra and classical optimization techniques. (A very brief review of probability distributions is appended to Chapter 5, the only place where this material is necessary.) An attempt has been made to present both the algebraic and the geometric logic of many of the concepts; an understanding of one often greatly facilitates comprehension of the other. More advanced or somewhat peripheral materials as well as many derivations or proofs of important statements (which will not interest all readers) have been put into appendices so as not to interrupt the text.

References for each chapter indicate my intellectual debt as well as sources of further information and detail for the interested reader. There are often specific citations in the chapter or chapters to which they apply.

I am grateful to Walter Isard and my other colleagues in the Regional Science Department, University of Pennsylvania, for helping to make possible an environment within which to work on this project, and especially to Nazir G. Dossani, whose thoughtful reading has eliminated a number of my awkward or outrageous statements. He is also responsible for a good many of the exercises. In addition, Judith Kelly typed the manuscript with what can only be termed astonishingly good humor as well as fantastic accuracy. Holt, Rinehart and Winston provided most helpful and understanding editorial assistance; I would particularly like to thank Robert Winkler, Robert Lentz and Sylvia Lang. Most of all I wish to acknowledge my debt to Richard E. Quandt of Princeton University, who read and commented on an entire draft of the manuscript and who is probably responsible for my original interest in these matters; beyond that, he should not be held accountable.

R. E. M.

Philadelphia, Pennsylvania
November 1971

Contents

Modern Mathematical Methods
for Economics and Business

I

MATRIX ALGEBRA

This chapter introduces the reader to a new kind of notation, one that encompasses groups or collections of elements (usually numbers), and presents for these groups of elements a series of definitions and operations that in many ways parallel those of ordinary numbers. The groups of numbers are called matrices—a single group is a matrix—and hence we have an algebra of matrices.

There are several reasons for developing this new notation and the rules for manipulating its symbols. It happens that many problems of the sort investigated in the later chapters of this book can be represented compactly in terms of the symbols of matrix algebra. Furthermore, we can often learn a great deal about the problem—for example, the kinds of solutions it has, or, indeed, whether or not it has any solutions at all—by studying the structure and properties of its matrix representation.

In order to take advantage of the insights provided by this kind of analysis, which is actually the subject matter of linear algebra, we need first to know the fundamental definitions and operations and how they are to be interpreted. These, therefore, are the topics of this chapter. In Chapter 2 we will examine equation systems in the light of this new terminology.

1.1. MATRICES: DEFINITION AND GENERAL REPRESENTATION

A matrix is an array of *elements* that has a particular shape. It is always a rectangular arrangement of elements in rows and columns. That is, each column has the same number of elements, say m, and each row has the same number of elements, say n. For example, two rows of three elements each is a matrix in which $m = 2$ and $n = 3$. If row 1 contained as elements the numbers 7, 8, and 9, and row 2 consisted of 4, 6, and 8, this matrix would be written

$$\begin{bmatrix} 7 & 8 & 9 \\ 4 & 6 & 8 \end{bmatrix}.$$

Square brackets are used to emphasize the notion of a *collection* of elements, and upper-case letters are usually used to denote an entire matrix. Thus, we could define the matrix A to be the two rows of three elements each shown above.

$$A = \begin{bmatrix} 7 & 8 & 9 \\ 4 & 6 & 8 \end{bmatrix}. \tag{1-1}$$

It is important to note that there cannot be any ragged edges in a matrix; each row (in this example) has three numbers in it, each column has two. This is necessary because of the definitions and the operations that have been developed for matrices—that is, because of the uses for which we need matrices and matrix algebra. Thus when the *dimensions* of a matrix are given—for example when we say that A is a 2-by-3 matrix (written 2×3)—this is understood to mean that it has two rows and three columns (the number of *rows* is always given first) and hence that it contains six elements in total. Some of the elements in a matrix may be zero, but none may be omitted or "left blank."

All of the uses for which we will need the notation and algebra of matrices in this book will require that the elements be either known ordinary numbers (as in A, above) or else unknown numbers whose values we want to determine. It is conventional in ordinary algebra and also in matrix algebra to use letters near the front of the alphabet as general representations for numbers whose values are known or given in any specific problem (the so-called *parameters* of the problem) and to use letters from near the end of the alphabet to represent *unknowns* or *variables* whose values are to be determined from the parameters and the relationships in the problem.

Each element of a given matrix sits in a unique position, relative to all others in the matrix—defined by the row and the column in which it is located. Thus we can refer to the 9 in matrix A above as the element in row 1 and column 3. We use two subscripts for this two-dimensional positioning scheme—the first for row location and the second for column. Using a's for the individual elements in the collection A, then in (1-1), for example, $a_{13} = 9$. Likewise, $a_{21} = 4$, $a_{22} = 6$, $a_{12} = 8$, and so on. We represent a general 2×3 matrix as follows:

$$A = \begin{bmatrix} a_{11} & a_{12} & a_{13} \\ a_{21} & a_{22} & a_{23} \end{bmatrix}. \tag{1-2}$$

Even more compactly

$$A = [a_{ij}],$$

where $i = 1, 2$ and $j = 1, 2, 3$. By selecting all possible combinations for the values of subscript i and subscript j, and then placing the resulting elements in correct order, we obtain the arrangement in (1-2). Finally, it is sometimes convenient to denote the dimensions of a matrix directly under the upper-case letter being used. In this case $\underset{(2\times3)}{A}$, without further information, would also represent the matrix in (1-2).

Thus, $\underset{(3\times4)}{B}$ or $[b_{ij}]$, $i = 1, \ldots, 3$; $j = 1, \ldots, 4$, are compact ways of indicating the arrangement:

$$B = \begin{bmatrix} b_{11} & b_{12} & b_{13} & b_{14} \\ b_{21} & b_{22} & b_{23} & b_{24} \\ b_{31} & b_{32} & b_{33} & b_{34} \end{bmatrix}.$$

When one of the two dimensions of a matrix is equal to 1, the matrix is given a special name; it is called a *vector*. This is only a matter of terminology; it is convenient because the name gives information about the specific shape of the matrix. For example, if C has three rows of one element each—that is, has dimensions 3×1—it will look just like a column of three numbers:

$$\underset{(3\times1)}{C} = \begin{bmatrix} c_{11} \\ c_{21} \\ c_{31} \end{bmatrix}.$$

Specifically, C is called a column vector. Similarly any matrix with one row of several elements, for example a 1×5 matrix, is called a row vector.[1]

$$\underset{(1\times5)}{D} = [1\ 4\ 3\ 2\ 5].$$

Thus vectors are simply matrices in which one of the dimensions has shrunk to 1. The ultimate in shrinkage has occurred when there is only one row and one column—that is, a matrix consisting of only one element. Thus, we have general $m \times n$ matrices (it is conventional to use m for the number of rows and n for the number of columns), special matrices of dimensions $m \times 1$ (column vectors), $1 \times n$ (row vectors), and 1×1. In studying the definitions and operations of matrix algebra we will find it generally not necessary or useful to distinguish between a 1×1 matrix and the ordinary number that is its single element; ordinary numbers are termed

---

[1] Sometimes commas are used between the elements of a row vector to avoid confusion. Here we could write $D = [1, 4, 3, 2, 5]$.

scalars in matrix algebra. When a matrix is *square* (when it has the same number of rows and columns—that is, $m = n$), it is often described as being of *order m*. The terminology simply helps us to visualize the shape.

1.2. THE ALGEBRA OF MATRICES

We now define a series of operations for matrices, representing collections of numbers, which are analogous to the operations for ordinary numbers. We will emphasize the points of similarity and also those of dissimilarity from ordinary algebra. Perhaps the easiest notion is that of equality.

DEFINITION 1.1: MATRIX EQUALITY. Two or more matrices are equal if they have the same dimensions and elements in corresponding positions are equal.

There are thus two essentials in the notion of matrix equality. The first is that the matrices involved must have exactly the same dimensions (note that this is a much stronger demand than just requiring that they contain the same numbers of elements); the second is that elements in corresponding positions must be identical. Despite the first—the so-called *conformability requirement for equality*—the definition is parallel to that for equality in ordinary algebra.

As an example, let

$$A = \begin{bmatrix} 1 & 3 & 5 \\ 2 & 4 & 6 \end{bmatrix} \quad \text{and} \quad B = \begin{bmatrix} 1 & 3 & 5 \\ 2 & 4 & 6 \end{bmatrix};$$

then clearly $A = B$, since $a_{ij} = b_{ij}$ for all i and j—that is, for $i = 1, 2$ and $j = 1, 2, 3$. However, if

$$C = \begin{bmatrix} 1 & 2 & 1 \\ 2 & 4 & 3 \end{bmatrix} \quad \text{and} \quad D = \begin{bmatrix} 1 & 2 \\ 2 & 4 \\ 1 & 3 \end{bmatrix}, \quad \text{then } C \neq D;$$

or, if

$$E = \begin{bmatrix} 1 & 2 \\ 2 & 4 \end{bmatrix}, \quad \text{then } C \neq E.$$

Neither $\underset{(2\times3)}{C}$ and $\underset{(3\times2)}{D}$ nor $\underset{(2\times3)}{C}$ and $\underset{(2\times2)}{E}$ are conformable for equality. Let

$$F = \begin{bmatrix} 2 & 4 \\ 2 & 1 \end{bmatrix}; \quad \text{then } \underset{(2\times2)}{E} \neq \underset{(2\times2)}{F},$$

although E and F do meet the conformability requirement and do each contain as elements a 1, two 2's, and a 4. The problem is that *all corresponding* elements are not equal. It is not enough that $e_{21} = f_{21}$, since, for the other elements in corresponding positions, $e_{11} \neq f_{11}$, $e_{12} \neq f_{12}$, and $e_{22} \neq f_{22}$.

We now consider for matrices the simplest of the four ordinary algebraic operations, addition.

OPERATION 1: MATRIX ADDITION. The sum of two or more $m \times n$ matrices is a matrix of the same dimension, each of whose elements is the sum of those in the corresponding positions of the matrices being added.

Let

$$A = \begin{bmatrix} a_{11} & a_{12} \\ a_{21} & a_{22} \end{bmatrix}, \qquad B = \begin{bmatrix} b_{11} & b_{12} \\ b_{21} & b_{22} \end{bmatrix}, \qquad C = \begin{bmatrix} c_{11} & c_{12} \\ c_{21} & c_{22} \end{bmatrix};$$

let D denote their sum. Then

$$D = A + B + C = \begin{bmatrix} a_{11} + b_{11} + c_{11} & a_{12} + b_{12} + c_{12} \\ a_{21} + b_{21} + c_{21} & a_{22} + b_{22} + c_{22} \end{bmatrix}.$$

Specifically, if

$$A = \begin{bmatrix} 2 & 0 \\ 1 & 1 \end{bmatrix}, \quad B = \begin{bmatrix} -1 & 2 \\ -3 & 4 \end{bmatrix}, \quad \text{and} \quad C = \begin{bmatrix} 5 & 5 \\ 4 & 4 \end{bmatrix},$$

$$\text{then } A + B + C = \begin{bmatrix} 6 & 7 \\ 2 & 9 \end{bmatrix}.$$

Thus, by the definition of this operation, the *conformability* requirement for matrix addition is the same as that for equality—namely, that all the matrices involved have exactly the same dimensions. Once this rule is met, we see that matrix addition is completely analogous to addition in ordinary algebra. It simply involves element-by-element addition. The operation maintains the commutative and associative properties of addition with ordinary numbers. That is, $A + B = B + A$ and $(A + B) + C = A + (B + C)$. Put somewhat loosely, the order in which the additions are done makes no difference.

OPERATION 2: MATRIX SUBTRACTION. The difference of two $m \times n$ matrices is a matrix of the same dimension, each of whose elements is the difference of those in the corresponding positions of the matrices being subtracted.

If

$$E = \begin{bmatrix} e_{11} & e_{12} \\ e_{21} & e_{22} \end{bmatrix} \quad \text{and} \quad F = \begin{bmatrix} f_{11} & f_{12} \\ f_{21} & f_{22} \end{bmatrix},$$

$$\text{then } E - F = \begin{bmatrix} e_{11} - f_{11} & e_{12} - f_{12} \\ e_{21} - f_{21} & e_{22} - f_{22} \end{bmatrix}.$$

The operation thus involves element-by-element subtraction and the same conformability requirement as that for equality and addition. (Clearly, as with subtraction of ordinary numbers, $E - F$ is generally different from $F - E$.)

An operation that has no parallel in ordinary algebra is that of transposition, which means interchanging rows and columns.

OPERATION 3: TRANSPOSITION. The transpose of an $m \times n$ matrix A, denoted A' (or A^T or A^t), is an $n \times m$ matrix whose rows are, in order, the columns of A.

For example, if

$$A = \begin{bmatrix} a_{11} & a_{12} & a_{13} \\ a_{21} & a_{22} & a_{23} \end{bmatrix}, \quad \text{then } A' = \begin{bmatrix} a_{11} & a_{21} \\ a_{12} & a_{22} \\ a_{13} & a_{23} \end{bmatrix}.$$

The transpose of an m-element row vector is an m-element column vector, and vice versa. If a matrix and its transpose are equal, the matrix is termed *symmetric*. Thus only square matrices can be symmetric; the property can be represented as $a_{ij} = a_{ji}$ for all i and j.

DEFINITION 1.2: IDENTITY ELEMENT FOR ADDITION—THE NULL MATRIX. The null (or zero) matrix, denoted O, contains only zeros as elements; $a_{ij} = 0$, for all i and j.

In ordinary algebra, the number 0 is formally termed the identity element for addition (and, actually, subtraction too). This means that adding it to (or subtracting it from) any number leaves the number unchanged; $5 \pm 0 = 5$ or $a \pm 0 = a$. It will be useful to have a similar concept in matrix algebra.

The null matrix has elastic dimensions; it always assumes the appropriate size to be conformable for the addition or subtraction operation in which it is involved. Thus one form in which the null matrix appears is $\underset{(2 \times 3)}{O}$ —that is, two rows of three zeros each. Then

$$\underset{(2 \times 3)}{A} + \underset{(2 \times 3)}{O} = \underset{(2 \times 3)}{A}.$$

However, if

$$B = \begin{bmatrix} 2 \\ 6 \\ 4 \\ 1 \end{bmatrix},$$

and we want the particular null matrix that can be added to B, we need

$$\underset{(4\times1)}{O} = \begin{bmatrix} 0 \\ 0 \\ 0 \\ 0 \end{bmatrix},$$

so that $B + O = B$. Note that we can always generate a null matrix of dimension $m \times n$ by subtracting any $m \times n$ matrix from itself. For example, let

$$\underset{(2\times4)}{A} = \begin{bmatrix} 1 & 0 & 4 & 5 \\ 2 & 3 & 5 & 5 \end{bmatrix}.$$

Then,

$$A - A = \begin{bmatrix} 0 & 0 & 0 & 0 \\ 0 & 0 & 0 & 0 \end{bmatrix} = \underset{(2\times4)}{O}. \qquad (1\text{-}3)$$

Using the definitions of (1) equality and (2) the identity element for addition (null matrix) and the operations of (1) addition and (2) subtraction, we can illustrate with an extremely (in fact, trivially) simple equation system one elementary application of matrix representations and matrix algebra.

Suppose we are given the following information—a very simple "set" of equations—and want to find the values of the unknown variables, x_1, x_2, and x_3.

$$\begin{aligned} x_1 + 1 &= 6, \\ x_2 + 7 &= 41, \\ x_3 + 5 &= 5. \end{aligned} \qquad (1\text{-}4)$$

(The fact that we can instantly write down the values of x_1, x_2, and x_3 for these equations should be ignored for the present.) We can define the following matrices (column vectors in this case):

$$X = \begin{bmatrix} x_1 \\ x_2 \\ x_3 \end{bmatrix}, \qquad A = \begin{bmatrix} 1 \\ 7 \\ 5 \end{bmatrix}, \qquad B = \begin{bmatrix} 6 \\ 41 \\ 5 \end{bmatrix}. \qquad (1\text{-}5)$$

Given these definitions, and given the definitions of matrix equality and the operation of matrix addition, we see that the three equations in (1-4) can be represented by the one *matrix* equation

$$X + A = B. \qquad (1\text{-}6)$$

To solve equations means to find the values of the unknown variables (here the x's) in terms of the known parameters (here the elements of A and B). Thus, in the representation of (1-6), we would like X alone on one side of the equality sign. This is easily accomplished in a very few steps, given the definitions and operations that we now have.

$$X + A - A = B - A, \tag{1-7}$$
$$X + O = B - A, \tag{1-8}$$
$$X = B - A. \tag{1-9}$$

In (1-7) we subtract A from both sides of (1-6). The conformability requirement is met, and, as in ordinary algebra, if equals are subtracted from equals, the results are equal. But we know, as in (1-3), that $A - A = O$; hence (1-8). And from the definition of the null matrix—that is, that it contributes nothing when it appears in a sum—we know it can be omitted; hence (1-9). Specifically,

$$X = \begin{bmatrix} 6 \\ 41 \\ 5 \end{bmatrix} - \begin{bmatrix} 1 \\ 7 \\ 5 \end{bmatrix} = \begin{bmatrix} 5 \\ 34 \\ 0 \end{bmatrix} \tag{1-10}$$

and from the definition of matrix equality (element-by-element equality) we know that this means $x_1 = 5$, $x_2 = 34$, and $x_3 = 0$.

In (1-6) through (1-9) the algebra necessary to solve this system has been done not on the system itself but rather on the matrix statement of the system, using matrix algebra. Finally, in (1-10) we have introduced the specific parameters that had been removed by the definitions of A and B in (1-5); this produces the necessary numerical result. The idea, to repeat, is to illustrate how we can manipulate the shorthand representation of the original problem in order to arrive at a solution (or, as we shall see later, in order to learn something about the nature or characteristics of the solution).

We turn now to operations that parallel multiplication in ordinary algebra. In view of the situations in which matrix representations of problems are useful, it is necessary to consider the multiplication operation in two parts: first, multiplication of a matrix by a scalar (by an ordinary number) and second, multiplication of two or more matrices.

OPERATION 4A: MATRIX MULTIPLICATION BY A SCALAR.   Multiplication of a matrix by a scalar is performed by multiplying each element in the matrix by the scalar.

This is straightforward. Let

$$A = \begin{bmatrix} a_{11} & a_{12} & a_{13} \\ a_{21} & a_{22} & a_{23} \end{bmatrix}.$$

Then the scalar 5 times the matrix A gives

$$5A = \begin{bmatrix} 5a_{11} & 5a_{12} & 5a_{13} \\ 5a_{21} & 5a_{22} & 5a_{23} \end{bmatrix}.$$

Note that the operation is commutative; $5A$ or $A5$ both denote the same operation: multiply each element in A by 5. If more than one *scalar* were involved, say 5 and 6, then $(5A)6$, $5(A6)$, $5(6A)$, $30A$, and a variety of other notations would all define operations whose ultimate effect is multiplication of each of the elements in A by 30. The operation, with one matrix and several scalars, is associative. It is usual to place the scalar before the notation for the matrix (and if several scalars are involved, to multiply them together); therefore $30A$ would be the customary notation for the example of 5 times 6 times A.

The definition of multiplication of two (or more) matrices is one of operational convenience—for example, because it facilitates operations with matrix representations of large systems of linear equations. This will become clear presently, but the reader should realize that there are several alternative ways in which the multiplication operation *could* have been defined for matrices. (One, for *vectors*, will be discussed later in this chapter.) At this point, we depart from the close analogy with ordinary algebra.

OPERATION 4B: MULTIPLICATION OF TWO MATRICES. Given matrices A $(m \times n)$ and B $(n \times p)$, the product AB is a matrix C $(m \times p)$ whose elements c_{ij} are defined as

$$c_{ij} = \sum_{k=1}^{n} a_{ik}b_{kj}, \qquad (i = 1, \ldots, m; j = 1, \ldots, p).$$

In words, the element in row i and column j of the *product* matrix is formed by summing a series of products of *pairs* of elements taken, in order, from across the ith *row* of A (the matrix on the left) and down the jth *column* of B (the matrix on the right). Because of this definition, we see that multiplication of two matrices involves a new conformability requirement. For two matrices to be *conformable for multiplication*, the number of *columns* in the matrix on the *left* must be the same as the number of *rows* in the matrix on the *right*.

For example, let

$$A_{(2\times2)} = \begin{bmatrix} a_{11} & a_{12} \\ a_{21} & a_{22} \end{bmatrix} \text{ and } B_{(2\times3)} = \begin{bmatrix} b_{11} & b_{12} & b_{13} \\ b_{21} & b_{22} & b_{23} \end{bmatrix}.$$

Then

$$C_{(2\times3)} = AB = \begin{bmatrix} (a_{11}b_{11} + a_{12}b_{21}) & (a_{11}b_{12} + a_{12}b_{22}) & (a_{11}b_{13} + a_{12}b_{23}) \\ (a_{21}b_{11} + a_{22}b_{21}) & (a_{21}b_{12} + a_{22}b_{22}) & (a_{21}b_{13} + a_{22}b_{23}) \end{bmatrix}.$$

$$(1\text{-}11)$$

The reader should visualize the process carefully. For each c_{ij} we move across a row in A and down a column in B, forming products of pairs of elements, then adding these products together. It is the fact that the second dimension of A (the number of columns) and the first dimension of B (the number of rows) are the same that *allows* us to write the product

$$\underset{(2\times\textcircled{2})\underline{}(\textcircled{2}\times3)}{A\qquad B}.$$

This assures us that as we select elements in order from any row, i, in the left-hand matrix (which means, after all, selecting elements from each of the *columns* in that row), there will be an element from the column, j, of the right-hand matrix, down which we are moving (hence selecting from each of the *rows* in that column).

Once we have established this conformability, we can find out how large the product matrix will be by observing the other two dimensions:

$$\underset{(\textcircled{2}\times\textcircled{3})}{C}\ =\ \underset{(\textcircled{2}\times2)\,(2\times\textcircled{3})}{A\qquad B}.$$

That is, because of the way in which matrix multiplication is defined, we see that the dimensions of the product matrix are given by the number of rows in the left-hand matrix, each of which can be selected to supply the a_{ik} in the product, as defined in Operation 4B, and the number of columns in the right-hand matrix, each of which can be selected to supply the b_{kj} in the same definition.

It is clear in this case that we cannot form the product BA, because of the way in which matrix multiplication has been defined. The conformability requirement is not met; the number of columns in B, 3, is not equal to the number of rows in A, 2. Thus, in contrast to ordinary algebra, order makes a difference—formally, matrix multiplication is *not* commutative. Even when the conformability requirement *is* met and the product in the reverse order *is* defined, it will (in general) be different from the original product. Two illustrations follow.

1. Suppose A is a 1×3 matrix (a three-element row vector) and B is a 3×1 matrix (a three-element column vector). Then *both* AB and BA are defined, but the former product is a matrix of one row and one column only and the latter is a 3×3 matrix.

For example, let

$$A = [2 \quad 5 \quad 3] \quad \text{and} \quad B = \begin{bmatrix} 1 \\ 4 \\ 7 \end{bmatrix}.$$

Then

$$AB = [2 \quad 5 \quad 3]\begin{bmatrix} 1 \\ 4 \\ 7 \end{bmatrix} = [43]$$

and

$$BA = \begin{bmatrix} 1 \\ 4 \\ 7 \end{bmatrix} [2 \quad 5 \quad 3] = \begin{bmatrix} 2 & 5 & 3 \\ 8 & 20 & 12 \\ 14 & 35 & 21 \end{bmatrix}.$$

2. Even when the dimensions of the matrices are such that multiplication can be done in either order *and* the product is a matrix of the *same* order, the results will (in general) differ.

Let

$$\underset{(2\times2)}{C} = \begin{bmatrix} 1 & 2 \\ 3 & 4 \end{bmatrix} \quad \text{and} \quad \underset{(2\times2)}{D} = \begin{bmatrix} 5 & 6 \\ 7 & 8 \end{bmatrix}.$$

Then CD and DC are both defined, and both products will be 2×2 matrices. But

$$CD = \begin{bmatrix} 1 & 2 \\ 3 & 4 \end{bmatrix} \begin{bmatrix} 5 & 6 \\ 7 & 8 \end{bmatrix} = \begin{bmatrix} 19 & 22 \\ 43 & 50 \end{bmatrix}$$

and

$$DC = \begin{bmatrix} 5 & 6 \\ 7 & 8 \end{bmatrix} \begin{bmatrix} 1 & 2 \\ 3 & 4 \end{bmatrix} = \begin{bmatrix} 23 & 34 \\ 31 & 46 \end{bmatrix}. \qquad (1\text{-}12)$$

(The reader should check his understanding of the multiplication operation by doing the products of both of these examples as exercises.)

We have said that the products in different orders (when defined) will *in general* differ. This is simply because there are some special cases in which the products will in fact be equal. For example:

$$\begin{bmatrix} 1 & 1 \\ 1 & 1 \end{bmatrix} \begin{bmatrix} 2 & 2 \\ 2 & .2 \end{bmatrix} = \begin{bmatrix} 4 & 4 \\ 4 & 4 \end{bmatrix} \quad \text{and} \quad \begin{bmatrix} 2 & 2 \\ 2 & 2 \end{bmatrix} \begin{bmatrix} 1 & 1 \\ 1 & 1 \end{bmatrix} = \begin{bmatrix} 4 & 4 \\ 4 & 4 \end{bmatrix},$$

$$\begin{bmatrix} 1 & 0 \\ 0 & 1 \end{bmatrix} \begin{bmatrix} 3 & 6 \\ 4 & 2 \end{bmatrix} = \begin{bmatrix} 3 & 6 \\ 4 & 2 \end{bmatrix} \quad \text{and} \quad \begin{bmatrix} 3 & 6 \\ 4 & 2 \end{bmatrix} \begin{bmatrix} 1 & 0 \\ 0 & 1 \end{bmatrix} = \begin{bmatrix} 3 & 6 \\ 4 & 2 \end{bmatrix}.$$

$$(1\text{-}13)$$

Such examples, where the order of multiplication does *not* matter, are exceptions to the general rule. Therefore the terms *premultiply* and *postmultiply* are used to indicate order. Thus, saying either that A premultiplies B or that B postmultiplies A denotes the product AB.

While the commutative property of ordinary multiplication no longer holds, matrix multiplication is associative. This means that provided the conformability requirements are met, the product ABC can actually be carried out by first multiplying AB and then *post*multiplying by C—that is, as $(AB)C$—or by first forming the product BC and then *pre*multiplying by A, $A(BC)$. Moreover, matrix multiplication (like ordinary multiplication) is distributive. That is (again, provided that all conformability requirements are met), $DE + DF = D(E + F)$. In words, we can premultiply both E and F by D and then sum, or we can sum E and F and then premultiply by D. These properties are used almost automatically in ordinary algebra, and we will have need for them also in matrix algebra operations. (The reader is encouraged to prove that these two properties hold for one or more general cases—for example, when all matrices involved are 2×2 or 3×3. The demonstration requires primarily an ability to copy subscripts properly from one line to the next. Specific illustrations are provided in Problems 6 and 7 to this chapter.)[2]

Partitioning

It is sometimes conceptually useful to subdivide a matrix into so-called submatrices. It is possible to carry out matrix algebraic operations on the larger matrices by considering the entire submatrices as single elements, providing that the conformability requirements for the operation are met. Suppose A and B are both 2×4 matrices. Their entries might represent dollar sales on two successive days (rows 1 and 2) of three nonfood items (columns 1, 2, and 3) and one food item (column 4) at two branches of a retail store (A and B). To sharpen the distinction between food and nonfood sales, A and B could be partitioned as follows:

$$A = \left[\begin{array}{ccc|c} a_{11} & a_{12} & a_{13} & a_{14} \\ a_{21} & a_{22} & a_{23} & a_{24} \end{array}\right] \quad \text{and} \quad B = \left[\begin{array}{ccc|c} b_{11} & b_{12} & b_{13} & b_{14} \\ b_{21} & b_{22} & b_{23} & b_{24} \end{array}\right] \quad (1\text{-}14)$$

or as

$$A = [A_{\mathrm{I}} \mid A_{\mathrm{II}}] \quad \text{and} \quad B = [B_{\mathrm{I}} \mid B_{\mathrm{II}}],$$

where

$$A_{\mathrm{I}} = \left[\begin{array}{ccc} a_{11} & a_{12} & a_{13} \\ a_{21} & a_{22} & a_{23} \end{array}\right], \quad A_{\mathrm{II}} = \left[\begin{array}{c} a_{14} \\ a_{24} \end{array}\right], \quad B_{\mathrm{I}} = \left[\begin{array}{ccc} b_{11} & b_{12} & b_{13} \\ b_{21} & b_{22} & b_{23} \end{array}\right],$$

$$B_{\mathrm{II}} = \left[\begin{array}{c} b_{14} \\ b_{24} \end{array}\right].$$

The dashed lines serve to indicate blocks of elements within the matrices. Then the total sales at both branches, by item, on each of the days, $A + B$, could be shown as

$$A + B = [A_{\mathrm{I}} + B_{\mathrm{I}} \mid A_{\mathrm{II}} + B_{\mathrm{II}}].$$

For addition or subtraction, partitioning provides no useful computational advantages, even though the submatrices are treated in the algebra as if they were single matrix elements. The sole purpose here is to indicate

---

[2] It is perhaps necessary to reemphasize that matrix multiplication (and hence, also, multiplication of a matrix by a vector) has been defined as indicated here precisely because of the use to which it will be put in the representation and study of linear equation systems. This will become clear by the end of Chapter 2.

logical divisions among the elements in a matrix; such divisions must always be made parallel to the edges.

For multiplication, however, there may well be a computational advantage. Suppose A, $m \times n$, and B, $n \times p$, are to be multiplied in the order AB and that they are both very large matrices. Then each element of the product will involve the sum of n products of pairs of elements. It is possible to partition A and B so that the multiplication can be carried out with smaller submatrices (that is, smaller *numbers* of pairs). Let A be partitioned as follows:

$$\underset{(m \times n)}{A} = m \left\{ \left[\begin{array}{c|c} A_{\mathrm{I}} & A_{\mathrm{II}} \\ \hline A_{\mathrm{III}} & A_{\mathrm{IV}} \end{array} \right] \right. \qquad (1\text{-}15)$$

$$\underbrace{}_{n}$$

where the dimensions are as follows:

Submatrix	Dimension
A_{I}	$q \times r$
A_{II}	$q \times (n - r)$
A_{III}	$(m - q) \times r$
A_{IV}	$(m - q) \times (n - r)$

Similarly, subdivide B into four matrices:

$$\underset{(n \times p)}{B} = n \left\{ \left[\begin{array}{c|c} B_{\mathrm{I}} & B_{\mathrm{II}} \\ \hline B_{\mathrm{III}} & B_{\mathrm{IV}} \end{array} \right] \right. \qquad (1\text{-}16)$$

$$\underbrace{}_{p}$$

with dimensions:

Submatrix	Dimension
B_{I}	$r \times s$
B_{II}	$r \times (p - s)$
B_{III}	$(n - r) \times s$
B_{IV}	$(n - r) \times (p - s)$

Then the matrix product AB can be shown as follows:

$$\left[\begin{array}{c|c} A_{\mathrm{I}} & A_{\mathrm{II}} \\ \hline A_{\mathrm{III}} & A_{\mathrm{IV}} \end{array} \right] \left[\begin{array}{c|c} B_{\mathrm{I}} & B_{\mathrm{II}} \\ \hline B_{\mathrm{III}} & B_{\mathrm{IV}} \end{array} \right]$$

$$= \left[\begin{array}{c|c} A_{\mathrm{I}}B_{\mathrm{I}} + A_{\mathrm{II}}B_{\mathrm{III}} & A_{\mathrm{I}}B_{\mathrm{II}} + A_{\mathrm{II}}B_{\mathrm{IV}} \\ \hline A_{\mathrm{III}}B_{\mathrm{I}} + A_{\mathrm{IV}}B_{\mathrm{III}} & A_{\mathrm{III}}B_{\mathrm{II}} + A_{\mathrm{IV}}B_{\mathrm{IV}} \end{array} \right]. \qquad (1\text{-}17)$$

The reader should check (1) that each of the eight products in (1-17) satisfies the conformability requirement for multiplication, and (2) that each of the four sums satisfies the conformability requirement for addition, and finally that the dimensions of the product matrix are indeed $m \times p$. Note now that none of the submatrix products involves a sum of n products of pairs of elements; either r or $(n - r)$ is required but never n. This size reduction may be helpful; moreover, in some situations (as will become clear later in this book) *logical* partitions are useful—for example, between zero-valued and positive-valued variables in linear programming problems.

We consider a small example for illustration. Let

$$A = \begin{bmatrix} 1 & 2 & 3 \\ 4 & 5 & 6 \\ 7 & 0 & 0 \end{bmatrix} \quad \text{and} \quad B = \begin{bmatrix} 1 & 1 & 1 & 1 \\ 2 & 2 & 3 & 1 \\ 1 & 1 & 2 & 1 \end{bmatrix}.$$

Partition A as in (1-15) into

$$A = \left[\begin{array}{cc|c} 1 & 2 & 3 \\ 4 & 5 & 6 \\ \hline 7 & 0 & 0 \end{array} \right]$$

—that is,

$$A_{\text{I}} = \begin{bmatrix} 1 & 2 \\ 4 & 5 \end{bmatrix}, \quad A_{\text{II}} = \begin{bmatrix} 3 \\ 6 \end{bmatrix}, \quad A_{\text{III}} = [7 \quad 0], \quad \text{and} \quad A_{\text{IV}} = [0].$$

Then B *must* be partitioned between rows 2 and 3 to allow the submatrix multiplication of (1-17); the column division (if any) is arbitrary. In this example we partition between columns 2 and 3. Thus, as in (1-16), let

$$B = \left[\begin{array}{cc|cc} 1 & 1 & 1 & 1 \\ 2 & 2 & 3 & 1 \\ \hline 1 & 1 & 2 & 1 \end{array} \right]$$

—that is,

$$B_{\text{I}} = \begin{bmatrix} 1 & 1 \\ 2 & 2 \end{bmatrix}, \quad B_{\text{II}} = \begin{bmatrix} 1 & 1 \\ 3 & 1 \end{bmatrix}, \quad B_{\text{III}} = [1 \quad 1], \quad \text{and} \quad B_{\text{IV}} = [2 \quad 1].$$

To summarize dimensions:

Submatrix	Dimension	Submatrix	Dimension
A_{I}	2×2	B_{I}	2×2
A_{II}	2×1	B_{II}	2×2
A_{III}	1×2	B_{III}	1×2
A_{IV}	1×1	B_{IV}	1×2

Thus the product AB can be found as the set of operations in (1-17):

$$A_I B_I = \begin{bmatrix} 1 & 2 \\ 4 & 5 \end{bmatrix} \begin{bmatrix} 1 & 1 \\ 2 & 2 \end{bmatrix} = \begin{bmatrix} 5 & 5 \\ 14 & 14 \end{bmatrix} \qquad A_I B_{II} = \begin{bmatrix} 1 & 2 \\ 4 & 5 \end{bmatrix} \begin{bmatrix} 1 & 1 \\ 3 & 1 \end{bmatrix} = \begin{bmatrix} 7 & 3 \\ 19 & 9 \end{bmatrix}$$

$$A_{II} B_{III} = \begin{bmatrix} 3 \\ 6 \end{bmatrix} [1 \ 1] = \begin{bmatrix} 3 & 3 \\ 6 & 6 \end{bmatrix} \qquad A_{II} B_{IV} = \begin{bmatrix} 3 \\ 6 \end{bmatrix} [2 \ 1] = \begin{bmatrix} 6 & 3 \\ 12 & 6 \end{bmatrix}$$

$$A_{III} B_I = [7 \ 0] \begin{bmatrix} 1 & 1 \\ 2 & 2 \end{bmatrix} = [7 \ 7] \qquad A_{III} B_{II} = [7 \ 0] \begin{bmatrix} 1 & 1 \\ 3 & 1 \end{bmatrix} = [7 \ 7]$$

$$A_{IV} B_{III} = [0] \ [1 \ 1] = [0 \ 0] \qquad A_{IV} B_{IV} = [0] \ [2 \ 1] = [0 \ 0]$$

and

$$\begin{bmatrix} A_I B_I + A_{II} B_{III} = \begin{bmatrix} 8 & 8 \\ 20 & 20 \end{bmatrix} & A_I B_{II} + A_{II} B_{IV} = \begin{bmatrix} 13 & 6 \\ 31 & 15 \end{bmatrix} \\ A_{III} B_I + A_{IV} B_{III} = [7 \ 7] & A_{III} B_{II} + A_{IV} B_{IV} = [7 \ 7] \end{bmatrix}.$$

$$(1\text{-}18)$$

Then

$$AB = \begin{bmatrix} 8 & 8 & 13 & 6 \\ 20 & 20 & 31 & 15 \\ \hline 7 & 7 & 7 & 7 \end{bmatrix}.$$

Since the dashed lines are only imaginary constructs, this product is indeed the 3 × 4 matrix AB. (The reader should check this by performing the multiplication directly.) Partitioning can also be a useful device in the matrix algebraic operation comparable to division, as we will see below.

Before turning to this last matrix algebraic operation—where we will find another departure from the concepts of ordinary algebra—we need to investigate the notion of an identity element for multiplication. The idea is the same as that of an identity element for addition and subtraction—namely, that when it multiplies a number, that number remains unchanged. In ordinary algebra this is, of course, the number 1. There is a similar concept in matrix algebra. The two examples (1-13), in which order did *not* make a difference, contained matrices that might seem logical as parallels in matrix algebra to the identity element for multiplication. The first matrix contains all 1's; the second has 1's on the main diagonal and 0's elsewhere. But we see, in (1-13), that a matrix of all 1's *does* change the matrix that it multiplies; however, the matrix with 1's and 0's appears to have the property. This turns out to be true in general.

DEFINITION 1.3: IDENTITY ELEMENT FOR MULTIPLICATION—THE IDENTITY MATRIX.   The identity (or unit) matrix, denoted I, is a square matrix with 1's on the main diagonal and zeros elsewhere;

$$I = [a_{ij}], \qquad \text{where } a_{ij} = \begin{cases} 1, & i = j, \\ 0, & i \neq j. \end{cases}$$

The identity matrix has flexible dimensions, although they are not quite so elastic as those of the null matrix; it must always remain square. However, this does not prevent the identity matrix from becoming conformable for any matrix *multiplication*. For example, if A had dimensions 2×4, then AI is possible for the 4×4 identity matrix, IA is possible for the 2×2 identity matrix, and in both cases the product will be simply A.

Let

$$A = \begin{bmatrix} 1 & 3 & 2 & 4 \\ 6 & 5 & 4 & 3 \end{bmatrix}.$$

Then

$$\underset{(2\times4)}{A} \ \underset{(4\times4)}{I} = \begin{bmatrix} 1 & 3 & 2 & 4 \\ 6 & 5 & 4 & 3 \end{bmatrix} \begin{bmatrix} 1 & 0 & 0 & 0 \\ 0 & 1 & 0 & 0 \\ 0 & 0 & 1 & 0 \\ 0 & 0 & 0 & 1 \end{bmatrix} = \begin{bmatrix} 1 & 3 & 2 & 4 \\ 6 & 5 & 4 & 3 \end{bmatrix}$$

and

$$\underset{(2\times2)}{I} \ \underset{(2\times4)}{A} = \begin{bmatrix} 1 & 0 \\ 0 & 1 \end{bmatrix} \begin{bmatrix} 1 & 3 & 2 & 4 \\ 6 & 5 & 4 & 3 \end{bmatrix} = \begin{bmatrix} 1 & 3 & 2 & 4 \\ 6 & 5 & 4 & 3 \end{bmatrix}.$$

The identity matrix is necessary for an understanding of the division operation in matrix algebra. There are several ways of looking at the concept of division in ordinary algebra. If we have an equation $ax = b$, where a and b are parameters, then the value of x can be found by *dividing* both sides of the equation by a (providing, of course, that $a \neq 0$)—that is, $x = b/a$. Equivalently, we could say that we find the value of x by multiplying both sides of the equation by $(1/a)$, the *reciprocal* of a, which can also be denoted by a^{-1}. Thus $(1/a)ax = (1/a)b$ or $x = (1/a)b = a^{-1}b$. Division of a by a and multiplication of a by its reciprocal are simply different ways of describing the same operation; they both achieve the same result of replacing the number a by 1, the identity element for multiplication. By definition, unity does not alter a multiplicative statement; hence it can be ignored. The steps, then—which we do automatically and without further thought—are really as follows:

$$ax = b,$$

$$\frac{ax}{a} = \frac{b}{a} \quad \text{or} \quad \left(\frac{1}{a}\right)ax = \left(\frac{1}{a}\right)b \quad \text{or} \quad a^{-1}ax = a^{-1}b, \qquad (1\text{-}19)$$

$$1x = \frac{b}{a},$$

and thus

$$x = \frac{b}{a},$$

Therefore division by a number can be thought of as multiplication by the reciprocal of that number; the defining property is that the product of a number and its reciprocal is unity. This is the most convenient way to think of the division operation in the algebra of matrices. For a given matrix A we define "division by A" as "multiplication by the reciprocal of A." We will carry over the notation of exponents in ordinary algebra and denote this reciprocal matrix by A^{-1}. And while the term reciprocal matrix is completely valid, it is more common to refer to A^{-1} as the *inverse* of A, or simply as A *inverse*.

It turns out to be useful to retain the commutative property for the reciprocal from ordinary algebra, so the inverse is defined only for square matrices as follows[3]

$$AA^{-1} = A^{-1}A = I \tag{1-20}$$

in complete analogy with the ordinary reciprocal. Thus A^{-1} is always a square matrix of the same order as A. Just as the number 0 has no reciprocal, so a square null matrix O, of any order, has no inverse. However, diverging from the algebra of numbers, we will find that many other matrices do not have inverses. Thus the question of the *existence* of an inverse for any square matrix is always relevant. The companion question of *uniqueness*, however, need not arise. If an inverse for a particular matrix exists, then it is unique.[4] We can learn a great deal about the elements in the inverse matrix from a careful examination of (1-20).

Consider the general 2×2 matrix A and, for notational simplicity, denote the inverse, A^{-1}, as the matrix X. Thus, from (1-20), $AA^{-1} = I$ or $AX = I$. Specifically for the 2×2 case:

$$\begin{bmatrix} a_{11} & a_{12} \\ a_{21} & a_{22} \end{bmatrix} \begin{bmatrix} x_{11} & x_{12} \\ x_{21} & x_{22} \end{bmatrix} = \begin{bmatrix} 1 & 0 \\ 0 & 1 \end{bmatrix}. \tag{1-21}$$

We assume a given A—that is, the elements a_{ij} are known; we are interested in the elements of A^{-1}, the x_{ij}'s. From our understanding of matrix multiplication and the meaning of matrix equality, we can make (1-21) even more explicit:

$$\begin{bmatrix} (a_{11}x_{11} + a_{12}x_{21}) & (a_{11}x_{12} + a_{12}x_{22}) \\ (a_{21}x_{11} + a_{22}x_{21}) & (a_{21}x_{12} + a_{22}x_{22}) \end{bmatrix} = \begin{bmatrix} 1 & 0 \\ 0 & 1 \end{bmatrix}$$

and finally, therefore,

---

[3] More modern work on "pseudo-inverses" for nonsquare matrices, with some of the properties of square-matrix inverses, need not concern us here. This will become clear in Chapter 2, where we have occasion to use, extensively, the concept of the inverse of a *square* matrix.

[4] The demonstration is as follows: Define B and C as inverses of A. This means $AB = BA = I = AC = CA$. Then $C(AB) = CI = C$. But since multiplication is associative, $(CA)B = C$ also. Since $CA = I$, therefore $IB = C$ and thus $B = C$.

$$a_{11}x_{11} + a_{12}x_{21} = 1, \qquad a_{21}x_{11} + a_{22}x_{21} = 0, \qquad \text{(1-22a)}$$
$$a_{11}x_{12} + a_{12}x_{22} = 0, \qquad a_{21}x_{12} + a_{22}x_{22} = 1. \qquad \text{(1-22b)}$$

Set (1-22a) contains two linear equations in the two unknowns x_{11} and x_{21}; (1-22b) involves only unknowns x_{12} and x_{22}. Each set can be solved by the simplest methods of ordinary algebra. From (1-22a), multiplying the left equation by a_{22} and the right one by a_{12}:

$$a_{11}a_{22}x_{11} + a_{12}a_{22}x_{21} = a_{22},$$
$$a_{12}a_{21}x_{11} + a_{12}a_{22}x_{21} = 0.$$

Thus, subtracting the lower from the upper equation,

$$(a_{11}a_{22} - a_{12}a_{21})x_{11} = a_{22}.$$

Similarly, multiplying the left equation in (1-22a) by a_{21} and the right equation by a_{11} and subtracting the left from the right equation gives

$$(a_{11}a_{22} - a_{12}a_{21})x_{21} = -a_{21}.$$

For convenience, let $(a_{11}a_{22} - a_{12}a_{21}) = d$.

Similarly, from (1-22b), $dx_{22} = a_{11}$ and $dx_{12} = -a_{12}$. Thus, as long as $d \neq 0$, we can find the values of the four unknowns; $x_{11} = a_{22}/d$, $x_{12} = -a_{12}/d$, $x_{21} = -a_{21}/d$, and $x_{22} = a_{11}/d$. The inverse elements, x_{ij}, are completely determined by the elements of A. Since each x_{ij} is divided by d (that is, multiplied by $1/d$), and since $1/d$ is a scalar, we can represent the inverse of A as the product of a scalar and a matrix:

$$A^{-1} = \frac{1}{a_{11}a_{22} - a_{12}a_{21}} \begin{bmatrix} a_{22} & -a_{12} \\ -a_{21} & a_{11} \end{bmatrix}. \qquad \text{(1-23)}$$

It is rather cumbersome, but a good test of the reader's facility with matrix multiplication, to check that in fact when the A of (1-21) is postmultiplied by A^{-1} in (1-23), the result is the 2×2 identity matrix.

From (1-23) we see that the existence of A^{-1} in this case must hinge on whether or not $(a_{11}a_{22} - a_{12}a_{21})$ is zero. If this expression is zero, its reciprocal is not defined, and we cannot perform the multiplication shown in (1-23). If the expression is not zero (whether positive or negative is of no importance), then a reciprocal exists and hence A^{-1} *must* exist. Put more formally, if A^{-1} exists, then $(a_{11}a_{22} - a_{12}a_{21}) \neq 0$ [that is, $(a_{11}a_{22} - a_{12}a_{21}) \neq 0$ is a *necessary* condition for A^{-1} to exist] and if $(a_{11}a_{22} - a_{12}a_{21}) \neq 0$, then A^{-1} exists [that is, $(a_{11}a_{22} - a_{12}a_{21}) \neq 0$ is a *sufficient* condition to insure that A^{-1} exists]. Thus $(a_{11}a_{22} - a_{12}a_{21}) \neq 0$ is both a necessary and sufficient condition for the existence of an inverse to A. We therefore have (at least for the general 2×2 case) a means of answering the existence question.

To illustrate, let

$$A = \begin{bmatrix} 1 & 3 \\ 4 & 14 \end{bmatrix}.$$

Does A^{-1} exist? Yes, since $a_{11}a_{22} - a_{12}a_{21} = (1)(14) - (3)(4) = 2$. Therefore

$$A^{-1} = \frac{1}{2} \begin{bmatrix} 14 & -3 \\ -4 & 1 \end{bmatrix} = \begin{bmatrix} 7 & -\frac{3}{2} \\ -2 & \frac{1}{2} \end{bmatrix}.$$

As a check:

$$AA^{-1} = \begin{bmatrix} 1 & 3 \\ 4 & 14 \end{bmatrix} \begin{bmatrix} 7 & -\frac{3}{2} \\ -2 & \frac{1}{2} \end{bmatrix} = \begin{bmatrix} 1 & 0 \\ 0 & 1 \end{bmatrix}.$$

(The reader should check that $A^{-1}A$ also gives I in this case.)

Because the definition of A^{-1} in (1-23) for the 2 × 2 case can be generalized to square matrices of any size, it is important to examine the scalar and the matrix parts of the product more carefully.

The denominator of the scalar in (1-23), the number that must not be zero if the matrix is to have an inverse, is called the *determinant* of A, usually written $|A|$ or det A. Formally, the determinant is a function that associates a *number* with a square matrix. It is a unique value, formed in the 2 × 2 case by subtracting from the product of the elements on the main diagonal

$$\left(\text{northwest to southeast,} \quad \begin{bmatrix} a_{11} & a_{12} \\ a_{21} & a_{22} \end{bmatrix} \right),$$

the products of the elements on the other diagonal

$$\left(\text{northeast to southwest,} \quad \begin{bmatrix} a_{11} & a_{12} \\ a_{21} & a_{22} \end{bmatrix} \right).$$

The *scalar* part of the definition for inverses of square matrices larger than 2 × 2 is always the reciprocal of the determinant of the matrix. It is therefore useful to extend the definition of a determinant to square matrices of any size; it is, unfortunately, also a bit involved.

The determinant when A is 3 × 3 can be formed by using a "diagonal" rule similar to that for the 2 × 2 case. For

$$A = \begin{bmatrix} a_{11} & a_{12} & a_{13} \\ a_{21} & a_{22} & a_{23} \\ a_{31} & a_{32} & a_{33} \end{bmatrix},$$

$$|A| = (a_{11}a_{22}a_{33} + a_{12}a_{23}a_{31} + a_{13}a_{21}a_{32}) - (a_{13}a_{22}a_{31} + a_{23}a_{32}a_{11} + a_{33}a_{12}a_{21}).$$

Schematically, there are three diagonals or "pseudo-diagonals" that contribute positive products and three that contribute negatively. Suppose we insert the first and second columns of A to the right of the third column, producing a 3×5 matrix Q.

$$Q = \begin{bmatrix} a_{11} & a_{12} & a_{13} & a_{11} & a_{12} \\ a_{21} & a_{22} & a_{23} & a_{21} & a_{22} \\ a_{31} & a_{32} & a_{33} & a_{31} & a_{32} \end{bmatrix}.$$

Then $|A|$ is the sum of the products of elements on the solid arrows less the sum of the products of elements on the dashed arrows.[5] For example, if

$$A = \begin{bmatrix} 1 & 1 & 1 \\ 2 & 0 & 6 \\ 3 & 7 & 1 \end{bmatrix},$$

then

$$|A| = 0 + 18 + 14 - (0 + 42 + 2) = -12. \qquad (1\text{-}24)$$

There is no similar, easily visualized diagonal rule for matrices larger than 3×3. It is necessary in larger cases to work with a more general definition of a determinant; this, however, requires some preliminary terminology.

DEFINITION 1.4: MINOR OF AN ELEMENT. The minor of an element a_{ij} in A, sometimes denoted $|a_{ij}|$, is the determinant of the matrix that is formed when row i and column j are deleted from A.

Thus, each element of a square matrix has a unique number associated with it, namely its minor.[6] For example, in the 3×3 matrix whose determinant is given in (1-24), the minor of the element 6—that is, the minor of a_{23}, denoted $|a_{23}|$—is the determinant of $\begin{bmatrix} 1 & 1 \\ 3 & 7 \end{bmatrix}$, the original A matrix with row 2 and column 3 gone. Thus $|a_{23}| = 4$. The concept of a minor is essential for the next definition.

DEFINITION 1.5: COFACTOR OF AN ELEMENT. The cofactor of an element a_{ij} in A, denoted A_{ij}, is the minor of a_{ij} multiplied by $(-1)^{i+j}$—that is, $A_{ij} = (-1)^{i+j}|a_{ij}|$.

---

[5] Although it involves bending the arrows, this 3×3 case is often shown as

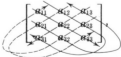

where, again, products of elements on the solid lines are added and those on the dashed lines are subtracted.

[6] Clearly only elements in *square* matrices have minors, since after one row and one column are removed it is necessary to find the *determinant* of the remaining matrix.

Thus, the cofactor of an element differs from the minor of the element at most by sign (hence it is termed the "signed minor"), and then only when the sum of a_{ij}'s row and column location is odd, since (-1) raised to an even power is $+1$, the identity element for multiplication. To continue with the previous example, A_{23}, the cofactor of a_{23} in the matrix of (1-24), is $(-1)^5(4)$—that is, -4. We are now prepared for a more general definition of the determinant of an $n \times n$ square matrix A.

DEFINITION 1.6: DETERMINANT OF A SQUARE MATRIX. The determinant of A, denoted $|A|$, is equal to

$$\text{(a)} \quad \sum_{j=1}^{n} a_{ij}A_{ij} \qquad \text{(for any } i)$$

or

$$\text{(b)} \quad \sum_{i=1}^{n} a_{ij}A_{ij} \qquad \text{(for any } j).$$

Part (a) says that the value of the determinant can be found by (1) selecting any row (any i) in A and (2) summing the products of each element in that row and its respective cofactor. Part (b) says that the same value can be found by (1) selecting any column (any j) in A and (2) summing the product of each element in that column and its respective cofactor.[7]
We already found in (1-24) that $|A| = -12$ for

$$A = \begin{bmatrix} 1 & 1 & 1 \\ 2 & 0 & 6 \\ 3 & 7 & 1 \end{bmatrix},$$

using the diagonal rule for 3×3 matrices. Applying part (a) of Definition 1.6 to row 3 requires that we calculate $a_{31}A_{31} + a_{32}A_{32} + a_{33}A_{33}$—more specifically, $(3)A_{31} + (7)A_{32} + (1)A_{33}$. Each of the three cofactors requires evaluation of a 2×2 determinant.

$$A_{31} = (-1)^4 \begin{vmatrix} 1 & 1 \\ 0 & 6 \end{vmatrix} = 6,$$

$$A_{32} = (-1)^5 \begin{vmatrix} 1 & 1 \\ 2 & 6 \end{vmatrix} = -4,$$

$$A_{33} = (-1)^6 \begin{vmatrix} 1 & 1 \\ 2 & 0 \end{vmatrix} = -2.$$

Therefore $|A| = (3)(6) + (7)(-4) + (1)(-2) = -12$, as before. Using part (b) of the definition for column 1, we find

[7] The reader who is interested in more details on the theory of determinants is referred to the books by Aitken [1], Hadley [3] or Perlis [4], listed at the end of this chapter.

$$|A| = a_{11}A_{11} + a_{21}A_{21} + a_{31}A_{31}$$
$$= (1)A_{11} + (2)A_{21} + (3)A_{31}$$
$$= (1)(-42) + (2)(6) + (3)(6) = -12.$$

Note that the general rules given in Definition 1.6 convert the problem of evaluating one $n \times n$ determinant into n calculations with determinants of size $(n-1) \times (n-1)$, since one row and one column are deleted in finding each of the cofactors along any row or down any column. Since there are simple diagonal rules for the 2×2 and 3×3 cases, one can in principle reduce the problem of evaluating a determinant of any size to a number of calculations involving evaluation of 3×3 (or 2×2) determinants. The number of such calculations becomes very large very quickly, however. A 6×6 determinant would break down into a sum involving 120 3×3 determinants. Judicious selection of the row or column along which to evaluate the determinant can save time and effort, since a large number of 0's or 1's in a row or column eliminates or reduces some of the calculations. In addition, computers can evaluate determinants of even large matrices quickly.

The second part of the definition of A^{-1} for the 2×2 case, in (1-23), is a matrix of the same size as A. This has a specific name and can also be generalized to larger cases.

DEFINITION 1.7: ADJOINT OF A SQUARE MATRIX. The adjoint of a square matrix A, denoted adj A, is a matrix that has for its element in row i and column j the *cofactor* of the element in A', the *transpose* of A, in row i and column j.

If we denote the elements of adj A as a_{ij}^*, then $a_{ij}^* = A_{ij}'$ or $a_{ij}^* = A_{ji}$, because of the way the transposition operation was defined (Operation 3). If A is an $n \times n$ matrix, to determine the elements of adj A we must evaluate n^2 determinants of size $(n-1) \times (n-1)$. For the general 3×3 matrix,

$$\text{adj } A = \begin{bmatrix} A_{11} & A_{12} & A_{13} \\ A_{21} & A_{22} & A_{23} \\ A_{31} & A_{32} & A_{33} \end{bmatrix}' = \begin{bmatrix} A_{11} & A_{21} & A_{31} \\ A_{12} & A_{22} & A_{32} \\ A_{13} & A_{23} & A_{33} \end{bmatrix}.$$

For example, the elements of the top row of adj A would be

$$(+) \begin{vmatrix} a_{22} & a_{23} \\ a_{32} & a_{33} \end{vmatrix}, \quad (-) \begin{vmatrix} a_{12} & a_{13} \\ a_{32} & a_{33} \end{vmatrix}, \quad \text{and} \quad (+) \begin{vmatrix} a_{12} & a_{13} \\ a_{22} & a_{23} \end{vmatrix}.$$

In the general 2×2 case,

$$\text{adj } A = \begin{bmatrix} a_{22} & -a_{12} \\ -a_{21} & a_{11} \end{bmatrix}.$$

Thus, (1-23) could be written $A^{-1} = (1/|A|)$ [adj A]. And this definition is completely general, as will be shown in the next section. [The reader should convince himself that the matrix on the right-hand side of (1-23), which was derived from the definition of the inverse for the 2×2 case, is indeed the adjoint of the general 2×2 matrix A.]

OPERATION 5: MATRIX DIVISION.   To divide by a square matrix is to multiply by its inverse (or reciprocal), denoted A^{-1}, and $A^{-1} = (1/|A|)$ [adj A].

1.3.   SYSTEMS OF LINEAR EQUATIONS: A PREVIEW

We saw earlier, in (1-4) through (1-10), how the solution to a particularly simple equation "system" could be obtained by operations on its matrix representation—that is, by applying matrix algebra. We now examine a less simple system of equations whose structure requires a different matrix representation; this will make clear the logic of the definition of matrix multiplication and the usefulness of the concept of the inverse. The concern of this chapter (and the next) is exclusively with *linear* equation systems. These are systems whose individual equations contain variables to the first power only; no x^2's, no products of variables, $x_i x_j$, no trigonometric, exponential, or more complicated functions of variables (such as $\log x$, $\cos x$) are allowed. Thus each equation can be represented geometrically by a straight line or plane or hyperplane;[8] none of them curves.

Suppose we have three linear equations involving three unknowns:

$$\begin{aligned} x_1 + \ x_2 + \ x_3 &= 18, \\ 2x_1 \qquad + 6x_3 &= \ 6, \\ 3x_1 + 7x_2 + \ x_3 &= 12. \end{aligned} \qquad (1\text{-}25)$$

(The second equation can be thought of as a function of x_1, x_2, and x_3; the coefficient multiplying x_2 is 0.)

These equations might have arisen in the following context. In a pre-election campaign a political candidate is deciding how to change, from week to week, his news media exposure to the voting public in a metropolitan area. He has 15-second spot announcements on radio (x_1) and on TV (x_3) and quarter-page evening newspaper advertisements (x_2); he is trying to decide how to *change* (if at all) his use of these media next week from the current week. He is at present concerned in particular about

---

[8] The prefix "hyper" is usually used to extend three-dimensional geometric concepts to higher-dimensional space—hyperline, hyperplane, and so on.

inroads that his opponent has made in three particular districts of the city (call them a, b, and c), and his campaign manager advises him that in the coming week he should try to *gain* 1800, 600, and 1200 voters, respectively, in these three critical districts. Moreover, a consulting firm has made estimates of the expected number of votes to be gained in each of the districts by each type of advertisement. From a 15-second radio spot announcement they estimate a probable gain of 100, 200, and 300 voters in districts a, b, and c, respectively. The coefficients associated with x_2 and x_3 in equations (1-25) should be interpreted similarly for newspaper ads and TV spot announcements; in particular, the $0x_2$ term in the second equation means that evening newspaper advertisements do nothing toward gaining voters in district b—perhaps because of literacy level or because of geographic location (out of the delivery area).

Thus the left-hand side of any equation in (1-25) gives the total voter gain to be expected in any one district for a particular set of x_1, x_2 and x_3; that is, for a set of decisions on changes in utilization of the citywide media an $x_2 = 5$ would mean that the candidate would buy five *more* evening newspaper advertisements next week than he did this week, an $x_1 = -4$ would mean use four *fewer* radio spots, and so on. The right-hand side of any equation gives his manager's assessment of needed voter support in one of the critical districts. (In all equations, both sides have been divided by 100 simply for convenience.) Hence the problem is to try to find a program of media utilization for the coming week that will achieve the desired increase in votes.

If we define

$$X = \begin{bmatrix} x_1 \\ x_2 \\ x_3 \end{bmatrix}, \qquad B = \begin{bmatrix} 18 \\ 6 \\ 12 \end{bmatrix}, \quad \text{and} \quad A = \begin{bmatrix} 1 & 1 & 1 \\ 2 & 0 & 6 \\ 3 & 7 & 1 \end{bmatrix}, \qquad (1\text{-}26)$$

and given the definitions of matrix multiplication and matrix equality, we see that the three equations in (1-25) can be represented by the one *matrix* equation

$$AX = B. \qquad (1\text{-}27)$$

The reader should note that the conformability requirement for multiplication is met by A and X, and he should convince himself that (1-27) actually *does* represent exactly the three-equation system in (1-25). In addition, he should compare this matrix equation and the system it represents with (1-6) and (1-4). It is precisely because of the way that matrix multiplication is defined that systems of linear equations such as (1-25) can be represented so compactly using matrices.

Therefore, to solve these equations for the values of the x's in terms of the known parameters (the elements of A and B), we utilize the concepts of the inverse and identity matrices.

$$A^{-1}AX = A^{-1}B, \tag{1-28}$$
$$IX = A^{-1}B, \tag{1-29}$$
$$X = A^{-1}B. \tag{1-30}$$

In (1-28) we *pre*multiply both sides of the equation by A^{-1}, *provided it exists*. The conformability requirement is met, and, as in ordinary algebra, if equals are multiplied by equals, the results are equal. But, by definition, $A^{-1}A = I$; hence (1-29). Note that it is not possible to *post*multiply both sides of (1-27) by A^{-1}; B is a 3×1 matrix, A^{-1} is 3×3, the same size as A, and hence BA^{-1} is not defined. And it would be pointless to multiply in that order in any case, since the object is eventually to have X alone on the left, which means to eliminate the A by "dividing through" by it. Because of the definition of I, (1-29) can be written as in (1-30). Thus, if any solution exists, it can be found as the product of two matrices (a matrix and a vector) whose values are known (B) or can be found (A^{-1}).

Since the coefficient matrix A for equation system (1-25) is exactly the 3×3 matrix whose determinant we found in (1-24) to be -12, we know that A^{-1} exists. Therefore, it is necessary to find adj A. In this case

$$\text{adj } A = \begin{bmatrix} -42 & 6 & 6 \\ 16 & -2 & -4 \\ 14 & -4 & -2 \end{bmatrix}$$

and, since $|A| = -12$,

$$A^{-1} = \begin{bmatrix} \frac{7}{2} & -\frac{1}{2} & -\frac{1}{2} \\ -\frac{4}{3} & \frac{1}{6} & \frac{1}{3} \\ -\frac{7}{6} & \frac{1}{3} & \frac{1}{6} \end{bmatrix}.$$

(The reader should derive at least some of the elements in adj A himself and also be convinced that $AA^{-1} = A^{-1}A = I$.) Therefore, from (1-30),

$$X = \begin{bmatrix} \frac{7}{2} & -\frac{1}{2} & -\frac{1}{2} \\ -\frac{4}{3} & \frac{1}{6} & \frac{1}{3} \\ -\frac{7}{6} & \frac{1}{3} & \frac{1}{6} \end{bmatrix} \begin{bmatrix} 18 \\ 6 \\ 12 \end{bmatrix} = \begin{bmatrix} 54 \\ -19 \\ -17 \end{bmatrix}, \tag{1-31}$$

or, more specifically, the values $x_1 = 54$, $x_2 = -19$, and $x_3 = -17$ will satisfy the system (1-25). Moreover, since we know that the inverse to a given matrix is unique, and since B is a vector of values particular to this system, the values for the unknown x's are unique; no other set of x_1, x_2, and x_3 will satisfy (1-25). In the context of the political candidate's problem, he should *reduce* his use of newspaper and TV spot announcements (by 19 quarter-page ads and 17 quarter-minute films, respectively) and concentrate heavily on radio announcements (54 *more* 15-second spots than the current week).

In this case, as earlier, we have found the values for the unknowns in the system by initially abstracting from the specific parameters, manipulating the matrix representation of the problem using the definitions and operations of matrix algebra, and then reintroducing the particular values after the general solution was found.[9]

Having gone through the algebra once, we now realize that a square linear equation system—one with the same number of variables as linear equations in those variables—of *any* size can be represented by the same matrix equation as in (1-27), namely $AX = B$. Only the dimensions of the matrices change (although X and B remain column vectors). And the unique solution to the system will *always* be given by $X = A^{-1}B$, provided that A does have an inverse. We therefore have an interest in recognizing whether or not a determinant is zero, since the nonzeroness of the determinant is both a necessary and a sufficient condition for the existence of the inverse. If the determinant of a matrix is *not* zero, the matrix is said to be *nonsingular;* thus, only nonsingular matrices have inverses. A *singular* matrix is one whose determinant *is* zero.

Several mathematical properties of determinants help to isolate cases in which the value of determinant is zero and hence in which the matrix is singular. They are therefore relevant for the analysis of square systems of linear equations, at least insofar as they help to establish when a system has a unique solution and when it does not.

Useful properties of determinants

PROPERTY 1. The determinant of a matrix A is equal to the determinant of the transpose of A—that is, $|A| = |A'|$. This follows directly from Definition 1.6, since the elements and their corresponding cofactors

---

[9] Note that, once matrix multiplication and division are defined, we can represent the original equation system (1-4) as in (1-27). If we let

$$A = \begin{bmatrix} 1 & 0 & 0 \\ 0 & 1 & 0 \\ 0 & 0 & 1 \end{bmatrix}, \quad X = \begin{bmatrix} x_1 \\ x_2 \\ x_3 \end{bmatrix}, \quad \text{and} \quad B = \begin{bmatrix} (6-1) \\ (41-7) \\ (5-5) \end{bmatrix} = \begin{bmatrix} 5 \\ 34 \\ 0 \end{bmatrix},$$

then $AX = B$ represents (1-4). Hence, since $|A| = 1$, the solution is given as in (1-30) by $X = A^{-1}B$. The identity matrix of any size is its own inverse (why?), and thus the solution is

$$X = IB = \begin{bmatrix} 5 \\ 34 \\ 0 \end{bmatrix},$$

exactly as in (1-10). This obviously should be true, since in defining B for the representation $AX = B$, we have performed the subtractions necessary to solve the system. The point is that the representation in (1-27) and the solution in (1-30) are perfectly general for n linear equations with n unknowns.

selected from *row i* of A will be identical to the elements and their cofactors[10] from *column i* of A'. Therefore, in the properties that follow, we may speak of row characteristics and column characteristics interchangeably.

PROPERTY 2.   If any column or row of a square matrix contains all 0's, the determinant of that matrix is 0. This is obvious from Definition 1.6. We can choose to expand along the column or row containing all 0 elements. Thus each cofactor will be multiplied by 0 and the sum will be 0.

PROPERTY 3.   Multiplication of the elements in any column or row of a square matrix by a constant, say c, multiplies the value of the determinant of the original matrix by the same amount, c. This is again obvious from the general definition. We can select the row or column that has been augmented as the one along which to expand, and the multiplier c can be factored out.

PROPERTY 4.   If any two rows or columns of a square matrix are interchanged, the value of the determinant of that matrix changes sign. This does not follow quite as directly from Definition 1.6 for a determinant,[11] but it leads immediately to two useful observations, both of which pertain to singular matrices:

PROPERTY 4(a).   If two (or more) rows or columns in a matrix are equal, the determinant of the matrix is 0. This follows since the interchange of two identical rows or columns would produce no discernible numerical change in the matrix, yet the sign of its determinant must reverse. The only case in which the positive value and the negative value of a number are the same is when the number is 0.

PROPERTY 4(b).   If two (or more) rows or columns in a matrix are proportional, the determinant of the matrix is 0. This is a direct result of Properties 3 and 4(a).

In particular, Properties 2, 4(a), and 4(b) give us some information on whether or not a matrix will have an inverse. For example, we know from Property 2 that if

---

[10] This property, $|A| = |A'|$, is easily demonstrated for the general 2×2 and 3×3 cases using parts (a) and (b) of Definition 1.6 (the reader should do this). In examining the property for the 4×4 case, the cofactors down column i of A' will involve determinants of 3×3 matrices that are the transposes of those in the cofactors of elements across row i of A. But from the general demonstration of $|A| = |A'|$ for the 3×3 case, these determinants will be identical. Hence the property follows for the 5×5, ..., $n \times n$ case.

[11] It relies on an even more general (but operationally less useful) definition of a determinant. Again, the interested reader should see Aitken [1], Hadley [3], or Perlis [4].

$$A = \begin{bmatrix} 1 & 2 & 3 \\ 0 & 0 & 0 \\ 4 & 6 & 2 \end{bmatrix},$$

there is no need to try to find A^{-1}; it does not exist, since $|A| = 0$. Similarly, if

$$B = \begin{bmatrix} 1 & 2 & 3 \\ 6 & 6 & 4 \\ 2 & 4 & 6 \end{bmatrix},$$

we know that B is singular (there is no B^{-1}), since rows 1 and 3 of B are proportional—Property 4(b). (The reader should convince himself that $|B| = 0$ by employing the diagonal rule for 3×3 matrices.) Therefore, if the coefficient (A) matrix in a system of n equations in n unknowns exhibits any of these properties, we know that it is impossible to obtain a solution to the system. It will be our interest in the next chapter to investigate more extensively the nature of the problem when a unique solution does not exist. Clearly there is something wrong with the system of equations; we want to be able to be more specific about what the trouble is.

One further mathematical property of determinants will enable us to show precisely why it is that $A^{-1} = (1/|A|)[\text{adj } A]$ in all cases. We derived the result for the 2×2 case and simply stated, in Operation 5, that it held for square matrices of any size.

PROPERTY 5. Expansion of a determinant by *alien cofactors* yields a value of zero. That is,

$$\text{(a)} \quad \sum_{j=1}^{n} a_{ij} A_{i'j} = 0 \qquad \text{(where } i \neq i')$$

and

$$\text{(b)} \quad \sum_{i=1}^{n} a_{ij} A_{ij'} = 0 \qquad \text{(where } j \neq j').$$

In part (a), Property 5 says that expansion along any row i [from part (a) of Definition 1.6] but using the cofactors from another row i' (which is what makes them "alien") necessarily gives a result of 0. And similarly for part (b) of Definition 1.6, using cofactors from some other column j'. (The reader can easily demonstrate that this is true for a small specific example.)

The proof relies on the fact that the alien cofactor expansion is equivalent to finding the determinant of a matrix with two rows (i and i') or two columns (j and j') that are equal. By Property 4(a) of determinants, we know that the value must be 0. Consider the general 3×3 case—that is,

$$A = \begin{bmatrix} a_{11} & a_{12} & a_{13} \\ a_{21} & a_{22} & a_{23} \\ a_{31} & a_{32} & a_{33} \end{bmatrix}.$$

Expanding as in (a) of Property 5—using elements from row 1 and cofactors from row 2—we have

$$a_{11}A_{21} + a_{12}A_{22} + a_{13}A_{23} = -a_{11}\begin{vmatrix} a_{12} & a_{13} \\ a_{32} & a_{33} \end{vmatrix} + a_{12}\begin{vmatrix} a_{11} & a_{13} \\ a_{31} & a_{33} \end{vmatrix} - a_{13}\begin{vmatrix} a_{11} & a_{12} \\ a_{31} & a_{32} \end{vmatrix}.$$

To show that this is exactly zero, we modify A so that row 1 replaces row 2. Thus we have a new matrix

$$\tilde{A} = \begin{bmatrix} a_{11} & a_{12} & a_{13} \\ a_{11} & a_{12} & a_{13} \\ a_{31} & a_{32} & a_{33} \end{bmatrix}.$$

Finding $|\tilde{A}|$ by *proper* expansion across row 2 will generate precisely the same expression as in the alien cofactor expression from A;

$$|\tilde{A}| = -a_{11}\begin{vmatrix} a_{12} & a_{13} \\ a_{32} & a_{33} \end{vmatrix} + a_{12}\begin{vmatrix} a_{11} & a_{13} \\ a_{31} & a_{33} \end{vmatrix} - a_{13}\begin{vmatrix} a_{11} & a_{12} \\ a_{31} & a_{32} \end{vmatrix}.$$

But we know $|\tilde{A}| = 0$ by Property 4(a) and hence $a_{11}A_{21} + a_{12}A_{22} + a_{13}A_{23} = 0$. This can be generalized to *any* pair of alien rows or columns in a square matrix of any size.

We now return to the problem of the inverse for a square matrix of any size. Given an $n \times n$ matrix A and its adjoint,

$$\text{adj } A = \begin{bmatrix} A_{11} & A_{21} & \cdots & A_{n1} \\ A_{12} & A_{22} & \cdots & A_{n2} \\ \vdots & & & \\ A_{1n} & A_{2n} & \cdots & A_{nn} \end{bmatrix},$$

we can form the product of A and its adjoint,

$$A[\text{adj } A] = \begin{bmatrix} \sum_{j=1}^{n} a_{1j}A_{1j} & \sum_{j=1}^{n} a_{1j}A_{2j} & \cdots & \sum_{j=1}^{n} a_{1j}A_{nj} \\ \sum_{j=1}^{n} a_{2j}A_{1j} & \sum_{j=1}^{n} a_{2j}A_{2j} & \cdots & \sum_{j=1}^{n} a_{2j}A_{nj} \\ \vdots & & & \\ \sum_{j=1}^{n} a_{nj}A_{1j} & \sum_{j=1}^{n} a_{nj}A_{2j} & \cdots & \sum_{j=1}^{n} a_{nj}A_{nj} \end{bmatrix}. \quad (1\text{-}32)$$

We have collected terms under summation signs to save space and also to focus sharply on the nature of these sums. The upper left sum is just

$|A|$, evaluated by Definition 1.6, part (a), along row 1. Similarly, the element in row 2, column 2 of the product is also $|A|$, using the same rule, from Definition 1.6, along row 2 of A. The same is true for all elements on the main diagonal of the product in (1-32). On the other hand, *all* off-diagonal elements in this product represent sums using elements from one row and cofactors from some other row—they are expansions by alien cofactors and hence equal 0. Thus,

$$A[\text{adj } A] = \begin{bmatrix} |A| & 0 & \cdots & 0 \\ 0 & |A| & \cdots & 0 \\ \vdots & & & \\ 0 & 0 & \cdots & |A| \end{bmatrix} = |A| \begin{bmatrix} 1 & 0 & \cdots & 0 \\ 0 & 1 & \cdots & 0 \\ \vdots & & & \\ 0 & 0 & \cdots & 1 \end{bmatrix} = |A|I.$$

(1-33)

But if $A[\text{adj } A] = |A|I$, then, dividing by $|A|$, which is a scalar,

$$A \left[\frac{\text{adj } A}{|A|} \right] = I,$$

(1-34)

and hence the matrix that postmultiplies A in (1-34) must be the inverse of A, since the product of the two gives the identity matrix:

$$A^{-1} = \left(\frac{1}{|A|} \right) [\text{adj } A].$$

(1-35)

Partitioned matrices and the inverse

The elements of the inverse matrix can also be found in blocks, using the concept of partitioning and the logic of the 2×2 case in (1-21) and (1-22), above. Let A be a square $n \times n$ matrix, partitioned into four general submatrices, as in (1-15), where A_I and A_IV are square.

$$\underset{(n \times n)}{A} = \begin{array}{c} q \ \{ \\ n - q \ \{ \end{array} \overbrace{\begin{bmatrix} \overbrace{A_\text{I}}^{q} & \overbrace{A_\text{II}}^{n-q} \\ \hline A_\text{III} & A_\text{IV} \end{bmatrix}}_{n} \Big\} \, n$$

where A_I has dimensions $q \times q$ and hence A_IV is $(n - q) \times (n - q)$; these two "on-diagonal" submatrices are intentionally made square. Denote the $n \times n$ inverse, A^{-1}, as the matrix R (for reciprocal) and let R be partitioned in the same way.

$$\underset{(n \times n)}{R} = \begin{array}{c} q \ \{ \\ n - q \ \{ \end{array} \begin{bmatrix} \overbrace{R_\text{I}}^{q} & \overbrace{R_\text{II}}^{n-q} \\ \hline R_\text{III} & R_\text{IV} \end{bmatrix},$$

with R_I a $q \times q$ matrix. It follows that the dimensions of the other submatrices in R are identical to those in corresponding locations in A. Then the defining relation for the inverse $AA^{-1} = AR = I$ can be shown as

$$\left[\begin{array}{c|c} A_I & A_{II} \\ \hline A_{III} & A_{IV} \end{array} \right] \left[\begin{array}{c|c} R_I & R_{II} \\ \hline R_{III} & R_{IV} \end{array} \right] = I. \tag{1-36}$$

The multiplication on the left can be carried out following (1-17) for the product of any pair of conformably partitioned matrices; the $n \times n$ identity matrix on the right can similarly be partitioned into

$$\underset{(n \times n)}{I} = \begin{array}{c} q \\ n - q \end{array} \begin{Bmatrix} \overbrace{}^{q} & \overbrace{}^{n-q} \\ \left[\begin{array}{c|c} I & O \\ \hline O & I \end{array} \right] \end{Bmatrix}.$$

Thus (1-36) can be looked at as the four *matrix* equations

$$(1) \quad A_I R_I + A_{II} R_{III} = I, \quad (2) \quad A_{III} R_I + A_{IV} R_{III} = O, \quad (1\text{-}37a)$$
$$(1) \quad A_I R_{II} + A_{II} R_{IV} = O, \quad (2) \quad A_{III} R_{II} + A_{IV} R_{IV} = I, \quad (1\text{-}37b)$$

just as the 2×2 case involved four simple algebraic equations (1-22). [The reader should convince himself that all products and terms in (1-37) meet the conformability requirements for multiplication, addition, and equality.] Recall that the a_{ij} are known, the r_{ij} are to be found. Assume that the inverse for A_{IV} exists and can be found. Then, from (1-37a)(2),

$$R_{III} = -A_{IV}^{-1} A_{III} R_I. \tag{1-38}$$

Substituting this relation into (1-37a)(1),

$$A_I R_I - A_{II} A_{IV}^{-1} A_{III} R_I = I,$$
$$(A_I - A_{II} A_{IV}^{-1} A_{III}) R_I = I,$$

and hence

$$R_I = (A_I - A_{II} A_{IV}^{-1} A_{III})^{-1} \tag{1-39}$$

From (1-37b)(2), multiplying by A_{IV}^{-1} again,

$$A_{IV}^{-1} A_{III} R_{II} + R_{IV} = A_{IV}^{-1},$$

and thus

$$R_{IV} = A_{IV}^{-1} - A_{IV}^{-1} A_{III} R_{II}. \tag{1-40}$$

Substituting into (1-37b)(1),

$$A_I R_{II} + A_{II}(A_{IV}^{-1} - A_{IV}^{-1} A_{III} R_{II}) = O$$

or

$$(A_I - A_{II} A_{IV}^{-1} A_{III}) R_{II} = -A_{II} A_{IV}^{-1},$$

but, using the result in (1-39), this becomes

$$R_{II} = -R_I A_{II} A_{IV}^{-1}. \tag{1-41}$$

Therefore, from (1-38) through (1-41) we see that it is possible to find all the elements of the inverse matrix R, provided that we solve equations in the correct order. First we must find A_{IV}^{-1}. Then (1) find R_I, using (1-39), which involves only the known A's; (2) use the result for R_I in (1-38) and (1-41) to find the elements of the "off-diagonal" blocks R_{III} and R_{II}; (3) finally, use R_{II} in (1-40) to derive R_{IV}. The process of "solving" these four matrix equations parallels exactly the logic used on the four regular equations in (1-22a) and (1-22b). There four elements a_{ij} were known and four unknown elements x_{ij} were to be determined. In the case above, four matrices A_i were known and four unknown matrices R_i were to be found.

We see that finding A^{-1} in this way requires finding inverses to two smaller matrices—A_{IV}, which is $(n-q) \times (n-q)$, and $(A_I - A_{II} A_{IV}^{-1} A_{III})$, which is $q \times q$—and performing several matrix multiplications. It is clear that for A matrices that are large, this approach may be easier than using the general definition (1-35), which requires the adjoint of the entire A matrix. For A matrices with particular structures, the solution via (1-38) through (1-41) may be especially simple. For example, suppose A can be partitioned into

$$\left[\begin{array}{c|c} I & A_{II} \\ \hline O & A_{IV} \end{array} \right].$$

Then the reader should use (1-38) through (1-41) to show that

$$A^{-1} = \left[\begin{array}{c|c} I & -A_{II} A_{IV}^{-1} \\ \hline O & A_{IV}^{-1} \end{array} \right]$$

—that is, that only one smaller inverse, A_{IV}^{-1}, needs to be found.

Cramer's rule

It will be useful in the analysis of equation systems, especially those in which the coefficient matrix A turns out to be singular, to recall another method for solving square systems of linear equations—namely Cramer's rule. The rule says that any x_i in an $n \times n$ system of linear equations $AX = B$ is given as the ratio of two determinants.

Specifically,

$$x_i = \frac{|A_{Bi}|}{|A|}. \tag{1-42}$$

The denominator is just the determinant of the matrix of coefficients from the equation system; the numerator is the determinant of a matrix formed from A by replacing its ith column (when solving for x_i) by the right-hand vector B.

We apply this solution rule to the 3 × 3 system in (1-25):

$$x_1 = \frac{|A_{B1}|}{|A|}, \qquad x_2 = \frac{|A_{B2}|}{|A|}, \qquad x_3 = \frac{|A_{B3}|}{|A|}.$$

Recall that the specifics of the problem were

$$A = \begin{bmatrix} 1 & 1 & 1 \\ 2 & 0 & 6 \\ 3 & 7 & 1 \end{bmatrix} \quad \text{and} \quad B = \begin{bmatrix} 18 \\ 6 \\ 12 \end{bmatrix}.$$

Since we have already found $|A| = -12$, only the numerators need to be evaluated. For x_1,

$$A_{B1} = \begin{bmatrix} 18 & 1 & 1 \\ 6 & 0 & 6 \\ 12 & 7 & 1 \end{bmatrix},$$

and therefore $|A_{B1}| = -648$, using the diagonal rule for 3 × 3 determinants. Similarly, $|A_{B2}| = 228$ and $|A_{B3}| = 204$, so that, by Cramer's rule,

$$x_1 = \frac{-648}{-12} = 54, \qquad x_2 = \frac{228}{-12} = -19, \qquad x_3 = \frac{204}{-12} = -17, \quad (1\text{-}43)$$

which is identical with the earlier results in (1-31).

This approach to equation solving involves evaluating $n + 1$ determinants of size $n \times n$ (for n equations in n unknowns), and since evaluation of larger size determinants using Definition 1.6 is rather tedious, Cramer's rule does not necessarily provide a method of great computational advantage for systems larger than 3 × 3 or 4 × 4. However, it will be useful analytically to visualize the solution values in a linear equation system as ratios of determinants, especially for equation systems in which a unique solution does not exist. In fact, it is clear that the requirement for the existence of A^{-1} is exactly the requirement that the denominators in each of the Cramer's-rule solutions—namely $|A|$—not be zero.

Using the matrix concepts that the reader now has, it is easy to see exactly why Cramer's rule works—why the ratios of determinants are the solution values for the unknown x's. Recall the completely general solution in (1-30): $X = A^{-1}B$. In (1-35) we generalized the definition of the inverse: $A^{-1} = (1/|A|)[\text{adj } A]$. Thus we may write the solution (1-35) as

$$X = A^{-1}B = \left(\frac{1}{|A|}\right)[\text{adj } A]B = \left(\frac{1}{|A|}\right)\begin{bmatrix} A_{11} & A_{21} & \cdots & A_{n1} \\ A_{12} & A_{22} & \cdots & A_{n2} \\ \vdots & & & \\ A_{1n} & A_{2n} & \cdots & A_{nn} \end{bmatrix}\begin{bmatrix} b_1 \\ b_2 \\ \vdots \\ b_n \end{bmatrix}.$$

$$(1\text{-}44)$$

Therefore, the value for a particular x_i (that is, the ith element in the column vector X) is given by $(1/|A|)$ times the product of the ith row of the adjoint and B.

$$x_i = \left(\frac{1}{|A|}\right)(A_{1i}b_1 + A_{2i}b_2 + \cdots + A_{ni}b_n). \qquad (1\text{-}45)$$

(Recall that the subscripts on the elements in the adjoint matrix are reversed from their usual order because we are dealing with cofactors of the *transpose* of A.)

Define the matrix A_{Bi} as the original A with the ith column replaced by B. That is,

$$A = \begin{bmatrix} a_{11} & a_{12} & \cdots & a_{1i} & \cdots & a_{1n} \\ a_{21} & a_{22} & \cdots & a_{2i} & \cdots & a_{2n} \\ \vdots & & & & & \\ a_{n1} & a_{n2} & \cdots & a_{ni} & \cdots & a_{nn} \end{bmatrix}$$

becomes

$$A_{Bi} = \begin{bmatrix} a_{11} & a_{12} & \cdots & b_1 & \cdots & a_{1n} \\ a_{21} & a_{22} & \cdots & b_2 & \cdots & a_{2n} \\ \vdots & & & & & \\ a_{n1} & a_{n2} & \cdots & b_n & \cdots & a_{nn} \end{bmatrix}.$$

Using part (b) of Definition 1.6, evaluate $|A_{Bi}|$ by expanding along the ith column.

$$|A_{Bi}| = b_1 A_{1i} + b_2 A_{2i} + \cdots + b_n A_{ni}. \qquad (1\text{-}46)$$

Since the sum on the right side of (1-46) appears in (1-45), we can condense (1-45) to read

$$x_i = \left(\frac{1}{|A|}\right)|A_{Bi}| = \frac{|A_{Bi}|}{|A|}, \qquad (1\text{-}47)$$

which is just Cramer's rule, (1-42).

Simple equation systems: solution possibilities

To illustrate the direction in which our study of equation systems will move, consider a trivially simple ordinary algebraic equation $ax = b$—for example, $3x = 12$. We know that $x = b/a$ (in the example, $x = 12/3 = 4$), whether we think of dividing by a or multiplying by a^{-1} or $1/a$—*provided that $a \neq 0$*. That is, if $a \neq 0$, a *unique* solution exists. If this requirement is not met, if $a = 0$, there is still something to be learned about the equation, not from the solution form $x = b/a$, but from the original statement $ax = b$. Specifically, we can distinguish the cases in which $b \neq 0$ from the case where $b = 0$. (These appear to be extremely trivial questions in this simple case, but they illustrate the kinds of possibilities that arise in square systems with any number of linear equations and unknowns.)

$a = 0$ *and* $b \neq 0$. For example, $0x = 12$. It is obvious that *no* value of x can be found for which this statement is true. The left-hand side of the statement is *inconsistent* with the right-hand side; 0 times anything cannot possibly equal 12. There is *no* solution.

a = 0 and b = 0. That is, $0x = 0$. In the one-variable, one-equation case this hardly merits discussion, but essentially the same situation will be encountered in larger systems, where it is much more meaningful. In this case, it is clear that *any* value of x will satisfy the equation; hence there are an *infinite* number of solutions.

Thus, when a *unique* solution does not exist, we can distinguish an inconsistent equation having *no* solutions from an equation with an *infinite number* of solutions. In the former case we might say that too much is required of the unknown (none can satisfy the equation), while in the latter case too little is required (too many unknowns can satisfy the equation). These distinctions hold for larger systems. In a particular situation it may be important to know, if a *unique* solution cannot be found, whether the reason is that there are no solutions at all or that there are too many. It is often preferable to learn that solutions exist (although they are not unique) rather than to learn that none can possibly be found.

The 2×2 case illustrates these possibilities with somewhat more generality. We supplement the algebra with a geometric picture of the equations involved in x_1, x_2 space, where we plot values of x_1 along one axis (usually the horizontal axis) and x_2 along a second (usually the vertical). This is termed "solution space" for the problems, because if one or more solutions exist they will appear as a point or points in this same figure. With two unknowns we (conveniently) need only two axes; hence the case is easily represented on paper.

CASE 1: UNIQUE SOLUTION

ALGEBRA

$$(1) \quad 3x_1 + 2x_2 = 7, \qquad (2) \quad 2x_1 + 5x_2 = 12. \qquad (1\text{-}48)$$

GEOMETRY

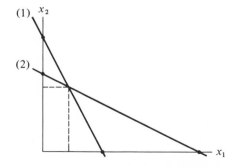

Figure 1.1. Solution-Space Representation of (1-48)

Geometrically, the straight lines representing the relations in equations (1) and (2) in (1-48) intersect in a single point. This point simultaneously satisfies both equations; hence its coordinates—the values of x_1 and x_2 that it represents—are the unique solution to the problem. In compact matrix form,

$$AX = B, \qquad A = \begin{bmatrix} 3 & 2 \\ 2 & 5 \end{bmatrix},$$

hence $|A| = 11 \neq 0$ and therefore we know that a *unique* solution $X = A^{-1}B$ can be found. (The reader should do this; the solution is $x_1 = 1$, $x_2 = 2$.)

CASE 2: NO SOLUTION

ALGEBRA

$$(1) \quad 3x_1 + 2x_2 = 7, \qquad (2) \quad 6x_1 + 4x_2 = 11. \tag{1-49}$$

GEOMETRY

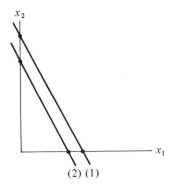

Figure 1.2. Solution-Space Representation of (1-49)

Geometrically, there is no intersection of the two lines in solution space; hence no values of x_1 and x_2 will satisfy both equations at the same time. The requirements on x_1 and x_2 are inconsistent.

$$A = \begin{bmatrix} 3 & 2 \\ 6 & 4 \end{bmatrix} \quad \text{and} \quad |A| = 0.$$

CASE 3: INFINITE NUMBER OF SOLUTIONS

ALGEBRA

$$(1) \quad 3x_1 + 2x_2 = 7, \qquad (2) \quad 6x_1 + 4x_2 = 14. \tag{1-50}$$

GEOMETRY

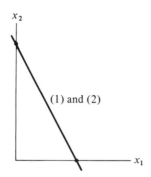

Figure 1.3.   Solution-Space Representation of (1-50)

In solution space the same line represents both equations (1) and (2); these two algebraic statements say exactly the same thing. Equation (2) is just twice equation (1). Therefore the coordinates of *any* point along the line (which extends infinitely far in both directions) will satisfy the requirements of the equations. Algebraically, as in Case 2, $|A| = 0$.

Thus with two linear equations and two unknowns, where we use matrix representations of the systems, it is clear that the absence of a unique solution is indicated by $|A| = 0$, just as in the simpler case $ax = b$ this was true when $a = 0$. Moreover, the distinction in the simple system between no solution and too many solutions depended on the right-hand side, b. In the 2×2 case we see that the right-hand side vector, B, is also crucial, since the equations in Cases 2 and 3 differ *only* in their right-hand sides. To understand completely the role of B in those cases where $|A| = 0$, it will be useful to employ the visual aid provided by the geometry of vectors, through which the notions of linear dependence and independence will be made clear. Then we will be able to classify all possible solution types for *any* linear equation system. This will occupy our attention in Chapter 2.

1.4.   THE GEOMETRY OF VECTORS

We concentrate in this section on a representation for two-element column vectors. The geometry would apply equally well to row vectors, and the logic of the representation can be extended to vectors with any number of elements—even though the geometry is impossible to show, since we will find that we use one axis for each element in vector space figures. We are concerned with *column* vectors, their representation, and operations on them because we will adopt a column-oriented approach for studying equation systems. Specifically, we will find it useful to think of the system $AX = B$ in a more disaggregated form, where A_i represents the ith *column* of A, as

$$A_1x_1 + A_2x_2 + \cdots + A_nx_n = B.$$

The reader should convince himself that this is in fact equivalent to $AX = B$ for the $n \times n$ case and that all conformability requirements are met.

A geometric picture can be associated with any two-element column vector

$$C = \begin{bmatrix} c_1 \\ c_2 \end{bmatrix}$$

Using a pair of axes like the horizontal and vertical in solution space, but without the x_1 and x_2 labels, measure a distance equal to c_1, the first element, along the horizontal axis and measure c_2, the second element, on the vertical axis. A point in this two-dimensional space with coordinates (c_1, c_2) relative to the origin of the two axes is uniquely associated with the vector C; the (algebraic) elements of C locate the (geometric) point in a figure whose horizontal and vertical axes are labeled "first element" (for which we use ϵ_1) and "second element" (ϵ_2), respectively. For later analysis it is convenient to connect the point to the origin $(0, 0)$ in the picture and to put an arrowhead at the point in question; this directed line is sometimes called a ray from the origin.

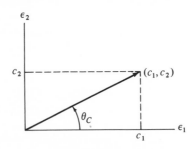

Figure 1.4. Vector-Space Representation of C

It is clear that any two-element vector can be completely described either by its *coordinates* in this geometric space (vector space) or by both its *length* and its *direction*, measured by the angle it makes with the horizontal axis. This angle is often designated θ_C. The algebraic elements of C thus have two geometric or spatial attributes.

1. *Length.* The length, or the *norm*, of a vector $\underset{(2 \times 1)}{C}$, often denoted

$\|C\|$ (or $|C|$, if no ambiguity with determinant notation is possible) is $\sqrt{c_1^2 + c_2^2}$. This is a straightforward application of the Pythagorean theorem. For an n-element vector, the norm is $\left(\sum\limits_{i=1}^{n} c_i^2\right)^{1/2}$.

2. *Direction.* The direction of C is given by the size of θ_C, which is measured by either of two trigonometric relations, its sine or its cosine. Specifically, $\sin \theta_C = c_2/\|C\|$ and $\cos \theta_C = c_1/\|C\|$.

With this correspondence between the algebraic and geometric representations for a two-element column vector, several matrix algebraic operations, when applied to vectors, have geometric interpretations that are useful. In particular, we examine the geometry of (1) multiplication by a scalar (Operation 4A) and (2) addition and subtraction (Operations 1 and 2), since these are the fundamental algebraic operations employed in linear combinations, a concept that we will meet in Section 1.5 and that will be used in the analysis of equation systems in Chapter 2.

The geometry of multiplication by a scalar

Multiplication of a vector by a scalar stretches or shrinks the vector.[12] For example, $2C$ doubles the length of the line representing C. It stretches the line to twice its original length; the *norm* is changed (doubled) but its direction, θ_{2C}, is unaltered. This is easily shown:

$$\|2C\| = \sqrt{(2c_1)^2 + (2c_2)^2} = 2\sqrt{c_1^2 + c_2^2} = 2\|C\|$$

but

$$\sin \theta_{2C} = \frac{2c_2}{2\|C\|} = \frac{c_2}{\|C\|} = \sin \theta_C.$$

Similarly $\frac{1}{3}C$ shrinks the line to one-third of its previous length, again with no change in direction. However, $-3C$ stretches the line to three times its original length *and* changes its orientation by 180 degrees—flips it over. The change in norm should be clear;

$$\|-3C\| = \sqrt{(-3c_1)^2 + (-3c_2)^2} = 3\sqrt{c_1^2 + c_2^2} = 3\|C\|.$$

The change (or reverse) in direction follows from the observation that

$$\sin \theta_{-3C} = \frac{-3c_2}{3\|C\|} = \frac{-c_2}{\|C\|} = -\sin \theta_C$$

and

$$\cos \theta_{-3C} = \frac{-3c_1}{3\|C\|} = \frac{-c_1}{\|C\|} = -\cos \theta_C,$$

---

[12] The fact that multiplication of a vector by an ordinary number only changes the *scale* of the vector is the origin of the term scalar for such a number in matrix algebra.

and the trigonometric fact that if $\sin x = -\sin y$ and $\cos x = -\cos y$, then angles x and y differ by 180 degrees.

Figure 1.5 gives the geometric representation.

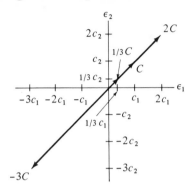

Figure 1.5.   Scalar Multiples of the Vector C

Thus a vector is stretched or shrunk depending on whether the absolute value of the scalar is greater or less than 1; the orientation in space is reversed or not depending on whether the sign of the scalar is negative or positive.

The geometry of addition (and subtraction)

The algebraic operation of addition of two vectors is also easily represented in vector geometry. If

$$C = \begin{bmatrix} c_1 \\ c_2 \end{bmatrix} \quad \text{and} \quad D = \begin{bmatrix} d_1 \\ d_2 \end{bmatrix},$$

we know that the vectors are conformable for matrix addition (both 2×1) and that their sum, S, will be a 2×1 column vector also; adding corresponding elements,

$$S = C + D = \begin{bmatrix} c_1 + d_1 \\ c_2 + d_2 \end{bmatrix}.$$

Geometrically, we know exactly the coordinates of the vector S, namely $(c_1 + d_1)$ units on the horizontal axis, $(c_2 + d_2)$ on the vertical. So we can easily show C, D, and S together (Figure 1.6).

We can visualize the process of "getting to S" from C and D in either of two ways. In Figure 1.7(a) we begin with C located and then, using (c_1, c_2) as the point of origin, add D—that is, add d_1 to the horizontal coordinate and d_2 to the vertical. In Figure 1.7(b) we imagine vector D located initially and then, from that point, add c_1 and c_2, respectively. Since

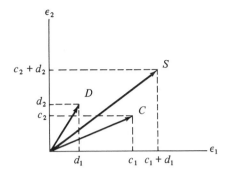

Figure 1.6.   The Sum (S) of Vectors C and D

addition is a commutative operation, the order in which the addition is performed makes no difference, and the coordinates of S are given by the sums of corresponding elements in the two vectors. By combining Figures 1.7(a) and (b), we see that vector addition involves the parallelogram-of-forces concept from physics, where, after all, a force was represented as a vector, since it has a magnitude (length) and a direction (angle). Clearly the sum of several two-element column vectors can be visualized as the formation of a series of parallelograms. The reader should add a third vector E to C and D in Figure 1.8.

Subtraction of vectors involves exactly the same principles. Considering only two-element column vectors, we indicate the geometry of the difference $F - G$. By the rules of matrix subtraction we know that the result will be a two-element column vector. Denoting this by H, we have the matrix statement $F - G = H$. We want to derive H from a vector-space picture of F and G only. Since the matrix statement can be rewritten as $F = G + H$, and we have just examined the geometry of vector addition, we realize that (geometrically) H must be one side of a parallelogram with

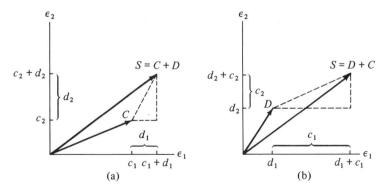

Figure 1.7.   (a) Adding D to C, (b) Adding C to D

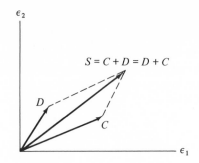

Figure 1.8.   The Sum (S) as the Parallelogram Diagonal

G as a side adjacent to it and F as the diagonal between them [Figure 1.9(a)]. The difference, $G - F$, call it J, would be a vector of the same length but pointing in the opposite direction [Figure 1.9(b)]. It is clear

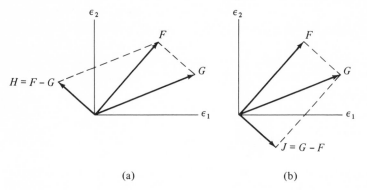

(a)   (b)

Figure 1.9.   (a) The Difference ($H = F - G$) as a Parallelogram Side, (b) the Difference ($J = G - F$) as a Parallelogram Side

that both H and J will be sides in a parallelogram opposite to the line connecting the endpoints of F and G, and hence that both H and J will be parallel to that line and also equal to it in length. Only orientation is governed by whether the statement is $F - G$ or $G - F$—that is, whether F is the diagonal and G is a side of the parallelogram, or vice versa.

Additional vector geometry

In order to exploit fully the visual aid that the geometry of vectors provides in the analysis of equation systems, it is useful to have several additional geometric concepts. These are stepping-stones along the way to a result of major importance—a definition of the area enclosed by two vectors (much as the concepts of a minor and a cofactor were needed for the generalized definition of the inverse). Our interest in the area enclosed by vectors, in turn, is prompted by the fact that it illustrates nicely the fundamental concept of linear independence, which is essential to a general analysis of linear equation systems and forms the subject matter of the next section. For ease of visualization, we will continue to emphasize two-element column vectors in the discussion; the generalization to n-element vectors should be obvious in each case.

DISTANCE BETWEEN TWO VECTORS

The distance between vectors

$$C = \begin{bmatrix} c_1 \\ c_2 \end{bmatrix} \quad \text{and} \quad D = \begin{bmatrix} d_1 \\ d_2 \end{bmatrix}$$

is the distance between their endpoints in vector space. By Pythagoras, this is $\sqrt{(c_1 - d_1)^2 + (c_2 - d_2)^2}$; refer, for example, to Figure 1.6. Since the terms are squared, the order of subtraction can always be written this way.[13] The geometric notion of *distance* between C and D is thus equivalent to the norm of the vector representing their *difference* and the notation $\|C - D\|$ is appropriate. (Recall from Figure 1.9 that H and J will have the same length; hence the norm of *either* would represent the distance between F and G on that figure.)

ANGLE INCLUDED BETWEEN TWO VECTORS

The size of the angle included between two two-element vectors C and D, denoted by ϕ, is measured by its cosine, which can be shown[14] to be

$$\frac{c_1 d_1 + c_2 d_2}{\|C\| \ \|D\|}.$$

[13] With a pair of three-element vectors (that is, three-dimensional vector space), the differences between coordinates on all three axes must be used. Hence, a term $(c_3 - d_3)^2$ would be added under the square root. (The reader who draws well in three dimensions should derive this result.) For n-dimensional vectors, n such differences are necessary—that is, $\left[\sum_{i=1}^{n} (c_i - d_i)^2 \right]^{1/2}$.

[14] The demonstration requires application of the law of cosines, from trigonometry, to the triangle formed by connecting points C and D. Refer again to Figure 1.6. Specifically,

$$2\|C\| \ \|D\| \cos \phi = \|C\|^2 + \|D\|^2 - \|C - D\|^2.$$

$\|C\| = \sqrt{c_1^2 + c_2^2}$, $\|D\| = \sqrt{d_1^2 + d_2^2}$, and $\|C - D\| = \sqrt{(c_1 - d_1)^2 + (c_2 - d_2)^2}$. Substitution and rearrangement gives the result in the text for $\cos \phi$. For two n-element vectors,

$$\cos \phi = \sum_{i=1}^{n} c_i d_i / \|C\| \ \|D\|.$$

The numerator, $c_1 d_1 + c_2 d_2$, is termed the *inner product* or *dot product* of vectors C and D, denoted $C \cdot D$ (hence the second name). This simply defines a different kind of matrix multiplication, one that is possible when the matrices involved are vectors.[15] Therefore, more compactly, $\cos \phi = C \cdot D / \|C\| \|D\|$ (in words, the dot product divided by the product of the norms).[16]

AREA ENCLOSED BY TWO VECTORS

Imagine the parallelogram formed by $C = \begin{bmatrix} c_1 \\ c_2 \end{bmatrix}$ and $D = \begin{bmatrix} d_1 \\ d_2 \end{bmatrix}$ (one of whose diagonals is their sum, as we have seen in Figure 1.8). Then the *area* of this figure can be shown[17] to be precisely $(c_1 d_2 - c_2 d_1)$.

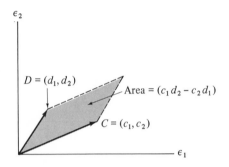

Figure 1.10.   Parallelogram as the Area between Vectors C and D

[15] The reader may wish to note that "ordinary" matrix multiplication and inner-product multiplication are related. For any two n-element column vectors E and F,

$$E \cdot F = \sum_{i=1}^{n} e_i f_i \quad \text{and} \quad E'F = \left[\sum_{i=1}^{n} e_i f_i \right];$$

the former is a number whereas the latter is a one-element matrix (that is, a 1×1 matrix). Except for matrix multiplication, the distinction is generally unimportant. The fact that $E \cdot F$ generates a scalar has led to the term *scalar product* as well for this operation.

[16] Since, for any $n \times 1$ vector E, $\|E\| = \sqrt{e_1^2 + e_2^2 + \cdots + e_n^2} = (E \cdot E)^{1/2}$, $\cos \phi$ can also be shown in several alternative ways. Note also that the distance between vectors E and F can be denoted by $[(E - F) \cdot (E - F)]^{1/2}$.

[17] The demonstration requires a few more trigonometric facts and algebraic manipulation. For any parallelogram, area = (base) (height). The base here can be thought of as $\|C\|$. Then the height is measured perpendicular to C; this height is given by $\|D\| \sin \phi$. Thus area = $\|C\| \|D\| \sin \phi$. Squaring both sides, using the fact that $\sin^2 + \cos^2 = 1$ and the fact that $\cos \phi = C \cdot D / \|C\| \|D\|$, and then extracting the positive square root gives the result in the text. It is more difficult to derive the generalization to n-element vectors. For $n = 3$, the relevant expression is for the *volume*. For $n > 3$, it would be an n-dimensional "hypervolume."

This is the important result. If we imagine a 2×2 matrix A made up of the columns C and D—that is, $A = [C \mid D]$—then this area is just $|A|$. Of particular interest is the case where the area is 0. Geometrically, no area means that vectors C and D are collinear, that they lie along the same ray, and hence that there is either no angle between them or else that the angle is 180 degrees. Since both C and D emanate from the origin, they are also termed parallel. In either case, no parallelogram can be formed, as Figures 1.11(a) and (b) illustrate.

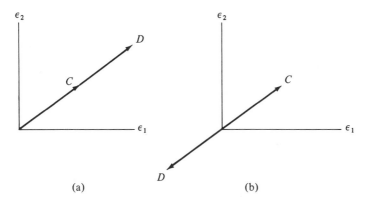

(a)   (b)

Figure 1.11.   (a) Angle of 0° between C and D, (b) Angle of 180° between C and D

For the 2×2 case, we have seen that when $|A| = 0$ the equation system $AX = B$ has no unique solution. Now the singularity of A is seen to have a particular geometric interpretation; its columns are collinear (parallel).

1.5.   LINEAR DEPENDENCE AND INDEPENDENCE

The relationships between algebraic statements and geometric representations will be useful in approaching the concepts of linear dependence and independence between vectors; these, in turn, provide a general framework within which to study linear equation systems of any size.

DEFINITION 1.8: LINEAR COMBINATION OF VECTORS.   Given n vectors $P_1, P_2, \ldots, P_n$ in m-dimensional vector space (that is, each having m elements) and given n scalars $\alpha_1, \alpha_2, \ldots, \alpha_n$, then

$$P_0 = \alpha_1 P_1 + \alpha_2 P_2 + \ldots + \alpha_n P_n = \sum_{i=1}^{n} \alpha_i P_i$$

is called a *linear combination* of the vectors $P_1, P_2, \ldots, P_n$. (Note that P_0 is itself an m-element vector.)[18]

A linear combination is seen to involve only the algebraic operations of multiplication of vectors by scalars and addition of vectors (or subtraction, if some scalars are negative). Therefore P_0 could also be written

$$\sum_{i=1}^{n} P_i \alpha_i,$$

since we have seen that multiplication of a vector by a scalar is a commutative operation. This definition is important, because linear equation systems can be thought of as linear combinations. The general system of two linear equations in two unknowns,

$$\begin{aligned}
a_{11}x_1 + a_{12}x_2 &= b_1, \\
a_{21}x_1 + a_{22}x_2 &= b_2,
\end{aligned} \tag{1-51}$$

in addition to its $AX = B$ form, can also be represented (partitioning A into its two columns, A_1 and A_2) as

$$[A_1 \mid A_2] \left[\frac{x_1}{x_2} \right] = B,$$

or

$$A_1 x_1 + A_2 x_2 = B, \tag{1-52}$$

or, in more explicit form,

$$\left[\begin{array}{c} a_{11} \\ a_{21} \end{array} \right] x_1 + \left[\begin{array}{c} a_{12} \\ a_{22} \end{array} \right] x_2 = \left[\begin{array}{c} b_1 \\ b_2 \end{array} \right].$$

This poses the problem of finding a solution to the system—that is of finding an x_1 and x_2 that satisfy (1-51)—in the following somewhat different form: can the right-hand side, B, be expressed as a *linear combination* of A_1 and A_2, and if so, what are the values of the scalar multipliers involved (the x's)? A_1, A_2, and B can all be represented in two-dimensional vector space. The form of the linear combination requires two operations: (1) possible stretching or shrinking of each vector (multiplication of each A_i by its x_i) and (2) adding these new vectors together. That is, (1) $A_1 x_1 = A_1^*$, $A_2 x_2 = A_2^*$ and then (2) $A_1^* + A_2^* = B$. It should be apparent that in a general two-dimensional case, such as that shown in Figure 1.12, *some* stretching and combining of A_1 and A_2 will lead to B. The solution values for x_1 and x_2 in equations (1-51) are just the amounts by which the lengths

---

[18] When all $\alpha_i \geq 0$, P_0 is termed a *nonnegative linear* combination of the P_i, and when, in addition to being nonnegative, $\sum_i \alpha_i = 1$, P_0 is called a *convex* (linear) combination.

We will meet this concept again in Chapter 4 and later, in dealing with convex sets.

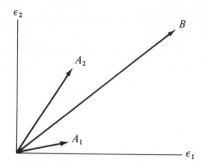

Figure 1.12.   Vector-Space Representation of (1-51)

of A_1 and A_2 must be multiplied. (Obviously an A_i may not need to change at all—$x_i = 1$—or some A_j may need to be reversed in direction—$x_j < 0$.) We may conclude from the geometry that *any pair* of A_1 and A_2 may be used to express any *B as long as A_1 and A_2 are not parallel*. (The reader should construct examples using other nonparallel A_1 and A_2 and other B vectors; a great deal of pushing and pulling may be necessary, but it will always be possible to get to B.) Figure 1.13 illustrates.

A pair of nonparallel two-element vectors is said to *span* the two-dimensional vector space; the vectors are called a *basis* for that space. These basis or spanning vectors may be thought of as a *set of axes* for the space. The fact that they are not necessarily perpendicular is not important for present purposes; what is important is that *any* other point (that is, vector) in two-dimensional vector space may be located using coordinates along these axes. The measures of unit length in the two directions are just the original norms of A_1 and A_2; the actual coordinates of the point (B) relative to the A_1, A_2 axis system are given by x_1 and x_2, the scalar multipliers in the linear combination. (Refer again to Figure 1.13.) In fact, as with "ordinary" axes and units of measure, any point B is located *uniquely*

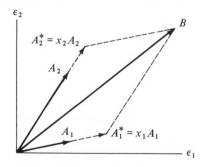

Figure 1.13.   Solution Values to (1-51) as Scalars in the Linear Combination (1-52)

relative to the axes formed by A_1 and A_2. Thus as long as A_1 and A_2 are not parallel, any B can be expressed as a unique linear combination of them. And if A_1 and A_2 are not parallel, then $|A_1 \mid A_2| = |A| \neq 0$. So the requirement of nonsingularity of A, which was a necessary and sufficient condition for the existence of A^{-1}, is equivalent to the requirement that the columns of A be nonparallel.

This is usually put differently: when $|A| \neq 0$, the columns of A are said to be *linearly independent*. The property of linear independence is defined in a more general way. For the present case, A_1 and A_2 would be termed linearly independent if the only x_1 and x_2 for which $A_1x_1 + A_2x_2 = O$ holds are $x_1 = 0$ and $x_2 = 0$. Conversely, if there exist an x_1 and x_2 *not both zero* for which $A_1x_1 + A_2x_2 = O$, then A_1 and A_2 are termed *linearly dependent*. Although the statement may appear cumbersome, it has a simple geometric interpretation. The right-hand side, O, is just $\begin{bmatrix} 0 \\ 0 \end{bmatrix}$ in this case. For linear *independence* of A_1 and A_2, the requirement is that the *only* way to express this particular point, which is the origin, $\begin{bmatrix} 0 \\ 0 \end{bmatrix}$, is by multiplying both vectors by 0—that is, by moving no distance at all along each of the new axes in two-dimensional vector space. If the two vectors are linearly *dependent*, however, the origin can be expressed in other ways in addition to $x_1 = 0$ and $x_2 = 0$. Figures 1.14(a) and 1.14(b) illustrate.

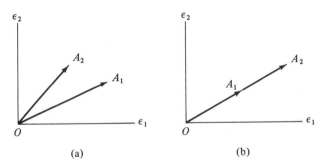

Figure 1.14.   (a) Linear Independence, (b) Linear Dependence

In Figure 1.14(a), the vectors A_1 and A_2 are not parallel—that is, they could be used to form a parallelogram with a positive amount of area. To describe the origin point, the *only* way in which we can stretch or shrink these vectors, before adding them together in a linear combination, is to shrink them both to zero. No other scalars will make the linear combination $A_1x_1 + A_2x_2$ equal to O. On the other hand, Figure 1.14(b) illustrates a pair of parallel vectors A_1 and A_2, which consequently cannot be used for adjacent sides in a parallelogram; there is no angle between them;

$|A_1 \vdots A_2| = 0$. It is clear that there are many ways (an infinite number, in fact) of stretching and shrinking A_1 and A_2 to reach the origin. For example, from the figure it appears that something like twice A_2 ($x_2 = 2$) added to four times A_1 *in the opposite direction* ($x_1 = -4$) would lead to $\begin{bmatrix} 0 \\ 0 \end{bmatrix}$; or twice A_1 ($x_1 = 2$) plus the negative of A_2 ($x_2 = -1$). (The reader should construct specific examples for illustration.) The logic is the same for any number of vectors with any number of elements each.

DEFINITION 1.9: LINEAR DEPENDENCE AND INDEPENDENCE. Vectors A_1, A_2, ..., A_n in m-dimensional vector space (that is, containing m elements each) are *linearly dependent* if there exist n scalars x_1, x_2, ..., x_n *not all zero* such that the linear combination of scalars and vectors equals the m-element null vector—that is, such that

$$x_1A_1 + x_2A_2 + \cdots + x_nA_n = O. \tag{1-53}$$

On the other hand, if the *only* set of x_i for which (1-53) holds is $x_1 = x_2 = \cdots = x_n = 0$, then the vectors A_1, A_2, ..., A_n are *linearly independent*.

To express the notion of linear dependence in a slightly different way, if a vector A_n is a linear combination of vectors A_1, A_2, ..., A_{n-1}, then the set of vectors A_1, A_2, ..., A_n is linearly dependent. This follows directly from Definitions 1.8 and 1.9. Let A_n be a linear combination of A_1, A_2, ..., A_{n-1}, that is,

$$A_n = x_1A_1 + x_2A_2 + \cdots + x_{n-1}A_{n-1},$$

where not all x_i are 0—for if they were, none of the A_i ($i = 1, \ldots, n - 1$) would appear in A_n, hence it would not be appropriate to define A_n as a linear combination of that particular set of A_i.[19] Then, rearranging,

$$x_1A_1 + x_2A_2 + \cdots + x_{n-1}A_{n-1} + (-1)A_n = O.$$

Since not all $x_i = 0$ ($i = 1, \ldots, n - 1$), and in particular $x_n = -1$, the requirement for linear dependence of the A_i is met (Definition 1.9). The converse is also straightforward.

Looked at from this point of view, it is clear that not more than two

---

[19] This is not strictly true, but it is a practical approach. Obviously if A_n is the m-element null vector, then the scalars in $A_n = \sum_{i=1}^{n-1} A_i x_i$ *may* all be zero and yet, since $A_1 x_1 + \cdots + A_{n-1}x_{n-1} + (-1)A_n = O$, the complete set of $A_i (i = 1, \ldots, n)$ will qualify as linearly dependent, since $x_n \neq 0$ in (1-53). This simply indicates the reasoning behind the convention that the null vector is considered a linear combination of any other vectors (of the same dimension) and hence any set of vectors that includes the null vector must necessarily be linearly dependent.

vectors can be linearly independent in two-dimensional vector space. [Refer to Figures 1.4(a) (b).] Once we have the two linearly independent vectors A_1 and A_2 in two-dimensional vector space, *any* other vector A_3 (that is, any point in that space) can be expressed as some linear combination of A_1 and A_2, a pair of basis vectors. Since a third vector must be a linear combination of A_1 and A_2, the three vectors are linearly dependent. The generalization is as follows: the maximum number of linearly independent vectors in m-dimensional vector space (m-element vectors) is m; more than m vectors in m-dimensional vector space must necessarily be linearly dependent.

The concept of linear dependence and independence provides a convenient framework within which to classify equation systems, which is still our primary objective. In that discussion, however, we will find extensive use for the concept of the *rank* of a matrix. Indeed, most analysis of linear equation systems is expressed in terms of ranks of the matrices involved, as we will see in Chapter 2.

DEFINITION 1.10: RANK OF A MATRIX. The rank of a matrix A, usually denoted $\rho(A)$, is defined as (1) the number of linearly independent columns in the matrix or (2) the size (dimension) of the largest matrix with a nonzero determinant that can be found in A.

From the discussion immediately above on linear dependence and independence, the reader should see that the two definitions are identical. For example, in the case of two-element vectors, which is easily shown geometrically, let

$$A = \begin{bmatrix} 1 & 2 & 3 \\ 2 & 7 & 1 \end{bmatrix}, \quad B = \begin{bmatrix} 1 & 2 & 2 \\ 2 & 7 & 4 \end{bmatrix}, \quad C = \begin{bmatrix} 1 & 2 & 3 \\ 2 & 4 & 6 \end{bmatrix},$$

$$D = \begin{bmatrix} 1 & 2 & 3 & 4 \\ 2 & 7 & 1 & 2 \end{bmatrix}, \quad E = \begin{bmatrix} 1 & 2 & 3 & 4 \\ 2 & 4 & 6 & 7 \end{bmatrix};$$

we examine each matrix for rank.

$\rho(A) = 2$:

1. A_1 and A_2 clearly are linearly independent, as are A_1 and A_3 or A_2 and A_3, using Definition 1.9. Each column in any pair in a linear combination must be multiplied by 0 for the combination to equal 0. Any pair in two-dimensional vector space has a nonzero included angle. Even though there are three pairs of independent two-element vectors, we know that all three cannot be linearly independent, since two linearly independent two-element vectors span two-dimensional vector space.

The reader should note that when we make the statement, as we might here, that "the columns of A are linearly dependent," this does not necessarily mean that all column vectors in A are parallel; it simply means that the column vectors in A are *not* linearly *independent*, as this example illustrates. (Compare with the example of matrix C, below.)

2. The determinant of the 2×2 matrix $[A_1 \mid A_2]$ is not zero. This is also true for $|A_2 \mid A_3|$ and $|A_1 \mid A_3|$. Since determinants are evaluated for square matrices only, we know that the *largest* possible rank for A is 2, the *smaller* of its two dimensions.

$\rho(B) = 2$:

1. B_1 and B_2 are linearly independent; this is sufficient to establish that the rank is 2. The rank is unaffected by the fact that, while B_2 and B_3 are linearly independent, B_1 and B_3 are not.
2. $|B_1 \mid B_2| \neq 0$. The fact that $|B_1 \mid B_3| = 0$ is not important; we have found one 2×2 submatrix in B with a nonzero determinant, so $\rho(B) = 2$.

$\rho(C) = 1$:

1. All combinations of two of the three columns of C are linearly dependent.[20] For example: $(2)C_1 + (-1)C_2 = O$ or $(-15)C_1 + (5)C_3 = O$.
2. No nonsingular 2×2 submatrix can be found among the elements of C. Since all (we need only one) of the elements themselves are nonzero, we *can* find a 1×1 nonsingular matrix—that is, a nonzero scalar. Hence, $\rho(C) = 1$.

$\rho(D) = 2$:

1. This is matrix A with one more column. The added column cannot change the rank at all, since *the matrix was already at maximum rank*.
2. Any pair of columns yields a nonsingular 2×2 matrix.

$\rho(E) = 2$:

1. This is matrix C with one more column. Since $\rho(C) = 1$, which is less than the maximum possible, the new column *can* increase the rank, provided it is linearly independent from the others. It is; hence $\rho(E) = 2$.
2. E_4 in combination with any one of columns 1, 2, or 3 yields a nonsingular 2×2 matrix.

---

[20] When the rank of a matrix A is 1, all of its columns are parallel; each is just a stretching or shrinking of any other (or others). Hence it may appear more correct to say that there are *no* linearly independent columns in A. However, given any *one* column, A_i, *any* other column in the matrix, A_j, is a linear combination of A_i. In that sense, the number of linearly *independent* columns in A may be considered to be 1.

Since the determinant of a matrix is the same as the determinant of its transpose, it is easy to show that the ranks of any matrix and its transpose are the same. Thus the number of linearly independent columns is the same as the number of linearly independent rows—a fact which is obvious by inspection for 2×2 matrices but is less easy to see when the matrix is larger.

SUMMARY

This chapter has presented the fundamental definitions and operations of matrix algebra. We have seen the relevance of these concepts for solution or analysis of systems of linear equations, largely through connections between the algebra and the geometry of some of the fundamentals. These applications will be explored further in the next chapter. Matrix notation will be used throughout this book, determinants are important in a study of maxima and minima for functions of many variables (Chapter 4), and the methods of linear systems analysis will be particularly relevant for linear programming models, especially in Chapter 6.

PROBLEMS

1. Construct matrix A, given that $a_{32} = 5, a_{11} = 11, a_{21} = 0, a_{12} = -1, a_{31} = -3$, and $a_{22} = 0$.
2. You want to add to the matrix in Problem 1 a matrix B for which $b_{i1} = 10$ (for all i) and $b_{i2} = -2$ (for all i).
   (a) What dimensions must B have?
   (b) Write out matrix B.
   (c) Perform the addition $A + B$.
3. Subtract from the sum $A + B$ in Problem 2 a matrix C for which
$$C' = \begin{bmatrix} -3 & 3 & 5 \\ 2 & -6 & -4 \end{bmatrix}.$$
4. Demonstrate the associative property of matrix addition using the following 1×4 matrices:
$$D = [\,4 \quad -5 \quad 3 \quad 1\,], \quad E = [\,1 \quad 1 \quad 0 \quad 1\,], \quad F = [\,6 \quad 5 \quad -4 \quad 1\,].$$
   That is, find $D + E + F$ as (a) $(D + E) + F$ and (b) $D + (E + F)$.
5. Given $A = [\,a_{ij}\,], i = 1, 2; j = 1, 2, 3$. In which of the following cases can B be premultiplied by A? In which can B be postmultiplied by A?

   (a) $B = \begin{bmatrix} 1 & 3 \\ 4 & 6 \end{bmatrix}.$
   (b) $B' = \begin{bmatrix} 4 & 6 & 8 \\ 2 & 2 & 3 \end{bmatrix}.$

   (c) $B = \begin{bmatrix} 4 \\ 1 \end{bmatrix}.$
   (d) $B = [b_{ij}\,], i = 1, 2, 3; j = 1, 2.$

   (e) $B = [\,b_{ij}\,], i = 1, 2; j = 1, 2, 3.$

6. For $A = \begin{bmatrix} 1 & 3 \\ 5 & 7 \end{bmatrix}$, $B = \begin{bmatrix} 2 & 2 & 4 \\ 5 & -6 & 9 \end{bmatrix}$, and $C = \begin{bmatrix} 0 & 6 & 6 \\ 4 & 1 & 2 \end{bmatrix}$, perform the operations AB, AC, and then $(AB) + (AC)$. Next perform the operations $B + C$, then $A(B + C)$. This illustrates the distributive law $A(B + C) = AB + AC$.

7. For $A = [5 \;\; -6]$, $B = \begin{bmatrix} 2 & 4 \\ 6 & 7 \end{bmatrix}$, and $C = \begin{bmatrix} 10 \\ 20 \end{bmatrix}$, form the product ABC by (a) premultiplying (BC) by A, and (b) postmultiplying (AB) by C. This illustrates the associative law $A(BC) = (AB)C$.

8. Consider

$$A = \begin{bmatrix} 1 & 2 & 5 \\ 4 & 6 & 7 \\ 1 & 0 & 0 \end{bmatrix} \quad \text{and} \quad B = \begin{bmatrix} 1 & 0 \\ 2 & 2 \\ 3 & 4 \end{bmatrix}.$$

Imagine A and B partitioned into four submatrices such that

$$A_{\mathrm{I}} = \begin{bmatrix} 1 & 2 \\ 4 & 6 \end{bmatrix} \quad \text{and} \quad B_{\mathrm{I}} = \begin{bmatrix} 1 \\ 2 \end{bmatrix}.$$

Find the product AB by multiplying and adding submatrices of A and B only [as in (1-17)]. Check your answer by multiplying AB directly.

9. Find $|A|$ in the following cases:

(a) $A = \begin{bmatrix} 1 & 2 \\ 3 & 4 \end{bmatrix}$.

(b) $A = \begin{bmatrix} 6 & 5 & 4 \\ 1 & 1 & 2 \\ 1 & 1 & 3 \end{bmatrix}$ (at least two different ways).

(c) $A = \begin{bmatrix} 6 & 5 & 4 & 3 \\ 1 & 1 & 2 & 0 \\ 1 & 1 & 3 & 0 \\ 4 & 3 & 1 & -1 \end{bmatrix}$ [evaluate down column 4, so as to make use of the result found in (b), above].

10. In each of the following cases, how do we know $|A| = 0$ without actually evaluating the determinant?

(a) $A = \begin{bmatrix} 1 & 1 \\ 1 & 1 \end{bmatrix}$.

(b) $A = \begin{bmatrix} 2 & 3 & 6 \\ 5 & 6 & 15 \\ 21 & 9 & 63 \end{bmatrix}$.

(c) $A = \begin{bmatrix} 1 & 2 & 3 \\ 4 & 5 & 6 \\ 0 & 0 & 0 \end{bmatrix}$.

(d) $A = \begin{bmatrix} 3 & 5 & 1 \\ 3 & 10 & 2 \\ 0 & 5 & 1 \end{bmatrix}$.

(e) $A = \begin{bmatrix} 5 & 4 & 1 \\ 6 & 3 & 2 \\ 5 & 4 & 1 \end{bmatrix}$.

11. Describe the kinds of solutions (unique, none, multiple) that each of the following equation systems has. (Use graphs and/or rules on the existence of an inverse.)

(a) $x_1 + 2x_2 = 3,$
    $4x_1 + 7x_2 = 1.$

(b) $x_1 + 2x_2 = 2,$
    $4x_1 + 7x_2 = 7.$

(c) $x_1 + 2x_2 = 3,$
    $4x_1 + 8x_2 = 12.$

(d) $x_1 + 2x_2 = 6,$
    $4x_1 + 8x_2 = 25.$

12. Consider the equation system
$$-x_1 + x_2 = 10,$$
$$-3x_1 + 2x_2 = 16.$$
   (a) Solve for x_1 and x_2 using ordinary algebra (substitution).
   (b) Write the system as $AX = B$ and find $A^{-1}B$.
   (c) Check that the answer in (b) is the same as that obtained in (a).
13. Find the inverse (if it exists) of each of the following matrices.

   (a) $A = \begin{bmatrix} 2 & -4 \\ 3 & 16 \end{bmatrix}$.   (b) $B = \begin{bmatrix} 2 & 4 \\ 3 & 6 \end{bmatrix}$.

   (c) $C = \begin{bmatrix} 1 & 0 & 0 \\ 0 & 1 & 0 \\ 0 & 0 & 2 \end{bmatrix}$.   (d) $D = \begin{bmatrix} 3 & 1 & 1 \\ 2 & -2 & 2 \\ 1 & 0 & 1 \end{bmatrix}$.

14. Determine the ranks of the following matrices.

   (a) $A = \begin{bmatrix} 1 & 2 & -2 \end{bmatrix}$.   (b) $B = \begin{bmatrix} 1 & 2 & -2 \\ 1 & 3 & 5 \end{bmatrix}$.

   (c) $C = \begin{bmatrix} 1 & 2 & 0 \\ 0 & 0 & 0 \end{bmatrix}$.   (d) $D = \begin{bmatrix} 1 & 2 \\ 3 & 6 \end{bmatrix}$.

   (e) $E = \begin{bmatrix} 1 & 2 & 0 \\ 3 & 6 & 1 \end{bmatrix}$.   (f) $F = \begin{bmatrix} 1 & 0 & 0 \\ 0 & 1 & 0 \\ 0 & 0 & 1 \end{bmatrix}$.

   (g) $G = \begin{bmatrix} 2 & 4 & 8 \\ 1 & 2 & 4 \\ 1 & 0 & 2 \end{bmatrix}$.

REFERENCES

1. Aitken, A. C., *Determinants and Matrices*, 9th ed. New York: Interscience Publishers, 1962.
2. Campbell, Hugh G., *An Introduction to Matrices, Vectors and Linear Programming*. New York: Appleton-Century-Crofts, 1965.
3. Hadley, G., *Linear Algebra*. Reading, Mass.: Addison-Wesley Publishing Company, Inc., 1961.
4. Perlis, Sam, *Theory of Matrices*. Reading, Mass.: Addison-Wesley Publishing Company, Inc., 1952.
5. School Mathematics Study Group, *Introduction to Matrix Algebra*, rev. ed. New Haven: Yale University Press, 1961.

2

SYSTEMS OF LINEAR EQUATIONS

In this chapter we extend the analysis of systems of linear equations that was begun in Section 1.3 for two equations and two unknowns. Initially we reexamine the 2×2 case using the vector concepts introduced in Sections 1.4 and 1.5. Next, we discuss the 3×3 case in some detail; certain complications exist only in systems of size 3×3 or larger. Then we cover the general $n \times n$ square case ("square" describes the shape of the coefficient matrix A). Finally we discuss the solution possibilities for nonsquare systems, with either fewer or more equations than unknowns. Since it is usual to speak of systems of m linear equations in n unknowns, we will initially be concerned with the $m = n$ case.

The reason that square systems are so fundamental is clear from both algebraic and geometric considerations. In the 1×1 case, $ax = b$, if $a \neq 0$ we have precisely enough information to find x uniquely; $x = a^{-1}b$. Any additional *variables* would generally place too great a demand on the information contained in a single equation; $a_1x_1 + a_2x_2 + a_3x_3 = b$ does not, in general, allow unique determination of x_1, x_2, and x_3. Similarly, again considering $ax = b$, additional *requirements* (that is, equations) would generally make it impossible to find a unique value of x satisfying all equations. If x must also satisfy $cx = d$ ($c \neq 0$), then for this equation alone $x = c^{-1}d$. If $a^{-1}b \neq c^{-1}d$, then *no* x can simultaneously satisfy both equations,[1] and the nonsquare system of more equations than unknowns is *inconsistent*. Should it happen that $a^{-1}b = c^{-1}d$, then indeed both equations can be satisfied by the same value of x, but either equation by itself would have been sufficient to find that value; one of the equations in the nonsquare system was unnecessary (redundant).

---

[1] For example, $3x = 9$ *and* $5x = 40$.

This same sort of reasoning holds for systems of any size. Beginning with a 2×2 system, the addition of a third variable increases the dimensionality of the solution-space picture by one, but this space contains only two planes (equations), for which a unique solution for all three variables would be impossible. Similarly, adding an equation only (having two variables and three equations) will mean three lines in the two-dimensional solution-space picture; in general these lines will not intersect in a single point. If they do, only two of them are necessary to define the point; if they do not, then the three-equation two-variable system has no solution; it is inconsistent. We will see in this chapter the circumstances under which square systems do not have a unique solution and also the kinds of solutions that can be salvaged in nonsquare cases.

2.1. THE 2×2 CASE AGAIN

The usefulness of the geometry of vectors and the concepts of linear dependence and independence is apparent if we look again at equation systems (1-48) through (1-50). If we view these sets of equations in their linear combination form, $A_1x_1 + A_2x_2 = B$, we can represent the systems in vector space.

CASE 1: UNIQUE SOLUTION

ALGEBRA

$$\begin{bmatrix} 3 \\ 2 \end{bmatrix} x_1 + \begin{bmatrix} 2 \\ 5 \end{bmatrix} x_2 = \begin{bmatrix} 7 \\ 12 \end{bmatrix}. \tag{2-1}$$

GEOMETRY

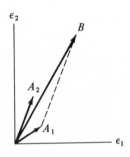

Figure 2.1. Vector-Space Representation of (2-1)

Geometrically, columns A_1 and A_2 are linearly independent, hence B can be expressed as a unique linear combination of them. In (1-48) we found

$x_1 = 1$ and $x_2 = 2$. The dashed line indicates the addition of $2A_2$ to $1A_1$—that is,

$$\begin{bmatrix} 3 \\ 2 \end{bmatrix} (1) + \begin{bmatrix} 2 \\ 5 \end{bmatrix} (2), \quad \text{which does indeed give } \begin{bmatrix} 7 \\ 12 \end{bmatrix}.$$

The representation in vector space, (2-1), does not necessarily lead to a better solution method than the solution-space approach of (1-48), provided that a unique solution exists. But it gives us a different framework for distinguishing the next two cases.

CASE 2: NO SOLUTION

ALGEBRA

$$\begin{bmatrix} 3 \\ 6 \end{bmatrix} x_1 + \begin{bmatrix} 2 \\ 4 \end{bmatrix} x_2 = \begin{bmatrix} 7 \\ 11 \end{bmatrix}. \tag{2-2}$$

GEOMETRY

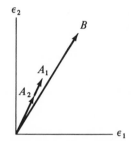

Figure 2.2. Vector-Space Representation of (2-2)

Since B is not on the same ray from the origin as the linearly dependent columns A_1 and A_2, it is impossible to describe the location of B along the $A_1 A_2$ axis; no amount of stretching or shrinking of A_1 and A_2 would lead to point B. It is linearly *independent* from the linearly *dependent* columns A_1 and A_2. An efficient way to describe this fact is to note that $\rho(A_1 \mid A_2) \equiv \rho(A) = 1$ whereas $\rho(A \mid B) = 2$. The matrix $[A \mid B]$, which attaches the right-hand vector to the matrix of coefficients from the equations, is called the *augmented matrix* of the equation system. It obviously has dimensions $m \times (n + 1)$; where $m = n$ (the square system), it is clear that $\rho(A \mid B)$ cannot be greater than this common value representing both the number of equations and the number of unknowns. Thus, Case 2 is characterized by two facts: (1) $\rho(A) = 1$, which is *less than* n, and (2) $\rho(A \mid B) = 2$, which is *different from* $\rho(A)$.

The fact that $\rho(A)$ is less than the number of variables, 2—that is, that the two columns in A are not linearly independent—means that the two variables are not sufficiently different to define a *pair* of axes in two-dimensional vector space. One variable alone is sufficient to contribute a column vector A_i that defines the direction given by both A_1 and A_2 in Figure 2.2. Thus we really have a case of *one* variable and two equations, where the two equations make conflicting demands on the single variable; it cannot satisfy both at once.

CASE 3: INFINITE NUMBER OF SOLUTIONS

ALGEBRA

$$\begin{bmatrix} 3 \\ 6 \end{bmatrix} x_1 + \begin{bmatrix} 2 \\ 4 \end{bmatrix} x_2 = \begin{bmatrix} 7 \\ 14 \end{bmatrix}. \tag{2-3}$$

GEOMETRY

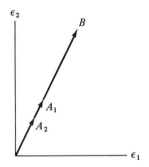

Figure 2.3.   Vector-Space Representation of (2-3)

In contrast to Case 2, B *is* on the ray defined by both A_1 and A_2, hence B's position can be described in an infinite number of ways, relative to the one axis and the lengths defined by A_1 and A_2. For example, $x_1 = 1$, $x_2 = 2$ will satisfy (2-3), as will $x_1 = -1$, $x_2 = 5$; $x_1 = -2$, $x_2 = 6\frac{1}{2}$; $x_1 = -3$, $x_2 = 8$; and so on. A_1, A_2, and B are linearly dependent; that is, $\rho(A \mid B) = 1$. We already know that $\rho(A) = 1$, since the coefficient matrices in Cases 2 and 3 are identical. Thus the facts of Case 3 are: (1) $\rho(A) = 1(<2)$ and (2) $\rho(A \mid B) = 1$, which is *the same as* $\rho(A)$.

Here we have a case in which the one variable-two equation situation of Case 2 has been reduced, in effect, to one variable and *one* equation. We have already seen (Case 2) that $\rho(A)$ gives the effective number of variables (the number of distinguishable axes provided in vector space by the A matrix). We now further observe that $\rho(A \mid B)$ gives the number of distinguishably different equations. Both of these observations generalize to larger systems.

The facts of rank for these three cases are summarized in Table 2.1.

Table 2.1.   Ranks in Cases 1–3 for $m = n = 2$

	Case 1	Case 2	Case 3
$\rho(A)$	2	1	1
$\rho(A \vdots B)$	2	2	1

This table suggests rules for establishing the *existence* and the *uniqueness* of solutions; these rules will turn out to be valid for square systems of any size and, with slight modification, for nonsquare systems as well. When $\rho(A) = \rho(A \vdots B)$ the equations are consistent—they have at least one solution (Cases 1 and 3). If the common rank is the maximum possible (which, for the $m = n$ case, is equal to the number of equations *and* the number of unknowns), a *unique* solution exists (Case 1). If the common rank is less than this maximum, *multiple* solutions exist (Case 3). When $\rho(A) \neq \rho(A \vdots B)$—note that this necessarily means $\rho(A) < \rho(A \vdots B)$—the system is inconsistent and *no* solution can be found that will simultaneously satisfy all of the equations (Case 2). Note that through the use of the *augmented matrix* for the equation system we have *explicitly* considered the structure of the right-hand side vector B; we realized at the end of our initial investigation of systems (1-48) through (1-50) in Chapter 1 that this was essential for distinguishing the two possible outcomes (Figures 1.2 and 1.3) when $|A| = 0$.

2.2.   THE 3×3 CASE

The examples above, equations (2-1) through (2-3), have shown how the three cases illustrated by equation systems (1-48) through (1-50) can be represented in vector space and classified according to certain rules of rank. The fundamental distinctions between systems with a unique solution, with no solution, and with multiple solutions have a clear vector-space meaning that can be expressed in the algebra of linear dependence and independence. Before we can generalize these ideas completely, however, it is necessary to recognize that in square linear equation systems of more than two variables and equations, further classification of solutions is possible. For an intuitive feeling of the nature of these new possibilities, consider three planes in three-dimensional solution space (that is, each plane involves variables x_1, x_2, and x_3).

(a)   All three planes may intersect in a unique point. That is, two planes intersect in a line and the third plane cuts through this line "at an angle." This corresponds to Case 1.

(b)   All three planes may be distinct, with each parallel to the other two. There is thus no solution possible; the equation system is inconsistent and only *one* equation at a time can be satisfied. This corresponds to Case 2.

(c)   The three planes may intersect in a common line [rather than in a point, as in (a), above], two equations may describe the same plane and the third intersect it, or, finally, the three equations may describe the same plane. In all of these cases, the equations are consistent but there are multiple solutions. This appears to correspond to Case 3, although clearly there are different "orders" of multiple solutions, some involving all points in a common plane, some allowing only those on a common line.

(d)   Two of the planes may be distinct and parallel and the third may "slice" through them, creating two parallel lines in three-dimensional space. Along each of these lines, *two* of the three equations are satisfied while the third is not. Or the planes may intersect in three parallel lines, and again there would be solutions for particular *pairs* of equations but not for all three. We may think of these cases as involving "lower-order" solutions in which not all of the equations can be satisfied simultaneously but subsets of more than one of them do have common solutions. Clearly, this possibility does not arise until more than two equations and more than two variables are involved. It is often important to distinguish this situation, where in effect too much is required of the variables (in terms of the number of equations to which they must conform). By judicious elimination of one or more of the equations, a solution becomes possible. When faced with a situation in which impossible requirements have been set up for the variables, it is useful to know whether only one equation at a time can possibly be met, as in (b), or whether several but not all can be satisfied, as in (d).

In the illustration for equations (1-25) in the preceding chapter, the right-hand side values (in matrix terms, the elements of B) were estimates made by a campaign manager; the coefficients attached to the x's (in matrix terms, the elements of A) were estimates made by a consulting firm. There is thus no particular reason why the resulting *equation system* $(AX = B)$ should necessarily be consistent or indeed even why the estimated figures on the vote-capturing power of advertisements in the various media in each district should lead to a nonsingular A matrix. (For example, if the consulting firm estimated the effects to be the same in each of two districts for radio, the same for newspapers, and the same for TV, then $|A|$ would be zero.) Moreover, it would be useful to know, in a case for which *no* solution could be found (inconsistent system), that for example by elimination of the district in which the smallest gain in voters was advised, the remaining (reduced) system *would* have a solution.

In order to distinguish the various possibilities completely, it is useful to examine several representative 3×3 cases, including one that corresponds to Case 2. We will need three-dimensional vector space for the geometry of the problem; axes are labeled ϵ_1, ϵ_2, and ϵ_3 for the first, second, and third elements in each column vector of A and in B.

CASE 2′: TOTAL INCONSISTENCY; COMPLETE PARALLELISM

ALGEBRA

$$\begin{aligned} x_1 + 2x_2 + 3x_3 &= 3, \\ 2x_1 + 4x_2 + 6x_3 &= 3, \\ 3x_1 + 6x_2 + 9x_3 &= 4. \end{aligned} \qquad (2\text{-}4)$$

GEOMETRY

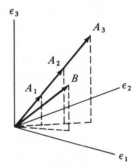

Figure 2.4.   Vector-Space Representation of (2-4)

The vectors A_1, A_2, and A_3 define only a single ray in three-dimensional vector space. Since B does not lie on that same ray, it is impossible to describe its position by some distance on that single axis. This is the obvious 3×3 analogue of Case 2. In three-dimensional solution space (one axis for each x_i), the system would be shown as three distinct and parallel planes. The ranks that are of interest are:

(a) $\rho(A) = 1$ (not only is $|A| = 0$, but there is not a single 2×2 sub-matrix in A with a nonzero determinant); and

(b) $\rho(A \vdots B) = 2$. Important information comes from (1) a comparison of these two ranks and (2) the amount by which $\rho(A)$ differs from n, the number of variables.

(1)   The fact that the ranks of A and the augmented matrix differ, $\rho(A \vdots B) \neq \rho(A)$, tells us that the equations are inconsistent and thus a solution cannot be found to satisfy them all simul-

taneously. This consistency test is relevant for square systems of any size. The reasoning is as follows. If the number of linearly independent columns of A—that is, $\rho(A)$—is not increased when B is adjoined to A, then, since $\rho(A)$ cannot be decreased, $\rho(A \mathrel{\vdots} B)$ must be the same as $\rho(A)$. But this says B is linearly dependent on the columns of A; therefore it can be described as a linear combination of some or all of the A_i. The scalars, x_i, in this linear combination are the solution values to the equation system, as we have seen. Hence the system is solvable—that is, consistent. Note that the consistency test deals with the question of the *existence* of a solution, not with *uniqueness;* the latter depends on whether or not *all* columns in A are needed to describe B.

(2) The fact that $\rho(A) < n$ tells us that a *unique* solution cannot exist, since A^{-1} cannot be found. This follows from Cramer's rule. It also follows from the general definitions of linear dependence and the rank of a matrix. Since $\rho(A) < n$, where n is the number of variables in the equation system, then not all n columns of A are linearly independent. Some of the columns are expressible as linear combinations of the others. Thus there is more than one way to select from the n columns of A a subset of less than n to act as a basis for—that is, to span—the vector space of dimension $\rho(A) < n$. For example,

$$\text{if } A = \begin{bmatrix} 1 & 4 & 6 \\ 2 & 5 & 9 \\ 3 & 2 & 8 \end{bmatrix}, \qquad \rho(A) = 2.$$

$A_3 = 2A_1 + A_2$; all three vectors lie in the same *plane* (two-dimensional space—less than n) in three-dimensional vector space. Thus, any *pair* of A_1, A_2, and A_3 would be sufficient to describe any other point in three-dimensional vector space that happens to lie on that plane. Consider a vector

$$B = \begin{bmatrix} 11 \\ 16 \\ 13 \end{bmatrix}.$$

Using A_1 and A_2, $B = 3A_1 + 2A_2$. Thus, a solution to $AX = B$ is $x_1 = 3$, $x_2 = 2$. But since $A_3 = 2A_1 + A_2$, A_2 is just $A_3 - 2A_1$, and thus

$$B = 3A_1 + 2(A_3 - 2A_1) = -A_1 + 2A_3,$$

and an equally valid solution is $x_1 = -1$, $x_3 = 2$. (A solution using only x_2 and x_3 can also be found.) Thus, the axes are not unique, and the coordinates—which are the x's—vary with the axes. Moreover, if, as in (2-4), $\rho(A) = 1$, we see that in solution space the planes are *all* parallel and that in vector space the number of linearly independent columns in A is just one (Figure 2.4); hence the columns of A define only one ray in vector space.

In the 2×2 case, the rank of the A matrix must be either 1 or 2; hence either there is a unique solution, $\rho(A) = 2$, or the two lines are parallel, $\rho(A) = 1$. The two kinds of "parallelism" were illustrated in (2-2) and (2-3) and were distinguishable by the consistency test, comparing $\rho(A)$ with $\rho(A \mid B)$. Either no solutions or an infinite number could be found to the entire system of equations. With square systems of size 3 or larger, it is clearly possible to fail the uniqueness test—that is, to have $\rho(A) < n$, and yet to have $\rho(A) > 1$. Two cases for a 3×3 system with $1 < \rho(A) < n$ will illustrate the nature of the possibilities. These are the cases of consistent and inconsistent systems.

CASE 3(A): CONSISTENT SYSTEMS; MULTIPLE SOLUTIONS

ALGEBRA

$$
\begin{aligned}
x_1 + 2x_2 + x_3 &= 10, \\
2x_1 + 4x_2 + 3x_3 &= 20, \\
3x_1 + 6x_2 + 4x_3 &= 30.
\end{aligned}
\tag{2-5}
$$

GEOMETRY

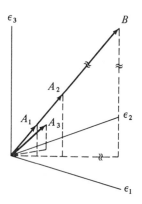

Figure 2.5. Vector-Space Representation of (2-5)

It is clear that B can be expressed using only A_1, or only A_2, or A_1 and A_2 in certain combinations.[2] Examining ranks, we find $\rho(A) = 2$, $\rho(A \mid B) = 2$.

---

[2] For example, $10A_1 + 0A_2 + 0A_3$, $0A_1 + 5A_2 + 0A_3$, $4A_1 + 3A_2 + 0A_3$, $2A_1 + 4A_2 + 0A_3$.

The first result tells us that there are not three but two linearly independent columns (by inspection these are either A_1 and A_3 or A_2 and A_3). The second result tells us that B is a linear combination of the columns of A. Thus the equations are consistent, which is always the interpretation of $\rho(A) = \rho(A \mid B)$.

Consider the picture in solution space; here we need one axis for each of the variables. It can be seen rather easily that each of the planes passes through the line $x_1 + 2x_2 = 10$ in the x_1, x_2 plane by simply setting each possible *pair* of variables from the set x_1, x_2, and x_3 equal to 0 in each equa-

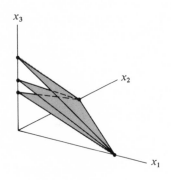

Figure 2.6. Solution-Space Representation of (2-5)

tion and finding the corresponding intercept on the other axis. Therefore this locus of solutions can be defined precisely by *any* two of the three equations in (2-5); put differently, any *one* of the three equations is *redundant*. For example, equation 3 is just equation 1 + equation 2.

Note that $[m - \rho(A \mid B)] = 1$; the difference between the number of equations and the rank of the augmented matrix is the same as the number of redundant equations again in this case, as it was above in Case 3 for the 2×2 system in (2-3). This is generally true; $[m - \rho(A \mid B)]$ or $[m - \rho(A)]$ gives the number of *unnecessary* equations in a *consistent* system.

A similar case is the following:

ALGEBRA

$$
\begin{aligned}
x_1 + x_2 + x_3 &= 10, \\
2x_1 + 2x_2 + 2x_3 &= 20, \\
7x_1 + 3x_2 + 3x_3 &= 10.
\end{aligned}
\tag{2-6}
$$

GEOMETRY

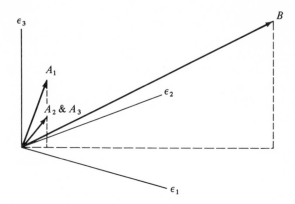

Figure 2.7.   Vector-Space Representation of (2-6)

Here, again, $\rho(A) = \rho(A \mid B) = 2$. It is not so obvious (visually) in the geometry of vector space that B lies in the *plane* generated by A_1 and A_2 (or A_1 and A_3). But by virtue of the ranks of A and $[A \mid B]$ we know that B can be described as (at least one) linear combination of the two linearly independent columns of A. However, in solution space, we recognize equation 2 as simply twice equation 1, and hence both describe the same plane. Therefore equation 1 *or* equation 2, plus equation 3, denote two intersecting planes; an entire line of points in solution space will satisfy the system. Thus, again, one equation is redundant $[m - \rho(A \mid B) = m - \rho(A) = 3 - 2 = 1]$; it need not be deleted, but it may be. Unlike the system in (2-5), however, not *any* one can be removed—only the first or the second; the third equation is essential.

This conclusion on the number of redundant equations in a consistent system of any size follows also from the interpretation of the rank of a matrix. Since the system of equations is consistent, $\rho(A) = \rho(A \mid B)$; B can be expressed as a linear combination of the A_i. However, the common rank is less than m, the number of equations. Let $\rho(A) = k$. This means that a subset of k of the equations contains all of the information of the entire m-equation system. If this were not true, then the addition of any one of the equations from the $(m - k)$ subset would either (a) add a new and inconsistent relation among the x's or (b) add a new and consistent relation among the x's—that is, add new information. The former is impossible, since the entire system of equations is *not* inconsistent—$\rho(A) = \rho(A \mid B)$. The latter is impossible, since if the new equation did add new information not contained in the k-equation subset, the rank of A would have to be at least $k + 1$.

CASE 3(B): INCONSISTENT SYSTEMS; "LOWER-ORDER" SOLUTIONS

ALGEBRA

$$x_1 + 2x_2 + 3x_3 = 3,$$
$$2x_1 + 4x_2 + 6x_3 = 3, \qquad (2\text{-}7)$$
$$x_1 + x_2 + x_3 = 3.$$

GEOMETRY

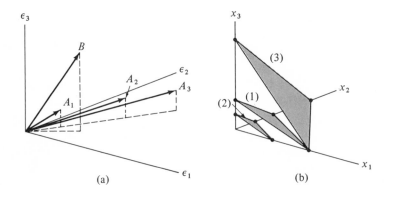

Figure 2.8. Representation of (2-7) in (a) Vector Space, (b) Solution Space

Equations 1 and 2 are distinct and parallel planes in three-dimensional solution space; equation 3 cuts them both. Once again, examining ranks, $\rho(A) = 2$, $\rho(A \mathbin{\vdots} B) = 3$. The difference between the two indicates an inconsistency; it is impossible to find any values of x_1, x_2, x_3 that simultaneously satisfy all three equations. B cannot be expressed as a linear combination of the A_i.

The rank of A is, as usual, the number of its linearly independent vectors; here that number is 2. In the case of a consistent system, the difference between the number of equations and the common rank of $(A \mathbin{\vdots} B)$ and A indicated the number of redundant equations. The important observation was on m and $\rho(A \mathbin{\vdots} B)$; in consistent systems, however, $\rho(A \mathbin{\vdots} B) = \rho(A)$. In the present case $[m - \rho(A \mathbin{\vdots} B)] = 3 - 3 = 0$. From this we conclude that the system contains *no* redundant or unnecessary equations; if any equations are disregarded, the resulting system will be different from that in (2-7). However, since $\rho(A)$ gives the number of linearly independent vectors in A, $[m - \rho(A)]$ gives the number of equations that would have to be *ignored* in the m-equation system in order to have a square system for which a solution could be found.

Here $[m - \rho(A)] = 3 - 2 = 1$. Hence there is at least one equation (say the ith) that, if disregarded, will allow solutions to the remaining system to be found. That is, in vector-space terms, if the ith element is removed from each of the columns of A, a basis for two-dimensional vector space could be found; that is what $\rho(A) = 2$ tells us. If the ith element is also removed from B, it becomes a two-element vector, and we could express it (indeed *any* two-element column vector) relative to the reduced basis derived from A.

For example, ignoring equation 1 in (2-7) leaves

$$2x_1 + 4x_2 + 6x_3 = 3,$$
$$x_1 + x_2 + x_3 = 3.$$

This is no longer a square system—we will deal explicitly with nonsquare systems in the next sections—but the reader should be convinced that solutions (infinitely many, in fact) are possible, since $\begin{bmatrix} 2 \\ 1 \end{bmatrix}$ and $\begin{bmatrix} 4 \\ 1 \end{bmatrix}$, for example, form a basis for two-dimensional vector space. A solution thus is

$$\left(\tfrac{9}{2}\right)\begin{bmatrix} 2 \\ 1 \end{bmatrix} + \left(-\tfrac{3}{2}\right)\begin{bmatrix} 4 \\ 1 \end{bmatrix} + (0)\begin{bmatrix} 6 \\ 1 \end{bmatrix} = \begin{bmatrix} 3 \\ 3 \end{bmatrix}$$

—that is, $x_1 = \tfrac{9}{2}$, $x_2 = -\tfrac{3}{2}$, $x_3 = 0$. Or equation 2 could be left out, giving the reduced system

$$\begin{bmatrix} 1 \\ 1 \end{bmatrix} x_1 + \begin{bmatrix} 2 \\ 1 \end{bmatrix} x_2 + \begin{bmatrix} 3 \\ 1 \end{bmatrix} x_3 = \begin{bmatrix} 3 \\ 3 \end{bmatrix}.$$

Since $\begin{bmatrix} 1 & 3 \\ 1 & 1 \end{bmatrix}$ is nonsingular, a solution is found by using $\begin{bmatrix} 1 \\ 1 \end{bmatrix}$ and $\begin{bmatrix} 3 \\ 1 \end{bmatrix}$ as the basis vectors, and setting $x_2 = 0$.

$$(3)\begin{bmatrix} 1 \\ 1 \end{bmatrix} + (0)\begin{bmatrix} 3 \\ 1 \end{bmatrix} = \begin{bmatrix} 3 \\ 3 \end{bmatrix}$$

—that is, $x_1 = 3$, $x_2 = 0$, $x_3 = 0$ is a solution to a different "lower-order" system.

One more algebraic example will complete the illustration of this "lower-order" solution possibility.

ALGEBRA

$$x_1 + x_2 + x_3 + x_4 = 10,$$
$$2x_1 + 2x_2 + 2x_3 + 3x_4 = 10,$$
$$3x_1 + 3x_2 + 3x_3 + 4x_4 = 10,$$
$$4x_1 + 4x_2 + 4x_3 + 5x_4 = 10.$$

(2-8)

GEOMETRY.   Both vector space and solution space require four dimensions.

Here $\rho(A) = 2$, $\rho(A \mid B) = 3$; the equation set is inconsistent. Since A has only two linearly independent columns, two elements of B (hence two equations) need to be removed in order for B to be expressible in terms of the basis for two-dimensional vector space that comes from A. This number of "excessive" equations is again $[m - \rho(A)]$—here $4 - 2$. Ignoring equations 3 and 4 in (2-8), for example, leaves

$$\begin{bmatrix} 1 \\ 2 \end{bmatrix} x_1 + \begin{bmatrix} 1 \\ 2 \end{bmatrix} x_2 + \begin{bmatrix} 1 \\ 2 \end{bmatrix} x_3 + \begin{bmatrix} 1 \\ 3 \end{bmatrix} x_4 = \begin{bmatrix} 10 \\ 10 \end{bmatrix},$$

for which possible solutions are $x_1 = 0$, $x_2 = 0$, $x_3 = 20$, $x_4 = -10$; $x_1 = 0$, $x_2 = 20$, $x_3 = 0$, $x_4 = -10$, and so on.

Summary of 2×2 and 3×3 solution possibilities

A consistent system is one in which $\rho(A) = \rho(A \mid B)$. Comparison of these ranks is thus the test for *existence* of a solution to the entire equation system. For such a system, the size of the rank of A relative to the number of variables, n, determines whether or not there is a *unique* solution. When $m = n$, as in all cases studied thus far, the *numerical* outcome is the same whether number of equations or number of variables is used. Logically, however, the question of *uniqueness* of the solution hangs on the number of linearly independent columns in A relative to the number of variables.

If there are multiple solutions in the consistent case, then clearly some of the equations are not providing new relationships among the variables; they are merely repeating the information contained in other equations. The number of such unnecessary or redundant equations is $[m - \rho(A)]$. For inconsistent systems, this same number indicates how many equations would have to be taken out of the system in order to remove the inconsistency. These observations are summarized in Table 2.2.

2.3.   THE $n \times n$ CASE

The extension to square linear systems ($n \times n$) of any size follows these same categories. The compact matrix notation remains $AX = B$; the vector form is

$$A_1 x_1 + A_2 x_2 + \cdots + A_n x_n = B.$$

When all elements on the right-hand side are zero, the equations are termed *homogeneous*, and it is useful to divide this final discussion of general $n \times n$ systems into homogeneous and nonhomogeneous classes.

Table 2.2. Rules of Rank for $m = n = 2$ or 3

	$\rho(A) = \rho(A \mid B)$ (Consistent system)	$\rho(A) \neq \rho(A \mid B)$ (Inconsistent system)
$\rho(A) = 1$	Multiple solutions, any $(m - 1)$ equations redundant. Case 3, equations (2-3).	Complete parallelism; only "lower-order" solution if a complete set of $(m - 1)$ equations is dropped. Cases 2 and 2', equations (2-2) and (2-4).
$1 < \rho(A) < n$	Multiple solutions; at least one set of $[m - \rho(A \mid B)] = [m - \rho(A)]$ equations redundant. Case 3(a), equations (2-5) and (2-6).	"Lower-order" solutions. At least one set of $[m - \rho(A)]$ equations must be dropped to produce a set of equations for which a solution is possible. Case 3(b), equations (2-7) and (2-8).
$\rho(A) = n$	Unique solution, $X = A^{-1}B$. Case 1, equations (2-1).	Impossible.

Homogeneous equations $(B = O)$[3]

CASE H1: $\rho(A) = n$. From Table 2.2 we recognize that the system should have a *unique* solution. Indeed, since A^{-1} exists [because $\rho(A) = n$], the solution is simply $X = A^{-1}B$, and since $B = O$, we recognize that $X = O$ is the only solution.

The existence of this all-zero solution follows directly from the definition of linear independence. The homogeneous equations are

$$A_1x_1 + A_2x_2 + \cdots + A_nx_n = O,$$

exactly the same as equation (1-53) in Definition 1.9. Since we are considering the case in which $|A| \neq 0$, the A_i must be linearly independent.

---

[3] The reader should recognize that homogeneous equation systems must be consistent, since adding a column of zeros to A cannot possibly alter its rank and hence $\rho(A) = \rho(A \mid B)$.

From Definition 1.9 we know that this requires that *all* $x_i = 0$. In the case of homogeneous equations, this is understandably called the *trivial* solution.

CASE H2: $\rho(A) < n$. From Table 2.2 we recognize that multiple solutions should exist. For *consistent* systems of equations, the distinction between the $\rho(A) = 1$ and $1 < \rho(A) < n$ cases is not really important; the nature of the outcome is the same for both. Since the columns of A are now linearly *dependent*, we know from Definition 1.9 that a solution exists in which not all x_i are zero. In fact, we know from the 2×2 and 3×3 cases that an infinite number of solutions can be found, including, of course, the one in which all x's are zero. The all-zero solution is *always* possible for homogeneous equations. Homogeneous equation systems of n equations and n variables will have a nontrivial solution if and only if $\rho(A) < n$; but then the solution is also not unique.

The geometry of the two homogeneous-equation-system cases (for two equations and two variables) is shown in the accompanying examples (Figures 2.9 and 2.10). The reader should note that there is nothing conceptually new in these figures; they parallel those for the 2×2 cases shown earlier except that in solution space the line or lines go through the origin and in vector space B is not shown as a distinct arrow since it is the point $\begin{bmatrix} 0 \\ 0 \end{bmatrix}$. [Compare Figure 2.9(a) with Figure 2.1, 2.9(b) with 1.1, 2.10(a) with 2.3, and 2.10(b) with 1.3.]

ALGEBRA

$$x_1 - 2x_2 = 0, \qquad (2\text{-}9)$$
$$x_1 + x_2 = 0.$$

GEOMETRY

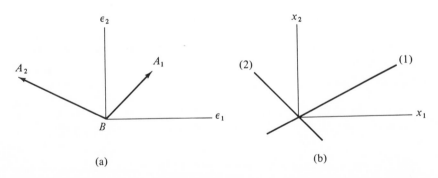

(a)

(b)

Figure 2.9. Representation of (2-9) in (a) Vector Space, (b) Solution Space

ALGEBRA

$$x_1 - x_2 = 0,$$
$$2x_1 - 2x_2 = 0. \tag{2-10}$$

GEOMETRY

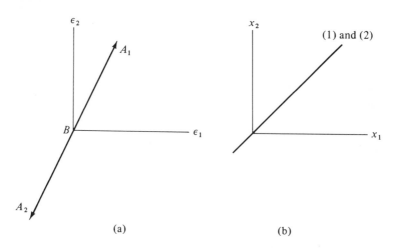

(a)   (b)

Figure 2.10. Representation of (2-10) in (a) Vector Space, (b) Solution Space

Nonhomogeneous equations $(B \neq O)$

Unlike the homogeneous case, nonhomogeneous equations may or may not pass the consistency test. These possibilities are considered in turn.

CONSISTENT SYSTEMS—$\rho(A) = \rho(A \mathbin{\vdots} B)$

CASE NHC1: $\rho(A) = n$. Since A is of full rank, addition of one more column cannot increase that rank; hence $\rho(A) = \rho(A \mathbin{\vdots} B)$. That is, an $n \times n$ system in which $\rho(A) = n$ is *always* consistent. In this case the unique solution exists, given by $X = A^{-1}B$. In the terminology of Cramer's rule, each x_i has a nonzero denominator; hence a unique set of values can be found by evaluating the determinant in each numerator. The 2×2 case is shown in Figure 1.1 accompanying equations (1-48) for solution space and in Figure 2.1 with equations (2-1) for vector space. This is the "well-behaved" case.

CASE NHC2: $\rho(A) < n$. Clearly a unique solution is impossible; A^{-1} does not exist. Yet the system is consistent. In the most extreme case $\rho(A) = 1$; *all* columns of A are linearly dependent. Since $\rho(A) = \rho(A \mathbin{\vdots} B)$,

B lies on the same ray in vector space defined by all of the A_i. The 2×2 case is illustrated by equations (1-50) and (2-3) and the corresponding Figures 1.3 and 2.3, in solution space and vector space, respectively. In the more likely case, $\rho(A) > 1$ (but less than n). Since the system is consistent, B lies on the line, in the plane, or, more generally, in the vector space of dimension $\rho(A)$ which is spanned by the A_i. Since $\rho(A) < n$, there is more than one set of columns in A that can be used to define B. Equations (2-5) and (2-6) and Figures 2.5, 2.6, and 2.7 illustrate the 3×3 case.

INCONSISTENT SYSTEMS—$\rho(A) \neq \rho(A \mid B)$

In this case it is impossible for the rank of A to be as large as n, since it is less than $\rho(A \mid B)$, which itself cannot exceed n. Thus there is no parallel in the inconsistent system to Case NHC1. We retain the numbering to facilitate comparison.

CASE NHI1: $\rho(A) = n$.   Not possible.

CASE NHI2: $\rho(A) < n$.   Again, it is quite generally possible that B will be independent of the columns of A (will *not* lie in the vector space spanned by the A_i, in contrast to Case NHC2), and no solution to the full set of equations is possible. "Lower-order" solutions can be found, but they require that some of the equations be ignored. Equation sets (2-7) and (2-8) provide examples.

In the case of an inconsistent system with $\rho(A) = 1$—that is, where *all* columns of A are linearly dependent, only *one* equation at a time can be satisfied. In solution space, the lines (planes, or hyperplanes) are distinct and parallel. Equations (2-4) and Figure 2.4 give a 3×3 example.

2.4.   FEWER EQUATIONS THAN UNKNOWNS $(m < n)$

The results of the discussion of $n \times n$ equation systems in Section 2.3 make it relatively easy to generalize to the cases of more equations than unknowns or more unknowns than equations. As before, m denotes the number of equations and n the number of variables; we examine the $m < n$ case in this section. The representation $AX = B$ is still appropriate; A becomes rectangular, $m \times n$, X is an n-element column vector and B contains m elements. The logic of the rules of rank still holds, however, since these rules are based on the fundamental concepts of linear dependence and independence, which are not concerned with any underlying "squareness."

In the political-candidate illustration, there is no particular reason for the number of critical districts and the varieties of news media available to him to be the same. We examine in this section the situation of fewer districts than news media $(m < n)$ and in Section 2.5 the opposite case—perhaps nearer to election day—in which there are more critical districts than media types $(m > n)$.

In cases involving more variables than equations, the coefficient matrix is "short and wide"; its greatest possible rank is m and hence it necessarily contains some linearly *dependent* columns. Unique solutions are *never* possible. As usual, the system may or may not be consistent.

Consistent systems—$\rho(A) = \rho(A \vdots B)$

CASE FC1: $\rho(A) = m$.   For the case of more variables than equations when A is of full rank, there is a systematic method for discarding $(n - m)$ extra variables (and thus producing a square $m \times m$ system). The solution of the reduced system is termed a *basic* solution, since the variables are eliminated in such a way that the remaining columns of A are linearly independent and hence form a *basis* in m-dimensional space. [This is obviously possible since $\rho(A) = m$.]

We select from A any set of m linearly independent columns from among the total number, n. (Recall that we are investigating the $m < n$ case in this section.) We denote the $m \times m$ *nonsingular* matrix composed of these columns A^M, and we know that at least one such A^M can be formed because we are considering here the particular case in which $\rho(A) = m$. Denote the $m \times (n - m)$ matrix of remaining columns from A by A^N. That is, we rearrange the columns of A and then consider its partitioned representation

$$A = [A^M \vdots A^N].$$

We also rearrange the elements in X so that

$$X = \left[\frac{X^M}{X^N} \right],$$

where X^M is a column vector of the m unknowns associated with the m columns in A^M, and X^N contains the $(n - m)$ remaining unknowns associated with the columns in A^N. Then $AX = B$ can be expressed as

$$[A^M \vdots A^N] \left[\frac{X^M}{X^N} \right] = B \quad \text{or} \quad A^M X^M + A^N X^N = B.$$

Then, since $(A^M)^{-1}$ exists (because of the way in which A^M was formed),

$$X^M = (A^M)^{-1}B - (A^M)^{-1}A^N X^N.$$

Thus, given *any* values of the $(n - m)$ variables in X^N, we can solve for the values of the remaining m variables in X^M. In particular, if we set each of the variables in X^N to zero, we have what is termed a *basic solution:*[4]

$$X^M = (A^M)^{-1}B. \tag{2-11}$$

Thus, a characteristic of a basic solution to m equations in n unknowns $(m < n)$ is that *no more than* m variables have a nonzero value. If some of the variables in the basic vector, X^M, are zero, the basic solution is termed *degenerate*. Thus a degenerate basic solution has less than m variables at nonzero value (out of the total of n). Recalling Cramer's rule for square equation systems, it is clear that a necessary and sufficient condition for a given basic solution (2-11) to be nondegenerate is the linear independence of B and every set of $(m - 1)$ columns from A^M.

Note that it is not possible to know exactly how many basic solutions a given system will have; we can only know the maximum number possible. Since a set of m columns is selected from the n in A, this can be done in a total of $C_m^n = n!/[m!(n - m)!]$ ways; some of these may not produce a nonsingular A^M, however.

For example:

$$\begin{aligned}
x_1 + 2x_2 + 3x_3 + 3x_4 &= 1, \\
3x_1 + 2x_2 + 3x_3 + 6x_4 &= 2,
\end{aligned} \tag{2-12}$$

$\rho(A) = 2$, $\rho(A \mid B) = 2$, $m = 2$, $n = 4$; thus we look for basic solutions, each involving two columns from A. A total of $C_2^4 = 6$ possible selections can be made, but one of these pairs, A_2 and A_3, produces a singular A^M. All other basic solutions are:

(1) A_1 and A_2: $X^M = \begin{bmatrix} x_1 \\ x_2 \end{bmatrix} = \begin{bmatrix} \frac{1}{2} \\ \frac{1}{4} \end{bmatrix}.$

(2) A_1 and A_3: $X^M = \begin{bmatrix} x_1 \\ x_3 \end{bmatrix} = \begin{bmatrix} \frac{1}{2} \\ \frac{1}{6} \end{bmatrix}.$

(3) A_1 and A_4: $X^M = \begin{bmatrix} x_1 \\ x_4 \end{bmatrix} = \begin{bmatrix} 0 \\ \frac{1}{3} \end{bmatrix}.$

---

[4] Consider two planes in three-dimensional solution space that intersect in a line (also in three-dimensional solution space). By setting, say, $x_1 = 0$, we find the point at which the line goes through the plane defined by the x_2 and x_3 axes (which is simply the plane defined by $x_1 = 0$ in three-dimensional solution space); by setting $x_2 = 0$, we find where the line meets the x_1, x_3 plane; and so on. Clearly, by setting x_1 (*or* x_2 *or* x_3) equal to any nonzero constant, we define a *different* plane and could find the point at which the line intersected it. Thus linear equation systems with fewer equations than variables have (generally) an infinite number of nonbasic solutions. Basic solutions, however, are of particular importance in linear programming, as we will see in Chapter 6.

(4) A_2 and A_4: $X^M = \begin{bmatrix} x_2 \\ x_4 \end{bmatrix} = \begin{bmatrix} 0 \\ \frac{1}{3} \end{bmatrix}$.

(5) A_3 and A_4: $X^M = \begin{bmatrix} x_3 \\ x_4 \end{bmatrix} = \begin{bmatrix} 0 \\ \frac{1}{3} \end{bmatrix}$.

Solutions (3), (4), and (5) are degenerate, since some (in these cases one) of the variables are in the basis at value zero.

CASE FC2: $\rho(A) = k$, $k < m$.   The analysis here parallels that for the $m = n$ case. Being consistent, some $(m - k)$ equations can be removed from the system with no loss of information. The solution is in no way affected, since the omitted equations describe exactly the same relations between the variables as those that are retained. When redundant equations have been removed, a consistent system results with n variables and a number of equations equal to $k = \rho(A)$; since $\rho(A) < n$, it is then possible to find *basic* solutions to this reduced system. We denote the $k \times n$ *reduced* system as $A^R X = B^R$. The geometry resembles that of the square-system case, except that, for $m < n$, vector space requires fewer dimensions than solution space. Two examples follow.

$$\begin{aligned} x_1 + 2x_2 + x_3 + 3x_4 &= 4, \\ 2x_1 + 4x_2 + 2x_3 + 6x_4 &= 8, \\ x_1 + x_2 + 3x_3 + 4x_4 &= 2. \end{aligned} \qquad (2\text{-}13)$$

$\rho(A) = 2$, $\rho(A \mid B) = 2$, $m = 3$, $n = 4$,   and $[m - \rho(A)] = 1$.

Equations 1 and 2 describe the same plane; either is therefore expendable. Removing equation 1 leaves a 2×4 system that is consistent and thus has *basic* solutions. We know that such solutions are possible, since $\rho(A) = 2$ and hence there must be at least one set of two linearly independent columns in the new 2×4 matrix, A^R. The point is that if we remove equations equal in number to $[m - \rho(A)]$, the number of equations remaining is exactly equal to $\rho(A)$; hence the reduced system will have basic solutions.

For example, if we partition A^R into $[A^M \mid A^N]$ as

$$\begin{bmatrix} 2 & 4 & \vdots & 2 & 6 \\ 1 & 1 & \vdots & 3 & 4 \end{bmatrix},$$

a basic solution is given by

$$\begin{bmatrix} x_1 \\ x_2 \end{bmatrix} = \begin{bmatrix} 2 & 4 \\ 1 & 1 \end{bmatrix}^{-1} \begin{bmatrix} 8 \\ 2 \end{bmatrix} = \begin{bmatrix} -\frac{1}{2} & 2 \\ \frac{1}{2} & -1 \end{bmatrix} \begin{bmatrix} 8 \\ 2 \end{bmatrix} = \begin{bmatrix} 0 \\ 2 \end{bmatrix}.$$

This happens to be a degenerate solution, since x_1 is in the basis at value zero; x_3 and x_4 have been set equal to zero in the partitioning of A^R—they are the $(4 - 2) = 2$ "extra" variables that have become constants, so that a 2×2 system with a unique solution is left. An equally valid partition of A^R would be

$$\left[\begin{array}{cc|cc} 2 & 6 & 2 & 4 \\ 3 & 4 & 1 & 1 \end{array}\right]$$

—that is, x_1 and x_2 are being set equal to zero and this 2×2 system has a solution:

$$\left[\begin{array}{c} x_3 \\ x_4 \end{array}\right] = \left[\begin{array}{cc} 2 & 6 \\ 3 & 4 \end{array}\right]^{-1}\left[\begin{array}{c} 8 \\ 2 \end{array}\right] = \left[\begin{array}{c} -2 \\ 2 \end{array}\right].$$

In the case where $\rho(A) = 1$, the picture is essentially identical to Figures 1.3 and 2.3 for the 2×2 case. In vector space, there would be more A_i but all would still be on the same ray. In two-dimensional solution space the one equation (line) would relate two variables; in three-dimensional solution space, the one or two equations would describe the same plane. Hence these particular equation systems are not very likely to occur in practice. For example:

ALGEBRA

$$\begin{aligned} x_1 + 2x_2 + x_3 &= 4, \\ 2x_1 + 4x_2 + 2x_3 &= 8. \end{aligned} \tag{2-14}$$

$$\rho(A) = 1, \quad \rho(A \mid B) = 1, \quad m = 2, \quad n = 3.$$

GEOMETRY

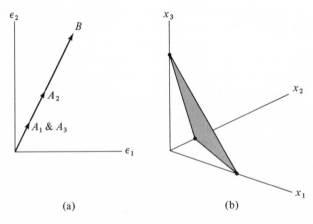

(a)   (b)

Figure 2.11.   Representation of (2-14) in (a) Vector Space, (b) Solution Space

Inconsistent systems—$\rho(A) \neq \rho(A \mid B)$

With m equations in n variables, and $m < n$, when the system is inconsistent, $\rho(A \mid B)$ is one larger than $\rho(A)$. Since $\rho(A \mid B) \leq m$, $\rho(A) < m$ and hence a case corresponding to FC1, above, cannot occur. We retain the numbering for consistency.

CASE FI1: $\rho(A) = m$.   Impossible.

CASE FI2: $\rho(A) < m$.   When $\rho(A) = k$, $k < m$, as in the $m = n$ case, only "lower-order" solutions are possible; these can be found only at the expense of *ignoring* equations in the system. There is at least one set of $(m - k)$ equations that, if dropped from the system, leaves k equations in n unknowns, $(k < n)$, for which basic solutions can be found. For example:

$$\begin{aligned} x_1 + 2x_2 + x_3 + 3x_4 &= 4, \\ 2x_1 + 4x_2 + 2x_3 + 6x_4 &= 5, \\ x_1 + x_2 + 3x_3 + 4x_4 &= 2. \end{aligned} \tag{2-15}$$

$\rho(A) = 2$, $\rho(A \mid B) = 3$, $m = 3$, $n = 4$, and $[m - \rho(A \mid B)] = 0$, $[m - \rho(A)] = 1$. Hence no equations are redundant, but lower-order solutions can be found to a reduced system when one equation is ignored. In four-dimensional solution space, equations 1 and 2 are parallel hyperplanes and equation 3 cuts through them; hence either equation 1 or 2 can be eliminated to produce a lower-order system with basic solutions. For example, without equation 1,

$$\begin{bmatrix} 2 \\ 1 \end{bmatrix} x_1 + \begin{bmatrix} 4 \\ 1 \end{bmatrix} x_2 + \begin{bmatrix} 2 \\ 3 \end{bmatrix} x_3 + \begin{bmatrix} 6 \\ 4 \end{bmatrix} x_4 = \begin{bmatrix} 5 \\ 2 \end{bmatrix}$$

Now, $\rho(A^R) = \rho(A^R \mid B^R) = 2$. Several basic solutions are: $x_1 = \frac{3}{2}$, $x_2 = \frac{1}{2}$, $x_3 = 0$, $x_4 = 0$; $x_1 = 0$, $x_2 = \frac{11}{10}$, $x_3 = \frac{3}{10}$, $x_4 = 0$; $x_1 = 4$, $x_2 = 0$, $x_3 = 0$, $x_4 = -\frac{1}{2}$, and so on. Here, all six (C_2^4) basic solutions exist. If the last column in A^R had been $\begin{bmatrix} 4 \\ 2 \end{bmatrix}$, then the basic solution involving only x_1 and x_4 would not have been possible, since $\begin{bmatrix} 2 \\ 1 \end{bmatrix}$ and $\begin{bmatrix} 4 \\ 2 \end{bmatrix}$ do not form a basis for two-dimensional vector space. Similarly, basic solutions can be found for the reduced system made up of only equations 1 and 3 from (2-15).

When $\rho(A) = 1$, all columns of A are linearly dependent and B does not lie on the single ray defined by the A_i in vector space. For example:

ALGEBRA

$$\begin{aligned} x_1 + 2x_2 + x_3 &= 4, \\ 2x_1 + 4x_2 + 2x_3 &= 5. \end{aligned} \tag{2-16}$$

GEOMETRY

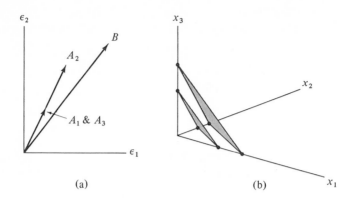

Figure 2.12.   Representation of (2-16) in (a) Vector Space, (b) Solution Space

$\rho(A) = 1$, $\rho(A \mid B) = 2$, $m = 2$, $n = 3$. The only "lower-order" solutions possible require that $[m - \rho(A)] = 1$ equation be ignored—that is, only *one* equation at a time can be satisfied. In solution space, all planes are parallel and distinct.

Summary: Fewer equations than unknowns

Basic solutions turn out to be of fundamental importance in the structure and solution of linear programming problems (Chapters 6 and 7). The essential problem of too many variables in $m < n$ linear equation systems is solved by fixing the values of some of the variables at zero; hence they cease to be unknowns.

If the system is inconsistent, then we know that some equations will have to be ignored before we can find "lower-order" solutions; once we have decided which equation or equations to ignore, the problem is one of finding basic solutions to the reduced system. To continue with the same illustration, the political candidate might have *four* media possibilities (for example, billboards also) and three critical districts and he may have been told that in districts a and b he needed to gain 400 and 500 votes, respectively. In addition, the coefficients for the x's in region a might be 2, 3, 3, and 4 and in region b 4, 6, 6, and 8. Irrespective of the details for region c, the three-equation, four-variable system will be inconsistent, since the equations for regions a and b are parallel planes in four-dimensional solution space. Thus he might ignore region a, where he needs to gain 400 votes, and concentrate on satisfying the requirements in regions b and c. If the system is consistent but has redundant equations, the same is true—we remove the redundant equations and then find basic solutions to the smaller system. If the campaign manager's estimate for needed new votes had been 400 and 800 for regions a and b, respectively, then the equation for either of these regions would be redundant, since both define the *same* plane. Hence either can be ignored; it will automatically be fulfilled by a solution to the smaller system. And if the equations are consistent and none are redundant, we find basic solutions to the entire system. The political candidate simply eliminates some of the advertising media from next week's plans.

Thus, once the excess equations are removed (either redundant and unnecessary or inconsistent and impossible), we have a system that necessarily satisfies the requirement that the rank of the coefficient matrix is equal to the number of (remaining) equations. Finding basic solutions is then a systematic way of disposing of the excess variables that are always present in the $m < n$ case.

2.5. MORE EQUATIONS THAN UNKNOWNS $(m > n)$

In these cases, the coefficient matrix is "tall and narrow"; its greatest possible rank is n and therefore unique solutions *are* possible, in contrast to the $m < n$ case in Section 2.4.

Consistent systems—$\rho(A) = \rho(A \mid B)$

CASE MC1: $\rho(A) = n$. The highest possible rank for A is n, which is the number of columns in A. Yet B, the right-hand side, is an m-element column vector. Since $m > n$, we know that the columns of A can never constitute a full basis in m-dimensional vector space; m linearly independent vectors are necessary for that purpose. Therefore, a unique solution could occur only if the consistent equation system had exactly $(m - n)$ *redundant* equations that could be removed without any loss of information. This is precisely the case when $\rho(A) = n$.

If $(m - n)$ redundant equations are removed, the remaining $n \times n$ system will have a unique solution, since all n of the (linearly independent) columns of the reduced coefficient matrix will be needed for the basis in n-dimensional space; B will be a unique combination of *all* of the columns of A^R. This is the "well-behaved" $n \times n$ case, once redundant equations are omitted.

ALGEBRA

$$\begin{aligned} x_1 + 0x_2 &= 2, \\ 0x_1 + x_2 &= 2, \\ x_1 + x_2 &= 4. \end{aligned} \qquad (2\text{-}17)$$

GEOMETRY

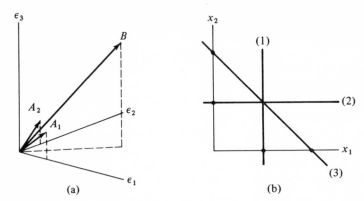

Figure 2.13.   Representation of (2-17) in (a) Vector Space, (b) Solution Space

Here $\rho(A) = 2$, $\rho(A \mid B) = 2$, $m = 3$, $n = 2$. The system is consistent, any $[m - \rho(A)] = 1$ equation can be considered redundant, and since $\rho(A) = n$, the 2×2 reduced system will have a unique solution. From the perspective of solution space it appears obvious that *any* equation can be dropped. We explore the consequences in vector space in Table 2.3.

CASE MC2: $\rho(A) = k$, $k < n$.   If $(m - k)$ of the redundant equations are removed, the new k-element right-hand side vector can be expressed as a linear combination of the k linearly independent columns in the coefficient matrix of the reduced system. This is identical to Case FC2, above. Both reduce to consistent $k \times n$ systems ($k < n$) and hence require basic solutions. An example will indicate the unlikelihood of this case.

$$\begin{aligned}
x_1 + 2x_2 + 2x_3 &= 1, \\
2x_1 + 4x_2 + 4x_3 &= 2, \\
x_1 + 3x_2 + 5x_3 &= 1, \\
3x_1 + 6x_2 + 6x_3 &= 3.
\end{aligned} \qquad (2\text{-}18)$$

$\rho(A) = k = 2$, $\rho(A \mid B) = 2$, $m = 4$, $n = 3$. Clearly, equations 1, 2, and 4 define the same plane in solution space. Equation 3 defines a plane that intersects it in a line. Hence the system is consistent; there are multiple solutions. Removing $[m - \rho(A)] = 2$ equations—for example, equations 1 and 4—leaves

$$\begin{aligned}
2x_1 + 4x_2 + 4x_3 &= 2, \\
x_1 + 3x_2 + 5x_3 &= 1,
\end{aligned} \quad \text{or} \quad \begin{bmatrix} 2 \\ 1 \end{bmatrix} x_1 + \begin{bmatrix} 4 \\ 3 \end{bmatrix} x_2 + \begin{bmatrix} 4 \\ 5 \end{bmatrix} x_3 = \begin{bmatrix} 2 \\ 1 \end{bmatrix},$$

$$A^R = \begin{bmatrix} 2 & 4 & 4 \\ 1 & 3 & 5 \end{bmatrix} \quad \text{and} \quad \rho(A^R) = 2.$$

The coefficient matrix of this reduced system, A^R, can be partitioned as

Table 2.3. Alternative Reductions of (2-17) to a 2 $\times$ 2 System

	(1)	*Equation dropped* (2)	(3)
Remaining system	$\begin{bmatrix} 0 \\ 1 \end{bmatrix} x_1 + \begin{bmatrix} 1 \\ 1 \end{bmatrix} x_2 = \begin{bmatrix} 2 \\ 4 \end{bmatrix}$	$\begin{bmatrix} 1 \\ 1 \end{bmatrix} x_1 + \begin{bmatrix} 0 \\ 1 \end{bmatrix} x_2 = \begin{bmatrix} 2 \\ 4 \end{bmatrix}$	$\begin{bmatrix} 1 \\ 0 \end{bmatrix} x_1 + \begin{bmatrix} 0 \\ 1 \end{bmatrix} x_2 = \begin{bmatrix} 2 \\ 2 \end{bmatrix}$
Rank of A^R	2	2	2
Unique solution	$x_1 = 2,\ x_2 = 2$	$x_1 = 2,\ x_2 = 2$	$x_1 = 2,\ x_2 = 2$

$$\begin{bmatrix} 2 & 4 & | & 4 \\ 1 & 3 & | & 5 \end{bmatrix}$$

and hence x_3 set to zero for the basic solution

$$(1)\begin{bmatrix} 2 \\ 1 \end{bmatrix} + (0)\begin{bmatrix} 4 \\ 3 \end{bmatrix} = \begin{bmatrix} 2 \\ 1 \end{bmatrix}.$$

Note that this basic solution

$$\begin{bmatrix} x_1 \\ x_2 \end{bmatrix} = \begin{bmatrix} 1 \\ 0 \end{bmatrix}$$

is degenerate, since x_2, a basis variable, has value zero. Other possible partitionings are

$$\begin{bmatrix} 2 & 4 & | & 4 \\ 1 & 5 & | & 3 \end{bmatrix} \quad \text{or} \quad \begin{bmatrix} 4 & 4 & | & 2 \\ 3 & 5 & | & 1 \end{bmatrix},$$

generating basic solutions

$$\begin{bmatrix} x_1 \\ x_3 \end{bmatrix} = \begin{bmatrix} 1 \\ 0 \end{bmatrix} \quad \text{or} \quad \begin{bmatrix} x_2 \\ x_3 \end{bmatrix} = \begin{bmatrix} \frac{3}{4} \\ -\frac{1}{4} \end{bmatrix},$$

respectively.

The very special case where $\rho(A) = 1$ is analogous to the same situation when $m = n$ or $m < n$. In the latter case [Equations (2-14), Figure 2.11] the dimensionality of vector space was less than that of solution space; here the opposite is true. The analysis is otherwise identical.

ALGEBRA

$$\begin{aligned} 2x_1 + x_2 &= 1, \\ 4x_1 + 2x_2 &= 2, \\ 6x_1 + 3x_2 &= 3. \end{aligned} \tag{2-19}$$

GEOMETRY

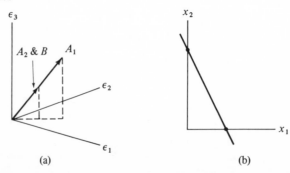

(a)   (b)

Figure 2.14.   Representation of (2-19) in (a) Vector Space, (b) Solution
Space

$\rho(A) = 1$, $\rho(A \mathbin{\vdots} B) = 1$, $m = 3$, $n = 2$. There are $[m - \rho(A)] = 2$ redundant equations. Since the system of equations is consistent, *any* two equations are redundant and can be removed without loss of information; one equation contains all that is known about the variables, hence an infinite number of solutions is possible.

Inconsistent systems—$\rho(A) \neq \rho(A \mathbin{\vdots} B)$

CASE MI1: $\rho(A) = n$. This parallels the same case for a consistent system in the sense that once the "extra" $(m - n)$ equations (here containing incompatible requirements on the variables) are removed, a *unique* solution for the reduced $(n \times n)$ system can be found. For example:

ALGEBRA

$$\begin{aligned}
x_1 + 0x_2 &= 2, \\
0x_1 + x_2 &= 2, \\
x_1 + x_2 &= 3.
\end{aligned} \tag{2-20}$$

GEOMETRY

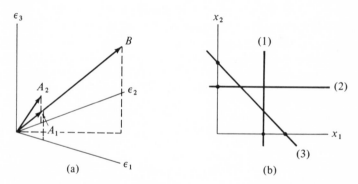

Figure 2.15. Representation of (2-20) in (a) Vector Space, (b) Solution Space

$\rho(A) = 2$, $\rho(A \mathbin{\vdots} B) = 3$, $m = 3$, $n = 2$. By removing one equation, we obtain a 2×2 system whose solution is indicated by one of the three intersections in the solution-space picture. For example, if we ignore equation 2,

$$A^R = \begin{bmatrix} 1 & 0 \\ 1 & 1 \end{bmatrix}, \qquad B^R = \begin{bmatrix} 2 \\ 3 \end{bmatrix},$$

and the solution to this lower-order system is

$$X^R = (A^R)^{-1}B^R = \begin{bmatrix} 1 & 0 \\ -1 & 1 \end{bmatrix}\begin{bmatrix} 2 \\ 3 \end{bmatrix} = \begin{bmatrix} 2 \\ 1 \end{bmatrix}.$$

CASE MI2: $\rho(A) = k$, $k < n$. This situation is identical in principle to that under Case MC2, above, except that in the present case when $(m - k)$ equations are omitted the system is changed; requirements on the variables are ignored. In the former case, $(m - k)$ equations were redundant and could be dropped without loss of information.

In (2-18), equations 1, 2, and 4 defined the same plane in solution space. In the following equations, they define three parallel planes. As before, equation 3 cuts them all.

$$\begin{aligned}
x_1 + 2x_2 + 2x_3 &= 1, \\
2x_1 + 4x_2 + 4x_3 &= 3, \\
x_1 + 3x_2 + 5x_3 &= 1, \\
3x_1 + 6x_2 + 6x_3 &= 8.
\end{aligned} \tag{2-21}$$

$\rho(A) = k = 2$; $\rho(A \mid B) = 3$; $m = 4$, $n = 3$. Basic (and hence nonunique) solutions can be found to various systems with two $[= (m - k)]$ equations, but at the expense of not meeting the requirements of the omitted equations. As usual with inconsistent systems, we achieve solutions only by throwing away equations.

The special case when $\rho(A) = 1$ is identical in principle to the $m = n$ and $m < n$ situations. Only the geometry changes slightly.

ALGEBRA

$$\begin{aligned}
x_1 + x_2 &= 10, \\
2x_1 + 2x_2 &= 16, \\
3x_1 + 3x_2 &= 21.
\end{aligned} \tag{2-22}$$

GEOMETRY

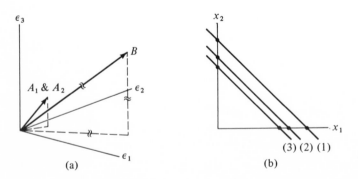

Figure 2.16.   Representation of (2-22) in (a) Vector Space, (b) Solution Space

$\rho(A) = k = 1$, $\rho(A \mid B) = 2$; $m = 3$, $n = 2$. The only solutions possible are when two equations $(m - k = 2)$ are ignored.

Summary: More equations than unknowns

Thus we see that in systems with more equations than unknowns we have, essentially, too much information about the variables. For a consistent system (one in which one or more solutions exist), at least $(m - n)$ equations must be redundant. If exactly $(m - n)$ may be removed, we have in fact a square system with a unique solution. If more may be removed, we have an "underdetermined" system with multiple solutions; this is the case of consistent systems with more variables than equations and hence with basic solutions. If none of the equations are unnecessary, or if less than $(m - n)$ of them may be removed, then the system is not consistent; no values of $x_1, \ldots, x_n$ can be found to satisfy all of the given equations. Then the only possibility is for "lower-order" solutions in which some of the equations are simply ignored. We have seen that it is necessary to ignore $[m - \rho(A)]$ of them. Thus, when $\rho(A) = 1$, we can cope with only one equation at a time; the higher the rank of A, the larger the number of equations that can be satisfied simultaneously. (The reader should be able to construct cases using the political candidate example—now with fewer advertising media than critical districts—to illustrate each of these possibilities.)

SUMMARY

Table 2.4 classifies solution possibilities for square and nonsquare systems.

Table 2.4. Classification of Solutions to m Linear Equations in n Unknowns $(AX = B)$

	Consistent system; $\rho(A) = \rho(A \vdots B)$		Inconsistent system; $\rho(A) \neq \rho(A \vdots B)$		
				"Lower-order" solutions	
	Unique solution $\rho(A) = n$	Multiple solutions $\rho(A) < n$	Total inconsistency; complete parallelism $\rho(A) = 1$	Unique solutions $\rho(A) = n$	Multiple solutions $1 < \rho(A) < n$
$m = n$	*Homogeneous system* Case H1 2×2 example Equations (2-9) Figure 2.9 *Nonhomogeneous system* Case NHC1 2×2 example Equations (1-48), (2-1) Figures 1.1, 2.1	*Homogeneous system* Case H2 2×2 example Equations (2-10) Figure 2.10 *Nonhomogeneous system* Case NHC2 2×2 example Equations (1-50), (2-3) Figures 1.3, 2.3 3×3 example Equations (2-5), (2-6) Figures 2.5, 2.6, and 2.7	Case NHI2 2×2 example Equations (1-49), (2-2) Figures 1.2, 2.2 3×3 example Equations (2-4) Figure 2.4	Impossible, since $\rho(A) \leq (n - 1)$	Case NHI2 3×3 example Equations (2-7) Figure 2.8 4×4 example Equations (2-8)

$m < n$	Impossible, since $\rho(A) \leq m < n$	Case FC 1 2 × 4 example Equations (2-12) Case FC 2 3 × 4 example Equations (2-13) 2 × 3 example Equations (2-14) Figure 2.11	Case FI2 2 × 3 example Equations (2-16) Figure 2.12	Impossible, since $\rho(A) < m < n$	Case FI2 3 × 4 example Equations (2-15)
$m > n$	Case MC1 3 × 2 example Equations (2-17) Figure 2.13	Case MC2 4 × 3 example Equations (2-18) 3 × 2 example Equations (2-19) Figure 2.14	Case MI2 3 × 2 example Equations (2-22) Figure 2.16	Case MI1 3 × 2 example Equations (2-20) Figure 2.15	Case MI2 4 × 3 example Equations (2-21)

PROBLEMS

1. Do the following sets of vectors form bases (in their relevant spaces)?

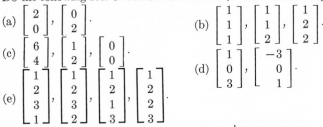

(a) $\begin{bmatrix} 2 \\ 0 \end{bmatrix}, \begin{bmatrix} 0 \\ 2 \end{bmatrix}.$

(b) $\begin{bmatrix} 1 \\ 1 \\ 1 \end{bmatrix}, \begin{bmatrix} 1 \\ 1 \\ 2 \end{bmatrix}, \begin{bmatrix} 1 \\ 2 \\ 2 \end{bmatrix}.$

(c) $\begin{bmatrix} 6 \\ 4 \end{bmatrix}, \begin{bmatrix} 1 \\ 2 \end{bmatrix}, \begin{bmatrix} 0 \\ 0 \end{bmatrix}.$

(d) $\begin{bmatrix} 1 \\ 0 \\ 3 \end{bmatrix}, \begin{bmatrix} -3 \\ 0 \\ 1 \end{bmatrix}.$

(e) $\begin{bmatrix} 1 \\ 2 \\ 3 \\ 1 \end{bmatrix}, \begin{bmatrix} 1 \\ 2 \\ 3 \\ 2 \end{bmatrix}, \begin{bmatrix} 1 \\ 2 \\ 1 \\ 3 \end{bmatrix}, \begin{bmatrix} 1 \\ 2 \\ 2 \\ 3 \end{bmatrix}.$

2. On the basis of observations on $\rho(A)$ and $\rho(A \mid B)$ describe the kinds of solutions (unique, none, multiple) that each of the following systems has.

(a) $- x_1 - 3x_2 = \quad 16,$
$3x_1 + 9x_2 = -25.$

(b) $x_1 + 2x_2 + 3x_3 = 0,$
$6x_2 + 9x_3 = 0.$

(c) $x_1 + 2x_2 + 2x_3 = \quad 3,$
$3x_1 + 4x_2 + 5x_3 = \quad 7,$
$4x_1 + 6x_2 + 7x_3 = 10.$

(d) $6x_1 + 2x_2 + 8x_3 = 4,$
$x_1 + x_2 + 2x_3 = 1,$
$3x_1 + 2x_2 + 5x_3 = 1.$

3. Find all the *basic* solutions to the following equations.

(a) $x_1 + x_2 + 4x_3 = 10,$
$2x_1 + 3x_2 + 8x_3 = 10.$

(b) $x_1 + 2x_2 + 2x_3 = \quad 3,$
$3x_1 + 4x_2 + 5x_3 = \quad 7,$
$4x_1 + 6x_2 + 7x_3 = 10.$

(c) $x_1 + 2x_2 + 3x_3 + 4x_4 = 10,$
$x_1 + 2x_2 + x_3 + 2x_4 = 10.$

4. What kinds of solutions are possible for the following equations? (If a unique solution exists, find it.)

(a) $x_1 + 2x_2 = 3,$
$4x_1 + 7x_2 = 1,$
$3x_1 + 6x_2 = 9.$

(b) $x_1 + 2x_2 = 3,$
$4x_1 + 7x_2 = 1,$
$3x_1 + x_2 = 6.$

(c) $x_1 + 2x_2 = 3,$
$4x_1 + 7x_2 = 1,$
$3x_1 + 6x_2 = 6.$

(d) $x_1 + 2x_2 = \quad 3,$
$4x_1 + 7x_2 = \quad 1,$
$x_1 + 3x_2 = 14.$

5. Do the following equation systems have unique solutions?

(a) $-4x_1 + x_2 + 3x_3 \qquad = 10,$
$2x_1 + 5x_2 - 7x_3 \qquad = 47,$
$x_1 - x_2 \qquad + 2x_4 = 39,$
$- 4x_2 + 4x_3 + x_4 = 16.$

(b) $x_1 \qquad + 3x_3 + 2x_4 = 4,$
$-2x_1 + x_2 + 6x_3 + x_4 = 7,$
$- x_1 + x_2 + 2x_3 - 4x_4 = 6,$
$- 3x_3 + 7x_4 = 0.$

(c) $x_1 + x_2 = 2; \quad 2x_3 + x_4 = 5; \quad x_1 + x_3 = 9; \quad x_3 + x_4 = 0.$

6. By using matrix *algebra*, the rules of rank, and so on, describe the *geometry* in solution space of each of the following:

(a) $3x_1 - x_2 + 2x_3 = 4,$
$x_1 + x_2 + x_3 = 10,$
$15x_1 - 5x_2 + 10x_3 = 18.$

(b) $x_1 + x_2 + x_3 = 1,$
$3x_1 + 3x_2 + 3x_3 = 3,$
$-5x_1 - 5x_2 - 5x_3 = 5.$

(c) $5x_1 - 10x_2 = 20,$
$-10x_1 + 5x_2 = 20,$
$x_1 - 2x_2 = 4.$

(d) $x_1 + x_2 = 4,$
$2x_1 + x_2 = 5,$
$4x_1 + 3x_2 = 1.$

(e) Left-hand side the same as in (a); right-hand side $= O.$

(f) $30x_1 + 5x_2 + 7x_3 = 100; 60x_1 + 10x_2 + 14x_3 = 200.$

(g) Left-hand side the same as in (f); right-hand side $= \begin{bmatrix} 100 \\ 100 \end{bmatrix}$.

7. Given the following pair of linear equations:

$$ax_1 + x_2 = 0, \qquad 10x_1 + bx_2 = c.$$

 (a) Discuss, for the homogeneous case, the conditions on a and b under which multiple solutions will exist.

 (b) In the nonhomogeneous case, under what conditions on a and b will the solution value for x_2 be zero?

8. Consider the following set of equations:

$$\begin{aligned} 2x_1 + ax_2 - x_3 &= 10, \\ bx_1 - 4x_2 + x_3 &= -30, \\ -x_1 + x_2 &= -20. \end{aligned}$$

For what values of a and b (a) will the system have a unique solution? (b) are the equations inconsistent? (c) are there infinitely many solutions?

REFERENCES

1. Campbell, Hugh G., *An Introduction to Matrices, Vectors and Linear Programming.* New York: Appleton-Century-Crofts, 1965.
2. Hadley, G., *Linear Algebra.* Reading, Mass.: Addison-Wesley Publishing Company, Inc., 1961.
3. Teichroew, D., *An Introduction to Management Science: Deterministic Models.* New York: John Wiley & Sons, Inc., 1964.

3

MAXIMIZATION AND MINIMIZATION
FOR FUNCTIONS OF ONE
AND TWO VARIABLES

This chapter assumes that the reader already has some acquaintance with the fundamental concepts of differential calculus. For functions of one variable this means essentially the notion of the derivative as the slope of a function (that is, the slope of its tangent) at a point, the obvious application that this has to the location of stationary points of the function (points at which the slope of the tangent is zero), and the classification of such points as maxima, minima, or neither (preferably through the use of the second derivative).[1] It will also help if the reader has been exposed to differential calculus with functions of two variables—that is, to the concepts of a partial derivative and of the total differential and to problems of maxima and minima for a function of two variables.

This chapter will review these fundamentals and present the (hopefully) familiar results on maximum and minimum points in a second and possibly less familiar form using differentials. This provides a foundation on which to construct the extensions of the theory when more (in general, n) variables are involved and when constraints or "side conditions" on some or all of the variables are also required. These more complicated issues are taken up in Chapter 4.

---

[1] Obviously an ability to apply the most basic rules of differentiation will also be assumed.

3.1. LIMITS AND DERIVATIVES FOR FUNCTIONS OF ONE VARIABLE

In dealing with functions of only one variable, it is customary to denote the dependent variable by y, the independent variable by x, and the function that transforms values of x into values of y by $f(x)$. Thus $y = f(x)$ is the general description of the functional relationship; a specific example is $y = f(x) = \frac{1}{2}x^2 - x + 1$.

Limits

Derivatives are of fundamental importance in maximization and minimization problems. Since the derivative is defined as a limiting process, it is useful to review briefly the concept of a limit. Consider the specific function $y = f(x) = \frac{1}{2}x^2 - x + 1$; at $x = 2$, $y = f(2) = 1$. For values of x "near to," but larger than, 2, $f(x)$ is "near to" 1; for example (all to three-decimal accuracy), at $x = 2.5$, $f(x) = 1.625$; at $x = 2.25$, $f(x) = 1.281$; at $x = 2.01$, $f(x) = 1.010$; and at $x = 2.001$, $f(x) = 1.001$. The sequence of values of x—2.5, 2.25, 2.01, 2.001—is said to approach 2 from the right (from values of x larger than 2). When $f(x)$ approaches a number, α^*, as x approaches a specific value, x_0, from the right, α^* is termed the *limit* of $f(x)$ as x approaches x_0 from the right [or the right-sided limit of $f(x)$ as x approaches x_0]. This is denoted

$$\lim_{x \to x_0^+} f(x) = \alpha^*.$$

(The $+$ superscript indicates that the values of x are larger than x_0.)

If we consider values of x "near to" but smaller than 2, $f(x)$, as defined above, is also "near to" 1. When $x = 1.5$, $f(x) = 0.625$; for $x = 1.75$, $f(x) = 0.781$; at $x = 1.99$, $f(x) = 0.990$; and at $x = 1.999$, $f(x) = 0.999$. The sequence 1.5, 1.75, 1.99, 1.999 approaches 2 from the left; as above, when $f(x)$ approaches a number α^{**} as x approaches x_0 from the left, α^{**} is termed the limit of $f(x)$ as x approaches x_0 from the left (or the left-sided limit).

$$\lim_{x \to x_0^-} f(x) = \alpha^{**}.$$

When, as in the example above, $\alpha^* = \alpha^{**}$ then this common value is termed the limit of $f(x)$ as x approaches x_0 (without reference to direction) and denoted

$$\lim_{x \to x_0} f(x) = \alpha^* \quad (\text{or } \alpha^{**}).$$

For $f(x) = \frac{1}{2}x^2 - x + 1$ the statement would be

$$\lim_{x \to 2^+} f(x) = \lim_{x \to 2^-} f(x) = \lim_{x \to 2} f(x) = 1.$$

The distinction between right- and left-sided limits is necessary for a number of rather special kinds of functions. Two illustrations are:

1. *Step functions.* Let

$$f(x) = \begin{cases} 1, & x \le 5, \\ 3, & x > 5; \end{cases}$$

this is shown in Figure 3.1. For $x_0 = 5$, the right-sided limit,

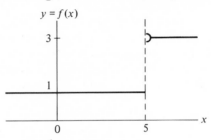

Figure 3.1. $f(x) = \begin{cases} 1, & x \le 5, \\ 3, & x > 5. \end{cases}$

$\lim_{x \to 5^+} f(x)$, is 3, while the left-sided limit, $\lim_{x \to 5^-} f(x)$, is 1. The right- and left-sided limits both exist, but since they are unequal, there is no single number that is $\lim_{x \to 5} f(x)$.

2. *Functions that have asymptotes.* The graph of

$$f(x) = \begin{cases} 1/(x - 1), & x > 1, \\ (x - 1)^2, & x \le 1, \end{cases}$$

is represented in Figure 3.2. For $x_0 = 1$, $\lim_{x \to 1^-} f(x) = 0$, while as x ap-

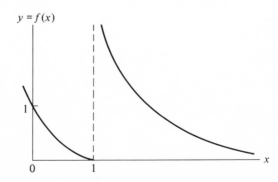

Figure 3.2. $f(x) = \begin{cases} 1/(x - 1), & x > 1, \\ (x - 1)^2, & x \le 1. \end{cases}$

proaches 1 from the right, $f(x)$ does not approach any finite number; it gets larger and larger.

In addition there may be points at which neither the right- nor the left-sided limit exists. This is true for

$$f(x) = \begin{cases} 1/x, & x > 0, \\ -1/x, & x < 0, \end{cases} \quad \text{at } x_0 = 0,$$

as Figure 3.3 suggests. Thus it may be that at one or more points neither

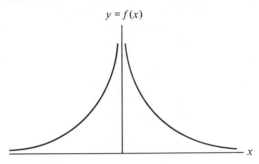

$y = f(x)$

Figure 3.3. $f(x) = \begin{cases} 1/x, & x > 0, \\ -1/x, & x < 0. \end{cases}$

one-sided limit of a function exists; one may exist but not the other; both may exist but their values may differ; or both may exist and have the same value.[2]

With these concepts in mind, the notion of *continuity* is easily defined. Formally, if

$$\lim_{x \to x_0} f(x) = f(x_0),$$

then $f(x)$ is said to be continuous at x_0. This simply says that at x_0 both right- and left-sided limits exist and have the same value, which is $f(x_0)$. If $f(x)$ is not continuous everywhere over the values of x on which it is defined, it is termed *discontinuous*. When $f(x)$ is continuous everywhere, its graph has no gaps or spaces in it; it can be drawn without lifting the pencil from the paper. The functions in Figures 3.1, 3.2, and 3.3 are discontinuous.

[2] More formally, the reader may recall that limits are usually defined using very small positive quantities δ and ϵ. The notation $\lim_{x \to x_0^+} f(x) = \alpha^*$ means that $|f(x) - \alpha^*|$, the absolute value of the difference between α^* and the function evaluated at x, is arbitrarily small for all x ($> x_0$) that are "sufficiently close" to x_0. Therefore *if* for all $\epsilon > 0$ we can find a $\delta > 0$ such that for all x in the range $x_0 < x < x_0 + \delta$, $|f(x) - \alpha^*| < \epsilon$, *then* $\lim_{x \to x_0^+} f(x) = \alpha^*$. Neither this formal definition nor the rules for finding limits for sums, products, or quotients of functions are essential for the material in this book.

The derivative (algebra)

The derivative of a function of one variable is defined in terms of limits. It can be described as the "instantaneous rate of change" of y, the dependent variable, *at a point*—that is, at a specific value of x, the independent variable. This concept is easily shown as the limit of the "average rate of change" of y *over an interval*—that is, over a range of values for x. At a specific value of x, say x_0, the dependent variable, y, takes on a value y_0, which equals $f(x_0)$, the function $f(x)$ evaluated at the point where $x = x_0$.

Consider some larger value of x, say x_1, near to x_0. The new value of y will be $f(x_1)$, which may be larger, smaller, or no different than $f(x_0)$. Then the "average rate of change" of y per unit of x is given by $[f(x_1) - f(x_0)]/(x_1 - x_0)$—simply the total change in y divided by the number of units that x changed. This is often shown as

$$\frac{\Delta y}{\Delta x} = \frac{f(x_1) - f(x_0)}{x_1 - x_0}. \tag{3-1}$$

If we let $x_1 = x_0 + \Delta x$, where $\Delta x > 0$, this average rate of change can also be written

$$\frac{\Delta y}{\Delta x} = \frac{f(x_0 + \Delta x) - f(x_0)}{\Delta x}. \tag{3-2}$$

We can imagine that the amount of change in x, over which this average is calculated, becomes very small. The limit, if it exists, would be denoted (since $\Delta x > 0$)

$$\lim_{\Delta x \to 0^+} \frac{\Delta y}{\Delta x} = \lim_{x_1 \to x_0^+} \frac{f(x_1) - f(x_0)}{x_1 - x_0} = \lim_{\Delta x \to 0^+} \frac{f(x_0 + \Delta x) - f(x_0)}{\Delta x}. \tag{3-3}$$

Similarly, for a value of x, say x_2, near to but smaller than x_0, we could find an average as shown in (3-1) or (3-2)—where $x_2 = x_0 + \Delta x$, and $\Delta x < 0$. In the limit, when x_2 becomes very close to x_0, we would have (now Δx is negative)

$$\lim_{\Delta x \to 0^-} \frac{\Delta y}{\Delta x} = \lim_{x_2 \to x_0^-} \frac{f(x_2) - f(x_0)}{x_2 - x_0} = \lim_{\Delta x \to 0^-} \frac{f(x_0 + \Delta x) - f(x_0)}{\Delta x} \tag{3-4}$$

When the limits in (3-3) and (3-4) are equal—that is, when

$$\lim_{\Delta x \to 0^+} \frac{\Delta y}{\Delta x} = \lim_{\Delta x \to 0^-} \frac{\Delta y}{\Delta x} = \lim_{\Delta x \to 0} \frac{\Delta y}{\Delta x},$$

this limit is termed the derivative of $f(x)$ at the point x_0 and is usually denoted $(dy/dx)_{x_0}$, $f'(x_0)$, or $df(x_0)/dx$, and read as "the derivative of y with respect to x, evaluated at $x = x_0$." Thus, for example

$$f'(x_0) = \lim_{\Delta x \to 0} \frac{f(x_0 + \Delta x) - f(x_0)}{\Delta x}. \tag{3-5}$$

Since the definition of the derivative rests on the existence of a limit, it is clear that functions such as those in Figures 3.1, 3.2, and 3.3 will not have derivatives everywhere; we have already seen that they do not have limits everywhere—that is, that they are discontinuous. Continuity of a function, however, is not enough to guarantee a derivative at every point, as the following example shows. Let $y = f(x) = 2 + |x|$—which means that y equals 2 plus the amount x without regard to sign—that is, $f(x) = 2 + x$ for $x \geq 0$, $f(x) = 2 - x$ for $x < 0$. Figure 3.4 illustrates.

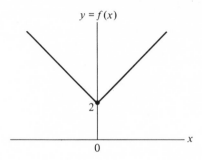

$$y = f(x)$$

Figure 3.4. $f(x) = 2 + |x|$

Consider $x_0 = 0$; clearly

$$\lim_{x \to 0^+} f(x) = 2, \qquad \lim_{x \to 0^-} f(x) = 2, \quad \text{and hence} \quad \lim_{x \to 0} f(x) = 2.$$

Moreover, $2 = f(0)$, so the function is continuous at $x = 0$—as is obvious when we have Figure 3.4 in front of us. Equally obvious is that, while continuous, the function at $x = 0$ has a kink, $f(x)$ is not "smooth" everywhere. The problem with the derivative becomes clear when we apply (3-3) and (3-4), at $x_0 = 0$. From (3-3)

$$\lim_{\Delta x \to 0^+} \frac{\Delta y}{\Delta x} = \lim_{\Delta x \to 0^+} \frac{f(x_0 + \Delta x) - f(x_0)}{\Delta x}$$

$$= \lim_{x_1 \to x_0^+} \frac{f(x_1) - f(x_0)}{x_1 - x_0} = \frac{2 + x_1 - 2}{x_1} = 1,$$

and from (3-4)

$$\lim_{\Delta x \to 0^-} \frac{\Delta y}{\Delta x} = \lim_{\Delta x \to 0^-} \frac{f(x_0 + \Delta x) - f(x_0)}{\Delta x}$$

$$= \lim_{x_2 \to x_0^-} \frac{f(x_2) - f(x_0)}{x_2 - x_0} = \frac{2 - x_2 - 2}{x_2} = -1.$$

Therefore

$$\lim_{\Delta x \to 0^+} \frac{\Delta y}{\Delta x} \neq \lim_{\Delta x \to 0^-} \frac{\Delta y}{\Delta x}$$

and hence $\lim\limits_{\Delta x \to 0} (\Delta y/\Delta x)$, the derivative, does not exist at $x = 0$. (We will soon have a geometric idea of the problem.)

Thus a function can be continuous at $x = x_0$ and not have a derivative at that point; if, however, there *is* a derivative at the point $x = x_0$, then we know that $f(x)$ is continuous there. A function that has derivatives for all values of x over which it is defined is termed everywhere differentiable[3] (or just differentiable, or simply "smooth," if there is no ambiguity).

One can in principle calculate the derivative for virtually any differentiable function at any value of x by using this fundamental "Δx" definition—that is, by using the so-called "delta process." For example, for the specific function $y = \frac{1}{2}x^2 - x + 1$, we may ask what its rate of change is right at the point where $x = 2$. For *any* x_0 and Δx,

$$f(x_0) = \tfrac{1}{2}x_0^2 - x_0 + 1,$$
$$f(x_0 + \Delta x) = \tfrac{1}{2}(x_0 + \Delta x)^2 - (x_0 + \Delta x) + 1$$
$$= \frac{x_0^2}{2} + x_0\,\Delta x + \frac{(\Delta x)^2}{2} - x_0 - \Delta x + 1.$$

Then

$$f(x_0 + \Delta x) - f(x_0) = x_0\,\Delta x + \frac{(\Delta x)^2}{2} - \Delta x$$

and, from (3-2),

$$\frac{\Delta y}{\Delta x} = x_0 + \frac{\Delta x}{2} - 1.$$

Therefore, as $\Delta x \to 0$, the second term becomes very very small and in the limit

$$\frac{dy}{dx} = \lim_{\Delta x \to 0} \frac{\Delta y}{\Delta x} = x_0 - 1.$$

That is, the rate of change of the function $y = \frac{1}{2}x^2 - x + 1$ can be found at *any* particular point x_0. For the question: what is the rate of change at $x_0 = 2$, we are now able to supply the answer: it is 1. It is only at the stage represented by dy/dx that the specific value of x is introduced. In terms of the derivative notation, we have found $f'(2) = 1$ or $(dy/dx)_{x=2} = 1$ or $df(2)/dx = 1$. It is from the fundamental logic of this "delta process" definition of the derivative that the basic rules for differentiation are derived for generalized functions of one variable.

The reader may wish to recall the most basic rules for differentiation:

---

[3] Or "continuously differentiable." Note that the property of "continuousness" refers to "differentiable" and *not* to "function."

1. If $y = x^n$, $dy/dx = nx^{n-1}$.
2. If $y = f(x) + g(x)$, $dy/dx = f'(x) + g'(x)$.
3. If $y = f(x)g(x)$, $dy/dx = f(x)g'(x) + f'(x)g(x)$.
4. If $y = f(x)/g(x)$, $dy/dx = [f'(x)g(x) - f(x)g'(x)]/[g(x)]^2$.
5. If $y = [f(x)]^n$, $dy/dx = n[f(x)]^{n-1}f'(x)$.

The derivative (geometry)

We also recall that the derivative in one-variable cases is easily shown geometrically as the slope of the tangent to the function at x_0, and the tangent is the limiting form of the secant line through $f(x_0)$ and $f(x_0 + \Delta x)$ on the function, as Δx gets small. Since only two variables, y and x, are involved, $f(x)$ can be represented in two dimensions; it is usual to put the independent variable on the horizontal axis and the dependent variable on the vertical axis. For the specific example $y = \frac{1}{2}x^2 - x + 1$, Figure 3.5 shows the curve representing values taken on by y over the range of the independent variable, x, from 1 to 4. Consider a line measuring the rate of change in y, from an initial point where $x_0 = 2$—that is, where $y_0 = f(2) = \frac{1}{2}(2)^2 - (2) + 1 = 1$—to the point where $x = 4$ (and $y = 5$). This is shown schematically in Figure 3.6.

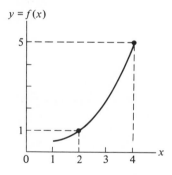

$y = f(x)$

Figure 3.5. $y = \frac{1}{2}x^2 - x + 1$, for $1 \leq x \leq 4$

The vertical displacement on Figure 3.6 (BC) is seen to be exactly the numerator of (3-2) and the horizontal displacement (AC) is exactly Δx, the change in the independent variable, which is the denominator of (3-2). This number is $(5 - 1)/(4 - 2) = 2$, the *average* number of units that y changes per unit of change in x *over the interval $x = 2$ to $x = 4$*. Thus the ratio in (3-2), $\Delta y/\Delta x$, is precisely the *slope* of the hatched line joining A and B. This line cuts the curve in two points and is called a secant to the curve.

Suppose now that Δx had been smaller than 2 (that is, $4 - 2$); if Δx had been only 1—that is, if x had changed from 2 to 3—this secant curve would

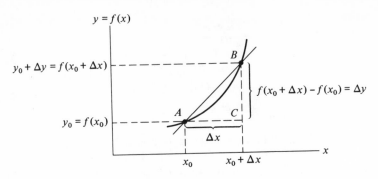

Figure 3.6.   Fundamental Geometry of the Delta Process

have sloped up less steeply and, visually, it would have been "closer" to the curve over the range $x = 2$ to $x = 3$. The ratio $\Delta y/\Delta x$ when $\Delta x = 1$ would be $(2\frac{1}{2} - 1)/(3 - 2) = 1\frac{1}{2}$; this is the average rate of change in y per unit of change in x over the interval from $x = 2$ to $x = 3$. It is different (here less) than the average rate of change over the wider interval $x = 2$ to $x = 4$. As one imagines smaller and smaller changes in x from $x = 2$, the point B rolls along the curve toward the point A. Let $\Delta x = \frac{1}{2}$, then $\Delta y/\Delta x = (\frac{5}{8})/(\frac{1}{2}) = 1.25$. Finally, if $\Delta x = 0.001$, $\Delta y/\Delta x = 1.0005$. Ultimately (in the limit) there is an interval Δx so close to zero that point B is indistinguishable from A; when this happens, the secant AB becomes the tangent to the curve $f(x)$ at the point A. Since this shrinkage of Δx toward zero is exactly the limiting process referred to in (3-5), the derivative of a function $y = f(x)$ at a point x_0 is the slope of the tangent to the function at x_0. Since $f(x)$ here is a "smooth" curve, we know that the limit in (3-5) exists; hence the right- and left-sided limits in (3-3) and (3-4) exist and are equal, and therefore we need only examine the case of an *increase* in x— that is, of $\Delta x > 0$ (the right-sided limit). The tangents to $y = (\frac{1}{2})x^2 - x + 1$ at $x = 2$ (point A), $x = 3$ and $x = 4$ (point B) are shown in Figure 3.7.

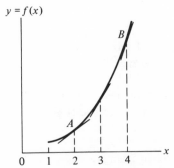

Figure 3.7.   Tangent Lines to $y = \frac{1}{2}x^2 - x + 1$ at $x = 2$, 3, and 4

3.2. REVIEW OF MAXIMUM AND MINIMUM CONDITIONS FOR FUNCTIONS OF ONE VARIABLE

Consider an interval of values of the independent variable x; $a \leq x \leq b$. The function $f(x)$ is said to take on its *absolute* (or *global*) maximum over the interval at x^0 ($a \leq x^0 \leq b$) if $f(x) \leq f(x^0)$ for all x in the interval. By contrast, the function is said to take on a *relative* (or *local*) maximum at x^* (where x^* is inside the interval from a to b) if there is a $\delta > 0$ such that for all x ($a \leq x \leq b$) whose distance from x^* is less than δ, $f(x) \leq f(x^*)$. This simply means that $f(x) \leq f(x^*)$ for all x very near to x^*. Absolute and relative minima are defined in a similar way; the only differences are $f(x) \geq f(x^0)$ and $f(x) \geq f(x^*)$, respectively.

Using the geometric interpretation of the derivative, and considering only smooth—that is, everywhere differentiable—functions in which x can take on all values from $-\infty$ to $+\infty$, it is clear that if $y = f(x)$ has a relative maximum or a minimum at a point x^*, it must necessarily be true that the derivative *evaluated at that point* must be zero. Clearly the tangent must be horizontal at either kind of stationary point.[4] Thus a *necessary condition* for a point to be a maximum *or* a minimum is that the derivative be zero at that point.[5] The condition is not enough to distinguish minima [Figure 3.8(a)] from maxima [Figure 3.8(b)]. Furthermore, it is not *sufficient* evidence that we have either a maximum or a minimum; a function may

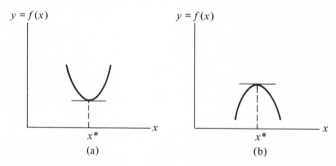

Figure 3.8. (a) Relative Minimum, (b) Relative Maximum

[4] Geometric intuition is consistent with analytic fact. Consider the definition of a relative maximum given above. For all Δx, $-\delta < \Delta x < \delta$, $f(x^* + \Delta x) \leq f(x^*)$—that is, $f(x^* + \Delta x) - f(x^*) \leq 0$. If $\Delta x > 0$ (but still less than δ), this means that $[f(x^* + \Delta x) - f(x^*)]/\Delta x \leq 0$. Since we are dealing exclusively with smooth functions, we know that $f'(x^*)$ exists and is equal to both the right- and left-sided limits, (3-3) and (3-4). Taking the right-sided limit, exactly as in (3-3)—with the reference point now denoted x^*—we have $f'(x^*) \leq 0$. (This relies on the fact that limits of nonpositive or nonnegative expressions are themselves nonpositive or nonnegative, respectively.) Similarly, if $\Delta x < 0$, $[f(x^* + \Delta x) - f(x^*)]/\Delta x \geq 0$. Taking the limit in (3-4), we have $f'(x^*) \geq 0$. Since $f'(x^*) \leq 0$ *and* $f'(x^*) \geq 0$, it follows that $f'(x^*)$ must be equal to 0. The same holds true for a relative minimum.

[5] Other ways of stating this *necessary* condition (again for continuously differentiable

be S-shaped and have a so-called point of inflection where the slope of the tangent may be zero. In Figure 3.9 the slope of the tangent to the curve gets smaller as one moves from x' toward x^*, where it becomes briefly zero and then begins increasing with movement toward x'', further to the right.[6]

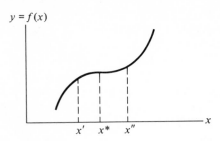

Figure 3.9.   Point of Inflection

Therefore by taking the derivative of a function and *imposing* the requirement that this derivative must be zero—that is, by setting $f'(x) = 0$—we find the value or values of x for which the necessary conditions for either a maximum or minimum are met. If there are no such x's, the function has no stationary point (for example, a straight line with a positive slope; $y = 3x + 2$, $dy/dx = 3$). If there is one such point (as with $y = 2x^2 - 8x + 10$, $dy/dx = 4x - 8$), it is generally important to know whether that point represents a maximum or a minimum (or neither). If there is more than one value of x for which the function is stationary (as with $y = x^3 - 4x^2 + 5x + 2$, $dy/dx = 3x^2 - 8x + 5$), it is also usually necessary to be able to distinguish maxima, minima, and points of inflection

Figure 3.10 represents a function that has three values of x for which $dy/dx = 0$. (That is, to the left of x_1 and to the right of x_5 the curve con-

---

functions only) are: (1) *if* a point is a maximum or a minimum, *then* the derivative evaluated at that point is zero; (2) a maximum or minimum point implies ($\Rightarrow$) a zero-valued derivative at that point; (3) a maximum or minimum is *sufficient* evidence that the derivative there is zero. The restriction to smooth functions is necessary to eliminate situations such as $x = 0$ in Figure 3.4, where the definition of a relative minimum is clearly satisfied but where the derivative is not defined.

[6] Consider the curve in Figure 3.8(a). For *any* x chosen near to x^*, if the tangent is drawn at that point, the curve lies *above* its tangent; the curve is described as convex downward (or concave upward). In Figure 3.8(b) the opposite is true; the curve lies everywhere *below* its tangent. It is concave downward (or convex upward). In Figure 3.9 the curve is convex downward to the left of x^* and convex upward to the right of x^*. Hence a point of inflection is one at which the orientation of the curve changes. Note that a point of inflection need not have a zero-valued derivative; the S-curve in Figure 3.9 could be "more vertical" and still have a point of inflection at x^*. Convexity and concavity of functions is covered in more detail in Section 4.7.

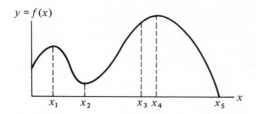

Figure 3.10.   Function with Several Stationary Points

tinues downward infinitely far; there are no additional values of x for which $dy/dx = 0$.) At x_1 the function has a relative maximum, since values of $y = f(x)$ *in the immediate neighborhood* of x_1 are less than at x_1. For similar reasons x_2 represents a relative minimum. Finally, x_4 is an absolute maximum. Note, however, that if one is concerned with the function for values of x within an interval smaller than the range from $-\infty$ to $+\infty$, maxima and minima may occur at endpoints of the interval where the slope of the function is not zero at all. For example, referring again to Figure 3.10, for the range of x from x_1 up to and including x_3—that is, $x_1 \leq x \leq x_3$—x_2 is still a global minimum and x_3 (an endpoint) is a global maximum. Similarly, for $x_3 \leq x \leq x_5$, the endpoint x_5 is a global minimum. In neither of these cases is $dy/dx = 0$. Thus when x is restricted to less than the entire range of real numbers, it is necessary to evaluate the function at *stationary points* (where $dy/dx = 0$) as well as at *endpoints* in order to find global maxima and minima.

For the moment we will be concerned with methods for (1) locating relative maxima and relative minima and (2) distinguishing the one from the other, for cases in which x can take on all values on the real number scale. This is all one needs in many cases. If the method isolates *both* x_1 and x_4 in Figure 3.10 and tells us that they are the only relative maxima in the problem, then by finding the value of the function at each of these points—that is, $f(x_1)$ and $f(x_4)$—we will observe that $f(x_4) > f(x_1)$ and hence know that x_4 represents the absolute maximum.[7]

Clearly, for the case of $y = f(x)$, if the curve only has *one* point at which $dy/dx = 0$, then we know that the relative maximum (or minimum) that it represents is also the absolute maximum (or minimum) for the function. In Chapter 4 we will see how such "well-behaved" functions can be characterized as strictly concave (or convex).

Thus the so-called "first-order" conditions (or *necessary* conditions) on

---

[7] Note that for an absolute maximum over $-\infty < x < +\infty$ it is also necessary to know that the curve does not turn up again, either to the left of x_1 or to the right of x_4. This information is provided by the fact that there is only one relative minimum point, namely x_2, and that it is between x_1 and x_4.

the derivative are not *sufficient* for the distinctions that need to be made between the cases illustrated in Figures 3.8 and 3.9. But they are conditions that we must initially impose—by setting the derivative equal to zero and solving for the critical x values for which this equality holds—to establish whether any maximum or minimum can possibly exist (as usual, for smooth functions). If one or more critical values of x can be found, then the geometric interpretation of the derivative as the slope of the tangent provides a means of making the distinction. Suppose that a point, x^*, has been found for which $f'(x^*) = 0$; the curve has zero slope at that value of x. Then evaluate the derivative at a point slightly to the *right* of x^*, say x_+^*; in particular, find the sign of $f'(x_+^*)$. Do the same for $f'(x_-^*)$—that is, $f'(x)$ evaluated at a point slightly to the *left* of x^*.

Then clearly the point x^* in Figure 3.8(a), the minimum, would be characterized by $f'(x_-^*) < 0$, $f'(x_+^*) > 0$. Schematically, we can sketch the general shape of the curve from these two derivatives (plus the one at x^*); this is done in Figure 3.11(a). Similarly, a maximum would have $f'(x_-^*) > 0$

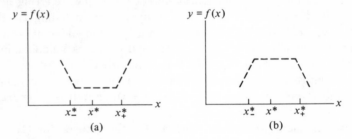

Figure 3.11.   (a) Minimum Point at x^*, (b) Maximum Point at x^*

and $f'(x_+^*) < 0$, as in Figure 3.11(b). (For the case in Figure 3.9, *both* derivatives would be positive; they could also both be negative, if the S-curve ran the other way, from upper left to lower right.) Thus maxima and minima *could* be found only through the use of the derivative dy/dx or $f'(x)$, evaluated at stationary points and on both sides.

The second derivative

The distinction between points that are maxima, minima, and neither, can also be established through use of the second derivative. The derivative that has been used thus far in this chapter to isolate stationary points— dy/dx or $f'(x)$—is in fact the *first* derivative of the function with respect to x. In general, since this derivative is itself a function of x, as in $y = \frac{1}{2}x^2 - x + 1$, it too can be sketched in two-dimensional space, with x on one axis and $f'(x)$ on the other. If it is continuous and smooth, it too has a tangent and hence a derivative at each value of x. (We will now be concerned exclusively with functions whose *first derivatives* are everywhere differentiable.)

The derivative of the derivative is logically termed the *second* derivative; it is obtained by differentiating the first derivative—hence the notation $d[dy/dx]/dx = d^2y/dx^2$, or y'', or $f''(x)$. Its relationship to the first derivative is exactly the same as that of the first derivative to the original function; hence it measures the rate of change of the first derivative at a point. The first derivative of $y = \frac{1}{2}x^2 - x + 1$ is $dy/dx = x - 1$; it too can be shown as a function of x (Figure 3.12), and *its* rate of change at any point x_0 is measured by *its* tangent at x_0. (In the present case the "curve" is a straight line; hence the tangent coincides with the function dy/dx at *any* value of x.)

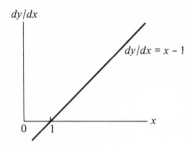

Figure 3.12. dy/dx as a Function of x

Maxima and minima with second derivatives

The second derivative provides a second way of distinguishing maxima from minima (from neither). If at a point, x^*, for which $f'(x^*) = 0$, the second derivative $f''(x^*) > 0$, this says that at x^* the first derivative is getting larger—its *rate of change* is positive. But at x^*, $f'(x^*) = 0$. Therefore, just to the left of x^*, $f'(x)$ must be negative, and just to the right of x^* it must be positive. That is, x^* is a point for which the general sketch in Figure 3.11(a) applies; it is a *minimum* point of $f(x)$. Conversely, if $f''(x^*) < 0$ at $f'(x^*) = 0$, then just prior to x^* the derivative is positive (since at x^* it is zero *and* getting smaller) and just beyond x^* it is negative. Then x^* looks like Figure 3.11(b) and hence represents a *maximum* of $f(x)$. These rules on the sign of the second derivative, the so-called "second-order" conditions, thus provide information sufficient to enable us to distinguish maxima from minima *for points where* $f'(x) = 0$. The distinction between the use of the first-order and second-order conditions should be clear. We *impose* the condition $f'(x) = 0$ to see whether or not there are any x_i^* to consider as maximum or minimum candidates. If there are no x_i^* for which $f'(x_i^*) = 0$, we can quit; the function has no maximum or minimum points. However, if one or more x_i^* are found for which $f'(x_i^*) = 0$, then we evaluate the sign of $f''(x_i^*)$—that is, of the second derivative at that one (or each of the) x_i^*. We are not imposing a further condition but rather only checking a sign. If $f''(x_i^*) > 0$, we *know* that x_i^* represents a minimum point; if $f''(x_i^*) < 0$, we *know* it is a maximum. If $f''(x_i^*) = 0$, we do not know what we have. It may be a maximum or a minimum point or neither. That is why the sign rules on $f''(x^*)$ by themselves are only *sufficient* conditions for a maximum or minimum, not *necessary* too.

The maximum and minimum points (x^*) of the function $y = f(x)$ can be classified as in Table 3.1. We immediately need to note one further case

Table 3.1. Characteristics of Maxima and Minima for $y = f(x)$

	Maximum	*Minimum*
First-order condition	$f'(x^*) = 0$	$f'(x^*) = 0$
Second-order condition	$f''(x^*) < 0$	$f''(x^*) > 0$

and one class of exceptions. The further case corresponds to Figure 3.9, where both $f'(x^*)$ and $f''(x^*)$ equal zero. That $f'(x^*) = 0$ is obvious; that $f''(x^*) = 0$ is clear from the movement of the tangent slope in Figure 3.9. Since it decreases as x^* is approached from the left and then increases beyond x^*, it must have been zero right at x^*. The first-derivative function, $f'(x)$, for the curve $y = f(x)$ in Figure 3.9 would have the general characteristics shown in Figure 3.13, and the tangent to *this* curve is d^2y/dx^2

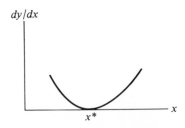

Figure 3.13. $f'(x)$ Near the Point of Inflection in Figure 3.9

[or $f''(x)$]. Clearly then a zero-valued first and second derivative *may* indicate a point of inflection, as in Figure 3.9.

As an example of the class of exceptions to the maxima and minima of Table 3.1, consider $y = f(x) = x^4 + 2$, for which $f'(x) = 4x^3$ and $f''(x) = 12x^2$. Imposing the first-order conditions (the *necessary* conditions) for either a maximum or a minimum gives $x^* = 0$; substituting into the second derivative gives $f''(x^*) = 0$. Yet the graphics [Figure 3.14(a)] indicate a minimum at $x = 0$.[8] Similarly, the rules of Table 3.1 break down for $y = f(x) = -3x^4 + 5$, for which $f'(x) = -12x^3$ and $f''(x) = -36x^2$, but which has a clear maximum at $x = 0$ [Figure 3.14(b)].

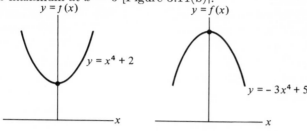

(a)   (b)

Figure 3.14.   Cases in which $f''(x^*) = 0$ at a Minimum or a Maximum

Therefore when $f''(x^*) = 0$, we *may* have a maximum or a minimum or a point of inflection. Note that if the power to which x was raised in either function in Figure 3.14 had been odd—for example, $y = x^3 + 2$—the curves would have had a point of inflection at $x = 0$. (The reader should sketch the function on both sides of $x = 0$ to see why.) This provides a clue to the rule required in these cases that do not conform to Table 3.1. Suppose we continue taking higher-order derivatives, as in Table 3.2.[9] Note

Table 3.2.   Higher-Order Derivatives for
Three Functions of x

$f(x)$	$x^4 + 2$	$-3x^4 + 5$	$x^3 + 2$
$f'(x)$	$4x^3$	$-12x^3$	$3x^2$
$f''(x)$	$12x^2$	$-36x^2$	$6x$
$f'''(x)$	$24x$	$-72x$	6
$f^{(4)}(x)$	24	-72	0
$f^{(5)}(x)$	0	0	0

that imposing the requirement $f'(x) = 0$ forces all three second derivatives (as well as those of higher order *that involve* x) to zero. But at some point for each function, just before the next higher derivative (and all higher)

[8] This shows why the second-order conditions are only sufficient, not necessary, for maxima and minima and thus why the first- and second-order conditions taken together, as in Table 3.1, do not constitute "necessary *and* sufficient" conditions.

[9] Since $f''(x)$ is generally a function of x, we can differentiate it, producing the third derivative $d[d^2y/dx^2]/dx \equiv d^3y/dx^3$ or $f'''(x)$. Similarly $d[d^3y/dx^3]/dx \equiv d^4y/dx^4$ or $f^{IV}(x)$ or, more usually, $f^{(4)}x$. Geometric analogies also persist; each derivative gives the rate of change of the next lower-order derivative.

becomes identically zero or "vanishes"—because it is the derivative of a constant—the x will disappear and that derivative will *not* be zero.

From the discussion of Figure 3.14 it seems clear that as long as these cases in which $f'(x^*) = 0$ because $x^* = 0$ involve an *even* power of x, they will represent true maxima or minima. But if even powers of x are involved, then the first nonvanishing derivative will be one of the even-numbered higher-order ones—$f^{(4)}, f^{(6)}$, and so on. Then the minimum case has a positive-valued number for that derivative, the maximum case has a negative-valued derivative. For a point of inflection—which we saw could be caused by either of these particular cases with x raised to an *odd* power—the first nonvanishing derivative (when evaluated at $x^* = 0$) will be one of the odd-numbered higher-order ones: $f''', f^{(5)}$, and so on.[10]

Therefore, functions for which (1) imposing $f'(x) = 0$ leads to $x^* = 0$ *and* (2) substitution into $f''(x)$ gives $f''(x^*) = 0$ can be classified according to the evenness or oddness of the first higher-order nonzero derivative. If even, then $x^* = 0$ represents a maximum or minimum as the sign of this derivative is negative or positive; if odd, $x^* = 0$ represents a point of inflection.

The differential

The derivative is obtained as the limit of the ratio $\Delta y/\Delta x$, as in (3-5). Thus for *very small* values of Δx we see that $\Delta y/\Delta x \cong dy/dx$, or

$$\Delta y \cong \frac{dy}{dx} \Delta x \qquad \text{or} \qquad \Delta y \cong f'(x) \Delta x. \qquad (3\text{-}6)$$

If the change in x is *very very small* (usually termed infinitesimal), we term it dx and hence label as dy the corresponding change in y. Then, from (3-6),

$$dy = \frac{dy}{dx} dx \qquad \text{or} \qquad dy = f'(x)\, dx. \qquad (3\text{-}7)$$

This expression is termed the *differential* of y; it is also denoted df, which is the form that we will use generally.

There is a straightforward and interesting interpretation for (3-7); it shows that the differential gives an *approximation* to the change in y for a given change in x. Consider again the function in Figure 3.5. Its derivative is $x - 1$; at $x = 2$, $f'(x) = 1$ and $y = f(x) = 1$. If we ask how much y changes as x changes from $x = 2$ to $x = 3$ $(dx = 1)$, we can obtain an approximation from (3-7). That is, at $x = 2$, $dy = f'(x)\, dx = (1)\,(1) = 1$.

---

[10] These rules are derived from the Taylor's series expansion of a function $f(x)$; this series is the sum of terms involving successively higher derivatives. The details are presented in Appendix 4.1, since they also pertain to functions of many variables.

$y = f(x)$

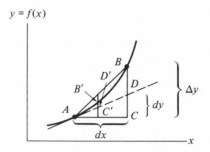

Figure 3.15. The Derivative and the Differential

Referring to Figure 3.15, the increase in y, BC, has been approximated as DC because the slope of the tangent at A—DC/AC—was used to approximate the slope of the function actually involved in the move from A to B, namely BC/AC. On this basis we would estimate the new value of y to be 2 at $x = 3$; in fact $y = 2.5$ at that point, and the error is due to the fact that the tangent line has been used to approximate the change in a curve. The differential provides a *linear approximation* and hence is more accurate, the smaller the change in x; this is behind the derivation of (3-7) from (3-6). Geometrically, if we change x from 2 to 2.01—that is, set $dx = 0.01$ (length AC')—then $dy = f'(x)\, dx = (1)(0.01) = 0.01$. The new value of y given by the linear approximation is $y = 1.01$ (length $D'C'$); the actual value $(B'C')$ is $f(2.01) = 1.01005$, and the error is, of course, much less—0.00005 rather than 0.5.

The expression for the differential, (3-7), when evaluated at a particular point, x_0, essentially gives the equation of the tangent to $f(x)$ at x_0. Recall that the general equation for a line is $ax + by = c$. [When we specify that x is the independent and y the dependent variable, we usually write $y = -(a/b)x + (c/b)$, where $-(a/b)$ is the *slope* of the line in xy space and (c/b) the *intercept* on the y axis. This is the so-called "slope-intercept" form for the equation of a line in two-dimensional space.] For any particular point (x_0, y_0) on the line, obviously $ax_0 + by_0 = c$. Subtracting the *particular* from the *general* equation,

$$a(x - x_0) + b(y - y_0) = 0 \qquad \text{or} \qquad (y - y_0) = -\frac{a}{b}(x - x_0).$$

Considering the tangent to a curve $y = f(x)$ at a point x_0, we clearly know y_0 $[= f(x_0)]$[11] *and* we know the slope of the tangent line at x_0, namely $(dy/dx)_{x=x_0} \equiv f'(x_0)$. Thus $f'(x_0) = -(a/b)$, and the equation of the line tangent to $y = f(x)$ at $x = x_0$ is

---

[11] That is, the curve and its tangent share one point in common, namely (x_0, y_0).

$$(y - y_0) = f'(x_0)(x - x_0),$$

where x_0, y_0, and $f'(x_0)$ are known. (Or, in slope-intercept form,

$$y = [f'(x_0)]x + [y_0 - f'(x_0)x_0].)$$

For a point (x, y) on the tangent line and *near to* (x_0, y_0) we can write

$$x = x_0 + dx, \qquad y = y_0 + dy,$$

and hence $(y - y_0) = f'(x_0)(x - x_0)$ could be read as $dy = f'(x_0)dx$—that is, the expression for the differential in (3-7).[12]

Maxima and minima with differentials

It should be clear that the conditions for maxima and minima can be stated in terms of the differential just as well as the derivative. That is, for arbitrary small changes dx, $dy = 0$ if and only if $f'(x) = 0$; this is clear from (3-7). Thus the first-order conditions for a maximum *or* a minimum point are that $dy \equiv df = 0$. Rules parallel to those using the second derivative to distinguish maxima from minima (from neither) can also be formulated using the second differential of y, namely $d(dy) \equiv d^2y$, or d^2f. The relationship between differentials of higher order is exactly the same as that between derivatives of higher order. The second differential estimates the change in the first differential just as the second derivative approximates the change in the first derivative. Therefore, if the second differential is positive at a point, x^*, where the first differential is zero, this means that the first differential is getting larger. Since it is zero at x^*, it was negative to the left of x^* and is positive to the right of x^*; hence x^* represents a minimum point. Table 3.1 could be rewritten in terms of differentials, where df^* and d^2f^* represent the first and second differential of $y = f(x)$ evaluated at x^*.

Table 3.3. Alternative Characterization of
Maxima and Minima for $y = f(x)$

	Maximum	*Minimum*
First-order condition	$df^* = 0$	$df^* = 0$
Second-order condition	$d^2f^* < 0$	$d^2f^* > 0$

[12] Since a function $f(x)$ may have the same slope at several points, it is of course necessary, when writing the equation of the tangent at a point, to specify precisely *which* point is involved. This information is lost in (3-7) but is present—that is, x_0 and y_0 appear explicitly—in either

$$(y - y_0) = f'(x_0)(x - x_0) \quad \text{or} \quad y = [f'(x_0)]x + [y_0 - f'(x_0)x_0].$$

This is equivalent to Table 3.1 because the rules for finding derivatives and those for finding differentials are really the same—hence the name *differentiation* covers both sets. For example, since dy was derived from y by the operation of taking the derivative with respect to x and multiplying by dx—$dy = (dy/dx)dx$—the notation $d(dy)$ indicates that this same operation should be done on dy to generate the second differential. Thus (using the product rule)

$$d^2y \equiv d(dy) = \frac{d[(dy/dx)(dx)]}{dx}(dx)$$

$$= \left[\frac{d(dy/dx)}{dx}(dx) + \frac{d(dx)}{dx}\left(\frac{dy}{dx}\right)\right](dx)$$

$$= \left[\left(\frac{d^2y}{dx^2}\right)(dx) + 0\left(\frac{dy}{dx}\right)\right](dx).$$

Finally, removing brackets,

$$d^2y = \left(\frac{d^2y}{dx^2}\right)(dx)^2 = f''(x)(dx)^2. \tag{3-8}$$

Note that since the arbitrary change in x, dx, is squared, the *sign* of d^2y is governed entirely by the *sign* of $f''(x)$. Hence the second-order conditions of Table 3.3 are identical to those of Table 3.1.

In fact, with functions of a single variable, x, there is no particular need to use the differential approach to maximum and minimum problems; first and second derivatives are quite sufficient. However, differentials facilitate the study of functions of several variables, to which we now turn.

3.3. MAXIMA AND MINIMA FOR FUNCTIONS OF TWO INDEPENDENT VARIABLES

We now consider the case in which y depends on the values taken by two independent variables, x_1 and x_2; that is, $y = f(x_1, x_2)$. Since only three dimensions are necessary, the conditions for maximum and minimum points are easily visualized. They then generalize easily to functions of any number of variables, which will be the topic of Chapter 4. Our concern throughout will be with functions that are smooth and continuous, so that differentiation is possible everywhere.[13] In general, we will require derivatives at least up to the second order, sometimes higher; hence we are interested in functions in which variables are at least squared or appear

---

[13] Also, we continue to assume that the independent variables can both range over the entire set of real numbers. In Chapter 4 we will deal explicitly with constraints and hence with the endpoint problem.

multiplied together. This is clearly logical, since otherwise the "curves" would have no curvature; they would be hyperplanes or hyperlines, and the search for maxima and minima via first-order conditions (tangent of zero slope) would generally be meaningless.

Partial derivatives

The reader may recall that with functions of two (or more) variables, the concept of a *partial derivative* is necessary. If $y = f(x)$, then dy/dx is un-ambiguously the derivative of the function with respect to the *only* independent variable x. When $y = f(x_1, x_2)$, a change in y may occur when *either one* of the independent variables changes while the other remains constant. Thus we need to specify which variable is changing and which one is not; this could be done by using dy/dx_1 and dy/dx_2. This notation, however, is reserved for the more specialized case in which the variables are not in fact independent—dy/dx_1 is used for $f(x_1, x_2)$ when x_2 is actually some further function of x_1. It is called the *total derivative*. We are at present interested in two *independent* variables x_1 and x_2, and the notation often used is $\partial y/\partial x_1$ and $\partial y/\partial x_2$, read as the *partial derivative* of y with respect to x_1 or x_2, respectively. The use of ∂ in place of d indicates the similarity of the concept; f_{x_1} and f_{x_2} are also sometimes used, but simpler yet are f_1 and f_2 to denote the partial derivatives of the function $y = f(x_1, x_2)$ with regard to x_1 and x_2, respectively. In general we will use this last version.

Since partial derivatives are designed to measure a change in y when all variables except one remain constant, the technique of partial differentiation is an extremely simple extension of ordinary differentiation. It requires only that the other x (or x's) be regarded as constants. For example, if

$$y = 3x_1^2 + 4x_1x_2 + x_2^3,$$

the two possible partial derivatives are

$$\frac{\partial y}{\partial x_1} \equiv f_1 = 6x_1 + 4x_2, \qquad \frac{\partial y}{\partial x_2} \equiv f_2 = 4x_1 + 3x_2^2. \qquad (3\text{-}9)$$

Note that in general both variables appear in both partial derivatives; in f_1 if a particular value for x_2, say x_2^0, is assumed, then f_1 (evaluated at x_2^0) is a function of x_1, the variable actually assumed to change. Similarly f_2 is a function of x_2 relative to some specific x_1^0. Since this is the case, it is easy to visualize the partial derivatives as curves in particular planes in three-dimensional x_1x_2y space. Figure 3.16 illustrates. Passing a plane through the surface perpendicular to the x_1x_2 plane and parallel to the x_1y plane at a particular value of x_2 (that is, disregarding x_2 as a variable) has the effect shown in Figure 3.16(b). Similarly, erecting a plane at some fixed value of x_1—that is, parallel to the x_2y plane—produces a curve

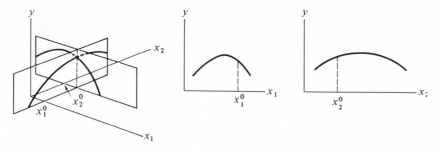

Figure 3.16.   (a) $y = f(x_1, x_2)$, (b) $y = f(x_1, x_2^0)$, (c) $y = f(x_1^0, x_2)$

such as that shown in Figure 3.16(c). Once y is reduced to a function of either x_1 or x_2 alone, then the (partial) derivative has exactly the same interpretation as did dy/dx in the one-variable case, namely the slope of the tangent to the curve.[14]

Higher-order partial derivatives can also be found. They are similar to higher-order derivatives in exactly the same way that $\partial y/\partial x_1$ was related to dy/dx. Thus $\partial^2 y/\partial x_1^2 = \partial(\partial y/\partial x_1)/\partial x_1$; the more convenient notation is $f_{x_1 x_1}$ or simply f_{11}—but *not* f_1^2, which denotes $(f_1)^2$, that is, $(\partial y/\partial x_1)^2$. From the first partials in (3-9), $f_{11} = 6$ and $f_{22} = 6x_2$. With functions of two or more variables, it is also possible to measure, for example, how the first partial derivative with respect to x_1 is itself affected by changes in x_2. Recall from (3-9) that x_2 entered into f_1; we must set it equal to some particular value, x_2^0, in order to examine the relationship between y and changes in x_1 alone. This is how Figure 3.16(b) was derived. The value x_2^0 simply determines the location of the $x_1 y$ plane. The notation for this *cross-partial* is $\partial(\partial y/\partial x_1)/\partial x_2$, $\partial^2 y/(\partial x_1 \partial x_2)$, $f_{x_1 x_2}$, or f_{12}. Note that the partial differentiation operations are carried out in the order of the subscripts.[15]

Maxima and minima with partial derivatives

This geometric analogy to the one-variable case makes clear that a set of *necessary* conditions for either a maximum or a minimum point (x_1^*, x_2^*) of a function of two variables is that both $\partial y/\partial x_1$ and $\partial y/\partial x_2$ be zero at that point. We denote these derivatives evaluated at (x_1^*, x_2^*) by f_1^* and f_2^*. The reader may then recall that, *provided a certain inequality is satisfied*, maxima are distinguished from minima by the sign of the second partial derivative

---

[14] The reader can convince himself of this by examining the geometry of the delta process to generate a change in either x_1 or x_2, forming $\Delta y/\Delta x_1$ or $\Delta y/\Delta x_2$ [as in (3-2), above], and taking limits.

[15] As a matter of fact, all of the smooth, continuous functions with which we will be dealing have the property that order makes no difference in cross-partials—that is, $f_{12} = f_{21}$.

with respect to *either* variable, evaluated at the same point (x_1^*, x_2^*). And the second partial sign rule is the same as the second derivative sign rule for $y = f(x)$, namely a maximum if

$$\left.\frac{\partial^2 y}{\partial x_1^2}\right|_{x_1^*, x_2^*} < 0 \qquad (\text{that is, } f_{11}^* < 0)$$

and a minimum if

$$\left.\frac{\partial^2 y}{\partial x_1^2}\right|_{x_1^*, x_2^*} > 0 \qquad (\text{that is, } f_{11}^* > 0).^{16}$$

The added requirement for *both* maxima and minima is that, at (x_1^*, x_2^*),

$$\left[\left(\frac{\partial^2 y}{\partial x_1^2}\right)\left(\frac{\partial^2 y}{\partial x_2^2}\right) - \left(\frac{\partial^2 y}{\partial x_1 \partial x_2}\right)^2\right] > 0, \qquad (3\text{-}10)$$

or, more simply, $[f_{11}^* f_{22}^* - (f_{12}^*)^2] > 0$. Only if (3-10) is satisfied by the point or points for which $f_1 = 0$ and $f_2 = 0$ is it necessary to examine the sign of the second partial. If (3-10) is not satisfied, the point cannot possibly be a maximum or a minimum.

Thus stationary points (x_1^*, x_2^*)—that is, *relative* maxima or *relative* minima—of the function $y = f(x_1, x_2)$ can be classified as in Table 3.4.

Table 3.4.   Characteristics of Maxima and
Minima for $y = f(x_1, x_2)$

	Maximum	*Minimum*
First-order condition	$f_1^* = f_2^* = 0$	$f_1^* = f_2^* = 0$
Second-order condition	$f_{11}^* < 0$ (or $f_{22}^* < 0$)	$f_{11}^* > 0$ (or $f_{22}^* > 0$)
provided that	$[f_{11}^* f_{22}^* - (f_{12}^*)^2] > 0$	in *either* case.

This is usually the point at which an introductory investigation of maximum and minimum problems stops. While two-variable functions are likely to arise in many more practical situations than only one-variable functions, it is still more likely that a particular dependent variable in which one is interested will depend on several (perhaps many) independent variables. Thus it is important to be able to extend the analysis of maxima and minima to functions of more than two variables. This is done most effectively by first reexamining the two-variable case using differentials rather than partial derivatives alone. In the process we will see where (3-10) comes from and why it is necessary for both maxima and minima.

---

^{16} Or $\partial^2 y / \partial x_2^2$ could be examined for sign, but it is unnecessary to look at the second partials with respect to *both* variables.

The total differential for functions of two variables

Since y now depends on the values taken by the two independent variables x_1 and x_2, it is clear that the differential of y, dy or df, must reflect the possibility of arbitrary small changes in both—that is, must include dx_1 and dx_2. Parallel to (3-7), and in view of our discussion of the meaning of partial derivatives, it is clear that the product $(\partial y/\partial x_1)\, dx_1$ (or $f_1\, dx_1$) would serve to transmit the small change in x_1, dx_1, to the function y. Similarly for independent changes in x_2; $(\partial y/\partial x_2)\, dx_2$ (or $f_2\, dx_2$) measures their impact on y. Since *both* x_1 and x_2 may change independently, the total effect on $y = f(x_1, x_2)$ is the sum of the two individual effects.[17]

$$dy \equiv df = \left(\frac{\partial y}{\partial x_1}\right) dx_1 + \left(\frac{\partial y}{\partial x_2}\right) dx_2 = f_1\, dx_1 + f_2\, dx_2. \qquad (3\text{-}11)$$

As in the case of the differential for a function of one variable, (3-11), when evaluated at a particular point (x_1^0, x_2^0), is essentially the equation of the tangent plane to $y = f(x_1, x_2)$ at (x_1^0, x_2^0). The reasoning is parallel to that on page 107 for $y = f(x)$, only slightly more involved. The general equation for a plane in $x_1 x_2 y$ space is $a_1 x_1 + a_2 x_2 + by = c$. (If the *dependent* variable is not made explicit—here as y—we write $a_1 x_1 + a_2 x_2 + a_3 x_3 = c$.) For a particular point (x_1^0, x_2^0, y^0) on the plane, of course, $a_1 x_1^0 + a_2 x_2^0 + by^0 = c$. As before, subtracting the particular from the general equation gives

$$a_1(x_1 - x_1^0) + a_2(x_2 - x_2^0) + b(y - y^0) = 0$$

or

$$y - y^0 = -\frac{a_1}{b}\,(x_1 - x_1^0) - \frac{a_2}{b}\,(x_2 - x_2^0).$$

We consider two particular *lines* that must lie in the tangent plane at the point (x_1^0, x_2^0, y^0). The first is the line tangent to $f(x_1, x_2)$ at that point and in the plane $x_2 = x_2^0$—that is, the plane that cuts $y = f(x_1, x_2)$ at (x_1^0, x_2^0) and is perpendicular to the x_2 axis at x_2^0. (Recall Figure 3.16.) We know that the *slope* of this tangent line is

$$\left.\frac{\partial y}{\partial x_1}\right|_{x_1 = x_1^0} \equiv f_1^0.$$

Since its equation is

(1) $x_2 = x_2^0$ and   (2) $a_1(x_1 - x_1^0) + b(y - y^0) = 0$,

we see that its slope is also $-(a_1/b)$. Similarly, the slope of the tangent line to $f(x_1, x_2)$ at (x_1^0, x_2^0) in the $x_1 = x_1^0$ plane (that is, perpendicular to the x_1 axis at x_1^0) is both

---

[17] This result can also be derived by using the delta process for Δy with both Δx_1 and Δx_2 and taking limits.

$$\frac{\partial y}{\partial x_2}\bigg|_{x_2=x_2^0} \equiv f_2^0 \quad \text{and} \quad -\frac{a_2}{b}.$$

Thus the equation for the tangent plane at x_1^0, x_2^0, and $y^0 \, [= f(x_1^0, x_2^0)]$ becomes

$$y - y^0 = f_1^0(x_1 - x_1^0) + f_2^0(x_2 - x_2^0).$$

As before, if x_1 and x_2 are points near to x_1^0 and x_2^0, we can write $x_1 = x_1^0 + dx_1$, $x_2 = x_2^0 + dx_2$, and $y = y^0 + dy$ and this equation becomes

$$dy = f_1^0 \, dx_1 + f_2^0 \, dx_2,$$

which is (3-11), evaluated at (x_1^0, x_2^0).[18]

As in the one-variable case, the total differential (3-11) gives a linear approximation to the change in the function for small changes in both independent variables. For $y = f(x)$, dy approximated the change by a tangent *line;* with $y = f(x_1, x_2)$, dy uses a tangent *plane* for the approximation. A clear illustration is that of the area (y) of a rectangle as a function of length (x_1) and width (x_2). The functional relationship is $y = f(x_1, x_2) = x_1 x_2$. Suppose $x_1 = 10$, $x_2 = 5$, $y = 50$. Let x_1 change to 10.5 and x_2 become 5.2, and use (3-11) to approximate the *change* in area. Taking partial derivatives, $f_1 = x_2$ and $f_2 = x_1$. Thus,

$$df = f_1 \, dx_1 + f_2 \, dx_2 = x_2 \, dx_1 + x_1 \, dx_2 = 5(0.5) + 10(0.2) = 4.5;$$

this is our estimate of the increase in area. We would approximate the *new* area as $50 + 4.5 = 54.5$. In fact it is $(10.5)(5.2) = 54.6$. Figure 3.17 illustrates the source of error. The two terms in the differential are the shaded areas; the error is thus caused by omitting the upper right area—$(dx_1)(dx_2)$. In this case, the error is $(0.5)(0.2) = 0.1$, as we saw; clearly, the smaller the changes in x_1 and x_2, the more accurate is the linear approximation given by the total differential (3-11).

The second total differential of a function of two variables is found, as before, by taking the differential of the first differential; $d(dy) \equiv d^2y$, or $d(df) \equiv d^2f$. The exact expression for d^2f can be derived using partial derivatives, exactly as derivatives were used for (3-8). Since the rules for dif-

---

[18] Also as above, the form in (3-11) loses information when there are (possibly) many points where the tangent plane has the same slope. Thus

$$y - y^0 = f_1^0(x_1 - x_1^0) + f_2^0(x_2 - x_2^0),$$

or, in slope-intercept form,

$$y = f_1^0 x_1 + f_2^0 x_2 + [y^0 - f_1^0 x_1^0 - f_2^0 x_2^0],$$

must be used, since x_1^0, x_2^0, and y^0 appear explicitly.

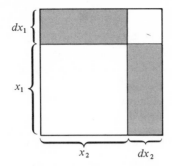

Figure 3.17.   Changes in Length, Width, and Area

ferentials parallel those for derivatives, they can also easily be applied to the first differential in (3-11).

$$
\begin{aligned}
d^2 f &= d(f_1 \, dx_1 + f_2 \, dx_2) \\
&= d(f_1 \, dx_1) + d(f_2 \, dx_2) \quad &&\text{[parallel to the rule for the derivative of a sum]} \\
&= d(f_1) \, dx_1 + d(dx_1) f_1 \\
&\quad + d(f_2) \, dx_2 + d(dx_2) f_2 \quad &&\text{[parallel to the rule for the derivative of a product].}
\end{aligned} \tag{3-12}
$$

In general, f_1 and f_2 are functions of both variables, x_1 and x_2. Thus

$$
d(f_1) = f_{11} \, dx_1 + f_{12} \, dx_2 \quad \text{and} \quad d(f_2) = f_{21} \, dx_1 + f_{22} \, dx_2;^{19}
$$

$d(dx_1)$ is just $d^2 x_1$ and $d(dx_2) \equiv d^2 x_2$. Hence

$$
d^2 f = (f_{11} \, dx_1 + f_{12} \, dx_2) \, dx_1 + f_1 \, d^2 x_1 + (f_{21} \, dx_1 + f_{22} \, dx_2) \, dx_2 + f_2 \, d^2 x_2.
$$

Since the functions with which we are concerned are still assumed to be "well behaved"—smooth and continuous second partials and cross-partials—the cross-partials will be identical; thus $f_{12} = f_{21}$, and

$$
d^2 f = f_{11}(dx_1)^2 + 2f_{12} \, dx_1 \, dx_2 + f_{22}(dx_2)^2 + f_1 \, d^2 x_1 + f_2 \, d^2 x_2. \tag{3-13}
$$

When x_1 and x_2 are *independent* variables, then dx_1 and dx_2 are arbitrary and unrelated small changes (that is, constants). This means that $d(dx_1) \equiv d^2 x_1 = 0$ and $d(dx_2) \equiv d^2 x_2 = 0$. Thus the second total differential for a function of two *independent* variables reduces to

$$
d^2 f = f_{11}(dx_1)^2 + 2f_{12} \, dx_1 \, dx_2 + f_{22}(dx_2)^2. \tag{3-14}
$$

---

[19] This is straightforward application of the rule in (3-11) to two new functions of x_1 and x_2.

Maxima and minima with differentials

As with functions of one variable, the conditions for stationary points and in particular for maxima and minima can be expressed using differentials rather than derivatives. In fact, the necessary condition with derivatives, that at a stationary point (x_1^*, x_2^*), $\partial y/\partial x_1 = 0 = \partial y/\partial x_2$, means that $df = 0$ at that point. It is clear that at a maximum or a minimum point the tangent plane should be horizontal—that is, the estimate given by df for an infinitesimal change in x_1 and x_2 should be zero. Also as with functions of one variable, d^2f measures the rate of change of df. Thus if $d^2f > 0$ at a point where $df = 0$, the tangent plane takes on a positive slope for slightly larger x_1 and x_2 and a negative slope at smaller x_1 and x_2, hence the stationary point is a minimum. The argument that $d^2f < 0$ distinguishes a maximum is similar.

Therefore the rules in Table 3.4 can be expressed in terms of differentials alone. A point (x_1^*, x_2^*) will be a maximum or a minimum of the function $y = f(x_1, x_2)$ according to the rules given in Table 3.5—where df^* and d^2f^* denote the first and second total differentials evaluated at (x_1^*, x_2^*). Observe that when differentials are used, the rules for maxima and minima in the two-variable case parallel exactly those for the single-variable case (Table 3.3). With derivatives, this was not true—compare Table 3.1 with Table 3.4, which was only valid if the inequality constraint held for (x_1^*, x_2^*).

Table 3.5. Alternative Characterization of
Maxima and Minima for $y = f(x_2, x_2)$

	Maximum	*Minimum*
First-order condition	$df^* = 0$	$df^* = 0$
Second-order condition	$d^2f^* < 0$	$d^2f^* > 0$

We have seen that the first-order conditions in Tables 3.5 and 3.4 are identical. We now want to see how the second-order condition in Table 3.5 is related to that condition in Table 3.4 *and the inequality qualification*.

To understand the connection, we look again at the form of d^2f for the case of two independent variables in (3-14). Because of the particular structure of (3-14) with respect to dx_1 and dx_2 (each is *squared* and their *product* appears once), it is possible to rewrite the expression in a different (and more cumbersome-looking) way.[20] This is called a "sum of squares":

$$d^2f = f_{11}\left[dx_1 + \left(\frac{f_{12}}{f_{11}}\right) dx_2 \right]^2 + \left(\frac{f_{11}f_{22} - f_{12}^2}{f_{11}}\right)(dx_2)^2. \qquad (3\text{-}15)$$

[20] The reader may convince himself that this is correct by multiplying out (3-15) to derive (3-14). The motivation for (3-15) will very soon be clear.

This is a convenient form only because the *sign* of d^2f is of interest in Table 3.5. Since the two terms that are added together in (3-15) involve products of two expressions, one of which is squared (hence this is a "sum of squares"), the sign of d^2f is obviously governed by the unsquared part of each term—that is, by f_{11} and by $[(f_{11}f_{22} - f_{12}^2)/f_{11}]$. (One obvious exception would be the rare case in which both squared terms happened to be zero; we can rule this out by specifying that not both dx_1 and dx_2 are zero, so that one of the squared terms is *always* strictly positive.) Specifically, we know that d^2f will *always* be positive if both of these are positive—that is, if (1) $f_{11} > 0$ and (2) $f_{11}f_{22} - f_{12}^2 > 0$; these are *sufficient* conditions to assure $d^2f > 0$. Similarly, to be certain that $d^2f < 0$, it is sufficient to require (1) $f_{11} < 0$ and (2) $f_{11}f_{22} - f_{12}^2 > 0$; note that the direction of the inequality is the *same* for condition (2) in both cases. This is because the second multiplier in (3-15) has f_{11} for the denominator; hence if the numerator is always positive, the sign of the fraction will be governed completely by the denominator, f_{11}. Therefore the sign of f_{11} separates maxima from minima, provided that condition (2) is met. This condition is exactly the inequality qualification of Table 3.4.[21] (The various implications of $f_{11}f_{22} - f_{12}^2 \leq 0$ are explored in Appendix 3.1 to this chapter for the interested reader.)

Let us summarize the case for $y = f(x_1, x_2)$. We *impose* the $df = 0$ condition, which means we solve the two (not necessarily linear) equations $f_1 = 0$ and $f_2 = 0$ for sets of critical values (x_1^*, x_2^*), if any exist. There may be no solution or one or several. Then this set of values (or these sets) are used to evaluate second partials and cross-partials in order to check whether: (a) $f_{11}^* > 0$ and $f_{11}^* f_{22}^* - f_{12}^{*2} > 0$, in which case $d^2f^* > 0$ and the critical point represents a minimum, or (b) $f_{11}^* < 0$ and $f_{11}^* f_{22}^* - f_{12}^{*2} > 0$, in which case $d^2f^* < 0$ and we have found a maximum. Any other combination of signs on f_{11}^* and $(f_{11}^* f_{22}^* - f_{12}^{*2})$ leaves us uncertain whether or not we have a true maximum or minimum. We may have—the d^2f conditions are only sufficient, not necessary—but further investigation, beyond the scope of this chapter, would be necessary.

SUMMARY

This chapter has guided the reader in recalling and reviewing (and perhaps clarifying) the fundamentals involved in using differential calculus in maximization or minimization problems for functions of first one and

---

[21] Note that the two conditions for $d^2f > 0$ assure that f_{22} *must be* positive and the two for $d^2f < 0$ assure a negative f_{22}. Note that if f_{11} were replaced by f_{22} in both conditions (1), the sign of d^2f would also be as required. Hence the sign of only one of the two second partials, f_{11} and f_{22}, needs to be specified. For reasons of symmetry in cases of more than two variables, f_{11} is preferred.

then two (independent) variables. The approach via differentials has been introduced and shown to parallel that using derivatives. This appears to offer no particular advantages in the one- and two-variable cases investigated here, but it becomes essential for a discussion of maxima and minima for functions of more than two variables. This is the subject matter of Chapter 4, and it provides the framework within which to study the more realistic constrained cases in which not only are several variables involved, but constraints or restrictions apply to the variables so that they no longer can be regarded as independent of one another; for example, if x_1 increases, then x_2 must decrease. We explore the ramifications of such restrictions in some detail in the next chapter.

APPENDIX 3.1

The Sign of d^2y when $y = f(x_1, x_2)$

We saw that the second total differential for a function of two independent variables can be expressed as in (3-14):

$$d^2f = f_{11}\, dx_1^2 + 2f_{12}\, dx_1\, dx_2 + f_{22}\, dx_2^2,$$

or as in (3-15):

$$d^2f = f_{11}\left[dx_1 + \left(\frac{f_{12}}{f_{11}}\right) dx_2 \right]^2 + \left(\frac{f_{11}f_{22} - f_{12}^2}{f_{11}}\right)(dx_2)^2.$$

For questions of maxima and minima we are interested in the conditions under which d^2f is unambiguously positive (minimum point) or unambiguously negative (maximum point). We explore all possibilities via the sign of $(f_{11}f_{22} - f_{12}^2)$.

CASE 1: $f_{11}f_{22} - f_{12}^2 > 0$

This is the case discussed in the text. When this term is positive, then the sign of d^2f—as expressed in (3-15)—is *completely determined* by the sign of f_{11}. We consider the possibilities: (1) $dx_1 \neq 0$, $dx_2 \neq 0$, (2) $dx_1 \neq 0$, $dx_2 = 0$, or $dx_1 = 0$, $dx_2 \neq 0$. Clearly it is not meaningful to set the changes in *both* variables equal to zero, since then $d^2f = 0$ by definition.

1. If both (independent) changes are nonzero, d^2f has the same sign as f_{11}. The first squared expression in (3-15) is nonnegative; it is generally

positive but could be zero if the sign and magnitude of f_{12}/f_{11} were just sufficient to make $dx_1 = (f_{12}/f_{11})\,dx_2$ for some changes dx_1 and dx_2. However, the second squared expression, dx_2, is strictly positive; therefore, since $f_{11}f_{22} - f_{12}^2$ is also strictly positive, the sum of both terms cannot be zero and it has the same sign as f_{11}.

2. If only x_1 changes, then from (3-14), $d^2f = f_{11}(dx_1)^2$ and the sign of d^2f is the same as that of f_{11}. If only x_2 changes, then $d^2f = f_{22}(dx_2)^2$; hence d^2f and f_{22} have the same sign. However, since $(f_{11}f_{22} - f_{12}^2) > 0$, $f_{11}f_{22} > f_{12}^2$ and hence f_{11} and f_{22} must have the same sign, since their product must be positive.

Thus when $f_{11}f_{22} - f_{12}^2 > 0$, the sign of d^2f is *always* the same as the sign of f_{11}.

CASE 2: $f_{11}f_{22} - f_{12}^2 < 0$

In this case, since $f_{11}f_{22} < f_{12}^2$, the two second partial derivatives may be of the same sign or they may not. Suppose that they are not; let f_{11} be positive and f_{22} negative. Then if we examine the curvature of the function in a plane parallel to the x_1y axis (that is, holding x_2 constant), we find that the slope of the tangent plane is increasing ($f_{11} > 0$). We conclude that the function was at a minimum in the x_1y plane (for some constant value of x_2).[22] Similarly, holding x_1 constant, $f_{22} < 0$ suggests a maximum of the function in the x_2y plane (for $x_1 =$ constant). Thus the function has a maximum from one point of view and a minimum from another point of view. This is termed a *saddle point*.

For example, $y = 1 + x_1^2 - x_2^2$. Then $f_1 = 2x_1$, $f_2 = -2x_2$; $f_{11} = 2$, $f_{22} = -2$, and $f_{12} = f_{21} = 0$. Hence $f_{11}f_{22} - f_{12}^2 = -4 < 0$. At $f_1 = 0$, $f_2 = 0$—that is, at $x_1 = 0$ and $x_2 = 0$—the function has a saddle point; Figure 3.18 illustrates.[23] This is enough to show that when $f_{11}f_{22} - f_{12}^2 < 0$, we may have neither a maximum nor a minimum point.[24]

CASE 3: $f_{11}f_{22} - f_{12}^2 = 0$

Here $f_{11}f_{22} = f_{12}^2$, and hence f_{11} and f_{22} must be of the same sign; the saddle-point possibility of Case 2 therefore does not arise. When either $dx_1 = 0$ or $dx_2 = 0$, the analysis is the same as under Case 1, using the expression for d^2f in (3-14). However, if both changes are nonzero, then from (3-15)

---

[22] Recall that we are dealing with the sign of d^2y at a point (or points) where $dy = 0$.

[23] The positioning of the x_1 and x_2 axes has been changed from earlier attempts at three-dimensional illustrations (for example, in Chapter 2) in order to emphasize the saddle shape.

[24] A $d^2f > 0$ *could* occur with $f_{11} > 0$ or $f_{11} < 0$ and $f_{11}f_{22} - f_{12}^2 < 0$, depending on the specific magnitudes of these functions and also on the sizes of the changes in x_1 and x_2. The same is true for a $d^2f < 0$. However, our interest is in conditions that assure the sign of d^2f for *general* functions evaluated at *any* stationary point for *any* small changes in x_1 and x_2—that is, in sufficient conditions for the general case.

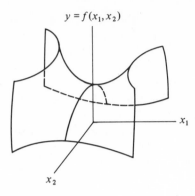

Figure 3.18. $y = 1 + x_1^2 - x_2^2$

$$d^2f = f_{11}\left[dx_1 + \left(\frac{f_{12}}{f_{11}}\right) dx_2 \right]^2.$$

Therefore, whenever the changes in dx_1 and dx_2 have the property that $dx_1 = -(f_{12}/f_{11})\, dx_2$, or $(dx_1/dx_2) = -(f_{12}/f_{11})$, then $d^2f = 0$. While in general the sign of d^2f will be the same as that of f_{11} (whenever $[dx_1 + (f_{12}/f_{11})\, dx_2]^2 > 0$), there will be a particular direction in the x_1x_2 plane along which $d^2f = 0$. Hence the function will have a "ridge line"—a "trough" or a "canopy"—along this direction.

For example, $y = -x_1^2 - x_2^2 + 2x_1x_2$. Then

$$f_1 = -2x_1 + 2x_2, \qquad f_2 = 2x_1 - 2x_2; \qquad f_{11} = f_{22} = -2.$$

Hence $f_{11}f_{22} - f_{12}^2 = 4 - 4 = 0$. When $f_1 = 0$ and $f_2 = 0$—that is, whenever $x_1 = x_2$—the first-order conditions $(df = 0)$ are clearly satisfied.[25] Figure 3.19 indicates the shape of $f(x_1, x_2)$.

The nature of the problem when $f_{11}f_{22} - f_{12}^2 = 0$ can also be illustrated for a general second-degree function of x_1 and x_2 using the analysis developed in Chapter 2 for systems of linear equations.[26] Let

$$y = f(x_1, x_2) = ax_1^2 + bx_1x_2 + cx_2^2 + dx_1 + ex_2 + f.$$

Then

$$f_1 = 2ax_1 + bx_2 + d \quad \text{and} \quad f_2 = bx_1 + 2cx_2 + e;$$

---

[25] These constitute a pair of homogeneous linear equations in two unknowns for which $\rho(A) = 0 < n$; hence nonunique, nontrivial solutions exist.

[26] A second-degree function is used in order that the resulting equation system be linear. Obviously the "trough" and "canopy" problem can exist in any number of dimensions—that is, for functions of more than two variables—as can saddle points. But as above, we illustrate that problems *do* arise by using a relatively simple general case.

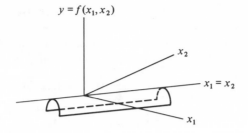

Figure 3.19. $y = -x_1^2 - x_2^2 + 2x_1x_2$

$f_{11} = 2a$, $f_{22} = 2c$, and $f_{12} = f_{21} = b$. Imposing the first-order condition that $f_1 = f_2 = 0$,

$$2ax_1 + bx_2 = -d, \qquad bx_1 + 2cx_2 = -e. \tag{3-16}$$

These two linear equations in x_1 and x_2 have a unique solution (that is, the function y has a unique stationary point) if and only if

$$\begin{vmatrix} 2a & b \\ b & 2c \end{vmatrix} \neq 0.$$

Conversely, if $[(2a)(2c) - b^2] = 0$, the equations have either an infinite number of solutions or no solution, depending on whether the ranks of the coefficient matrix and the augmented matrix in (3-16) are the same or different.

The determinant of the coefficient matrix in (3-16) is just $f_{11}f_{22} - f_{12}^2$, since the coefficient matrix for the case considered here is exactly

$$\begin{bmatrix} f_{11} & f_{12} \\ f_{21} & f_{22} \end{bmatrix}.$$

Thus if $f_{11}f_{22} - f_{12}^2 \neq 0$, we have either the maximum or minimum case (Case 1) or the saddle-point situation (Case 2). If $f_{11}f_{22} - f_{12}^2 = 0$ and if the right-hand column vector in (3-16) is linearly *dependent* on the columns $\begin{bmatrix} f_{11} \\ f_{21} \end{bmatrix}$ and $\begin{bmatrix} f_{12} \\ f_{22} \end{bmatrix}$, then an infinite number of points satisfy (3-16)—that is, $f(x_1, x_2)$ has an infinite number of stationary points. For example, let

$$y = f(x_1, x_2) = 8x_1^2 + 8x_1x_2 + 2x_2^2 + 6x_1 + 3x_2.$$

Here

$$f_1 = 16x_1 + 8x_2 + 6, \qquad f_2 = 8x_1 + 4x_2 + 3; \qquad f_1 = 2f_2.$$

Setting $f_1 = f_2 = 0$ for the necessary conditions for a stationary point,

$$\rho \begin{bmatrix} 16 & 8 \\ 8 & 4 \end{bmatrix} = \rho \begin{bmatrix} 16 & 8 & -6 \\ 8 & 4 & -3 \end{bmatrix} = 1,$$

the number of linearly independent columns *or rows*. Here we see that row 1 is just twice row 2. Therefore, as long as $8x_1 + 4x_2 + 3 = 0$, or $x_1 = -\frac{1}{2}x_2 - \frac{3}{8}$, the *necessary* conditions for a stationary point for the function will hold. There are thus infinitely many such points.

Suppose, however, that $f_{11}f_{22} - f_{12}^2 = 0$ and that the right-hand side of (3-16) is linearly *independent* of $\begin{bmatrix} f_{11} \\ f_{21} \end{bmatrix}$ and $\begin{bmatrix} f_{12} \\ f_{22} \end{bmatrix}$. That is, the rank of the augmented matrix is greater than the rank of $\begin{bmatrix} f_{11} & f_{12} \\ f_{21} & f_{22} \end{bmatrix}$. Then *no* points can be found to satisfy the necessary first-order conditions for a maximum or minimum. For example, let

$$y = f(x_1, x_1) = 8x_1^2 + 8x_1x_2 + 2x_2^2 + 6x_1 + 4x_2.$$

Then

$$f_1 = 16x_1 + 8x_2 + 6, \qquad f_2 = 8x_1 + 4x_2 + 4; \qquad f_1 = 2f_2 - 2.$$

Setting $f_1 = f_2 = 0$ leads to the inconsistent linear system

$$16x_1 + 8x_2 = -6,$$
$$8x_1 + 4x_2 = -4,$$

in which

$$\rho \begin{bmatrix} 16 & 8 \\ 8 & 4 \end{bmatrix} = 1, \qquad \rho \begin{bmatrix} 16 & 8 & -6 \\ 8 & 4 & -4 \end{bmatrix} = 2.$$

Hence the number of linearly *independent* columns *and rows* in the augmented matrix is two, the maximum possible. From the linear independence of f_1 and f_2 ($f_1 = 2f_2 - 2$) it is clear that f_1 and f_2 can never *simultaneously* be zero. The necessary conditions for a stationary point cannot be fulfilled.

PROBLEMS

1. Find the derivative of each of the following functions using the "delta process." Check your answer by finding the derivative exactly.
   (a) $y = 4x^2 + 2x + 1$.   (b) $y = 12x + 15$.
   (c) $y = 1/x^2$.
2. Examine the following functions for maxima, minima, and points of inflection, without using the second derivative.
   (a) $y = 3x^2 + 12x + 10$.   (b) $y = 3x^2 - 12x + 10$.
   (c) $y = -3x^2 + 12x + 10$.
3. Write the equation for the tangent line to the function in the following:
   (a) Problem 2(a), above, at $x = 10$.   (b) Problem 2(b), above, at $x = 2$.
   (c) Problem 2(c), above, at $x = 4$.

4. Find maxima and/or minima for each of the following functions, using both first and second derivatives. Indicate in each case whether the points so found are relative (local) or absolute (global) maxima or minima.
   (a) $y = 2x^3 + 3x^2 - 12x - 15$.   (b) $y = 3x^4 - x^3 + 2$.
   (c) $y = x^3$ (d) $y = 3x^2 + 12x + 10$.
   (e) $y = 8x^3 - 9x^2 + 1$.
5. (a) Find the number that, when diminished by its square, is a maximum.
   (b) Find two numbers whose sum is 40 and whose product is as large as possible.
6. Find maxima and/or minima for each of the following functions.
   (a) $y = x_1^2 + x_1 x_2 + x_2^2 - x_2$.
   (b) $y = x_1^2 + x_2^2 + (3x_1 + 4x_2 - 26)^2$.
   (c) $y = 9x_1^2 - 18x_1 - 16x_2^2 - 64x_2 - 55$.
   (d) $y = 16 - 2(x_1 - 3)^2 - (x_2 - 7)^2$.
   (e) $y = -2x_1^3 + 6x_1 x_2 - x_2^2 - 4x_2 + 100$.
7. If $z = xy/(x + y)$, show that $x(\partial z/\partial x) + y(\partial z/\partial y) = z$.
8. Costs (y) have been found to depend in the following way on x_1 and x_2, total outputs of products 1 and 2, respectively:
$$y = x_1^2 + 4x_2^2 - 40x_1 + 500.$$
   (a) What amount of 1 and 2 should be produced in order to minimize costs?
   (b) What amount of each should be produced if there is an upper limit of 12 on x_1?
9. Suppose that the cost function of Problem 8 has been incorrectly estimated; it is discovered actually to be
$$y = x_1^2 + 4x_2^2 - 40x_1 + 500 - 2x_1 x_2.$$
   How would you answer the question in Problem 8(a), above?
10. Suppose that, in the function in Problem 9, y represented *profits* as a function of x_1 and x_2.
   (a) What amount of 1 and 2 should be produced to maximize profits?
   (b) How much of product 2 should be produced if it is established that (for other, external, reasons) x_1 must be exactly 12?
   (c) How would you answer (b) if x_2 could not exceed 5?
11. The management of a single-product firm know that their annual distribution costs (D) are related to annual production (Q) in the following way:
$$D = -2Q^2 + 90Q + 600.$$
   They maintain no inventory, so negative output is not possible; moreover, their facilities are such that production of more than 50 units a year is impossible. They wish to minimize annual distribution costs. How much would you advise them to produce? Would you advise the firm differently if their capacity limited them to no more than 40 units per year?

REFERENCES

1. Baumol, W. J., *Economic Theory and Operations Analysis*, 2d ed. Englewood Cliffs, N.J.: Prentice-Hall, Inc., 1965.
2. Chiang, A. C., *Fundamental Methods of Mathematical Economics*. New York: McGraw-Hill, Inc., 1967.

3. Draper, J. E., and J. S. Klingman, *Mathematical Analysis: Business and Economic Applications*. New York: Harper & Row, Publishers, 1968.
4. Hadley, G., *Elementary Calculus*. San Francisco: Holden-Day, 1968.
5. Teichroew, D., *An Introduction to Management Science: Deterministic Models*. New York: John Wiley & Sons, Inc., 1964.
6. Yamane, T., *Mathematics for Economists: An Elementary Survey*. Englewood Cliffs, N.J.: Prentice-Hall, Inc., 1962.

4

MULTIVARIABLE OPTIMIZATION

This chapter will extend the "classical" (that is, differential calculus) analysis of maximum and minimum problems to the much more realistic situations where the functions depend on *many* independent variables. In this investigation, compact matrix notation will be useful, and an introduction to the structure and properties of quadratic forms will facilitate discussion of second differential conditions. After this, we will introduce the complication of first one and then several side conditions in the form of equations that express necessary relations among the variables. These constraints may or may not affect the location (and the size) of the maximum or minimum for the function, but a systematic way of dealing with them is necessary. Finally, we expand the problem to allow for one or more inequality constraints that set upper or lower limits for functions of the variables, rather than imposing strict equalities only. In many problems this kind of constraint is much more realistic than a strict equality, and we need a procedure for taking inequalities into account.

The material of this chapter, therefore, comprises classical methods for unconstrained or constrained maximization or minimization problems with functions of many variables—that is, for optimization problems. A large set of such problems forms the material of mathematical programming, of which linear programming is one special, very important, extremely useful branch. This chapter puts mathematical programming in its general, classical setting and provides a background for the more modern approaches discussed in Chapters 6 through 9. Of course, classical optimization methods are useful in their own right, as Chapter 5 illustrates.

Specifically, Section 4.1 develops a consistent mathematical terminology for generalizing the discussion of Chapter 3, especially Section 3.3, to maxima and minima for functions of any number of independent variables. The generalization is accomplished in Section 4.2. Similarly, Section 4.3 introduces the complication of *dependence* between the variables into the mathematical terminology developed in Section 4.1, allowing discussion of problems of maxima and minima for functions of nonindependent variables (variables subject to side conditions in the form of equations). This is done in Sections 4.4, 4.5, and 4.6, first for two and then for any number of variables subject to first one and then any number of constraint equations. The third of the primarily mathematical sections, Section 4.7, provides the terminology within which *inequality* constraints among the variables can be discussed. This terminology is applied, in Section 4.8, to maximum and minimum problems in which the variables are required to conform to one or more constraints of this type, rather than equations.

4.1. QUADRATIC FORMS

The conditions shown in Table 3.5 on the first and second total differentials for maxima and minima extend to functions of any number of variables. The logic with respect to rates of change of the function in particular directions and slopes of tangent hyperplanes parallels that for $f(x_1, x_2)$. All that is necessary is an understanding of the structure of df and d^2f for the n-variable case. For the first total differential, this is straightforward, as we shall see in Section 4.2. For the second total differential, an introduction to the concept of quadratic forms is necessary; this will also be helpful when the assumption of independence between the variables is removed and it makes clear the "sum of squares" form of d^2f in (3-15).

Basic structure of quadratic forms

A quadratic form of, say, two variables, x_1 and x_2, is any function of x_1 and x_2 in which each of the variables may appear in only two ways: (1) squared and (2) multiplied by the other variable. For example: $2x_1^2 + 6x_1x_2 + 5x_2^2$ is a quadratic form in x_1 and x_2. The name simply describes a particular algebraic structure. A quadratic form may be a function of any number of variables, as we shall see below. Using elementary rules of matrix multiplication, the reader should convince himself that this function of x_1 and x_2 can be written as

$$[x_1 \quad x_2] \begin{bmatrix} 2 & 3 \\ 3 & 5 \end{bmatrix} \begin{bmatrix} x_1 \\ x_2 \end{bmatrix},$$

where the 3 is $\frac{6}{2}$—that is, one-half of the coefficient attached to x_1x_2.

The general quadratic form for two variables, $Q(x_1, x_2)$, can be represented as

$$Q(x_1, x_2) = a_{11}x_1^2 + (a_{12} + a_{21})x_1x_2 + a_{22}x_2^2. \tag{4-1}$$

Since any parameter multiplying the x_1x_2 term can always be represented as the sum of two equal terms, this could as well be written for the general case as

$$Q(x_1, x_2) = a_{11}x_1^2 + 2a_{12}x_1x_2 + a_{22}x_2^2. \tag{4-2}$$

In matrix terms:

$$\begin{bmatrix} x_1 & x_2 \end{bmatrix} \begin{bmatrix} a_{11} & a_{12} \\ a_{12} & a_{22} \end{bmatrix} \begin{bmatrix} x_1 \\ x_2 \end{bmatrix}, \tag{4-3}$$

or, letting $X = \begin{bmatrix} x_1 \\ x_2 \end{bmatrix}$ and denoting by A the *symmetric* matrix

$$\begin{bmatrix} a_{11} & a_{12} \\ a_{21} & a_{22} \end{bmatrix}$$

—that is, $a_{12} = a_{21}$, (4-3) is just

$$X'AX. \tag{4-4}$$

The beauty of (4-4) is that it represents a quadratic form of any number of variables; nothing changes but the dimensions of the matrices involved. Thus

$$Q(x_1, x_2, x_3) = X'AX,$$

where

$$X = \begin{bmatrix} x_1 \\ x_2 \\ x_3 \end{bmatrix} \quad \text{and} \quad A = \begin{bmatrix} a_{11} & a_{12} & a_{13} \\ a_{21} & a_{22} & a_{23} \\ a_{31} & a_{32} & a_{33} \end{bmatrix}$$

and A is symmetric. One final representation is

$$Q(x_1, x_2, x_3) = \sum_{i=1}^{3} \sum_{j=1}^{3} a_{ij}x_ix_j;$$

this makes clear the quadratic nature of the function. When $i = j$, a variable is squared; otherwise (when $i \neq j$) *pairs* of variables are multiplied together. (The number of variables influences only the range of the subscripts i and j.)

For n variables,

$$Q(x_1, \ldots, x_n) = \sum_{i=1}^{n} \sum_{j=1}^{n} a_{ij}x_ix_j = X'AX,$$

where X is an n-element column vector of the variables and A is an $n \times n$ symmetric matrix of the coefficients a_{ij}.

Rewritten structure of quadratic forms

Consider $Q(x_1, x_2)$ as written in (4-2):

$$a_{11}x_1^2 + 2a_{12}x_1x_2 + a_{22}x_2^2.$$

Suppose that we were trying to determine conditions on the values of the a_{ij} under which this expression would *always* be positive or *always* be negative, regardless of the values of x_1 and x_2. To anticipate the discussion below, second total differentials for functions of any number of variables can be written as quadratic forms. We saw in Chapter 3 that the sign of the second total differential was useful for distinguishing maxima from minima. This is true for functions of n variables and is precisely the reason for the investigation of signs of quadratic forms. In the form of (4-2) the question could not be answered. The middle term, $2a_{12}x_1x_2$, would take on differing signs depending on the signs of x_1 and x_2, even though $a_{11}x_1^2$ and $a_{22}x_2^2$ present no problem. What is needed, then, is an expression in which the x's all appear in terms that are squared; this removes any ambiguity about signs. We thus want to modify (4-2), and specifically we employ the device of "completing the square." Consider the first two terms—$a_{11}x_1^2 + 2a_{12}x_1x_2$. If $(a_{12}^2/a_{11})x_2^2$ were added to these terms, the entire expression would be

$$a_{11}x_1^2 + 2a_{12}x_1x_2 + \left(\frac{a_{12}^2}{a_{11}}\right)x_2^2 = a_{11}\left[x_1^2 + 2\left(\frac{a_{12}}{a_{11}}\right)x_1x_2 + \left(\frac{a_{12}^2}{a_{11}^2}\right)x_2^2\right]$$

$$= a_{11}\left[x_1 + \left(\frac{a_{12}}{a_{11}}\right)x_2\right]^2.$$

But then the added term $(a_{12}^2/a_{11})x_2^2$ must also be subtracted from (4-2), if the expression is to remain unchanged. Thus the third term in (4-2), $a_{22}x_2^2$, must absorb the loss of $(a_{12}^2/a_{11})x_2^2$;

$$a_{22}x_2^2 - \left(\frac{a_{12}^2}{a_{11}}\right)x_2^2 = \left(a_{22} - \frac{a_{12}^2}{a_{11}}\right)x_2^2 = \left(\frac{a_{11}a_{22} - a_{12}^2}{a_{11}}\right)x_2^2.$$

Therefore (4-2) is now

$$Q(x_1, x_2) = a_{11}\left[x_1 + \left(\frac{a_{12}}{a_{11}}\right)x_2\right]^2 + \left(\frac{a_{11}a_{22} - a_{12}^2}{a_{11}}\right)(x_2)^2 \qquad (4\text{-}5)$$

—that is, a *sum of squares.*[1] The sign of $Q(x_1, x_2)$ for cases in which x_1 and x_2 are both nonzero thus depends entirely on the two terms multiplying the squared expressions.

Recall the A matrix in (4-3) and (4-4). The first critical term in (4-5) is

---

[1] The reader may note a similarity between (4-5) and the rewritten form of d^2f in (3-15). This is the whole point of our interest in quadratic forms.

just a_{11}, the element in the upper left corner of A. The second critical term is the ratio of the *determinant* of A divided by a_{11}. Since the determinant of the 1×1 matrix $[a_{11}]$ is just a_{11}, we could represent the critical terms as $|a_{11}|$ and $|A|/|a_{11}|$, respectively. These determinants have a particular name; they are called the *principal minors* of A. The first principal minor of a square matrix A is the determinant of the matrix formed by deleting *all but* the first row and column from A; that is, it is always simply a_{11}. It is denoted[2] $|A_1|$. The second principal minor, $|A_2|$, is the determinant of the matrix formed by removing all but the first *two* rows and columns of A. Thus

$$|A_2| = \begin{vmatrix} a_{11} & a_{12} \\ a_{21} & a_{22} \end{vmatrix} = a_{11}a_{22} - a_{12}a_{21};$$

for a symmetric matrix this is also $a_{11}a_{22} - a_{12}^2$. For an $n \times n$ matrix, therefore, the nth principal minor is the determinant of the entire matrix; for the 2×2 case here, $|A_2| = |A|$. Thus (4-5) may be written

$$Q(x_1, x_2) = |A_1| \left[x_1 + \left(\frac{a_{12}}{a_{11}} \right) x_2 \right]^2 + \left(\frac{|A_2|}{|A_1|} \right) x_2^2. \qquad (4\text{-}6)$$

Although the process of completing squares is more involved, the general quadratic form for three variables can be shown to be

$$Q(x_1, x_2, x_3) = |A_1|(\cdot)^2 + \frac{|A_2|}{|A_1|}(\cdot)^2 + \frac{|A_3|}{|A_2|}(\cdot)^2. \qquad (4\text{-}7)$$

The squared terms contain functions of the x's and a's, which, from the point of view of the *sign* of (4-7), are unimportant. And for n variables,

$$Q(x_1, \ldots, x_n) = |A_1|(\cdot)^2 + \frac{|A_2|}{|A_1|}(\cdot)^2 + \cdots + \frac{|A_n|}{|A_{n-1}|}(\cdot)^2. \qquad (4\text{-}8)$$

The sign of a quadratic form

The following terminology is in general use for describing quadratic forms. If a quadratic form Q is always positive ($Q > 0$) for *any* values that the x's assume, except when all x's are zero, it is termed *positive definite*.[3] If Q is always negative ($Q < 0$) except when all x's are zero, it is *negative definite*. If Q is either positive or zero ($Q \geq 0$) for all values of x, except when all are zero (that is, $Q = 0$ for some set of x_i not all zero), it is termed

---

[2] The vertical bars tell us that we are dealing with a determinant and hence with a square matrix; A_1 alone would still denote the first column of the matrix A. As anticipated in Chapter 1, we have found another use for determinants, quite independent of their role in analysis of equation systems and Cramer's rule.

[3] "Definitely positive" would seem to be more logical, and just "positive" would be in keeping with the "greater than zero" notation in general use in algebra.

positive semidefinite.[4] And if the inequality is reversed ($Q \leq 0$), it is said to be *negative semidefinite.* For example:

(a) $x_1^2 + 6x_2^2$ is positive definite.
(b) $-x_1^2 - 6x_2^2$ is negative definite.
(c) $x_1^2 - 4x_1x_2 + 4x_2^2 + x_3^2 = (x_1 - 2x_2)^2 + x_3^2$ is positive semidefinite. (It is never negative, but equals zero at $x_1 = 2$, $x_2 = 1$, $x_3 = 0$; $x_1 = 10$, $x_2 = 5$, $x_3 = 0$, and so on.)
(d) $-(x_1 - 2x_2)^2 - x_3^2$ is therefore negative semidefinite.
(e) $x_1^2 - 6x_2^2$ cannot be classed as either definite or semidefinite; it is *indefinite.*

For the general quadratic form of two variables, $Q(x_1, x_2)$, to be *positive definite* it is therefore both necessary and sufficient that the coefficients on both squared terms be strictly positive—that is, from (4-6), that (1) $|A_1| > 0$ and (2) $|A_2|/|A_1| > 0$. Since the denominator in (2) is covered by the rule in (1), this can be put simply as (1) $|A_1| > 0$ and (2) $|A_2| > 0$. Similarly (4-6) will be *negative definite* if and only if (1) $|A_1| < 0$ and (2) $|A_2|/|A_1| < 0$ or, more simply, (1) $|A_1| < 0$ and (2) $|A_2| > 0$, since if the numerator of a fraction is always positive, the sign of the fraction will be governed by the denominator.

Because of the generalization of the sum-of-squares form in (4-7) and (4-8), it is clear that:

A quadratic form of n variables, $Q(x_1, \ldots, x_n)$, will be (a) *positive definite* if and only if all principal minors of A are positive (that is, $|A_1| > 0$, $|A_2| > 0$, $\ldots$, $|A_n| > 0$) and (b) *negative definite* if and only if the principal minors of A *alternate* in sign, *beginning negative* (that is, $|A_1| < 0$, $|A_2| > 0$, $\ldots$, $|A_n| < 0$ if n is odd and $|A_n| > 0$ if n is even).   (4-9)

To return to the previous examples, where

$$X = \begin{bmatrix} x_1 \\ x_2 \end{bmatrix} \text{ or } \begin{bmatrix} x_1 \\ x_2 \\ x_3 \end{bmatrix},$$

as appropriate:

(a) $x_1^2 + 6x_2^2 = X' \begin{bmatrix} 1 & 0 \\ 0 & 6 \end{bmatrix} X$; $|A_1| = 1 > 0$, $|A_2| = 6 > 0$, thus positive definite.

---

[4] Again, "nonnegative" would seem to do as well.

(b) $-x_1^2 - 6x_2^2 = X' \begin{bmatrix} -1 & 0 \\ 0 & -6 \end{bmatrix} X; |A_1| = -1 < 0; |A_2| = 6 > 0$, thus negative definite.

(c) $x_1^2 - 4x_1x_2 + 4x_2^2 + x_3^2 = X' \begin{bmatrix} 1 & -2 & 0 \\ -2 & 4 & 0 \\ 0 & 0 & 1 \end{bmatrix} X; |A_1| = 1 > 0, |A_2| = $

$0; |A_3| = 0$; thus this is *neither* positive definite nor negative definite. [Note that the general rule in (4-9) on signs of principal minors is relevant only for definiteness, not for *semi*definiteness.]

(d) $-x_1^2 + 4x_1x_2 - 4x_2^2 - x_3^2 = X' \begin{bmatrix} -1 & 2 & 0 \\ 2 & -4 & 0 \\ 0 & 0 & -1 \end{bmatrix} X; |A_1| = -1 < 0,$

$|A_2| = 0$, $|A_3| = 0$, and, again, this is neither positive nor negative definite.

(e) $x_1^2 - 6x_2^2 = X' \begin{bmatrix} 1 & 0 \\ 0 & -6 \end{bmatrix} X; \quad |A_1| = 1 > 0, \quad |A_2| = -6 < 0,$ so

neither.

The reader will recognize that the rules on signs of principal minors, (4-9), may allow early judgment that a quadratic form of n variables is neither positive definite nor negative definite. For example, if $|A_1| < 0$ and $|A_2| < 0$, we can stop; also, if $|A_1| > 0$ and $|A_2| < 0$, we can stop. If $|A_1| > 0$, then *no change* of sign of higher principal minors is allowed, whereas if $|A_1| < 0$, then signs *must alternate* continuously from that point onward. Hence in (c) and (d) above it would have been sufficient, in examining for positive or negative *definiteness*, to stop at $|A_2|$ in both cases.

The sign of d^2f for $y = f(x_1, x_2)$

The general form of the second total differential for a function of two independent variables was shown in equation (3-14):

$$d^2f = f_{11}(dx_1)^2 + 2f_{12} \, dx_1 \, dx_2 + f_{22}(dx_2)^2.$$

We now recognize that this is a quadratic form in the variables dx_1 and dx_2, the independent small changes in x_1 and x_2. Thus, for $y = f(x_1, x_2)$, we can use the generalized notation for quadratic forms:

$$d^2f = \begin{bmatrix} dx_1 & dx_2 \end{bmatrix} \begin{bmatrix} f_{11} & f_{12} \\ f_{21} & f_{22} \end{bmatrix} \begin{bmatrix} dx_1 \\ dx_2 \end{bmatrix}. \tag{4-10}$$

Letting

$$dX = \begin{bmatrix} dx_1 \\ dx_2 \end{bmatrix} \quad \text{and} \quad H = \begin{bmatrix} f_{11} & f_{12} \\ f_{21} & f_{22} \end{bmatrix}$$

(where H is symmetric, since we are dealing with functions for which $f_{ij} = f_{ji}$—that is, for which order of differentiation in cross-partials makes no difference), this is

$$d^2f = [dX]'[H][dX]. \tag{4-11}$$

For $d^2f > 0$—that is, for the quadratic form to be positive definite, we know that the principal minors of H must all be positive—$|H_1| > 0$ and $|H_2| > 0$. That is, $f_{11} > 0$ and $f_{11}f_{22} - f_{12}^2 > 0$. For the form to be negative definite, $d^2f < 0$, the requirements are $|H_1| < 0$ and $|H_2| > 0$—that is, $f_{11} < 0$ and $f_{11}f_{22} - f_{12}^2 > 0$. Thus the problem of establishing the sign of the second total differential is just a particular case of the general problem of determining the sign of a quadratic form. This is the entire reason for examining the structure of quadratic forms in this section. For the second total differential, the variables are dx's and the symmetric matrix of coefficients is composed of second partial and cross-partial derivatives. This matrix is termed the *Hessian* of the function f, which is why H was used to denote it; H_f is also used. The sign of d^2f thus depends on the signs of the principal minors of the Hessian.[5]

4.2. MAXIMA AND MINIMA FOR FUNCTIONS OF n INDEPENDENT VARIABLES

We now use the discussion on quadratic forms and their signs to generalize results on maxima and minima for functions of any number of independent variables. Consider $y = f(x_1, \ldots, x_n)$; letting $X = \begin{bmatrix} x_1 \\ \vdots \\ x_n \end{bmatrix}$,

[5] Note the distinction between (1) the sign rule on principal minors, which is both *necessary* and *sufficient* to establish positive or negative definiteness of the quadratic form, and (2) the sign rule on the second total differential, which is *sufficient* only to differentiate maxima from minima. The former rule tells us unambiguously when and only when we will *always* have $Q > 0$ or $Q < 0$. The *always* is important; it is explicit in the definition of positive and negative definiteness. The fact that Q may be positive for some values of the variables—case (e), for example—is not enough; it must be so for all values (except all zero). When the quadratic form is d^2f, we therefore know when and only when $d^2f > 0$ or $d^2f < 0$. This depends *exclusively* on the values of the second partials and cross-partials evaluated at a stationary point where $df = 0$. If we carry out the evaluation and $d^2f > 0$, we are *assured* that the point is a minimum; if $d^2f < 0$, a maximum. However, if the test on the sign of d^2f fails, we do not know for certain that we do not have a maximum or minimum, since rule (2) is not necessary, only sufficient.

we may denote this alternatively as $y = f(X)$. A point $X^* = [x_1^*, \ldots, x_n^*]'$ will be a relative maximum or a relative minimum of the function $y = f(X)$ according to the rules given in Table 4.1. This is virtually identical to

Table 4.1. Characteristics of Maxima and Minima for $y = f(X)$

	Maximum	*Minimum*
First-order condition	$df^* = 0$	$df^* = 0$
Second-order condition	$d^2f^* < 0$	$d^2f^* > 0$

Table 3.5, for $f(x_1, x_2)$; all that is required is a thorough understanding of the structure of df and d^2f for a function of n variables.

First-order conditions

The logic by which df was seen in (3-11) to equal $f_1\,dx_1 + f_2\,dx_2$ for the two-variable case can be extended to any number of variables. Changes in each of the independent variables, dx_i, are transmitted to the function y via the respective first partial derivatives, f_i. Thus

$$df = f_1\,dx_1 + f_2\,dx_2 + \cdots + f_n\,dx_n. \tag{4-12}$$

Exactly as before, $df = 0$ for independent small changes in $dx_1, \ldots, dx_n$ (not all zero) if and only if $f_1 = f_2 = \cdots = f_n = 0$. This is then the first-order condition that any stationary point for a function of n variables must satisfy.

Second-order conditions

The second-order condition, on the sign of d^2f, was established for the two-variable case in the preceding section, as was the condition for positive or negative definiteness for a quadratic form of *any* number of variables. The second total differential for $y = f(x_1, \ldots, x_n)$ is exactly as in (4-11), where

$$dX = \begin{bmatrix} dx_1 \\ \vdots \\ dx_n \end{bmatrix} \quad \text{and} \quad H = \begin{bmatrix} f_{11} & f_{12} & \cdots & f_{1n} \\ f_{21} & f_{22} & \cdots & f_{2n} \\ \vdots & & & \\ f_{n1} & f_{n2} & \cdots & f_{nn} \end{bmatrix}.$$

Thus $d^2f < 0$ (a maximum) if and only if $|H_1| < 0$, $|H_2| > 0$, $|H_3| < 0$, $\ldots$, $|H_n| < 0$ if n is odd and $|H_n| > 0$ if n is even. For $d^2f > 0$ (a minimum) we must have $|H_1| > 0$, $|H_2| > 0$, $\ldots$, $|H_n| > 0$. To examine the second-order condition of Table 4.1, we evaluate the principal minors of H^*, the Hessian matrix in which f_{ij} for all i and j are evaluated at the one or more $X^* = [x_1^*, \ldots, x_n^*]'$, where $df = 0$. The rules for maxima and minima of functions of one or of two variables can now be looked upon as special cases of the general results of this section.

Example

We conclude with a specific example. Examine the stationary points of

$$y = f(x_1, x_2, x_3) = 5x_1^2 + 2x_2^2 + x_3^4 - 32x_3 + 6x_1x_2 + 5x_2$$

for maxima and minima. The first-order condition, $df = 0$, requires that the three first partial derivatives be set equal to zero. Since $f_1 = 10x_1 + 6x_2$, $f_2 = 4x_2 + 6x_1 + 5$, and $f_3 = 4x_3^3 - 32$, the necessary conditions are

$$\begin{aligned} 10x_1 + 6x_2 &= 0, \\ 6x_1 + 4x_2 &= -5, \\ 4x_3^3 - 32 &= 0. \end{aligned} \qquad (4\text{-}13)$$

The first two equations can be solved for x_1 and x_2; the third equation contains only information about x_3. For the system

$$\begin{aligned} 10x_1 + 6x_2 &= 0, \\ 6x_1 + 4x_2 &= -5, \end{aligned}$$

the determinant of the coefficient matrix is 4; thus a unique solution for x_1 and x_2 can be found. For example, using Cramer's rule,

$$x_1^* = \frac{\begin{vmatrix} 0 & 6 \\ -5 & 4 \end{vmatrix}}{4} = \frac{30}{4} = 7\tfrac{1}{2}; \qquad x_2^* = \frac{\begin{vmatrix} 10 & 0 \\ 6 & -5 \end{vmatrix}}{4} = -\frac{50}{4} = -12\tfrac{1}{2}.$$

From the third equation, $4x_3^3 = 32$; that is, $x_3^* = 2$. Therefore

$$X^* = \begin{bmatrix} 7\tfrac{1}{2} \\ -12\tfrac{1}{2} \\ 2 \end{bmatrix}$$

satisfies the conditions for a stationary point in equations (4-13).

To construct the Hessian, we need all second partial derivatives and all cross-partials. For this problem, $f_{11} = 10$, $f_{22} = 4$, $f_{33} = 12x_3^2$; $f_{12} = f_{21} = 6$, $f_{13} = f_{31} = 0$, $f_{23} = f_{32} = 0$. That is:

$$H = \begin{bmatrix} 10 & 6 & 0 \\ 6 & 4 & 0 \\ 0 & 0 & 12x_3^2 \end{bmatrix}$$

The principal minors are $|H_1| = 10 > 0$, $|H_2| = 4 > 0$, $|H_3| = 4(12x_3^2)$; hence the sign of $|H_3|$ depends on x_3. Since $x_3^* = 2$, $|H_3| = 192 > 0$, so X^* represents a minimum point, since $df^* = 0$ and $d^2f^* > 0$.

We are now able to investigate functions of any number of independent variables for their maximum and minimum points. Our next concern, therefore, is with cases in which not all of the variables are independent of one another—that is, where there are further conditions relating some or all of the variables to each other. To anticipate the complications involved with the sign of the second total differential under these conditions, we must turn once again to the underlying theory of quadratic forms.

4.3.   QUADRATIC FORMS WITH SIDE CONDITIONS

Consider again $Q(x_1, x_2) = a_{11}x_1^2 + 2a_{12}x_1x_2 + a_{22}x_2^2$ for the case in which x_1 and x_2 are not independent variables but rather must conform to the added condition[6] that $c_1x_1 + c_2x_2 = 0$. Because of the particularly simple form of the relation between the two variables, we can observe that $x_2 = -(c_1/c_2)x_1$, and thus that the quadratic form reduces, through substitution and algebra, to a function of x_1 alone:

$$Q(x_1) = (a_{11}c_2^2 - 2a_{12}c_1c_2 + a_{22}c_1^2)\left(\frac{x_1^2}{c_2^2}\right). \qquad (4\text{-}14)$$

Therefore, the sign of $Q(x_1, x_2)$ with the side condition taken explicitly into account, (4-14), hinges on the sign of $(a_{11}c_2^2 - 2a_{12}c_1c_2 + a_{22}c_1^2)$. It may not be obvious until one sees it for the first time, but this expression is precisely the negative of the determinant of a matrix, $\bar{A}$, whose particularly appealing structure is made more apparent by partitioning. Let

$$\bar{A} = \left[\begin{array}{c|cc} 0 & c_1 & c_2 \\ \hline c_1 & a_{11} & a_{12} \\ c_2 & a_{12} & a_{22} \end{array}\right];$$

then the expression multiplying (x_1^2/c_2^2) in (4-14) is just $-|\bar{A}|$. That is, $Q(x_1) = -|\bar{A}|(x_1^2/c_2^2)$. Thus, $Q > 0$ if and only if $-|\bar{A}| > 0$ or $|\bar{A}| < 0$; $Q < 0$ if and only if $|\bar{A}| > 0$. The structure of $\bar{A}$ should be clear; it consists of the original (symmetric) matrix of coefficients, A, from the quadratic form, bordered by the coefficients of the linear relation between the

---

[6] This is a very specific and not at all general kind of side condition; we introduce it in this way here precisely because it appears in this form when we consider d^2f for a function with a *general* type of dependence among the variables.

variables, $c_1 x_1 + c_2 x_2 = 0$.[7] Letting $C = [c_1, c_2]$ and denoting by A the *symmetric* matrix

$$\begin{bmatrix} a_{11} & a_{12} \\ a_{21} & a_{22} \end{bmatrix}, \qquad \bar{A} = \left[\begin{array}{c|c} 0 & C \\ \hline C' & A \end{array} \right].$$

It is much more complicated to show the case for $Q(x_1, x_2, x_3)$ subject to $c_1 x_1 + c_2 x_2 + c_3 x_3 = 0$. By virtue of the side relation, one of the variables can be eliminated from $Q(x_1, x_2, x_3)$. It then becomes a quadratic form in the two remaining *independent* variables, similar in structure to (4-2) except that a_{11}, a_{12}, and a_{22} are replaced by much more complex expressions. It too can then be written as a sum of squares as in (4-5). The result is that for positive definiteness of $Q(x_1, x_2, x_3)$ with a relationship among the variables, $c_1 x_1 + c_2 x_2 + c_3 x_3 = 0$, the *last two*[8] principal minors of $\bar{A}$ in the three-variable case:

$$\bar{A} = \left[\begin{array}{c|ccc} 0 & c_1 & c_2 & c_3 \\ \hline c_1 & a_{11} & a_{12} & a_{13} \\ c_2 & a_{21} & a_{22} & a_{23} \\ c_3 & a_{31} & a_{32} & a_{33} \end{array} \right] = \left[\begin{array}{c|c} 0 & C \\ \hline C' & A \end{array} \right],$$

must be *negative*, where A is symmetric and $C = [c_1, c_2, c_3]$. That is,

$$|\bar{A}_3| = \begin{vmatrix} 0 & c_1 & c_2 \\ c_1 & a_{11} & a_{12} \\ c_2 & a_{21} & a_{22} \end{vmatrix} < 0 \quad \text{and} \quad |\bar{A}_4| = |\bar{A}| = \begin{vmatrix} 0 & c_1 & c_2 & c_3 \\ c_1 & a_{11} & a_{12} & a_{13} \\ c_2 & a_{21} & a_{22} & a_{23} \\ c_3 & a_{31} & a_{32} & a_{33} \end{vmatrix} < 0.$$

For negative definiteness, $Q(x_1, x_2, x_3) < 0$, the signs of these two determinants must alternate, beginning *positive*.

For $Q(x_1, \ldots, x_n)$ subject to $c_1 x_1 + \cdots + c_n x_n = 0$, the results are a direct extension of the three-variable case. Let A be the $n \times n$ symmetric matrix associated with the quadratic form and C be the row vector of coefficients $c_1, \ldots, c_n$ in the constraint. Then

$$\bar{A} = \left[\begin{array}{c|cccc} 0 & c_1 & c_2 & \cdots & c_n \\ \hline c_1 & a_{11} & a_{12} & \cdots & a_{1n} \\ \vdots & & & & \\ c_n & a_{n1} & a_{n2} & \cdots & a_{nn} \end{array} \right] = \left[\begin{array}{c|c} 0 & C \\ \hline C' & A \end{array} \right].$$

[7] Using a modified A reminds us that it is a matrix formed from A, and the bar provides a visual suggestion of one of the two borders.

[8] The *number* of principal minors is derived from the number of variables (n) and the number of equations to which they must conform (m); it is $n - m$, which for this case is $3 - 1 = 2$.

For $Q > 0$ (positive definite) subject to $c_1 x_1 + \cdots + c_n x_n = 0$, it is both necessary and sufficient that the last $n - 1$ principal minors (that is, starting with the third) of $\bar{A}$ be *negative;* $|\bar{A}_3| < 0$, $|\bar{A}_4| < 0$, ..., $|\bar{A}_n| < 0$. $Q < 0$ (4-15)
(negative definite), subject to the same side relation, if and only if these same principal minors alternate in sign, beginning *positive.*[9]

The generalization, finally, to more than one linear relation of the sort

$$\sum_{i=1}^{n} c_i x_i = 0$$

is a more or less straightforward extension of the rules given in (4-15), although it is much more difficult to derive. Let $CX = O$ represent a system of m linear homogeneous equations in n variables $(m < n)$ with $\rho(C) = m$. Then

For $Q(x_1, \ldots, x_n)$ to be positive definite $(Q > 0)$ subject to $CX = O$, it is both necessary and sufficient that the last $n - m$ principal minors of the $(m + n) \times (m + n)$ matrix $\bar{A}$, where

$$\bar{A} = \left[\begin{array}{c|c} O & C \\ \hline C' & A \end{array} \right],$$ (4-16)

have the sign of $(-1)^m$. Q is negative definite $(Q < 0)$ if and only if these same principal minors alternate in sign, beginning with the sign of $(-1)^{m+1}$.

The reader can see that the rules in (4-15) for $m = 1$ and the $(n + 1) \times (n + 1)$ matrix $\bar{A}$ used there are a special case of the rules in (4-16).

---

[9] The reader will note that these rules differ from those for the unconstrained-quadratic-form case (Section 4.1) in two respects. First, the *signs* of the rules are just reversed. This is because the rewritten sums-of-squares expressions for the quadratic forms, taking into account the constraints, involve squared terms multiplied by the *negative* of principal minors of $\bar{A}$. Second, not all of the principal minors of $\bar{A}$ are involved. Since, in the n-variable case, any one variable can be removed because of the side relation, the unconstrained quadratic form has $n - 1$ independent variables. It thus can be written as the sum of $n - 1$ squared terms, each multiplied by a coefficient that, except for the first term, is the ratio of two successive principal minors. Thus $n - 1$ principal minors are needed. Since $\bar{A}$ is $(n + 1) \times (n + 1)$, it has a total of $n + 1$ principal minors; if two are ignored, exactly the right number will remain. From the algebra of the sum-of-squares expression we can deduce that $|\bar{A}_1|$ and $|\bar{A}_2|$ should be eliminated.

4.4. MAXIMA AND MINIMA FOR FUNCTIONS OF TWO DEPENDENT VARIABLES

We are now in a position to develop rules for maximum and minimum problems in which the variables are not independent of one another—that is, in which side conditions relate some or all of them. We will begin with the simplest constrained optimization problem, involving a function of two variables subject to one constraint in the form of an equation. Then (Section 4.5) we will extend to more variables (in the same manner as we have done above for the unconstrained optimum problem) and also to more constraints (Section 4.6). Finally, after some convex set theory (Section 4.7), we examine in Section 4.8 the case in which the constraints are *inequalities* rather than equations, setting upper or lower limits on some combinations of the variables. Unless otherwise noted, the rules will isolate relative (that is, local) maxima and minima; this may be troublesome, as we shall see. These topics constitute the remainder of this chapter.

First-order conditions: differentials

Consider $y = f(x_1, x_2)$, where, in addition, x_1 and x_2 must satisfy the completely general relation $h(x_1, x_2) = 0$. If the constraint is $g(x_1, x_2) = c$, then $h(x_1, x_2) \equiv g(x_1, x_2) - c = 0$. For example, if $x_1 + 3x_2 = 10$, this can be written

$$h(x_1, x_2) = x_1 + 3x_2 - 10 = 0;$$

if $3x_1^2 + 17 = 2x_1x_2 + 4x_2^2$, this can be expressed as

$$h(x_1, x_2) = 3x_1^2 - 2x_1x_2 - 4x_2^2 + 17 = 0.$$

We assume, throughout this section, that both variables appear in the constraint. (If they did not—for example, if the constraint were $3x_1 = 9$, or $x_1 = 3$—then we would actually have an unconstrained problem with only one variable, x_2.)

Geometrically, we are now looking for a maximum or minimum on the surface $y = f(x_1, x_2)$ only above the line or curve in x_1x_2 space that represents $h(x_1, x_2) = 0$. Figure 4.1 illustrates for a maximum problem in which $f(x_1, x_2)$ has the general shape of an inverted bowl and the constraint, $h(x_1, x_2) = 0$, is a straight line in x_1x_2 space. The linear constraint has the effect of building a wall on the x_1x_2 plane that passes through the surface $f(x_1, x_2)$; the constrained maximum point must be found on the trace of the $f(x_1, x_2)$ surface on this plane. [When $h(x_1, x_2) = 0$ is not a linear function, the surface will be cut by a curved wall.]

It is still appropriate to impose the customary necessary condition that the first total differential be zero—that is, that for a maximum or a minimum

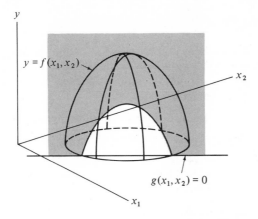

Figure 4.1. Illustration of Equality-constrained Maximization Problem

$$df = f_1\, dx_1 + f_2\, dx_2 = 0 \qquad (4\text{-}17)$$

provided that account is taken of the influence of the constraining side condition. Because $h(x_1,\ x_2) = 0$, x_1 and x_2 are no longer independent; hence dx_1 and dx_2 in df, (4-17), are no longer independent either. The nature of their dependence can be made explicit by taking the total differential of both sides of the constraint equation $h(x_1,\ x_2) = 0$. (Here $h_1 \equiv \partial h/\partial x_1$, $h_2 \equiv \partial h/\partial x_2$, completely analogous to f_1 and f_2; both h_1 and h_2 will be different from zero since we assume that both variables appear in the constraining equation):

$$h_1\, dx_1 + h_2\, dx_2 = 0. \qquad (4\text{-}18)$$

Note that the left-hand side is just the total differential of the function $h(x_1,\ x_2)$; the right-hand side is the differential of zero. The origins of the equations in (4-17) and (4-18) should be clearly distinguished. The zero on the right-hand side of (4-17) is an *external* condition, imposed because we are interested in maxima and minima. The zero on the right-hand side of (4-18) is simply a reflection of the constraint; it is *internal* to the problem. Thus, for example, from (4-18), $dx_2 = -(h_1/h_2)\, dx_1$. This shows precisely how the changes in x_1 and x_2 must be related, owing to the constraint. Thus, df in (4-17) can be rewritten as a function of either dx_1 or dx_2 alone. For example, taking account of the relationship between dx_1 and dx_2, (4-17) can be written

$$df = f_1\, dx_1 + f_2\left(-\frac{h_1}{h_2}\right)dx_1 = 0,$$

from which it follows that

$$\frac{f_1}{f_2} = \frac{h_1}{h_2} \quad \text{or} \quad \frac{f_1}{h_1} = \frac{f_2}{h_2}. \tag{4-19}$$

In taking the first total differential of $h(x_1, x_2)$ in order to establish the relationship between dx_1 and dx_2 in (4-18), we may have lost some information from the constraint, namely the magnitude of the constant term, if there was one. For example, both

$$x_1^2 + 3x_1x_2 + 4x_2^2 = 2 \quad \text{and} \quad x_1^2 + 3x_1x_2 + 4x_2^2 = 700,$$

expressed as $h(x_1, x_2) = 0$ by taking the constant term to the left-hand side, have $dh = (2x_1 + 3x_2)\, dx_1 + (3x_1 + 8x_2)\, dx_2$. Therefore, to the necessary conditions in (4-19) we must add the original statement of the constraint to recapture the lost constant term.[10] The conditions that must hold at a stationary point of $f(x_1, x_2)$ subject to $h(x_1, x_2) = 0$ are thus:

$$\text{(a)} \quad \frac{f_1}{h_1} = \frac{f_2}{h_2} \quad \text{and} \quad \text{(b)} \quad h(x_1, x_2) = 0. \tag{4-20}$$

We can derive the same results somewhat differently, in a manner that draws heavily on our study of equation systems in Chapter 2 and that lends itself to generalization: to more variables and more constraints. Consider again equations (4-17) and (4-18):

$$\begin{aligned} f_1\, dx_1 + f_2\, dx_2 &= 0, \\ h_1\, dx_1 + h_2\, dx_2 &= 0. \end{aligned} \tag{4-21}$$

This is a pair of homogeneous linear equations in the variables dx_1 and dx_2. We know from Chapter 2 that for this system to have a solution other than the trivial one where $dx_1 = 0$ and $dx_2 = 0$, the matrix of coefficients multiplying the variables must be singular—that is,

$$\begin{vmatrix} f_1 & f_2 \\ h_1 & h_2 \end{vmatrix} = 0. \tag{4-22}$$

We use the notion of the differential in first-order conditions to examine the effect on the function f of small changes in one or more variables; it is only useful if any or all dx_i can be nonzero—that is, small changes in any or all x_i are allowed. Hence the determinant in (4-22) must vanish so that values other than zero for both dx_1 and dx_2 can satisfy (4-21). But (4-22) means that $f_1 h_2 = f_2 h_1$; that is, $f_1/h_1 = f_2/h_2$ or $f_1/f_2 = h_1/h_2$, exactly as in (4-19).

---

[10] Since information loss occurs between $h(x_1, x_2)$ and dh, the reader might ask: why use the differential form? Why not use the information in $h(x_1, x_2)$ directly? The reason is that the first-order condition is on df, which is a function of dx_1 and dx_2; by using dh, which is *always* of the form $h_1\, dx_1 + h_2\, dx_2$, we have immediately the necessary relationship between the changes in x_1 and x_2. As some of the examples in the text show, it may not be an easy task to solve $h(x_1, x_2)$ for one of the variables in order to substitute into $f(x_1, x_2)$.

We recall from Chapter 2 that this can also be expressed by saying that the rows of $\begin{bmatrix} f_1 & f_2 \\ h_1 & h_2 \end{bmatrix}$ must be linearly dependent; that is, $[f_1, \ f_2] = \alpha[h_1, \ h_2]$, where α is the factor of proportionality. If we consider the transpose of these row vectors, the relationship remains the same:

$$\begin{bmatrix} f_1 \\ f_2 \end{bmatrix} = \alpha \begin{bmatrix} h_1 \\ h_2 \end{bmatrix};$$

in two-dimensional vector space, α is the scalar by which the point $\begin{bmatrix} h_1 \\ h_2 \end{bmatrix}$ must be stretched or shrunk to reach $\begin{bmatrix} f_1 \\ f_2 \end{bmatrix}$.

We could therefore also describe the condition on this determinant by saying

$$\begin{array}{ccccc} f_1 = \alpha h_1, & & f_1 - \alpha h_1 = 0, & & f_1/h_1 = \alpha, \\ & \text{or} & & \text{or} & \\ f_2 = \alpha h_2, & & f_2 - \alpha h_2 = 0, & & f_2/h_2 = \alpha. \end{array} \qquad (4\text{-}23)$$

This undetermined scalar α could have appeared explicitly in (4-20)(a) as the common value for the two ratios that are required to be equal. However, its interpretation as the scalar showing the relationship between the two rows of the coefficient matrix in (4-21) would not have been clear. As before, the original constraint $h(x_1, \ x_2) = 0$ must be added to (4-23) because of the information lost in taking differentials. Thus the necessary conditions for a stationary point can also be written as

$$\text{(a)} \quad f_1 - \alpha h_1 = 0, f_2 - \alpha h_2 = 0 \quad \text{and} \quad \text{(b)} \quad h(x_1, \ x_2) = 0. \quad (4\text{-}20')$$

First-order conditions: Lagrange multipliers

The method of Lagrange multipliers[11] is just a systematic way of generating the conditions in (4-20'). Form the so-called Lagrangean function, L, by subtracting the constraint, multiplied by an unknown new variable, λ, from $f(x_1, \ x_2)$:

$$L = f(x_1, \ x_2) - \lambda[h(x_1, \ x_2)]. \qquad (4\text{-}24)$$

L is thus a function of three variables—x_1, x_2, and λ. Note that as long as x_1 and x_2 satisfy the constraint—that is, $h(x_1, \ x_2) = 0$—then the Lagrangean function L is exactly the same as $f(x_1, \ x_2)$. Take the three first partial derivatives of L *as if* all variables were independent and set them equal to zero. This just sets up the necessary conditions for a stationary point as if

---

[11] After Count Joseph Louis Lagrange (or La Grange), 1736–1813, a French mathematician and astronomer.

L were a function of three independent variables—that is, $dL = 0$—as in Table 4.1.

$$\frac{\partial L}{\partial x_1} \equiv L_1 = f_1 - \lambda h_1 = 0,$$

$$\frac{\partial L}{\partial x_2} \equiv L_2 = f_2 - \lambda h_2 = 0, \tag{4-25}$$

$$\frac{\partial L}{\partial \lambda} \equiv L_\lambda = -h(x_1, x_2) = 0.$$

(The reader should be certain that he understands each of these partial derivatives; we will use the Lagrange approach extensively in succeeding sections.)

The equations involving derivatives with regard to x_1 and x_2, the original variables, reproduce exactly conditions (4-20')(a), with $\lambda = \alpha$. The last equation, from the partial derivative with regard to the new variable λ, simply reproduces the original constraint—after both sides are multiplied by (-1); this is (4-20')(b). Therefore, constructing the Lagrangean function, taking partial derivatives as if all variables were independent, and setting all first partials equal to zero is just a simple and automatic way of generating the first-differential (necessary) conditions for a maximum or minimum of $f(x_1, x_2)$ subject to $h(x_1, x_2) = 0$.[12] How difficult these conditions are to solve depends entirely on how complex the first derivative functions are. For a function f that includes one or more x_i cubed (or raised to a power higher than three), these necessary conditions will involve nonlinear equations.

Second-order conditions

Once the point or points satisfying (4-20)—or (4-20') or (4-25)—have been found, we want to be able to distinguish maxima from minima. For this we used the sign of the second total differential in the case of independent variables (Table 4.1). It is equally appropriate now. Consider again the general expression for d^2f, (3-13):

$$d^2f = f_{11}(dx_1)^2 + 2f_{12}\, dx_1\, dx_2 + f_{22}(dx_2)^2 + f_1\, d^2x_1 + f_2\, d^2x_2.$$

When x_1 and x_2 (and hence dx_1 and dx_2) were independent, we saw that d^2x_1 and d^2x_2 were both zero, and the last two terms were dropped, resulting

---

[12] From the point of view of the necessary conditions, the expression $\lambda[h(x_1, x_2)]$ could as well be *added* to $f(x_1, x_2)$ to produce the Lagrangean. This would simply define $L_1 = f_1 + \lambda h_1$ and $L_2 = f_2 + \lambda h_2$ in (4-25) and it would generate $h(x_1, x_2) = 0$ directly, without multiplication by (-1). It is subtracted here to maintain consistency with the discussion of the determinental condition (4-23) and because of later interpretations we will make of λ.

in (3-14). Now, by virtue of $h(x_1, x_2) = 0$, the variables are dependent; either one may be considered the (single) independent variable. Suppose we consider x_1 as the independent variable; dx_1 can be arbitrarily chosen, but dx_2 is then determined through the functional relationship from (4-18), $dx_2 = -(h_1/h_2)\, dx_1$. Therefore, while $d^2x_1 \equiv d(dx_1)$ is still zero in (3-13), $d^2x_2 \equiv d(dx_2)$ is not; it depends on dx_1. The second total differential now has one more term than previously in (3-14):

$$d^2f = f_{11}(dx_1)^2 + 2f_{12}\, dx_1\, dx_2 + f_{22}(dx_2)^2 + f_2\, d^2x_2. \qquad (4\text{-}26)$$

This is unfortunate; d^2f is no longer a quadratic form in dx_1 and dx_2, because of the new last term in (4-26). The rules of sign for quadratic forms from Section 4.1 cannot be applied, and yet it is the sign of d^2f that distinguishes maxima from minima.

The d^2x_2 term spoils the symmetry. If it could be replaced by terms with only $(dx_1)^2$, $dx_1\, dx_2$, and $(dx_2)^2$, (and d^2x_1, which is equal to zero), (4-26) could be rewritten as a quadratic form. Consider for this purpose the equation involving the second differential of the constraint [obtained by taking the total differential of $h(x_1, x_2) = 0$ twice].[13]

$$h_{11}(dx_1)^2 + 2h_{12}\, dx_1\, dx_2 + h_{22}(dx_2)^2 + h_1\, d^2x_1 + h_2\, d^2x_2 = 0. \qquad (4\text{-}27)$$

Since $d^2x_1 = 0$,

$$d^2x_2 = -\frac{1}{h_2}\left[h_{11}(dx_1)^2 + 2h_{12}\, dx_1\, dx_2 + h_{22}(dx_2)^2\right]$$

by ordinary algebra. Putting this into (4-26)—note that it is multiplied by f_2—and then collecting terms on $(dx_1)^2$, $dx_1\, dx_2$, and $(dx_2)^2$ gives

$$d^2f = \left[f_{11} - \left(\frac{f_2}{h_2}\right)h_{11}\right](dx_1)^2 + 2\left[f_{12} - \left(\frac{f_2}{h_2}\right)h_{12}\right] dx_1\, dx_2$$

$$+ \left[f_{22} - \left(\frac{f_2}{h_2}\right)h_{22}\right](dx_2)^2. \qquad (4\text{-}28)$$

This is admittedly more complicated than (3-14), but the important point is that it is now a *quadratic form* in dx_1 and dx_2. It is, however, a quadratic form of two *dependent* variables, and the exact nature of the dependence between dx_1 and dx_2 is given by (4-18)—that is, $h_1\, dx_1 + h_2\, dx_2 = 0$. We are interested therefore, for second-order conditions, in the sign of the quadratic form (4-28) when the variables in that form are subject to a particular linear constraint (4-18). This was exactly the subject matter of Section 4.3, and the results in (4-15) are therefore of interest here. It is because of the particularly simple structure of the first total differential

[13] The left-hand side of (4-27), for the function h, is identical to (3-13) for the function f.

of $h(x_1, x_2) = 0$ that a side condition of the form $c_1x_1 + c_2x_2 = 0$ was studied in that section.

Let $v_{jk} = f_{jk} - (f_2/h_2)h_{jk}$, where, as usual, v_{jk}^* indicates evaluation at a point satisfying the first-order conditions for a maximum or a minimum. The structure of d^2f^* is given in (4-28). For d^2f^* to be positive definite ($d^2f^* > 0$) and thus designate a minimum point, we require (from Section 4.3) that the determinant of

$$\bar{V}^* = \begin{bmatrix} 0 & h_1^* & h_2^* \\ h_1^* & v_{11}^* & v_{12}^* \\ h_2^* & v_{21}^* & v_{22}^* \end{bmatrix} \tag{4-29}$$

be negative. For $d^2f^* < 0$—that is, a maximum—$|\bar{V}^*|$ must be positive. Since the determinant is evaluated at $X^* = [x_1^*, x_2^*]'$, where $df = 0$, f_2^*/h_2^* could be replaced by f_1^*/h_1^* or by λ^* throughout the v_{jk}^*, because of (4-20′)(a) and (4-23).

Example

Examine $y = f(x_1, x_2) = 6x_1x_2$ for maxima and minima if the variables are also required to satisfy the relation $2x_1 + x_2 = 10$.[14] By straightforward application of (4-20) we see that we need, initially, $f_1 = 6x_2$, $f_2 = 6x_1$, $h_1 = 2$, $h_2 = 1$. Using (4-20)(a), part of the necessary condition is that $6x_2/2 = 6x_1/1$, or $x_2 = 2x_1$. Putting this relationship into the constraint (4-20)(b):

$$2x_1 + 2x_1 = 10,$$
$$x_1^* = 2\tfrac{1}{2},$$

therefore

$$x_2^* = 5.$$

The point $x_1^* = 2\tfrac{1}{2}$, $x_2^* = 5$ may be a maximum, a minimum, or neither. We turn to the sufficient conditions, the sign of d^2f^* as given by (4-29). Here[15] $f_{11} = 0$, $f_{22} = 0$, $f_{12} = f_{21} = 6$; $h_{11} = 0$, $h_{22} = 0$, $h_{12} = h_{21} = 0$. Since, at $x_1^* = 2\tfrac{1}{2}$, $x_2^* = 5$,

$$\frac{f_1^*}{h_1^*} = \frac{f_2^*}{h_2^*} = 15, \qquad v_{jk} = f_{jk} - (15)h_{jk};$$

---

[14] Obviously, in this simple case we could solve $2x_1 + x_2 = 10$ for either x_1 or x_2 and substitute into $6x_1x_2$, making it a function of one variable only. We are interested here in more general procedures for the cases in which it is not easy—or indeed impossible—to eliminate one of the variables this way.

[15] All second partials and cross-partials are constants. Therefore their value at (x_1^*, x_2^*) is the same as at any other combination of x_1 and x_2. We have omitted the asterisk superscripts for notational simplicity, since $f_{jk}^* = f_{jk}$ and $h_{jk}^* = h_{jk}$ for all j and k in this example.

but since all second partials and cross-partials of the constraint are zero, it happens in this example that $v_{jk} = f_{jk}$. Thus the bordered Hessian in question is

$$|\bar{V}| = |\bar{V}^*| = \begin{vmatrix} 0 & 2 & 1 \\ 2 & 0 & 6 \\ 1 & 6 & 0 \end{vmatrix} = 12 + 12 = 24 > 0.$$

Therefore $d^2f < 0$, and the point $x_1^* = 2\frac{1}{2}$, $x_2^* = 5$ represents a *maximum* of the function subject to the constraint.

If we use the Lagrange method on this problem, (4-25), we construct[16]

$$L = 6x_1x_2 - \lambda(2x_1 + x_2 - 10)$$

and then take all three first partial derivatives and set them equal to zero:

$$L_1 = 6x_2 - 2\lambda = 0,$$
$$L_2 = 6x_1 - \lambda = 0,$$
$$L_\lambda = -(2x_1 + x_2 - 10) = 0.$$

The partials with respect to x_1 and x_2 lead to

$$6x_2 = 2\lambda \qquad \text{and} \qquad 6x_1 = \lambda.$$

Therefore $3x_2 = 6x_1$ or $x_2 = 2x_1$; this result put into L_λ gives, as before, $2x_1 + 2x_1 = 10$, $x_1^* = 2\frac{1}{2}$ and thus $x_2^* = 5$.

This second approach adds one piece of information that direct application of (4-20) does not provide; this is the value of λ at the maximum or minimum point, λ^*. Although λ is not one of the variables whose optimum values are of *direct* interest in the problem, it does turn out that λ^* provides possibly useful information about the constraint, $h(x_1, x_2) = 0$. In this example $\lambda^* = 6x_2^*/2 = 15 \ (= 6x_1^*/1)$. Note that $f(x_1^*, x_2^*) = f^* = 75$.

Suppose now that the constraint had read $2x_1 + x_2 = 11$, rather than 10—that is, that the right-hand side had increased by one unit.[17] Clearly the relationships from (4-20)(a) will not change, since the constant term in the constraint is in no way involved in h_1 or h_2. Substituting $x_2 = 2x_1$ into the new constraint gives the new values $x_1^{**} = 2\frac{3}{4}$, $x_2^{**} = 5\frac{1}{2}$, and $f^{**} = 90\frac{3}{4}$. The change in the value of f, $f^{**} - f^*$, is $15\frac{3}{4}$; λ^* was 15. This is no accident; the value of λ evaluated at a stationary point gives an *approximation* to the amount that the optimum value of f will change for a *unit* change in the constraint. Even more simply (and importantly for the later discussion of inequality constraints in Section 4.8), the *sign* of λ^* tells the

---

[16] On the form of the constraint in L, as well as the use of $-\lambda$, see the final subsection of this section.

[17] Since X^* represents a maximum, it is clear that the larger the value of $2x_1 + x_2$ allowed, the larger the value of f^*. Hence we could also say that the constraint was *relaxed* by one unit.

direction of the change. A positive λ^* means that if the right-hand side of the constraint increases, so does f^*; $\lambda^* < 0$ means that an increase in the constraint constant is accompanied by a decrease in f^*. The value of λ^* is, in fact, the partial derivative of f, evaluated at X^*, with respect to the right-hand side of the constraint.[18] If we write the constraint for this problem in general as $2x_1 + x_2 = c$, then $\lambda^* = \partial f^*/\partial c$.

A note on the form of the Lagrangean function

In writing L, we have chosen the format $L = f(X) - \lambda[g(X) - c]$. Notice that this has involved two choices: (1) the operation attaching the second term—$\lambda[g(X) - c]$—was subtraction; (2) in rearranging the constraining equation to be equal to zero, the right-hand side, c, was moved to the left.

Clearly the $\partial L/\partial x_j = 0$ conditions on the function with $\lambda[g(X) - c]$ added, $L = f(X) + \lambda[g(X) - c]$, would produce exactly the same necessary relationships between the x_j's, only the definition of λ in terms of the x_j would be opposite in sign to that derived from (4-25). The $\partial L/\partial \lambda$ expression would reproduce the original constraint exactly, instead of its negative, as in (4-25). Therefore the X^* found as the stationary point (or points) would be the same. However, since λ, and in particular λ^*, would be of *opposite* sign, then $\lambda^* = -(\partial f^*/\partial c)$ or $(\partial f^*/\partial c) = -\lambda^*$. This distinction will turn out to be particularly important when we come to consider inequality constraints in Section 4.8. We prefer the form in which the constraint term is subtracted, because then λ^* and $\partial f^*/\partial c$ are of the *same* sign.

In attaching the constraint, it would also have been possible to use $[c - g(X)]$, since for X satisfying $g(X) = c$, this would also be zero. The form $L = f(X) - \lambda[c - g(X)]$ will generate the same necessary relationships from $\partial L/\partial x_j$, except that, again, λ will be defined with a sign opposite to that in (4-25). Therefore, in this form, $\lambda^* = -(\partial f^*/\partial c)$, as with $L = f(X) + \lambda[g(X) - c]$.

Finally, if L is formed as $f(X) + \lambda[c - g(X)]$, then the $\partial L/\partial x_j$ will be identical to those in (4-25), and the original constraint will be exactly reproduced by $\partial L/\partial \lambda$; multiplication by (-1), as in (4-25), will not be necessary.

Therefore, for either

---

[18] Recall that the form of the constraint used in the Lagrangean function is $h(X) \equiv g(X) - c = 0$. From the point of view of the original constraint, $g(X) = c$, the right-hand side constant is moved to the left (with changed sign). From (4-24), at X^* and λ^*, $L^* = f^* - \lambda^*[h(X^*)]$ or $L^* = f^* - \lambda^*[g(X^*) - c]$. If we consider the possibility of a *change* in the size of c and want its impact on L^*, we want $\partial L^*/\partial c$, which is λ^*. Since at optimum the constraint $h(X^*) = 0$, $L^* = f^*$ and hence $\partial f^*/\partial c = \lambda^*$ also.

$$L = f(X) - \lambda[g(X) - c] \qquad \text{or} \qquad L = f(X) + \lambda[c - g(X)],$$

the property $\lambda^* = \partial f^*/\partial c$ holds. Since the $[g(X) - c]$ form of the constraint involves less movement of terms and hence less sign change, we prefer it and use the first form of the Lagrangean function throughout. The second-order conditions are unchanged, whatever form the Lagrangean function takes.

4.5. EXTENSION TO MORE DEPENDENT VARIABLES

First-order conditions

Consider $y = f(x_1, \ldots, x_n)$ subject to one equality constraint $h(x_1, \ldots, x_n) = 0$. The necessary conditions are best found as a direct extension of $(4\text{-}20')(a)$, now using λ, from the Lagrange multiplier approach, in place of α:

$$\text{(a)} \quad f_1 - \lambda h_1 = \cdots = f_n - \lambda h_n = 0,$$

and   (4-30)

$$\text{(b)} \quad h(x_1, \ldots, x_n) = 0.$$

These conditions are derived from the fact that, as before, we require $df = 0$ subject to the relationships between the dx_j $(j = 1, \ldots, n)$ given by taking the total differential of both sides of the constraint. Thus we have two homogeneous linear equations in dx_j:

$$\begin{aligned} f_1 \, dx_1 + f_2 \, dx_2 + \cdots + f_n \, dx_n = 0, \\ h_1 \, dx_1 + h_2 \, dx_2 + \cdots + h_n \, dx_n = 0. \end{aligned} \qquad (4\text{-}31)$$

For these two homogeneous equations in n unknowns to have nontrivial basic solutions—that is, to allow variation in all of the x_j through $dx_j \neq 0$—it is necessary that *all* 2×2 submatrices of the form

$$\begin{bmatrix} f_j & f_k \\ h_j & h_k \end{bmatrix}, \qquad (j, k = 1, \ldots, n; j \neq k),$$

be singular. This means proportionality between the rows of the coefficient matrix

$$\begin{bmatrix} f_1 & f_2 & \cdots & f_n \\ h_1 & h_2 & \cdots & h_n \end{bmatrix} \quad \text{—that is,} \quad [f_1 \ \ f_2 \ \ \cdots \ \ f_n] = \lambda[h_1 \ \ h_2 \ \ \cdots \ \ h_n],$$

which, from scalar multiplication and matrix equality, means exactly $(4\text{-}30)(a)$.

These conditions can also be generated directly by partial differentiation of the Lagrangean function, which in this case is

$$L = f(x_1, \ldots, x_n) - \lambda[h(x_1, \ldots, x_n)],$$

and setting $L_j = 0$ $(j = 1, \ldots, n)$ and $L_\lambda = 0$.

When dealing with functions of many variables it is clear that the first part of the necessary conditions—as in (4-30)(a)—must be stated as $f_j - \lambda h_j = 0$ (or as $f_j = \lambda h_j$) for $j = 1, \ldots, n$, rather than in ratio form as $f_j/h_j = \lambda$. Not *all* variables x_j need appear in the constraint and hence some h_j may be zero. This makes them unacceptable as denominators in an f_j/h_j expression but does not affect their usefulness in a statement of the sort $f_j - \lambda h_j = 0$.

Second-order conditions

Sufficient conditions for distinguishing maxima from minima for a function of n variables subject to one constraint parallel those for determining the sign of the general quadratic form $Q(x_1, \ldots, x_n)$ subject to $c_1 x_1 + \cdots + c_n x_n = 0$; this was discussed in Section 4.3. Let

$$U = \left[\frac{\partial h}{\partial x_1}, \ldots, \frac{\partial h}{\partial x_n} \right] \equiv [h_1, \ldots, h_n]$$

and V be the $n \times n$ matrix of elements $v_{jk} = f_{jk} - \lambda h_{jk}$. Thus the matrix

$$\bar{V} = \begin{bmatrix} 0 & h_1 & \cdots & h_n \\ \hline h_1 & v_{11} & \cdots & v_{1n} \\ \vdots & & & \\ h_n & v_{n1} & \cdots & v_{nn} \end{bmatrix} \quad \text{can be represented as} \quad \bar{V} = \left[\begin{array}{c|c} 0 & U \\ \hline U' & V \end{array} \right].$$

As usual, asterisks as superscripts denote that these derivatives are evaluated at $X^* = [x_1^*, \ldots, x_n^*]'$, a point that satisfies the necessary conditions for a maximum or a minimum. Then, from (4-15), for a minimum—that is, for $d^2f^* > 0$—all principal minors, beginning with the third, of

$$\bar{V}^* = \left[\begin{array}{c|c} 0 & U^* \\ \hline U^{*\prime} & V^* \end{array} \right] \tag{4-32}$$

must be *negative*. For $d^2f^* < 0$ and hence a maximum, these same principal minors must *alternate*, beginning *positive*. This is straightforward application of the quadratic form analysis to the bordered Hessian-like matrix V, which governs the sign of d^2f.

Example

We add a third variable to the example of the last section. Let the function be $f(x_1, x_2, x_3) = 6x_1 x_2 - 10x_3^2$, where the variables are subject to $2x_1 + x_2 + 3x_3 = 10$. Here

$$f_1 = \quad 6x_2, \quad h_1 = 2,$$
$$f_2 = \quad 6x_1, \quad h_2 = 1,$$
$$f_3 = -20x_3, \quad h_3 = 3,$$

and using (4-30)(a), $6x_2 - 2\lambda = 6x_1 - \lambda = -20x_3 - 3\lambda = 0$. From these we find that $x_2 = 2x_1$ and $x_3 = -\frac{9}{10}x_1$. Substituting into the constraint,

$$2x_1 + 2x_1 - \frac{27}{10}x_1 = 10, \quad x_1^* = \frac{100}{13},$$

and therefore $x_2^* = \frac{200}{13}$ and $x_3^* = -\frac{90}{13}$.

For the sufficiency test we also need

$$f_{11} = \quad 0, \quad f_{12} = f_{21} = 6, \quad h_{11} = 0, \quad h_{12} = h_{21} = 0,$$
$$f_{22} = \quad 0, \quad f_{13} = f_{31} = 0, \quad h_{22} = 0, \quad h_{13} = h_{31} = 0,$$
$$f_{33} = -20, \quad f_{23} = f_{32} = 0, \quad h_{33} = 0, \quad h_{23} = h_{32} = 0.$$

Since the second partials and cross-partials are constants, $f_{jk}^* = f_{jk}$ and $h_{jk}^* = h_{jk}$ for all j and k throughout. Thus we omit asterisks wherever possible. Furthermore, $\lambda^* = 6x_1^* = (6)\left(\frac{100}{13}\right) = \frac{600}{13}$. However, since all second partials and cross-partials of the constraint are zero, $v_{jk} = f_{jk}$ for this example. Thus

$$\bar{V} = \bar{V}^* = \begin{bmatrix} 0 & 2 & 1 & 3 \\ \hline 2 & 0 & 6 & 0 \\ 1 & 6 & 0 & 0 \\ 3 & 0 & 0 & -20 \end{bmatrix},$$

$$|\bar{V}_3| = \begin{vmatrix} 0 & 2 & 1 \\ 2 & 0 & 6 \\ 1 & 6 & 0 \end{vmatrix} = 12 + 12 = 24 > 0;$$

$$|\bar{V}_4| = |\bar{V}| = (-3)\begin{vmatrix} 2 & 0 & 6 \\ 1 & 6 & 0 \\ 3 & 0 & 0 \end{vmatrix} + (-20)\begin{vmatrix} 0 & 2 & 1 \\ 2 & 0 & 6 \\ 1 & 6 & 0 \end{vmatrix}$$

$$= 324 - 480 = -156 < 0.^{19}$$

Since the correct principal minors alternate in sign, beginning positive, the point $x_1^* = \frac{100}{13}$, $x_2^* = \frac{200}{13}$, and $x_3^* = -\frac{90}{13}$ represents a maximum for $6x_1x_2 - 10x_3^2$ subject to $2x_1 + x_2 + 3x_3 = 10$.

4.6. EXTENSION TO MORE CONSTRAINTS

The nature of the dependence among the variables may be expressed by more than one side restriction. Consider $y = f(x_1, \ldots, x_n)$ with m constraining equations $h_1(x_1, \ldots, x_n) = 0, \ldots, h_m(x_1, \ldots, x_n) = 0$. It is ap-

---

[19] By expansion of the determinant down the fourth column. Recall Definition 1.6.

propriate to assume that there are fewer constraints than variables ($m < n$) because of the structure of the first differential conditions, shown below. We saw in Section 2.5 that the existence of more (linear) equations than variables always implies either redundant equations (which can be dropped) or an inconsistent system in which not all equations can be met simultaneously. We denote $\partial h_i / \partial x_j$ by h_j^i, the partial derivative of the ith constraint with respect to the jth variable.

First-order conditions

The first differential conditions are the same; we impose the requirement that $df = 0$, subject to the relationships between the dx_j ($j = 1, \ldots, n$) that are implicit in each of the $h_i(x_1, \ldots, x_n) = 0$ ($i = 1, \ldots, m$).

$$
\begin{aligned}
df &= f_1 \ dx_1 + f_2 \ dx_2 + \cdots + f_n \ dx_n = 0, \\
dh_1 &= h_1^1 \ dx_1 + h_2^1 \ dx_2 + \cdots + h_n^1 \ dx_n = 0, \\
&\vdots \\
dh_m &= h_1^m \ dx_1 + h_2^m \ dx_2 + \cdots + h_n^m \ dx_n = 0.
\end{aligned}
\tag{4-33}
$$

This set of $m + 1$ homogeneous linear equations in the n variables $dx_1, \ldots, dx_n$ parallels (4-21) for the two-variable, one-constraint case in Section 4.5. The system of equations is always consistent, as we saw in Chapter 2. For nontrivial solutions to all square $(m + 1) \times (m + 1)$ subsystems of (4-33)—that is, to all *basic* systems—the rank of the coefficient matrix must be less than $m + 1$. In fact, if any redundant constraints have been eliminated, the rank will be m. Then, for example, the first row of

$$
\begin{bmatrix}
f_1 & f_2 & \cdots & f_n \\
h_1^1 & h_2^1 & \cdots & h_n^1 \\
\vdots & & & \\
h_1^m & h_2^m & \cdots & h_n^m
\end{bmatrix}
$$

can be expressed as a linear combination of the remaining m (linearly independent) rows. That is:

$$
\text{row } 1 = \lambda_1(\text{row } 2) + \lambda_2(\text{row } 3) + \cdots + \lambda_m(\text{row } m + 1),
$$

or

$$
[f_1, \ldots, f_n] = \sum_{i=1}^{m} \lambda_i [h_1^i, \ldots, h_n^i].
$$

Thus

$$
f_j = \lambda_1 h_j^1 + \lambda_2 h_j^2 + \cdots + \lambda_m h_j^m = \sum_{i=1}^{m} \lambda_i h_j^i
$$

or

$$f_j - \sum_{i=1}^{m} \lambda_i h_j^i = 0.$$

These, plus the constraints, constitute the necessary conditions.

$$\text{(a)} \quad f_1 - \sum_{i=1}^{m} \lambda_i h_1^i = \cdots = f_n - \sum_{i=1}^{m} \lambda_i h_n^i = 0,$$

and   (4-34)

$$\text{(b)} \quad h_i(X) = 0 \qquad (i = 1, \ldots, m).$$

As before, the Lagrange approach, setting first partials equal to zero, generates exactly the conditions in (4-34). For this most general case with n variables, x_j, and m equations, h_i (of which all preceding cases in Sections 4.4 and 4.5 were only specific examples), the Lagrangean function is

$$L(x_j, \lambda_i) = f(X) - \sum_{i=1}^{m} \lambda_i [h_i(X)],$$

from which the first partial derivatives give

$$L_{x_j} = f_j - \sum_{i=1}^{m} \lambda_i h_j^i = 0 \qquad (j = 1, \ldots, n),$$

$$L_{\lambda_i} = -h_i(X) = 0 \qquad (i = 1, \ldots, m).$$

The first n equations are exactly the requirements set forth in (4-34)(a); the last m equations just reproduce the constraints, as in (4-34)(b)—except for sign, which is easily eliminated by multiplying through by (-1).

Second-order conditions

The sufficient conditions require positive definiteness or negative definiteness of a more widely bordered Hessian-like matrix. These conditions parallel the results in Section 4.3, specifically in (4-16), for a quadratic form in $x_1, \ldots, x_n$ subject to m linear homogeneous equations $CX = O$ $(m < n)$. Obviously, for problems in which m and n are large, the work involved in evaluating $(n - m)$ principal minors becomes immense, both because each determinant is large and because there may be many of them. The size of the determinants depends on the sizes of m and n (the *last* principal minor is always a determinant of size $m + n$), whereas the number that must be evaluated depends on the difference between the two. We present these conditions here to indicate the symmetry with all that has gone before and also so that the reader will have an appreciation for the simplicity of the methods developed later to deal with both linear and nonlinear programming problems involving large numbers of variables (n) and constraints (m), although the latter are generally inequalities.

The Jacobian matrix of the system of constraints $h_i(X) = 0$ is defined as

$$
J = \begin{bmatrix} \partial h_1/\partial x_1 & \cdots & \partial h_1/\partial x_n \\ \partial h_2/\partial x_1 & \cdots & \partial h_2/\partial x_n \\ \vdots & & \\ \partial h_m/\partial x_1 & \cdots & \partial h_m/\partial x_n \end{bmatrix} = \begin{bmatrix} h_1^1 & \cdots & h_n^1 \\ h_1^2 & \cdots & h_n^2 \\ \vdots & & \\ h_1^m & \cdots & h_n^m \end{bmatrix}. \tag{4-35}
$$

This is sometimes shown as $J = [\partial(h_1, \ldots, h_m)/\partial(x_1, \ldots, x_n)]$. Consider the partitioned and more widely bordered Hessian-like matrix

$$
\bar{V} = \left[\begin{array}{c|c} O & J \\ {\scriptstyle (m \times m)} & {\scriptstyle (m \times n)} \\ \hline J' & V \\ {\scriptstyle (n \times m)} & {\scriptstyle (n \times n)} \end{array} \right].
$$

The upper left is the null matrix. The off-diagonal blocks are the Jacobian and its transpose, a logical extension of the single row and column border in (4-32). The elements of V are expansions of the bracketed terms in expression (4-28) for the second total differential when only two variables and one constraint were considered. That is,

$$
V = [v_{jk}], \qquad \text{where } v_{jk} = f_{jk} - \sum_{i=1}^{m} \lambda_i h_{jk}^i
$$

—the second partials ($j = k$) and cross-partials ($j \neq k$) of f less the sum of those same partials or cross-partials *in each of the constraints* (i), each multiplied by the λ for that constraint. Thus, following (4-16), the rank of the Jacobian matrix must be m. Then for $d^2 f^* > 0$ (that is, for X^* to represent a minimum point), the last $n - m$ principal minors of $\bar{V}^*$ must be of sign $(-1)^m$. For $d^2 f^* < 0$ and hence a maximum at X^*, these same principal minors must alternate in sign, with the first having the sign $(-1)^{m+1}$. (As usual, asterisks denote that elements of the matrix are evaluated at the point or points that satisfy the first-order conditions.)

Example

We add a second equality constraint to the example of the preceding section. We now want to maximize $f(x_1, x_2, x_3) = 6x_1 x_2 - 10x_3^2$, where the variables are subject to $2x_1 + x_2 + 3x_3 = 10$ (as in Section 4.5) and also $x_1 + x_2 + 2x_3 = 8$. Thus

$$
\begin{array}{lll}
f_1 = 6x_2, & h_1^1 = 2, & h_1^2 = 1, \\
f_2 = 6x_1, & h_2^1 = 1, & h_2^2 = 1, \\
f_3 = -20x_3, & h_3^1 = 3, & h_3^2 = 2,
\end{array}
$$

and, using (4-34), we have

$$
\text{(a)} \quad
\begin{cases}
6x_2 - 2\lambda_1 - \lambda_2 = 0, \\
6x_1 - \lambda_1 - \lambda_2 = 0, \\
-20x_3 - 3\lambda_1 - 2\lambda_2 = 0,
\end{cases}
$$

$$
\text{(b)} \quad
\begin{cases}
2x_1 + x_2 + 3x_3 = 10, \\
x_1 + x_2 + 2x_3 = 8.
\end{cases}
$$

From the first equation in (a), $\lambda_2 = 6x_2 - 2\lambda_1$; putting this result into the other two equations in (a), and rearranging, gives $6x_1 + 6x_2 + 20x_3 = 0$. When this is combined with the other two equations in x_1, x_2, and x_3 in part (b), we have a system of three linear equations in three unknowns whose coefficient matrix is nonsingular; hence a unique solution exists. Either Cramer's rule or the use of A^{-1} leads to $x_1^* = 8$, $x_2^* = 12$ and $x_3^* = -6$.

For the sufficiency test we also need

$$
\begin{aligned}
f_{11} &= 0, & f_{12} = f_{21} &= 6, \\
f_{22} &= 0, & f_{13} = f_{31} &= 0, \\
f_{33} &= -20, & f_{23} = f_{32} &= 0, & \text{and all } h_{jk}^1 \text{ and } h_{jk}^2 = 0.
\end{aligned}
$$

Since all second partials and cross-partials are constants, and since all h_j^1 and h_j^2 ($j = 1, 2, 3$) are constants, in this case all elements in $\bar{V}^*$ are constants; hence we need not use the asterisks. Moreover, since all h_{jk}^1 and h_{jk}^2 are zero, $v_{jk} = f_{jk}$ for this example. Thus

$$
\bar{V} = \bar{V}^* =
\left[
\begin{array}{cc|ccc}
0 & 0 & 2 & 1 & 3 \\
0 & 0 & 1 & 1 & 2 \\
\hline
2 & 1 & 0 & 6 & 0 \\
1 & 1 & 6 & 0 & 0 \\
3 & 2 & 0 & 0 & -20
\end{array}
\right],
$$

and the sign of the last $n - m = 3 - 2 = 1$ principal minor—that is, the sign of $|\bar{V}^*|$—is of interest. For a minimum, the sign must be that of $(-1)^2$—positive; for a maximum it must be the same as $(-1)^3$—negative. Straightforward application of the general definition of the determinant (along row 2 is a good choice because of the small size of the nonzero elements) gives $|\bar{V}^*| = -8$. Thus the solution $x_1^* = 8$, $x_2^* = 12$, and $x_3^* = -6$ represents a maximum for $6x_1x_2 - 10x_3^2$ subject to $2x_1 + x_2 + 3x_3 = 10$ *and* $x_1 + x_2 + 2x_3 = 8$.

4.7. CONVEX SETS; CONVEX AND CONCAVE FUNCTIONS

Before extending the investigation of optimization problems to those with inequality constraints, it is useful to have available some of the terminology of convex set theory. This terminology is also fundamental to the discussion of the general linear and nonlinear programming problems in later chapters, and it provides us with a geometric interpretation of the sign requirements on the principal minors of the Hessian matrix that constituted the sufficiency conditions in the preceding sections.

Convex sets

The adjective *convex* may be applied to collections or sets of points. The defining property is intuitively simple: a set is convex if and only if the straight line joining any two points that are in the set lies entirely in the set also.

DEFINITION 4.1: CONVEX SET OF POINTS. A set of points, S, is convex if and only if, for any two points X' and X'' that are in the set S, the convex combination $\alpha X' + (1 - \alpha)X''$, for all α in the interval $0 \leq \alpha \leq 1$, is also in the set S.

Figure 4.2 illustrates several convex and several nonconvex sets.

Figure 4.2.   Convex Sets (top), Nonconvex Sets (bottom)

Intuitively, a nonconvex set has dents or holes in it. The *intersection* of two or more *convex* sets—that is, the points simultaneously included in both (or all) sets—is also a convex set. The intersection of two or more *nonconvex* sets may be a convex set and it may be a nonconvex set. For example, from the general shapes in Figure 4.2 we can imagine several intersections (Figure 4.3).

Consider several ordinary geometric figures. In two-dimensional space, a *line* is a relation between x_1 and x_2 of the sort $a_1x_1 + a_2x_2 = b$, where a_1, a_2, and b are constants. In three-dimensional space, $a_1x_1 + a_2x_2 + a_3x_3 = b$ defines a *plane*. In more (that is, n) dimensions, the term is *hyperplane* and the extension is $a_1x_1 + a_2x_2 + \cdots + a_nx_n = b$. Using matrix notation, define a row vector $a = [a_1, \ldots, a_n]$ and a column vector

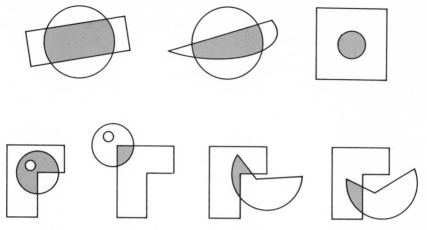

Figure 4.3.   Intersections of Convex Sets (top), Intersections of Nonconvex Sets (bottom)

$$X = \begin{bmatrix} x_1 \\ \vdots \\ x_n \end{bmatrix} ;$$

then a hyperplane in n-dimensional space is defined[20] as $aX = b$. When $n = 2$ or 3, we have a line or plane. It is easy to show, using the fundamental definition of convexity, that a hyperplane is a convex set. We will demonstrate why this is true and ask the reader to prove similar statements that will be made below for other figures.

Let

$$X' = \begin{bmatrix} x_1' \\ \vdots \\ x_n' \end{bmatrix} \quad \text{and} \quad X'' = \begin{bmatrix} x_1'' \\ \vdots \\ x_n'' \end{bmatrix}$$

be *any* two (distinct) points that lie on the hyperplane; that is, $aX' = b$ and $aX'' = b$. Define X''' as the convex combination of these two points; $X''' = \alpha X' + (1 - \alpha)X''$. We want to show that X''' is also on the hyperplane. Since α is a scalar,

$$\begin{aligned} aX''' &= a[\alpha X' + (1 - \alpha)X''] \\ &= \alpha aX' + (1 - \alpha)aX'' \\ &= \alpha b + (1 - \alpha)b = b. \end{aligned}$$

---

[20] Note that a and X are vectors, hence their product is the scalar b. This is to be distinguished from the matrix representation of a *set* of linear equations—that is, a *set* of hyperplanes—$AX = B$, where A is a matrix (which can be viewed as composed of *several* row vectors) and B a vector. In Chapter 2 we saw that such a set of equations has a unique solution if and only if the hyperplanes have one common point.

Thus a hyperplane is a convex set. Thus, also, the points that simultaneously satisfy several hyperplanes (that is, their intersection) form a convex set.

Consider a linear inequality $a_1x_1 + a_2x_2 + \cdots + a_nx_n \leq b$. An inequality is in either strong or weak form. A *strong* inequality, $<$ (or $>$), allows only "less than" (or "greater than"). A *weak* inequality, $\leq$ (or $\geq$), allows both "less than" and "equal to" (or "greater than" and "equal to"). Weak inequalities set boundaries that may be touched; strong inequalities set boundaries that may not be touched.

In two dimensions $a_1x_1 + a_2x_2 \leq b$ defines a line and all points on one side of it. For example, in Figure 4.4 the shaded area represents $2x_1 + x_2 \leq 10$.

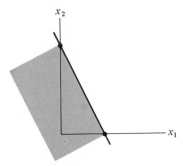

Figure 4.4. $2x_1 + x_2 \leq 10$

This area defined by the inequality is called a *half-space*. When the inequality is weak, the half-space is termed *closed*. This simply means that the boundary (here the line $2x_1 + x_2 = 10$) is included. If the inequality is strong, the corresponding half-space is *open*. Note that *open* and *closed* refer to whether or not the bounding function is included; the terms say nothing about the *extent* of the region. The closed half-space shown in Figure 4.4 is termed *unbounded* because it extends infinitely far in the left and downward directions. Half-spaces (either open or closed) are also convex sets, as the reader can show by an argument similar to that for hyperplanes, above. Therefore, points that satisfy several linear inequalities simultaneously (that is, their intersection) form a convex set.

Convex and concave functions of one variable

We will use the definition of convex sets in discussing convexity and concavity of *functions*. The distinction between local and global maxima (and minima) is frequently discussed in terms of the curvature of the function involved. In footnote 6 on page 100 we described concavity and convexity of a function by means of the position of the tangent relative to the function. A curve that lies everywhere below its tangent was described as either concave downward or convex upward. We adopt the usual convention of viewing the function from below; hence it would simply be called concave. Correspondingly, a function that lies everywhere above its tangent is convex. Figures 3.8(a) and (b) illustrated convex and concave functions, respectively.

For $y = f(x)$, the sign of the second derivative gives us exactly the convexity-concavity information. It is intuitively clear that if $d^2y/dx^2 > 0$ over the entire range of x, which is to say that the slope of the function (that is, the slope of its tangent) is increasing, then the curve is everywhere above its tangent and hence convex. If $d^2y/dx^2 > 0$ over some particular interval $c \leq x \leq d$, the curve is convex over that interval. If fact, when $d^2y/dx^2 > 0$, the curve is said to be *strictly* convex. If $d^2y/dx^2 = 0$ over some part or parts of an interval and $d^2y/dx^2 > 0$ over the remainder of the interval, which means that the tangent slope remains *constant* over some parts of the interval and hence the curve *coincides* with its tangent over that range, it is said to be convex. Figures 4.5(a) and (b) illustrate the possi-

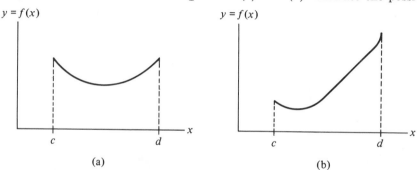

Figure 4.5.   (a) Strictly Convex over $c \leq x \leq d$, (b) Convex over $c \leq x \leq d$

bilities. Conversely, a function is concave or strictly concave if $d^2y/dx^2 \leq 0$ or $d^2y/dx^2 < 0$, respectively. (Note that a linear function is *both* concave and convex, although neither *strictly*.)

This test for concavity and convexity *may* in certain cases be easy to apply, but it is restricted to functions that have derivatives (the first two) over the entire range of interest. A second definition is therefore sometimes used. At first glance it may appear to lack appeal (algebraically), but it has a very straightforward geometric interpretation. For this reason we state it first for a function of one variable and then extend it to functions of n variables. Since the description of concavity and convexity is one of shape, the range over which the description is valid must be specified. For that reason, we think of a function of x defined over a continuous interval $c \leq x \leq d$, where clearly c and d may be $-\infty$ and $+\infty$, respectively. That is, x can take on all values $c \leq x \leq d$. Hence $f(x)$ ranges over the line on the x axis connecting $x = c$ and $x = d$; this, as we have seen, is a convex set of points. An interval that includes its endpoints—that is, where weak inequalities are used to define boundaries—is termed a *closed* interval and is sometimes denoted $[c, d]$. There should be no confusion with a two-element row vector in the context of the problem.

DEFINITION 4.2: CONVEX FUNCTION $f(x)$.   A function $f(x)$ is said to be *convex* over a convex set of points $c \leq x \leq d$ if for every α in the closed interval $[0, 1]$ and every pair of points (x_1, x_2) in the interval $[c, d]$,

$$f[\alpha x_1 + (1 - \alpha)x_2] \leq \alpha f(x_1) + (1 - \alpha)f(x_2).$$

The function is strictly convex if $\leq$ is replaced by $<$ *and* α is in the open interval $0 < \alpha < 1$.

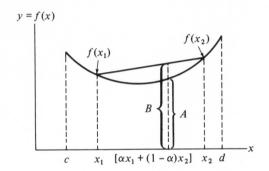

Figure 4.6.   A Convex Function over the Interval $[c, d]$

Consider the geometry of this definition, using Figure 4.6. Along the horizontal axis there are three points of interest in the interval $[c, d]$; these are: the point x_1, the point x_2, and the point represented by the combination $\alpha x_1 + (1 - \alpha)x_2$. Since $0 \leq \alpha \leq 1$, this point must lie in the closed interval $[x_1, x_2]$—if $\alpha = 0$, the point is at x_2; if $\alpha = 1$, the point is at x_1, and any other α will describe a point between x_1 and x_2. The length A is simply the value of $f(x)$ for that particular position on the x axis; thus $A = f[\alpha x_1 + (1 - \alpha)x_2]$. This is the left-hand side of the inequality in Definition 4.2. At x_1 and x_2 the function takes on the values $f(x_1)$ and $f(x_2)$, respectively. The line joining these two points is just the convex combination $\alpha f(x_1) + (1 - \alpha)f(x_2)$, for all α in the interval $[0, 1]$. In particular, when the weights α and $(1 - \alpha)$ in this combination are the same as those in $\alpha x_1 + (1 - \alpha)x_2$, then the location so defined on the line is that point directly above $\alpha x_1 + (1 - \alpha)x_2$—that is, the length B.[21] This is the right-

---

[21] This can be shown by straightforward application of the proportional-side property of similar triangles, drawing a line parallel to the x-axis through $f(x_1)$.

hand side of the inequality in Definition 4.2. Thus $f(x)$ is convex in the interval $[c, d]$ if for any x_1 and x_2 in the interval and any α, $0 \leq \alpha \leq 1$, $A \leq B$; it is strictly convex if $A < B$.[22]

DEFINITION 4.3: CONCAVE FUNCTION $f(x)$.   A function $f(x)$ is said to be *concave* over a convex set of points $c \leq x \leq d$ if for every α in the closed interval $[0, 1]$ and every pair of points (x_1, x_2) in the interval $[c, d]$,

$$f[\alpha x_1 + (1 - \alpha)x_2] \geq \alpha f(x_1) + (1 - \alpha)f(x_2).$$

The function is strictly concave if $\geq$ is replaced by $>$ *and* α is in the open interval $0 < \alpha < 1$.

Definitions 4.2 and 4.3 are often preferred because they are valid for functions whether or not they have derivatives throughout the range in question. The function in Figure 4.7(a) is seen to be concave by Definition 4.3, even though a derivative does not exist at the point x_0 in the interval $[0, d]$.

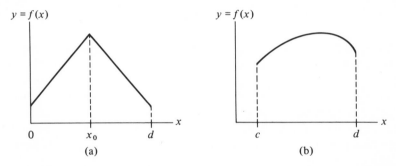

Figure 4.7.   (a) Concave Function over $[0, d]$, (b) Concave Function over $[c, d]$

Maxima and minima of $f(x)$

Consider the problem of finding the *maximum* of a function $f(x)$ over a continuous interval $[c, d]$. If we know, or can deduce, that the function is *strictly concave* over $[c, d]$, then we know that there is *at most* one maximum point and that if a *relative* maximum is found, it is the *absolute* maximum of $f(x)$ in the interval $c \leq x \leq d$. Figure 4.7(b) illustrates.

Completely analogously, a *strictly convex* function over $[c, d]$ has at most

---

[22] Recall that in discussing the derivative for a function of x we saw the tangent to be the limit of a series of secant lines. We may define a function of x as convex in an interval when it is everywhere *above* its tangents in that interval, or equivalently (see Figure 4.6) when it is everywhere *below* its secants in the interval. Definitions 4.2 and 4.3 make statements of location relative to secant lines.

one minimum point; the *relative* minimum, if found, is an *absolute* minimum in the interval $c \leq x \leq d$.

If a function is just concave or convex, not *strictly* so, then a maximum or minimum may or may not be unique. Figures 4.8(a) and (b) illustrate the possibilities for a concave function.

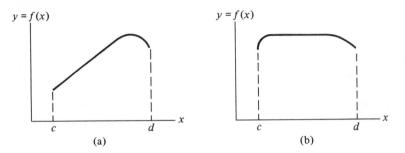

Figure 4.8.   (a) Unique Maximum in $[c, d]$, (b) Nonunique Maximum in $[c, d]$

Thus, for functions that are strictly concave or convex throughout the entire range of x, we know that a maximum or minimum point, if found, is the *absolute* maximum or minimum for the function.[23] We know even more than this. Consider a point x^* that satisfies the first-order requirement for maxima and minima—that is, $df^* = 0$. If $f(x)$ is concave *in the neighborhood*[24] of x^*, then we know that the point *must* represent a relative maximum of $f(x)$. Similarly, if $f(x)$ is convex in the neighborhood of x^*, then x^* *must* be a relative minimum. Examination of the second derivative (or second differential) at the point x^* is precisely an examination of the concavity or convexity of the function at that point. This was exactly the problem of Section 3.2, the unconstrained maximum or minimum of $y = f(x)$, where it was implicitly assumed that x could take on any value in the range $-\infty$ to $+\infty$; hence the region for $f(x)$ was the entire line defined by the x axis (a convex set).

If the second derivative (or second differential) of $f(x)$ is *independent* of x^*—that is, if it is a *constant*, k—then the function is concave (if $k < 0$) or convex (if $k > 0$) *over its entire range*. For maximum problems with concave functions over the entire range of x and minimum problems with convex

---

[23] The reader may also observe that *minima* of concave functions [for example, Figures 4.7(a) and (b)] and *maxima* of convex functions must occur at endpoints of the interval $[c, d]$—that is, on the boundary, if one exists.

[24] That is, concave over the range $x^* - \delta < x^* < x^* + \delta$, for some $\delta > 0$. We used this concept in defining a relative maximum at the beginning of Section 3.2.

functions over the entire range, the first-order conditions are *both necessary and sufficient*.[25] If a function is strictly concave or strictly convex, then the maximum or minimum is unique.

Convex and concave functions of many variables

For $f(x_1, \ldots, x_n)$, the sign of the second total differential at a point tells us where the function lies in relation to the tangent plane (or hyperplane) at that point. It is a test for concavity or convexity of the function at that point in the same way that the second derivative is for functions of one variable. It requires, however, the existence of all second partial derivatives and cross-partials. Definitions 4.2 and 4.3 can be easily extended to functions of n variables to avoid this requirement.

In the definitions of convexity and concavity of $f(x)$ over an interval $c \leq x \leq d$, it was implicitly assumed that x could range *continuously* over all possible values beginning with c and ending with d. This is important; if there were gaps between c and d where x was not allowed, then we would be unable to evaluate $f(x)$ in those gaps and hence could not be sure of the shape of the function there. A similar requirement is necessary when we consider functions of many variables. We avoid the gaps problem by defining concavity or convexity of $f(x_1, \ldots, x_n)$ over a convex set, as in the $f(x)$ case.[26]

DEFINITION 4.4: CONVEX FUNCTION $f(x_1, \ldots, x_n)$. A function $f(x_1, \ldots, x_n)$ is *convex* over a convex set of points X if for every α in $[0, 1]$ and every pair of points $X' = [x_1', \ldots, x_n']'$ and $X'' = [x_1'', \ldots, x_n'']'$, in the set X,

$$f[\alpha X' + (1 - \alpha)X''] \leq \alpha f(X') + (1 - \alpha)f(X'').$$

As before, for *strict convexity* the $\leq$ is replaced by $<$, and the range of α is $0 < \alpha < 1$.

DEFINITION 4.5: CONCAVE FUNCTION $f(x_1, \ldots, x_n)$. A function $f(x_1, \ldots, x_n)$ is *concave* over a convex set of points X if for every α in $[0, 1]$ and every pair of points $X' = [x_1', \ldots, x_n']'$ and $X'' = [x_1'', \ldots, x_n'']'$ in the set X,

$$f[\alpha X' + (1 - \alpha)X''] \geq \alpha f(X') + (1 - \alpha)f(X'').$$

As before, for *strict concavity* the $\geq$ is replaced by $>$, and the range of α is $0 < \alpha < 1$.

[25] The connection between concavity and convexity of a function and the second-order conditions on the sign of d^2f is most easily seen by using the Taylor series expansion of the function. This is done for the interested reader in Appendix 4.1.

[26] Requiring in the one-variable case that x can take on all values from c to d, including endpoints, is exactly the same as requiring that the segment of the x axis from $x = c$ to $x = d$ be a convex set.

The fact that convex and concave functions are defined over convex sets serves to assure that, if X' and X'' are in the set, so is $\alpha X' + (1 - \alpha)X''$, for $0 \leq \alpha \leq 1$. The interpretation of convexity and concavity is similar to that for the case $y = f(x)$. If the n-variable function f is convex, then all points along the convex combination joining any two points on the hypersurface $f(x_1, \ldots, x_n)$ never underestimate the value of the function; if the function is *strictly* convex, all these points overestimate the value of f. If the function is concave or strictly concave, the terms overestimate and underestimate are interchanged.

Maxima and minima of $f(x, \ldots, x_n)$

Consider again the unconstrained maximization or minimization problem of Sections 3.3 [for $y = f(x_1, x_2)$] and 4.2 [for $y = f(x_1, \ldots, x_n)$]. It was implicitly assumed throughout the discussion of those sections that each of the x variables could take on any value in the entire range from $-\infty$ to $+\infty$. Thus, for example, the region over which $f(x_1, x_2)$ was defined was the entire plane formed by the x_1 and x_2 axes (a convex set).

Maxima are separated from minima by the shape of the function f. We have seen that this can be done by using the second total differential. Investigation of the signs of the principal minors of the Hessian matrix of second partial derivatives *evaluated at* X^* (where $df = 0$) is precisely an investigation of the function for convexity or concavity *in the neighborhood* of X^*. So, if a point X^* is found for which $df^* = 0$, and if it is known that f is a concave function in the neighborhood of X^*, then we know that X^* represents a relative *maximum*. Thus the first-order condition $df = 0$ becomes both necessary and sufficient for finding *maxima* for *concave* functions. It is clearly also necessary and sufficient for finding *minima* of *convex* functions.[27]

Consider a function for which the elements of the Hessian are independent of X^*—that is, where the second partial derivatives and cross-partials are all constants. Then if the sign rules establish concavity (convexity), this property holds over the entire range of the function, and a *relative* maximum (minimum) is also the *absolute* maximum (minimum).

Nonlinear inequalities defining convex sets

With the definitions of convex and concave functions, we are now able to prove the important property of convexity for the sets of points defined by two basic nonlinear inequalities. These are of fundamental importance in the next section.

---

[27] These relationships are shown in Appendix 4.1 through the use of Taylor's series. The material in Appendix 4.1 is not essential to an understanding of the preceding (or following) sections of this chapter, but it does serve to tie the various concepts together.

Consider an inequality of the form $h(x_1, \ldots, x_n) \leq 0$ where the function $h(X)$ is specified to be convex. Let $X' = [x'_1, \ldots, x'_n]'$ and $X'' = [x''_1, \ldots, x''_n]'$ be two points that satisfy the inequality; that is, $h(X') \leq 0$ and $h(X'') \leq 0$. Furthermore, let $h(X') \leq h(X'')$; this is completely general. Consider the convex combination of X' and X''; $X''' = \alpha X' + (1 - \alpha)X''$, for $0 \leq \alpha \leq 1$. We wish to show that X''' also satisfies the inequality—that is, that $h(X''') \leq 0$. Since $h(X)$ is convex, from Definition 4.4 we know that

$$h(X''') = h[\alpha X' + (1 - \alpha)X''] \leq \alpha h(X') + (1 - \alpha)h(X'').$$

However, since $h(X') \leq h(X'') \leq 0$,

$$\alpha h(X') + (1 - \alpha)h(X'') \leq \alpha h(X'') + (1 - \alpha)h(X'') = h(X'') \leq 0,$$

and hence $h(X''') \leq h(X'') \leq 0$.

Therefore points satisfying the inequality defined by the *convex* function $h(X) \leq 0$ constitute a convex set.[28] The same would be true of points satisfying several such constraints $h_i(X) \leq 0$ simultaneously, provided all $h_i(X)$ are convex; this is true because the intersection of convex sets is itself a convex set.

Finally the reader can show by a similar argument (using Definition 4.5) that if an area is defined by $h(X) \geq 0$, where $h(X)$ is *concave*, that area is a convex set. The same would be true for the set comprised of points that simultaneously satisfy several constraints $h_i(X) \geq 0$, provided that all $h_i(X)$ are concave. Thus if $h(X)$ is convex, $h(X) \leq 0$ defines a convex region; if $h(X)$ is concave, $h(X) \geq 0$ defines a convex region.[29]

4.8.   MAXIMA AND MINIMA WITH INEQUALITY CONSTRAINTS

It very often is the case that the variables in a problem are not related by means of one or more equations but rather by one or several inequalities. A standard example is the problem of enclosing a rectangular area that is

---

[28] Note that with functions of two variables, the shape of the function in x_1x_2 space must not be interpreted as it was for the two-dimensional representations of $y = f(x)$, as in Figures 4.5 and 4.6 for convex functions and Figures 4.7 and 4.8 for concave functions. For example, consider the inequality $4x_1^2 + x_2^2 \leq 16$ or $h(X) \leq 0$, where $h(X) = 4x_1^2 + x_2^2 - 16$. Here $h(X)$ is a convex function—by Definition 4.4 or the Hessian principal minor test in Appendix 4.1—but the representation of the boundary $h(X) = 0$ in x_1x_2 space is an ellipse centered on the origin. Hence above the x_1 axis it "looks" concave. In three-dimensional space, with an axis for $h(x_1, x_2)$, the boundary defines a bowl-like shape whose minimum point is at $x_1 = 0$, $x_2 = 0$, and $h(x_1, x_2) = -16$. Points on the boundary or inside the bowl constitute a convex set.

[29] This can also be seen as follows. The negative of a convex function is concave; if $h(X)$ is convex, $-h(X)$ is concave. Thus if $h(X)$ is convex and $h(X) \leq 0$ defines a convex region, then (multiplying by -1) $-h(X) \geq 0$ defines a convex region also—and $-h(X)$ is concave.

as large as possible with the limitation that there is a fixed perimeter c (for example, a given amount of fencing). This can be stated as

$$\text{maximize:} \quad lw$$
$$\text{subject to:} \quad 2l + 2w = c,$$

where the two variables represent the unknown length and width. This lends itself to standard Lagrange multiplier analysis.

In this particular problem it is clear that to maximize the area, all of the fencing would be used; if any of the amount c were left idle—not used in the fence—then the area (lw) would have to be smaller, since both area and perimeter $(2l + 2w)$ are positive functions of l and w. Conceptually, however, the fixed amount c really only sets an *upper limit* on the number of running feet that the fence can contain. Logically, the constraint seems to make more sense as a weak inequality: $2l + 2w \leq c$. In this case we know that an optimal solution will always consume all of c, that the weak inequality will be met as an equality.

Obviously this is not always true. With more variables and more complex inequalities—perhaps several of them—it is by no means clear that the maximum or minimum will involve using all of what we might term the scarce resource (or resources). Yet there are many problems in which it is much more realistic to state the constraining relations as inequalities. We consider the implications of this on the methods for locating maxima and minima. Geometrically, we are restricting our interest not to just that part of the surface $f(X)$ above a *line* or *curve* (as in Figure 4.1) but rather to that part of $f(X)$ above an entire *area*, as in Figure 4.9. We consider alternative ways of dealing with first one and then several inequality constraints.

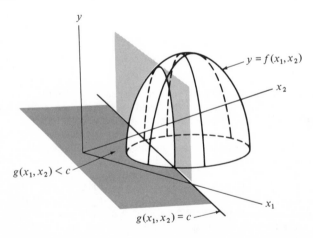

Figure 4.9. Inequality-constrained Maximization Problem

The completely unconstrained approach

Consider the problem of finding a maximum to $y = f(x_1, \ldots, x_n)$ subject to the qualification that $g(x_1, \ldots, x_n) \leq c$. One way to deal with the inequality constraint is simply to ignore it completely. That is, find the unconstrained maximum of $f(X)$—if one exists—and see whether or not this point satisfies the constraint. If it does, the problem is solved. If it does not—that is, if the maximum is outside of the boundary, as it would be in the example shown in Figure 4.9—then it would seem that the problem should be done again, this time with the constraint considered as a strict equation. This is then a straightforward *equality*-constrained problem. The logic is that in moving toward the absolute maximum (which cannot be attained, because of the constraint) we would be willing to stop only when the boundary is hit—that is, when the inequality is met as an equation.

Unfortunately, as we will see in the examples later in this chapter, this logic is not valid when more than one constraint is involved. Of course, we can always first try the unconstrained approach. If we are lucky, the global maximum will satisfy all constraints. If it does not, however, we cannot conclude that all violated constraints should therefore be imposed as equalities. That is, we gain no information about the relative importance of violated constraints when the unconstrained maximum does not satisfy all of the inequalities. However, we *do* learn, by solving the completely unconstrained problem first, whether or not the function in fact has a finite absolute maximum. If it does not, the following two approaches can lead us somewhat astray, as we will see below.

The direct Lagrange multiplier approach

In the preceding paragraphs we dealt with the inequality constraint by ignoring it completely. A second approach to the problem of finding a maximum to $y = f(X)$ subject to $g(X) \leq c$ is to use the necessary conditions from the method of Lagrange multipliers *as if* the constraint were an equality. This was the procedure first discussed in Section 4.4. Having the point or points X^* for which the necessary conditions are fulfilled, evaluate λ at that point (or at those points, if there is more than one). Recall the discussion of the Example in Section 4.4 on the interpretation of λ^* as the change in f^* for a small change in the constraining constant c. Suppose that we have treated the constraint as an equality and have found [via the approach of (4-30)] an X^* for which $df^* = 0$ [that is, $df(X^*) = 0$]; furthermore, suppose that the second-order conditions [on the relevant principal minors, as in (4-32)] indicate that this represents a maximum of $f(x_1, \ldots, x_n)$—subject to $g(x_1, \ldots, x_n) = c$. Then evaluate λ at X^*; we may find that $\lambda^* > 0$—that is, that $\partial f^*/\partial c > 0$. In words, more c would mean a larger value of f^*. If this is true, then clearly, since we are dealing with a *maximization* problem *and* are at the *maximum* point along the constraint equation, we would want to use all available c. The approach of reading the constraint as if it were an equation was correct; the maximum occurs *on the boundary* $g(x_1, \ldots, x_n) = c$. Viewed from a position at the origin, the boundary set by the constraint cuts the $f(x_1, \ldots, x_n)$ surface on the "near side" of the hilltop—again, as illustrated in Figure 4.9.

Alternatively, suppose $\lambda^* \equiv \partial f^*/\partial c < 0$. This tells us that the problem is structured in such a way that *more c* would *decrease* the value of f^*. Hence, for the maximization problem the optimum point is interior to the constraint line, *away from the boundary*. We were wrong to consider the constraint as an equation; in fact it is wrong (or at least unnecessary) to consider the constraint at all. Viewed from the origin, the boundary lies on the "far side" of the hill. The problem must be redone, ignoring the constraint; we want to find the maximum to $f(X)$ as if the variables were *independent*. This was the subject matter of Section 4.2.

Note that this reasoning is sound *only* after we have established, via the second-order conditions, that X^* is indeed a maximum and not a minimum to the equality-constrained version of the problem. If X^* were a minimum, then the fact that $\partial f^*/\partial c > 0$—that this minimum value of the function f would increase for a small increase in c—tells us nothing about the location of the *maximum* to the inequality-constrained problem. Figure 4.10 indicates the general ideas involved for $f(x_1, x_2)$ and a linear constraint.

Imagine that T represents a mountain top and B the bottom of a valley. For simplicity imagine that beyond the outermost contours for the mountain and the valley the surface is flat. Then consider the problem: maximize $f(x_1, x_2)$ subject to a linear constraint $a_1 x_1 + a_2 x_2 \leq c$. Let the boundary

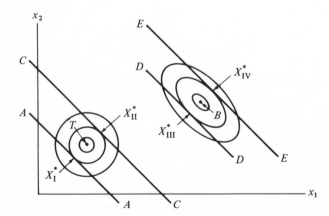

Figure 4.10. $f(x_1, x_2)$ with Alternative Inequality Constraints

(the upper limit on values of x_1 and x_2) be located as indicated by AA and treat the problem as if the constraint were an equality. X_I^* represents a maximum along AA; at that point $\lambda_I^* > 0$, and clearly it was correct to consider the constraint as an equation. [The contour of the surface on a plane perpendicular to the x_1x_2 plane along AA would appear as in Figure 3.8(b).] The same approach, were the constraint in fact positioned as in CC, would find an X_{II}^* that is the maximum point along CC; there, $\lambda_{II}^* < 0$, and the point T will be found by ignoring the constraint.

On the other hand, for the same maximization problem the constraint might be located as in DD or EE. The reader should be clear that at X_{III}^* or X_{IV}^*, the minima along those lines, the values of λ^* will be negative and positive, respectively. [The contour at either point would be as in Figure 3.8(a).] The latter, $\lambda_{IV}^* > 0$ at X_{IV}^*, does *not* mean that it was correct to treat the constraint as an equality, precisely because X_{IV}^* is a *minimum* and not a *maximum* point.

Finally, it may happen that $\lambda^* = 0$; that is, an infinitesimal change in the amount of c does nothing to f^*. Thus the maximum of f must occur exactly on the constraint $g(X) = c$—that is, *on the boundary*. The boundary cuts through the top of the hill exactly.[30] Note that in the $\lambda^* = 0$ case the same optimum is achieved with *or* without the constraint considered explicitly. However, since the value of λ^* is only found *after* assuming that the constraint is $g(X) = c$, it is appropriate to leave X^* at the value (or values) found in this manner. Doing the problem again, ignoring the constraint, would lead to exactly the same X^*.

The rule for the problem: maximize $f(X)$ subject to $g(X) \leq c$, is therefore as follows: Solve the problem as if the constraint were an equality using both first- and second-order conditions; then

(a) if $\lambda^* \geq 0$, the maximum is on the boundary; therefore X^* found by assuming $g(X) = c$ is correct;

(b) if $\lambda^* < 0$, the maximum is interior to the boundary;   (4-36) therefore redo the problem ignoring the constraint completely.

Examples of the direct Lagrange multiplier approach

To illustrate the various sign possibilities for λ^*, consider the following problems.

Maximize

$$y = f(x_1, x_2) = -x_1^2 - x_2^2 + 4x_1 + 6x_2$$

---

[30] Or, in terms of Figure 4.10, the bottom of the valley. Hence, again, it is necessary to be certain, first of all, that X^* is indeed a *maximum* point along the constraint as an equation.

subject to three different inequality constraints, which we will consider in turn: (a) $x_1 + x_2 \leq 2$; (b) $x_1 + x_2 \leq 10$; (c) $x_1 + x_2 \leq 5$. These are illustrated in Figure 4.11.

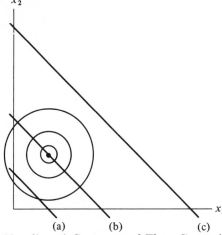

Figure 4.11. $f(x_1, x_2)$ Contours and Three Constraint Boundaries

CASE (A). Maximize $y = -x_1^2 - x_2^2 + 4x_1 + 6x_2$ subject to $x_1 + x_2 \leq 2$

Assume that the constraint is an equality. Then the Lagrangean function is

$$L = -x_1^2 - x_2^2 + 4x_1 + 6x_2 - \lambda(x_1 + x_2 - 2)$$

and

$$\frac{\partial L}{\partial x_1} \equiv L_1 = -2x_1 + 4 - \lambda = 0,$$

$$\frac{\partial L}{\partial x_2} \equiv L_2 = -2x_2 + 6 - \lambda = 0,$$

$$\frac{\partial L}{\partial \lambda} \equiv L_\lambda = -(x_1 + x_2 - 2) = 0,$$

are the first-order conditions. Therefore, from L_1 and L_2,

$$-2x_1 + 4 = -2x_2 + 6$$

or

$$x_1^* = x_2^* - 1.$$

Substituting into L_λ:

$$(x_2^* - 1) + x_2^* = 2,$$
$$2x_2^* = 3,$$
$$x_2^* = \tfrac{3}{2};$$

therefore

$$x_1^* = \tfrac{1}{2}.$$

The relevant bordered Hessian-like matrix requires further partial and cross-partial derivatives; here

$$f_{11} = -2, \quad f_{22} = -2, \quad f_{12} = f_{21} = 0;$$
$$h_1 = 1, \quad h_2 = 1, \quad h_{11} = h_{22} = h_{12} = h_{21} = 0.$$

Thus, from (4-32),

$$\bar{V}^* = \begin{bmatrix} 0 & 1 & 1 \\ 1 & -2 & 0 \\ 1 & 0 & -2 \end{bmatrix}$$

and $|\bar{V}_3^*| = |\bar{V}^*| = 2 + 2 = 4 > 0$. Thus $d^2 f^*$ is negative and X^* represents a maximum.[31]

Importantly,

$$\lambda^* = -2x_1^* + 4 \text{ (from } L_1) = -2x_2^* + 6 \text{ (from } L_2),$$
$$\lambda^* = 3 > 0.$$

Thus, since X^* is a maximum point and $\lambda^* > 0$, we conclude that it was correct to treat the constraint as an equality; $f^* = L^* = 8\frac{1}{2}$ and $x_1^* + x_2^* = \frac{1}{2} + \frac{3}{2} = 2$.

CASE (B). Maximize $y = -x_1^2 - x_2^2 + 4x_1 + 6x_2$ subject to $x_1 + x_2 \leq 10$

Clearly L_1 and L_2 will be the same as in Case (a), above, from which it follows that $x_1^* = x_2^* - 1$, as before. Only L_λ has changed.

$$L_\lambda = -(x_1 + x_2 - 10) = 0$$

and therefore

$$(x_2^* - 1) + x_2^* = 10$$
$$x_2^* = \tfrac{11}{2},$$

and consequently

$$x_1^* = \tfrac{9}{2}.$$

Note that the elements of $\bar{V}^*$ are identical to those in Case (a), and hence X^* is again a maximum point. Here, however, $\lambda^* = -5 < 0$.

From this we conclude that the point $x_1^* = \frac{9}{2}$, $x_2^* = \frac{11}{2}$, on the boundary given by $x_1 + x_2 = 10$, where $f^* = \frac{1}{2}$, is *not* a maximum. On the contrary, we should redo the problem, without considering the constraint at all. The first-order condition ($df^* = 0$), Table 3.5 or 4.1, means

---

[31] The rule is, of course, that for $d^2 f^* < 0$, the principal minors of $\bar{V}^*$, beginning with the third, must alternate, starting positive. Since the third principal minor is the last one in a 3×3 matrix, alternation cannot occur.

$$f_1 = -2x_1 + 4 = 0,$$
$$f_2 = -2x_2 + 6 = 0.$$

Therefore $x_1^* = 2$, $x_2^* = 3$.

The check to assure that this is a maximum comes from Table 3.5 or 4.1 also; it involves elements of the Hessian *without* borders. Recall that $f_{11} = -2$, $f_{22} = -2$, and $f_{12} = f_{21} = 0$; hence $f_{11}^* f_{22}^* - f_{12}^{*2} = 4 > 0$, or, more generally,

$$H = H^* = \begin{bmatrix} -2 & 0 \\ 0 & -2 \end{bmatrix},$$

and thus $|H_1^*| = -2 < 0$, $|H_2^*| = 4 > 0$, the correct sequence for a maximum at $x_1^* = 2$, $x_2^* = 3$. Note that here $f^* = 13$; when the constraint was imposed as an equality, $f^* = \frac{1}{2}$.

CASE (C). Maximize the same function, subject to $x_1 + x_2 \leq 5$

As before $x_1^* = x_2^* - 1$, and this, when substituted into

$$L_\lambda = -(x_1 + x_2 - 5) = 0,$$

gives $x_1^* = 2$, $x_2^* = 3$, which is a maximum point; $f^* = 13$, and $\lambda^* = 0$. Therefore, considering the constraint as an equality and using the Lagrange multiplier technique gave the same result as if it had been ignored completely, as in Case (b).

The problem of maximizing $f(x_1, \ldots, x_n)$ subject to $g(x_1, \ldots, x_n) \leq c$ is perfectly general in the sense that

1. a minimization problem can be converted to a maximization one by changing the sign of the function involved; the minimum of $f(x_1, \ldots, x_n)$ occurs at the same point (or points) as the maximum of $-f(x_1, \ldots, x_n)$, and
2. the direction of any inequality can be reversed by multiplying both sides by (-1); $g(x_1, \ldots, x_n) \geq c$ is the same as $-g(x_1, \ldots; x_n) \leq -c$.

Logically, however, we *generally* expect that, in its natural form, the constraint on a maximum problem will set an upper limit—$g(x_1, \ldots, x_n) \leq c$—and that the minimization problem will be bounded from below—$g(x_1, \ldots, x_n) \geq c$—keeping the variables from becoming extremely small. We will consider these the *standard forms* for the general optimization problem with one inequality constraint. Since $\partial f^*/\partial c = \lambda^*$ in the formulation of L that has been used in this and previous sections, it should be clear that the sign rules on λ^* in (4-36) for the inequality-constrained maximization problem are identical for the inequality-constrained *minimization* problem *in standard form*—minimize $f(x_1, \ldots, x_n)$ subject to $g(x_1, \ldots, x_n) \geq c$. Solve the problem as if the constraint were an equality, using both first- and second-order conditions; then

(a) if $\lambda^* \geq 0$, the minimum is on the boundary; therefore
     the X^* found by assuming $g(x_1, \ldots, x_n) = c$ is correct;

(b) if $\lambda^* < 0$, the minimum is inside the boundary; there-   (4-37)
     fore redo the problem ignoring the constraint
     completely.[32]

From the discussion at the end of Section 4.4, it is clear that these same
rules will hold for the case in which the Lagrangean is formed (schematically) as $L = f(X) + \lambda[c - g(X)]$, and on the other hand that the sign
rules on λ^* for both maximum and minimum problems will be reversed for
either of the alternative formulations $L = f(X) - \lambda[c - g(X)]$ and $L =
f(X) + \lambda[g(X) - c]$. All of the rules are entirely consistent, once a par-
ticular form for the Lagrangean function has been selected. As before, we
prefer $L = f(X) - \lambda[g(X) - c]$, for which (4-36) and (4-37) apply.[33]

The Kuhn-Tucker approach

Consider again the problem of finding a maximum to $y = f(x_1, \ldots, x_n)$
subject to the qualification that $g(x_1, \ldots, x_n) \leq c$. Let $h(x_1, \ldots, x_n) \equiv
g(x_1, \ldots, x_n) - c$; then the constraint is expressible as $h(x_1, \ldots, x_n) \leq 0$.[34]
Suppose that we add a variable to the left-hand side of this inequality to
convert it to an equation—that is, add a so-called "slack" variable equal to
the difference between 0 and $h(x_1, \ldots, x_n)$ for any values of $x_1, \ldots, x_n$.
Since this difference, $0 - h(x_1, \ldots, x_n)$, must be either zero or positive
(that is, nonnegative), the added variable must also be nonnegative. If we
denote the added term by s^2, we are certain that it will have the proper
sign. Thus

$$h(x_1, \ldots, x_n) + s^2 = 0,$$

and the optimization problem can now be expressed as

[32] The reader should convince himself that he understands why these statements are
correct by doing (or at least thinking through) each of the three cases in the Example
above, as if $f(x_1, x_2)$ were to be *minimized* and each of the inequalities in Cases (a), (b),
and (c) were reversed; that is, set lower limits on $x_1 + x_2$. Figure 4.11 still applies,
except that we are looking down into a bowl rather than onto a mountain.

[33] We emphasize this point precisely because of the lack of consistency in the literature
and the consequent apparent contradictions between various authors—for example, in
the interpretation of λ^*.

[34] It should be clear that subtraction of a constant term from a concave (convex)
function leaves a concave (convex) function. Only position, not shape, has been changed.
Thus, since we define $h(X) \equiv g(X) - c$, the concavity (convexity) of either $h(X)$ or
$g(X)$ implies the concavity (convexity) of the other; they have the *same* shape. Note
that if we had defined $h(X) \equiv c - g(X)$, the functions $h(X)$ and $g(X)$ would have been
of *opposite* shape. This is another point of inconsistency in the literature.

$$\text{maximize } y = f(x_1, \ldots, x_n)$$

subject to the qualification that $h(x_1, \ldots, x_n) + s^2 = 0$.

This is a straightforward *equality*-constrained maximization problem involving $n + 1$ variables (the n x's and one s) and one constraint.[35] Therefore the approach of Section 4.5 can be utilized. Form the Lagrange function in the standard way:

$$L = f(x_1, \ldots, x_n) - \lambda[h(x_1, \ldots, x_n) + s^2], \qquad (4\text{-}38)$$

and consider the first-order conditions, as in Section 4.5, that can be derived from setting all first partial derivatives of L equal to zero.

(a) $\dfrac{\partial L}{\partial x_j} \equiv L_j = f_j - \lambda h_j = 0 \qquad (j = 1, \ldots, n),$

(b) $\dfrac{\partial L}{\partial \lambda} \equiv L_\lambda = -[h(x_1, \ldots, x_n) + s^2] = 0, \qquad (4\text{-}39)$

(c) $\dfrac{\partial L}{\partial s} \equiv L_s = -2\lambda s = 0.$

There are $n + 2$ equations now: $n + 1$ from the variables in the problem (x's and s) and one from the Lagrange multiplier λ.

Consider (4-39)(c). The implication of this equation is that either $\lambda = 0$ or $s = 0$, or both. If $s = 0$, then from (4-39)(b), after multiplying through by (-1), $h(x_1, \ldots, x_n) = 0$. Therefore s, which was added to the problem only to convert it to equality-constraint form, can be eliminated from the first-order conditions (4-39). The results in (4-39)(b) and (c) can be reexpressed in terms of λ and $h(X)$ only:

(d) $\lambda[h(x_1, \ldots, x_n)] = 0.$ \qquad (4\text{-}39)

Thus the n equations in (4-39)(a) and the one in (4-39)(d) contain the remaining first-order conditions in terms of the original variables x_j and the Lagrange multiplier λ. In this process, however, the *direction* of the inequality has been lost, and so $h(x_1, \ldots, x_n) \leq 0$ must be reintroduced as an explicit requirement. The first-order conditions are therefore:

(a) $\qquad f_j - \lambda h_j = 0,$
(b) $\quad \lambda[h(x_1, \ldots, x_n)] = 0, \qquad (4\text{-}40)$
(c) $\qquad h(x_1, \ldots, x_n) \leq 0,$

and we know, furthermore, from earlier discussion, that in these necessary conditions for a local maximum we must have $\lambda^* \geq 0$, since we employed

---

[35] Note that, had only s been added, it would have then been necessary to append a new constraint requiring that $s \geq 0$, and there would thus still be an inequality constraint in the full statement of the problem.

the Lagrange multiplier approach on an equality constraint. These results, known as the Kuhn-Tucker conditions,[36] are often stated as follows:

> The necessary conditions for a point $X^* = [x_1^*, \ldots, x_n^*]'$ to be a relative maximum of $f(X)$ subject to $h(X) \leq 0$ are that   (4-41) a nonnegative λ exists such that it and X^* satisfy (4-40).

These necessary conditions, as stated in (4-41), differ in two respects from the necessary conditions given in Sections 4.2 and 4.5, for either the unconstrained or the equality-constrained cases; they primarily affect the method of solution.

1. In addition to equations, the conditions also include an inequality. The solution procedure, therefore, is to find the value (or values) of the variables that satisfy the *equations* in (4-40) and then check it (or them) in the *inequality*.
2. The equation $\lambda[h(X)] = 0$ requires that one find the solutions implied by (a) setting $\lambda = 0$ and (b) setting $h(X) = 0$. In general, then, there will be more than one set of X^* to check in the inequality constraint.

Using the notions of convexity and concavity developed in Section 4.7, we can make a more powerful statement:

> If $f(X)$ is *concave* and the constraint $h(X) \leq 0$ is a *convex* function, then conditions (4-41) are also *sufficient* for a   (4-42) local maximum.

That is, the Kuhn-Tucker conditions become *both* necessary and sufficient for a maximum; a point satisfying them is a maximum, and if a point is a maximum, it must satisfy them.[37] Finally, if f is *strictly* concave, the maximum will be an *absolute* one.

Example

The example in Section 4.4 involved $f(x_1, x_2) = 6x_1x_2$, subject to $2x_1 + x_2 = 10$. There we found a *maximum* at $x_1^* = 2\frac{1}{2}$, $x_2^* = 5$. Suppose that the constraint had been an inequality: $2x_1 + x_2 \leq 10$ (or $2x_1 + x_2 - 10 \leq 0$).

If we ignore the constraint completely, we find $f_1 = 6x_2$ and $f_2 = 6x_1$; that is, $x_1^* = 0$, $x_2^* = 0$, the origin, is the only point satisfying the first-order conditions. Moving to the second-order conditions, however, shows

---

[36] Named for H. Kuhn and A. Tucker, who first presented them in this general form for inequality-constrained optimization problems. We will be concerned with these conditions in more detail in subsequent chapters, especially Chapter 8.

[37] Alternatively, provided the concavity-convexity requirements on $f(X)$ and $h(X)$ are met, a point is a maximum to $f(x_1, \ldots, x_n)$ subject to $h(x_1, \ldots, x_n) \leq 0$ *if and only if* conditions (4-41) are met.

$$H^* = \begin{bmatrix} 0 & 6 \\ 6 & 0 \end{bmatrix}; \qquad |H_1^*| = 0, \quad |H_2^*| = -36 < 0.$$

In fact, the origin represents a saddle point for $6x_1x_2$; in the quadrants where both variables are positive or both negative, $f(X)$ takes on positive values; in those quadrants where one variable is positive and the other negative, it takes on negative values. There is clearly no finite absolute maximum, since, for example, increasingly large negative values for both x_1 and x_2 produce increasingly large values for $f(X) = 6x_1x_2$ while still satisfying the inequality constraint $2x_1 + x_2 \leq 10$.

If we were to use the Lagrange multiplier approach of the present section, we would examine λ^* at the point satisfying the first-order conditions, replacing the inequality by an equality. This, of course, is exactly what the calculations in Section 4.4 did. There we found $\lambda^* > 0 \ (= 15)$; hence a relative maximum is in fact on the boundary.

The Kuhn-Tucker approach can also be used. Conditions (4-40) applied to this problem are:

$$
\begin{array}{ll}
\text{(a)} & \begin{cases} 6x_2 - 2\lambda = 0, \\ 6x_1 - \lambda = 0, \end{cases} \\
\text{(b)} & \lambda(2x_1 + x_2 - 10) = 0, \\
\text{(c)} & (2x_1 + x_2 - 10) \leq 0.
\end{array}
\qquad (4\text{-}43)
$$

From (4-43)(a)

$$6x_2 = 2\lambda, \quad 6x_1 = \lambda, \quad \text{therefore} \quad x_2^* = 2x_1^*. \qquad (4\text{-}44)$$

From (4-43)(b), either $\lambda^* = 0$ or $\lambda^* \neq 0$. We examine the implications of both possibilities. In particular: (1) if $\lambda^* = 0$, does (4-43)(c) hold? and (2) if $\lambda^* \neq 0$, is $\lambda^* > 0$? For each alternative that *does* meet all the relevant conditions, evaluate $f(x_1^*, x_2^*)$; then select that point for which f^* is larger (or largest). Remember, however, that only when the proper convexity of the function can be established are we assured that these conditions are sufficient as well.

CASE 1.   Set $\lambda^* = 0$. Then from (4-44), $x_1^* = x_2^* = 0$. Constraint (4-43)(c) becomes $0 + 0 - 10$, which clearly is < 0. Thus $x_1^* = 0$, $x_2^* = 0$ satisfies all requirements of (4-41), the Kuhn-Tucker *necessary* conditions for a maximum; $f(0, 0) = 6(0)(0) = 0$. This is the saddle point.

CASE 2.   If $\lambda^* \neq 0$, then $(2x_1 + x_2 - 10) = 0$, from (4-43)(b). From (4-44), $x_2^* = 2x_1^*$, hence $2x_1^* + 2x_1^* = 10$; $x_1^* = 2\frac{1}{2}$, and $x_2^* = 5$. Again, from (4-44), $\lambda^* = 6x_1^* = 15$, which is > 0, as required. Moreover, $f(X^*) = f(2\frac{1}{2}, 5) = 75$. From this we conclude that $x_1^* = 2\frac{1}{2}$, $x_2^* = 5$ represents a *local* (that is, a relative) maximum.[38] This is certainly true; small deviations

---

[38] Note that (4-42) does not apply, since $f(x_1, x_2) = 6x_1x_2$ is not convex. As discussed in Appendix 4.1, we need all positive principal minors of H^* for a convex function; here, as we have seen, $|H_1^*| = 0$ and $|H_2^*| = -36$.

(while still satisfying the constraint) around this point give smaller values to $6x_1x_2$.

The reader should note that, as is always the case with first-order conditions, the equations involved may or may not be easily solved; this depends on the extent to which nonlinearities are present. However, in using the Kuhn-Tucker approach for inequality constraints, the presence of a condition of the form $\lambda[h(X)] = 0$ means that two sets of answers must be explored—one in which $\lambda = 0$ and one in which $h(X) = 0$.

Several inequality constraints

The generalization to more than one inequality constraint follows that in the equality-constrained cases. In the Lagrange multiplier approach, each constraint has an associated λ. These must be evaluated at the point or points that satisfy the first-order conditions for the equality-constrained problem—(4-34) of Section 4.6—and maxima, minima, and neither must be separated by the more cumbersome determinantal rules at the end of Section 4.6. The constraints associated with those $\lambda_i^* < 0$ are then dropped and the problem is done again, including as equalities only those constraints for which $\lambda_i^* \geq 0$. This is generally, therefore, a detailed, two-stage process. As will become clear below, for the Kuhn-Tucker approach it is no longer necessary to assume that $m < n$—that there are fewer constraints than variables.

The Kuhn-Tucker conditions become:

The necessary conditions for a point $X^* = [x_1^*, \ldots, x_n^*]'$ to be a relative maximum of $f(x_1, \ldots, x_n)$ subject to $h_i(x_1, \ldots, x_n) \leq 0$ are that nonnegative λ_i exist such that they and X^* satisfy

$$
\begin{aligned}
&\text{(a)} && f_j - \sum_{i=1}^{m} \lambda_i h_j^i = 0 && (j = 1, \ldots, n), \\
&\text{(b)} && \lambda_i[h_i(x_1, \ldots, x_n)] = 0 && (i = 1, \ldots, m), \\
&\text{(c)} && h_i(x_1, \ldots, x_n) \leq 0 && (i = 1, \ldots, m).
\end{aligned}
\tag{4-45}
$$

As before, these are also sufficient conditions for a maximum if $f(x_1, \ldots, x_n)$ is a *concave* function and all of the constraints $h_i(x_1, \ldots, x_n)$ $(i = 1, \ldots, m)$ are *convex* functions. If f is *strictly* concave, the maximum is an *absolute* one.

Example

Consider maximizing $f(x_1, x_2, x_3) = -x_1^2 - x_2^2 - x_3^2 + 4x_1 + 6x_2$ subject to two constraints: (a) $x_1 + x_2 \leq 2$ and (b) $2x_1 + 3x_2 \leq 12$. We illustrate both the direct Lagrange and the Kuhn-Tucker approaches to the problem.

1. THE DIRECT LAGRANGE MULTIPLIER APPROACH

Form the Lagrangean function as if both constraints were equalities.

$$L = -x_1^2 - x_2^2 - x_3^2 + 4x_1 + 6x_2 - \lambda_1(x_1 + x_2 - 2) - \lambda_2(2x_1 + 3x_2 - 12).$$

The first-order conditions are therefore:

$$\begin{aligned}
L_1 &= -2x_1 + 4 - \lambda_1 - 2\lambda_2 = 0, \\
L_2 &= -2x_2 + 6 - \lambda_1 - 3\lambda_2 = 0, \\
L_3 &= -2x_3 \qquad\qquad\quad\ = 0, \\
L_{\lambda_1} &= -(x_1 + x_2 - 2) \qquad = 0, \\
L_{\lambda_2} &= -(2x_1 + 3x_2 - 12) \ = 0.
\end{aligned} \qquad (4\text{-}46)$$

The last two equations in (4-46) are simply

$$x_1 + x_2 = 2, \qquad 2x_1 + 3x_2 = 12.$$

Since, in $AX = B$ terms, $|A| \neq 0$, we know a unique solution exists, and it can be found in any of several ways, as we saw in Chapter 2. For a 2×2 problem, Cramer's rule is efficient.

$$x_1^* = \begin{vmatrix} 2 & 1 \\ 12 & 3 \end{vmatrix} \bigg/ \begin{vmatrix} 1 & 1 \\ 2 & 3 \end{vmatrix} = -\frac{6}{1} = -6,$$

$$x_2^* = \begin{vmatrix} 1 & 2 \\ 2 & 12 \end{vmatrix} \bigg/ \begin{vmatrix} 1 & 1 \\ 2 & 3 \end{vmatrix} = \frac{8}{1} = 8.$$

Clearly $x_3^* = 0$.

The second-order conditions, from Section 4.6, require additional derivatives:

$$\begin{aligned}
f_{11} &= -2, & f_{12} &= f_{21} = 0, & h_1^1 &= 1, & h_1^2 &= 2, \\
f_{22} &= -2, & f_{23} &= f_{32} = 0, & h_2^1 &= 1, & h_2^2 &= 3, \\
f_{33} &= -2, & f_{31} &= f_{13} = 0, & h_3^1 &= 0, & h_3^2 &= 0,
\end{aligned}$$

and all second partials h_{jk}^i for $i = 1, 2$ and $j, k = 1, 2, 3$ are zero. In this case

$$\bar{V} = \begin{bmatrix}
0 & 0 & 1 & 1 & 0 \\
0 & 0 & 2 & 3 & 0 \\
1 & 2 & -2 & 0 & 0 \\
1 & 3 & 0 & -2 & 0 \\
0 & 0 & 0 & 0 & -2
\end{bmatrix},$$

and X^* will represent a maximum point if the last $[(n - m) = (3 - 2) = 1]$ principal minor of $\bar{V}$ has a negative sign $[(-1)^{m+1} = (-1)^3 = -1]$. Here, evaluating $|\bar{V}_5| = |\bar{V}|$ down the fifth column and the resulting 4×4 determinant down its first column, we find $|\bar{V}_5| = |\bar{V}| = -2$; hence $x_1^* = -6$, $x_2^* = 8$, $x_3^* = 0$ is a maximum subject to the two equality constraints.

We now evaluate λ_1^* and λ_2^* via the first two equations in the first-order conditions (4-46):

$$\lambda_1 + 2\lambda_2 = 16, \qquad \lambda_1 + 3\lambda_2 = -10.$$

Again, this is a pair of linear equations in two variables. The determinant of the coefficient matrix is nonzero, and Cramer's rule gives the unique values of λ_1 and λ_2 implied by x_1^* and x_2^* from the first-order conditions.

$$\lambda_1^* = \begin{vmatrix} 16 & 2 \\ -10 & 3 \end{vmatrix} \bigg/ \begin{vmatrix} 1 & 2 \\ 1 & 3 \end{vmatrix} = \frac{68}{1} = 68,$$

$$\lambda_2^* = \begin{vmatrix} 1 & 16 \\ 1 & -10 \end{vmatrix} \bigg/ \begin{vmatrix} 1 & 2 \\ 1 & 3 \end{vmatrix} = -\frac{26}{1} = -26.$$

In particular: $\lambda_1^* \geq 0$, $\lambda_2^* < 0$. Therefore it is correct to treat the first constraint as an equality—the constrained maximum point will be on that boundary. But it is incorrect to require equality in the second constraint—the maximum will be inside that boundary, so the second constraint can and should be ignored. As a matter of curiosity, the reader may note that at $x_1^* = -6$, $x_2^* = 8$, $x_3^* = 0$, the function $f(x_1^*, x_2^*, x_3^*) = -76$.

Thus the problem must be done again, with only $x_1 + x_2 = 2$ as a constraint. Now

$$L = -x_1^2 - x_2^2 - x_3^2 + 4x_1 + 6x_2 - \lambda(x_1 + x_2 - 2),$$

for which the first-order conditions are

$$\begin{aligned} L_1 &= -2x_1 + 4 - \lambda &= 0, \\ L_2 &= -2x_2 + 6 - \lambda &= 0, \\ L_3 &= -2x_3 &= 0, \\ L_\lambda &= -(x_1 + x_2 - 2) &= 0, \end{aligned}$$

from which

$$-2x_1 + 4 = -2x_2 + 6 \quad \text{or} \quad x_1^* = x_2^* - 1 \quad \text{and} \quad x_3^* = 0.$$

This is substituted into L_λ to give

$$x_1^* = \tfrac{1}{2}, \qquad x_2^* = \tfrac{3}{2}.$$

Now $f(x_1^*, x_2^*, x_3^*) = 8\frac{1}{2}$. Clearly constraint (a), $x_1 + x_2 \leq 2$, is met as an equality; constraint (b), $2x_1 + 3x_2 \leq 12$, is indeed a strict inequality—$2(\frac{1}{2}) + 3(\frac{3}{2}) = 5\frac{1}{2} < 12$—exactly as we deduced from observation on λ_2^* in the first phase of the solution. The relevant principal minors of the bordered matrix (which is $\bar{V}$ from above, with the second row and column removed) alternate, beginning positive, and hence this is a true maximum (Section 4.5).

The reader could easily find that the completely unconstrained maximum occurs at $x_1^* = 2$, $x_2^* = 3$, and $x_3^* = 0$. There $f(x_1^*, x_2^*, x_3^*) = +13$, but *both* constraints are violated. As we have just seen, we could not conclude from this result that *both* constraints should therefore be imposed as equalities. A simple geometric illustration makes this clear.

Suppose, for graphic simplicity, that we ignore x_3 in the current problem; thus we have a function of only two variables, whose contours can be drawn in an $x_1 x_2$ plane. In this same plane we draw the boundaries formed by the constraints in their equality form, as in Figure 4.12. (The shaded

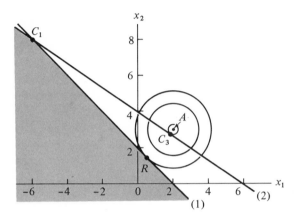

Figure 4.12. Unconstrained and Constrained Maxima

area designates points satisfying both inequalities.) The reader can easily see that the unconstrained maximum for this smaller problem remains at the point $x_1^* = 2$, $x_2^* = 3$ (point A, for absolute maximum, in the figure). The inequality-constrained maximum will be at $x_1^* = \frac{1}{2}$, $x_2^* = \frac{3}{2}$ (point R in the figure),[39] where constraint (1) is met as an equation and constraint (2) is a strict inequality.

2. THE KUHN-TUCKER APPROACH

It is unnecessary to form the Lagrangean function, including the new variables s_1 and s_2 that convert the constraints to equalities. We have done this for the general case with one constraint and derived the first-order conditions (4-40) and, through our knowledge of the interpretation of λ^*, the statement in (4-41). The extension in (4-45) to more than one constraint can be made specific here for the case of two inequalities. It is:

---

[39] Points designated C_1 and C_3 will be discussed below.

$$\text{(a)} \quad \begin{cases} -2x_1 + 4 - \lambda_1 - 2\lambda_2 = 0, \\ -2x_2 + 6 - \lambda_1 - 3\lambda_2 = 0, \\ -2x_3 \qquad\qquad\quad = 0; \end{cases}$$

$$\text{(b)} \quad \begin{cases} \lambda_1(\ x_1 + \ x_2 - \ 2) = 0, \\ \lambda_2(2x_1 + 3x_2 - 12) = 0; \end{cases} \qquad\qquad (4\text{-}47)$$

$$\text{(c)} \quad \begin{cases} x_1 + \ x_2 - \ 2 \le 0, \\ 2x_1 + 3x_2 - 12 \le 0. \end{cases}$$

As in the Kuhn-Tucker approach to the one-constraint problem in (4-43), we begin with the implications of the relations in the nonlinear equations (4-47)(b).

CASE 1: $\lambda_1 \ne 0$, $\lambda_2 \ne 0$.   Then

$$x_1 + \ x_2 = \ 2,$$
$$2x_1 + 3x_2 = 12,$$

from which we have already found $x_1^* = -6$ and $x_2^* = 8$ (and, of course, $x_3^* = 0$) and, more importantly, $\lambda_1^* = 68$ but $\lambda_2^* = -26$. Hence for the case in which both λ_1 and λ_2 are nonzero, one of them must necessarily be negative; this violates the Kuhn-Tucker requirement that we find all nonnegative λ's satisfying (4-47). Thus this X^* is rejected.

CASE 2: $\lambda_1 = 0$, $\lambda_2 = 0$.   Then, from (4-47)(a),

$$-2x_1 = -4, \qquad x_1^* = 2,$$
$$-2x_2 = -6, \qquad x_2^* = 3.$$

Checking the inequality constraints (4-47)(c), we find *both* are violated; $x_1^* = 2$ and $x_2^* = 3$ satisfy neither of them. Therefore $X^* = [2, \ 3, \ 0]'$ must be rejected as well.

CASE 3: $\lambda_1 = 0$, $\lambda_2 \ne 0$.   Since $\lambda_2 \ne 0$, from (4-47)(b) we know that $2x_1 + 3x_2 = 12$. Since $\lambda_1 = 0$, we find from (4-47)(a) that

$$-2x_1 + 4 = 2\lambda_2,$$
$$-2x_2 + 6 = 3\lambda_2,$$

or, multiplying the first equation by 3 and the second by 2,

$$-6x_1 + 12 = -4x_2 + 12 \quad \text{---that is,} \quad -6x_1 + 4x_2 = 0.$$

We therefore have two equations in x_1 and x_2:

$$2x_1 + 3x_2 = 12,$$
$$-6x_1 + 4x_2 = \ 0.$$

The coefficient matrix is nonsingular, and from Cramer's rule we find that

$$x_1^* = \begin{vmatrix} 12 & 3 \\ 0 & 4 \end{vmatrix} \bigg/ \begin{vmatrix} 2 & 3 \\ -6 & 4 \end{vmatrix} = \frac{48}{26} = \frac{24}{13},$$

$$x_2^* = \begin{vmatrix} 2 & 12 \\ -6 & 0 \end{vmatrix} \bigg/ \begin{vmatrix} 2 & 3 \\ -6 & 4 \end{vmatrix} = \frac{72}{26} = \frac{36}{13}.$$

Since we have assured that λ_1 is of the correct sign and the second inequality is met, it is necessary to check on the first inequality in (4-47)(c) and the nonnegativity of λ_2. For $x_1^* = \frac{24}{13}$ and $x_2^* = \frac{36}{13}$, the first inequality is violated. This is enough evidence to eliminate these values of x_1 and x_2. Note that, from (4-47)(a), the value of λ_2 is found to be $\frac{2}{13}$ (>0), which is of correct sign. But since one of the constraints is violated, this solution is invalidated.

CASE 4: $\lambda_1 \neq 0$, $\lambda_2 = 0$. The procedure here is the same as in Case 3, above. Since $\lambda_1 \neq 0$, from (4-47)(b) we know that $x_1 + x_2 = 2$. Since $\lambda_2 = 0$, from (4-47)(a) we find

$$-2x_1 + 4 = \lambda_1,$$
$$-2x_2 + 6 = \lambda_1,$$

and therefore $-2x_1 + 2x_2 = 2$. The unique values of x_1 and x_2 implied by the assumptions that $\lambda_1 \neq 0$ and $\lambda_2 = 0$ come from

$$x_1 + x_2 = 2,$$
$$-2x_1 + 2x_2 = 2.$$

Using Cramer's rule again,

$$x_1^* = \begin{vmatrix} 2 & 1 \\ 2 & 2 \end{vmatrix} \bigg/ \begin{vmatrix} 1 & 1 \\ -2 & 2 \end{vmatrix} = \frac{2}{4} = \frac{1}{2},$$

$$x_2^* = \begin{vmatrix} 1 & 2 \\ -2 & 2 \end{vmatrix} \bigg/ \begin{vmatrix} 1 & 1 \\ -2 & 2 \end{vmatrix} = \frac{6}{4} = \frac{3}{2}.$$

The first constraint is met, since $\lambda_1 \neq 0$ means that $x_1 + x_2 = 0$. Is the second constraint also met? From (4-47)(c),

$$2x_1^* + 3x_2^* - 12 = 2(\tfrac{1}{2}) + 3(\tfrac{3}{2}) - 12 = 5\tfrac{1}{2} - 12 = -6\tfrac{1}{2} < 0.$$

This test is passed. What about the nonnegativity of the λ^*'s? We know about λ_2^*; by assumption it is zero. From (4-47)(a),

$$-2(\tfrac{1}{2}) + 4 = \lambda_1^*; \qquad \lambda_1^* = 3 > 0.$$

Therefore $x_1^* = \tfrac{1}{2}$, $x_2^* = \tfrac{3}{2}$, $x_3^* = 0$, $\lambda_1^* = 3$, and $\lambda_2^* = 0$ satisfy the Kuhn-Tucker necessary conditions for a maximum to

$$f(x_1, x_2, x_3) = -x_1^2 - x_2^2 - x_3^2 + 4x_1 + 6x_2$$

subject to (a) $x_1 + x_2 \leq 2$ and (b) $2x_1 + 3x_2 \leq 12$. Since

$$H = \begin{bmatrix} -2 & 0 & 0 \\ 0 & -2 & 0 \\ 0 & 0 & -2 \end{bmatrix},$$

the principal minors alternate, beginning negative, and therefore (Appendix 4.1) $f(X)$ is a concave function. The constraints are linear and hence convex. Thus, from (4-45), the Kuhn-Tucker conditions in (4-47) are also sufficient for a maximum.

Again, the ease of solution of each of the possible cases depends entirely on the structure of the first partial derivative equations. The reader may note that in the Kuhn-Tucker approach each constraint contributes an equation of the form of (4-45)(b); and for each such equation the *two* options $\lambda_i = 0$ and $\lambda_i \neq 0$ must be examined. Hence if there are m constraints, there will be 2^m cases to be examined individually. (In the immediately preceding example with two constraints, each of the $2^2 = 4$ cases was shown explicitly.)

The four cases have straightforward geometric interpretations. We can continue to use Figure 4.12, since x_3 plays essentially no role in the constrained maximization. In Case 1, when both λ's are required to be nonzero, both constraints are being imposed as equalities and the value of $f(X)$ is found at the point where the equations intersect. This is the point labeled C_1 in the figure. In Case 2, with both λ's set equal to zero, the completely unconstrained maximum is found; this is point A, as before. In Case 3, when $\lambda_1 = 0$ but $\lambda_2 \neq 0$, we are in effect finding the maximum along the boundary given by the second constraint and ignoring the first constraint entirely—point C_3. In Case 4, when $\lambda_1 \neq 0$ and $\lambda_2 = 0$, the reverse is true; we are maximizing subject to the first constraint alone—point R, as before. That is, the various combinations of λ_1 and λ_2 equal to and not equal to zero allow exploration along the boundaries for local maxima. In each case, once that particular maximum is found, we then see whether or not it satisfies all other constraints in the Kuhn-Tucker necessary conditions. This means considering both original constraints as well as the nonnegativity requirements on the resulting λ's.

Minimization problems using the Kuhn-Tucker approach

In view of the discussion leading up to the results in (4-37) for minimization problems, we can analyze such problems subject to inequality constraints in the same (Kuhn-Tucker) manner. The only (but important) requirement is that they be in *standard form*. That is, minimize $f(x_1, \ldots, x_n)$ subject to $g(x_1, \ldots, x_n) \geq c$. Let $h(x_1, \ldots, x_n) \equiv g(x_1, \ldots, x_n) - c$; then the constraint can be expressed as $h(x_1, \ldots, x_n) \geq 0$. Form the Lagrangean function after *subtracting* a nonnegative variable from the left-hand side of the constraint to make it an equality:

$$L = f(x_1, \ldots, x_n) - \lambda[h(x_1, \ldots, x_n) - s^2].$$

Parallel to (4-39), we have

(a) $\dfrac{\partial L}{\partial x_j} \equiv L_j = f_j - \lambda h_j = 0 \qquad (j = 1, \ldots, n),$

(b) $\dfrac{\partial L}{\partial \lambda} \equiv L_\lambda = -[h(x_1, \ldots, x_n) - s^2] = 0,$ \hfill (4-48)

(c) $\dfrac{\partial L}{\partial s} \equiv L_s = 2\lambda s = 0,$

from which conditions exactly analogous to (4-40) can be deduced (except, of course, for the direction of the inequality):

(a) $\qquad f_j - \lambda h_j = 0 \qquad (j = 1, \ldots, n),$

(b) $\quad \lambda[h(x_1, \ldots, x_n)] = 0$ \hfill (4-49)

(c) $\quad h(x_1, \ldots, x_n) \quad \geq 0$

Hence the Kuhn-Tucker conditions:

The necessary conditions for a point $X^* = [x_1^*, \ldots, x_n^*]'$ to be a relative minimum of $f(x_1, \ldots, x_n)$ subject to $h(x_1, \ldots, x_n) \geq 0$ are that a nonnegative λ exists such that it and X^* satisfy (4-49). \hfill (4-50)

The generalization to m constraints is identical to the statement in (4-45), except, again, for the direction of the inequalities in conditions (c)

For the minimization problem, these Kuhn-Tucker necessary conditions are also sufficient if $f(x_1, \ldots, x_n)$ is a *convex* function and the constraint $h(x_1, \ldots, x_n)$ [or constraints, $h_i(X)$] are *concave*, so that the region defined by them is a convex set. And the minimum will be an *absolute* one if f is *strictly* convex.

For example, consider the problem of minimizing $f(x_1, x_2, x_3) = x_1^2 + x_2^2 + x_3^2$ subject to (a) $x_1 + x_2 + x_3 \geq 0$ and (b) $2x_1 + 2x_3 \geq 2$—that is, $2x_1 + 2x_3 - 2 \geq 0$. We need the following derivatives:

$$\begin{array}{lll} f_1 = 2x_1, & h_1^1 = 1, & h_1^2 = 2, \\ f_2 = 2x_2, & h_2^1 = 1, & h_2^2 = 0, \\ f_3 = 2x_3, & h_3^1 = 1, & h_3^2 = 2. \end{array}$$

Following (4-45), reversing the direction of the inequalities in (c)—parallel to (4-49) for the single-constraint case:

(a) $\begin{cases} 2x_1 - \lambda_1 - 2\lambda_2 = 0, \\ 2x_2 - \lambda_1 \qquad\quad = 0, \\ 2x_3 - \lambda_1 - 2\lambda_2 = 0; \end{cases}$

(b) $\begin{cases} \lambda_1(\ x_1 + x_2 + x_3) = 0, \\ \lambda_2(2x_1 + 2x_3 - 2\ ) = 0; \end{cases}$ \hfill (4-51)

(c) $\begin{cases} x_1 + x_2 + x_3 \geq 0, \\ 2x_1 + 2x_3 - 2 \geq 0. \end{cases}$

As in the previous maximization problem, we begin with the implications of the relations in (4-51)(b).

CASE 1: $\lambda_1 \neq 0$, $\lambda_2 \neq 0$. Then $x_1 + x_2 + x_3 = 0$ and $2x_1 + 2x_3 = 2$. From the first equation, $x_1 = -x_2 - x_3$; substituting into the second equation, $x_2^* = -1$, and therefore $x_1 = 1 - x_3$. From the second equation in (a) we find that this means $\lambda_1^* = -2$, which violates the nonnegativity requirement on the λ_i.

CASE 2: $\lambda_1 = 0$, $\lambda_2 = 0$. Then, from (4-51)(a), $x_1 = x_2 = x_3 = 0$ and the second inequality in (4-51)(c) is violated.

CASE 3: $\lambda_1 = 0$, $\lambda_2 \neq 0$. From (4-51)(a), this means $2x_1 = 2\lambda_2$; $2x_2 = 0$—that is, $x_2 = 0$; and $2x_3 = 2\lambda_2$, or $x_1 = x_3$. From the second relation in (b), since $\lambda_2 \neq 0$, $2x_1 + 2x_3 = 2$, or $4x_1 = 2$, $x_1^* = \frac{1}{2}$ and therefore $x_3^* = \frac{1}{2}$. As a consequence $\lambda_2^* = \frac{1}{2} > 0$ and the first inequality in (4-51)(c) is satisfied.

CASE 4: $\lambda_1 \neq 0$, $\lambda_2 = 0$. From (a), $2x_1 = \lambda_1$, $2x_2 = \lambda_1$, $2x_3 = \lambda_1$—that is, $x_1 = x_2 = x_3$. Since, from (b), $x_1 + x_2 + x_3 = 0$, this means $x_1^* = x_2^* = x_3^* = 0$, which violates the second constraint in (4-51)(c).

Hence the results in Case 3, $x_1^* = \frac{1}{2}$, $x_2^* = 0$, and $x_3^* = \frac{1}{2}$, are the only ones that satisfy all the Kuhn-Tucker necessary conditions for a minimum to $x_1^2 + x_2^2 + x_3^2$ subject to $x_1 + x_2 + x_3 \geq 0$ and $2x_1 + 2x_3 \geq 2$. Since

$$H = \begin{bmatrix} 2 & 0 & 0 \\ 0 & 2 & 0 \\ 0 & 0 & 2 \end{bmatrix},$$

$|H_1| = 2 > 0$, $|H_2| = 4 > 0$, and $|H_3| = |H| = 8 > 0$, the function $f(x_1, x_2, x_3)$ is convex. Moreover, since both constraints are linear and hence concave, we know that these conditions are also sufficient for a minimum.

SUMMARY

In this chapter we have seen how the fundamental logic of the calculus rules for finding stationary points of a simple function of one or two variables—$y = f(x)$ or $y = f(x_1, x_2)$—and distinguishing maxima from minima (from neither) can be extended to more realistic problems. Initially this means to a function of many independent variables, $y = f(x_1, \ldots, x_n)$. For this purpose, the concept of the total differential of y was essential, and for the question of separating the maxima from the minima—that is, establishing the sign of the second total differential of y—it was necessary to introduce the concepts and terminology of quadratic forms.

The next extension was to remove the independence among the variables in $f(x_1, \ldots, x_n)$ by at first one and then several constraints in the form of equations. The first-order conditions, necessary for any kind of stationary point, were seen to involve a proportionality requirement between the first partial derivatives of f and those of the constraint h (or constraints h_i), plus the constraint or constraints considered explicitly. We saw that the method of Lagrange multipliers is simply an easily remembered procedure for generating the first-order requirements. An analysis of second-order conditions—to determine what kinds of stationary points had been found—required that we establish the sign of a quadratic form whose variables are subject to a particular linear relation (or set of relations); this was the second differential test.

Finally, we considered the implications of inequalities rather than equations as constraints on the variables in $f(x_1, \ldots, x_n)$. We found that the fundamental definitions of convexity and concavity of functions and the basic content of convex set theory helped us understand the implications of inequality constraints. Three approaches to the many-variable, many-inequality constraint problem were investigated; two of them rely on the methods developed for equality constraints, although the rationale differs.

Initially the constraints can be ignored completely; with luck the absolute maximum or minimum will satisfy all constraints. If it does, the problem is solved; if it does not, we must move on to either of the next two methods.

The direct Lagrange multiplier approach to inequality constraints is straightforward: ignore the fact that they are inequalities—go right ahead as if they were all equations. The extent to which this turns out to be proper procedure is then measured by the signs of the Lagrange multipliers associated with each of the constraints. The problem generally then must be redone, ignoring some of those constraints that were explicitly included as equations, since a "better" result can be obtained if they are strict inequalities.

The Kuhn-Tucker approach to inequality constraints is to convert them to equalities by explicit addition (or subtraction, depending on the direction of the inequality) of a slack variable whose function is simply to make up the difference (if any) between one side of the constraint and the other. The problem then is exactly in a form for which Lagrange multipliers are suited, and it turns out that the slack variables can easily be eliminated from the first-order conditions. The relations that remain in the necessary conditions, however, are somewhat more complicated than in the case where the constraints are equalities from the beginning, and finding values of the x's and λ's to satisfy them is less straightforward.

The question of maximum versus minimum via second-order conditions becomes even more complicated, and when possible an appeal to the concavity-convexity properties of the function f and the constraints h_i settles the matter.

Also, it should be emphasized that necessary conditions by themselves *can* be very useful. They allow us to eliminate points as possible maxima or minima if it can be demonstrated that those points cannot fulfill the conditions. Even though a point that meets the necessary conditions *may not* be a maximum (for example), a point that does not satisfy the conditions *cannot* be a maximum. Moreover, the necessary conditions sometimes have an interesting interpretation in the context of the problem being dealt with; they may serve to characterize the stationary points in a way that provides useful insight into the nature of the optimum, even if it cannot easily be found.

In later chapters we will see how the addition of one more set of inequality constraints converts the problem of Section 4.8 into the completely general *mathematical programming* problem; in view of the relative complexity of the results of Section 4.8, the monumental simplifications that are possible for the all-linear case—a *linear programming* problem—are particularly appealing. We will also see that in certain less simple cases—for example, for *quadratic programming* problems—the general Kuhn-Tucker approach leads to a *relatively* simple set of necessary conditions.

APPENDIX 4.1

Taylor's Series, Convexity and Concavity, and the Sign of the Second Total Differential

Taylor's series or Taylor's expansion for a function $y = f(x)$ says that an approximation to the value of the function in the neighborhood of a particular point $x = x_0$ can be found to any degree of accuracy required, provided that the values of $f(x)$ *and its derivatives* are known at the point $x = x_0$. Denote the "nearby" value of the independent variable by $x_0 + dx$. Then the Taylor expansion is [40]

---

[40] The notation $n!$ (read "n factorial") means $(n)(n - 1)(n - 2)\cdots(3)(2)(1)$; that is, it is the product of all integers from n down to 1.

$$f(x_0 + dx) = f(x_0) + f'(x_0) \, dx + \left(\frac{1}{2!}\right) f''(x_0)(dx)^2 + \left(\frac{1}{3!}\right) f'''(x_0)(dx)^3$$

$$+ \cdots + \left(\frac{1}{n!}\right) f^{(n)}(x_0)(dx)^n + \cdots. \tag{4-52}$$

That is, the value of the function at a point near x_0 is the sum of a series of terms involving progressively higher-order derivatives evaluated at x_0 multiplied by dx raised to ascending powers. If dx—the difference between the new value and the old value of the independent variable—is very small, then higher powers of dx will become negligible, especially when divided by correspondingly higher-order factorials.[41] Thus a *first approximation* to the *difference* in the value of the function at x_0 and at $x_0 + dx$ is given by

$$f(x_0 + dx) - f(x_0) = f'(x_0) \, dx + \tfrac{1}{2}f''(x_0)(dx)^2. \tag{4-53}$$

Suppose now that x_0 represents a stationary point—one at which $f'(x)$ is zero. Then clearly the *sign* of the change in the value of the function given in (4-53) depends entirely on the sign of $f''(x_0)$, since $f'(x_0) = 0$ and both $\tfrac{1}{2}$ and $(dx)^2$ are necessarily positive. Hence if $f''(x_0) < 0$, $f(x_0)$ is larger than $f(x_0 + dx)$ for *any* small change in x, and x_0 must represent a maximum. Put differently, the function $f(x)$ is strictly *concave* in the neighborhood of x_0. Similarly, if $f''(x_0) > 0$, x_0 represents a minimum point, since the function is larger for any variation dx; the function is therefore strictly *convex* in the neighborhood of x_0. Thus the convexity or concavity of $f(x)$ in the neighborhood of x_0 is established through the sign of $f''(x_0)$. This corresponds exactly to our intuitive understanding in Section 3.2.

Taylor's expansion can be extended to a function of n variables. Let $X^* = [x_1^*, \ldots, x_n^*]'$ be a point at which the first total differential of the function is zero—that is, $df^* = 0$; and let $(X^* + dX)$ represent the "nearby" point $[x_1^* + dx_1, \ldots, x_n^* + dx_n]'$. The n-variable statement corresponding to (4-52) is

$$f(X^* + dX) = f(X^*) + df^* + \left(\frac{1}{2!}\right) d^2 f^* + \left(\frac{1}{3!}\right) d^3 f^*$$

$$+ \cdots + \left(\frac{1}{n!}\right) d^n f^* + \cdots, \tag{4-54}$$

and the approximation to the change in the function as a result of the displacement dX, parallel to (4-53), is

$$f(X^* + dX) - f(X^*) = df^* + \tfrac{1}{2}d^2 f^*. \tag{4-55}$$

Again, since X^* has been chosen such that $df^* = 0$—so that necessary conditions for a maximum or minimum are satisfied—the sign of the change

---

[41] For example: $3! = 6$, $4! = 24$, $5! = 120$, $6! = 720$, $\ldots$, $10! = 3,628,800$. (!)

in the value of $f(x_1, \ldots, x_n)$ depends entirely on the sign of d^2f^*, the second total differential evaluated at X^*. But we have seen (Sections 4.1 and 4.2) that the second total differential is a quadratic form in $dx_1, \ldots, dx_n$, and we have, in (4-9) of Section 4.1, rules for establishing the signs of quadratic forms. For d^2f, these depend on the principal minors of the Hessian matrix evaluated at X^*:

$$H^* = \begin{bmatrix} f_{11}^* & f_{12}^* & \cdots & f_{1n}^* \\ f_{21}^* & f_{22}^* & \cdots & f_{2n}^* \\ \vdots & & & \\ f_{n1}^* & f_{n2}^* & \cdots & f_{nn}^* \end{bmatrix}.$$

Specifically, if the principal minors alternate, beginning negative, then $d^2f^* < 0$ and, from (4-55), the function is larger at X^* than at $X^* + dX$. Hence X^* represents a local maximum; the function is *concave* in the neighborhood of X^*. If the principal minors of H^* are all positive, then $d^2f^* > 0$ and X^* represents a local minimum, since $f(X^*)$ is smaller than $f(X^* + dX)$. The function is thus *convex* in the neighborhood of X^*.

Reference to (4-52) shows that the Taylor expansion provides a criterion to cover the case in which *both* $f'(x_0)$ and $f''(x_0)$ are zero. The value of the difference, $f(x_0 + dx) - f(x_0)$, then depends on the sign of $f'''(x_0)$ or, should that also be zero, on the sign of the first nonzero higher-order derivative. However, the $(dx)^3$, $(dx)^4$, $\ldots$, $(dx)^n$ terms in (4-52) add a complication. Clearly, if the first nonzero derivative is of *even* power—$f^{(4)}(x_0), f^{(6)}(x_0), \ldots$— then, since $(dx)^4, (dx)^6, \ldots$ are necessarily positive, the sign of $f(x^* + dx) - f(x^*)$ is the same as the sign of that derivative. If the first nonzero derivative is of *odd* power, however—such as $f'''(x_0)$ or $f^{(5)}(x_0)$—then the sign of $(dx)^3$ or $(dx)^5$ will depend on whether dx is positive or negative and cannot be established unambiguously in advance. Hence the following general rule:

If $f'(x_0) = f''(x_0) = \cdots = f^{(n-1)}(x_0) = 0$ and $f^{(n)}(x_0) \neq 0$, then $f(x)$ has a stationary value at x_0 that is a *point of inflection* if n is odd and that is a maximum if n is even and $f^{(n)}(x_0) < 0$ or a minimum if n is even and $f^{(n)}(x_0) > 0$.   (4-56)

The necessary conditions and the sufficient conditions for a function of one variable set out in Table 3.3 for the unconstrained maximum or minimum problems in the text follow from (4-56) when $f^{(n)}(x_0) \equiv f''(x_0) \neq 0$. Thus the criteria in (4-56) are both necessary and sufficient for isolating maxima and minima; they have simply taken care of the ambiguous cases such as those in Figures 3.9, 3.14(a), and 3.14(b) in the text.

In exactly the same way, (4-54) provides criteria for the n-variable case when $d^2f^* = 0$; we must examine the signs of higher-order total differentials evaluated at $X^* = [x_1^*, \ldots, x_n^*]$. Since the structure of d^3f, d^4f, and so on becomes much more complex, and since such cases are not often met in practice, we will not pursue this possibility further.

PROBLEMS

1. Decide whether each of the following quadratic forms is (1) positive definite, (2) negative definite, or (3) neither.
   (a) $-x_1^2 - x_2^2 - 4x_3^2 + x_1x_2 + 2x_2x_3$.
   (b) $2x_1^2 + 6x_2^2 - 6x_1x_2$.
   (c) $x_1^2 + x_2^2 + x_3^2 - x_1x_2 - x_2x_3 - x_1x_3$.
2. (a) Maximize $6x_1^2 + 5x_2^2$ subject to the constraint that $x_1 + 5x_2 = 3$.
   (b) Minimize the same function subject to the same constraint.
3. Find the maximum or minimum of

$$y = -x_1^2 - x_2^2 - x_3^2 + 4x_1 + 6x_2 + 2x_3$$

   subject to $2x_1 + 3x_2 + x_3 = 10$.
4. Maximize or minimize $y = 5x_1^2 + 6x_2^2 - 3x_1x_2$ subject to $2x_1 + 3x_2 = 58$.
5. Maximize or minimize $4x_1^2 + 2x_2^2 + x_3^2 - 4x_1x_2$ subject to the following two constraints: $x_1 + x_2 + x_3 = 15$ and $2x_1 - x_2 + 2x_3 = 20$.
6. Find the maximum or minimum of y in Problem 3, subject to both $2x_1 + 3x_2 + x_3 = 10$ and $x_1 + 2x_2 + 4x_3 = 7$.
7. Minimize $6x_1^2 + 5x_2^2$ (a) subject to the constraint that $x_1 + 5x_2 \leq 3$, (b) subject to the constraint that $x_1 + 5x_2 \geq 3$.
8. Find the maximum of $2x_1^2 + 12x_1x_2 - 7x_2^2$ (a) subject to $2x_1 + 5x_2 = 98$, (b) subject to $2x_1 + 5x_2 \leq 98$.
9. Do Problem 3 as if the constraint were $2x_1 + 3x_2 + x_3 \leq 10$.
10. Do Problem 6 as if both constraints were "less than or equal to" inequalities.

REFERENCES

1. Allen, R. G. D., *Mathematical Analysis for Economists*. London: Macmillan & Co., Ltd., 1938. (Also Papermac No. 34, 1964.)
2. Chiang, A. C., *Fundamental Methods of Mathematical Economics*. New York: McGraw-Hill, Inc., 1967.
3. Courant, R., *Differential and Integral Calculus*, trans. E. J. McShane. New York: Interscience Publishers, Inc., vol. I, 2d ed., 1937, vol. II, 1936.
4. Draper, J. E., and J. S. Klingman, *Mathematical Analysis: Business and Economic Applications*. New York: Harper & Row, Publishers, 1968.
5. Hadley, G., *Linear Algebra*. Reading, Mass.: Addison-Wesley Publishing Company, Inc., 1961.
6. ———, *Nonlinear and Dynamic Programming*. Reading, Mass.: Addison-Wesley Publishing Company, Inc., 1964.
7. Teichroew, D., *An Introduction to Management Science: Deterministic Models*. New York: John Wiley & Sons, Inc., 1964.
8. Yamane, T., *Mathematics for Economists: An Elementary Survey*. Englewood Cliffs, N.J.: Prentice-Hall, Inc., 1962.

5

OPTIMIZATION IN INVENTORY
AND QUEUING MODELS

In this chapter we explore the fundamental structure of two models taken from the field of operations research. The object is to illustrate how, ultimately, the problem becomes one of optimization—perhaps with several variables and perhaps with constraints. The reader should gain a feeling for the levels of complexity in such problems that can be handled with the optimization techniques presented thus far in this book, and he should also realize that more complex and hence probably more realistic situations will require, for example, an ability to deal with many inequality constraints, including, perhaps, nonnegativity requirements on the variables. The more modern techniques presented in the next four chapters are designed for precisely this kind of problem.

In presenting typical but very simple inventory and queuing models here, we explain briefly the logic of the setting within which the optimization problems arise. The reader whose interest is aroused should turn to any good operations research textbook,[1] since these models themselves are not our primary interest here. The reader who is more interested in the development of further techniques for more complex constrained optimization problems can proceed directly to Chapter 6.

[1] Several are listed among the references at the end of this chapter; Hillier and Lieberman [8] and Wagner [22] are especially recommended. Even further detail is provided in the various books listed that deal with inventory and/or queuing theory and problems.

5.1. INVENTORY MODELS: INTRODUCTION

The fundamental approach employed in inventory models is useful for analyzing and solving a wide variety of business problems; the essence of these problems is that a decision must be made on how much of something to undertake (produce, purchase, stockpile) when faced with two or more kinds of costs that push in opposite directions—that is, when there are both economies and diseconomies of large undertakings. The fundamental problem typically arises in situations dealing with inventory decisions, and this becomes a useful framework within which to discuss the approach.

A manufacturer uses several inputs, which he may either purchase from one or several suppliers or produce himself. The inputs are used only as quickly as production occurs—one foil container is needed to package each frozen cheesecake turned out, four jet engines are used on each Boeing 747 aircraft. Yet in many situations it is cheaper (per unit) to buy or produce in large quantity—for example, because the supplier offers price discounts on large orders or because of setup costs involved in preparing to produce the part supplied. The machine that stamps and molds foil cheesecake containers may also produce packages of other sizes and shapes, a certain time being required to adjust and convert from one style to another. From that point of view it is more economical to produce a large number once a month than a small number every few days. On the other hand, large inventories (items waiting to be used) can be costly in many ways. They may be bulky, thus taking up space and getting in the way; they may be valuable and require heavy insurance; they may be subject to damage and/or deterioration; and of course they represent tied-up capital.

In this chapter we will see how a family of models can be developed to find the best "trade-offs" between these various costs. We will see that it is necessary to distinguish cases in which the demand for the final product (such as cheesecakes or Boeing 747's) is assumed known in advance with certainty from those in which it is only estimated or forecast and hence known in advance only probabilistically. Clearly both situations arise in practice—in the former case, for example, the manufacturer only produces when he has a fixed number of orders on hand; in the latter case he tries to anticipate demand by producing in advance. The models themselves are extremely simple in concept, involving basically the areas of common geometric figures, and in the certain-demand case simple calculus is sufficient. For the uncertain-demand case we will need a few elementary principles from the calculus of finite differences and a new rule for differentiating a particular kind of function. These are presented in the sections in which they are needed. We also explore the question of the sensitivity of some of the results—that is, the way in which they are affected by changes in the known parameters in the problem. This kind of question can also be answered through the use of fairly elementary calculus.

5.2. SIMPLE INVENTORY MODELS WITH KNOWN DEMAND

The fundamental economic lot size problem

Consider a manufacturer who is faced with the problem of balancing the two kinds of costs mentioned above. Assume in fact that he himself produces the input item (say, a molded plastic carrying case for a portable typewriter) as well as the final product (the typewriter). The larger the number of cases stamped out at one time on the case machine, the smaller the setup or changeover costs per time period, but the higher the inventory (or holding) costs per time period.[2] Let Q denote the lot size—that is, the number of cases produced in one run—and let D be the number of final products (typewriters) produced per time period. For convenience we let the time period be one year, simply so that we can speak of *annual* demand, production, and so on. Note that D is a known number (demand is assumed to be known with certainty). If there are d days per year on which typewriters can be produced, and since each typewriter uses one case, then D/d cases will be needed each day.

The fundamental situation can be shown on an inventory-time diagram, with Q on the vertical axis and time on the horizontal axis. If the manufacturer produced (provided that it was possible) all cases for a year's production of typewriters at one time, Q would be equal to D. Then an approximation to the inventory level over time would appear as in Figure 5.1. Actually the one-year interval on the time axis is divided into d equal

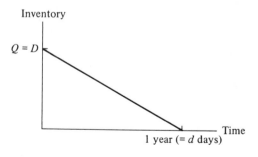

Figure 5.1.   Once-a-year Production for Inventory

[2] Production of one million cases in one "run" would spread the setup costs (incurred only once) over one million cases and also over a very long time period, but the inventory on hand would be excessive for quite a while.

parts, representing the production days, and the sloping line can be thought of as connecting d different vertical heights, showing inventory remaining at a given point in each day. It is thus an approximation to a step function in which there is a reduction of D/d cases from inventory during the course of each day.

If less than the entire yearly amount D is produced in a run, then several batches will be needed over a year's time, and the picture will be as shown schematically in Figure 5.2. If Q are produced for inventory each time a

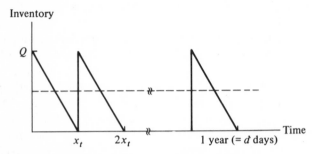

Figure 5.2.   Several Production Runs for Inventory

batch is made, the number of such production runs per year will be D/Q. (If n cases were used for each finished product, the number of runs would be nD/Q.) It should be clear that the *average* amount of inventory on hand on any given day is just $\frac{1}{2}Q$, shown as the dotted horizontal line in Figure 5.2. Geometrically, the total inventory (measured in item-days) over the period x_t days is the area of the first triangle—$\frac{1}{2}Qx_t$. Thus the average inventory on any given day in the x_t period is just $(\frac{1}{2}Qx_t)/x_t = \frac{1}{2}Q$ items. Since each of the triangles in the one-year period looks the same, this is the average amount of inventory on each day during the entire year. Let the costs associated with holding item in inventory for one year be c_1 (the units are dollars/item-year); then $f(Q) = c_1Q/2$ represents annual inventory holding costs. Since $c_1 > 0$, annual inventory costs are clearly a linear function of Q with a positive slope; the smaller the average inventory, the lower are these costs (Figure 5.3).

A very low average inventory would result if Q were equal to D/d—that is, if each run produced just enough for one day's production. In terms of Figure 5.2, x_t would equal 1 day, and there would be $D/Q = D/(D/d) = d$ small triangles, each with a height of only D/d units. However, since there would necessarily be d production runs, the setup costs over the year would be high. Let c_2 represent the setup cost for one run (the units are simply dollars); annual costs associated with runs of size Q are $g(Q) = c_2(D/Q)$. Clearly, these costs decrease as Q increases, in contrast to the inventory holding costs (Figure 5.4).

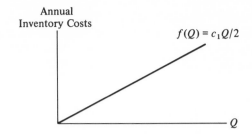

Figure 5.3.   Annual Inventory Holding Costs

In this initial simplified problem, we assume that the inventory decision—the size of Q—is to be made on the basis of these two kinds of costs
alone. Thus, let c_A be total annual costs; these can be represented as follows:

$$c_A = f(Q) + g(Q) = \frac{c_1 Q}{2} + \frac{c_2 D}{Q}, \qquad (5\text{-}1)$$

where c_1, c_2, and D are known. We take the minimization of these annual
costs to be the policy objective; this is to be achieved through appropriate
selection of Q. Since c_A is a function of only one variable, Q, the calculus is
extremely straightforward (see Section 3.2). The necessary condition on
the first derivative is that $dc_A/dQ = c_1/2 - c_2 D/Q^2 = 0$; therefore $c_1/2 =
c_2 D/Q^2$ or $Q^2 = 2c_2 D/c_1$ and[3]

$$Q^* = \sqrt{\frac{2c_2 D}{c_1}}. \qquad (5\text{-}2)$$

This result is known as the economic (optimum) lot size formula; it is
relevant only in situations for which c_1, c_2, and D are known. Note that in
arriving at (5-2) we learn from the *necessary* condition that a characteristic

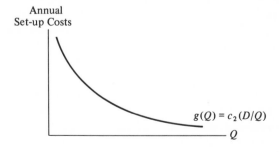

Figure 5.4.   Annual Setup Costs

[3] The second-order condition is that the second derivative be positive for a minimum.
Here $d^2 c_A/dQ^2 = 2c_2 D/Q^3$, which is positive for positive c_2, D, and Q. Thus Q^* in (5-2)
represents a minimum.

of the minimum will be $c_1/2 = c_2D/Q^2$. Multiplying by Q gives $c_1Q/2 = c_2D/Q$ or $f(Q) = g(Q)$; that is, the minimum must necessarily occur where the two cost curves intersect (Figure 5.5). By substitution into (5-1) and algebra, it follows then that the minimum annual cost is

$$c_A^* = \sqrt{2c_1c_2D}. \tag{5-3}$$

This represents the total annual cost associated with holding inventory and setting up the machine when the optimum lot size, Q^*, is produced in each run.

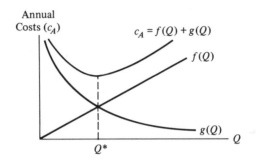

Figure 5.5.   Annual Inventory and Setup Costs

Several characteristics of this extremely simplified representation should be made explicit. In Figure 5.2, the fact that each of the triangles has a right angle (that is, that its left-hand side parallels the vertical axis) means that all inventory in each batch is assumed to be available at the same time. If the items are *purchased* in lots from a supplier, this assumption is realistic. If they are manufactured by the final-product producer, it may be an oversimplification. Later we will relax the assumption by allowing the inventory amount Q to build up *over a period* of time rather than appearing *at an instant* of time. This will alter the left-hand sides of the triangles.

In Figure 5.2 it is also assumed that inventory items are used at a *constant rate* per day. This is what allows us to draw the hypotenuses of these figures as straight lines. Although this assumption seems less offensive than the previous one, the reader should note that a policy of irregular inventory item use would lead to *curves* rather than straight lines connecting the heights Q and the widths x_t. If the rate of use were greater at the beginning of each period (for example, a decreasing function of time), the curves would be convex; if the rate of use were heavier at the end of each period (for example, an increasing function of time), the curves would be concave.

In either case, integral calculus for the areas under curves would replace the simple formula for the areas of the triangles that are needed for the average inventory in $f(Q)$.

Introduction of shortage costs

If we consider the possibility of shortages of the item in question—that is, of *negative inventories*—we see that this has the effect of changing the *position* but not the *basic shape* of the triangles in Figure 5.2. In essence, the horizontal (time) axis is simply shifted upward, as in Figure 5.6(a). Over the period x_t there are now two kinds of days [see Figure 5.6(b)].

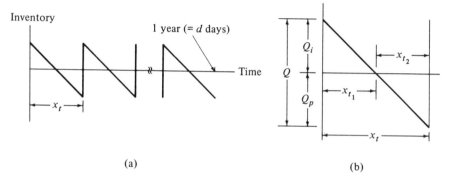

(a)   (b)

Figure 5.6.   (a) Several Production Runs for Inventory; Shortages Allowed; (b) Detail from (a)

During those in the interval x_{t_1}, the items are drawn from inventory as needed; during the days in the interval x_{t_2}, orders for the item are being accumulated but not filled. (For example, the typewriters are completed *except for* their carrying cases.) Then, at the end of the interval x_t ($= x_{t_1} + x_{t_2}$) an amount Q is produced (or delivered). Unlike the preceding example, in which *all* of Q went into inventory (and hence contributed to the inventory costs), the amount Q is now divided between that which goes into inventory, Q_i (the height *above* the horizontal axis), and that which is immediately taken to satisfy past orders or unfilled demand, Q_p (the height *below* the horizontal axis). Assume that it is possible to obtain an estimate of the cost of being without one item for one day. This may be made up of penalty costs in a contract (if the item is purchased from a supplier); estimates of costs of downtime on a production line, if production is actually halted; loss of customer goodwill for delays in delivery; and so on. Denote this cost by c_3, after converting it to the same units as c_1—since c_1 was dollars per item-year, we therefore put shortage cost per item-day on the same basis by multiplying by d, the numbers of days in a production year.[4]

The problem now has two facets; along with deciding how large each production run Q should be (which is, in fact, the decision on how often to produce), we must now also decide how each production run will be divided between inventory (Q_i) and satisfaction of past demand (Q_p).[5] When $Q_p = 0$, we have the situation of the example in Figure 5.2. If $Q_i = 0$ (highly unlikely), the entire amount in each run would be used for past unfilled orders, and the figure corresponding to 5.2 or 5.6 would have a series of triangles entirely *below* the horizontal axis with the right angle in their upper right corners.

In this new problem we therefore are concerned with the areas of triangles (1) above the time axis (representing items in inventory) and (2) below the same axis (representing items in shortage). The total amount of *inventory* over each period x_t is $\frac{1}{2}Q_i x_{t_1}$ (formula for the area of a triangle). Thus, the *average* daily inventory over the period (x_t days) is $(\frac{1}{2}Q_i x_{t_1})/x_t$. As before, this is typical for any day in any of the x_t-day periods during the year; it is the average daily inventory over the year. Thus *annual* inventory costs are $c_1(\frac{1}{2}Q_i x_{t_1})/x_t$. Similarly the total amount of *shortage* over each x_t period is $\frac{1}{2}Q_p x_{t_2}$; *average* daily shortage is $(\frac{1}{2}Q_p x_{t_2})/x_t$. This represents every day in the year and thus *annual* shortage costs are $c_3(\frac{1}{2}Q_p x_{t_2})/x_t$. Finally, since (D/Q) runs must be produced during the year, *annual* setup costs are $c_2(D/Q)$. The sum of these three different kinds of costs incurred over a year is thus

$$c_A = \frac{c_1(\frac{1}{2}Q_i x_{t_1})}{x_t} + c_2\left(\frac{D}{Q}\right) + \frac{c_3(\frac{1}{2}Q_p x_{t_2})}{x_t}. \tag{5-4}$$

It is these costs that we wish to minimize by the choice of a correct inventory policy—that is, by a choice of *both* Q_i and Q_p. Clearly, the variables in (5-4) are not all independent. First,

$$Q = Q_i + Q_p \tag{5-5}$$

(so that, for example, the choice can also be stated as that of finding both Q and Q_i or both Q and Q_p). Second, Figure 5.6 indicates the nature of the

---

[4] In terms of consistency of the cost functions, it is immaterial whether a day, week, month, or year is used as the time unit. What is necessary is that c_1 and c_3 be quoted for the same time period, which must also be that of the demand figure, D. However, since the basis of inventory analysis is to consider holding items *over a period*, it makes sense to select a time unit that is "relatively long"—so that, for example, more than one run can occur and thus the impact of setup costs is made clearer.

[5] This is often termed an (s, S) policy in inventory model literature, where s is what we have termed Q_p and S is the same as Q_i [refer to Figure 5.6(b)]. The policy is then as follows: when the inventory level reaches s, order an amount equal to $S + s$ (or $S - s$, if one uses the convention of measuring shortages, s, as negative amounts).

dependence between Q_i, Q_p, x_{t_1}, and x_{t_2}. The larger Q_i relative to Q, the larger x_{t_1} relative to x_t. The exact relationship between these variables can be obtained from a simple observation about similar triangles,[6] namely that their corresponding sides are proportional. In particular

$$\frac{x_{t_1}}{x_t} = \frac{Q_i}{Q} \quad \text{or} \quad x_{t_1} = \frac{x_t Q_i}{Q}$$

and   (5-6)

$$\frac{x_{t_2}}{x_t} = \frac{Q_p}{Q} \quad \text{or} \quad x_{t_2} = \frac{x_t Q_p}{Q}.$$

[Note that (5-5) and (5-6) together imply $x_{t_1} + x_{t_2} = x_t$, which clearly also must hold; requiring only $Q_i + Q_p = Q$ and $x_{t_1} + x_{t_2} = x_t$ would not be enough, however, since it fails to capture the relationships between the Q's and the x's.]

The problem of minimization of (5-4) subject to the equality constraints in (5-5) and (5-6) can be approached in either of two ways. If we rewrite c_A as a function of Q and Q_i only, utilizing the relationships required in (5-5) and (5-6), then the techniques of Section 3.3 for a function of two independent variables are relevant. We do this below. Identical results can be obtained via the Lagrange multiplier method (Section 4.6), which here would involve a function of nine variables—the original six (Q_i, Q_p, Q, x_{t_1}, x_{t_2}, x_t) and one Lagrange multiplier for each of the three equality constraints in (5-5) and (5-6). Hence there are nine equations in the first-order Lagrangean conditions—six for the partial derivatives with respect to the six original variables and three from the λ_i ($i = 1, 2, 3$). Since direct substitution is easily done, it is the simpler of the two alternatives here.

Rewriting (5-4), utilizing the relationships in (5-5) and (5-6),

$$c_A = \frac{1}{2} c_1 \left(\frac{Q_i^2}{Q} \right) + c_2 \left(\frac{D}{Q} \right) + \frac{1}{2} c_3 \left[\frac{(Q - Q_i)^2}{Q} \right], \qquad (5\text{-}7)$$

which, for known demand and costs, is a function of Q_i and Q only—that is, $c_A = f(Q_i, Q)$. Minimization thus requires that the two partial derivatives $\partial c_A / \partial Q_i \equiv f_{Q_i}$ and $\partial c_A / \partial Q \equiv f_Q$ be set equal to zero to fulfill the first-order conditions for any kind of stationary point. The first, $f_{Q_i} = 0$, leads to

$$Q_i = \frac{c_3 Q}{c_1 + c_3}, \qquad (5\text{-}8)$$

and the second, $f_Q = 0$, gives[7]

---

[6] Right triangles are similar if their other two angles are the same. It is easy to show that the triangle that includes sides Q and x_t is similar to the one with sides Q_i and x_{t_1} as well as the one with sides Q_p and x_{t_2}.

[7] Once the partial derivatives have been written down, the expressions in (5-8) and especially (5-9) result from a good deal of algebra and rearrangement.

$$Q = \sqrt{\frac{2c_2 D + c_1 Q_i^2}{c_3} + Q_i^2}.$$ (5-9)

This leads to (again after considerable algebra)

$$Q_i^* = \sqrt{\frac{2c_2 D}{c_1}} \cdot \sqrt{\frac{c_3}{c_1 + c_3}},$$ (5-10)

and hence

$$Q^* = \sqrt{\frac{2c_2 D}{c_1}} \cdot \sqrt{\frac{c_1 + c_3}{c_3}}.$$ (5-11)

These are the fundamental results, since they show the two decision variables completely determined by known quantities—the costs and annual demand. In addition

$$Q_i^* = \left(\frac{c_3}{c_1 + c_3}\right) Q^*.$$ (5-12)

To be certain that these are cost-minimizing quantities, not cost-maximizing ones, the second-order conditions from Section 3.3 must be checked.[8] By substitution of (5-10) and (5-11) into (5-7), the minimum annual costs for this model that allows shortages can be shown to be

$$c_A^* = \sqrt{2c_1 c_2 D} \cdot \sqrt{\frac{c_3}{c_1 + c_3}}.$$ (5-13)

The reader should compare (5-10) and (5-11) with (5-2), which gave the optimum Q in the case where shortages were not allowed. This is the same as assuming that shortage costs, c_3, are infinitely large. When this is the case, both $\sqrt{(c_1 + c_3)/c_3}$ [in (5-11)] and $\sqrt{c_3/(c_1 + c_3)}$ [in (5-10)] are unity; or, from (5-12), the entire production lot (Q^*) goes to inventory (Q_i^*). Comparison of (5-13) with (5-3) shows that the costs are correctly shown in either formula. That is, the problem analyzed earlier in this section is just a special case of the more general one dealt with now.

The results in (5-10), (5-11), and (5-12) show how the decision between production for inventory, Q_i, and that for past shortages, Q_p, is affected by the relative sizes of c_1 and c_3. The "limiting cases" can be examined,

---

[8] $f_{Q_i Q_i} = (c_1 + c_3)/Q; f_{QQ} = [Q_i^2(c_1 + c_3) + 2c_2 D]/Q^3;$ and $f_{Q_i Q} = -Q_i(c_1 + c_3)/Q^2.$ Thus

$$[f_{Q_i Q_i} \cdot f_{QQ} - f_{Q_i Q}^2] = \frac{2(c_1 + c_3)c_2 D}{Q^4}.$$

For positive costs, demand, and lot size (Q), both numerator and denominator are positive; hence (5-10) and (5-11) represent a *minimum* of c_A.

both as a check on the logic of these results and also for the insights that they provide into the balancing of costs that inventory problems require.

1. *Shortages prohibited.* Here $c_1 > 0$, $c_3 = \infty$, and, as we saw above, $Q_i^* = Q^* = \sqrt{2c_2D/c_1}$. Each batch Q^* is used entirely for inventory.

2. *Inventory prohibited.* In this unlikely case, $c_1 = \infty$ and $c_3 > 0$. From (5-10), $Q_i^* = 0$, and from (5-11), $Q^* = \sqrt{2c_2D/c_3}$. Each batch is used only to fill back orders.

3. *Shortage costs negligible.* This can be represented as $c_1 > 0$, $c_3 \to 0$. Then $Q_i^* \to 0$ and $Q^* \to \infty$. This only represents the logical result that the smaller shortage costs are, the larger should be the lot size (to be used for back orders) and the less should be the amount put into inventory.

4. *Inventory costs negligible.* $c_1 \to 0$, $c_3 > 0$. Note that here, as in case 3, above, $Q^* \to \infty$, but now $Q_i^* \to \infty$ also [that is, $Q_i^* \to Q^*$, from (5-12)]. Thus as inventory costs become very small, increasingly large batches should be produced and used entirely as inventory for future demands.

These examples show that the relationships obtained in the case where three kinds of costs are involved produce logical results for certain "extreme" cases. In fact, this kind of logical pretesting of results is very often useful before one goes on to apply new results to a particular problem. Consider one further case:

5. *Inventories and shortages are equally costly.* That is, $c_1 = c_3$. At first glance, one might decide that the producer should be indifferent between putting a unit into inventory or using it to satisfy a past shortage; since it costs the same for a unit to be above the horizontal axis (in inventory) for a day as it does to be below the axis (in shortage), it seems to make no difference how Q^* is divided. This is in fact wrong; the crucial observation is on the total number of inventory-days (multiplied by c_1) and the total number of shortage-days (multiplied by c_3). These totals, we have seen, are equal to the areas included in the basic triangles, and as Figure 5.7 shows, the areas vary with the distribution between Q_i and Q_p, even though the weights put on the areas (c_1 and c_3) are the same. The value of Q is the same in all three cases, and thus the shaded areas in Figures 5.7(a) and (c) are the same size. Clearly, however, the shaded area in 5.7(b) is less than either of these; hence the total costs are smaller. [The costs are, of course, equal in 5.7(a) and (c), since $c_1 = c_3$.]

   Figure 5.7 suggests that equal division between Q_i and Q_p would minimize total costs. This is true, as can be easily seen from (5-12);

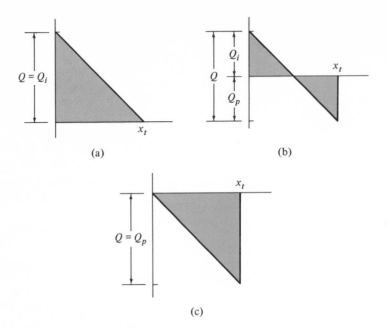

Figure 5.7. Alternative Divisions between Q_i and Q_p

since $c_3/(c_1 + c_3) = \frac{1}{2}$ when $c_1 = c_3$, it follows that $Q_i^* = \frac{1}{2}Q^*$. Moreover, from (5-11) we see that

$$Q^* = \sqrt{\frac{2c_2D}{c_1}} \cdot \sqrt{2} = 1.414 \sqrt{\frac{2c_2D}{c_1}}$$

—that is, the lot size is 1.414 times as large as it was earlier when no shortages were allowed. Thus the *relative* sizes of c_1 and c_2 determine, via (5-12), the *proportions* of each batch that are put into inventory and used to satisfy past shortages, but the *absolute* size of each batch, Q^*, is determined when all three costs and also the size of total demand are taken into account.

Production over a period

Especially when the manufacturer is producing the required items himself, it is more realistic to assume that units come into inventory over a period of time rather than instantaneously, as has been assumed above. This modification alters the fundamental triangle picture, but the basic approach remains the same. We consider again the case described early in this section, where no shortages are allowed. Our aim is to focus on the impact of noninstantaneous delivery of items; the reader can easily extend to the later case in which shortages were included explicitly.

To return to the example, we assume that production of a run of Q cases takes place over a period during which they are being added to inventory at a constant rate per day, while at the same time the inventory of cases is being run down, owing to continuing production of typewriters. Assume

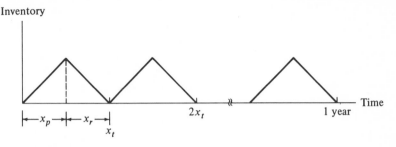

Figure 5.8.   Inventory Build-up over a Period

that the cases are produced at a rate of p per day during the interval x_p and used for typewriters at a rate of r per day over the entire period x_t, where $p > r$. Then, during x_p, inventory is building up at a rate of $(p - r)$ units per day; during x_r $(= x_t - x_p)$, the inventory is being reduced at the rate of r per day, since $p = 0$ during x_r. The problem is similar to the first one considered in this section; for known total demand, setup and inventory costs, and production and use rates, p and r, how large should each run, Q, be? The difference is that now a run Q is done over x_p days. The analysis involves areas of triangles, exactly as before.

Each of the triangles that covers a period x_t has an altitude (the dotted line in the first triangle) that indicates the total accumulation of inventory items; this is just daily accumulation, $(p - r)$, times the number of days that amount is going into inventory, x_p. The base of the triangle is x_t. Hence the area is $\frac{1}{2}(p - r)x_p x_t$. This is the total inventory holding during x_t days; the average per day is thus $\frac{1}{2}(p - r)x_p$. Moreover, since production is done at a rate p for x_p days, the total run $Q = px_p$. Thus $x_p = Q/p$ and the average inventory can be expressed without x_p as

$$\frac{\frac{1}{2}(p - r)Q}{p} = \frac{Q}{2}\left(\frac{p - r}{p}\right).$$

With only inventory (c_1) and setup (c_2) costs (as before, for D/Q runs), annual costs will be

$$c_A = \frac{c_1 Q}{2}\left(\frac{p - r}{p}\right) + \frac{c_2 D}{Q}. \tag{5-14}$$

Since c_1, c_2, r, p, and D are known, $c_A = f(Q)$. Thus the size of Q is found from the first- and second-order conditions for the minimum of a function of one variable (Section 3.2). From $dc_A/dQ = 0$ we find that

$$Q^* = \sqrt{\frac{2c_2 D}{c_1}} \cdot \sqrt{\frac{p}{p - r}} \cdot \qquad (5\text{-}15)$$

Since it is easily shown that $d^2 c_A / dQ^2 > 0$ for c_2, Q, and $D > 0$, this represents the cost-minimizing lot size; consequently, substituting into (5-14),

$$c_A^* = \sqrt{2c_1 c_2 D} \cdot \sqrt{\frac{p - r}{p}} \cdot \qquad (5\text{-}16)$$

Again, comparison with (5-2) and (5-3) shows consistency with our original results; the analysis at the opening of this section assumed that p was infinitely large. Note also the logical implications of (5-15) and (5-16) as $r \to p$—for example, as the rate of use of cases approaches the rate at which they can be produced, Q^*, the lot size, gets larger and larger, since in the limit production of cases must occur continuously; hence one "batch" goes on forever, with items being used up just as fast as they are produced. Thus over any slice of time there are *no* setup costs and *no* items in inventory, and c_A as defined in this section is zero; (5-16) confirms this for the situation in which $p \to r$.

5.3. SENSITIVITY ANALYSIS

In general terms, by sensitivity analysis we mean here the investigation of how much the value of a variable is affected by small changes in one or more of the variables on which it depends—that is, how sensitive it is to changes in these variables. There are two fundamentally different approaches in sensitivity analysis, and we illustrate both by returning to the initial results of Section 5.2—the basic cost equation (5-1) and the *optimizing* lot size (5-2) that leads to *minimum* annual costs (5-3).

We consider the following question: how sensitive is the optimum lot size to errors in the measurement (in this case, probably the *estimation*) of the costs involved, c_1 and c_2? In many cases it is possible that demand may be known accurately, whereas estimates of the annual cost of having an item in inventory or the actual cost of setting up a machine to produce it may be much more difficult to pin down. It is thus very relevant to ask how important variations (that is, errors) in these figures are for the problem of interest to us; the answer would clearly influence decisions on such matters as expending more effort and money on accurate estimation of the costs.

The magnitude of the influence on a dependent variable of small changes in one or more of the variables of which it is a function is precisely what the total differential of a function approximates (Chapter 3). Since the optimum lot size in (5-2) is a function of c_1, c_2, and D, we can show this influence explicitly as

$$dQ^* = \frac{\partial Q^*}{\partial c_1} dc_1 + \frac{\partial Q^*}{\partial c_2} dc_2 + \frac{\partial Q^*}{\partial D} dD. \tag{5-17}$$

Assume that $dD = 0$—that is, that demand is known accurately. Then, taking partial derivatives of Q^* in (5-2) with respect to c_1 and c_2 and rearranging, we have

$$dQ^* = \frac{1}{2}\sqrt{\frac{2c_2 D}{c_1}}\left(\frac{dc_2}{c_2} - \frac{dc_1}{c_1}\right) = \frac{1}{2}Q^*\left(\frac{dc_2}{c_2} - \frac{dc_1}{c_1}\right). \tag{5-18}$$

Thus, for example, if only c_2 is uncertain, $dQ^*/Q^* = \frac{1}{2}(dc_2/c_2)$, which is to say (multiplying both sides by 100 to convert to percentage terms) that if c_2 is underestimated by two percent, Q^* will be underestimated by one percent. Since c_2 represents setup costs, this result is logical; when setup costs are underestimated, the result would be to produce smaller amounts (that is, underestimate Q^*) more frequently (thus incurring the underestimated setup costs more often). In Figure 5.9(b) the dashed curve represents the "true" setup cost function (when c_2 is correctly estimated) and the solid curve shows the estimated function (an underestimate of c_2). If we assume that c_1 is correct, then the solid curve in Figure 5.9(a) represents the true inventory cost function, and hence the intersection of the solid line in Figure 5.9(c) with the dashed curve shows the best inventory decision (point $Q_{c_2}^*$), whereas the intersection of the solid line and solid curve (point Q^*) indicates the (smaller) amount chosen because of the underestimate of c_2.

On the other hand, if only c_1 is in error, $dQ^*/Q^* = -\frac{1}{2}(dc_1/c_1)$, and thus a two percent *under*estimate of c_1 will lead to a one percent *over*estimate in Q^*. Again, this is logical. If inventory costs are underestimated, the result would be to produce larger amounts (and hence put more into inventory each time). In this case, Figure 5.9(a) shows "true" (dashed line) and estimated (solid line) inventory cost functions, $f(Q)$, while the solid curve in Figure 5.9(b) is both the actual and estimated function $g(Q)$. Hence, in Figure 5.9(c), $Q_{c_1}^*$ is the inventory that should be selected, while Q^* is the (larger) amount decided upon because of the underestimate of c_1. Clearly if both c_1 and c_2 are underestimated, the Q^* actually selected may be more than, less than, or the same as it would be if the functions were correctly estimated; Q_b^* (for "both") shows one possibility. [The vertical sum of $f(Q)$ and $g(Q)$—the function c_A—is shown only for the solid line $f(Q)$ and solid curve $g(Q)$. Clearly either one (or both) of the dashed functions will lead to a c_A function that is higher in Figure 5.9(c).]

Thus we see from (5-18) and Figure 5.9 that: (1) the *direction* of error is the same for c_2 and Q^* and *opposite* for c_1 and Q^*; (2) the absolute magnitude of the effect on Q^* is the same for both c_2 and c_1; and (3) in particular, the effect on Q^* is a diminished one (in both cases cut in half) rather than an explosive one. For the economic lot size in (5-2), then, it is possible for

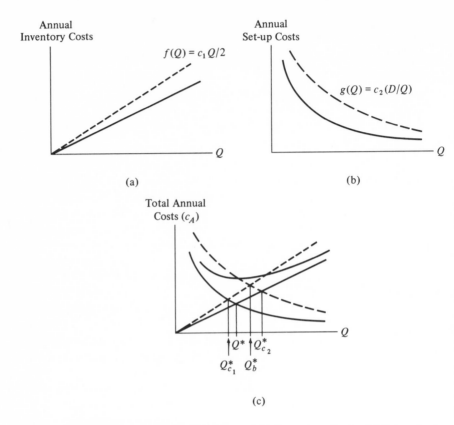

Figure 5.9. Actual and Estimated (a) Inventory Costs, (b) Setup Costs, (c) Total Costs

errors to be "compensating" in the sense that if both costs are misestimated by the same percentage amount and in the same direction (both underestimated by two percent, for example), there will be no effect on Q^*—the errors will cancel out. [It is also possible to show that $dQ^*/Q^* = \frac{1}{2}(dD/D)$; that is, the effect of errors in total demand alone is the same as for errors in setup costs alone.]

Since c_A^*, the minimum annual costs in (5-3), are also a function of c_1, c_2, and D, we may also ask what the impact of errors in any of these is on c_A^*. Again, supposing that demand is accurately estimated ($dD = 0$), we find the total differential for c_A^* to be

$$dc_A^* = \frac{\partial c_A^*}{\partial c_1} dc_1 + \frac{\partial c_A^*}{\partial c_2} dc_2 + 0.$$

Taking partial derivatives from (5-3), substituting, and rearranging gives

$$\frac{dc_A^*}{c_A^*} = \frac{1}{2}\left[\frac{dc_1}{c_1} + \frac{dc_2}{c_2}\right].$$

Thus in the case of minimum costs (as opposed to optimum lot size), percentage errors in either c_1 or c_2 are transmitted to percentage deviations in optimum cost in the *same* direction (although diminished by one-half, as before).

An entirely different kind of question is the following: if the lot size produced is "wrong," *for whatever reason,* how much are annual costs affected by this error? That is, how much do they differ from c_A^*, the minimum costs when each run consists of the optimal amount Q^*? Note that this is *not* a question of how c_A^* is influenced by the cost parameters c_1 or c_2, or by the demand figure D. The relationship between costs and lot size is, of course, that of (5-1); it was illustrated in Figure 5.5 for the case of inventory and setup costs only. Precisely because the optimum size of the decision variable Q was found *so as to minimize c_A* in (5-1)—that is, so that $dc_A/dQ = 0$; or, in terms of differentials, so that $dc_A = 0$—it is clear that the differential approach used above is of no use, since the differential approximation around Q^* will show $dc_A^* = 0$; the tangent is horizontal at $Q = Q^*$. Thus, if we do not wish to (or cannot) specify that the error in Q is a result of c_1, c_2, or D, we must relate the error in Q to c_A in a different way. The question, however, may be equally important: how sensitive are annual costs (which are probably our real interest) to deviations around the optimum value of the decision variable Q? Specifically, are errors (measured in percentages) magnified or dampened, and are they in the same or opposite direction?

We utilize what is essentially a "delta" approach very similar to that used in deriving the notion of the derivative in Section 3.1. Instead of Q^*, imagine that an amount $Q^* + \Delta Q^*$, or $(1 + \Delta)Q^*$, is actually produced in each lot. Thus, if $\Delta = .10$, the lot size is 10 percent above Q^*; if $\Delta = -.30$, the lot size is 30 percent below Q^*; and so on. Then *actual* annual costs are [from (5-1)]

$$c_A^a = c_1\frac{(1 + \Delta)Q^*}{2} + \frac{c_2 D}{(1 + \Delta)Q^*}.$$

Substituting Q^* from (5-2) and c_A^* from (5-3) gives

$$c_A^a = \left[\frac{(1 + \Delta)^2 + 1}{2(1 + \Delta)}\right]c_A^* = \left[1 + \frac{\frac{1}{2}\Delta^2}{(1 + \Delta)}\right]c_A^*, \qquad (5\text{-}19)$$

and, when $\Delta = 0$, or the correct lot size, Q^*, is produced, $c_A^a = c_A^*$, the desired minimum cost. Since 100Δ measures percentage error in Q, we want a measure in similar terms for actual annual costs. That is, we want to relate $[(c_A^a - c_A^*)/c_A^*] \times 100$ to various Δ's. This is precisely the reason for the second form of the expression in (5-19); $[\frac{1}{2}\Delta^2/(1 + \Delta)] \times 100$ gives the percentage deviations in annual costs from the minimum, c_A^*. We can evaluate this expression for various values of Δ (that is, for various errors in Q) as shown in Table 5.1.

Table 5.1.   Percentage Errors in Q and c_A

Percentage error in Q $(= 100\Delta)$	10	30	60	100	−10	−30	−60
Percentage error in c_A $(= 100[\frac{1}{2}\Delta^2/(1 + \Delta)])$	.5	3.5	11	25	.6	6.4	45

For example, if Q is 30 percent *above* the optimum Q^*, costs will be only 3.5 percent *higher* than c_A^*; if Q is 10 percent *below* its cost-minimizing value, c_A^a will be .6 percent *above* the smallest value, c_A. It appears that costs are rather *insensitive* to variations in Q, at least over a rather wide range around Q^*. In general this is a good kind of result; it reflects characteristics of both the shape and the location of the cost curve [Figure 5.9(c)]. Insensitivity of costs around Q^* indicates a relatively flat curve in the neighborhood of the minimum point and/or a curve that is "high" relative to distance "to the right," so that large (percentage) movements in the horizontal (Q) direction produce small (percentage) increases in the vertical (c_A) direction. (The actual position and shape of the function is also influenced, of course, by the units of measurement along both axes.)

To summarize: errors in the parameters c_1, c_2, or D may divert the quantity actually produced from the optimum quantity, Q^*, in *either* direction. However, this deviation from Q^* must lead to increases in actual annual cost over the minimum possible, c_A^*. Thus, the same parameter variations that lead to either a larger or smaller lot size than Q^* always generate costs *larger* than c_A^*. The distinction is that between shifts *of* a curve (or curves) and shifts *on* a curve (or curves).

Considering the solid total-cost curve in Figure 5.9 (or in Figure 5.5), it is clear that any deviation of Q from Q^*, the minimum point on the total-cost curve, will by definition lead to higher costs c_A. This is a question of the effect on the vertical axis of a change in the value of the independent variable (measured on the horizontal axis). For this kind of sensitivity analysis, the "delta" process is needed.

On the other hand, changes in the underlying parameters (the independent variables) in the problem lead to shifts of the functions—the solid and dashed lines in Figures 5.9(a) and/or (b) and consequently (c). This shift (or these shifts) may or may not alter Q^* and hence the actual annual costs. For this kind of question the total differential is completely appropriate. This is precisely because, in terms of Figures 5.9, the errors are not in terms of the decision variable (or variables)—in this case Q—with respect to which the optimization was originally carried out.

5.4. UNCERTAIN DEMAND

The discrete case

In the preceding sections it was assumed that demand for the period was known with certainty. In the cost functions (5-1), (5-7), and (5-14) D was considered a constant, for example, when differentiating. It appears in the optimal lot sizes, Q^*, in (5-2), (5-10), (5-11), and (5-15) as a parameter whose value must be supplied. Since a demand figure of this sort is generally a forecast, it is much more likely that several possible values will be estimated, each with some probability of occurrence. We might expect an amount D_1 with probability $p(D_1)$, D_2 with probability $p(D_2)$, ..., and D_n with probability $p(D_n)$, where of course all possibilities must be accounted for, so

$$\sum_{i=1}^{n} p(D_i) = 1.$$

Obviously one approach to this case would be to use the mean value of demand

$$E(D) = \sum_{i=1}^{n} D_i p(D_i)$$

as a single known figure, D, for the formulas in earlier sections. The mean, however, being a measure of central tendency for a variable, fails to take account of the spread or dispersion of the values of the variable, is strongly influenced by values far from the mean, and so on. In some cases, then, either the median or the mode might better serve as the single-number summary of the discrete distribution. On the other hand, there is a simple method that takes the entire distribution much more explicitly into account. To indicate the variety possible in the general category of inventory problems, we pose a somewhat different situation from those in the preceding sections.

Assume that demand is known as a discrete random variable; that is, with each possible value, D_i, we have the probability of that demand's occurring, $p(D_i)$.[9] Assume that the problem is such that the D_i are only whole numbers and never negative. Penalty costs are associated with pro-

---

[9] A brief review of discrete and continuous random variables and their associated probability functions is provided in Appendix 5.1.

ducing Q, which is less than the amount actually demanded; we term these shortage costs and designate by c_s the unit cost of *under*supplying. This may be made up of loss of goodwill, costs of a special order for each missing item, contract penalties for failure to deliver, and so on. Similarly, assume that penalty costs are associated with *over*supply—producing an amount Q that is larger than demand. Denote these by c_0—the unit cost of overproducing. For example, extra items might have to be sold at a loss, held by the producer at a cost, and so on. Clearly, these two costs are very similar to the shortage and inventory costs used earlier; in the present example we have simply abstracted from the time dimension by assuming that the inventory items are produced by a supplier who disposes of the entire amount Q each time it is produced. The costs depend entirely on how closely Q matches the demand and, when there is a discrepancy, on whether it is an under- or an oversupply. When actual demand, D, is less than Q, the difference $(Q - D)$ generates a cost $c_0(Q - D)$; when the demand is greater, the cost is $c_s(D - Q)$. But of course the values of demand are known in advance only probabilistically. For the oversupply possibilities, we need to match each possible value of D_i that is less than Q with its probability $p(D_i)$; the *expected* size of the oversupply is thus

$$\sum_{D_i=0}^{Q} (Q - D_i)p(D_i).$$

On each unit in this amount a cost of c_0 is incurred; thus

$$c_0 \sum_{D_i=0}^{Q} (Q - D_i)p(D_i)$$

represents the *expected* costs of overproduction. Similarly

$$c_s \sum_{D_i=Q+1}^{\infty} (D_i - Q)p(D_i)$$

gives the *expected* costs of underproduction. Thus expected costs associated with producing an amount Q when facing a demand known only as a discrete random variable are

$$c_Q = c_0 \sum_{D_i=0}^{Q} (Q - D_i)p(D_i) + c_s \sum_{D_i=Q+1}^{\infty} (D_i - Q)p(D_i). \quad (5\text{-}20)$$

The problem now is to find the Q that minimizes (5-20). It is clear that this function differs from those seen in Chapters 3 and 4; D in (5-20) is a variable in the sense that it ranges over a set of values according to a probability distribution; it is a so-called "random variable." This serves to distinguish it from the *independent* variables in many of the functions of

Chapters 3 and 4 whose values could be completely decided by the decision maker with some particular objective such as minimum costs. Moreover, since D takes only a limited number of values, Q will also range over those same values. Recall that development of the first-order and second-order conditions using calculus depended on the continuity of the functions involved; c_Q in (5-20) is not a continuous function. We develop a method that looks much more complicated in the explaining than it actually is. The logic, in fact, is completely parallel to that involved in isolating maxima from minima for functions of one variable in the continuous case by evaluating the first derivative slightly to the left and slightly to the right of the stationary point at which $dy/dx = 0$. It is known, formally, as the calculus of finite differences.[10]

Consider the costs [as given in (5-20)] if an amount $Q + 1$ were produced. We would have (replacing Q by $Q + 1$ everywhere)

$$c_{Q+1} = c_0 \sum_{D_i=0}^{Q+1} (Q + 1 - D_i)p(D_i) + c_s \sum_{D_i=Q+2}^{\infty} [D_i - (Q + 1)]p(D_i). \quad (5\text{-}21)$$

Our object is now to rearrange this expression to relate it more easily to c_Q in (5-20). The algebra is in Appendix 5.2; the important result is below:

$$c_{Q+1} = c_Q + (c_0 + c_s) \sum_{D_i=0}^{Q} p(D_i) - c_s. \quad (5\text{-}22)$$

Alternatively, since $\displaystyle\sum_{D_i=0}^{Q} p(D_i)$ is the sum of the probabilities that D_i takes

on all values up to and including Q—that is, $p(D_i \leq Q)$—we can express c_{Q+1} as

$$c_{Q+1} = c_Q + (c_0 + c_s)p(D_i \leq Q) - c_s. \quad (5\text{-}22')$$

Similarly, by substitution of $(Q - 1)$ for Q in (5-20), we can obtain (as shown in Appendix 5.2):

$$c_{Q-1} = c_Q - (c_0 + c_s)p(D_i \leq Q - 1) + c_s. \quad (5\text{-}23)$$

Suppose now that we found a Q^* having the property that (a) $c_{Q*} < c_{Q*+1}$ *and* (b) $c_{Q*} < c_{Q*-1}$. That is, (5-20) evaluated at Q^* was less than when evaluated on either side of Q^*, namely at $Q^* \pm 1$. Then Q^* would clearly represent a local minimum point of c_Q. Define Δc_{Q*} as the *difference* between the cost for Q^* and for the next *higher* value, $Q^* + 1$—that is, $\Delta c_{Q*} =$

---

[10] Complete statements of first- and second-order conditions for relative and absolute maxima and minima will not be presented here. Further discussion can be found in Sasieni, Yaspan, and Friedman [17, app. 1].

$c_{Q^*+1} - c_{Q^*}$. Then property (a), above, can be expressed as $\Delta c_{Q^*} > 0$; property (b) can be expressed as $\Delta c_{Q^*-1} < 0$. Thus Q^* is a local minimum if $\Delta c_{Q^*} > 0 > \Delta c_{Q^*-1}$.

From (5-22') we see that $\Delta c_{Q^*} > 0$ means $(c_0 + c_s)p(D_i \leq Q) - c_s > 0$; from (5-23) $\Delta c_{Q^*-1} < 0$ means $(c_0 + c_s)p(D_i \leq Q - 1) - c_s < 0$. Thus for the problem at hand $\Delta c_{Q^*} > 0 > \Delta c_{Q^*-1}$ requires that

$$(c_0 + c_s)p(D_i \leq Q) - c_s > 0 > (c_0 + c_s)p(D_i \leq Q - 1) - c_s$$

or

$$p(D_i \leq Q) > \frac{c_s}{c_0 + c_s} > p(D_i \leq Q - 1). \qquad (5\text{-}24)$$

This is a very useful result. It says that, given the known costs c_s and c_0, the optimum quantity (for which costs c_Q will be minimized) is the one at which the (known) value of the cumulative probability distribution exceeds the ratio $c_s/(c_0 + c_s)$. That is, we find Q^* by comparing a cost ratio with probability figures.

For example, suppose the possible values for demand and their probabilities are as given in Table 5.2.

Table 5.2. Hypothetical Probability Table for D

D_i	$p(D_i)$
10	.05
11	.15
12	.40
13	.20
14	.10
15	.05
16	.05

Since possible Q will be limited to the relevant range of possible D_i, we can form Table 5.3.

Table 5.3. Derived Probability Table and Cumulative Distribution for Q

Q	$p(D_i = Q)$	$F(Q) = p(D_i \leq Q)$
10	.05	.05
11	.15	.20
12	.40	.60
13	.20	.80
14	.10	.90
15	.05	.95
16	.05	1.00

Suppose that the two costs are $c_s = \$12.50$ and $c_0 = \$2.50$; then

$$\frac{c_s}{c_0 + c_s} = \frac{5}{6} = .833,$$

and we find that

$$p(D_i \leq 14) > \frac{c_s}{c_0 + c_s} > p(D_i \leq 13);$$

that is, $.90 > .83 > .80$. Thus $Q^* = 14$ is the optimum batch size to produce when faced with the demand distribution and costs given above. Expected costs for $Q = 14$, from (5-20), will be \$6. (As a check, the reader can show that costs for $Q = 15$ are \$7 and for $Q = 13$ they are \$6.50.) Note that the mean value of demand for this distribution, $E(D)$, is 12.5; rounding upward and producing $Q = 13$ gives an expected cost of \$6.50; rounding downward and making $Q = 12$ has an associated cost of \$10; both are inferior to production of $Q = 14$.

We can illustrate this procedure on the usual step-function representation of cumulative probability functions for discrete variables. In Figure 5.10

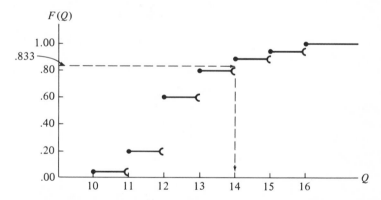

Figure 5.10.   Optimal Q for the Example in Table 5.3

(where each horizontal part of the function extends up to but does not include the next value of Q), we utilize the information from the last column of Table 5.3. Finding the value of $c_s/(c_0 + c_s)$ on the vertical axis, which ranges from 0 to 1 for the cumulative probability function,[11] and

---

[11] Note that, for $c_s \geq 0$, $c_0 \geq 0$ (but not *both* c_s and $c_0 = 0$, since then there would be no costs and hence no problem):

$$1 \geq \frac{c_s}{c_0 + c_s} \geq 0.$$

The ratio is 1 when $c_s > 0$, $c_0 = 0$, and 0 when $c_s = 0$, $c_0 > 0$. These are logical results: if $c_0 = 0$, make Q^* as large as might possibly be demanded; if $c_s = 0$, produce nothing until you see how large demand turns out to be.

projecting horizontally (as if the cumulative function had vertical portions) gives the optimal Q. Note that there is no reason here to draw the cumulative function and use this geometric approach, since to do so requires knowledge of the cumulative probabilities, and once $c_s/(c_0 + c_s)$ is also calculated, Q^* can be found directly from the $p(D_i \leq Q)$ column.

Clearly, since there is a finite number of possible values for D_i in the discrete variable case, one could always calculate expected costs for all possibly relevant Q from (5-20) and then select the one for which these costs were lowest. But once the derivation of (5-24) has been done, it is far easier to compare the cost ratio $c_s/(c_0 + c_s)$ with successive values of the cumulative probability distribution for D_i.

The continuous case

If the demand is estimated as a continuous probability distribution, then the cost function analogous to (5-20) has integrals instead of summation signs, and the small interval probabilities $f(D) \, dD$ for the continuous probability function replace the $p(D_i)$ terms in the discrete case.[12]

$$c_Q = c_0 \int_0^Q (Q - D) f(D) \, dD + c_s \int_Q^\infty (D - Q) f(D) \, dD. \qquad (5\text{-}25)$$

Again, we have costs as a function of Q, a random variable D is also present, and our interest is in finding the value of Q that minimizes these costs. However, (5-25) is now a continuous function; we are faced with the problem of differentiating a function with integrals and a random variable. All that is needed is an additional rule for the process of differentiation. The basic rule is stated, without proof,[13] and then we apply it to the problem of minimizing c_Q in (5-25).

If $g(z) = \int_{h(z)}^{k(z)} f(z, x) \, dx$, then

$$\frac{dg(z)}{dz} = \int_{h(z)}^{k(z)} \frac{\partial f}{\partial z} \, dx + f(z, k(z)) \frac{dk(z)}{dz} - f(z, h(z)) \frac{dh(z)}{dz}.$$

We are dealing with a function g that involves an *independent* variable z and a *random* variable x. We wish to differentiate g with respect to z, the variable whose value we can set. The function is integrated between two limits, which themselves may be functions of z, $h(z)$, and $k(z)$.[14] The presence of x in $f(z, x)$ and the dx term indicate the random variable for which the continuous probability distribution (density function) is known.

---

[12] See Appendix 5.1 for further details.

[13] The interested reader is referred to Courant [4] for a derivation of these results, and to Sasieni, Yaspan, and Friedman [17] for some additional details.

[14] Of course, they need not be functions of z. If the lower limit, for example, is 0, then $h(z) = 0$—that is, a constant.

Note that if $g(z)$ takes the form

$$\int_0^{k(z)} f_1(z, x) \, dx + \int_{k(z)}^\infty f_2(z, x) \, dx,$$

then

$$\frac{dg(z)}{dz} = \int_0^{k(z)} \frac{\partial f_1}{\partial z} \, dx + \int_{k(z)}^\infty \frac{\partial f_2}{\partial z} \, dx + \frac{dk(z)}{dz} [f_1(z, k(z)) - f_2(z, k(z))]. \quad (5\text{-}26)$$

This form of $g(z)$ parallels the structure of c_Q in (5-25). Thus, applying (5-26), we find that

$$\frac{dc_Q}{dQ} = c_0 \int_0^Q f(D) \, dD - c_s \int_Q^\infty f(D) \, dD + [(Q - Q)f(Q) - (Q - Q)f(Q)]$$

or

$$\frac{dc_Q}{dQ} = c_0 \int_0^Q f(D) \, dD - c_s \int_Q^\infty f(D) \, dD. \quad (5\text{-}27)$$

For the continuous random variable D, the cumulative probability of D between 0 and Q (the distribution function) is represented as

$$F(Q) = \int_0^Q f(D) \, dD;$$

that is, this is $p(D \le Q)$. As in the discrete case

$$p(D > Q) = \int_Q^\infty f(D) \, dD = 1 - p(D \le Q) = 1 - F(Q).$$

Thus, from (5-27),

$$\frac{dc_Q}{dQ} = c_0 F(Q) - c_s[1 - F(Q)] = (c_0 + c_s)F(Q) - c_s, \quad (5\text{-}28)$$

and the first-order condition for a minimum is that $dc_Q/dQ = 0$.[15] Thus, setting (5-28) equal to zero,

$$p(D \le Q) \equiv F(Q) = \frac{c_s}{c_0 + c_s}. \quad (5\text{-}29)$$

This says that the best quantity to produce is that for which the value of the cumulative probability distribution for D is just equal to $c_s/(c_0 + c_s)$. Recall that this same ratio was of critical importance in the discrete variable case earlier in this section. In the discrete case it is (in general) impossible to find a value of the cumulative probability function that matches this ratio exactly; in the continuous case one can find such a value. Also, unlike the discrete case, the graphic approach is more generally useful. Schematically, if we have the distribution function for D,

---

[15] Reapplication of (5-26) to the first derivative in (5-27) gives $d^2c_Q/dQ^2 = 2f(Q)$, which is nonnegative, since f is a probability distribution.

$$F(Q) = \int_0^Q f(D) \, dD = p(D \leq Q)$$

—Figure 5.11—we find the value of $c_s/(c_0 + c_s)$ on the vertical axis, exactly as in Figure 5.10 for the discrete case, project horizontally to $F(Q)$ and then drop to the horizontal axis.

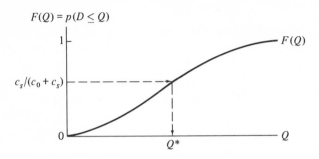

Figure 5.11. Optimum Q for the Continuous Probability Distribution Case

5.5. QUEUING (WAITING LINE) MODELS: INTRODUCTION

As in inventory models, the basic problem in waiting line or queuing models is one of balance between two kinds of costs that tend to work in opposite directions. The fundamental queuing situation is one in which items arrive at a facility for processing; depending on the size of the facility and the nature of the distribution of arrivals, queues may or may not form. If they do, the items in the line may incur a cost due to waiting. This general description covers a wide variety of actual phenomena. Each of the following is a queuing situation: airplanes wanting to land at an airport; customers at the tellers' windows in a bank, at check-out counters in a supermarket, ticket counters at an airport, train, or bus station; patients at a clinic; ships waiting to unload cargo at a port; jobs to be processed at a computer center; automobiles waiting to pay at toll booths on highways and at bridges and tunnels.

Clearly, if the service facility is very large relative to the number of customers at any one time (hundreds of check-out counters in a supermarket, dozens of piers in a port), then the probability of a waiting line's forming is very small and so also is the probability that an item (customer, ship) will be forced to wait. Thus (1) the cost of waiting will not be incurred and (2) provision for physical accommodation of waiting units need not be extensive (a line of five customers in a bank may not be disruptive to normal operations anyway, while five ships waiting for piers in a narrow harbor might be). Of course there are costs associated with large service facilities, both in terms of investment in space and equipment and in terms of idle capacity (rent, utilities, insurance, and so on on a larger bank building; electronic communication devices from each teller's window to a computerized central data file; tellers with nothing to do; piers with cranes and other ship unloading equipment; facilities for short-term cargo storage). These costs obviously decrease with fewer (and smaller) facilities; one teller or one pier in operation would allow a minimal amount of processing, and while facility cost would be low, time spent by customers or ships waiting would tend to be very long, as would the length of the waiting line. The problem then is to achieve an optimum balance between the costs associated with idle time (excess service facility or too little demand) and with waiting time (excess demand or not enough servicing facility).

To study queuing phenomena it is necessary to know (or specify an assumption about):

1. The way in which items arrive for service—that is, the average time between arrivals, the distribution of times between arrivals, and so on.
2. The size of the service facility—that is, the number of "channels" available to an arriving unit—and the nature of service priority. Two common approaches are first-in, first-out (service in order of appearance) and least-work, first-out (service "next" the item in line that requires least service, from among those in line).[16]
3. The rate at which items are processed or "serviced."

Clearly if arrivals are completely regular—such as one banking customer exactly every 10 minutes or one cargo ship exactly every 20 days—then there is no problem in matching service facilities to demand. A common characteristic of the queuing examples given above is that the time between arrivals at the servicing facility is a *random variable*—which is simply to say that arrivals do not occur at evenly spaced points in time; rather they are "bunched" or "clustered."[17] Similarly, it is *usually* true that the amount of time taken to process or service the item is also a random variable (not all customers want the same banking service from a teller; ships vary in size and in amount of cargo to be unloaded at a particular pier). Thus, in studying queuing situations, it is first necessary to indicate the nature of

---

[16] This policy is used at certain machine repair facilities, for example, to keep the average number of machines out of service at a minimum.

[17] Events that occur "randomly" in time will necessarily appear clustered or bunched. Events that happen at evenly spaced intervals are anything but random.

the randomness in times between arrivals and in servicing times; to state simply that "arrivals occur at random," for example, is insufficient information on which to build a model. Rather, we need a specification of the probabilities associated with all possible values of the variable "time between arrivals"—that is, a probability density function.[18]

We will see that once the probabilities have been specified for arrival and service characteristics, we can derive from these functions relations that show exactly how system phenomena—such as the average amount of time a unit spends waiting, the average amount of time a service facility is idle, the average queue length, and so on—depend on the parameters of the arrival and service probability distributions. It is through these relations that the effects of changes in arrival or service characteristics can be related to system phenomena; hence the costs of such changes can be compared with the savings (if any) expected to result.

The most basic waiting line models have been developed on the assumptions that (1) arrival *rates* follow a Poisson distribution and (2) service *times* follow a negative exponential distribution. In the next sections of this chapter we will see exactly what these two assumptions mean. In later sections we will use them explicitly to derive characteristics of the queuing process. We will begin with a single-station situation and then extend the basic results to multiple-station systems. We will also see how the system characteristics are utilized in cost functions which can serve as the basis for cost-minimizing decisions.

5.6. A GENERALIZED "POISSON PROCESS"

The Poisson distribution

The number e, which acts as the base for the "natural" system of logarithms, is defined as the limit of a particular function:

$$e = \lim_{k \to \infty} \left(1 + \frac{1}{k}\right)^k. \tag{5-30}$$

Table 5.4 shows this expression for different values of k. For larger and larger k, the expression approaches 2.71828.... The limit in (5-30) can be expressed as a so-called infinite series (because there are infinitely many terms):

$$e = 1 + 1 + \frac{1}{2!} + \frac{1}{3!} + \frac{1}{4!} + \cdots, \tag{5-31}$$

[18] See Appendix 5.1.

where $n!$ (read "n factorial") denotes the product of all whole numbers from n down to 1; that is,

$$n! \equiv n \cdot (n - 1) \cdot (n - 2) \cdots (3)(2)(1).$$

Table 5.4. $[1 + (1/k)]^k$ for Various k

k	$[1 + (1/k)]^k$
1	2
2	2.25
3	2.37037...
4	2.44141...
⋮	⋮
10	2.59374...

Although unnecessary for (5-31), it is useful to note that the series expression in (5-31) is for e to the first power (e^1) and that the series is actually

$$e^1 = \frac{1^0}{0!} + \frac{1^1}{1!} + \frac{1^2}{2!} + \frac{1^3}{3!} + \cdots = \sum_{x=0}^{\infty} \frac{1^x}{x!}. \tag{5-32}$$

Since anything raised to the zeroth power is defined to be 1, since 0! is defined to be 1, and since 1 raised to any power is still 1, (5-32) and (5-31) are identical. Both, however, are particularizations of the more general series

$$e^z = \frac{z^0}{0!} + \frac{z^1}{1!} + \frac{z^2}{2!} + \frac{z^3}{3!} + \cdots = \sum_{x=0}^{\infty} \frac{z^x}{x!} \tag{5-33}$$

The Poisson probability distribution is *defined* as follows:

$$p(x) = e^{-z} \left(\frac{z^x}{x!} \right) \tag{5-34}$$

for $x = 0, 1, \ldots, \infty$. That is, (5-34) gives the probabilities associated with each value that x may assume (nonnegative integers), once the single parameter of the function, z, is specified. Because of (5-33) the reader can easily show that $p(x)$ in (5-34) has one of the required characteristics of any probability distribution, namely that the sum of the probabilities over all possible values of the variable must be unity:

$$\sum_{x=0}^{\infty} p(x) = 1.$$

Nor is it difficult to show[19] that the mean of the Poisson distribution is just the parameter z;

$$E(x) = z. \tag{5-35}$$

The Poisson distribution is of interest here because it provides a good approximation to the probabilities of the numbers of occurrences of such isolated events in a continuous span of time as goals in a football game, lightning flashes during a thunderstorm, and flaws in daily production runs of electrical cable. The parameter z [$= E(x)$] must be obtained by observation of one or more samples of the event that is of interest. The reader may recall that the *binomial* distribution also provided information about probabilities of numbers of occurrences of events, such as heads in flips of a coin or, say, 5's in rolls of a die. The crucial difference between the situations in which these distributions are relevant is that for the *binomial*, the number of "trials" is specified; and hence we know exactly the number of times the event (heads or a 5 on the die) *did not occur*. The probability of exactly 21 rolls showing 5 in 100 rolls of a fair die is $C_{21}^{100}(\frac{1}{6})^{21}(\frac{5}{6})^{79}$; there are 100 times when either a 5 or some other face of the die may show, and thus if we are asking for 21 5's, we must necessarily have 79 non-5's. Given the probability of occurrence, p, and hence the probability of non-occurrence, $(1 - p)$, the binomial provides answers. But with flashes of lightning or football goals or flaws in wire we really do not know how many "trials" there were and hence how many times the event did *not* happen. For these cases, the Poisson distribution is relevant.

As an indication of the "fit" of the Poisson distribution to a particular set of isolated events in time, the following data are often cited. Consider the records over a ten-year period of twenty corps of the Prussian Cavalry. For each of the 200 corps-years, a statistic is recorded: number of men in that corps in that year who died as a result of being kicked by a horse. The data might be presented in a 10 × 20 table, as in Table 5.5.

Thus a table of relative frequencies for the variable x = deaths per corps-year can be formed. Actual observations on this variable and its

---

[19] From Appendix 5.1, $E(x) = \displaystyle\sum_{x=0}^{\infty} xp(x)$. For the Poisson,

$$E(x) = \sum_{x=0}^{\infty} xe^{-z}\left(\frac{z^x}{x!}\right) = e^{-z}\sum_{x=0}^{\infty}\frac{xz^x}{x!} = e^{-z}\sum_{x=1}^{\infty}\frac{z^x}{(x-1)!}$$

$$= e^{-z}z\sum_{x=1}^{\infty}\frac{z^{(x-1)}}{(x-1)!} = e^{-z}\cdot z\cdot e^{z} = z.$$

The variance of the Poisson distribution can also be shown to be z.

Table 5.5. Fatal Kicks

		Corps					
		A	B	C	.	.	.	T
Year	1	0	2	...			
	2	1	0				
	:	:	:				
	10	0	1				

frequencies per 200 corps-years are given in Table 5.6.[20] The mean is given by

$$\bar{x} = (0)(\tfrac{109}{200}) + (1)(\tfrac{65}{200}) + \cdots + 4(\tfrac{1}{200}) + 5(0) + 6(0) = .61.$$

(That is, there was an average of .61 deaths from kicking in each of the 200 corps-years observed.) Suppose we use .61 as the mean (and hence the parameter z) in a Poisson function:

$$p(x) = \frac{e^{-.61}(.61)^x}{x!} = \frac{(.543)(.61)^x}{x!}$$

and find the probabilities of 0, 1, ..., 6 "events" using $p(x)$ (Table 5.7).

Even without employing any particular measure of "goodness of fit" the reader will see that the Poisson function with $z = .61$ describes well the distribution of occurrences of this event. Observations on the one parameter, the *actual* mean number of events per unit of time, when used in the Poisson distribution, generate a (discrete) probability function for all possible values of the variable. In this section we investigate the characteristics of a "Poisson process," which is fundamental in queuing situations.

Table 5.6. Observations on Fatal Kicks

Number of deaths per corps-year	Relative frequency in 200 corps-years
0	109/200 = .545
1	65/200 = .325
2	22/200 = .110
3	3/200 = .015
4	1/200 = .005
5	0/200 = .000
6	0/200 = .000

[20] Cited in Wilks [24, p. 143].

Table 5.7.   Poisson Probabilities and Occurrences for Deaths by Kicking and Actual Probabilities and Occurrences

x:	0	1	2	3	4	5	6
$p(x)$	.543	.331	.101	.021	.003	.000	.000
Observed relative frequencies	.545	.325	.110	.015	.005	.000	.000
Poisson occurrences in 200 corps-years	108.6	66.2	20.2	4.2	0.6	0	0
Observed occurrences in 200 corps-years	109	65	22	3	1	0	0

The Poisson process

Without specifying, for the moment, what the "events" are, consider a phenomenon for which, beginning at some initial time of observation, $t_0 = 0$, we count the *number of events*, n, occurring between t_0 and some general terminal time, t. Denote by $p_n(t)$ the probability that n events occur between t_0 and t—that is, over an interval of length t. Suppose that the following three (plausible) hypotheses are made:

1. $p_n(t)$ is homogeneous (or stationary) in time; this means that the probability $p_n(t)$ depends on the *length* of the interval, t, and not on the initial point.
2. The probability that the "event" will occur *more than once* in a "suitably defined" *small* time interval Δt is very, very (in fact, infinitesimally) small, relative to Δt. (That is, for a small enough Δt, the probability of two or more events occurring in Δt is effectively zero.)
3. The probability of an event's occurring once in the time interval Δt is *proportional* to Δt; the constant of proportion can be written as π. Thus $p_1(\Delta t) = \pi(\Delta t)$. For example, if an event occurs at a rate of four per hour, or four each 60 minutes, or one each 15 minutes, then, letting $\Delta t = .05$ minute, $\pi(\Delta t) = (\frac{4}{60})(.05) = .003$—the probability of one event's occurring in a time interval of .05 minute.[21]

The fact is that an event characterized by the three assumptions above can be described as a "Poisson process," precisely because for such an event

---

[21] Note that the third assumption means that the occurrence of the event is *equally likely* over the time interval Δt.

$$p_n(t) = \frac{e^{-\pi t}(\pi t)^n}{n!}, \tag{5-36}$$

which is exactly (5-34) for $z = \pi t$ and $n = x$. We examine the result in (5-36) more closely.

For the specific small time interval Δt, with $n = 1$, we know from assumption 3 that $p_1(\Delta t) = \pi(\Delta t)$. We also know, (from assumption 2), that

$$1 - p_0(\Delta t) - p_1(\Delta t) = p_2(\Delta t) + \cdots + p_\infty(\Delta t)$$

$$= \sum_{i=2}^{\infty} p_i(\Delta t) = 0;$$

thus $1 - p_0(\Delta t) = p_1(\Delta t)$ or

$$p_0(\Delta t) = 1 - p_1(\Delta t) = 1 - \pi(\Delta t). \tag{5-37}$$

This describes the probability of *no* events during the time interval Δt. Suppose we now examine the ways in which n events can happen in an *interval of length* t. To do so we will investigate a very slightly *longer* interval of length $t + \Delta t$, and then send $\Delta t \to 0$; this in many ways is parallel to the basic "delta process" reasoning that we used in Chapter 3. In the time from $t_0 = 0$ to $t + \Delta t$ we can have: (a) n events during t, none in Δt; (b) $n - 1$ in t, 1 in Δt; (c) $n - 2$ in t, 2 in Δt; and so on. But recall (from assumption 2) that the probability of more than one event in a suitably small interval Δt is assumed to be zero. Hence, adding (a) and (b) only, which represent the two *mutually exclusive* ways that the event can happen:

$$p_n(t + \Delta t) = p_n(t) \cdot p_0(\Delta t) + p_{n-1}(t) \cdot p_1(\Delta t). \tag{5-38}$$

From (5-37) this is

$$p_n(t + \Delta t) = p_n(t)(1 - \pi \, \Delta t) + p_{n-1}(t)(\pi \, \Delta t)$$

or

$$p_n(t + \Delta t) - p_n(t) = [p_{n-1}(t) - p_n(t)](\pi \, \Delta t),$$

or, finally, dividing by Δt and taking the limit as $\Delta t \to 0$, we have the probability for the time interval t:

$$\lim_{\Delta t \to 0} \left[\frac{p_n(t + \Delta t) - p_n(t)}{\Delta t} \right] \equiv \frac{dp_n(t)}{dt} \equiv p_n'(t) = \pi[p_{n-1}(t) - p_n(t)]. \tag{5-39}$$

This is, formally, a *differential equation*, which describes how the rate of change of $p_n(t)$ depends on the time *interval* t; from (5-39) we see that this derivative depends on two probabilities and the parameter, π, from assumption 3. While (5-39) is *generally* true, it cannot hold for the *particular* case when $n = 0$, since then the p_{n-1} term has no meaning. For $n = 0$, the only possibility is *no* events during t and *none* during Δt; that is,

$$p_0(t + \Delta t) = p_0(t) \cdot p_0(\Delta t) = p_0(t)(1 - \pi \, \Delta t)$$

and

$$p_0(t + \Delta t) - p_0(t) = -p_0(t)(\pi \, \Delta t),$$

or, dividing by Δt and letting $\Delta t \to 0$,

$$\lim_{\Delta t \to 0} \left[\frac{p_0(t + \Delta t) - p_0(t)}{\Delta t} \right] \equiv p_0'(t) = -\pi p_0(t). \qquad (5\text{-}40)$$

Now (5-39) and (5-40) are two (differential) equations that come from the hypotheses about the probabilities of events. Moreover, we know certain "boundary" conditions. For example: $p_0(0) = 1$; that is, the probability is 1 (certainty) that no events occur during a time interval of length zero. This information can help us to "solve" (5-39) and (5-40), which means finding the underlying function of t that has the first derivative properties shown in the two equations. (This *general* problem—finding solutions to "differential equations"—is an entire subject itself.)

Consider the requirements stated in (5-40). We must find a function having the property that when its derivative is divided by itself, the result is a constant, $-\pi$. Suppose we try

$$p_0(t) = k e^{-\pi t}, \qquad (5\text{-}41)$$

where k is any constant. This has exactly the property required. However, by considering the "boundary condition" that $p_0(0) = 1$, we see that k must equal 1 in (5-41). Hence, specifically

$$p_0(t) = e^{-\pi t}. \qquad (5\text{-}41')$$

What about the more general statement in (5-39), for $n > 0$? This must *also* be satisfied by any acceptable $p(t)$. Again, suppose[22] we try

$$p_n(t) = \frac{e^{-\pi t}(\pi t)^n}{n!}. \qquad (5\text{-}42)$$

[For $n = 0$, this indeed reduces to $p_0(t)$ in (5-41').] Differentiating (using the product rule), we find that the ratio of $p_n'(t)$ to $[p_{n-1}(t) - p_n(t)]$ is exactly π, as required by (5-39). And, finally, the additional "boundary condition," for $n \neq 0$, that $p_n(0) = 0$, *is* satisfied by (5-42).

Thus, (5-42) represents a Poisson distribution, (5-34), with the single parameter $z = \pi t$ and $x = n$. We may, therefore, describe the "occurrences" or "events" about which we made the three assumptions above as being a "Poisson process," since their probabilities follow a Poisson function.

---

[22] The functions can be "found" through an elementary knowledge of differential equations, but this is not essential here.

5.7. TOWARD A QUEUING PROCESS: THE DISTRIBUTION OF ARRIVALS OR OF COMPLETED SERVICES

Arrival distribution

Suppose we let the "event" in Section 5.6 be "arrival" at a service facility; we then speak of a queuing situation with "Poisson arrivals." This means that the random variable "arrivals per unit of time"—the arrival *rate*—obeys a Poisson distribution. Consider the three underlying hypotheses behind a Poisson process—assumptions 1 to 3 in the preceding section (replacing π in assumption 3 by λ for the case where the variable is arrivals).[23] Thus (1') the probability of n arrivals during t, $p_n(t)$, is homogeneous in time, (2') the probability of more than one arrival in Δt is negligibly small, and (3') the probability of one arrival in Δt, $p_1(\Delta t)$, is given by $\lambda \Delta t$. In this case, λ is usually termed the "mean arrival rate." Thus,

$$p_n(t) = \frac{e^{-\lambda t}(\lambda t)^n}{n!} \tag{5-43}$$

gives the probability of n arrivals during a time interval of length t; this is, of course, a Poisson distribution, as in (5-34), with parameter λt. Specifically,

$$p_0(t) = e^{-\lambda t} \tag{5-44}$$

gives the probability of *no* arrivals during t.

Consider a related random variable, T, the time between (consecutive) arrivals. On the basis of the Poisson assumption about arrivals per unit time, from which (5-44) results, the probability that the time between arrivals, T, is greater than some particular interval τ (for example, 15 minutes) is

$$p(T > \tau) = e^{-\lambda \tau}, \tag{5-45}$$

since $e^{-\lambda \tau}$ is the probability that an interval of length τ elapses *without* an arrival. Thus

$$p(T \leq \tau) = 1 - p(T > \tau) = 1 - e^{-\lambda \tau} \tag{5-46}$$

represents the probability of a time between arrivals of τ or less. Expression (5-46) is a cumulative probability function, or distribution function.[24] We know that the distribution function for a continuous random variable—

---

[23] This is standard in queuing literature; it should not be confused with the Lagrange multipliers of Chapter 4.

[24] See Appendix 5.1.

denote it here by $G(\tau)$—is simply the integral of its probability density function, denoted here by $g(T)$. In particular

$$G(\tau) = p(T \le \tau) = \int_0^\tau g(T) \, dT. \tag{5-47}$$

But from (5-46) we know that this is $(1 - e^{-\lambda \tau})$. To find $g(T)$, therefore, we need to find the function that, when integrated between 0 and τ, gives $(1 - e^{-\lambda \tau})$; that is, we want the derivative of $(1 - e^{-\lambda \tau})$. Thus[25]

$$g(T) = \lambda e^{-\lambda T}. \tag{5-48}$$

The functions in (5-45), (5-46), and (5-48) are generally described as *negative exponential* distributions simply because they involve the random variable as a negative exponent of e.

Knowing this much about the distribution of arrival times, it is easy to obtain, for example, the system characteristic "mean time between arrivals." This is simply the mean of the (continuous) random variable T whose probability density function is given in (5-48). Thus[26]

$$E(T) = \int_0^\infty T(\lambda e^{-\lambda T}) \, dT = \frac{1}{\lambda}. \tag{5-49}$$

Thus, *for the Poisson case*, the mean time between arrivals is the reciprocal of the mean arrival rate, λ.

The distribution of completed services

Returning to the generalized Poisson process of Section 5.6, suppose the "event" in question had been "completion of service on an item"—that is, departure from (rather than arrival at) the service facility. Once again, the hypotheses or assumptions at the beginning of that section could be reinterpreted, this time for the event "completion of service"; in general (in the queuing literature) μ replaces π in assumption 3—so $\mu \, \Delta t$ represents the probability of service completion during Δt and hence μ is the mean service (completion) rate. As above, the distribution for n services in time t would be

$$q_n(t) = \frac{e^{-\mu t}(\mu t)^n}{n!} \tag{5-50}$$

---

[25] The reader may wish to integrate $g(T)$ between 0 and τ to convince himself that the result is $1 - e^{-\lambda \tau}$. The function also meets the "sums to one" requirement of all probability density functions, since

$$\int_0^\infty \lambda e^{-\lambda T} \, dT = -e^{-\lambda T} \Big]_0^\infty = 0 + 1 = 1.$$

[26] The reader familiar with integral calculus is encouraged to derive this result. The rule for "integration by parts" is recommended.

(using q to denote probabilities of service completions to distinguish them from p, the probabilities of arrivals). Going through an analysis similar to that for the times between arrivals, it is relatively easy to show that if we let s be the random variable "times between service completion," then its probability density function is

$$h(s) = \mu e^{-\mu s} \tag{5-51}$$

(using h to distinguish from g, above), and, in particular $E(s) = 1/\mu$. In words, the mean time between service completions (the "mean service time") is the reciprocal of the mean service completion rate.

5.8. ARRIVALS AND SERVICES: THE QUEUING SITUATION (ONE STATION)

Our object is now to combine the arrivals with the servicings. When the Poisson distribution (Section 5.6) can be said to underlie both facets,[27] we speak of a queuing situation with "Poisson arrivals" [as in (5-43)] and "exponential service times" [as in (5-51)]. It turns out that for these (relatively realistic) cases, the resulting system characteristics—in which a decision maker's interest lies—can be expressed as functions that are not too complex.[28] Our ultimate interest is in using the relevant system descriptors in functions (usually cost) that we wish to optimize. Our object now is to show how these characteristics can be derived from the assumptions and functions of Section 5.7. Here we investigate one line served by one facility—the so-called *single-station* case.

Number of items in the system: n

Consider now a random variable that is neither number of arrivals nor number of service completions (departures) per unit time. Rather let the variable be the *number of items in the system* (in line or being serviced). The object is to derive expressions for $p_n(t)$ in terms of *both* λ and μ, the arrival and service rates, when the underlying description of both aspects of the queuing situation is a Poisson process. More specifically, the object is to derive distributions (frequency functions or probability density

---

[27] Considerable evidence indicates that this is a reasonable assumption in many real-world situations, especially for arrivals. We explore alternatives for the servicing distribution in later sections.

[28] Some queuing situations generate such a complicated series of functions for system characteristics that simulation (generally on a computer) is virtually the only way to approach the decision-making (for example, cost-minimizing) problem. The student interested in the simulation approach is referred, again, to any of the operations research texts listed at the end of this chapter.

functions) and hence to find means (expected values) for several measures related to the entire system. It is to these expected values of the various measures that costs may be assigned, and this is our entire purpose in deriving the distributions. We must assume throughout that $\lambda < \mu$—that is, that infinitely long lines do not form, since the service rate exceeds the arrival rate; this is often expressed as $\lambda/\mu < 1$.

Consider now the ways in which there can be n units in a single-station queuing system (in line or in service).[29] As before, we first let n be strictly greater than 0. The probability of n items in the system at $t + \Delta t$ is the sum of the probabilities of four mutually exclusive events. These are described in turn; we now let $p_n(t)$ denote the probability of n items in the system at time[30] t. We maintain, parallel to assumption 1, above, that this is independent of t and hence can be shown as p_n and thought of as the probability of n items in the system at *any* time t.

1. n in the system at t, none arrive during Δt, none leave during Δt:
    (a) p_n,
    (b) $1 - \lambda \Delta t$,
    (c) $1 - \mu \Delta t$;

or

2. $(n + 1)$ in the system at t, none arrive during Δt, one leaves during Δt:
    (a) p_{n+1},
    (b) $1 - \lambda \Delta t$,
    (c) $\mu \Delta t$;

or

3. $(n - 1)$ in the system at t, one arrives during Δt, none leave during Δt:
    (a) p_{n-1},
    (b) $\lambda \Delta t$,
    (c) $1 - \mu \Delta t$;

or

4. n in the system at t, one arrives during Δt, one leaves during Δt:
    (a) p_n,
    (b) $\lambda \Delta t$,
    (c) $\mu \Delta t$.

Thus the probability of n units $(n > 0)$ in the system (at *any* time t) is the sum of the probabilities of each of these compound events:

---

[29] This is parallel to (but broader than) the analysis behind (5-39) and (5-40).

[30] In the discussions above, $p_n(t)$ was used for the probability of n "occurrences" over an *interval* of length t. Our analysis would in no way be affected if we here used, for example, $_np(t)$ to emphasize the distinction. The fundamental Poisson process assumptions specify what happens during Δt in the analysis that follows.

$$p_n = p_n(1 - \lambda \, \Delta t)(1 - \mu \, \Delta t) + p_{n+1}(1 - \lambda \, \Delta t)\mu \, \Delta t + p_{n-1}(1 - \mu \, \Delta t)\lambda \, \Delta t$$
$$+ p_n \lambda \mu (\Delta t)^2, \quad (5\text{-}52)$$

or, rewriting,

$$0 = p_n[-\lambda \, \Delta t - \mu \, \Delta t + \lambda \mu (\Delta t)^2] + p_{n+1}(1 - \lambda \, \Delta t)\mu \, \Delta t$$
$$+ p_{n-1}(1 - \mu \, \Delta t)\lambda \, \Delta t + p_n \lambda \mu (\Delta t)^2.$$

Dividing by Δt, and eliminating further terms in Δt (since they become negligible for very small Δt, and the size of Δt can be as small as we wish),

$$(\lambda + \mu)p_n = \mu p_{n+1} + \lambda p_{n-1} \quad \text{or} \quad p_{n+1} = \left(\frac{\lambda + \mu}{\mu}\right)p_n - \left(\frac{\lambda}{\mu}\right)p_{n-1}. \quad (5\text{-}53)$$

For the $n = 0$ case, there are fewer possible alternatives:

5.   none in the system at t and none arrives during Δt:
    (a) p_0,
    (b) $1 - \lambda \, \Delta t$;
6.   one in the system at t, no arrivals in Δt, one leaves in Δt:
    (a) p_1,
    (b) $1 - \lambda \, \Delta t$,
    (c) $\mu \, \Delta t$.

Therefore, for $n = 0$, p_n is the sum of the probabilities in alternatives 5 and 6:

$$p_0 = p_0(1 - \lambda \, \Delta t) + p_1(1 - \lambda \, \Delta t)\mu \, \Delta t, \quad (5\text{-}54)$$

and, rearranging, dividing by Δt, and eliminating further Δt terms,

$$\lambda p_0 = \mu p_1 \quad \text{or} \quad p_1 = \left(\frac{\lambda}{\mu}\right)p_0. \quad (5\text{-}55)$$

Now (5-53) and (5-55) provide the following set of relations:

$$p_0 = p_0,$$
$$p_1 = \left(\frac{\lambda}{\mu}\right)p_0,$$
$$p_2 = \left(\frac{\lambda + \mu}{\mu}\right)p_1 - \left(\frac{\lambda}{\mu}\right)p_0 = \left(\frac{\lambda + \mu}{\mu} - 1\right)\left(\frac{\lambda}{\mu}\right)p_0$$
$$= \left(\frac{\lambda}{\mu}\right)\left(\frac{\lambda}{\mu}\right)p_0 = \left(\frac{\lambda}{\mu}\right)^2 p_0, \quad (5\text{-}56)$$
$$\vdots \quad \vdots$$
$$p_n = \left(\frac{\lambda}{\mu}\right)^n p_0.$$

The problem is to establish p_0, after which all else is determined. Consider the *sum* of both sides of (5-56). On the left,

$$\sum_{i=0}^{\infty} p_i = 1,$$

by definition, since these are probabilities. On the right, the sum is

$$p_0 \sum_{i=0}^{\infty} \left(\frac{\lambda}{\mu}\right)^i$$

Recall that we have assumed $(\lambda/\mu) < 1$. Thus[31]

$$p_0 \sum_{i=0}^{\infty} \left(\frac{\lambda}{\mu}\right)^i = p_0 \left[\frac{1}{1 - (\lambda/\mu)}\right],$$

and hence

$$1 = p_0 \left[\frac{1}{1 - (\lambda/\mu)}\right], \tag{5-57}$$

or

$$p_0 = 1 - \frac{\lambda}{\mu}. \tag{5-58}$$

This is the type of result we want: p_0 is defined in terms of the known system parameters λ and μ. Thus, inserting (5-58) in the last equation of (5-56):

$$p_n = \left(\frac{\lambda}{\mu}\right)^n \left(1 - \frac{\lambda}{\mu}\right). \tag{5-59}$$

We now have all the information possible about the (discrete) random variable n, the number of items in the system (queue plus service); we know that n can take on integral values 0, 1, ... and we know, in (5-59), the probabilities of each of these values. Thus, for example, we can find $E(n)$, the average number of items in the system (a value which might be useful, for example, in making decisions about physical size and arrangement at the service facility). We let $N \equiv E(n)$ for notational simplicity in later formulas.

$$N \equiv E(n) = (0)p_0 + (1)p_1 + \cdots + (n)p_n + \cdots = \sum_{n=0}^{\infty} (n)p_n.$$

This works out to be[32]

---

[31] This is a fundamental result for infinite series, provided that the ratio involved is strictly less than 1.

[32] The details of this and several other results are shown in Appendix 5.3 for the interested reader; they are not our primary concern in this chapter.

$$N = \frac{\lambda/\mu}{1 - (\lambda/\mu)} \quad \text{or} \quad \frac{\lambda}{\mu - \lambda} \cdot \qquad (5\text{-}60)$$

Thus, for a single-station system with a mean arrival rate (λ) of 10 items per hour and a mean service rate (μ) of 20 items per hour, we can immediately calculate that the expected number of items in the system is $N = 10/(20 - 10) = 1$ item.

Our object in the remainder of this section will be to select other variables that describe characteristics of the queuing system, derive the probabilities associated with values of the variables—that is, find their frequency function (discrete variables) or probability density function (continuous variables)—and then calculate the *means* of these functions to gain an idea of the average characteristics to be expected. There are two general classes of queue variables. One deals with *numbers* of items, such as items in the system, length of the waiting line, and so on; these are discrete variables. The other class consists of variables measuring *time*, such as the time an item spends waiting, the total time spent in the system (waiting plus service), and so on; these are continuous variables. We examine several from each class.

Queue length (number of items waiting in line): m

Consider the discrete variable m = queue length. For the single-station case, queue length is related very simply to the number of items in the system, n; clearly $m = n - 1$, for $n > 0$. To find the average queue length we want

$$E(m) = \sum_{m=0}^{\infty} (m)p_m.$$

[Again, for later convenience we let $M \equiv E(m)$.] Note, however, that the first term in this summation is just 0—$(0)p_0$; hence writing

$$M = \sum_{m=1}^{\infty} (m)p_m$$

is just as accurate. We have not derived the values p_m, but we *do* know the probabilities p_n from (5-59) *and* we know how m and n are related. Thus

$$M = \sum_{m=1}^{\infty} (m)p_m = \sum_{n=2}^{\infty} (n - 1)p_n. \qquad (5\text{-}61)$$

We have converted the right-hand side to elements concerned *exclusively* with n. All that is needed now is a certain amount of algebra and application of our fundamental knowledge of p_n. (The interested reader may refer to Appendix 5.3.) The result of importance is

$$M = N - \frac{\lambda}{\mu} = \frac{\lambda^2}{\mu(\mu - \lambda)}. \tag{5-62}$$

Again an average characteristic of the queue is found to be a straightforward function of the governing parameters: mean arrival rate and mean service rate. For the system with $\lambda = 10$ and $\mu = 20$, for which $N = 1$, we see that $M = 1 - \frac{1}{2} = (10)(10)/(20)(10) = \frac{1}{2}$. Since $\lambda/\mu = \frac{1}{2}$ represents the expected number of items *in service* at any time, it is logical that $M = N - (\lambda/\mu)$.

Length of nonempty queues: m_c

In general in a queuing situation there will be times when no items are waiting—that is, when a queue of zero length exists. However, in many decisions involving the planning of facilities space, and in particular in planning for the amount of room to allot for items in line (for example, the safety aspect involved with airplanes stacked over an airport), it is much more relevant to weight in the average measure *only* those cases in which the waiting line is strictly greater than zero.[33]

Precisely because we saw that the range of the random variable m could in fact be assumed to begin at unity (and not zero), we see that the range of summation for m_c is just that of m. However, in each case the accompanying probability must be conditional ("given that $m > 0$—that is, that $n > 1$"). Thus, since the *range* of summation is correct, all that is necessary to convert the derivation for $E(m)$ to that for $E(m_c) \equiv M_c$ is to divide each of the probabilities, p_m, by $p(m > 0)$, to make them *conditional* probabilities. Since $p(m > 0) = p(n > 1)$, we are in fact dividing by

$$(1 - p_0 - p_1) = 1 - \left(1 - \frac{\lambda}{\mu}\right) - \frac{\lambda}{\mu}\left(1 - \frac{\lambda}{\mu}\right) = \left(\frac{\lambda}{\mu}\right)^2.$$

Thus (again, Appendix 5.3 gives details):

$$M_c = \frac{M}{(\lambda/\mu)^2} = \frac{\mu}{\mu - \lambda}. \tag{5-63}$$

Considering once again the example where $\lambda = 10$ and $\mu = 20$, $M_c = 2$. While $M = \frac{1}{2}$, $p_0 = 1 - (\lambda/\mu) = \frac{1}{2}$ indicates the proportion of time in which *no* items are expected to be in the system (and hence in line) and $p_1 = (\lambda/\mu)[1 - (\lambda/\mu)] = \frac{1}{4}$ indicates the proportion of time with only *one* item in the system (and hence in service, meaning *none* in line). Thus 3/4

---

[33] To illustrate by an extreme example, if a line had *no* items 90 percent of the time and *100* items the other 10 percent, the average queue length would be $(0)(.90) + (100)(.10) = 10$, yet provision may need to be made for those 100 items that are expected to be present 10 percent of the time.

of the times (that is, of the "weightings") used in calculating M involve *no* items in line. Hence M_c could be found from the logical relation $\frac{3}{4}(0) + \frac{1}{4}(x) = \frac{1}{2}$, where $x =$ average length of nonempty queues; clearly $x = 2 = M_c$, as found above.

Waiting time of an arrival: w

Random variables concerned with *times* spent by an arrival in waiting, in the system, and so on are of course *continuous* variables, for which probability densities rather than frequency functions are relevant. If we denote this density function by $\psi(w)$, then we attach to the expression $\psi(w)\,dw$ the interpretation:[34] the probability that the variable "waiting time" is between w and $w + dw$. Our interest, therefore, is in deriving the function $\psi(w)$.

Clearly the probability of *no* waiting time is just the probability of *no* units in the system:

$$p(w = 0) = 1 - \frac{\lambda}{\mu}. \tag{5-64}$$

For values of the variable w that are greater than zero, we see that the following three events are necessary in order that an item arriving at any time t_0, waits for an interval of time $w + dw$:

1. there must be n items in line and none in service at t_0;
2. $n - 1$ of these must be serviced during the time interval w;
3. one must be serviced during the interval dw.

In this way, the item entering the line at t_0 will be entering service after a wait of $w + dw$. Figure 5.12 illustrates. We know the probabilities of each of these three events from earlier discussion:

1. $p_n = (\lambda/\mu)^n[1 - (\lambda/\mu)]$; this is (5-59).
2. $p(n - 1 \text{ services during } w) = e^{-\mu w}(\mu w)^{n-1}/(n - 1)!$; this comes directly from (5-50).
3. $p(1 \text{ service in } dw) = \mu\,dw$; this is the third hypothesis that underlies both the arrival and the service descriptions.

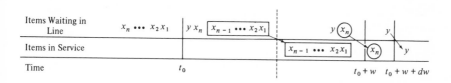

Figure 5.12.   Schematic Representation for Waiting Time of $w + dw$

[34] Again, refer to Appendix 5.1.

Thus the product of these three probabilities,

$$\left(\frac{\lambda}{\mu}\right)^n \left(1 - \frac{\lambda}{\mu}\right) \frac{e^{-\mu w}(\mu w)^{n-1}}{(n-1)!} \mu \, dw,$$

gives the probability that an arrival at t_0 waits in line for a period $(w + dw)$—*for a specified n*. That is, the three probabilities listed above are valid for *any* $n > 1$; hence the item arriving at t_0 will wait $w + dw$ if $n = 1$ and none are serviced in w, if $n = 2$ and 1 is serviced in w, and so on. Thus, this product (of the three individual probabilities) must be *summed* over all possible values of n; these represent the mutually exclusive ways in which the item arriving at t_0 will have to wait $w + dw$. This sum will give the function $\psi(w) \, dw$ for the case $w > 0$. It works out to be (the details are in Appendix 5.3):

$$\psi(w) \, dw = \left(1 - \frac{\lambda}{\mu}\right) \lambda e^{(\lambda - \mu)w} \, dw. \qquad (5\text{-}65)$$

We now can ask, what is the expected amount of time an arrival spends waiting in line in a single-station service facility with parameters μ and λ? For the continuous-variable case, we know (Appendix 5.1) that

$$E(w) \equiv W \equiv \int_0^\infty w\psi(w) \, dw.$$

The function in (5-65) is valid for $w > 0$; but (5-64) gave the probability for $w = 0$. Hence what we appear to want is something like

$$(0)p_0 + \int^\infty w\psi(w) \, dw,$$

where the lower bound on the integral is just above zero. But clearly (1) omitting a $(0)p_0$ term leaves nothing out and (2) since the product $w\psi(w) \, dw$ is under the integral sign, the $w = 0$ contribution drops out in any case. Thus we can write

$$W = \int_0^\infty w\psi(w) \, dw = \int_0^\infty w \left(1 - \frac{\lambda}{\mu}\right) \lambda e^{(\lambda - \mu)w} \, dw \qquad (5\text{-}66)$$

[from (5-65)]. By moving constant terms outside the integral sign and applying the "integration by parts" rule to what remains, we obtain (remembering that $\mu > \lambda$),

$$W = \frac{\lambda}{\mu(\mu - \lambda)}. \qquad (5\text{-}67)$$

Again, from the $\lambda = 10$ and $\mu = 20$ example, the expected *waiting time* is $(10)/(20)(10) = \frac{1}{20}$ hour or 3 minutes.

Waiting time of an arrival who waits: w_c

As above, where we distinguished queues in general from nonempty ones, we may also wish to distinguish average waiting time in general, W, from average waiting time for those who have to wait at all. That is, we may wish to abstract from the possibility of no waiting and simply average the waiting times to be expected, *given* that an item has to wait at all for service. As before, we want to convert the probabilities in a calculation such as (5-61) or (5-66) to *conditional* ones; here the condition is "given that a person has to wait"—that is, $w > 0$. Thus, we need only divide each of the probabilities in (5-66) by the probability of the event on which they are conditional—that is, by $p(w > 0) = 1 - p(w = 0) = 1 - [1 - (\lambda/\mu)] = (\lambda/\mu)$. Therefore, letting $E(w_c) \equiv W_c$,

$$
\begin{aligned}
W_c &= \int_0^\infty w \, \frac{[1 - (\lambda/\mu)]\lambda e^{(\lambda-\mu)w}}{\lambda/\mu} \, dw \\
&= (\mu - \lambda) \int_0^\infty w e^{(\lambda-\mu)w} \, dw \\
&= (\mu - \lambda) \left[\frac{1}{(\lambda - \mu)^2} \right] \\
&= (\mu - \lambda) \left[\frac{1}{(\mu - \lambda)^2} \right],
\end{aligned}
$$

or, directly through division of W in (5-67) by λ/μ,

$$
W_c = \frac{1}{\mu - \lambda}. \tag{5-68}
$$

Thus, for the system with $\lambda = 10$ and $\mu = 20$, the expected waiting time of an arrival, given that he has to wait at all, is $W_c = \frac{1}{10}$ hour or 6 minutes. Again, this result is consistent with the earlier one, $W = 3$. Since, with $\lambda = 10$ and $\mu = 20$, the probability of no waiting—that is, the probability of no items in the system—is $p_0 = 1 - (\lambda/\mu) = \frac{1}{2}$, then the *overall* average waiting time will be

$$(0)[p(w = 0)] + (W_c)[p(w \neq 0)] = (0)(\tfrac{1}{2}) + (6)(\tfrac{1}{2}) = 3 \text{ minutes,}$$

as we found above.

Total time in the system: v

Consider now another possibly relevant queue characteristic, namely, total time that an item spends in the system—waiting in line plus being serviced. As in the case immediately above, we are concerned with establishing a probability density function for the continuous variable v; let

$$\theta(v)\, dv = (v < \text{waiting} + \text{service time} < v + dv).$$

The conditions necessary for an item arriving at t_0 to spend a total time of $v + dv$ in the system are:

1. n in line before arrival at t_0; for this $p_n = (\lambda/\mu)^n[1 - (\lambda/\mu)]$;
2. n serviced during the interval v; the probability of this is $q_n = e^{-\mu v}(\mu v)^n/n!$;
3. one (the unit arriving at t_0) serviced during the time interval dv; this probability is $\mu\, dv$.

As in the analysis for waiting time, w, we need the products of these three probabilities, summed over all alternatives for n (here $n = 0$, 1, ..., ∞, since condition 2 requires n services, not $n - 1$ as in the case of w). The final outcome (again, Appendix 5.3 gives details) is

$$\theta(v)\, dv = (\mu - \lambda)e^{(\lambda - \mu)v}\, dv. \tag{5-69}$$

As always, our interest is fundamentally in the expected or average value of this characteristic of the queue, total time in the system. As is usual with continuous probability distributions,

$$V \equiv E(v) = \int_0^{\infty} v\, \theta(v)\, dv = \int_0^{\infty} v(\mu - \lambda)e^{(\lambda - \mu)v}\, dv. \tag{5-70}$$

When constant terms are moved out from under the integral sign, this becomes

$$V = (\mu - \lambda) \int_0^{\infty} ve^{(\lambda - \mu)v}\, dv,$$

which has exactly the same structure as the integral for W_c prior to (5-68), once its constant terms are placed outside the integral. Thus, utilizing the earlier results for W_c:

$$V = (\mu - \lambda) \left(\frac{1}{(\lambda - \mu)^2} \right) = \frac{1}{\mu - \lambda}. \tag{5-71}$$

Therefore, in the $\lambda = 10$, $\mu = 20$ example, both expected total time in the system, V, and expected waiting time of a unit that waits, W_c, are $\frac{1}{10}$ hour or 6 minutes.[35] Note that $V = W + (1/\mu)$, which is logical; average total time is average waiting time plus average time in service.

---

[35] Again, this result makes sense. Either an arrival waits or it does not: (1) if it does not, the total expected system time is just expected service time, $1/\mu$, or in this example $\frac{1}{20}$ hour or 3 minutes; this occurs with probability $p_0 = \frac{1}{2}$; (2) if it does wait, the expected system time is expected waiting (W_c) plus expected service times, 6 minutes + 3 minutes = 9 minutes; this occurs with probability $1 - p_0 = \frac{1}{2}$. Thus $V = (3)(\frac{1}{2}) + (9)(\frac{1}{2}) = 6$ minutes.

Summary of single-station system characteristics

The relevant characteristics for a single-station queuing system are collected here for easy reference; the numbering is that of the original statement:

The probability of having n units in the system at any time is

$$p_n = \left(\frac{\lambda}{\mu}\right)^n \left(1 - \frac{\lambda}{\mu}\right) ; \qquad (5\text{-}59)$$

the average number of items in the system is

$$E(n) \equiv N = \frac{\lambda}{\mu - \lambda} ; \qquad (5\text{-}60)$$

the average queue length is

$$E(m) \equiv M = \frac{\lambda^2}{\mu(\mu - \lambda)} ; \qquad (5\text{-}62)$$

the average length of nonempty queues is

$$E(m \mid m > 0) \equiv M_c = \frac{\mu}{\mu - \lambda} ; \qquad (5\text{-}63)$$

the average waiting time (time in the queue) is

$$E(w) \equiv W = \frac{\lambda}{\mu(\mu - \lambda)} ; \qquad (5\text{-}67)$$

the average waiting time of an arrival who has to wait is

$$E(w \mid w > 0) \equiv W_c = \frac{1}{\mu - \lambda} ; \qquad (5\text{-}68)$$

and, finally, the average time spent in the system (waiting *and* service) is

$$E(v) \equiv V = \frac{1}{\mu - \lambda}. \qquad (5\text{-}71)$$

The reader should realize that these average system characteristics depend precisely on the forms of the distributions used to describe arrivals and service times; in this case on the assumptions of "Poisson arrivals and negative exponential services." The derivations in Appendix 5.3 and the integrations for the average values of the continuous random variables all involve the probability functions directly and explicitly. The important outcome is that these average characteristics are relatively simple functions of the two system parameters over which the decision maker may have some control. Thus, he is able to know how changes in either or both of the rates will be reflected in the system.

5.9. OPTIMUM SERVICE RATE FOR A SINGLE-STATION MODEL

Consider the problem of repairing certain types of machines as they break down in a large factory in which many such machines are in operation daily. There are essentially two costs associated with a machine that breaks down; one is the cost of repairing it, the second is the cost of the production time lost while the machine is inoperative. Assume that we can establish an average cost of repairing a machine, c_1. (The dimensions are money/item.) Although the times taken to make a complete repair may vary—indeed we assume they follow a negative exponential distribution with a parameter μ that can be estimated through observation—we can still derive an average cost of repair per item from past records. Similarly, assume that we can estimate the cost per unit of time of a machine's being inoperable; call this c_2. (The dimensions are money/item-time—for example, dollars per machine-hour.)

Thus $c_1\mu$ represents total servicing cost per time interval (since μ gives the number of services completed in some selected time interval), and c_2N or, from (5-60), $c_2[\lambda/(\mu - \lambda)]$ gives total "downtime cost" for the same time interval. (All that is necessary is that the time dimensions of μ, λ, and c_2 be the same.) Thus the cost per time interval (say one hour) of maintaining a service rate μ per hour when faced with costs c_1 and c_2 and an arrival rate of λ per hour is

$$c_h = c_1\mu + c_2\left(\frac{\lambda}{\mu - \lambda}\right). \qquad (5\text{-}72)$$

Assume that management has little or no control over λ (in many situations they might, in which case c_h could be considered a function of two independent variables) and thus their interest is in establishing a service rate μ that minimizes the hourly costs shown in (5-72). Note that the two terms in c_h behave in much the same way as the two components of inventory cost in the simple model with holding and setup costs only [see (5-1) and Figure 5.5, above]. The influence of $c_1\mu$ is toward a decision for a *lower* μ; the second term, $c_2[\lambda/(\mu - \lambda)]$, gives weight to a *larger* μ. The cost-minimizing service rate can be found through calculus. From (5-72)

$$\frac{dc_h}{d\mu} = c_1 - \frac{c_2\lambda}{(\mu - \lambda)^2},$$

and setting the first derivative equal to zero gives, after some rearrangement,

$$\mu^* = \lambda + \sqrt{\frac{c_2}{c_1}\lambda}. \qquad (5\text{-}73)$$

(The second-derivative check shows this to represent a minimum of c_h, as desired.) If the service rate is adjusted to conform to this result, the *minimum* cost will be

$$c_h^* = c_1\mu^* + c_2\left(\frac{\lambda}{\mu^* - \lambda}\right) = c_1\lambda + 2\sqrt{c_1 c_2 \lambda}. \tag{5-74}$$

Clearly many more complex functions of queuing system characteristics may be derived for the single-station case, and it may be necessary or important to incorporate constraints in the optimization problem. The reader should appreciate that the queue reasoning takes place within a framework similar to (but generally more complicated than) that in Section 5.8. The optimization then proceeds along the lines of Chapter 4, or, in cases constrained by many inequalities and nonnegativity requirements on the variables, via the programming methods discussed in the next four chapters. We conclude this chapter with two extensions of the fundamental queuing model of Section 5.8.

5.10. THE QUEUING SITUATION (MULTIPLE STATIONS)

Consider now the system in which items arrive and wait (if necessary) in a single line to receive service at any one of k stations—for example, ships waiting for an empty dock in a harbor, any "over-the-counter" situation where customers wait (knowing their order of arrival, even if a single, well-behaved line does not exist) for any one of several sales or service personnel, and so on. In the development of Section 5.8, we needed the assumption that $\lambda/\mu < 1$—that is, that $\lambda < \mu$—intuitively, to assure that an infinitely long line did not occur, mathematically to derive the fundamental infinite-series result for p_0 in (5-58). Now for similar reasons we impose the condition that $\lambda/k\mu < 1$ or $\lambda < k\mu$.

The k-station situation involves another variation from the development in Section 5.8. It is necessary, in developing p_n, to distinguish the case in which $n \leq k$ from that in which $n > k$—as well as the $n = 0$ case, as before. This is because the probability of a service completion during Δt is directly influenced by the number of stations *relative to* the number of units in the system. Thus, while $\lambda \Delta t$ still represents the probability of an arrival during Δt, the probability that one serviced item will be turned out during Δt is

0	if there were no units in the system at t,
$\mu \Delta t$	if there was one unit in the system at t,
$2\mu \Delta t$	if there were two units in the system at t,
$\vdots$	$\vdots$
$n\mu \Delta t$	if there were n units in the system at t,

provided that $n \leq k$. The reader should be clear what this means. Even with multiple stations, the probability of *more than one* item's completing service during Δt will be proportional to Δt squared (or raised to some higher power) and thus will be considered negligible. However, for example, if $k = 5$, then the probability of one item's completing service during Δt when $n = 3$ is $3\mu \Delta t$; if $n = 5$, this probability is $5\mu \Delta t$; if $n = 10$, this probability is still $5\mu \Delta t$, since there are only five stations at which servicing can be done.[36] Thus, for $n < k$, the service probabilities are $n\mu \Delta t$, for $n > k$ they are $k\mu \Delta t$, and for $n = k$ either $n\mu \Delta t$ or $k\mu \Delta t$ expresses the same probability.

We therefore consider *three* cases: (1) $n = 0$, (2) $1 \leq n < k$, and (3) $n \geq k$.

1. For $n = 0$, the derivation of p_n is identical to that for the single-station case in Section 5.8. The two mutually exclusive possibilities are: (a) none in the system at t and no arrivals in Δt, (b) one in the system at t, no arrivals and one service in Δt. The probabilities of these two events, as before, must be added:

$$p_0 = p_0(1 - \lambda \Delta t) + p_1(1 - \lambda \Delta t)\mu \Delta t,$$

which, after removing parentheses, subtracting p_0 from both sides, dropping $(\Delta t)^2$ terms, and dividing by Δt, gives the result in (5-55), which is repeated here with the numbering of this section:

$$p_1 = \left(\frac{\lambda}{\mu}\right) p_0. \tag{5-75}$$

2. For $1 \leq n < k$, we consider the alternatives that leave n in the k-station system after an interval Δt:

   (a) $(n - 1)$ in the system at t, one arrival and no services in Δt; the probability of this event is $p_{n-1}(\lambda \Delta t)(1 - n\mu \Delta t)$.
   (b) $(n + 1)$ in the system at t, no arrivals and one service during Δt; the probability of this event is $p_{n+1}(1 - \lambda \Delta t)[(n + 1) \mu\Delta t]$.
   (c) n in the system at t, and either no arrivals and no services completed or one arrival and one service during Δt; these probabilities are $p_n(1 - \lambda \Delta t)(1 - n\mu \Delta t)$ and $p_n(\lambda \Delta t)(n\mu \Delta t)$, respectively.

The reader should note that the description of these alternative events for p_n is the same as before (Section 5.8); only the probabilities associated with services have changed to reflect the multichannel character of the system. Parallel to (5-53) we now have

---

[36] Recall that Δt is chosen sufficiently small so that probabilities of more than one arrival or service are infinitely small. It is also possible to select Δt so that, in the k-station case, $k\mu \Delta t < 1$, as we expect of probabilities. This is essentially no different than the situation of $\lambda = 10$ per hour; if Δt is chosen to be $\frac{1}{2}$ hour, $\lambda \Delta t = 5$. However, with a Δt of $\frac{1}{2}$ minute, $\lambda \Delta t = \frac{1}{12}$.

$$(\lambda + n\mu)p_n = \lambda p_{n-1} + (n + 1)\mu p_{n+1}$$

or

$$p_{n+1} = \left[\frac{\lambda + n\mu}{(n + 1)\mu}\right] p_n - \left[\frac{\lambda}{(n + 1)\mu}\right] p_{n-1}. \qquad (5\text{-}76)$$

3. For $n \geq k$, the same four alternative events are relevant; only the probabilities change. They now are

(a) $p_{n-1}(\lambda \, \Delta t)(1 - k\mu \, \Delta t)$,
(b) $p_{n+1}(1 - \lambda \, \Delta t)(k\mu \, \Delta t)$,
(c) $p_n(1 - \lambda \, \Delta t)(1 - k\mu \, \Delta t)$ and $p_n(\lambda \, \Delta t)(k\mu \, \Delta t)$.

From this we derive

$$(\lambda + k\mu)p_n = \lambda p_{n-1} + k\mu p_{n+1}$$

or

$$p_{n+1} = \left(\frac{\lambda + k\mu}{k\mu}\right) p_n - \left(\frac{\lambda}{k\mu}\right) p_{n-1}. \qquad (5\text{-}77)$$

The recursive nature of (5-76) and (5-77) [parallel to (5-53)], along with the initial relation (5-75), provides the result

$$p_0 = p_0,$$
$$p_n = \frac{(\lambda/\mu)^n}{n!} p_0 \qquad \text{for } 1 \leq n < k, \qquad (5\text{-}78)$$
$$p_n = \frac{(\lambda/\mu)^n}{k!k^{n-k}} p_0 \qquad \text{for } n \geq k.$$

As before, we can now find p_0 explicitly as a function of the system parameters by summing both sides of (5-78). From the left-hand side:

$$p_0 + \sum_{n=1}^{\infty} p_n = 1.$$

The right-hand sides for p_n, summed over their appropriate ranges of n, are complicated-looking expressions:

$$\sum_{n=0}^{k-1} \frac{(\lambda/\mu)^n}{n!} p_0 + \sum_{n=k}^{\infty} \frac{(\lambda/\mu)^n}{k!k^{n-k}} p_0.$$

The second sum can be simplified (see Appendix 5.3), and the resulting expression for p_0 (still not simple) is

$$p_0 = \frac{1}{\displaystyle\sum_{n=0}^{k-1} \frac{(\lambda/\mu)^n}{n!} + \frac{(\lambda/\mu)^k}{k!\left(1 - \dfrac{\lambda/\mu}{k}\right)}}. \qquad (5\text{-}79)$$

With these probabilities, we can now derive system characteristics as the average values of the random variables and their underlying probability distributions—either discrete frequency functions or continuous probability density functions. The reader is familiar with the logic of the derivations from Section 5.8; we summarize the results here. A k-station system, with Poisson arrivals and negative exponential service times, has the following system characteristics:

The probability of n units in the system at any time is given for $n = 0$ in (5-79) and for both $1 \leq n < k$ and $n \geq k$ in (5-78); these latter two (p_n) require p_0 from (5-79) as well; the average number of items in the system is

$$E(n) \equiv N = \frac{\lambda\mu(\lambda/\mu)^k}{(k-1)!(k\mu - \lambda)^2} p_0 + \frac{\lambda}{\mu} ; \qquad (5\text{-}80)$$

the average queue length[37] is

$$E(m) \equiv M = \frac{\lambda\mu(\lambda/\mu)^k}{(k-1)!(k\mu - \lambda)^2} p_0; \qquad (5\text{-}81)$$

the average waiting time (time in the queue) is

$$E(w) \equiv W = \frac{\mu(\lambda/\mu)^k}{(k-1)!(k\mu - \lambda)^2} p_0; \qquad (5\text{-}82)$$

and the average time spent in the system[38] (waiting and service) is

$$E(v) \equiv V = \frac{\mu(\lambda/\mu)^k}{(k-1)!(k\mu - \lambda)^2} p_0 + \frac{1}{\mu}. \qquad (5\text{-}83)$$

Again, the average characteristics are seen to depend—although in a far less straightforward way—on the same two system parameters, λ and μ, and on k, the number of service facilities. (For $k = 1$, these results reduce exactly to those in Section 5.8.) Thus the effect of decisions to alter one or more of these parameters can be determined relatively easily, and hence the expected benefits from proposed changes can be compared with expected costs involved.

5.11. A MORE GENERAL DISTRIBUTION OF COMPLETED SERVICES

The probability density function for times between service, s, in (5-51), $h(s) = \mu e^{-\mu s}$ [and the underlying Poisson distribution of service completions in (5-50)] has been used throughout the preceding sections. It has

[37] Although it is a much more involved proof, it can be shown (again, see Appendix 5.3) that in the k-station model the expected number of items in service is (λ/μ)—exactly (and perhaps surprisingly) as in the single-station model. Thus $M = N - (\lambda/\mu)$, as before, which is how (5-81) can be derived from (5-80).

[38] As with N and M, the relationship between W and V is the same in the k-station case as when there is only one service facility.

generally been found that the underlying Poisson distribution is a better assumption for arrivals than for service completions. For this reason a more general theory for service distributions is also available.[39] Consider the Erlang distribution of service times, s:

$$h(s) = \frac{(\mu r)^r}{(r-1)!} s^{r-1} e^{-r\mu s}. \tag{5-84}$$

This is a two-parameter distribution; values taken by s generate values for $h(s)$ *given* both μ and r. In particular, for $r = 1$, (5-84) reduces to the negative exponential distribution in (5-51). Thus the results in Section 5.8 are for a *particular* Erlang function. The mean and variance of the Erlang distribution are $(1/\mu)$ and $(1/r\mu^2)$, respectively. Therefore, when $r = \infty$, the mean is $(1/\mu)$ and the variance is *zero;* this represents the case of *constant service time.*

The Erlang distribution in (5-84), precisely because it has the added flexibility of a second parameter, r, can often be used to provide a more accurate description of an observed distribution of service times than would be possible using $h(s)$ in (5-51) only. Moreover, there is a somewhat different type of queuing situation in which the form of $h(s)$ in (5-84) can be used. Consider a multistage service situation (say r stages) in which time in each stage is independent of the others (for example, various tests in a clinic). If service time in each stage follows a common exponential distribution with mean time $1/r\mu$, then total service time will follow an Erlang distribution as given by (5-84) with parameters r and μ. For example, consider a series of three tests given to incoming patients at a clinic, each of which takes an average of 12 minutes (although the distribution of actual times within each test is exponential). Let $s_i =$ time spent in test i ($i = 1, 2, 3$); and let s_t be total time spent in the tests: $s_t = s_1 + s_2 + s_3$. Then s_t follows an Erlang distribution with $r = 3$ (three stages to the incoming tests) and, since $1/3\mu = 12$ minutes, $\mu = \frac{1}{36}$ and $1/\mu = 36$ minutes,

$$h(s_t) = \left(\frac{1}{3456}\right) s_t^2 e^{-(1/12)s_t}.$$

For the general Erlang distribution, it is also possible (and even more complicated) to derive average system characteristics. They are as follows (for the rth Erlang distribution) *for the single-station case.*

The average number of items in the system is

$$E(n) \equiv N = \left(\frac{r+1}{2r}\right)\frac{\lambda^2}{\mu(\mu-\lambda)} + \frac{\lambda}{\mu}; \tag{5-85}$$

as usual, the average queue length is just $N - \lambda/\mu$;

---

[39] Due largely to A. K. Erlang, who pioneered queuing analysis, in particular for problems at telephone central offices.

$$E(m) \equiv M = \left(\frac{r+1}{2r}\right) \frac{\lambda^2}{\mu(\mu - \lambda)} \; ; \qquad (5\text{-}86)$$

the average waiting time is

$$E(w) \equiv W = \left(\frac{r+1}{2r}\right) \frac{\lambda}{\mu(\mu - \lambda)} \; ; \qquad (5\text{-}87)$$

and the average time spent in the system is, as before, $W + 1/\mu$;

$$E(v) \equiv V = \left(\frac{r+1}{2r}\right) \frac{\lambda}{\mu(\mu - \lambda)} + \frac{1}{\mu}. \qquad (5\text{-}88)$$

The reader will see that these differ from the results in Section 5.8 only by the multiplicative factor $(r + 1)/2r$, which equals unity for $r = 1$. For the case of *constant* service time at a single-station facility ($r = \infty$), the average system characteristics are:

$$E(n) \equiv N = \frac{\lambda^2}{2\mu(\mu - \lambda)} + \frac{\lambda}{\mu}, \qquad (5\text{-}89)$$

$$E(m) \equiv M = \frac{\lambda^2}{2\mu(\mu - \lambda)}, \qquad (5\text{-}90)$$

$$E(w) \equiv W = \frac{\lambda}{2\mu(\mu - \lambda)}, \qquad (5\text{-}91)$$

$$E(v) \equiv V = \frac{\lambda}{2\mu(\mu - \lambda)} + \frac{1}{\mu}. \qquad (5\text{-}92)$$

SUMMARY

In this chapter we investigated initially the fundamentals of the class of problems for which inventory models are appropriate. The reader will have seen that the "models" as such are nothing particularly new: they involve selection of a policy to minimize a particular cost function, where the costs are related to overproduction, underproduction, shortages, inventories, and so on, of a particular item. In the case of known demand, the common thread that may be said to run through the approach is a simple geometric concern with areas of variously constructed triangles, which represent overall amounts of inventory and shortage.

In the case of uncertain (probabilistically known) demand, in order to take completely into account the information in the probability distribution governing the expected amounts to be demanded, we have seen that a cost function results that involves either summation signs or integrals and a random as well as an independent variable. In the discrete case, because of the lack of continuity in the function, the method of finite differences was seen to provide criteria for a minimum point. In the continuous case, the principles of differential calculus were relevant, except that a new rule was required to cover the problem of differentiating a function involving a random variable and integrals. Obviously, possibilities for more complicated problems are numerous: interest costs on capital tied up in inventory can be explicitly considered, quantity discounts or alternate prices for different-sized orders can be introduced, and so forth. However, the concern of this chapter has been to present the underlying and basic structure common to all inventory problems.

Second, we were concerned with the basic elements of models for analyzing several different waiting line situations. Once the average values of various queue characteristics have been derived—such as expected queue length or average time spent in the system—the actual use of these averages is quite straightforward. In general some sort of cost function is associated with one or more of the queue characteristics, and to the extent that λ or μ (or k, in the multiple-station case) is under a decision maker's control, the methods of calculus can be used to find the optimum (cost-minimizing) values of these variables.

When the student appreciates fully the implications of assumptions about arrival and service distributions, then, in any given situation, he is better equipped to judge between possible assumptions—some of which will naturally be more realistic but at the same time less manageable. Initially, our discussion made specific the nature of the "randomness" of the random variables (1) arrival rates and (2) service times—that is, specified their probability distributions. Then the simplest case of a one-station situation with Poisson arrivals and negative exponential service times was studied in detail to emphasize exactly how the underlying distributions (the assumptions or hypotheses about the arrivals and services) affect the average characteristics of the system. Next the more complex k-station situation was developed (of which the earlier single-station model was a special—the simplest—case). Finally the more general family of Erlang distributions was presented to cover a wider range of service-time assumptions. In each case it is ultimately the average characteristics of the system that are of interest, since they indicate precisely how the system depends on its parameters; and it is these parameters that one may be able to change to optimize some aspect of system performance. Clearly, side conditions that may arise within the context of the queuing problem—in the form of equality or inequality constraints on some or all of the variables—will further complicate the optimization procedure. In some cases, the methods of Chapter 4 will still be appropriate. In others, new techniques will be needed. These are the subject matter of the remainder of this book.

APPENDIX 5.1

Discrete and Continuous Probability Distributions

When a variable takes on different specific values with known probabilities, it is generally known as a "random variable." If the variable can take on only a finite number of specific values (for example, the outcome of the roll of one die), it is called a *discrete* random variable.[40] If, on the other hand, the values of the variable are continuous (at least over some range), it is called a *continuous* random variable. Real-world measurements are always discrete—this is inherent in the nature of measuring devices—but it is often convenient to use continuous models to represent the underlying phenomena.

For a discrete random variable, we refer to a listing of the possible values of the variable x and the probabilities with which they occur, $f(x)$, as a probability table. (Its graph is generally termed a probability function or probability distribution.) Table 5.8 and Figure 5.13 illustrate. The most

Table 5.8.   Probability Table for the Random Variable x = Outcome of One Roll of a Fair Die

x	1	2	3	4	5	6
$f(x)$	$\frac{1}{6}$	$\frac{1}{6}$	$\frac{1}{6}$	$\frac{1}{6}$	$\frac{1}{6}$	$\frac{1}{6}$

common measure of central tendency is the mean or "expected value"; for such functions, where x_i represents a particular possible value of the random variable and $f(x_i)$ the probability with which that value occurs, the mean is given by

$$E(x) = \sum_{i=1}^{n} x_i f(x_i), \qquad (5\text{-}93)$$

[40] This is somewhat confusing, since "discrete" is used in the mathematical programming literature to mean whole number or integer. However, the variable that is one-half of the number that shows on the roll of one die is a noncontinuous (and hence discrete) random variable that takes on values $\frac{1}{2}$, 1, $\frac{3}{2}$, 2, $\frac{5}{2}$, 3 with known probabilities.

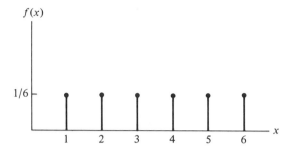

Figure 5.13.   Probability Distribution for x = Outcome of One Role of a Fair Die

where the range of summation is designed to cover all possible values that x_i may take. The standard measure of dispersion, the variance (formally: the second moment around the mean) is given by

$$\text{Var } (x) = \sum_{i=1}^{n} [x_i - E(x)]^2 f(x_i), \qquad (5\text{-}94)$$

which, for purposes of calculation, is equivalent to

$$\text{Var } (x) = \sum_{i=1}^{n} x_i^2 f(x_i) - [E(x)]^2 \qquad (5\text{-}94')$$
$$= E(x^2) - [E(x)]^2.$$

The standard deviation is the square root of the variance. Since the variance calculation in (5-94) squares each deviation from the mean (to eliminate a distinction between positive and negative deviations), the standard deviation measure attempts to compensate by taking the square root of the variance.

Assume that the possible values of the discrete random variable x have been arranged in order from the smallest, x_1, to the largest, x_n. Then the cumulative probability function, or the *distribution* function, is defined, for any particular number c, as the probability that x takes on a value less than or equal to c—that is, as $f(x \leq c)$. If we use capital letters to denote cumulative functions, then

$$F(c) = f(x \leq c) = \sum_{i=1}^{j} f(x_i) \qquad \text{for } x_j \leq c < x_{j+1}.$$

Thus the distribution function is composed of sums of probabilities, from that associated with the smallest x, x_1, to that associated with the x nearest to (and below) or at $x = c$. For the die example (if it is a fair one), the probabilities associated with the six possible outcomes for one roll—1, 2, 3,

4, 5, or 6—are all $\frac{1}{6}$; that is, $f(1) = f(2) = \cdots = f(6) = \frac{1}{6}$. The distribution function, say $F(4) = f(1) + f(2) + f(3) + f(4) = \frac{4}{6}$, is simply the cumulative probability that the outcome of one roll is anything up to and including a 4. For discrete variables, the cumulative probabilities are step functions with horizontal bars that extend up to but do not include the next highest value of x, as illustrated for a fair die in Figure 5.14.

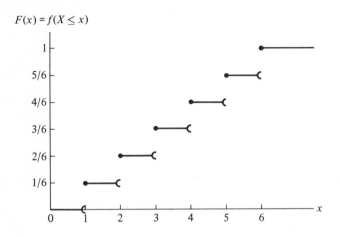

Figure 5.14. Distribution Function (Cumulative Probability) for $x =$ Outcome of One Roll of a Fair Die

For continuous distributions, the usual terms are *density function*, $f(x)$ (in place of frequency function in the discrete case), and *distribution function*, $F(x)$, as before. Because a continuous random variable can (at least theoretically) take on an infinite number of different values, we cannot speak of the probability that the variable takes on *a* specific value—this probability would obviously be infinitely small. Rather we consider the probability that the variable falls within a particular interval, where the interval may be defined so that it is *very* small. From the fundamental interpretation of the definite integral as the area under the curve $f(x)$ between two points, we see that the probability that the continuous random variable x is in the interval between $x = a$ and $x = b$ (put exactly, $a < x \leq b$) is given by the definite integral $\int_a^b f(x)\,dx$. That is,

$$p(a < x \leq b) = \int_a^b f(x)\,dx.$$

By straightforward application of the "delta process" reasoning that we used early in Chapter 3, it is possible to show that $f(x)\, dx$ can be regarded as an estimate of the probability that the random variable takes on a value between x and $x + dx$.[41] The concepts of central tendency and dispersion follow those of the discrete case. As before, the mean is the sum, over the entire range, of each value times its probability. The ranges on the integral signs are shown as negative and positive infinity; when a continuous variable is defined over a narrower range, of course, these limits can be altered (for example, careful measurements on elapsed time to complete a standard task; the variable "elapsed time" can never be negative).

$$E(x) = \int_{-\infty}^{\infty} xf(x)\, dx. \tag{5-95}$$

[Compare with (5-93), above.]

Similarly, the variance is defined as

$$\text{Var } (x) = \int_{-\infty}^{\infty} [x - E(x)]^2 f(x)\, dx, \tag{5-96}$$

or, for easier calculation,

$$\begin{aligned}\text{Var } (x) &= \int_{-\infty}^{\infty} x^2 f(x)\, dx - [E(x)]^2 \\ &= E(x^2) - [E(x)]^2.\end{aligned} \tag{5-96'}$$

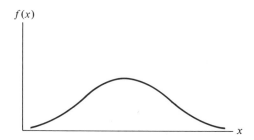

Figure 5.15.   Density Function for a Continuous Variable x

---

[41] Consider a specific example. Let $f(x) = 2x + 6$. We know that $\int_{x_0}^{x_0+\Delta x} (2x + 6)\, dx$ is the probability that x lies in the range $x_0 < x \le (x_0 + \Delta x)$. Performing the integration, this probability is

$$x^2 + 6x \Big]_{x_0}^{x_0+\Delta x} = (x_0 + \Delta x)^2 + 6(x_0 + \Delta x) - x_0^2 - 6x_0.$$

Omitting the $(\Delta x)^2$ term, this reduces to $(2x_0 + 6)\, \Delta x$. Thus, for *any* x (not specifically x_0) the probability of being in the interval between x and $x + \Delta x$ is $(2x + 6)\, \Delta x$. Let the interval shrink; $\Delta x \to dx$. Hence $(2x + 6)\, dx$ is an approximation to this probability when Δx gets small; this is just $f(x)\, dx$.

For the continuous case the cumulative (distribution) function $f(x \leq c)$ is

$$f(x \leq c) \equiv F(c) = \int_{-\infty}^{c} f(x)\, dx \qquad (5\text{-}97)$$

—that is, the "sum" of all probabilities from the lower limit of the variable x up to c. Figures 5.15 and 5.16 give a general illustration for the continuous case.

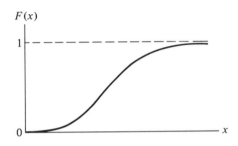

Figure 5.16.   Distribution Function for a Continuous Variable x

APPENDIX 5.2

Supporting Calculations for the Finite Difference Analysis

For c_{Q+1}, substitution into (5-20) produced

$$c_{Q+1} = c_0 \sum_{D_i=0}^{Q+1} (Q + 1 - D_i)p(D_i) + c_s \sum_{D_i=Q+2}^{\infty} [D_i - (Q + 1)]p(D_i)$$

$$(5\text{-}21)$$

The first term can be split into a $\sum\limits_{D_i=0}^{Q}$ part and the final $D_i = Q + 1$ part.

Thus

$$c_0 \sum_{D_i=0}^{Q+1} (Q + 1 - D_i)p(D_i) = c_0 \sum_{D_i=0}^{Q} (Q + 1 - D_i)p(D_i)$$
$$+ c_0[Q + 1 - (Q + 1)]p(Q + 1)$$

and the second term on the right-hand side is zero.

Similarly, the second term in (5-21) can be re-expressed as a $\sum\limits_{D_i=Q+1}^{\infty}$ term if the $D_i = Q + 1$ addition to the lower end of the summation is also subtracted. Thus

$$c_s \sum_{D_i=Q+2}^{\infty} [D_i - (Q + 1)]p(D_i) = c_s \sum_{D_i=Q+1}^{\infty} [D_i - (Q + 1)]p(D_i)$$
$$- c_s[Q + 1 - (Q + 1)]p(Q + 1)$$

The second term here is also zero.

Collecting these results and rearranging

$$c_{Q+1} = c_0 \sum_{D_i=0}^{Q} (Q - D_i)p(D_i) + c_0 \sum_{D_i=0}^{Q} p(D_i) + c_s \sum_{D_i=Q+1}^{\infty} [D_i - Q]p(D_i)$$
$$- c_s \sum_{D_i=Q+1}^{\infty} p(D_i) \quad (5\text{-}21')$$

Since $\sum\limits_{D_i=0}^{\infty} p(D_i) = 1$, $\sum\limits_{D_i=Q+1}^{\infty} p(D_i) = 1 - \sum\limits_{D_i=0}^{Q} p(D_i)$.

Thus, since the first and third terms in (5-21') constitute exactly c_Q in (5-20), we have

$$c_{Q+1} = c_Q + (c_0 + c_s) \sum_{D_i=0}^{Q} p(D_i) - c_s. \quad (5\text{-}22)$$

For c_{Q-1}, substitution into (5-20) gives

$$c_{Q-1} = c_0 \sum_{D_i=0}^{Q-1} (Q - 1 - D_i)p(D_i) + c_s \sum_{D_i=Q}^{\infty} [D_i - (Q - 1)]p(D_i).$$

The first term can be rewritten as

$$c_0 \sum_{D_i=0}^{Q} (Q - 1 - D_i)p(D_i) - c_0(Q - 1 - Q)p(Q)$$

or

$$c_0 \sum_{D_i=0}^{Q} (Q - D_i)p(D_i) - c_0\left[\sum_{D_i=0}^{Q} p(D_i) - p(Q)\right]$$

and finally

$$c_0 \sum_{D_i=0}^{Q} (Q - D_i)p(D_i) - c_0 \sum_{D_i=0}^{Q-1} p(D_i).$$

The second term is

$$c_s \sum_{D_i=Q+1}^{\infty} [D_i - (Q - 1)]p(D_i) + c_s[Q - (Q - 1)]p(Q)$$

or

$$c_s \sum_{D_i=Q+1}^{\infty} (D_i - Q)p(D_i) + c_s\left[\sum_{D_i=Q+1}^{\infty} p(D_i) + p(Q)\right]$$

and again, since

$$\sum_{D_i=0}^{\infty} p(D_i) = 1, \qquad \sum_{D_i=Q+1}^{\infty} p(D_i) = 1 - \sum_{D_i=0}^{Q} p(D_i),$$

this is also

$$c_s \sum_{D_i=Q+1}^{\infty} (D_i - Q)p(D_i) + c_s - c_s\left[\sum_{D_i=0}^{Q} p(D_i) - p(Q)\right]$$

and finally

$$c_s \sum_{D_i=Q+1}^{\infty} (D_i - Q)p(D_i) + c_s - c_s \sum_{D_i=0}^{Q-1} p(D_i).$$

Thus, collecting the rewritten expressions of the first and second terms,

$$c_{Q-1} = c_Q - (c_0 + c_s) \sum_{D_i=0}^{Q-1} p(D_i) + c_s, \qquad (5\text{-}23)$$

and the summation of probabilities from $p(0)$ to $p(Q - 1)$ is just the cumulative probability that $D_i \leq Q - 1$—that is, $p(D_i \leq Q - 1)$.

APPENDIX 5.3

Derivations of Queue Characteristics

AVERAGE NUMBER OF ITEMS IN THE SYSTEM: N

From first principles:

$$N = \sum_{n=0}^{\infty} (n)p_n = \sum_{n=0}^{\infty} (n) \left(\frac{\lambda}{\mu}\right)^n \left(1 - \frac{\lambda}{\mu}\right)$$

$$= \sum_{n=0}^{\infty} (n) \left(\frac{\lambda}{\mu}\right)^n - \sum_{n=0}^{\infty} (n) \left(\frac{\lambda}{\mu}\right)^{n+1}$$

$$= \left[1\left(\frac{\lambda}{\mu}\right) + 2\left(\frac{\lambda}{\mu}\right)^2 + 3\left(\frac{\lambda}{\mu}\right)^3 + \cdots \right]$$

$$- \left[1\left(\frac{\lambda}{\mu}\right)^2 + 2\left(\frac{\lambda}{\mu}\right)^3 + 3\left(\frac{\lambda}{\mu}\right)^4 + \cdots \right]$$

$$= \frac{\lambda}{\mu} + \left(\frac{\lambda}{\mu}\right)^2 + \left(\frac{\lambda}{\mu}\right)^3 + \cdots$$

$$= \left(\frac{\lambda}{\mu}\right) \left[1 + \frac{\lambda}{\mu} + \left(\frac{\lambda}{\mu}\right)^2 + \cdots \right]$$

$$= \frac{\lambda}{\mu} \sum_{n=0}^{\infty} \left(\frac{\lambda}{\mu}\right)^n,$$

but we saw that this sum, for $\lambda/\mu < 1$, is just $1/[1 - (\lambda/\mu)]$. Thus,

$$N = \frac{\lambda/\mu}{1 - (\lambda/\mu)} = \frac{\lambda}{\mu - \lambda}.$$

AVERAGE QUEUE LENGTH: M

$$M = \sum_{m=0}^{\infty} (m)p_m = \sum_{m=1}^{\infty} (m)p_m$$

$$= \sum_{n=2}^{\infty} (n - 1)p_n = \sum_{n=2}^{\infty} (n)p_n - \sum_{n=2}^{\infty} p_n.$$

Considering each of these two summations in turn,

$$\sum_{n=2}^{\infty} (n)p_n = \sum_{n=0}^{\infty} (n)p_n - \sum_{n=0}^{1} (n)p_n$$
$$= N - (0 + p_1),$$
$$\sum_{n=2}^{\infty} p_n = \sum_{n=0}^{\infty} p_n - \sum_{n=0}^{1} p_n$$
$$= 1 - (p_0 + p_1).$$

Thus, combining these results,

$$M = N - (0 + p_1) - [1 - (p_0 + p_1)] = N - 1 + p_0$$
$$= N - 1 + \left(1 - \frac{\lambda}{\mu}\right) = N - \frac{\lambda}{\mu}.$$

Note the logic of the result at this point: the average queue length, M, is equal to the average number of items in the system, N, less the average number being serviced, which is just what (λ/μ) is.[42] Finally, since $N = \lambda/(\mu - \lambda)$,

$$M = \frac{\lambda}{\mu - \lambda} - \frac{\lambda}{\mu} = \frac{\lambda^2}{\mu(\mu - \lambda)}.$$

AVERAGE LENGTH OF NONEMPTY QUEUES: M_c

$$M_c = \sum_{m=1}^{\infty} (m)\left(\frac{p_m}{p_{m>0}}\right) = \sum_{n=2}^{\infty} (n-1)\left(\frac{p_n}{p_{n>1}}\right)$$
$$= \frac{\lambda^2/\mu(\mu - \lambda)}{1 - [1 - (\lambda/\mu)] - (\lambda/\mu)[1 - (\lambda/\mu)]} = \frac{\lambda^2/\mu(\mu - \lambda)}{(\lambda/\mu)^2},$$
$$M_c = \frac{\mu}{\mu - \lambda}.$$

[42] If $\lambda = 10$ and $\mu = 20$, then *on average* the single service facility is working on an item one-half of the time, which is to say that one-half an item is in service *at any time*. More formally, let s = number in service; then

$$E(s) = \sum_{s=0}^{\infty} (s)p_s.$$

For $s = 0$, p_s is just the probability of none in the system, $1 - (\lambda/\mu)$. Since s cannot exceed 1, the probability of $s = 1$ is $1 - p\{s = 0\} = \lambda/\mu$. Hence

$$E(s) = (0)\left(1 - \frac{\lambda}{\mu}\right) + 1\left(\frac{\lambda}{\mu}\right) = \frac{\lambda}{\mu}.$$

DERIVATION OF $\psi(w)\,dw$ FOR $w > 0$

$$\psi(w)\,dw = \sum_{n=1}^{\infty} \left(\frac{\lambda}{\mu}\right)^n \left(1 - \frac{\lambda}{\mu}\right) \frac{e^{-\mu w}(\mu w)^{n-1}}{(n-1)!}\, \mu\,dw$$

$$= \left(1 - \frac{\lambda}{\mu}\right) e^{-\mu w}\,dw \sum_{n=1}^{\infty} \frac{(\lambda/\mu)^n (\mu w)^{n-1} \mu}{(n-1)!}$$

$$= \left(1 - \frac{\lambda}{\mu}\right) e^{-\mu w}\,dw \sum_{n=1}^{\infty} \frac{\lambda^n w^{n-1}}{(n-1)!}.$$

This sum is as follows:

$$\lambda + \lambda^2 w + \frac{\lambda^3 w^2}{2!} + \frac{\lambda^4 w^3}{3!} + \cdots.$$

Recall that $e^z = 1 + z + (z^2/2!) + (z^3/3!) + \cdots$; therefore,

$$e^{\lambda w} = 1 + \lambda w + \frac{\lambda^2 w^2}{2!} + \frac{\lambda^3 w^3}{3!} + \cdots$$

and

$$\lambda(e^{\lambda w}) = \lambda + \lambda^2 w + \frac{\lambda^3 w^2}{2!} + \frac{\lambda^4 w^3}{3!} + \cdots,$$

which is just the sum we have in $\psi(w)\,dw$. Therefore,

$$\psi(w)\,dw = \left(1 - \frac{\lambda}{\mu}\right) e^{-\mu w}\,dw\, \lambda e^{\lambda w}$$

$$= \left(1 - \frac{\lambda}{\mu}\right) \lambda e^{(\lambda-\mu)w}\,dw,$$

which is (5-65) in the text.

DERIVATION OF $\theta(v)\,dv$

1. $p_n = (\lambda/\mu)^n [1 - (\lambda/\mu)]$.
2. $q_n = e^{-\mu v}(\mu v)^n/n!$.
3. $p\{1 \text{ service in } dv\} = \mu\,dv$.

The product of these,

$$\left(\frac{\lambda}{\mu}\right)^n \left(1 - \frac{\lambda}{\mu}\right) \frac{e^{-\mu v}(\mu v)^n}{n!}\, \mu\,dv,$$

must be summed over all possible values of n, from 0 to ∞, to cover the mutually exclusive ways in which the total time in the system can be between v and $v + dv$. Thus,

$$\theta(v)\, dv = \sum_{n=0}^{\infty} \left(\frac{\lambda}{\mu}\right)^n \left(1 - \frac{\lambda}{\mu}\right) \frac{e^{-\mu v}(\mu v)^n}{n!}\, \mu\, dv$$

$$= \left(1 - \frac{\lambda}{\mu}\right) e^{-\mu v}\mu\, dv \sum_{n=0}^{\infty} \frac{(\lambda/\mu)^n (\mu v)^n}{n!}$$

$$= \left(1 - \frac{\lambda}{\mu}\right) e^{-\mu v}\mu\, dv \sum_{n=0}^{\infty} \frac{\lambda^n v^n}{n!}.$$

But

$$\sum_{n=0}^{\infty} \frac{\lambda^n v^n}{n!} = 1 + \lambda v + \frac{\lambda^2 v^2}{2!} + \frac{\lambda^3 v^3}{3!} + \cdots,$$

which is just $e^{\lambda v}$. Thus,

$$\theta(v)\, dv = \left(1 - \frac{\lambda}{\mu}\right) e^{-\mu v}\mu\, dv\, e^{\lambda v}$$

$$= \left(1 - \frac{\lambda}{\mu}\right) \mu e^{(\lambda - \mu)v}\, dv$$

$$= (\mu - \lambda)e^{(\lambda - \mu)v}\, dv,$$

which is (5-69) in the text.

p_0 IN THE k-STATION CASE

The first term multiplying p_0 in the summation of the right-hand sides of (5-78)

$$\sum_{n=0}^{k-1} \frac{(\lambda/\mu)^n}{n!},$$

cannot be simplified. The second

$$\sum_{n=k}^{\infty} \frac{(\lambda/\mu)^n}{k!\, k^{n-k}},$$

can. This can be expressed as

$$\frac{(\lambda/\mu)^k}{k!}\left[1+\frac{\lambda/\mu}{k}+\frac{(\lambda/\mu)^2}{k^2}+\frac{(\lambda/\mu)^3}{k^3}+\cdots\right]=\frac{(\lambda/\mu)^k}{k!}\sum_{i=0}^{\infty}\left(\frac{\lambda}{k\mu}\right)^i.$$

And since it has been assumed that $\lambda/k\mu < 1$, this is

$$=\frac{(\lambda/\mu)^k}{k!}\left[\frac{1}{1-(\lambda/k\mu)}\right]$$

$$=\frac{(\lambda/\mu)^k}{k!\left(1-\frac{\lambda/\mu}{k}\right)}.$$

Thus, from (5-78),

$$1=\sum_{n=0}^{k-1}\frac{(\lambda/\mu)^n}{n!}\,p_0+\frac{(\lambda/\mu)^k}{k!\left(1-\frac{\lambda/\mu}{k}\right)}\,p_0,$$

from which (5-79) follows.

AVERAGE NUMBER IN SERVICE IN THE k-STATION CASE: S

$$S=(0)p_0+(1)p_1+\cdots+(k-1)p_{k-1}+(k)p_k+(k)p_{k+1}+\cdots$$

$$=\sum_{n=0}^{k-1}(n)p_n+k\sum_{n=k}^{\infty}p_n$$

$$=\sum_{n=0}^{k-1}(n)p_n+k\left(1-\sum_{n=0}^{k-1}p_n\right).$$

But, from (5-78) this is

$$=k-p_0\left(k\sum_{n=0}^{k-1}\frac{(\lambda/\mu)^n}{n!}-\sum_{n=0}^{k-1}n\frac{(\lambda/\mu)^n}{n!}\right).$$

Consider p_0 as defined in (5-79):

$$p_0=\frac{1}{\displaystyle\sum_{n=0}^{k-1}\frac{(\lambda/\mu)^n}{n!}+\frac{(\lambda/\mu)^k}{k!\left(1-\frac{\lambda/\mu}{k}\right)}}.$$

With a little algebra, this can be shown to be

$$= \frac{k - (\lambda/\mu)}{k \sum_{n=0}^{k-1} \frac{(\lambda/\mu)^n}{n!} - \frac{\lambda}{\mu} \sum_{n=0}^{k-1} \frac{(\lambda/\mu)^n}{n!} + \frac{k(\lambda/\mu)^k}{k!}}$$

and, manipulating the sums in the denominator,

$$= \frac{k - (\lambda/\mu)}{k \sum_{n=0}^{k-1} \frac{(\lambda/\mu)^n}{n!} - \sum_{n=0}^{k} \frac{n(\lambda/\mu)^n}{n!} + \frac{k(\lambda/\mu)^k}{k!}},$$

so that, finally,

$$p_0 = \frac{k - (\lambda/\mu)}{k \sum_{n=0}^{k-1} \frac{(\lambda/\mu)^n}{n!} - \sum_{n=0}^{k-1} \frac{n(\lambda/\mu)^n}{n!}}$$

Therefore,

$$S = k - \left(k - \frac{\lambda}{\mu}\right) = \frac{\lambda}{\mu}.$$

PROBLEMS

1. A manufacturer of various kinds of passenger seats for commercial airplanes has agreed, by contract, to supply a particular style of seat to an airplane company at a constant daily rate during the production year. The seats are of molded plastic and can be produced in huge quantities (hundreds per day), once the stamping and finishing machinery has been set up for their manufacture. This is expensive to do, however; it costs $750. The company estimates that a chair produced but not yet delivered costs on average $20 per year for storage. If the contract specifies 4800 seats per year and has a no-shortage clause, how often per year should these seats be produced and how many should be made each time if the seat manufacturer wants to minimize his annual setup and holding costs?

2. The airplane company in Problem 1 offers to remove the no-shortage clause from the contract, specifying instead that the manufacturer will be charged for shortages at a rate of $80 per item per year (that is, if there was a shortage of 100 chairs for three months, the charge would be $2000). They offer to do this, however, only for the additional consideration of a flat deduction of $500 from their total (annual) bill for the seats. Should the seat manufacturer accept the offer and, if so, how would his production pattern for these particular seats differ from that in Problem 1, if at all?

3. Suppose that the seat manufacturer in Problems 1 and 2 found that, because of

a newly discovered quirk in his machinery, he had to produce lots of 620 seats each time. Under these added conditions, should he accept the airplane company's offer for removal of the no-shortage clause (as outlined in Problem 2)? If so, how would the runs of 620 be divided between production for inventory and production to meet back demand?

4. Consider an inventory problem within the airplane manufacturing company of the preceding problems. A particular division produces the landing-gear assemblies for the company's aircraft as well as doing subcontracting for other manufacturers. When the division is set up to produce these landing-gear units, they can turn out, on average, nine every two days; switching over from their other subcontracting projects to landing-gear production costs on average $100. Having the finished assemblies in inventory, waiting to be used, costs the company $10 per assembly per year. Each airplane requires one landing-gear assembly, and 120 airplanes are produced each year, which consists of 240 production days. How often should landing-gear assemblies be produced, and in runs of what size?

5. Management of the company in Problem 4 is considering increasing production to 180 airplanes per year (over the same 240 production days).
   (a) *Estimate* the change in their annual inventory and setup costs.
   (b) Find these new costs *exactly* and compare your result with those in (a).
   (c) Suppose that management were considering doubling output per year. Estimate the change in costs and also find the new costs exactly. Discuss the discrepancy.

6. A florist has observed that the daily demand for bunches of red roses at his shop is uniformly distributed over an interval beginning at five bunches and extending through 14. On the assumption that he wants to minimize his under- and oversupply costs, how many bunches should he have available each morning if:
   (a) He estimates that not having a bunch of roses available for a customer is twice as costly to him as having an extra bunch at the end of the day to be disposed of?
   (b) He estimates that a shortage of one unit is only one-half as costly to him as having a bunch left over at the end of the day?
   (c) Both costs are the same?

7. Suppose that the florist of Problem 6 also stocks carnations, for which he observes the daily demand (per dozen) to range from one through eight, with three through six equally likely *and* four times as probable (each) as one, two, seven, or eight dozen. Again, assume that he wants to minimize the inventory costs associated with carnations.
   (a) How many dozen should he stock each morning if $c_0 = \$3$ and $c_s = \$2$?
   (b) If he thinks that $c_0 = \$10$ and estimates that the right number of (dozens of) carnations is three, within what range of c_s will his estimate be correct?

8. The arrivals of freighters at a single port facility follow a Poisson distribution, with an average of three arrivals per working day. Ships can be unloaded (one at a time) at an exponential rate averaging four per day. The cost of an idle ship is $2000 per day; the port operates eight hours per day, five days a week, 50 weeks

per year. The port authority is considering two possible improvements in the facility:

(a) Replacement of the present dock arrangement with a new unloading facility that could provide, on average, an exponential service rate of six ships per day. It is estimated that this would cost $300,000 per year over its life, including maintenance and interest charges.

(b) Containerization equipment on each ship that would make all unloading times constant, at one hour and 20 minutes, rather than exponentially distributed. This equipment, for the entire fleet, and including depreciation and maintenance, would cost the authority $400,000 annually.

Which improvement (if either) should be introduced and why? [*Note:* A ship is considered idle whether it is waiting in line or actually being unloaded.]

9. A theater ticket office has two windows: one sells tickets for the current day only, the other handles only advance sales. At either window, service times have been found to be exponentially distributed with a mean of four minutes per customer. Arrivals are found to be Poisson distributed; for current ticket sales the mean arrival rate is twelve per hour, for advance sales it is nine per hour. The theater's management is sensitive to customer waiting times; they would like the average wait to be no more than 10 minutes for current day customers and only half of that for advance sales customers. Are they presently meeting this goal? What would be the effect on average waiting time of restructuring the ticket selling facility so that either window could handle both kinds of sales, current and advance?

10. The owner-driver of a rental limousine estimates that his average earnings are $40 per hour. He must take the car frequently to a nearby automatic washing installation, which has only one line of service. Cars arrive there at the rate of 18 per hour; the distribution of arrivals is observed to follow a Poisson function. Service times are exponentially distributed and the machines can process cars at the rate of 20 per hour. He has found, however, that he can bribe people to stay out of line. In particular, a bribe of $10 is just sufficient to reduce the mean arrival rate by one car per hour. How many bribes should he give (at $10 each) each time he goes to the car wash in order to minimize (on the average) his total car washing costs (lost time plus bribes)?

11. A different automatic car washing and waxing installation has two complete channels; it can turn out two shining automobiles simultaneously. At present, however, only one line is being utilized. Output is exponentially distributed with a mean service time of five cars per hour. Arrivals are Poisson distributed. A customer becomes dissatisfied and leaves the line without having his car washed if he is forced to wait more than one hour before his car enters the process. The loss in profits for each dissatisfied customer is estimated at $25 (loss of goodwill, reputation, and so on). How large must the expected arrival rate be before it becomes just profitable for the second channel to be opened if it costs $50 per hour to run?

12. The ticket counter for Bluebird Airlines in a small upstate airport currently has only one sales line; they are open from 8 A.M. to 6 P.M. The length of time necessary to complete a sale has been observed to be exponentially distributed

with a mean of ten minutes per customer. Customer arrivals are approximately Poisson distributed with a mean arrival rate of four per hour. Management has observed a rather consistent loss of customers.

(a) What is the probability that a person will have to wait to be served?

(b) A questionnaire survey suggests that if a person must wait 12 minutes or longer to get to the counter, there is a probability of .5 that he will give his future business to Hawkair, a competitor. How many customers per day are being lost to Hawkair?

(c) If a completely modernized electronic reservation hookup and other facilities were installed, the average customer service time could be cut in half. This would cost the airline an additional $50 per day. If they estimate their profit per customer per day at $10, should they install the new equipment?

(d) How much should Bluebird be willing to pay per day for an advertising campaign that increases their customers by ten per day, if they have installed the new equipment?

REFERENCES

1. Ackoff, R. L., and M. W. Sasieni, *Fundamentals of Operations Research*. New York: John Wiley & Sons, Inc., 1968.

2. Arrow, K. J., S. Karlin, and H. E. Scarf, eds., *Studies in the Mathematical Theory of Inventory and Production*. Stanford: Stanford University Press, 1958.

3. Buffa, E. S., *Production-Inventory Systems: Planning and Control*. Homewood, Ill.: Richard D. Irwin, Inc., 1968.

4. Courant, R., trans. E. J. McShane, *Differential and Integral Calculus*, vol. II. New York: Interscience Publishers, Inc., 1936.

5. Cox, D. R., and W. L. Smith, *Queues*. New York: John Wiley & Sons, Inc., 1961.

6. Gue, R. L., and M. E. Thomas, *Mathematical Methods in Operations Research*. New York: The Macmillan Company, 1968.

7. Hadley, G., and T. M. Whitin, *Analysis of Inventory Systems*. Englewood Cliffs, N.J.: Prentice-Hall, Inc., 1963.

8. Hillier, F. S., and G. J. Lieberman, *Introduction to Operations Research*. San Francisco: Holden-Day, 1967.

9. Kaufmann, A., *Methods and Models of Operations Research*. Englewood Cliffs, N.J.: Prentice-Hall, Inc., 1963.

10. Lee, A. M., *Applied Queueing Theory*. New York: St. Martin's Press, Inc., 1966.

11. Morse, P. M., *Queues, Inventories and Maintenance: The Analysis of Operations Systems with Variable Demand and Supply*. New York: John Wiley & Sons, Inc., 1958.

12. Naddor, E., *Inventory Systems*. New York: John Wiley & Sons, Inc., 1966.

13. Panico, J. A., *Queuing Theory: A Study of Waiting Lines for Business, Economics and Science*. Englewood Cliffs, N.J.: Prentice-Hall, Inc., 1969.

14. Prabhu, N. U., *Queues and Inventories: A Study of Their Basic Stochastic Processes*. New York: John Wiley & Sons, Inc., 1965.

15. Richmond, S. B., *Operations Research for Management Decisions*. New York: The Ronald Press Company, 1968.
16. Saaty, T. L., *Elements of Queueing Theory with Applications*. New York: McGraw-Hill, Inc., 1961.
17. Sasieni, M., A. Yaspan, and L. Friedman, *Operations Research—Methods and Problems*. New York: John Wiley & Sons, Inc., 1959.
18. Scarf, H. E., D. Gilford, and M. W. Shelly, eds., *Multistage Inventory Models and Techniques*. Stanford: Stanford University Press, 1963.
19. Starr, M. K., *Production Management Systems and Synthesis*. Englewood Cliffs, N.J.: Prentice-Hall, Inc., 1964.
20. Starr, M. K., and D. W. Miller, *Inventory Control: Theory and Practice*. Englewood Cliffs, N.J.: Prentice-Hall, Inc., 1962.
21. Takács, L., *Introduction to the Theory of Queues*. Oxford: Oxford University Press, 1962.
22. Wagner, H. M., *Principles of Operations Research*. Englewood Cliffs, N.J.: Prentice-Hall, Inc., 1969.
23. ———, *Statistical Management of Inventory Systems*. New York: John Wiley & Sons, Inc., 1962.
24. Wilks, S. S., *Elementary Statistical Analysis*. Princeton: Princeton University Press, 1948.

6

LINEAR PROGRAMMING MODELS—
I: FUNDAMENTALS

In Chapter 4 we saw how the general conditions for maximization or minimization problems involving many variables could be formulated through extensions of the logic for a function of one variable—using the concept of the total differential. Second-order conditions depended upon an understanding of the rules for determining the sign of a quadratic form. *Equality* constraints removed the independence between all variables and required, in turn, a further examination of quadratic forms for dependent variables. The basic approach, however, was essentially the same: first differentials had to be set equal to zero, the resulting equations solved, and then maxima, minima, or neither distinguished by the sign of the second total differential.

Inequality constraints posed a somewhat different problem, since the nature of the dependence between the variables is specified less exactly in an inequality than in an equation. The more complex results of Section 4.8 (building on the convex set theory of Section 4.7) reflect this; it seems clear that for many-variable, many-constraint problems, the approach of that section would generally be unworkable. Then, in Chapter 5, we saw that one of the *basic* mathematical tools used in inventory or waiting line problems came from the calculus—for example, in minimizing an inventory cost function or minimizing system cost in a queuing situation. Construction of the function to be minimized required a rather detailed examination of the fundamentals of the process in order to be able to express system characteristics—the average amount of inventory, the average waiting time of an item, and so on—in terms of the relevant variables or system parameters. However, only relatively simple optimization problems were investigated.

In this chapter we consider a different class of problems in which the function to be maximized or minimized is relatively easily constructed— that is, is a simple function of system variables, but where the simple calculus criteria for maxima and minima cannot be used. There are two reasons for this. The first is that we will be dealing in this chapter with (usually many) variables that not only enter into an *objective function*—the function to be maximized or minimized—but also are subjected, individually and in combination, to (usually many) *inequality constraints*. Thus we have the difficulties of Section 4.8. The second reason, which makes even the complex criteria of Chapter 4 inappropriate for the class of problems to be discussed in this chapter, is that both the objective function and *all* of the constraints will be assumed to be *linear* functions of the variables whose values are to be determined. The reader may recall the requirement on existence of first and second partial derivatives for the function to be maximized (or minimized) and on the constraints from Chapter 4; this was necessary to allow development of first- and second-order conditions. If all functions are linear, all first partial derivatives are constants and this development is not generally valid. Only when the objective function and all of the constraining inequalities are linear functions of the variables do we have a *linear* programming model, or simply a linear program; thus the *linear* part of the name is an exact description of the mathematical properties of all of the functions involved. *Programming*, on the other hand, is used only to denote "planning" or "scheduling" of activities. This is illustrated in the following extremely simple and rather artificial example of a linear programming problem.

Assume that a business has just been inherited by a person—we refer to him as the producer. The company produces two items, and to do so it utilizes three inputs—two raw materials and labor. We assume that the producer has inherited certain amounts of the raw materials stored in a warehouse and also a certain amount of prepaid labor, but *no cash*. His interest is in maximizing the profit that comes from producing the two products in his newly-acquired business. Assume that his is a small company that can sell any amount it can possibly produce at a fixed price, and that from past experience on input costs, there are estimates of the profit to be derived from production of each item; denote these unit profit figures by p_1 and p_2. Thus, in planning his production—in scheduling or *programming* what he should do—the producer wants to find production quantities x_1 and x_2 such that $p_1x_1 + p_2x_2$ is maximized. This is his objective function; it is a linear function of the variables x_1 and x_2. (Considering each of the x_j's as a one-element column vector, the objective function is a linear combination of the x_j; see Section 1.5.)

Obviously, producing extremely large amounts of any or all items would bring him a very large profit.[1] He is prevented from doing so because of the limited availabilities of the three inputs or resources that he has inherited and that are used in manufacturing. Denote these upper limits by r_i ($i = 1, 2, 3$). In addition, he knows the way in which inputs are combined to produce outputs; specifically, he knows how much of each resource i is needed *per unit* of product j ($j = 1, 2$). These so-called "technical coefficients," a_{ij}, can be represented in column vectors for each product;

$$\begin{bmatrix} a_{1j} \\ a_{2j} \\ a_{3j} \end{bmatrix}$$

indicates inputs from the three resources per unit of output of j. The total use of resource 1 in production of item 1 is $a_{11}x_1$—input per unit times number of units; for product 2 it is $a_{12}x_2$. Thus, total use of resource 1 in producing amounts x_1 and x_2 is $a_{11}x_1 + a_{12}x_2$; since an amount r_1 is available, the variables are restrained by the linear inequality $a_{11}x_1 + a_{12}x_2 \leq r_1$. There are similar inequalities—involving a_{2j}'s and a_{3j}'s—for r_2 and r_3.[2] This set of resource constraints can be written in linear combination form as

$$\begin{bmatrix} a_{11} \\ a_{21} \\ a_{31} \end{bmatrix} x_1 + \begin{bmatrix} a_{12} \\ a_{22} \\ a_{32} \end{bmatrix} x_2 \leq \begin{bmatrix} r_1 \\ r_2 \\ r_3 \end{bmatrix},$$

or even more compactly in matrix form. Let

$$A = \begin{bmatrix} a_{11} & a_{12} \\ a_{21} & a_{22} \\ a_{31} & a_{32} \end{bmatrix}, \quad X = \begin{bmatrix} x_1 \\ x_2 \end{bmatrix}, \quad \text{and} \quad R = \begin{bmatrix} r_1 \\ r_2 \\ r_3 \end{bmatrix};$$

then the constraint set is $AX \leq R$. If we also make explicit the condition that neither x_j be negative, we summarize this requirement in the set of linear inequalities $X \geq 0$.

The linear programming problem for the producer in this example is thus to find that best combination of production of his two alternatives—the

---

[1] This assumes that neither p_j is negative or zero, which is reasonable in this illustration. If either of them were, the producer would simply drop that item from his production line.

[2] Note that each row may involve different units of measurement. Resource 1 may be measured in pounds, resource 2 in gallons, and resource 3 in man-hours of skilled labor. The technical coefficients for each *row* relate inputs of the material on the right-hand side (in units measuring availability of that resource) to outputs of final product (measured in units appropriate for the x's)—for example, a_{12} might be in terms of "pounds per case."

combination that maximizes $\displaystyle\sum_{j=1}^{2} p_j x_j$—subject to the three linear inequality constraints summarized as $AX \leq R$ and the two nonnegativity conditions implied by the matrix statement $X \geq 0$.

Specifically, suppose that production of a unit of output 1 requires 1, 3, and 1 units from resources 1 (a raw material), 2 (a second raw material), and 3 (labor), respectively. Similarly, a unit of the second item uses the three resources in amounts 2, 2, and 10. That is, the columns of technical coefficients are

$$A_1 = \begin{bmatrix} 1 \\ 3 \\ 1 \end{bmatrix} \quad \text{and} \quad A_2 = \begin{bmatrix} 2 \\ 2 \\ 10 \end{bmatrix},$$

so that

$$A = [A_1 \mid A_2] = \begin{bmatrix} 1 & 2 \\ 3 & 2 \\ 1 & 10 \end{bmatrix}.$$

If the inherited amounts of resources available to the producer are $r_1 = 10$, $r_2 = 24$, and $r_3 = 40$—that is,

$$R = \begin{bmatrix} 10 \\ 24 \\ 40 \end{bmatrix},$$

and if his estimates of per-unit profit are $p_1 = \$2$ and $p_2 = \$5$, or

$$P = \begin{bmatrix} 2 \\ 5 \end{bmatrix},$$

then his problem is to

$$
\begin{aligned}
\text{maximize:} \quad & 2x_1 + 5x_2 \\
& x_1 + 2x_2 \leq 10, \\
\text{subject to:} \quad & 3x_1 + 2x_2 \leq 24, \\
& x_1 + 10x_2 \leq 40, \\
\text{and} \quad & x_1 \geq 0, \quad x_2 \geq 0.
\end{aligned}
$$

In this chapter we will see that, precisely because of the linearities, the problem is greatly simplified; complications suggested by the rules for the more general case in Section 4.8 are completely avoided, and the actual calculations involved in solving a linear programming problem are the simplest kind of arithmetic,[3] based on the study of equation systems in

---

[3] Although they are simple, they may also be numerous; this makes them obvious candidates for solution on a computer.

Chapter 2. Initially, we will review and extend some of the fundamental convex set theory from Chapter 4, specifically Section 4.7. We will see how this leads directly to theorems that enable us to relate the linear programming problem to one of selection from among *basic* solutions to an *equation* system formed from the constraints (Section 2.4). Because of the added presence of an objective function, efficient arithmetic procedures for this solution process can be developed. Finally, in this chapter we will see that all linear programs come in pairs and that the two problems have certain mathematical connections that may provide additional insight into the optimal solution.

6.1. FUNDAMENTAL STRUCTURE, ALGEBRA AND GEOMETRY

The maximization problem: algebra

The manufacturer's linear programming problem can be represented in its most compact form as

$$\text{maximize:} \quad P'X$$
$$\text{subject to:} \quad AX \leq R \qquad (6\text{-}1)$$
$$\text{and} \qquad X \geq O.$$

The dimensions of A (3×2 in the illustration) completely define the size of the problem; rows of A represent the inequality constraints, exclusive of nonnegativities, and columns of A represent variables. (In the example each column was essentially a production function or recipe for that variable, showing how inputs were used to produce one unit of output.) Clearly, this form (as well as others to be presented below) is possible only because all functions involved are linear.

Thus, if we assign to A the dimensions $m \times n$—and, as a consequence, P, X, and O become n-element column vectors while R has m elements— we have in (6-1) the *general* linear programming maximization problem with n nonnegative variables subject to m linear inequality constraints.[4] Note that the objective is to *maximize* a linear function subject to a set of m linear constraints (in addition to the nonnegativities) that establish *upper* bounds. The left-hand side must be no more than the value on the right-hand side. If all parameters in the problem are positive, this is the

---

[4] Whenever reference is made to the number of constraints, this will exclude the nonnegativity requirements, unless otherwise specified. That is, it will refer to the number of rows in A in the $AX \leq R$ set. Note that we have used R (for "resources") for the right-hand sides of the inequality constraints rather than C, for "constraints," as in Chapters 3 and 4. This may help the reader to bear in mind that throughout this chapter we are dealing with linear functions.

logical direction for the inequalities; they keep the variables and hence the value of the objective function from becoming infinitely large. More generally, some parameters in a problem may be negative and some inequalities may initially run in the other direction. These inequalities can be converted to "less than or equal to" form by multiplying through by -1; hence $AX \leq R$ is perfectly general.[5]

In order that the reader be completely familiar with alternative statements of the fundamental linear programming maximization problem, several less aggregate statements of (6-1) for m constraints and n variables are presented:

$$\text{maximize:} \quad \sum_{j=1}^{n} p_j x_j$$

$$\text{subject to:} \quad \sum_{j=1}^{n} a_{ij} x_j \leq r_i \quad (i = 1, \ldots, m) \tag{6-2}$$

$$\text{and} \quad x_j \geq 0 \quad (j = 1, \ldots, n),$$

or, in linear combination form, letting A_j represent the jth column of A,

$$\text{maximize:} \quad \sum_{j=1}^{n} p_j x_j$$

$$\text{subject to:} \quad \sum_{j=1}^{n} A_j x_j \leq R \tag{6-3}$$

$$\text{and} \quad x_j \geq 0 \quad (j = 1, \ldots, n),$$

and, in its most explicit form,

$$
\begin{aligned}
\text{maximize:} \quad & p_1 x_1 + \cdots + p_n x_n \\
\text{subject to:} \quad & a_{11} x_1 + \cdots + a_{1n} x_n \leq r_1 \\
& \quad \vdots \qquad\qquad \vdots \qquad \vdots \\
& a_{m1} x_1 + \cdots + a_{mn} x_n \leq r_m \\
\text{and} \quad & x_1 \geq 0, \ldots, \quad x_n \geq 0.
\end{aligned} \tag{6-4}
$$

The minimization problem: algebra

The approach of Chapters 3 and 4 was relevant for both maximization and minimization problems. A similar pairing can be found with linear programs. A problem with a linear objective function to be *minimized*, subject to a set of constraints that set *lower* limits, as well as requirements that the variables be nonnegative, is also called a linear program. A clas-

---

[5] Inclusion of equality constraints as well as inequalities will be discussed in the next chapter.

sic example is the so-called diet problem. Assume the calorie contents, c_j, of unit amounts (however defined) of various food items are known. Suppose one is planning a menu (for a week)—that is, deciding on amounts of various foods to consume, y_j. Subject to certain *minimum* levels of other food essentials, such as vitamins and minerals, the objective is to select a combination of foods that minimizes (weekly) calorie intake. Let C and Y be the (column) vectors of unit calorie content and amounts of food items and E be a vector of minimum levels of food essentials. Finally, let a matrix K contain elements k_{ij} that represent content of food essential i (say, vitamin B_1) per unit of food item j (cupful of rice, for example). Then the diet problem is

$$\begin{aligned} \text{minimize:} \quad & C'Y \\ \text{subject to:} \quad & KY \geq E \\ \text{and} \quad & Y \geq O. \end{aligned} \qquad (6\text{-}1')$$

The reader should think through the more disaggregate forms, parallel to (6-2) through (6-4) for the maximum problem.

The point is that any problem of the general form of (6-1) or (6-1') is termed a linear program. In both problems the variables are required to be nonnegative,[6] and a linear function of those variables is to be maximized or minimized subject to a set of linear inequality constraints that set upper or lower limits, respectively.

The maximization problem: geometry

We now consider the geometric implications of the algebraic structure of the linear programming maximization problem. With linear inequalities, as with linear equations, we have a choice of solution space or vector space (see Chapters 1 and 2). For present purposes we will use solution space. This is most easily done with two variables ($n = 2$). Consider again the producer's two-variable, three-constraint linear programming problem:

$$\begin{aligned} \text{maximize:} \quad & 2x_1 + 5x_2 \\ \text{subject to:} \quad & \begin{cases} (1) \quad x_1 + 2x_2 \leq 10, \\ (2) \quad 3x_1 + 2x_2 \leq 24, \\ (3) \quad x_1 + 10x_2 \leq 40, \end{cases} \\ \text{and} \quad & x_1 \geq 0, \quad x_2 \geq 0. \end{aligned} \qquad (6\text{-}5)$$

[6] More correctly, this is *customarily* required. Allowing some or indeed all of the variables to take on negative values as well as positive would not destroy all of the important mathematical characteristics of linear programs, as subsequent sections will show; it would, however, complicate the computational procedure. In any case, in the great majority of linear programming applications, negative values for the variables are meaningless in the context of the actual problem.

Recall that a weak linear inequality defines a closed half-space (Section 4.7) and hence is shown geometrically as the boundary plus everything on one side of it. In two dimensions the boundary is a line. We shade the area defined by each of the three constraints separately [Figures 6.1(a), (b), and (c)] and then show their intersection—the area common to all three [Figure 6.1(d)]. Note that, because of the conditions $x_1 \geq 0$ and $x_2 \geq 0$, we can restrict our pictures to the nonnegative quadrant, "above and to the right" of the origin. (In multidimensional problems, the area within which no variables are less than zero is called the nonnegative orthant.)

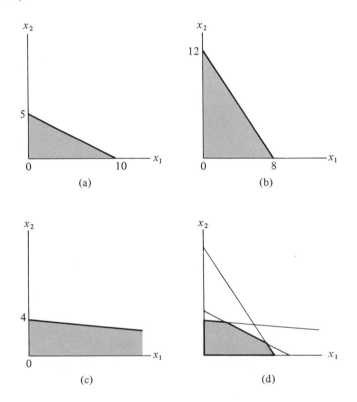

Figure 6.1.   (a) Constraint 1, (b) Constraint 2, (c) Constraint 3, (d) all three constraints

Points in the shaded area inside the dark boundaries, as well as all points on the boundaries themselves, satisfy all three constraints of (6-5) and the nonnegativity requirements. Such points (representing specific values of x_1 and x_2) are called *feasible solutions* to the linear program in (6-5); the shaded region, with its boundaries, is termed the *feasible region* for the program. We notice, as a direct consequence of the fact that the inequality constraints are linear, that the boundaries of the feasible region are all straight lines. Moreover, it is clear that adding a new constraint to the problem will either "cut away" at the feasible region, adding a new segment to its boundary, or else have no effect whatsoever, if the added constraint is less severe than those already in the picture. The latter is termed *redundant;* its addition does not change the solution-space picture at all. For example, consider a fourth inequality $x_1 + 5x_2 \leq 80$. As the reader can easily see for himself, this constraint lies completely above and to the right of the shaded feasible region in Figure 6.1(d); hence all feasible solutions to the original problem (6-5) *will automatically satisfy* $x_1 + 5x_2 \leq$ 80 and it is unnecessary to include it at all in the statement of the problem. In terms of the solution-space picture, then, *constraints* (usually) add sides to the feasible region and *variables* add dimensions to the space in which the feasible region is represented.

Consider now the objective function in (6-5); denote it as $\pi = 2x_1 + 5x_2$. Clearly for any specific set of values, x_1^0 and x_2^0, this function assumes a particular value π^0. On the other hand, the function can be partially represented in solution space, since the relation between x_1 and x_2—that is, the *slope* of the function—is given unambiguously by the coefficients of x_1 and x_2. In slope-intercept form, the objective function can be written $x_2 = -\frac{2}{5}x_1 + (\pi/5)$. While the (vertical axis) *intercept*—$\pi/5$—depends on the particular values of x_1 and x_2 and thus is not determined until they are, the *slope* of the function in solution space, regardless of its location, will be $-\frac{2}{5}$. Therefore the "contour lines" for various values of π can be represented in Figure 6.1(d) by a series of parallel lines with slope $-\frac{2}{5}$; a set of five such lines, labeled $\pi_1, \ldots, \pi_5$, is shown in Figure 6.2.

Since the intercept on the x_2 axis is a direct function of π, namely $\pi/5$, it is clear that the higher the intercept—the farther it is from the origin— the larger is π. From among the five lines in Figure 6.2, π_5 is best from this point of view. But none of the combinations of x_1 and x_2 along this line are

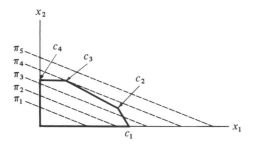

Figure 6.2.   Feasible Region and Objective Function Contours

in the feasible region. Hence the linear programming problem can be seen to be one of finding an objective function contour line that is as far as possible from the origin (measured upward along the x_2 axis) while still having *at least one* point in the feasible region. Visually, in Figure 6.2, π_4 is such a line. Objective function values associated with π_1, π_2, and π_3 are clearly inferior; they intercept the x_2 axis below π_4; π_5 has a higher objective function value but is inadmissible because it violates the feasibility requirement. The coordinates of the *corner* point, c_3, at which the objective function is tangent to the feasible region, thus represent the values of x_1 and x_2 that maximize $2x_1 + 5x_2$ while also satisfying the constraints defining the feasible region. This is the *optimal solution*. If we consider carefully the implications of Figure 6.2, we see that the linearity of the objective function and all of the constraints assures that the optimal solution to a linear program will *always* be at a corner of the feasible region. The only slight variant of this result occurs when the objective function happens to be *parallel* to one of the constraints; in that case (in the two-variable example) *two* corners *and* all points along the edge joining them will be "equally optimal." (Imagine that the objective function lines are parallel to the edge connecting corners c_2 and c_3; then both c_2 and c_3 and all points on the boundary between them will be optimal.)[7] The linearity, which invalidated any approach utilizing calculus and the Lagrange multiplier or Kuhn-Tucker results of Chapter 4, thus assures that a corner solution will always be the best for a linear program. Therefore, any solution procedure that examines *only* corners of the feasible region is assured of finding the optimum.

Since corners will be crucial in linear programming calculations, we examine their characteristics in more detail. It is often useful to express a linear program in *augmented* form, in which each inequality is converted to an equation by the addition of a so-called *slack* variable. Consider again (6-5). Suppose we add to the left-hand side of the first constraint a nonnegative variable, s_1, which serves the function of taking up the slack or balancing the difference between the two sides. Since 10 is never less than $x_1 + 2x_2$, s_1 must necessarily be nonnegative. The first constraint is now $x_1 + 2x_2 + s_1 = 10$. Similarly, different slack variables can be added to the left-hand sides of constraints 2 and 3. (In the production example, the slack variables represent the difference between the fixed amounts of each resource and the amount used by a particular production decision—that is, by given values of x_1, and x_2.) Thus the equality (augmented) form of the constraints is

$$(1')\quad x_1 + 2x_2 + s_1 = 10,$$
$$(2')\quad 3x_1 + 2x_2 + s_2 = 24,$$
$$(3')\quad x_1 + 10x_2 + s_3 = 40,$$

---

[7] We consider this special case in some detail in Chapter 7.

which is a set of three equations in five unknowns—the two original variables (x_1 and x_2) and the three additional slack variables (s_1, s_2, and s_3). Since the slack variables are added for computational convenience and have nothing to contribute to the objective function of the problem, they can, for purposes of symmetry, be thought of as appearing in the objective function with coefficients of zero. Also for the sake of symmetry, the equality constraints can be written as below, in the fully augmented form of problem (6-5).

$$
\begin{array}{ll}
\text{Maximize:} & 2x_1 + 5x_2 + 0s_1 + 0s_2 + 0s_3 \\
\text{subject to:} & x_1 + 2x_2 + s_1 + 0s_2 + 0s_3 = 10, \\
& 3x_1 + 2x_2 + 0s_1 + s_2 + 0s_3 = 24, \qquad (6\text{-}6) \\
& x_1 + 10x_2 + 0s_1 + 0s_2 + s_3 = 40, \\
\text{and} & x_1 \geq 0, \quad x_2 \geq 0; \quad s_1 \geq 0, \quad s_2 \geq 0, \quad s_3 \geq 0.
\end{array}
$$

It should be clear that the matrix form of the augmented general linear programming maximization problem is

$$
\begin{array}{ll}
\text{maximize:} & P'X + O'_m S \\
\text{subject to:} & AX + IS = R, \qquad (6\text{-}7) \\
& X \geq O_n, \quad S \geq O_m,
\end{array}
$$

where S is an m-element column vector of slack variables, O'_m is an m-element null (row) vector, I is the $m \times m$ identity matrix, and O_n is an n-element null (column) vector. [Compare with (6-1).] The augmented problem can also be written in other forms, parallel to (6-2), (6-3), and (6-4). The important point is that the constraints of the general augmented problem will *always* be a set of m *equations* in $m + n$ variables, since one slack variable for each constraint—of which there are m—is added to the original x's—which are n in number. Since the constraints now consist of a set of fewer equations than unknowns, we know (Section 2.4), if the equation system is not inconsistent, that by systematically eliminating "extra" variables, so that $m \times m$ equation systems remain, we can find a series of *basic* solutions—solutions in which at least n of the $m + n$ variables are equal to zero.[8]

Referring again to Figure 6.2, consider the values of x_1 and x_2 and the slack variables s_1, s_2, and s_3 at several of the corners of the feasible region. At the origin, $x_1 = x_2 = 0$ and clearly, from (6-6), each slack variable is positive—$s_1 = 10$, $s_2 = 24$, and $s_3 = 40$. At c_1, x_1 has become positive and the slack variable associated with constraint 2, the constraint that contributed the edge $c_1 c_2$ (see Figure 6.1), has become zero. Clearly, c_1 is defined as the point at which constraint 2 intersects the x_1 axis; thus by definition at that point (and all along the edge $c_1 c_2$) $s_2 = 0$. At the same time it is clear that s_1, associated with constraint 1, is positive, since the

---

[8] The reader may find it useful to review Section 2.4 at this point.

intersection of that constraint with the x_1 axis is further out than c_1 [extend c_2c_3 downward to the x_1 axis in Figure 6.2 or refer to Figure 6.1(a) and (b)]. Similarly, s_3 is positive, as reference to Figure 6.1(a) and (c) will show. Finally, consider c_3. At that corner, both x_1 and x_2 have positive values while the slack variables associated with constraints 1 (edge c_2c_3) and 3 (edge c_3c_4) are necessarily zero; those two constraints hold as strict *equalities* at c_3. At the same time, extension of c_1c_2 upward toward the x_2 axis shows that s_2 must be positive. Table 6.1 summarizes these results for the three corners examined and also for c_2 and c_4.

Table 6.1.   Positive and Zero-Valued Variables at Corners of the Feasible Region

	Corner				
	Origin	c_1	c_2	c_3	c_4
Positive-valued variables	s_1, s_2, s_3	x_1, s_1, s_3	x_1, x_2, s_3	x_1, x_2, s_2	x_2, s_1, s_2
Zero-valued variables	x_1, x_2	x_2, s_2	s_1, s_2	s_1, s_3	x_1, s_3

The extremely important point is that each of the corners has three of the five variables at positive value and two at value zero; hence each corner corresponds to a *basic solution* to the constraint equations in (6-6). Since there are three equations in five unknowns, we know that altogether $C_3^5 = 10$ possible basic solutions exist, yet the feasible region has only five corners; thus five $[= (10 - 5)]$ basic solutions are lost in this case when we look only at the corners of the feasible region. The missing basic solutions are those in which at least one of the basic variables would necessarily be strictly *negative*. These basic solutions would be associated with the following (infeasible) intersections in Figure 6.2 (the reader should examine which variables are zero, which positive, and which negative in each case):[9]

1. constraint 1 and the x_1 axis,
2. constraint 3 and the x_1 axis,
3. constraint 1 and the x_2 axis,
4. constraint 2 and the x_2 axis,
5. constraints 2 and 3.

Therefore, a possible method of solution for a linear programming prob-

[9] Remembering that for points along the x_1 axis, $x_2 = 0$, and vice versa, while for points along a constraint line the slack variable *for that constraint* is zero.

lem would appear to be one in which all nonnegative basic solutions to the augmented constraint set—basic solutions in which no variable is negative—were found, the objective function evaluated for each, and that solution for which the objective function was largest chosen as optimal.[10] We present a variant of this idea after making somewhat more precise the algebraic-geometric results that appear obvious in the case of two-dimensional solution space.

6.2. CONVEX SET THEORY AGAIN

At this point it is useful to recall several results that were presented in Section 4.7.

1. A linear inequality defines a half-space; if the inequality is weak ($\geq$ or $\leq$), the half-space is closed (which means that its boundary line— or plane or hyperplane—is included in the half-space).

2. A closed half-space is a convex set; formally, the line joining any two points in the set lies entirely within the set. Less formally, a convex set has no holes and its boundaries have no dents.

3. Points that satisfy several linear inequalities simultaneously—that is, points in the intersection of the half-spaces defined by the inequalities— form a convex set. Therefore, the x's that simultaneously satisfy the weak inequalities $AX \leq R$ and $X \geq O$ form a closed convex set.

We have seen in the preceding section that corners of the feasible region are particularly important in linear programming problems, since the optimal solution is to be found among the corners. It will be useful to have an unambiguous definition of a "corner" or "vertex" or *extreme point* of a convex set in solution space of any number of dimensions.

DEFINITION 6.1: EXTREME POINT.   A point P_0 is an extreme point of a convex set if and only if there do not exist two distinct points P_1 and P_2 in the set such that $P_0 = \alpha P_1 + (1 - \alpha)P_2$ for $0 < \alpha < 1$—that is, for α in the *open* interval between 0 and 1.

The definition simply means that P_0 is an extreme point of a particular convex set if and only if it cannot be expressed as a convex combination of some two other points—that is, if it is not "between" some two other points—in the set.

---

[10] There is the obvious drawback that problems with *many* constraints and *many* variables—problems that have a many-sided and multidimensional feasible region—will have *many* corners and hence many nonnegative basic solutions. The reader who visualizes well in three dimensions should imagine a set of axes (the corner of a room often does well for the origin), introduce one constraint (a plane), then a second, then a third, and so on, counting the number of corners in each case.

The following theorem is essential for the underlying computational method that will be presented for solving linear programs via basic solutions to the augmented constraints. It will not be proved.

THEOREM 6.1.   The intersection of a finite number of closed half-spaces is a closed convex set with a *finite* number of extreme points.[11]

This means that the feasible region to a linear programming problem has a finite number of corners. If the intersection described in Theorem 6.1 is *bounded*, which means that any point in the set is a finite distance from the origin, then the figure is described as a *convex polyhedron*. Figure 6.3 illus-

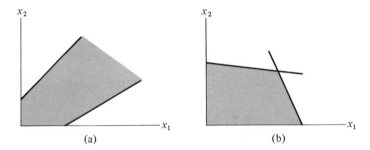

Figure 6.3.   (a) Unbounded, Closed Convex Region, (b) Bounded, Closed Convex Region

trates bounded and unbounded convex regions; note that both regions are closed, since the constraints are weak inequalities.

Another useful theorem (proved in Appendix 6.1 for the interested reader) is the following:

THEOREM 6.2.   Any point inside a closed, bounded convex set can be expressed as a convex combination of the extreme points of the set.

The following theorems (also proved in Appendix 6.1) establish the connection between optimal solutions, corners of the feasible region, and basic solutions to the constraint set of the augmented problem, for a problem of any size. That is, they generalize the geometrical results for two-variable problems of the last section.

---

[11] Intuitively this makes sense. Consider the two-dimensional case. A single closed half-space has *no* extreme points. The intersection of *two* such spaces has at most one extreme point (it may have none if the boundaries are parallel). Addition of a third closed half-space produces a region with at most three extreme points, and addition of the nth closed half-space generates an (at most) n-cornered region. Hence if n is finite, so is the number of extreme points. The reader should convince himself of this with pencil and paper.

THEOREM 6.3.   If the objective function takes on a maximum value somewhere in the feasible region, then it takes on this value at an extreme point of the region.

This states as a theorem the fact that was observed to be true in the small example of Figure 6.2. Note that there are two cases in which the objective function may not have a maximum value in the feasible region; one is when the region is empty, the other is when it is unbounded.

(a) *No feasible region.* Consider a linear programming problem with two constraints:

ALGEBRA

$$
\begin{aligned}
(1) \quad & 2x_1 + x_2 \le & 50, \\
(2) \quad & -x_1 & \le -30,
\end{aligned}
$$

and $x_1 \ge 0$, $x_2 \ge 0$.

GEOMETRY

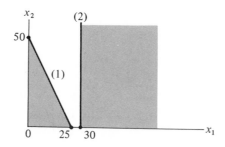

Figure 6.4.   Empty Feasible Region

A nonnegative point satisfying (1) *must* lie in the triangle at the left; a nonnegative point satisfying (2) *must* lie in the shaded area on the right. Hence no point can *simultaneously* satisfy (1) and (2) and be nonnegative. Thus the feasible region, which is the intersection of (1) and (2), contains no points or is empty.

(b) *Unbounded feasible region.* Consider the following pair of constraints.

ALGEBRA

$$
\begin{aligned}
(1) \quad & -x_1 + x_2 \le 10, \\
(2) \quad & -x_1 + 2x_2 \le 40,
\end{aligned}
$$

and $x_1 \ge 0$, $x_2 \ge 0$.

GEOMETRY

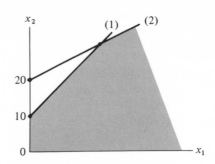

Figure 6.5. Unbounded Feasible Region

The feasible region is unbounded; it extends infinitely far in an east-northeasterly direction. Any objective function whose contour lines are downward sloping—that is, having positive coefficients for both x_1 and x_2—will have no finite maximum value.

Provided that neither of these two cases applies (which is the condition expressed in the first clause of Theorem 6.3), the objective function achieves a maximum value at a corner of the feasible region in a linear program of any size.

THEOREM 6.4.   If the objective function takes on a maximum value at *more than one* extreme point of the feasible region, then it has that same maximum value at every convex combination of those extreme points.

As we could visualize in Figure 6.2, if the objective function happened to be parallel to a side—for example, that given by constraint 1—then two corners, c_2 and c_3, and all points on the line connecting them (that is, their convex combination, which is an edge of the feasible region) would be equally optimal. There are infinitely many such points. In solution space of more than two dimensions, the convex combination may consist of two extreme points, in which case the objective function is parallel to an edge of the feasible region, or it may contain three or more extreme points, in which case the objective function is parallel to a face of the feasible region. In either case, we say that the programming problem has *multiple optima* or *alternative optima*.

To establish the connection between extreme points of the feasible region and basic solutions, we must of course consider the augmented form of the constraints. For the sake of generality we rewrite $AX + IS = R$ from (6-7). Suppose we redefine A to be an $m \times (n + m)$ matrix containing the original $m \times n$ matrix of coefficients a_{ij} and the identity matrix associated with the slack variables. Also, redefine $s_1, s_2, \ldots, s_m$ as $x_{n+1}, x_{n+2}, \ldots, x_{n+m}$. Then let X be an $(n + m)$-element column vector of both original variables and slack variables. The constraints as equalities can then be expressed as $AX = R$. This is done simply for terminological convenience. The next two theorems refer to the augmented form of the general linear programming maximization problem.

THEOREM 6.5. If a nonnegative basic solution can be found to the m-equation, $(n + m)$-variable system, $AX = R$, say $A_1 x_1^* + \cdots + A_k x_k^* = R$ (where $k \leq m$ and $x_1^* > 0, \ldots, x_k^* > 0$), then the $(n + m)$-element column vector $X^* = [x_1^*, \ldots, x_k^*, 0, \ldots, 0]'$ is an extreme point of the feasible region for the augmented problem.

Put loosely, this says that to every nonnegative basic solution there corresponds an extreme point. In Appendix 6.1 the relationship between the feasible regions for the inequality form and the augmented form of the problem is investigated; the important result is that extreme points in the augmented problem correspond precisely to extreme points in the original problem. The relevance of the theorem should be clear; if we find nonnegative basic solutions to $AX = R$ and find the value of the objective function at each such solution, we are in fact evaluating the objective function at extreme points of the feasible region. The only question remaining is whether *every* corner of the feasible region has a corresponding nonnegative basis. Theorem 6.5 tells us that to every nonnegative basis there corresponds an extreme point; is it also true that to every extreme point there corresponds a nonnegative basis? Theorem 6.6 provides an affirmative answer.

THEOREM 6.6. If $X^* = [x_1^*, \ldots, x_k^*, 0, \ldots, 0]'$ is an extreme point of the feasible region of the augmented problem, then the column vectors $A_1, \ldots, A_k$ from A that correspond to the positive x_i^* in X^* are linearly independent.

When $k = m$, these columns form a basis; when $k < m$, other columns from A must be added. (The latter represents a degenerate basic solution.) Nonetheless, in either case, since (1) an optimum, if it exists, will be at an extreme point, of which there are a finite number, (2) each extreme point is represented by a nonnegative basic solution to $AX = R$, and (3) each non-negative basis corresponds to an extreme point, then a solution procedure that evaluates the objective function for each nonnegative basic solution to $AX = R$ will always find the optimum and will do so in a finite number of steps. The *simplex method* is precisely such a procedure; it is the subject matter of the next section.[12]

---

[12] Consider $n + 1$ points in n-dimensional space, not all of which lie on the same hyperplane (or plane, if $n = 3$; line, if $n = 2$). The set of all convex combinations of these $n + 1$ points is called a *simplex*. For $n = 2$, the two-dimensional simplex is a triangle and its interior. (The set of all convex combinations of a set of points is termed the *convex hull* of the points.) The term is applied to the solution method for linear programs because of the geometry of the operations as they appear in vector space, not in the solution space that we have chosen to use.

6.3. THE SIMPLEX METHOD

Although the number of extreme points for any feasible region is finite, it still may be very large. Instead of evaluating the objective function for each corner in turn, a much more efficient method would, at any particular corner, only next examine a "better" corner—one for which it was known in advance that the objective function would have a larger value. This would have the effect, generally, of eliminating extreme points from possible consideration with each move from one corner to a better one, and once eliminated, they would never again be worth considering. The method therefore requires (1) a procedure for finding a starting or initial basic feasible solution and (2) a procedure for moving from a given basic feasible solution to a better one—one for which the objective function value will be larger.

In small problems with two or three variables (and hence two- or three-dimensional feasible regions) the optimum can easily be found geometrically; for the general n-variable, m-constraint case we need a completely algebraic solution procedure. In this chapter we present a method for linear programming maximum problems. Because of the relationships to be explored in Section 6.4, however, we will see that this also equips us to solve minimization problems.

The simplex criterion

If the origin is included among the extreme points of the feasible region, it provides a convenient starting point, since it is completely described by letting the slack variable for each constraint take on the entire right-hand side value.[13] This will generally take care of the first requirement above. For the second requirement the *simplex criterion* provides a means of ranking other corners relative to the current one in terms of their marginal contribution to the current objective function value. This will become clear in what follows. Consider the augmented problem as in the preceding section:

$$\text{maximize:} \quad P'X$$
$$\text{subject to:} \quad AX = R \qquad (6\text{-}8)$$
$$\text{and} \qquad X \geq O,$$

where the X vector has been enlarged to include slack variables and P and A correspondingly changed. Suppose that a basic feasible solution has been found and that it involves the first m variables (renumbered, if necessary). The equation system is

---

[13] This means that $R \geq O$ so that in the initial basic solution (where $S = R$) all slack variables will be nonnegative, as required in (6-7). We will see in Chapter 7 how an initial basis can be found when the condition $R \geq O$ does not hold.

$$A_1x_1 + \cdots + A_mx_m = R, \tag{6-9}$$

and let the solution values to (6-9) be $x_1^*, \ldots, x_m^*$. The associated value of the objective function is $P'X^* = p_1x_1^* + \cdots + p_mx_m^*$. We now want to consider the impact on the objective function of bringing a currently excluded variable into the solution. There are $(m + n) - m = n$ such variables. Suppose we consider having x_q in the solution; suppose furthermore that we want the new solution to be *basic* as well as feasible. This means that, when x_q comes into the solution, one variable from among those m currently in the solution—$x_1, \ldots, x_m$—will have to become zero and thus drop out. Only in this way will the proper number for a basic solution, m, remain.

By definition, the column vectors $A_1, \ldots, A_m$ form a basis in the m-dimensional vector space of the equation set $AX = R$. Therefore *any* other column in A (not in the basis) can be expressed uniquely in terms of the basis $A_1, \ldots, A_m$. (See Section 1.5.) Let A_q, the coefficients associated with x_q, be such a column; then we know that y_{iq}'s can be found such that

$$A_1y_{1q} + \cdots + A_my_{mq} = A_q. \tag{6-10}$$

These y's are simply the coordinates of A_q relative to the $A_1, \ldots, A_m$ basis; assume that at least one of these coordinates is positive.

Consider first the *feasibility* problem. New values of the x_i^* ($i = 1, \ldots, m$)—call them x_i^{**}—and x_q must still satisfy the constraints. Thus

$$A_1x_1^{**} + \cdots + A_mx_m^{**} + A_qx_q = R \tag{6-11}$$

must hold. Since $x_1^*, \ldots, x_m^*$ previously satisfied (6-9)—that is, used up all of the resources R—it is clear that the introduction of another variable that also uses resources must be accompanied by a *reduction* in the sizes of at least some of the $x_1^*, \ldots, x_m^*$; the question is, which ones and by how much?[14]

Note that (6-10) expresses the resource-use column for x_q in terms of those for $x_1, \ldots, x_m$, the variables presently in the basis. Multiplying both sides by x_q gives

$$A_1y_{1q}x_q + \cdots + A_my_{mq}x_q = A_qx_q, \tag{6-12}$$

which indicates, on the right-hand side, the *total* use of resources for any amount, x_q. Thus $x_1^*, \ldots, x_m^*$ must be adjusted so as to release just this amount from their previous consumption; only in this way will a solution with x_q still be feasible—that is, satisfy $AX = R$. Thus, subtracting (6-12) from (6-9), and rearranging, we have

---

[14] Clearly, if there were a variable whose column in the A matrix—for example, in (6-1)—contained all negative or zero entries [that is, that either *produced* resources (rather than consuming them) or else used none at all as it was made larger and larger], then this variable could be increased without limit from the point of view of the constraints. The feasible region would be *unbounded*.

$$A_1(x_1^* - x_q y_{1q}) + \cdots + A_m(x_m^* - x_q y_{mq}) + A_q x_q = R. \qquad (6\text{-}13)$$

This has the same structure as (6-11); it simply shows exactly how the x_i^{**} are related to the original x_i^*.

For the variables in (6-13) to provide a *basic* solution (at most m variables nonzero), at least one of the $(x_i^* - x_q y_{iq})$ terms $(i = 1, \ldots, m)$ must become zero. Moreover, to maintain feasibility, we must be certain that none of the new x_i^{**} is negative; $X \geq O$, from (6-8). If $y_{1q} > 0$, then a large x_q could make x_1^{**} $(= x_1^* - x_q y_{1q})$ negative and thus infeasible. Therefore, to assure that the new solution in (6-13) remains feasible, an *upper limit* on the size of x_q is necessary; in words, x_q must be small enough that no x_i^{**} is negative. The problem arises only for those y_{iq} that are positive. Since the minimum for a new variable, x_i^{**}, is zero, at that minimum

$$x_i^{**} = (x_i^* - x_q y_{iq}) = 0 \qquad \text{or} \qquad x_q = \frac{x_i^*}{y_{iq}}.$$

Thus, the *largest* value that x_q can have is the *smallest* of the ratios x_i^*/y_{iq} from among those y_{iq} that are positive. That solution for x_q will send to zero the previously included variable; all others will still be positive.[15] If two or more ratios x_i^*/y_{iq} are *tied* for the smallest value, then more than one previously included variable will become zero and the new basic feasible solution will also be degenerate (Section 2.4). We consider the computational implications of degeneracy in Chapter 7.

We now see *how* we could bring an x_q into the basis; the question that remains is: do we want to? The answer obviously depends on what happens to the objective function if we do; we gain an amount $p_q x_q$ but we lose something because $x_1^*, \ldots, x_m^*$ are, in general, *smaller* than they were without x_q. Specifically, the objective function in the new situation (with x_q in the basis) is

$$\begin{aligned} P'X^{**} &= p_1 x_1^{**} + \cdots + p_m x_m^{**} + p_q x_q \\ &= p_1(x_1^* - x_q y_{1q}) + \cdots + p_m(x_m^* - x_q y_{mq}) + p_q x_q \\ &= P'X^* + x_q \left(p_q - \sum_{i=1}^{m} p_i y_{iq} \right). \end{aligned} \qquad (6\text{-}14)$$

Thus the *change* associated with introducing x_q into the solution and making the necessary compensating changes to insure basic feasibility is given by

---

[15] If all $y_{iq} \leq 0$ [but at least one strictly less than zero; otherwise A_q in (6-10) would just be the zero vector], then from (6-13) we see that a *feasible* solution could be found in which the x_i^{**} corresponding to $y_{iq} < 0$ could be arbitrarily large and hence the objective function would be unbounded. [See (6-14), below.]

the second term, $x_q \left(p_q - \sum_{i=1}^{m} p_i y_{iq} \right)$. Consider the parenthetical part only; this is the so-called *simplex criterion*.

$$p_q - \sum_{i=1}^{m} p_i y_{iq}. \tag{6-15}$$

If (6-15) is positive, x_q should enter the solution, since $P'X^{**} > P'X^*$—that is, the objective function has a larger value with x_q in the solution; if negative, x_q should not be brought in; and if the term is zero, the objective function value is unchanged if x_q is brought into the solution. This term, (6-15), has a very logical interpretation. The y_{iq} represent the amounts by which currently included variables x_i must be reduced per unit of x_q introduced in the solution; this follows from (6-10). The p_i are per unit "profits" associated with x_i. Thus, $\sum_{i=1}^{m} p_i y_{iq}$ is the total *reduction* in the value of the objective function because of introduction of one unit of x_q into the solution; p_q is the total *increase* in objective function value for a unit of x_q. The difference between the two, (6-15), is thus the unit (marginal) gain or loss from introduction of one unit of x_q into the basis; when multiplied by x_q this is the *total* gain or loss. Precisely because the objective function is *linear*, it is adequate to examine the *marginal* impact of a proposed new variable, since there cannot be increasing or decreasing returns. If the marginal gain exceeds the marginal loss, the variable should be in the basis; put differently, a variable should enter the basis if the *net marginal gain* is positive.

Simplex arithmetic

The steps, then, are:

1. Find a basic feasible solution.
2. Examine the simplex criterion for variables excluded from that basis. Transform the present basis by introducing a previously excluded variable and removing (by sending to zero) a currently included one. Any variable with a positive simplex criterion may be introduced into the basis; an effective rule is to bring in that variable with the *largest* positive net marginal gain.
3. Repeat until no further transformation of basic solutions is profitable.

Each transformation—bringing in a new variable and removing an old one—is called an *iteration*. Iterations, then, correspond to finding basic solutions of the augmented constraint set $AX = R$.

We repeat the small sample problem (6-5), above.

$$\begin{aligned}
\text{Maximize:} \quad & 2x_1 + 5x_2 \\
\text{subject to:} \quad & x_1 + 2x_2 \le 10, \\
& 3x_1 + 2x_2 \le 24, \\
& x_1 + 10x_2 \le 40, \\
\text{and} \quad & x_1 \ge 0, \quad x_2 \ge 0.
\end{aligned}$$

Converted to equations, using s_1, s_2, and s_3 for slack variables, we have

$$\begin{aligned}
\text{maximize:} \quad & 2x_1 + 5x_2 \\
\text{subject to:} \quad & x_1 + 2x_2 + s_1 = 10, \\
& 3x_1 + 2x_2 + s_2 = 24, \qquad (6\text{-}16) \\
& x_1 + 10x_2 + s_3 = 40, \\
\text{and} \quad & x_1, x_2, s_1, s_2, \text{ and } s_3 \ge 0.
\end{aligned}$$

Rearranging the constraints gives

$$\begin{aligned}
s_1 &= 10 - x_1 - 2x_2, \\
s_2 &= 24 - 3x_1 - 2x_2, \qquad (6\text{-}17) \\
s_3 &= 40 - x_1 - 10x_2.
\end{aligned}$$

This simple algebraic rearrangement puts the constraints into a particularly useful form. By setting $x_1 = x_2 = 0$, we obtain instantly an initial basic feasible solution, namely $s_1 = 10$, $s_2 = 24$, and $s_3 = 40$; this is, of course, the origin, where all original variables (x's) are zero and all resources are consumed exclusively and entirely by slack variables (s's).[16] Since slack variables do not contribute to the objective function, its value at this point is $2(0) + 5(0) = 0$.

Note that the form of (6-17) expresses the values of the variables in the current basis as (linear) functions of the variables not in the current basis (and hence at value zero). Since we know that all basic solutions to this problem will have three variables included (number of constraining equations) and two omitted (total number—original plus slack—less number of constraints), we can adopt a format within which to record this and any further basic solutions. Rewrite (6-17) as

---

[16] If the origin is not a feasible solution, one or more of the s_i at this point will be negative, which simply means that one or more of the right-hand sides was negative in the original problem, (6-5) or (6-16). For such problems, a modification of the beginning steps is necessary. This will be discussed in Chapter 7.

		x_1	x_2
s_1	10	-1	-2
s_2	24	-3	-2
s_3	40	-1	-10

where the double vertical line can be read as "equals." The bottom line, for example, summarizes exactly the last equation in (6-17); the coefficients simply have been detached from their respective nonbasic variables. It says: "s_3 equals 40 plus the next coefficient (-1) times the variable at the top of that column (x_1) plus the next coefficient (-10) times the variable at the top of that column (x_2)." Since $x_1 = x_2 = 0$, by virtue of their *exclusion* from the current basis, this table really says: $s_1 = 10$, $s_2 = 24$, $s_3 = 40$. The leftmost (or "zeroth") column of numbers thus records the values of the basic variables listed at the far left. A *new* basis, then, will need a table (tableau) of exactly the same shape, with one of the left-column variable labels exchanged for one of those currently excluded—that is, along the top row.

If the table could be expanded to include information on the objective function also, it would be complete. If, as before, we denote the current value of the objective function at any basic solution by π—that is, $\pi = 2x_1 + 5x_2$—then in (6-16) the objective function can be expressed, in a manner analogous to the constraints, as $-2x_1 - 5x_2 + \pi = 0$,[17] and, parallel to the rewritten form in (6-17), as $\pi = 0 + 2x_1 + 5x_2$. Therefore we can add one more row to the top of the table in which the objective function coefficients and value appear.

		x_1	x_2
π	0	2	5
s_1	10	-1	-2
s_2	24	-3	-2
s_3	40	-1	-10

(6-18)

---

[17] That is, π is rather like a slack variable, measuring the difference between (the negative of) a current value of the objective function (for a particular set of x_1 and x_2 values) and zero.

This top line (the "zeroth" row) can now be read exactly as any of the others, which represent the constraints, and the current value of the objective function is in the upper left corner of the numbers (zeroth column and zeroth row). At this stage, with *no* x variables in the basis, the p_1 and p_2 from the objective function give the net marginal gains associated with having x_1 or x_2 in the basis. The zeroth-row numbers (except for the left-most) thus contain (in the initial table) the value of the simplex criterion for each of the x's. So much for the initial basis (the origin; see Table 6.1).

To move to a new basis means putting either x_1 or x_2 into the solution and removing one of the three slack variables. We can look at this transformation as a three-part operation:

1. Decide which variable, from among those listed above the top row, to bring into the basis.
2. Decide which variable, from among those listed at the left side, to remove from the basis.
3. Express each of the variables in the new basic solution as linear functions of the nonbasic ones; that is, generate a new set of numbers (coefficients) to fill the bottom three rows of the tableau. Find the value of the simplex criterion for each of the variables excluded from the new basis; this puts new numbers in the top row.

Repeat until all top-row values, except the leftmost, are negative (or negative and zero). When that happens, there is no point in changing basic solutions further; no change would increase the value of the objective function, and the solution at that point is optimal. We consider each operation.

VARIABLE TO ENTER THE BASIS

In (6-18) it is clear that either x_1 or x_2 would improve the value of the objective function. A good rule is to bring in that variable with the *largest* positive top-row coefficient (net marginal gain).[18] If several are tied, any one of them will do. Thus, in the present example, we want the label x_2

[18] This rule is not always most efficient in terms of leading to the optimum in the fewest number of operations, but it is easy to apply and logical. Consider the following problem with only one constraint: maximize $100x_1 + 2x_2$, subject to $500x_1 + 4x_2 \leq 100$ and $x_1, x_2 \geq 0$. If only x_1, with a much larger *marginal* gain, is brought into the basis, the *total* value of the objective function becomes $100(\frac{1}{5}) + 2(0) = 20$, since x_1 uses the scarce resource so heavily. However, if only x_2, with a smaller marginal value, is introduced into the basis, the objective function becomes $100(0) + 2(25) = 50$, since x_2 is (relatively) more economical in its use of the scarce resource. Thus a larger *total* gain on that iteration comes from bringing in the variable with the smaller simplex criterion.

to move from the top row to the side column. The next two operations are discussed in reverse order, for reasons that will become obvious.

EXPRESSING NEW BASIC VARIABLES AS FUNCTIONS OF NON-BASIC ONES

Imagine a generalization of the table in (6-18) in which the elements of the table are denoted a_{ij}, $i = 0, 1, \ldots, m$ and $j = 0, 1, \ldots, n$, where subscripts 0 denote zeroth row or column, where the variables in the current basis (down the left side) are denoted $x_1^*, \ldots, x_m^*$, and those currently excluded (nonbasic) are labeled $x_1^{nb}, \ldots, x_n^{nb}$. Assume that x_q^{nb} has been selected to *enter* the basis and x_p^* is the variable *leaving* the basis. The row and the column associated with the variables leaving and entering the basis are sometimes referred to as the *pivot* row and *pivot* column. The entire operation of moving from one basic solution to another is often termed pivoting, and in particular the a_{ij} element at the intersection of the pivot row and pivot column is called, not surprisingly, the pivot element. Consider the linear equation that related x_p^* to the nonbasic variables:

$$x_p^* = a_{p0} + a_{p1}x_1^{nb} + \cdots + a_{pq}x_q^{nb} + \cdots + a_{pn}x_n^{nb}. \qquad (6\text{-}19)$$

We now want x_p^* to act as a nonbasic variable and x_q^{nb} to become basic; hence we want to express x_q^{nb} as a linear function of the old nonbasic variables *and* x_p^*, which has just become nonbasic. But from (6-19), this is simple algebra, giving, after rearrangement,

$$x_q^{nb} = -\frac{a_{p0}}{a_{pq}} - \frac{a_{p1}}{a_{pq}}x_1^{nb} - \cdots + \frac{1}{a_{pq}}x_p^* - \cdots - \frac{a_{pn}}{a_{pq}}x_n^{nb}. \qquad (6\text{-}20)$$

Thus the rule for transforming elements in the pivot row—the row whose label has been replaced by that of the variable entering the basis—is extremely simple. The pivot element, a_{pq}, is replaced by its reciprocal. All other elements in the pivot row are divided by the pivot element and have their sign changed. In particular, the numerical value of the variable that has just entered the basis is $-a_{p0}/a_{pq}$. Since $a_{p0} \geq 0$ (the current basis is feasible) and we require $-a_{p0}/a_{pq} \geq 0$ (the next basis shall be feasible), it is clear that the pivot element, a_{pq}, *must be negative*.

Consider any one of the variables that remain in the basis, say $x_i^*(i \neq p)$. Before pivoting,

$$x_i^* = a_{i0} + a_{i1}x_1^{nb} + \cdots + a_{iq}x_q^{nb} + \cdots + a_{in}x_n^{nb}. \qquad (6\text{-}21)$$

Since x_i^* remains in the basis and x_q^{nb} has become basic, we must replace x_q^{nb} in (6-21) by its expression in terms of nonbasic variables, which is precisely what (6-20) gives. Substitution and rearrangement leads to

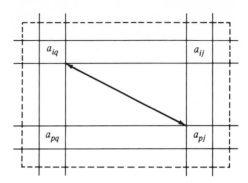

Figure 6.6.   Location of Elements for "Corner Product" Rule

$$x_i^* = \left(a_{i0} - \frac{a_{iq}a_{p0}}{a_{pq}}\right) + \left(a_{i1} - \frac{a_{iq}a_{p1}}{a_{pq}}\right)x_1^{nb} + \cdots + \frac{a_{iq}}{a_{pq}}\,x_p^*$$

$$+ \cdots + \left(a_{in} - \frac{a_{iq}a_{pn}}{a_{pq}}\right)x_n^{nb}. \qquad (6\text{-}22)$$

Rules for the new elements in the pivot column (except for the pivot itself) and elsewhere in the matrix are made explicit in (6-22). For the pivot column, the old element is simply divided by the pivot (in contrast to the pivot row, the sign is not changed). Finally, all other elements have subtracted from them: (1) the element in the same column, pivot row, times (2) the element in the same row, pivot column, divided by (3) the pivot element. If the reader examines the structure of this transformation, he will see that for each nonpivot-row, nonpivot-column element, the a's that are used come from the opposite corners of an imaginary rectangle, as Figure 6.6 illustrates. We summarize these pivoting rules in Table 6.2. It remains to be shown that the zeroth-row elements can be transformed

Table 6.2.   Summary of Simplex Arithmetic

Old basis	New basis
Pivot element	Reciprocal of pivot element
Pivot-column elements	Old element/pivot element
Pivot-row elements	$-$(Old element)/pivot element
All other elements	Old element $- \left(\dfrac{\text{``corner product''}}{\text{pivot element}}\right)$

in the same manner as those in any of the constraint rows. We illustrate with a small but general example that these pivoting rules, when applied to *top-row elements*, provide exactly the *simplex criterion*—the evaluation of net marginal gain that would result from bringing currently excluded variables into the basis. Consider the initial table for a three-variable, two-constraint maximization problem, shown below.

		x_1	x_2	x_3
π	0	p_1	p_2	p_3
s_1	r_1	$-a_{11}$	$-a_{12}$	$-a_{13}^*$
s_2	r_2	$-a_{21}$	$-a_{22}$	$-a_{23}$

$$(6\text{-}23)$$

Assume that when the rules for pivot column and row choice are applied, x_3 will enter the basis and s_1 go out, hence $-a_{13}$ is starred as the pivot element. Using the rules just developed, the next basic solution will be as follows (where blanks are left in cells that are not of interest)[19]:

		x_1	x_2	s_1
π	①$0 + p_3 r_1/a_{13}$	③$p_1 - (a_{11}/a_{13})p_3$	⑥$p_2 - (a_{12}/a_{13})p_3$	
x_3	②$+r_1/a_{13}$	④$-a_{11}/a_{13}$	⑦$-a_{12}/a_{13}$	
s_2		⑤$-a_{21} + (a_{11}/a_{13})a_{23}$	⑧$-a_{22} + (a_{12}/a_{13})a_{23}$	

$$(6\text{-}24)$$

The new value in cell ③—in the top row under x_1: $p_1 - (a_{11}/a_{13})p_3$—shows the *net* value of a unit of x_1 entering the basis, now that x_3 is there, and using up all of resource 1. To free some of this resource, in order for x_1 to take on a positive value, requires that x_3 decrease; and the new coefficient in the x_3-row, x_1-column, the cell numbered ④, shows exactly the *rate of exchange* of resource 1 between product 3 and product 1. For example, if $a_{11} = 30$ and $a_{13} = 15$, the ratio is -2; this says that from the point of view of resource 1, each unit of 1 that might be produced "costs" two units of 3

---

[19] Since $(-a_{13})$ has been chosen as the pivot, it must be negative; hence a_{13} is positive.

that must be foregone. Thus ③ values this cost by the unit contribution of product 3 to the objective function and nets it out of p_1. The first two elements in the next column, cells ⑥ and ⑦, have the same interpretations for x_2.

The last element under x_1, in cell ⑤, similarly alters the coefficient relating use of resource 2 to production of 1. In particular, $(a_{11}/a_{13})a_{23}$ shows the amount of resource 2 *freed* when x_3 is *decreased* by an amount (a_{11}/a_{13})—which is necessary for a unit *increase* in x_1. Thus, a_{21} alone no longer measures the net use of resource 2 by x_1. Similarly, cell ⑧ indicates how a_{22} must be changed.

If all elements in (6-24) are now written as a'_{ij}, and if we assume that the pivot column rules dictate that x_2 next comes into the basis, replacing s_2, it is easy to show that the elements in the next table, call them a''_{ij}, bear the same relationship to the a'_{ij} as the a'_{ij}—in (6-24)—do to the original elements in (6-23). Thus in particular, after a second pivot (bringing x_2 into the basis),

$$
\begin{aligned}
a''_{01} &= a'_{01} - \left(\frac{a'_{21}}{a'_{22}}\right) a'_{02} \\
&= p_1 - \left(\frac{a_{11}}{a_{13}}\right) p_3 - \left(\frac{a'_{21}}{a'_{22}}\right)\left[p_2 - \left(\frac{a_{12}}{a_{13}}\right) p_3 \right] \\
&= p_1 - \left\{ \left(\frac{a'_{21}}{a'_{22}}\right) p_2 + \left[\left(\frac{a'_{21}}{a'_{22}}\right)\left(\frac{a_{12}}{a_{13}}\right) - \left(\frac{a_{11}}{a_{13}}\right)\right] p_3 \right\}.
\end{aligned}
\tag{6-25}
$$

This is in the form of (6-15), the simplex criterion, except that y_{21} and y_{31} are made explicit for the case in which x_3 and x_2 have entered the basis, replacing s_1 and s_2, respectively. Thus, we can treat the elements in the zeroth row in the same way as those in any other row; the simplex arithmetic will generate current net marginal gains for currently excluded variables.

Consider finally the objective function value itself, a_{00}. After the first iteration, from (6-23) to (6-24), this is $(0 + p_3 r_1/a_{13})$—cell ① in (6-24). The new basis contains x_3 at a level equal to r_1/a_{13}—cell ② in (6-24). Since $-a_{13}$, the pivot, is negative, and since $r_1 \geq 0$ and $p_3 \geq 0$, $p_3(r_1/a_{13})$ is the value to the objective function of having (r_1/a_{13}) units of product 3 in the basis. This amount is added to 0, the previous objective function value, in ①. In each succeeding iteration the level of the newly included basic variable (zeroth column element divided by pivot and sign changed) is multiplied by the net marginal gain for the new variable *at that point* (zeroth row element in pivot column, which is always chosen to be positive), and this is added to the current value of the objective function. Thus the general simplex arithmetic automatically gives us, in the upper left, the current objective function value.

VARIABLE TO LEAVE THE BASIS

The table in (6-18) has been constructed with one row for each constraint (ignoring the zeroth row), and thus the left-hand column will always show the correct *number* of variables in a solution to keep it basic. To assure feasibility as well, it is necessary that none of the zeroth-column numbers become negative.

Our study of the arithmetic of the simplex method facilitates development of a rule to insure nonnegativity of the new basic variables. We have established that the pivot must be negative. Thus, only basic variables whose pivot column coefficients are currently negative are candidates for leaving the basis.[20] But which one? The answer has already been established in the rule for the *size* of the variable entering the basis that was used to derive the simplex criterion. We found (page 280) that the new basic variable should have a value equal to the smallest x_i^*/y_{iq} from among the y_{iq} that were positive. The x_i^* are current values of basic variables—now denoted in the tables as a_{i0}. The y_{iq} related amounts of i given up or consumed (whether a basic variable or a resource) to unit production of q. These were just the a_{iq} in the original statement of the problem or the $-a_{iq}$ in the initial table (6-18), where they appeared with changed sign. And in further tables these modified coefficients still represent amounts by which currently included variables must be altered per unit of the new variable introduced, except for sign. Thus a search among *positive* y_{iq} is a search among *negative* a_{iq}. The critical ratios, then, are the a_{i0}/a_{iq}—zeroth-column element divided by pivot-column element—in which a_{iq} is negative. And the value of the new basic variable, call it a_{p0}/a_{pq}, is the smallest of these ratios, *ignoring sign*. Thus, x_p^* leaves the basis. The rule is simply this: From among those elements in the pivot column, a_{iq}, that are negative, form the absolute values of ratios of zeroth column element to pivot column element; that is, ignore the negative signs. The variable that *must* leave the basis is the one for which this ratio, a_{i0}/a_{iq}, is *smallest*. (If several are tied at smallest, any one can be selected.)[21] This rule must be followed to assure nonnegativity of all variables in the new basic solution.

---

[20] This makes sense from the point of view of the initial table, such as (6-18), in which the signs of the a_{ij} coefficients in $AX = R$ all have been reversed (since the constraints are written as $s_i = a_{i0} - a_{i1}x_1 - \cdots - a_{in}x_n$). Hence a negative coefficient in (6-18) indicates in the original constraint, a *positive* use of resource i by product j. If a coefficient a_{ij} were either zero or negative in the *original* constraint (meaning that production of j did not use or even freed or generated resource i), it would be zero or positive in the initial table for the problem. In that case, r_i would never be critical for j; s_i would never become zero (leave the basis) because of production of j.

[21] As noted earlier, such a tie is a signal that the next basic feasible solution will be degenerate. This is not usually of any importance. We consider this further in Chapter 7.

EXAMPLE

We now apply these rules to problem (6-5), which is repeated here.

$$\text{Maximize:} \quad 2x_1 + 5x_2$$
$$\text{subject to:} \quad x_1 + 2x_2 \leq 10,$$
$$3x_1 + 2x_2 \leq 24,$$
$$x_1 + 10x_2 \leq 40,$$
$$\text{and} \quad x_1 \geq 0, \quad x_2 \geq 0.$$

The initial table was shown in (6-18) and is repeated here; the picture was

		x_1	x_2
π	0	2	5
s_1	10	-1	-2
s_2	24	-3	-2
s_3	40	-1	-10^*

shown in Figure 6.2. From (6-18) we know that the first basic feasible solution is the origin, namely $s_1 = 10$, $s_2 = 24$, $s_3 = 40$, where $x_1 = x_2 = 0$ by exclusion from the basis. The next basic feasible solution will contain *either* x_1 or x_2 and will have lost s_1, s_2, or s_3; hence it will be a corner *adjacent to* the origin (c_1 or c_4 in Figure 6.2 and Table 6.1). In fact, since the simplex method moves from basis to basis in steps that transfer a single variable in (and out) each time, it moves around the boundary of the feasible region going from one extreme point to an *adjacent* one, always in the direction of improving the objective function.[22]

The rule for incoming variables dictates that x_2 be selected (both 2 and 5 are positive, 5 is the larger). From among the negative elements associated with constraints in the x_2 column (all three are negative), we form the ratios of zeroth-column to pivot-column elements, ignore sign, and choose the smallest. Here these are $10/2 = 5$, $24/2 = 12$, and $40/10 = 4$; thus s_3 *must* leave the basis.[23] Hence -10, which has been starred, is the pivot element. We now: (1) interchange labels and then (2) transform the basis to that in (6-26). (The reader should do this, using the rules summarized in Table 6.2.)

---

[22] In a two-variable problem, once the origin has been left behind there is always only *one* adjacent corner, other than the one that has just been deserted, to consider. In a larger problem, of course, there may be many choices at each pivot.

[23] These ratios have a simple geometric interpretation. They are the intercepts of the three constraints on the axis of x_2, the variable entering the basis. Thus the rule of selecting the smallest simply makes certain that we stop moving out along the x_2 axis when we hit the first boundary imposed by a constraint.

		x_1	s_3
π	20	$\frac{3}{2}$	$-\frac{1}{2}$
s_1	2	$-\frac{8}{10}{}^{*}$	$\frac{2}{10}$
s_2	16	$-\frac{28}{10}$	$\frac{2}{10}$
x_2	4	$-\frac{1}{10}$	$-\frac{1}{10}$

(6-26)

The new basic feasible solution (corresponding to c_4 in Figure 6.2 and Table 6.1) is $s_1 = 2$, $s_2 = 16$, $x_2 = 4$; $s_3 = x_1 = 0$ by exclusion, from the basis. Now the objective function has a value (a_{00}) of 20, which is easily checked—$2(0) + 5(4) = 20$.

A value of 20 is better than nothing, but we can do better still. At this point the rule for entering variables dictates that x_1 should be introduced into the basis. Since the relevant ratios are now $20/8$, $160/28$, and $40/1$, the first row *must* be used for pivoting. The new pivot element, to transform (6-26) further, is starred. Changing labels and using the same four pivoting rules gives (again the reader should check *all* these numbers):

		s_1	s_3
π	$23\frac{3}{4}$	$-\frac{15}{8}$	$-\frac{1}{8}$
x_1	$2\frac{1}{2}$	$-\frac{10}{8}$	$\frac{1}{4}$
s_2	9	$\frac{28}{8}$	$-\frac{1}{2}$
x_2	$3\frac{3}{4}$	$\frac{1}{8}$	$-\frac{1}{8}$

(6-27)

We see, from Table 6.1, that this is the extreme point labeled c_3, which is indeed the only relevant corner adjacent to c_4 (when movement is away from the origin). Moreover, the entering variable test tells us that this is the optimal solution; at this point one unit of either of the currently excluded variables contributes negatively to the value of the objective function.

Thus $x_1^0 = 2\frac{1}{2}$, $x_2^0 = 3\frac{3}{4}$ represents the optimal combination of these variables, given the objective function and the constraints they face. The objective function has grown to $23\frac{3}{4}$ and cannot be larger unless at least one of the constraints is violated. In the context of a manufacturing problem, optimal production quantities should be $x_1 = 2\frac{1}{2}$ and $x_2 = 3\frac{3}{4}$;

if these amounts are produced, total profit will be maximized at $23\frac{3}{4}$ and none of the scarce resources will be required in amounts greater than their availabilities. At this basic feasible solution, constraints 1 and 3 are met as equalities—those resources are completely used up—($s_1^0 = s_3^0 = 0$ by exclusion from the current basis) and there are 9 units of resource 2 remaining ($s_2^0 = 9$). The reader should check the optimal values in each of the constraints to confirm these results.

6.4. DUALITY

Mathematical relationships and interpretation

Suppose the producer whose problem occupied our attention earlier were given the following alternative. One or more offers are made to buy his recently inherited stock of resources; instead of making money by producing, he has the option of selling his resource inputs and thus producing nothing. Consider how he might approach the problem of deciding how to put a value on his stock of resources—that is, establishing their worth to him—so he can judge whether or not any particular offer that is made to him is an attractive one.

Let v_1 be the unit valuation that he assigns to resource 1 and v_2 and v_3 be the same for resources 2 and 3. Therefore $10v_1 + 24v_2 + 40v_3$ will be the total value of his stock of the three resources. In order to avoid refusing what is actually a good offer, he wants this total value to be as *small* as possible, consistent with lower limits of the following sort: the valuations must not give him less than he can get from the resources if he uses them for production of 1 and 2. Consider the first product; its resource content (per unit) is shown by the elements a_{11}, a_{21}, and a_{31} in column 1 of the A matrix in (6-5)—that is, by 1, 3, and 1. Thus the *value* of a unit of 1 in terms of resources used to produce it is $v_1 + 3v_2 + v_3$; a produced unit of 1 brings a return of 2. Therefore, the v_i's should be such that the valuation of the resource content of a unit of 1 is *no less than* the amount that he can gain by producing a unit of 1—that is, $v_1 + 3v_2 + v_3 \geq 2$. And the same argument can be used for a unit of 2. Hence the producer's resource valuation problem is the following linear program:

$$
\begin{aligned}
\text{minimize:} \quad & 10v_1 + 24v_2 + 40v_3 \\
\text{subject to:} \quad & v_1 + 3v_2 + v_3 \geq 2, \\
& 2v_1 + 2v_2 + 10v_3 \geq 5,
\end{aligned}
\tag{6-28}
$$

where it is also logical to assume that the valuations will never be negative—that is, v_1, v_2, and $v_3 \geq 0$. The v_i are thus the values that can be earned with one unit of each resource i; they therefore can be thought of as the *maximum* price that the producer would be willing to pay for an additional unit of resource i. For this reason they are sometimes called "shadow prices" of the resources. We present the two problems, (6-5) and (6-28), side by side, to show their complete symmetry.

Maximize:	$2x_1 + 5x_2$	Minimize:	$10v_1 + 24v_2 + 40v_3$
subject to:	$x_1 + 2x_2 \leq 10,$	subject to:	$v_1 + 3v_2 + v_3 \geq 2,$
	$3x_1 + 2x_2 \leq 24,$		$2v_1 + 2v_2 + 10v_3 \geq 5,$
	$x_1 + 10x_2 \leq 40,$		
and	$x_1, x_2 \geq 0.$	and	$v_1, v_2, v_3 \geq 0.$

$$(6\text{-}29)$$

This is shown even more clearly in matrix notation.

Maximize:	$P'X$	Minimize:	$R'V$	
subject to:	$AX \leq R,$	subject to:	$A'V \geq P,$	$(6\text{-}30)$
and	$X \geq 0.$	and	$V \geq 0.$	

Specifically:

1. One is a maximization problem, the other a minimization one;
2. the constraints in the maximum problem set *upper* bounds (aside from nonnegativity of the variables), in the minimum problem they set *lower* bounds;
3. the coefficient matrices in the two constraint sets are transposes of one another; and
4. the objective function coefficients of one problem become the right-hand sides of the constraints of the other.

When two problems are related in this mathematical way, they are said to be *dual* to one another (or *mutually dual*), or, in this case, the minimization problem would be termed the *dual* to the maximization problem; this is because the maximization problem was in fact the problem of primary concern and the minimization problem was (perhaps somewhat artificially) constructed second. The problem of *primary* concern is then termed the *primal*.[24]

Because of certain mathematical relationships that exist between the optimal values of primal and dual variables, the optimal dual *variables* may be of interest in a particular situation, even though the dual *problem* itself may appear to be somewhat artificial. Moreover, it turns out that the final simplex table—(6-27), above—contains the optimal values for *both*

---

[24] In any pair of mutually dual problems, then, the "more important" of the two is termed the primal and the other is the dual. Either a maximization problem or a minimization problem can be the primal; it depends entirely on the context in which they arise. Note that the dual of the dual problem is just the primal.

problems; hence in solving a maximization problem one also automatically solves the related minimization problem.[25] We therefore present several important primal-dual relationships.

Consider first the structure of the two problems in augmented form, where S and T are the vectors of nonnegative slack variables for each problem and O is used in each case to denote a null vector (either column or row) of appropriate size:

$$
\begin{array}{llll}
\text{maximize:} & \pi = P'X + OS & \text{minimize:} & \Delta = R'V + OT \\
\text{subject to:} & AX + S = R & \text{subject to:} & A'V - T = P \qquad (6\text{-}31) \\
\text{and} & X, S \geq O, & \text{and} & V, T \geq O,
\end{array}
$$

where π and Δ are used as mnemonic shorthand devices for the values of the primal and dual objective functions. We now do some algebra, in matrix form. If we multiply both sides of each constraint, i, in the maximum problem by its associated v_i and each constraint, j, in the minimum problem by its associated x_j, we have $V'AX + V'S = V'R$ and $X'A'V - X'T = X'P$. But the product of the two vectors $V'R$ and $R'V$ must be the same;[26] similarly for $X'P$ and $P'X$. Hence, $\pi = X'A'V - X'T$ and $\Delta = V'AX + V'S$. But $X'A'V = (AX)'V = V'AX$ (see the last footnote); therefore,

$$
\Delta - \pi = V'S + X'T. \qquad (6\text{-}32)
$$

Since feasible solutions to the primal and dual require nonnegativity of all the variables, Theorem P-D1 follows:

THEOREM P-D1.   For any feasible solutions to the primal and dual problems, $\Delta \geq \pi$.

This follows since the difference in (6-32) is made up entirely of nonnegative terms. The theorem is important because it says that the value of the objective function of the minimization problem puts an *upper limit* on the objective function for the maximization problem; viewed differently, the value of the maximization problem's objective function sets a *lower limit* for that of the minimum problem. Thus:

THEOREM P-D2.   Consider a pair of *feasible* solutions, X^* and V^*, with objective functions $\pi^* = P'X^*$ and $\Delta^* = R'V^*$. If $\pi^* = \Delta^*$, these solutions are optimal.

This follows immediately from (6-32) and the preceding theorem, as does

---

[25] For this reason our maximization-oriented simplex method is not as restrictive as it appears. If we have a minimization linear program to solve, we write down the dual maximum problem and solve it. The optimum to the minimum problem is then to be found in the final simplex tableau but not in the zeroth column, as we are about to see.

[26] The transpose of a product is the product of the transposed matrices, in reverse order—$(AB)' = B'A'$, and the transpose of a scalar is the scalar itself.

THEOREM P-D3. A pair of feasible solutions has $\pi = \Delta$ if and only if $V'S = 0$ and $X'T = 0$.

Explicitly, since $V'S = v_1 s_1 + \cdots + v_m s_m$ and $X'T = x_1 t_1 + \cdots + x_n t_n$, this means that $\pi = \Delta$ if and only if $v_i s_i = 0$ for $i = 1, \ldots, m$ and $x_j t_j = 0$ for $j = 1, \ldots, n$. In this form, this theorem has an interesting interpretation. Each s_i is a primal slack variable—

$$s_i = r_i - \sum_{j=1}^{n} a_{ij} x_j$$

—the difference between the fixed amount of resource i and the amount consumed by a particular solution x_j $(j = 1, \ldots, n)$. Thus from Theorem P-D3, for an optimal solution

$$v_i^0 s_i^0 = v_i^0 \left(r_i - \sum_{j=1}^{n} a_{ij} x_j^0 \right) = 0 \qquad (i = 1, \ldots, m). \tag{6-33}$$

Similarly the dual slack variables are t_j—

$$t_j = \sum_{i=1}^{m} a_{ij} v_i - p_j$$

—the difference between the valuation of resources in a unit of x_j and its objective function profit. Again from Theorem P-D3, at optimum

$$x_j^0 t_j^0 = x_j^0 \left(\sum_{i=1}^{m} a_{ij} v_i^0 - p_j \right) = 0 \qquad (j = 1, \ldots, n). \tag{6-34}$$

Specifically:

1. If $v_i^0 > 0$, then $s_i^0 = 0$. If, in the optimal solution, the valuation placed on the ith resource is positive, this means that in that solution all of the ith resource was used up.
2. If $x_j^0 > 0$, then $t_j^0 = 0$. If a positive amount of x_j is produced in the optimal solution, then the imputed value of resources embodied in x_j is just equal to p_j, the per-unit profit.
3. If $s_i^0 > 0$, then $v_i^0 = 0$. A resource that is not fully consumed in the optimal solution is valued at zero; it is in excess supply.
4. If $t_j^0 > 0$, then $x_j^0 = 0$. If the imputed value of resources in a unit of x_j is greater than its per-unit profit, x_j is not produced in the optimal solution.

Note, by the way, that the inference cannot be made in the reverse direction: if a particular s^0, t^0, v^0, or x^0 is zero, the associated variable may or may not be zero. $V'S = 0$ and $X'T = 0$ require *at least* one of each pair of terms to be zero.

Thus, the mathematical relationships between primal and dual problems that must hold at an optimal solution may have useful interpretations in the context of the problem. Before turning to an even closer relation between primal and dual optima, we note

THEOREM P-D4. If both problems have feasible solutions, then both have optimal solutions.

This may not sound terribly useful, but it sometimes makes possible an easy investigation of the question of the *existence* of an optimum to either problem—a question that may be worth answering *before* time and effort are expended in trying to find the optimum. (For example, the origin is often easily established to be a feasible solution to a maximum problem; a problem has no feasible solution if and only if its feasible region is empty—that is, the constraints are contradictory—as we saw with regard to Theorem 6.3, above.) Once feasibility for both problems is established, optimality follows from Theorem P-D1, since feasibility means that a ceiling (Δ) exists on the value of the objective function in the maximum problem and a floor (π) exists on the value of the objective function in the minimization problem.

Further, and perhaps even more importantly:[27]

THEOREM P-D5. $\partial \pi^0 / \partial r_i = v_i^0$.

In words, the optimal value of the ith dual variable is a measure of the amount by which the optimal value of the primal objective function can be expected to change for a small (marginal) change in the amount of the ith resource, all others remaining constant. This follows from Theorem P-D2. Since

$$\pi^0 = P'X^0 = R'V^0 = v_1^0 r_1 + \cdots + v_m^0 r_m, \qquad \partial \pi^0 / \partial r_i = v_i^0.$$

Thus the dual variables in a linear programming problem have characteristics that parallel those of the Lagrange multipliers that were first introduced in Section 4.4. That is, there is one associated with each constraint, and their optimal values measure the contribution of marginal changes in the right-hand sides of the constraints. (We will explore and utilize a similar connection for the case of duality in nonlinear programming problems in Chapter 9.)

This interpretation of the optimal dual variables as marginal values of the primal constraint quantities is one of the major reasons for interest in the linear programming dual. There are very often problems in which the

---

[27] Provided that the proper right- and left-side limits exist and are equal so that the derivative is defined; see Chapter 3. We will see in Chapter 7 that degeneracy of an optimal solution may invalidate this theorem for some of the constraints.

marginal worth of each of the resources to the primal objective function is an important piece of information—for example, in making decisions about the acquisition of more of the resources. However, the marginal nature of this valuation also means that it can be misleading, since it is only valid over a particular range of change in resource amount. For this reason we turn now to first locating the optimal dual values in the final simplex tableau and then establishing ranges of relevance for each of them.

Dual values in the simplex tables

Consider a primal optimal tableau in which, say, the primal variables s_1 and x_2 (among others) are in the top row and hence absent from the primal optimum. Figure 6.7 represents this schematically. Since $s_1^0 = 0$ (it is absent

	•••	s_1	•••	x_2	•••
π^0	•••	$-k_1$	•••	$-k_2$	•••

Figure 6.7. Part of the Top Row and its Labels for a Primal Optimal
Tableau

from the primal optimal basis), the first primal constraint is met as an equality—in the production example, the first resource is completely used up. But we also know that for *any* tableau, including the optimal one, and for any row, including the top one, the coefficients express the variable at the left as a linear function of the currently excluded primal variables whose labels appear along the top. Thus, in particular, $\partial\pi^0/\partial s_1 = -k_1$; in words, if we had to have a unit of s_1 in the final solution, the optimal value of π would *decrease* by k_1. But one unit of s_1 in a solution means one unit of r_1 unused, since s_1 is the *slack* in constraint 1. Hence $-k_1$ really represents the loss to the primal optimum of having one less unit of resource 1 to use; that is, it measures the marginal value of resource 1, which we have denoted v_1^0.

Similarly, $\partial\pi^0/\partial x_2 = -k_2$ tells us that if we were forced to have a unit of x_2 in the optimal solution, the value of π^0 would *decrease* by k_2; that is, x_2 is, in the production scheme of the primal optimum, an *unprofitable* activity. This means that, relative to the per-unit profits and resource uses of other x's, x_2 would cost more (in resources taken away from other production) than it would contribute (in profit). But this per-unit *loss* for x_2 is just what the second dual slack variable, t_2, measures, as we saw in the augmented formulation of the general dual problem (6-31) and in the discussion following Theorem P-D3.

Recall the initial summary tableau for the primal problem, (6-18):

	x_1	x_2
π	0	2	5
s_1	10	-1	-2
s_2	24	-3	-2
s_3	40	-1	-10

In (6-29) and (6-30) we saw that the primal and dual problems were essentially transposes of one another. By viewing this table as if it were rotated clockwise 90°, we have essentially all of the information on the dual in exactly the same way as all primal information is incorporated in its normal position. The one exception is that, since the nonnegative dual slack variables must be *subtracted* from the left-hand side of the dual constraints, the signs in all columns (which represent rows for the dual) except the zeroth are reversed. We can add one more labeling row and column. Associated with each s_i is the corresponding v_i; with each x_j we pair a $-t_j$ to take account of this sign problem. Thus the next table (6-35) more explicitly shows both the primal and the dual information. Taking the "rotated" point of view (for the dual), the last column says $-t_2 = 5 - 2v_1 - 2v_2 - 10v_3$; that is, the second dual constraint is $2v_1 + 2v_2 + 10v_3 - t_2 = 5$, or $2v_1 + 2v_2 + 10v_3 \geq 5$.

		Δ	$-t_1$	$-t_2$
			x_1	x_2
	π	0	2	5
v_1	s_1	10	-1	-2
v_2	s_2	24	-3	-2
v_3	s_3	40	-1	-10

(6-35)

The optimal solution to the dual

Recall the second and the last simplex tableaux associated with the small problem solved in the last section. They are repeated here with the dual labels explicit.

		Δ	$-t_1$	$-v_3$
			x_1	s_3
	π	20	$\frac{3}{2}$	$-\frac{1}{2}$
v_1	s_1	2	$-\frac{8}{10}$	$\frac{2}{10}$
v_2	s_2	16	$-\frac{28}{10}$	$\frac{2}{10}$
t_2	x_2	4	$-\frac{1}{10}$	$-\frac{1}{10}$

(6-36)

		Δ	$-v_1$	$-v_3$
			s_1	s_3
	π	$23\frac{3}{4}$	$-\frac{15}{8}$	$-\frac{1}{8}$
t_1	x_1	$2\frac{1}{2}$	$-\frac{10}{8}$	$\frac{1}{4}$
v_2	s_2	9	$\frac{28}{8}$	$-\frac{1}{2}$
t_2	x_2	$3\frac{3}{4}$	$\frac{1}{8}$	$-\frac{1}{8}$

(6-37)

Since the signal to stop the simplex arithmetic is that all top-row elements (except the primal objective function value) are nonpositive, as in (6-37), it is clear that from the point of view of the dual those values are nonnegative, since the dual labels are all preceded by a minus sign. Thus, for example, the solution in (6-35) in which $v_1 = v_2 = v_3 = 0$, by their absence from the top row, which contains the *dual* basis, is infeasible, since it requires $-t_1 = 2$ and $-t_2 = 5$, or $t_1 = -2$ and $t_2 = -5$, violating the nonnegativity requirements on dual variables, both regular and slack. Similarly, the dual solution in (6-36) is infeasible. It requires $v_1 = v_2 = 0$, $v_3 = \frac{1}{2}$, $t_2 = 0$, but $t_1 = -\frac{3}{2}$. In fact *only* when the primal *optimal* solution is reached will the corresponding dual basic solution be *feasible*, as in (6-37).

The question then is, will this solution be an optimal one for the dual? It is clear that the correct variables will appear in the dual solution, because of the labeling procedure we have adopted. A variable *in* the dual basis— that is, in the top row—automatically has its corresponding primal variable *excluded* from the primal basis (the left-hand column). Thus it is assured that Theorem P-D3 will hold. But then $\Delta = \pi$. Then, by Theorem P-D2, both solutions are optimal ones.

Therefore, from (6-37), the optimal solution to the dual linear programming minimization problem in (6-29) is: $v_1^0 = \frac{15}{8}$, $v_3^0 = \frac{1}{8}$; $v_2^0 = t_1^0 = t_2^0 = 0$ by their exclusion from the top row (dual basis). The reader can check that the dual objective function also has a value of $23\frac{3}{4}$ at this point and that both dual constraints are met as equalities.

Valid range of a dual variable

In Theorem P-D5 we saw that the optimal value of a dual variable, v_i^0, measures the marginal effect on the optimal value of the primal objective function of a small (infinitesimal) change in the right-hand side of the ith primal constraint; $\partial \pi^0 / \partial r_i = v_i^0$. Being a partial derivative, this is strictly a *ceteris paribus* concept; everything else—specifically the values of all r_j ($j \neq i$)—must remain unchanged.

Consider again the geometry of the problem of this chapter, specifically Figure 6.2, the essentials of which are repeated in Figure 6.8. We have seen that $v_2^0 = 0$, which is consistent with the figure; a small change in the amount of r_2, which means the position of constraint 2, will not alter the optimum at all. However, a small change (say an increase) in either r_1 or r_3 *will* have the effect of moving the optimal extreme point outward, away from the origin. This will result in an *increased* primal objective function value.

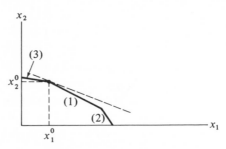

Figure 6.8.   Feasible Region and Objective Function Contours

If only (1) moves outward, the optimal corner will creep out along the extension of (3), until such time as it bumps into (2), also extended. Further outward movement of (1) will not affect the feasible region. It will then be completely defined by (2) and (3). The dual valuation on resource 1, $v_1^0 = \frac{15}{8}$, is thus valid along that range of increase of r_1 up to the point where another corner is hit—that is, until constraint 2, in this case, becomes binding. It turns out that the optimal tableau, (6-37), contains all the information we need to establish the range of increase over which $\frac{15}{8}$ ($= 1\frac{7}{8}$) is a valid measure of the worth of r_1.

Algebraically, adding units of capacity to r_1 is equivalent to allowing the slack variable in that primal constraint, s_1, to become negative. This means that variables that are currently in the primal basis and that have *positive* coefficients in the s_1 ($= -v_1$) column will become *smaller* for increasingly negative values of s_1.[28] Therefore, among the *positive* coefficients in the s_1 column we must find the smallest ratio of zeroth-column to s_1-column elements, since this will be precisely the variable in the current optimum that hits zero first. In this case we compare $9/\frac{28}{8} = \frac{18}{7}$ (s_2 row) and $\frac{15}{4}/\frac{1}{8} = 30$ (x_2 row) and select the smaller (in general, with more than

---

[28] Recall that for any tableau the coefficients express basic primal variables as linear functions of nonbasic ones. From (6-37), for example, $s_2 = 9 + \frac{28}{8}s_1 - \frac{1}{2}s_3$. Beyond a particular negative value of s_1, s_2 would turn negative, if s_3 remains zero. This critical value is just where $9 + \frac{28}{8}s_1 = 0$—that is, at $s_1 = -9/\frac{28}{8} = -\frac{18}{7}$.

two choices, the smallest). Thus s_2 will become zero before any of the other currently included basic variables as s_1 becomes negative; it will do so at $s_1 = -\frac{18}{7} = -2\frac{4}{7}$, and hence $2\frac{4}{7}$ units is the maximum that r_1 can *increase* before another corner (constraint) is hit in the feasible region. Referring to Figure 6.8, this will happen when (1) moves out until constraints 3 and 2 intersect. Thus in this case the *marginal* valuation on resource 1 is valid for a *unit* increase in r_1 or even if r_1 goes up by 2 units, but not if it increases 3 or more units.

The curious reader may wish to solve several new linear programs, identical to (6-5) except for a change in the 10 in constraint 1.

(a) If the 10 becomes 11 (thus within the range of validity of v_1^0), so that constraint 1 intersects the x_2 axis at $5\frac{1}{2}$, rather than at 5, the new optimal solution is $x_1^0 = 3\frac{3}{4}$, $x_2^0 = 3\frac{5}{8}$, and the objective function is $25\frac{5}{8}$, which is exactly the old value $(23\frac{3}{4})$ plus $(\Delta r_1)v_1^0 = (1)(1\frac{7}{8})$.

(b) If the 10 becomes 12 (still within the range of validity for v_1^0), the new optimum is at $x_1^0 = 5$, $x_2^0 = 3\frac{1}{2}$, with an objective function value of $27\frac{1}{2}$, which is the original value $(23\frac{3}{4})$ plus $(\Delta r_1)v_1^0 = (2)(1\frac{7}{8})$.

(c) However, if 10 changes to 13 in the first constraint (beyond the $2\frac{4}{7}$ range for v_1^0), the new solution is $x_1^0 = 5\frac{5}{7}$, $x_2^0 = 3\frac{3}{7}$, with an objective function value of $28\frac{4}{7}$, which is *less* than $23\frac{3}{4} + (3)(1\frac{7}{8})$.

The geometry of the three new positions for constraint 1 and hence the optimum is shown in the various parts of Figure 6.9. The changes in (a) and (b), for which v_1^0 is a correct measure of change in the objective function, involve movement of the optimal extreme point out along the line representing constraint 3. The last move, in (c), takes constraint 1 beyond the point of intersection of the lines for constraints 2 and 3; hence the first constraint is now *redundant*, since the feasible region defined by constraints 2 and 3 lies entirely within the half-space of constraint 1. Thus movement along the line for constraint 3 is stopped short by the presence of constraint 2; therefore the increase in the objective function is less than in the move from the original problem to position (a) or from (a) to (b). Since constraint 2 was not binding in the original solution $(s_2^0 > 0)$, that resource was given no value $(v_2^0 = 0)$, and so we have no information, from our optimal tableau, on the value of resource 2 once it does become critical.

A similar calculation shows the range over which $v_3^0 = \frac{1}{8}$ is a correct valuation on resource 3 to be 10 units; that is, for each one-unit increase in the right-hand side of constraint 3—up to 10 units more (up to a total of 50)—the value of the objective function will increase by $\frac{1}{8}$. From Figure 6.9, we see that this is the range over which constraint 3 contributes something to the boundary of the feasible region. Above $x_1 + 10x_2 \leq 50$ the constraint is redundant; the feasible region is then defined *entirely* by constraints 1 and 2.

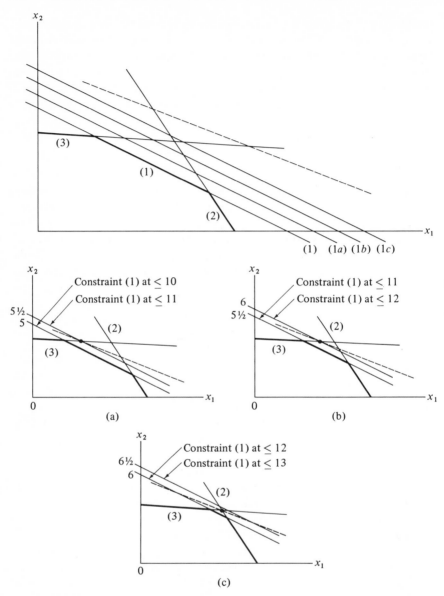

Figure 6.9. Three (Unit) Changes in Location of Constraint 1, (a) Unit Change from 10 to 11, (b) Unit Change from 11 to 12, (c) Unit Change from 12 to 13

We see, then, that the linearity of the sides of the feasible region has two influences on the marginality interpretation of the optimal dual variables, $v_i^0 = \partial\pi^0/\partial r_i$. First, it means that there may be a range much larger than the infinitesimal one implied by the partial derivative over which the value v_i^0 is valid. Second, however, at some point the dual valuations become totally invalid, since beyond that range increases in the amount of that resource alone either are less profitable (because new constraints become binding)[29] or are completely useless (as in Figure 6.9, for eventual changes in r_1).[30]

SUMMARY

This chapter has introduced the reader to linear programming models. We have seen how this particular variation of the general inequality-constrained optimization problem of Chapter 4 is saved by the very characteristics that invalidate the calculus approach, via either Lagrange multipliers or the Kuhn-Tucker method. Precisely because (geometrically) the objective function and the sides of the feasible region are linear or (algebraically) the augmented problem consists of a set of linear equations with more unknowns than equations, we can utilize an efficient solution procedure for examining objective function values associated with basic solutions to the equations. This is the simplex method.

We have seen that linear programs always come in pairs, and that after the one that is of interest in a particular situation (the primal) has been formulated and solved, there may or may not be relevant information in the optimal values of the associated (dual) problem.

In the next chapter we investigate several additional topics in linear programming. Some are particular problems that can arise in the simplex arithmetic owing to special characteristics of the problem that are easily shown geometrically. Others are cases where the algebraic structure of a variant of the form we have presented in this chapter allows a special (simpler) solution procedure.

---

[29] The reader might try to visualize this; it requires at least a three-dimensional feasible region.

[30] The concept of the total differential (Chapter 3) has relevance here also. That is, the increase in the optimal value of the objective function for a *simultaneous* change of one unit in resources 1 and 3 is given by

$$d\pi^0 = \left(\frac{\partial\pi^0}{\partial r_1}\right)dr_1 + \left(\frac{\partial\pi^0}{\partial r_3}\right)dr_3 = v_1^0(1) + v_3^0(1) = \frac{15}{8} + \frac{1}{8} = 2.$$

Geometrically, the optimal corner is moving out along a line with a slope that lies between that of constraints 1 and 3 in Figure 6.9. Eventually either constraint 2 or the x_2 axis will be hit. The reader may wish to practice his simplex arithmetic here too. If the original problem is altered so that constraint 1 reads ≤ 11 and constraint 3 is ≤ 41, the new optimum is $x_1^0 = 3\frac{1}{2}$, $x_2^0 = 3\frac{3}{4}$, and the objective function is $25\frac{3}{4}$ ($= 23\frac{3}{4} + 2$).

APPENDIX 6.1

Proofs and Derivations

THEOREM 6.2.   Any point inside a closed, bounded convex set can be expressed as a convex combination of the extreme points of the set.

Consider a perfectly general closed, bounded, convex set with four extreme points $E_1, \ldots, E_4$ (Figure 6.10). Select a point P_0 anywhere inside the

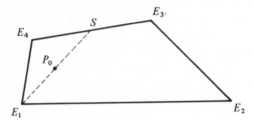

Figure 6.10. P_0 Inside the Convex Set with Extreme Points $E_1, \ldots, E_4$

set. We wish to show that P_0 can be expressed as a convex combination of the four extreme points—that is, that

$$P_0 = \sum_{i=1}^{4} \alpha_i E_i, \qquad \text{where } \alpha_i \geq 0 \text{ and } \sum_{i=1}^{4} \alpha_i = 1.$$

1. Connect *any* extreme point with P_0 and extend to the opposite side. (Here E_1 was selected.)
2. Label the intersection of the E_1-P_0 line and the opposite side S.
3. Then $P_0 = \beta_1 E_1 + (1 - \beta_1)S$, for $0 \leq \beta_1 \leq 1$. That is, P_0 lies on the line between E_1 and S.
4. But $S = \beta_2 E_3 + (1 - \beta_2)E_4$, for $0 \leq \beta_2 \leq 1$. That is, S lies on the line between E_3 and E_4.
5. Then, from (3) and (4),

$$\begin{aligned} P_0 &= \beta_1 E_1 + (1 - \beta_1)[\beta_2 E_3 + (1 - \beta_2)E_4] \\ &= \beta_1 E_1 + (1 - \beta_1)\beta_2 E_3 + (1 - \beta_1)(1 - \beta_2)E_4. \end{aligned}$$

6. Let $\alpha_1 = \beta_1$, $\alpha_2 = 0$, $\alpha_3 = (1 - \beta_1)\beta_2$ and $\alpha_4 = (1 - \beta_1)(1 - \beta_2)$. Then

$$P_0 = \alpha_1 E_1 + \alpha_2 E_2 + \alpha_3 E_3 + \alpha_4 E_4 = \sum_{i=1}^{4} \alpha_i E_i.$$

7. The question is: is this a true convex combination? (a) Are all $\alpha_i \geq 0$? The answer is yes, from their definition in terms of the β's and the ranges on the β's given in (3) and (4). (b) Does $\sum_{i=1}^{4} \alpha_i = 1$? Again, the answer is yes.

$$\sum_{i=1}^{4} \alpha_i = \beta_1 + 0 + (1 - \beta_1)\beta_2 + (1 - \beta_1)(1 - \beta_2) = 1.$$

Therefore any point inside a closed, bounded convex set is expressible as a convex combination of the extreme points of the set.

THEOREM 6.3. If the objective function takes on a maximum value at some point in the feasible region, it does so at an extreme point of the region.

Let the objective function $P'X$ have a maximum at X^0; that is, $P'X^0 \geq P'X$ for all X in the feasible region. Denote by $C_1, \ldots, C_k$ the extreme points of the feasible region—its corners. If X^0 is an extreme point, the theorem is true. Suppose X^0 is not an extreme point. Then, from Theorem 6.2, X^0 can be expressed as a convex combination of the C_i $(i = 1, \ldots, k)$;

$$X^0 = \sum_{i=1}^{k} \alpha_i C_i \quad \text{for } \alpha_i \geq 0 \text{ and } \sum_{i=1}^{k} \alpha_i = 1.$$

From among the k extreme points find that one for which $P'C_i$ is maximum; denote it by C^0. Thus $P'C^0 = \max [P'C_1, P'C_2, \ldots, P'C_k]$. Since $P'C^0$ is a particular (maximum) value, and since $\sum_{i=1}^{k} \alpha_i = 1$,

$$\sum_{i=1}^{k} \alpha_i P'C^0 = P'C^0 \sum_{i=1}^{k} \alpha_i = P'C^0. \tag{6-38}$$

Moreover,

$$\sum_{i=1}^{k} \alpha_i P'C^0 \geq \sum_{i=1}^{k} \alpha_i P'C_i \tag{6-39}$$

because of (6-38) and the way C^0 was selected. Since $X^0 = \sum_{i=1}^{k} \alpha_i C_i$,

$$P'X^0 = P' \sum_{i=1}^{k} \alpha_i C_i = \sum_{i=1}^{k} \alpha_i P'C_i \tag{6-40}$$

by substitution and because the P' (a vector of constants) can appear either outside or inside the linear combination.

Therefore, from these three results $P'C^0 \geq P'X^0$. But X^0 was defined so that $P'X^0 \geq P'X$ for *all* points in the feasible region; this includes the extreme points, $C_1, \ldots, C_k$, of which C^0 is one. Hence, in particular, $P'X^0 \geq P'C^0$. Therefore $P'X^0 = P'C^0$: the objective function attains its maximum value at at least one extreme point.

THEOREM 6.4.   If the objective function takes on a maximum value at *more than one* extreme point of the feasible region; then it has that same maximum value at every convex combination of those extreme points.

Let the maxima occur at extreme points, $C_1, C_2, \ldots, C_j$ $(j \leq k)$. That is,

$$P'C_1 = P'C_2 = \cdots = P'C_j = \pi^0 = \max [P'C_1, \ldots, P'C_k].$$

Consider a convex combination of these extreme points

$$\hat{C} = \sum_{i=1}^{j} \beta_i C_i, \qquad \text{where } \beta_i \geq 0 \text{ and } \sum_{i=1}^{j} \beta_j = 1.$$

Then the value of the objective function at $\hat{C}$ is

$$P'\hat{C} = \sum_{i=1}^{j} P'\beta_i C_i = \sum_{i=1}^{j} \beta_i P'C_i = \pi^0 \sum_{i=1}^{j} \beta_i = \pi^0.$$

That is, the value is the same as it was at any one of the extreme points where the maximum occurred.

Feasible regions for the augmented and original problems

The feasible region defined by $AX \leq R$ and $X \geq O$ is the part of the intersection of the m half-spaces in $AX \leq R$ that is in the nonnegative orthant $(X \geq O)$. When the $AX \leq R$ part is converted to equalities, the region is that part of the intersection of m hyperplanes in $(n + m)$-dimensional space that lies in the nonnegative orthant.

The *dimensionality* of a figure is, essentially, the number of dimensions needed to represent it. Thus a general plane in three-dimensional space really "takes up" only two dimensions; by proper rotation and shifting of the three orthogonal axes for three-dimensional space, the plane could be embedded in an x_1,x_2 plane only, for example. Similarly a line in $x_1 x_2$ space has a dimensionality of one. This is expressed formally by the statement: a hyperplane in r-dimensional space is a linear manifold (vector space) of dimensionality $(r - 1)$. It can be shown that the intersection of k linearly independent hyperplanes in r-dimensional space is a linear manifold of dimension $r - k$—for example, two planes in three-dimensional space intersect in a line (dimensionality $3 - 2 = 1$). Therefore m linearly independent hyperplanes in $(n + m)$-dimensional space intersect in a linear manifold of dimensionality n. This describes the feasible region (constraints) of the augmented problem (when all equations are independent).

The dimensionality of the feasible region in the inequality form is just that of the solution space, n. Hence, the two regions have the same dimensionality. It is also possible to show the correspondence of extreme points in the two feasible regions. The following (small) example is the largest that can be done without exceeding three-dimensional geometry. Let the original linear programming problem have only one constraint $3x_1 + 2x_2 \leq 12$ and the nonnegativity requirements $x_1 \geq 0$ and $x_2 \geq 0$. Let the slack variable be denoted x_3; the augmented form of the constraints is thus $3x_1 + 2x_2 + x_3 = 12$, x_1, x_2 and $x_3 \geq 0$. Clearly C_3 in the augmented problem (defined as the point corresponding to $x_1 = x_2 = 0$ or as the point

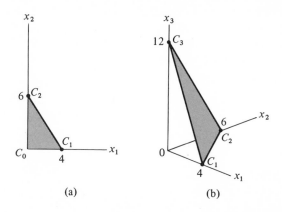

Figure 6.11.   (a) Feasible Region, Original Problem, (b) Feasible Region, Augmented Problem

where the slack variable is 10) corresponds to C_0 in the two-dimensional picture. Since the extreme points of the two feasible regions have the same characteristics, especially in terms of the values of the n original x-variables, examining the extreme points of the feasible region to the augmented problem (equality form) is equivalent to examining the extreme points of the feasible region of the original problem (inequality form).

THEOREM 6.5.   If a nonnegative basic solution can be found to the m-equation, $(n + m)$-variable system $AX = R$, say $A_1 x_1^* + \cdots + A_k x_k^* = R$ (where $k \leq m$ and $x_i^* > 0$, $i = 1, \ldots, k$), then the $(n + m)$-element vector $X^{*\prime} = [x_1^*, \ldots, x_k^*, 0, \ldots, 0]$ is an extreme point of the feasible region for the augmented problem.

The theorem can be proved by contradiction. We assume that $X^{*\prime}$ is *not* an extreme point and then show that this assumption must be false. If $X^{*\prime}$ is not an extreme point, it can be expressed as a convex combination of two other points in the feasible region, call them X_a and X_b with coordinates $(x_1^a, \ldots, x_k^a)$ and $(x_1^b, \ldots, x_k^b)$.   Thus $X^* = \alpha X_a + (1 - \alpha)X_b$,   for $0 < \alpha < 1$. Since X_a and X_b are feasible,

$$A_1 x_1^a + \cdots + A_k x_k^a = R \quad \text{and} \quad A_1 x_1^b + \cdots + A_k x_k^b = R.$$

Subtracting the latter from the former,

$$A_1(x_1^a - x_1^b) + \cdots + A_k(x_k^a - x_k^b) = O.$$

This is a set of m homogeneous equations in the k $(\le m)$ variables $x_i \equiv x_i^a - x_i^b$. Since the column vectors $A_1, \ldots, A_k$ form a basis (that is, are independent), the only solution is the trivial one $x_i \equiv x_i^a - x_i^b = 0$ for $i = 1, \ldots, k$. The implication of this is that $x_i^a = x_i^b$ $(i = 1, \ldots, k)$ and thus $X_a = X_b$. But then these are *not* two distinct points in the feasible region. Hence, the assumption that $X^{*\prime}$ is *not* an extreme point must be false; it cannot be expressed as a convex combination of two distinct points in the feasible region.

THEOREM 6.6.   If $X^{*\prime} = [x_1^*, \ldots, x_k^*, 0, \ldots, 0]$ is an extreme point of the feasible region of the augmented problem, then the column vectors $A_1, \ldots, A_k$ from A that correspond to the positive x_i^* in $X^{*\prime}$ are linearly independent.

Again the proof is by contradiction. We assume that the $A_1, \ldots, A_k$ are *not* independent and then show that this assumption is false. If $A_1, \ldots, A_k$ are dependent, then we could find a set of multipliers, y_i, *not all zero*, for which $A_1 y_1 + \cdots + A_k y_k = O$. (For a set of homogeneous equations to have a nontrivial result, the columns of the coefficient matrix must be linearly dependent.) Multiplying both sides by a constant θ gives

$$A_1 \theta y_1 + \cdots + A_k \theta y_k = O. \tag{6-41}$$

Since $X^{*\prime}$ is an element of the feasible region,

$$A_1 x_1^* + \cdots + A_k x_k^* = R. \tag{6-42}$$

Subtracting (6-41) from (6-42) gives

$$A_1(x_1^* - \theta y_1) + \cdots + A_k(x_k^* - \theta y_k) = R. \tag{6-43}$$

Moreover, adding (6-41) and (6-42) gives

$$A_1(x_1^* + \theta y_1) + \cdots + A_k(x_k^* + \theta y_k) = R. \tag{6-44}$$

Thus, the $(x_i^* - \theta y_i)$ in (6-43) and the $(x_i^* + \theta y_i)$ in (6-44), for $i = 1$, ..., k, constitute two feasible solutions to the augmented problem.[31] That is, the following are feasible solutions:

$$X_I' = [(x_1^* - \theta y_1), \ldots, (x_k^* - \theta y_k), 0, \ldots, 0]$$

and

$$X_{II}' = [(x_1^* + \theta y_1), \ldots, (x_k^* + \theta y_k), 0, \ldots, 0].$$

But $X^{*\prime} = \frac{1}{2}X_I' + \frac{1}{2}X_{II}'$; that is, $X^{*\prime}$ is expressible as a convex combination of X_I' and X_{II}', two distinct points in the feasible region. Hence, $X^{*\prime}$ cannot be an extreme point; but it must be, by the assumption of the theorem. Thus the $A_1, \ldots, A_k$ can *not* be dependent.

PROBLEMS

1. Maximize $3x_1 + 2x_2 + 15x_3$, subject to $x_1 + x_2 + x_3 \le 12$ and $2x_1 + x_2 + 5x_3 \le 18$, as well as $x_1, x_2, x_3 \ge 0$.

2. Minimize $6x_1 + 8x_2$, subject to $2x_1 + 7x_2 \ge 12$ and $2x_1 + x_2 \ge 1$, as well as nonnegativity of the two variables.

3. Solve the following problem:
   minimize: $5x_1 + 9x_2$
   subject to: $3x_1 + 4x_2 \ge 2$,
                $x_1 + 4x_2 \ge 6$,
   and $x_1 \ge 0, \quad x_2 \ge 0$.

4. Maximize: $x_1 + 8x_2 + 10x_3 + 9x_4$
   subject to: $2x_1 \qquad + \quad x_3 \qquad \le 10$,
                $\qquad 2x_2 + 2x_3 + 5x_4 \le 30$,
   and $x_1, x_2, x_3, x_4 \ge 0$.

5. Maximize $x_1 + 2x_2$, subject to $-x_1 + x_2 \le 6$ and $-x_1 + 2x_2 \le 16$, and x_1 and x_2 nonnegative.

6. Write down the dual linear program for Problems 1 through 5. In each case:
   (a) What is the optimal solution to this dual problem?
   (b) Show that all of the "complementary slackness" relations of Theorem P-D3 hold.

7. Consider two linear programs that differ only in that one of the constraints in one of them is a constant, k, times the corresponding constraint in the other problem. How would the optimal values of the dual variables in these two problems differ?

8. Consider a maximization problem where per-unit profits in the objective function are expressed in hundreds of dollars (for example, $2x_1$ in the objective function means that a unit amount of product 1 generates \$200 in profits).

---

[31] Since all $x_i^* > 0$, θ can be chosen sufficiently small that none of the $(x_i^* - \theta y_i)$ in (6-43) becomes zero or negative.

Suppose that you reexpressed the objective function profits in thousands of dollars.

(a) How would this affect the optimal values of the variables in the primal?

(b) How would the optimal values of the dual variables be affected?

9. Show how the conversion of a primal maximization linear programming problem from inequality to equality form (that is, conversion to the augmented problem) assures the nonnegativity of the dual variables.

10. Show that the dual to the following linear programming problem has no feasible solution.

Maximize: $2x_1 + 3x_2 + x_3$

subject to: $-5x_1 + x_2 + x_3 \leq 20,$

$-x_1 + 2x_2 \qquad \leq 50,$

and $x_1, x_2 \geq 0.$

11. A pleasure boat manufacturer produces two basic lines—a standard model (the Cruiser) and a more luxurious version (the Clipper). These are sold to dealers at a profit of $200 per Clipper and $100 per Cruiser. A Clipper requires, on the average, 150 man-hours for assembly, 50 man-hours for painting and finishing, and 10 man-hours for checking out and testing. A Cruiser averages 60 man-hours for assembly, 40 for painting and finishing, and 20 man-hours for checkout and testing. During each production run, there are 30,000 man-hours available in the assembly shops, 13,000 in the painting and finishing shops, and 5000 in the checking and testing division. How many of each model should the manufacturer schedule for each production run in order to realize the greatest possible profit from each production run?

12. In Problem 11, what would be the most profitable production program if both Clippers and Cruisers were sold to the dealers at the same profit of $100 per boat?

13. A bottling plant turns out two basic products, Regular and Extra Smooth Draft. The operations carried out at the plant are done in two separate divisions. Division 1, which does the basic bottling operation, requires 5 minutes of machine time for each case of Extra Smooth Draft (because of more careful pouring) and 2 minutes of machine time for each case of Regular. In Division 2, where labels are attached and packaging is done, 3 minutes of labor are required for a case of either kind of brew. Three identical machines in Division 1 are available for bottling. There are three men in the Labeling Division, but for obvious reasons (such as fume inhalation, spillage), they can each work only 45 minutes out of any particular hour. Management estimates that profit averages $3 per case on Extra Smooth Draft and $2 per case on Regular.

(a) What is the optimal hourly production schedule for this plant from the point of view of maximizing profits?

(b) Suppose that bottling technology does not change but that, by varying the market price of Regular, the plant is able to increase the profit per case on Regular. The profit on Extra Smooth Draft remains the same. At what figure of profit per case of Regular would management be indifferent (in terms of maximizing profit) between (1) producing any one of a number of combinations of the two products and (2) producing only Regular?

(c) This plant is later given an additional operation, prior to the bottling, in which the bottles are sterilized. This is accomplished on one of seven sterilizers, and requires 7 minutes for a case of bottles to be used for Regular and 10 minutes for a case to be used for Extra Smooth Draft (because of their more complicated shape). How would the optimal production schedule from (a) be altered?

(d) How much should the plant pay for: (1) an additional man in the Labeling Division? (2) an additional sterilizing machine?

14. Regions A and B can both produce Miniautos. However, different technologies are used in the two regions. It is estimated that each unit produced in A contributes \$30 to that region's income, while each unit in B contributes \$70 to B's income. Skilled labor is freely mobile between regions. Production of a Miniauto in A requires 30 man-hours of skilled labor, while production in B requires 100 man-hours. The total pool of skilled labor available is 3000 man-hours per day. However, unskilled labor is also required, and this is immobile between regions. Production of one Miniauto in A requires 20 man-hours of unskilled labor; in B it requires 15 man-hours. Total available supplies of unskilled labor are 800 man-hours per day in A and 360 in B. Finally, production of each Miniauto requires one enginette; these are produced at a factory on the border (the regions are contiguous) and are available the next day in either region. The factory produces 60 enginettes a day.

(a) An Interregional Council wants to set production in both regions so as to maximize the total regional income (income in A plus income in B). What should the Council recommend?

(b) What is the value to the two-region system of: (1) an additional man-hour of skilled labor? (2) an additional 40 man-hours?

(c) If an additional 8 man-hours of labor (unskilled) per day could be made available from outside the system in either A or B, where should it be used?

REFERENCES

1. Baumol, W. J., *Economic Theory and Operations Analysis*, 2d ed. Englewood Cliffs, N.J.: Prentice-Hall, Inc., 1965.
2. Campbell, Hugh G., *An Introduction to Matrices, Vectors and Linear Programming*. New York: Appleton-Century-Crofts, 1965.
3. Chung, A., *Linear Programming*. Columbus: C. E. Merrill Books, Inc., 1963.
4. Dantzig, G. B., *Linear Programming and Extensions*. Princeton: Princeton University Press, 1964.
5. Gass, S. I., *Linear Programming*, 3d ed. New York: McGraw-Hill, Inc., 1969.
6. Hadley, G., *Linear Programming*. Reading, Mass.: Addison-Wesley Publishing Company, Inc., 1962.
7. Karlin, S., *Mathematical Methods and Theory in Games, Programming and Economics*, vol. I. Reading, Mass.: Addison-Wesley Publishing Company, Inc., 1959.
8. Metzger, R. W., *Elementary Mathematical Programming*. New York: John Wiley & Sons, Inc. (Science Editions), 1963.

9. Simonnard, M., *Linear Programming*, trans. W. S. Jewell. Englewood Cliffs, N.J.: Prentice-Hall, Inc., 1966.
10. Spivey, W. A., *Linear Programming, an Introduction*. New York: The Macmillan Company, 1963.
11. Vajda, S., *Mathematical Programming*. Reading, Mass.: Addison-Wesley Publishing Company, Inc., 1961.

LINEAR PROGRAMMING MODELS—
II: SPECIAL TOPICS AND EXTENSIONS

The fundamental structure and computational approach to linear programming problems was presented in the preceding chapter. Because of the wide application that programming models have found—in such diverse fields as equipment scheduling for an airline and security portfolio analysis in investment banking—our discussion of this topic is continued in the present chapter. Initially we investigate the implications of several special features that a linear programming problem may have. Then we briefly examine two particular variations on the general programming theme, each of which has generated its own computational methods. Next we explore the effects on the geometry and the simplex arithmetic of adding the requirement that the variables in the solution be whole numbers; this is the *discrete* or *integer programming* problem. Finally, we introduce the topic of game theory and explore its relationship to linear programming models.

7.1. MULTIPLE OPTIMA AND DEGENERACY

Consider the following problem:

$$
\begin{aligned}
\text{maximize:} \quad & 6x_1 + 4x_2 \\
\text{subject to:} \quad & -2x_1 + x_2 \leq 2, \\
& x_1 - x_2 \leq 2, \\
& 3x_1 + 2x_2 \leq 9, \\
\text{and} \quad & x_1, x_2 \geq 0.
\end{aligned}
\tag{7-1}
$$

Using the simplex arithmetic of Section 6.3, the reader would find the following tableau after two iterations (he should carry through the calculations for practice):

		s_2	s_3
π	18	0	-2
s_1	$6\frac{3}{5}$	$-1\frac{2}{5}$	$-\frac{1}{5}$
x_1	$2\frac{3}{5}$	$-\frac{2}{5}$	$-\frac{1}{5}$
x_2	$\frac{3}{5}$	$\frac{3}{5}$	$-\frac{1}{5}$

(7-2)

Looking at the simplex criterion elements in the zeroth row, we see that while neither of the excluded variables would *increase* the value of the objective function (no positive elements), introduction of s_2 into the basis would leave the objective function unchanged. Iteration rules compel us to remove s_1 from the basis when bringing s_2 in ($\frac{3.3}{7} < \frac{1.3}{2}$). The new tableau is

		s_1	s_3
π	18	0	-2
s_2	$4\frac{5}{7}$	$-\frac{5}{7}$	$-\frac{1}{7}$
x_1	$\frac{5}{7}$	$\frac{2}{7}$	$-\frac{1}{7}$
x_2	$3\frac{3}{7}$	$-\frac{3}{7}$	$-\frac{2}{7}$

(7-3)

[The reader should convince himself that pivoting again in the s_1 column of (7-3) will lead back to (7-2).] The two alternative optima given by these tableaux are shown in Table 7.1. In both cases, the objective function value

Table 7.1. Alternative Optima (Primal Problem)

	Included in Optimal Basis	Excluded from Optimal Basis
(7-2)	$x_1 = 2\frac{3}{5}$, $x_2 = \frac{3}{5}$, $s_1 = 6\frac{3}{5}$	$s_2 = 0$, $s_3 = 0$
(7-3)	$x_1 = \frac{5}{7}$, $x_2 = 3\frac{3}{7}$, $s_2 = 4\frac{5}{7}$	$s_1 = 0$, $s_3 = 0$

is 18. Since $s_3^0 = 0$ in both solutions, but s_1 is in one basis and s_2 in the other, it appears that (7-2) represents one endpoint of constraint 3 (its intersec-

tion with constraint 2, since $s_2 = 0$) and (7-3) represents the other endpoint of constraint 3 (the intersection with constraint 1). These points are "equally optimal," which suggests that the objective function contours must be parallel to constraint 3. Looking back at the original statement of the problem, in (7-1), we see that this is the case. It is also clear from solution-space geometry. Solutions I and II are shown in Figure 7.1. It is

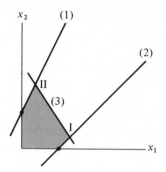

Figure 7.1. Multiple Optima

clear that when parallelism of this kind occurs, there will be more than one *basic* optimal solution and also an infinite number of *nonbasic* optima, namely all points on the convex combination of solutions I and II—that is, along the edge of the feasible region defined by constraint 3.

Therefore, the appearance of one or more zeros in a top row with otherwise negative elements means that the primal problem has multiple (or alternative) optima. The relevance of the simplex method—which looks only at basic solutions—is not affected, however, since among the multiple optima there will be at least two that are at corners of the feasible region and hence are basic.

Consider the dual optimal solutions in (7-2) and (7-3). Making the appropriate labeling changes, using v's for dual variables and t's for dual slacks, we have the results shown in Table 7.2. Thus, in either case, the optimal dual v's are: $v_1^0 = 0$, $v_2^0 = 0$, $v_3^0 = 2$, *even though* (7-2) and (7-3) have

Table 7.2. Dual Values Associated with Primal Alternative Optima

	Included in Optimal Basis	Excluded from Optimal Basis
(7-2)	$v_2 = 0$, $v_3 = 2$	$v_1 = 0$, $t_1 = 0$, $t_2 = 0$
(7-3)	$v_1 = 0$, $v_3 = 2$	$v_2 = 0$, $t_1 = 0$, $t_2 = 0$

a different pair of dual variables in the basis (top-row labels). This is, of course, because the dual optima are *degenerate* (one or more variables in the basis at value zero). Clearly a primal problem has multiple optima only if one or more zeros appear in an otherwise negative top row;[1] but since the top-row elements are also dual optimal values, the dual optimum must be degenerate. Multiple optima in one problem thus imply a degenerate but unique optimum in the other. When we refer to a problem as being degenerate, we will mean degeneracy in the *optimal* basis. Degeneracy at corners "along the way" to the optimum presents only minor computational problems and is of no particular theoretical interest. We will see in the following problem that degeneracy of the *next* solution is signaled by the equality of two or more ratios $|a_{i0}/a_{iq}|$ in the *current* pivot-choice calculations. That is, two or more rows are equally qualified to be pivot rows, which is to say that two or more variables in the current basis could be removed.[2]

The following problem exhibits degeneracy in the primal optimum:

$$
\begin{aligned}
\text{maximize:} \quad & x_1 + 2x_2 \\
\text{subject to:} \quad & x_2 \leq 3, \\
& x_1 \leq 2, \\
& 3x_1 + 2x_2 \leq 12, \\
\text{and} \quad & x_1, x_2 \geq 0.
\end{aligned}
\tag{7-4}
$$

[1] This is *almost* an "if and only if" statement. The "only if" part should be clear; one or more zeros in an otherwise negative top row are obviously *necessary* for multiple optima in the primal. There are two ways in which this would not also be *sufficient* (the "if" part); one is impossible and the other unlikely. We consider them in turn.

1. If all columns with a zero at the top had no negative elements (that is, pivot candidates) elsewhere in the column, it would be impossible to pivot in any of these columns. This would signal an *unbounded* primal, as we saw in Chapter 6. However, an unbounded primal is impossible, since both primal and dual problems have feasible solutions (the reader should convince himself that this is true) and hence, from Theorem P-D4, both must have optimal solutions.

2. If the primal optimum were degenerate (one or more variables in the basis at value zero) *and* the zero column (or columns) had negative elements in the row or rows of those primal variables that were zero, and hence would be (or would be tied for, if there were more than one) the pivot row, then pivoting would not lead to a distinguishably different primal optimum. Since a_{p0} would be zero, the "corner product" in the rule that would apply to transforming all other elements in the zeroth column (Table 6.2) would be zero; hence no primal variable values would be changed. This is a rather specialized situation that need not concern us further.

[2] While virtually *any* method for choosing among the tied rows is generally valid (for example, choose completely randomly), there is at least a theoretical possibility that a problem with degeneracy characteristics may *cycle* among a sequence of basic solutions without ever reaching an optimum. A perturbation technique may be used, in which the constraints at the degenerate corner are altered slightly (by amounts ϵ_i, hence this is sometimes called the ϵ-technique) so that they do not all meet at the same point. Details are to be found, for example, in Hadley [10, chap. 6].

After one iteration we have the next tableau (7-5). Clearly x_1 should come

	x_1	s_1	
π	6	1	-2
x_2	3	0	-1
s_2	2	-1^a	0
s_3	6	-3^b	2

$$(7\text{-}5)$$

into the basis, but the criterion for choosing the variable to leave the basis (that is, the choice of a pivot row) indicates that s_2 and s_3 are equally good. (In both cases the relevant ratio is equal to 2, and no other elements in this column can be pivot candidates.) The results for the two possible pivot selections, labeled a and b in (7-5), are shown in (7-6) and (7-7).

Either choice produces an optimal solution in one additional pivot—from (7-5) to (7-6) or from (7-5) to (7-7). The primal optima are (1) degenerate and (2) the same in both cases (Table 7.3).

	s_2	s_1
π	8	-1	-2
x_2	3	0	-1
x_1	2	-1	0
s_3	0	3	2

$$(7\text{-}6)$$

	s_3	s_1
π	8	$-\frac{1}{3}$	$-\frac{4}{3}$
x_2	3	0	-1
s_2	0	$\frac{1}{3}$	$-\frac{2}{3}$
x_1	2	$-\frac{1}{3}$	$\frac{2}{3}$

$$(7\text{-}7)$$

Pivot a   Pivot b

In moving *from* (7-5)—that is, in introducing x_1 into the solution that already includes x_2—constraints 2 and 3 are hit simultaneously. This is the implication of the equality of the ratios in (7-5) for the s_2 and s_3 rows.

Table 7.3. Degenerate Optima (Primal Problem)

	Included in Optimal Basis	Excluded from Optimal Basis
(7-6)	$x_1 = 2, x_2 = 3, s_3 = 0$	$s_1 = 0, s_2 = 0$
(7-7)	$x_1 = 2, x_2 = 3, s_2 = 0$	$s_1 = 0, s_3 = 0$

Normally, in a pivoting operation, one moves along an edge of the feasible region until a corner is reached—along a constraint until it intersects a new one. Here, however, *two* new constraints define the same stopping point. Either one would be sufficient to define the corner, and one of the two constraints is redundant in the problem.[3] This is clearly illustrated by the solution-space geometry. Tableau (7-5) represents the situation at point I in Figure 7.2. Introduction of x_1 at that point involves movement

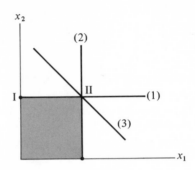

Figure 7.2.   Degenerate Optimum

along constraint 1, and *either* constraint 2 *or* 3 would serve to define corner II, the stopping point in the x_1 direction. From the point of view of the problem, however, only constraint 3 is redundant, since its removal would not alter the feasible region, whereas removal of constraint 2 would change the shape of the region.

Although the optimal values of the primal variables are unaffected by the pivot choice in (7-5), it is clear from (7-6) and (7-7) that the values of the dual variables do differ. After appropriate labeling, the alternative basic dual solutions are shown in Table 7.4.

Therefore, although degeneracy at a primal optimum point does not affect the solution values in the primal, it *does* mean that the optimal

Table 7.4.   Dual Values Associated with Primal
Degenerate Optima

	Included in Optimal Basis	*Excluded from Optimal Basis*
(7-6)	$v_1 = 2, v_2 = 1$	$v_3 = 0, t_1 = 0, t_2 = 0$
(7-7)	$v_1 = \frac{4}{3}, v_3 = \frac{1}{3}$	$v_2 = 0, t_1 = 0, t_2 = 0$

---

[3] That is, its absence from the original statement (7-4) would in no way change the feasible region and hence the optimum.

values of the dual variables are not unique. This is important in applications in which optimal dual variables (shadow prices) are used in a normative sense and compared with "real-world" prices or valuations; the dual variables used as the norm for comparison will depend on the rule used to choose among the equally valid pivot elements, as in (7-5).[4]

Degeneracy and multiple optima are seen to be essentially opposite sides of the same coin, but their implications are quite different. If a linear programming primal problem has multiple optima, then its dual *must* be degenerate.[5] Conversely, if a dual problem is degenerate, then the corresponding primal optimum is usually nonunique; that is, the primal has multiple optima. And because of the complete symmetry between a primal problem and its dual (the dual to the dual is the primal), the terms "primal" and "dual" can be interchanged throughout these statements.

7.2. ARTIFICIAL VARIABLES

The discussion in Chapter 6 of the simplex method for examining successively "more optimal" basic solutions was seen to be valid for (1) maximization problems with (2) nonnegative numbers on the right-hand sides of each of the constraints.[6] The duality properties of a linear programming problem and the structure of the simplex tableaux assure that a minimization problem can be handled by solving its dual, which is a maximization problem.[7] The requirement that right-hand sides of the constraints be nonnegative simply assures that the origin is a corner of the feasible region. It is easy to imagine, however, that there may be actual problems in which

---

[4] The interested reader may wish to observe that at a degenerate corner, such as II in Figure 7.2, the effects of marginal increases and decreases are *different* for some of the constraints; that is, their right- and left-sided derivatives at that point will differ and hence $\partial \pi / \partial r_i$ will not exist. For example, a unit *increase* (upward movement) in constraint 1 leads to an increase in the objective function that is smaller than the (absolute value of the) decrease associated with a unit *decrease* in constraint 1. Or, again, an *increase* (outward movement) in constraint 3 does nothing to the objective function value; a *decrease*, however, reduces this value. Thus Theorem P-D5 of the last chapter is strictly true only for nondegenerate optima.

[5] The chain of reasoning is: if multiple optima, then at least one zero-valued simplex criterion in the top row, and if a zero-valued simplex criterion, then degeneracy in the basis represented by the top row.

[6] When all constraints are weak inequalities reading "less than or equal to." The direction of any inequality can always be reversed by multiplying both sides by -1.

[7] As a matter of fact, it is easy to modify the rules of Chapter 6 so that minimization problems can be handled directly. The interested reader should try this, after noting the sign differences necessary because nonnegative slack variables must be *subtracted* from the left-hand sides of "greater than or equal to" inequalities, which is the standard form for a linear programming minimization problem.

the origin will be excluded.[8] It is convenient if the origin is a corner of the feasible region, because it makes the selection of an initial basic feasible solution such a simple matter. Setting each x variable equal to zero (and hence defining the coordinates of the origin) is accomplished by setting each slack variable equal to the entire right-hand side of the constraint, so that there is no opportunity, in any constraint, for any of the x's to take on a nonzero value. And if all right-hand sides of the constraints are non-negative, then all the slack variables at the origin will have nonnegative values, which is required of *all* variables in a linear programming problem.

When the origin is not available as an initial feasible basis, the problem can be resolved by addition of one or more so-called *artificial* variables. Consider problem (6-5) from Chapter 6, with the direction of the third inequality reversed.

$$
\begin{aligned}
\text{Maximize:} \quad & 2x_1 + 5x_2 \\
\text{subject to:} \quad & x_1 + 2x_2 \leq 10, \\
& 3x_1 + 2x_2 \leq 24, \\
& x_1 + 10x_2 \geq 40, \\
\text{and} \quad & x_1, x_2 \geq 0.
\end{aligned}
\tag{7-8}
$$

Rewriting, so that all constraints have the proper direction, we have

$$
\begin{aligned}
\text{maximize:} \quad & 2x_1 + 5x_2 \\
\text{subject to:} \quad & x_1 + 2x_2 \leq 10, \\
& 3x_1 + 2x_2 \leq 24, \\
& -x_1 - 10x_2 \leq -40, \\
& x_1, x_2 \geq 0.
\end{aligned}
\tag{7-8'}
$$

The feasible region (shaded) and objective function contours are shown in Figure 7.3, which should be compared with Figure 6.2 for problem (6-5) in

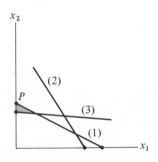

Figure 7.3. Feasible Region for Problem (7-8)

[8] For example, if a maximization problem includes the constraint $-x_1 - 4x_2 \leq -7$ (that is, $x_1 + 4x_2 \geq 7$), this sets a lower limit on nonnegative values of x_1 and x_2 that disallows $x_1 = 0$ *and* $x_2 = 0$ (the origin).

the preceding chapter. Note in particular that the origin is no longer in the feasible region for the problem. The effect of a negative right-hand side shows up clearly when the constraints of (7-8') are written as equalities, as in (7-9).

$$\text{Maximize:} \quad 2x_1 + 5x_2 + 0s_1 + 0s_2 + 0s_3$$
$$\text{subject to:} \quad x_1 + 2x_2 + s_1 = 10,$$
$$3x_1 + 2x_2 + s_2 = 24, \qquad (7\text{-}9)$$
$$-x_1 - 10x_2 + s_3 = -40,$$
$$\text{and} \quad x_1, x_2, s_1, s_2, s_3 \geq 0.$$

When x_1 and x_2 are zero, $s_3 = -40$, and this violates nonnegativity of the slack variables.

Suppose then that for the moment we let s_3 be zero also and alter the third constraint further by *subtracting* a new variable, s_a. Thus this constraint becomes $-x_1 - 10x_2 + s_3 - s_a = -40$. Clearly, an initial feasible solution with all nonnegative variables will be $s_1 = 10$, $s_2 = 24$, $s_a = 40$; $x_1 = x_2 = s_3 = 0$. Now, if s_a can also be included in the original objective function, then we can construct an initial simplex tableau and proceed with the simplex arithmetic. Since we have added a *variable*, s_a, we know that the tableaux for this problem will all have an additional *column*. Since s_a has no meaning in the problem and is introduced only to facilitate "starting up" the simplex arithmetic, we want to insure that this artificial variable is *immediately* removed from the basic solution and does not return to any future basis. For this purpose we assign it a very very large *negative* value in the objective function that we want to *maximize*. In fact, we can simply give it a coefficient of $-K$, where we understand K to be an immense number.[9]

Thus the final version of the problem is

$$\text{maximize:} \quad 2x_1 + 5x_2 + 0s_1 + 0s_2 + 0s_3 - Ks_a$$
$$\text{subject to:} \quad x_1 + 2x_2 + s_1 = 10,$$
$$3x_1 + 2x_2 + s_2 = 24, \quad (7\text{-}10)$$
$$-x_1 - 10x_2 + s_3 - s_a = -40,$$
$$\text{and} \quad x_1, x_2; s_1, s_2, s_3; s_a \geq 0.$$

We know that x_1, x_2, and s_3 will be zero in the initial tableau; hence they will be the column labels. We also know from constraint 3 that $s_a = 40 - x_1 - 10x_2 + s_3$. This provides us with the numbers for the bottom row of the initial tableau, the coefficients that relate the currently included variable (s_a) to the currently excluded ones (x_1, x_2, and s_3). *Moreover*, since s_a is totally artificial from the point of view of the objective function, this rearrangement of constraint 3 allows us to *eliminate* s_a from the objective function; it becomes

---

[9] Often M is used, which has led to the name "the big M method" for this procedure.

$$2x_1 + 5x_2 + 0s_1 + 0s_2 + 0s_3 - K(40 - x_1 - 10x_2 + s_3),$$

or

$$(2 + K)x_1 + (5 + 10K)x_2 + 0s_1 + 0s_2 + (0 - K)s_3 - 40K.$$

In the initial tableau, with $s_1 = 10$, $s_2 = 24$, and $s_a = 40$, the value of the objective function is seen to be $-40K$, which is correct. This is shown in (7-11), which should be read in exactly the same way as all other linear programming tableaux.

		x_1	x_2	s_3	
π	$-40K$	$(2 + K)$	$(5 + 10K)$	$(0 - K)$	
s_1	10	-1	-2	0	(7-11)
s_2	24	-3	-2	0	
s_a	40	-1	-10	1	

Since $-40K$ is not a very satisfactory maximum, and since both x_1 and x_2 have positive coefficients for the objective function at this point, this basic solution can be improved upon by the usual rules of simplex arithmetic. In the first iteration, x_2 will be introduced into and s_a removed from the basis; thus the first pivot element is -10. Then, in the second pivot operation, x_1 comes in and s_1 leaves the basis. Finally, s_3 moves into the basic solution, replacing x_1 (which just came in on the previous pivot step). After three iterations, the simplex tableau is as shown in (7-12).[10] Therefore, the optimal primal solution is $x_1^0 = 0$, $x_2^0 = 5$, at which point the objective

		s_1	s_a	x_1	
π	25	$-\frac{5}{2}$	$-K$	$-\frac{1}{2}$	
s_3	10	-5	1	-4	(7-12)
s_2	14	1	0	-2	
x_2	5	$-\frac{1}{2}$	0	$-\frac{1}{2}$	

[10] The reader should carry through the intervening steps for practice in general and especially to see how the K's disappear from all columns except that for s_a.

function has a value of 25, the first constraint is met as an equality ($s_1^0 = 0$, by exclusion from the primal basis), and the slacks needed for constraints 2 and 3 are 14 and 10, respectively. The optimum corresponds, of course, to point P in Figure 7.3.

The artificial-variable technique can be used for a linear programming maximum problem with any number of constraints having negative right-hand sides. If the ordinary rules of pivoting produce a unique optimal solution in which not all artificial variables have been removed from the basis, then the original problem has no feasible solution.

An essentially identical approach is the so-called two-phase procedure. After adding artificial variables, exactly as above, to each constraint with a negative right-hand side—denoting by s_{a_i} the artificial variable for constraint i—the Phase I problem seeks to minimize the sum of the artificial variables, $\sum_i s_{a_i}$, subject to the (enlarged) constraints of the original problem. Since these variables are also required to be nonnegative, the minimum of this sum is obviously zero—except in the rare case where there is no feasible solution at all. When this optimal Phase I solution is reached, the resulting values for x's and s's constitute an initial basic feasible solution to the original linear program. Phase II then begins with this solution as a starting point for the simplex calculations on the original problem. In other words, Phase I establishes an alternative to the (excluded) origin from which to begin the real work.

7.3. EQUATIONS AS CONSTRAINTS

We saw in Chapter 4 that problems of maximization or minimization of a function subject to constraints that are equations can be approached using Lagrange multipliers. We also saw that inequalities are a different matter, and the development of the simplex arithmetic in Chapter 6 depended on constraints in the form of weak linear inequalities. In this section we note that linear *equations* as constraints can also be handled by the simplex method. This means that the calculation procedures of Chapter 6 can be used for a problem with some inequality and some equality constraints, thus increasing the generality of the method.[11] Again, we consider two related approaches.

---

[11] The reader should recall that the Lagrange multiplier approach to constrained optimization problems is not generally valid for *linear* functions because of the use made of first and second partial derivatives, which must generally be functions of the variables and not constants.

The first is extremely simple; it involves nothing more than converting each of the linear equations to *two* linear inequalities. Consider $2x_1 + 3x_2 = 10$. If we require (1) $2x_1 + 3x_2 \geq 10$ *and* (2) $2x_1 + 3x_2 \leq 10$, we have exactly the same result as the single equation. If this equation appeared in a maximization problem, then, since all inequalities should read "less than or equal to," we would rewrite (1), above, as $-2x_1 - 3x_2 \leq -10$. This, plus (2), would be the pair of inequalities that expressed the relation shown originally in the single equation.

Computationally, since one of the two right-hand sides will automatically be negative, artificial variables will generally be necessary, but otherwise, from the point of view of the primal problem, there is nothing new. Each equation is replaced by two inequalities.[12] There is, however, a consequence for the *dual* that may be of interest, depending on the use (if any) to which the optimal values of the dual variables are put. Since a dual *variable* is associated with each primal *inequality constraint*, each primal equation, when rewritten in double-inequality form, will generate *two* dual variables. In fact, however, these two dual variables can be combined into one (which is more logical, since they are associated with what is fundamentally one primal constraint), but this dual variable will be unrestricted in sign—that is, it can no longer be required to be nonnegative. This is easily illustrated by a small example; the reader should carry out the demonstration for a more general case.

Let the primal be

$$
\begin{aligned}
\text{maximize:} \quad & x_1 + 6x_2 \\
\text{subject to:} \quad & 3x_1 + 4x_2 \leq 5, \\
& 2x_1 + 8x_2 = 7, \\
\text{and} \quad & x_1, x_2 \geq 0.
\end{aligned}
\tag{7-13}
$$

In all-inequality form, this becomes

---

[12] If there are *several* equations, it is in fact not necessary to retain *both* inequality forms of each equation. Rather (in a maximization problem, for example) it is sufficient to retain the "$\leq$" form of *each* equation plus *one* more that is the *sum* of all "$\geq$" inequalities. For example, given the two planes $2x_1 + x_2 + x_3 = 10$ and $x_1 + x_2 + x_3 = 3$ as constraints, their intersection (common points) is a line. Convert each to a pair of inequalities. It is clear that the half-spaces $2x_1 + x_2 + x_3 \leq 10$ and $x_1 + x_2 + x_3 \leq 3$ define a convex set having this same line as an edge; and if

$$(2x_1 + x_2 + x_3) + (x_1 + x_2 + x_3) \geq 10 + 3$$

that is, $3x_1 + 2x_2 + 2x_3 \geq 13$, or $-3x_1 - 2x_2 - 2x_3 \leq -13$—is also required, the *only* points that these *three* half-spaces have in common lie along that same line. (The reader should convince himself that this is true for small examples that he can draw accurately.) This, of course, has implications for the dual—it adds in fact only *one* dual variable.

$$\text{maximize:} \quad x_1 + 6x_2$$
$$\text{subject to:} \quad 3x_1 + 4x_2 \le \quad 5,$$
$$2x_1 + 8x_2 \le \quad 7, \qquad (7\text{-}14)$$
$$-2x_1 - 8x_2 \le -7,$$
$$\text{and} \qquad x_1, x_2 \ge \quad 0.$$

The dual to (7-14) is, following the general rules of Chapter 6,

$$\text{minimize:} \quad 5v_1 + 7v_2 - 7v_3$$
$$\text{subject to:} \quad 3v_1 + 2v_2 - 2v_3 \ge 1,$$
$$4v_1 + 8v_2 - 8v_3 \ge 6, \qquad (7\text{-}15)$$
$$\text{and} \qquad v_1, v_2, v_3 \ge 0.$$

But this is equivalent to

$$\text{minimize:} \quad 5v_1 + 7(v_2 - v_3)$$
$$\text{subject to:} \quad 3v_1 + 2(v_2 - v_3) \ge 1,$$
$$4v_1 + 8(v_2 - v_3) \ge 6,$$
$$\text{and} \qquad v_1, v_2, v_3 \ge 0.$$

Therefore, define $v_d \equiv v_2 - v_3$ (the subscript d reminds us that it is a *difference* between two variables), and the problem becomes

$$\text{minimize:} \quad 5v_1 + 7v_d$$
$$\text{subject to:} \quad 3v_1 + 2v_d \ge 1,$$
$$4v_1 + 8v_d \ge 6, \qquad (7\text{-}16)$$
$$\text{and} \qquad v_1 \ge 0$$
$$\text{but} \qquad v_d \gtrless 0,$$

since the difference between two nonnegative variables (v_2 and v_3) can be of either sign, or zero. Hence, in the final form of (7-16) we have one dual variable for each of the original primal constraints—in (7-13)—but the variable associated with the primal equation is unrestricted in sign.

The second approach to equality constraints is exactly the two-phase procedure described in the preceding section for inequality constraints with negative right-hand sides. Artificial variables can be added to each *equation;* that is, it can be treated as if it were an inequality. Then in Phase I one seeks to minimize the sum of the added *artificial* variables, subject to the revised constraint equations that include these variables. Except in unusual circumstances, as above, the minimum will be zero, and this optimum to the Phase I problem becomes the initial basic feasible solution for the Phase II simplex computations on the problem of original interest.

7.4. THE TRANSPORTATION PROBLEM

The name *transportation problem* denotes a class of linear programming models with a structure that allows computational streamlining. It is a framework of quite wide applicability. The model can be introduced in the following setting, which explains its name. Consider the problem of distributing units of a homogeneous product from places where they are produced—the origins, m in number—to places where they are consumed—the destinations, n in number. Suppose that each origin i ($i = 1, \ldots, m$) has a known capacity or number of units produced, c_i, and each destination j ($j = 1, \ldots, n$) has a known demand or number of units needed, d_j, and that production has already been planned so that demand is exactly met—that is,

$$\sum_{i=1}^{m} c_i = \sum_{j=1}^{n} d_j.$$

The only problem is to decide which destinations to serve from which origins and in what amounts; assume that the object is to distribute items in such a way that total cost of transporting them is minimized. Let x_{ij} denote the amount of product sent from origin i to destination j, and k_{ij} be the unit transportation cost associated with the i-j route. The objective function is then to minimize

$$\sum_{i=1}^{m} \sum_{j=1}^{n} k_{ij}x_{ij}.$$

In addition to nonnegativity requirements on the x_{ij}, there are two classes of constraints; one concerns each of the origins, the other each of the destinations. Specifically, shipments *out of* any origin must equal the production (supply) at that origin:

$$\sum_{j=1}^{n} x_{ij} = c_i \qquad \text{for each origin } i, \tag{7-17}$$

and shipments *into* any destination must equal the demand at that destination:

$$\sum_{i=1}^{m} x_{ij} = d_j \qquad \text{for each destination } j. \tag{7-18}$$

Thus, the problem is

$$\text{minimize:} \quad \sum_{i=1}^{m} \sum_{j=1}^{n} k_{ij} x_{ij}$$

$$\text{subject to:} \begin{cases} (1) \quad \sum_{j=1}^{n} x_{ij} = c_i \quad \text{for } i = 1, \ldots, m, \\ (2) \quad \sum_{i=1}^{m} x_{ij} = d_j \quad \text{for } j = 1, \ldots, n, \end{cases} \quad (7\text{-}19)$$

$$\text{and} \qquad\qquad x_{ij} \geq 0.$$

Note that constraint sets (1) and (2) in (7-19) have a particularly simple structure. Not only are they equations, but also all the coefficients on the x's are either 0 (absence of that particular x_{ij}) or 1 (presence of that x_{ij}). This is more easily seen if we write out a small example completely. Let there be two origins [say (1) = New York and (2) = Philadelphia] and three destinations [(1) = Chicago, (2) = Seattle, and (3) = San Francisco]. The constraints are therefore

$$\begin{aligned} x_{11} + x_{12} + x_{13} & & = c_1, \\ & x_{21} + x_{22} + x_{23} & = c_2, \\ x_{11} \qquad\qquad + x_{21} & & = d_1, \\ x_{12} \qquad\qquad + x_{22} & & = d_2, \\ x_{13} \qquad\qquad + x_{23} & = d_3. \end{aligned} \quad (7\text{-}20)$$

The first equation, for example, says that shipments from New York to Chicago, to Seattle, and to San Francisco (the three possible destinations) must exhaust New York's production; the last constraint says that the amounts coming into San Francisco from New York and from Philadelphia (the only origins in the problem) must just satisfy San Francisco's demand.

The matrix of coefficients has the following particularly simple structure:

$$\mathop{A}_{(5\times 6)} = \begin{bmatrix} 1 & 1 & 1 & 0 & 0 & 0 \\ 0 & 0 & 0 & 1 & 1 & 1 \\ 1 & 0 & 0 & 1 & 0 & 0 \\ 0 & 1 & 0 & 0 & 1 & 0 \\ 0 & 0 & 1 & 0 & 0 & 1 \end{bmatrix}.$$

Consider the rank of this matrix. It cannot exceed 5 (the smaller of its two dimensions). However, removing *any* column leaves a 5×5 submatrix whose determinant is zero; this is because there is linear dependence among the rows—

$$(\text{row 1}) + (\text{row 2}) = (\text{row 3}) + (\text{row 4}) + (\text{row 5})$$

—both in A and in any 5×5 submatrix in A. The rank of A is 4, since a 4×4 matrix from A necessarily has one of the rows of A missing; hence the linear dependence among the rows is removed. Since $c_1 + c_2 = d_1 +$

$d_2 + d_3$, the same linear dependence exists in the augmented matrix $[A \mathbin{\vdots} B]$ as in A, and therefore (7-20) represents a consistent set of *four* linearly independent equations. Thus the transportation problem consists of $m \cdot n$ variables and $(m + n - 1)$ independent constraints in the form of equations.[13] An optimal solution will therefore contain at most $(m + n - 1)$ variables in the basis at positive value. Variants of the simplex method, programmed to deal exclusively with equations, can be used. However, we now investigate a method of calculation that takes particular advantage of the structure of the constraints in a transportation problem; it has come to be known as the "stepping-stone" method.

Looking again at equations (7-20), which form the constraints, we see that an initial basic solution can be written down very easily. Each x_{ij} appears only twice—and in the same column. Let the "leftmost" variable, x_{11}, be equal to either c_1 or d_1, whichever is smaller. Assume $c_1 < d_1$. Then (1) set $x_{11} = c_1$; this means $x_{12} = x_{13} = 0$, which in turn means (2) $x_{22} = d_2$ and $x_{23} = d_3$. Now (1) implies (from the equation for d_1) that $x_{21} = d_1 - x_{11} = d_1 - c_1$; (2) means that (from the equation for c_2) $x_{21} = c_2 - d_2 - d_3$. But since $c_1 + c_2 = d_1 + d_2 + d_3$, the expressions for x_{21} are equal.

This step (and the full solution procedure) can be very nicely carried out in a condensed format. Since the number of possible variables involved is the product of the number of origins and the number of destinations, we construct a matrix with each origin as a row, each destination as a column, and the unit costs, k_{ij}, inside the matrix (in the *upper* triangle in each cell). Since there is a column for each destination, one "extra" row can be used to record the demands, d_j. Similarly, an additional column can contain the c_i figures. Then all the data of the problem are summarized in an $(m + 1) \times (n + 1)$ matrix. This is shown for the general 2×3 problem in (7-21).

Origins \ Destinations	1	2	3	Capacities
1	k_{11} / x_{11}	k_{12} / x_{12}	k_{13} / x_{13}	c_1
2	k_{21} / x_{21}	k_{22} / x_{22}	k_{23} / x_{23}	c_2
Demands	d_1	d_2	d_3	

(7-21)

For a specific 2×3 example, let the data be as follows:

[13] Except for the trivial cases in which $m = 1$ or $n = 1$ (or both), there will be more unknowns than equations; hence we must look for *basic* solutions, as usual.

Origins \ Destinations	1	2	3	Capacities	
1	3 /	4 /	2 /	10	(7-22)
2	4 /	1 /	6 /	15	
Demands	8	12	5		

Now the general approach suggested above, for writing down an initial feasible solution, is easily carried out in this condensed framework. Begin in the x_{11} cell, the "northwest corner." Insert, for the value of x_{11}, the *smaller* of the two marginal totals—c_1 or d_1 in general, 8 or 10 in the specific example. This is done in (7-23), where the k_{ij} have been omitted.

O \ D	1	2	3	c_i	
1	8			10	(7-23)
2				15	
d_j	8	12	5		

O \ D	1	2	3	c_i	
1	8	2		10	(7-24)
2				15	
d_j	8	12	5		

Thus column 1 is complete (that is, x_{21} must be zero, since x_{11} has exhausted the demand of destination 1). Then move to the next cell in *row* 1 (since *column* 1 is complete) and examine marginal totals again, this time taking account of what is *already entered* in row 1. That is, compare 12 with $(10 - 8) = 2$, and enter the *smaller* in cell $(1, 2)$. This is shown in (7-24), and row 1 is now *also* complete. Then move *down* column 2, this time comparing 15 (row 2 total) with $(12 - 2) = 10$ (column 2 modified total) and enter the smaller—as in (7-25)—completing column 2. Now the final move

O \ D	1	2	3	c_i	
1	8	2		10	(7-25)
2		10		15	
d_j	8	12	5		

O \ D	1	2	3	c_i	
1	8	2		10	(7-26)
2		10	5	15	
d_j	8	12	5		

(rightward in row 2) will *always* complete the final row and column simultaneously, precisely because

$$\sum_j d_j = \sum_i c_i;$$

here the total from column 3 is 5 and the modified total from row 2 is $(15 - 10) = 5$. Hence (7-26) represents an initial basic feasible solution: $x_{11} = 8$, $x_{12} = 2$, $x_{22} = 10$, and $x_{23} = 5$; all other $x_{ij} = 0$. What has been done, in effect, is to construct a path from the northwest to the southeast corner by making a connected chain (filling *adjacent* cells)—hence the name "stepping-stone" method.

If a row and column are *simultaneously* satisfied (prior to the last cell), we are unable to move either horizontally (the row requirement is already satisfied) or vertically (the column requirement is also satisfied). In order to keep our initial stepping-stone path somewhat connected, we therefore move diagonally, one square downward *and* one square to the right. Each time this happens there is one *less* stone than in a normal path (one *more* variable equal to zero); hence the resulting solution will be degenerate.

The total cost associated with the initial feasible solution in (7-26) is easily found as the sum of the products of the k_{ij} and x_{ij} in the four cells in which $x_{ij} \neq 0$; here this is $(3)(8) + (4)(2) + (1)(10) + (6)(5) = 72$. Note that in the initial assignment no attention was paid at all to costs. An initial variable, x_{11}, was selected to become nonzero—in fact, to become as positive as possible—and from then on the implications of this choice were carried through via the stepping-stone approach. The initial path is complete in (7-26). The question now is: could the row and column totals be satisfied at a lower total cost? The answer is to be found from figures that we calculate for each presently unoccupied cell (that is, where $x_{ij} = 0$). These express, much like the simplex criteria from Chapter 6, the (marginal) cost associated with introducing a unit amount of flow in that cell. If any presently unoccupied cell has a negative marginal cost, that x_{ij} should become positive. Since this is a *linear* program, and the cost function is

$$\sum_i \sum_j k_{ij}x_{ij},$$

it obviously pays to make that x_{ij} as large as possible. The limits will again come from the row and column totals.

Calculation of this cost for presently unoccupied cells requires that we make explicit the compensating changes that would necessarily accompany an increase in one of the cells. Since the final tableau, (7-26), is completely "in balance," a number of entries will have to change if a current x_{ij} that is 0 becomes 1. In the present case there are two such variables. Consider x_{13}. If x_{13} becomes 1, then x_{23} must decrease by 1 to maintain balance in column 3; but then x_{22} must go up by 1 to maintain balance in row 2. Finally, because of this (*and* because of the initial change in x_{13}), x_{12} must go down by 1. To summarize, when x_{13} goes from 0 to 1, x_{23} and x_{12} must decrease by 1, x_{22} must increase by 1 unit. The *cost* implications are clear: a unit of x_{13} costs 2, a unit of x_{22} costs 1; these make positive contributions to the change in total costs, since they are associated with *increased* flows. At the same time, a unit of x_{23} costs 6 and a unit of x_{12} costs 4; these are subtractions from total costs, since they are attached to flows that decrease. Hence the *net* change in total costs accompanying the introduction of a unit flow from origin 1 to destination 3 and the compensating changes that follow is $+(2 + 1) - (6 + 4) = -7$. A similar analysis for x_{21} shows a net cost change of $+4$. We add this information to (7-26), filling its two empty cells as shown in (7-27).

O \ D	1	2	3	c_i	
1	8	2	$\boxed{-7}$	10	(7-27)
2	$\boxed{+4}$	10	5	15	
d_j	8	12	5		

When the net change in costs has been calculated for each currently unoccupied cell, we select the one that has the largest negative value.[14] The next question is: how large can this x_{ij} (in the example, x_{13}) be made? The answer is that it can be as large as the smallest (here the smaller since there are only two) of the x_{ij} that *decrease* in the adjustment process, since none of the flows that are reduced can become negative, and one must become zero to maintain the correct number for a basic solution. The two decreasing variables in this case are x_{23} (present value $= 5$) and x_{12} (present value $= 2$). Therefore the four variables in question can change as shown in Table 7.5.

Table 7.5.   Possible Changes in Tableau (7-27)

	Variable			
	x_{13}	x_{23}	x_{22}	x_{12}
Old value	0	5	10	2
New value	2	3	12	0

---

[14] The logic here is exactly the same as selecting the largest positive top-row element for the pivoting operation in the simplex calculations for a maximization problem.

The new basic solution is shown in (7-28); the total cost is now [going

D ⟍ O	1	2	3	c_i	
1	8		2	10	(7-28)
2		12	3	15	
d_j	8	12	5		

across rows, using the k_{ij} from (7-22)]:

$$(3)(8) + (2)(2) + (1)(12) + (6)(3) = 58,$$

which is indeed $72 - (2)(7)$. (The stepping-stone path has been disturbed in the process, but this is unimportant; it is only a useful device for getting started.) The new solution has a lower total cost, but there is no assurance that it is the lowest possible. It is now necessary again to calculate the new net change in costs for each unoccupied cell. Note that now the compensating changes for x_{21} involve x_{11}, x_{13} and x_{31}. It can be shown that for each unoccupied cell in any basic feasible solution there is a *unique* set of cells through which the compensating changes are made.[15] The new net cost values are circled in (7-29). Now we see that *at this point* it pays to

D ⟍ O	1	2	3	c_i	
1	8	(+7)	2	10	(7-29)
2	(−3)	12	3	15	
d_j	8	12	5		

bring x_{21} into the basis; each unit sent from origin 2 to destination 1 will save \$3 in costs, once all other cells are properly altered. In this case this implies the changes shown in Table 7.6.

---

[15] In larger problems the "linkage" may be more subtle. The fundamental principle is that each cell changed in the compensation process must be in a row *and* column with at least one other positive flow. Degeneracy introduces additional difficulties.

Table 7.6.   Possible Changes in Tableau (7-29)

	Variable			
	x_{21}	x_{23}	x_{13}	x_{11}
Old value	0	3	2	8
New value	3	0	5	5

Thus (7-29) becomes

D ⟍ O	1	2	3	c_i	
1	5	$\boxed{+4}$	5	10	(7-30)
2	3	12	$\boxed{+3}$	15	
d_j	8	12	5		

with a total cost of $(3)(5) + (2)(5) + (4)(3) + (1)(12) = 49$, exactly $58 - (3)(3)$. Net cost changes from this solution are shown circled in the two unoccupied cells; since both are positive, no further cost reduction is possible. The optimum is thus

$$x_{11} = 5, \quad x_{12} = 0, \quad x_{13} = 5,$$
$$x_{21} = 3, \quad x_{22} = 12, \quad x_{23} = 0,$$

for which total transportation cost is 49 and all origin and destination constraints are met.

The stepping-stone method can be used for transportation problems of any size. The arithmetic involved is even simpler than that in the general simplex method; no division is ever required. Note that in problems in which the row and column totals are whole numbers, the x_{ij} in all basic feasible solutions, including the optimum, will also be whole numbers. It is possible to calculate optima to transportation problems by converting the constraints to pairs of inequalities (Section 7.3) and then using artificial variables (Section 7.2), or, indeed, by using the two-phase approach directly. Because of the extreme simplicity of the problem structure, however, this is generally inefficient, at least for purposes of hand calculation.

The point of the "stepping-stone" analogy is that it gives a straightforward method for generating an *initial* feasible solution. The path is no longer connected (in terms of *adjacent* cells from upper left to lower right) in (7-29) or (7-30), the optimum. Obviously, then, one could use other rules for filling the cells of a transportation-problem tableau. For example, since the problem is one of cost minimization, one could begin by entering a positive shipment (x_{ij}) in the cell with minimum unit transport cost (k_{ij}) and then go on to fill cells in order (more or less) of increasing cost, always observing the upper limits imposed by row and column totals.[16]

If a transportation-problem situation contains unequal supply and demand, it is easily converted to the form of the model discussed here. Suppose more is produced than is demanded—that is,

$$\sum_{i=1}^{m} c_i > \sum_{j=1}^{n} d_j.$$

Then, while the destination constraints would still be equations,

$$\sum_{i=1}^{m} x_{ij} = d_j,$$

those for the origins would be inequalities,

$$\sum_{j=1}^{n} x_{ij} \leq c_i.$$

However, since the amount of excess productive capacity,

$$\sum_{i=1}^{m} c_i - \sum_{j=1}^{n} d_j,$$

is known, a *dummy* destination, $j = n + 1$, with precisely this demand, can be added, with the property that costs from *any* origin to it are zero. Thus,

$$\sum_{i=1}^{m} c_i = \sum_{j=1}^{n+1} d_j, \qquad k_{i,n+1} = 0 \qquad \text{for all } i,$$

and the problem can be handled exactly as the example of this section. The amounts in the dummy destination (added column) at optimum indicate the unused capacity at each of the origins (rows).

In exactly the same way, excess total demand

$$\sum_{i=1}^{m} c_i < \sum_{j=1}^{n} d_j$$

would mean,

---

[16] In the example of this section, this approach would have produced the optimal solution in the first tableau, as the reader can easily check.

$$\sum_{i=1}^{m} x_{ij} \le d_j,$$

even though shipments out of each origin would remain equalities. This can be handled by a dummy origin, $i = m + 1$, with zero transport costs to all destinations and capacity equal to the difference between total demand and total capacity. At optimum, the entries in this added row indicate the magnitudes of undersupply for each destination.

For example, suppose in (7-22) (the original data of the sample problem above) that the capacity of origin 1 had been 12. Then total capacity (27) exceeds total demand (25). The initial tableau would be modified by adding a fourth destination to "absorb" the excess supply, as in (7-31).

O \ D	1	2	3	4	c_i	
1	3	4	2	0	12	(7-31)
2	4	1	6	0	15	
d_j	8	12	5	2		

The reader should use the stepping-stone method to generate the optimum shown in Tableau (7-32).

O \ D	1	2	3	4	c_i	
1	7		5		12	(7-32)
2	1	12		2	15	
d_j	8	12	5	2		

With this solution—that is,

$$x_{11} = 7, \qquad x_{12} = 0, \qquad x_{13} = 5,$$
$$x_{21} = 1, \qquad x_{22} = 12, \qquad x_{23} = 0,$$

and with two units of capacity at origin 2 left unused ($x_{24} = 2$), the total transportation cost is 47. Note that this is *less* than the optimal cost in the original problem, (7-30). This happens because the added capacity of two units at origin 1 allows that origin to ship two units more of destination 1's total demands, and it is advantageous to do so, since origin 1 is cheaper than origin 2 as a supplier of destination 1's needs. Thus the excess capacity in the system is left at origin 2.[17]

On the other hand, if, in the problem of (7-22), the demand at destination 2 had been 16, so that there was excess demand in the system (total demand = 29, total capacity = 25), the reader should show that the optimal solution is that shown in (7-33), where a third (dummy) origin has been added.

D O	1	2	3	c_i	
1	5		5	10	
2		15		15	(7-33)
3	3	1		4	
d_j	8	16	5		

Now

$$x_{11} = 5, \quad x_{12} = 0, \quad x_{13} = 5,$$
$$x_{21} = 0, \quad x_{22} = 15, \quad x_{23} = 0,$$

and neither destination 1 nor destination 2 has its demands fully met— $x_{31} = 3$ and $x_{32} = 1$. Total transportation cost is 40. Compared with (7-30), the capacity of origin 2 is now used exclusively for demand at destination 2, since that is the cheapest route in the system; the three units formerly comprising x_{21} in (7-30) are shifted to x_{22}, and then the unfilled demand is distributed in the dummy origin (zero transport cost) row to bring column sums into balance.

It should be clear that a *maximization* problem with the same structure— in particular with constraints of the form of (7-17) and (7-18)—could also be solved by the procedures of this section, the difference being that the

---

[17] The reader should not be confused by the fact that it was at origin 1 that the extra capacity was created, in transforming from the problem in (7-22) to that in (7-31). Once there are two units of excess capacity in the total *system*—27 > 25—the stepping-stone method leads us to an optimum in which the excess capacity is left unused at the optimal place.

unoccupied cell with the most *positive* simplex criterion would receive a positive x_{ij} in the next tableau.[18]

We indicate two further variations on the basic transportation problem format. These incorporate features that make them often more realistic frameworks for analysis of actual problems. The *capacitated transportation problem* has exactly the structure of (7-19), the original problem of this section, with the added set of constraints $x_{ij} \leq u_{ij}$ for some or all of the i-j arcs. The u_{ij}'s are upper limits or capacities on the arcs (for example, maximum possible flow per minute in a pipeline; maximum number of flights per hour over a particular air route—limited partly by takeoff and landing capabilities and required spacings). Essentially all that is necessary is that one include the u_{ij} information (along with k_{ij} and the current x_{ij}) in each cell of the tableaux such as (7-21) *and* not violate any of these upper bounds in making an initial solution or subsequent improvements. Unfortunately this latter is not always as easy as it sounds; the presence of u_{ij} for some or all of the possible routes *can* complicate the solution a great deal.[19]

The *transshipment problem* format allows the possibility of sending units from their origin to their destination via one or more intermediate points—that is, via transshipment points. For example, air passengers from Philadelphia to Seattle may travel via Chicago or via St. Louis; bulk inventory shipments may be sent from New York to San Francisco where they are then broken down to smaller lots and sent on to various California destinations; and so on.

The basic transportation model structure, (7-19), can be enlarged to encompass this kind of shipment. Consider that model, with the origins now labeled $i = 1, \ldots, m$, as before, and the destinations labeled $j = m + 1, \ldots, m + n$. This allows the possibility of shipments from one origin (i) to another "origin" (i') en route to a final destination (j), or indeed en route to a "destination" point (j') from which to be shipped to

---

[18] The interested reader may also wish to examine the dual to the general transportation problem, whose constraints can be written as

$$\sum_{i=1}^{m} x_{ij} \geq d_j \quad \text{and} \quad \sum_{j=1}^{n} x_{ij} \leq c_i.$$

If $\sum_{j} d_j = \sum_{i} c_i$, then all constraints *must* hold as equalities, and we are back to the problem in (7-19). The variables in the dual (maximization) problem are necessarily spatially oriented; they are associated with primal capacity or demand constraints that relate to a particular point. It is possible to interpret the dual objective function and constraint relations in terms of the economist's concept of location rents.

[19] Most books dealing exclusively with linear programming cover this topic in more detail. The reader should refer to Dantzig [7, chap. 18] or Hadley [10, sec. 11-8].

the final destination (j). We expand the cost matrix of (7-21)—omitting the flows, x_{ij}—using k'_{ij}'s for the new intraorigin or intradestination costs (where, generally, k'_{ii} and k'_{jj} will be zero), and simply referring to either origins or destinations as points. Recall that previously 1, 2 were origins and 3, 4, and 5 (that is, $2 + 1$, $2 + 2$, $2 + 3$) were destinations; hence the original costs, k_{ij}, are in the northeast corner of this expanded table.[20]

Points

		1	2	3	4	5	Capacities
	1	k'_{11}	k'_{12}	k_{11}	k_{12}	k_{13}	a_1
	2	k'_{21}	k'_{22}	k_{21}	k_{22}	k_{23}	a_2
Points	3	k'_{31}	k'_{32}	k'_{33}	k'_{34}	k'_{35}	0
	4	k'_{41}	k'_{42}	$\ldots$			0
	5	k'_{51}	k'_{52}				0
Demands		0	0	b_1	b_2	b_3	

$$(7\text{-}34)$$

In this form there is clearly no change in the problem of (7-21), since only points 1 and 2 have capacities and only points 3, 4, and 5 have demands. To allow a shipment from, say, point 1 to 3, then from 3 to 5, we would need a "capacity" at 3. If we knew in advance exactly how much was to be transshipped in this way through point 3, we could add that amount to both the "capacity" and the "demand" for that point and proceed as with the general transportation problem. But, obviously, these transshipment amounts are part of the *solution* to the problem, not the data. The best we can do is set an upper bound of t, the total capacity ($=$ total demand)[21] in the system; that is,

$$t = \sum_{i=1}^{m} a_i = \sum_{j=1}^{n} b_j.$$

Then the capacity column and demand row in (7-34) are increased by these fictitious stockpiles, as below.

[20] The costs in the lower left part of the table may be the same (although transposed) as the original ones in the upper right if the *direction* of flow along an arc does not affect its cost. If one were measuring time, not cost, this would clearly not be the case for, say, all air routes, where the direction of prevailing headwinds affects flying times.

[21] The form of transshipment problem outlined here requires this equality of total capacity and total demand.

						and	Capacities
Demands	t	t	$b_1 + t$	$b_2 + t$	$b_3 + t$		$a_1 + t$
							$a_2 + t$
							t
							t
							t

This then can be handled by exactly the same procedures as discussed above for the regular transportation problem.[22]

7.5. THE ASSIGNMENT PROBLEM

In this section we describe a particular form of the transportation problem, which, because of its very special structure, allows a different solution procedure and has a name of its own—the assignment problem.[23] Suppose that a certain number of jobs or tasks, say n, are to be accomplished and the same number of men are available to do them; each man is capable of performing each task, but their efficiencies differ. This difference is reflected in the known costs—or times, or some other measure—for each man at each job; let these known figures be denoted by k_{ij}. The object is to assign people to jobs so that total cost (or time) to accomplish all jobs is minimized. Let x_{ij} be a variable that can take on only two values—0 if man i is *not* assigned to task j and 1 if he *is* assigned; this is termed a 0-1 variable. Then the objective is to minimize

$$\sum_{i=1}^{n} \sum_{j=1}^{n} k_{ij}x_{ij}.$$

Without constraints (if the $k_{ij} > 0$) the minimum is zero, which is achieved when no assignments are made and no jobs are done. To avoid this we require that: (1) each job is accomplished by one man; that is,

$$\sum_{i=1}^{n} x_{ij} = 1 \quad \text{for each } j.$$

[22] Again, the reader interested in details might consult Dantzig [7, chap. 16] or Hadley [10, sec. 10-13].

[23] As with the transportation problem, the assignment problem name is used to describe any problem that has the structural characteristics of the example of this section. The problem arises naturally in making decisions about certain kinds of "assignments," but the framework is relevant to a much broader range of situations.

This assures that no job is left undone; it does not prevent the assignment of one man to more than one task, however. For this purpose, we also require that:[24] (2) each man is assigned to only one task; that is,

$$\sum_{j=1}^{n} x_{ij} = 1 \quad \text{for each } i.$$

The problem is therefore

minimize:
$$\sum_{i=1}^{n} \sum_{j=1}^{n} k_{ij} x_{ij}$$

subject to:
$$\begin{cases} (1) & \sum_{i=1}^{n} x_{ij} = 1 \quad \text{for } j = 1, \ldots, n, \\ (2) & \sum_{j=1}^{n} x_{ij} = 1 \quad \text{for } i = 1, \ldots, n, \end{cases}$$
(7-35)

and
$$x_{ij} = 0, 1 \quad \text{for all } i \text{ and } j.$$

If we adopt the schematic approach of the transportation problem as it is set up for the stepping-stone method, letting individuals represent origins and tasks be destinations, we have the arrangement in (7-36). The form of

Men \ Jobs	1	2	3	Capacities
1	k_{11}	k_{12}	k_{13}	1
2	k_{21}	k_{22}	k_{23}	1
3	k_{31}	k_{32}	k_{33}	1
Demands	1	1	1	

(7-36)

(7-35) and the structure in (7-36) make clear that the assignment problem is a very specialized transportation model. Because of this, and our discussion in Section 7.4, we realize that it is sufficient to specify $x_{ij} \geq 0$ in the problem statement (7-35). The results will always be integers, and the row and column totals make clear that nonzero x_{ij}'s will always be equal to one.

---

[24] The skeptical reader should write out the constraints for a 3 × 3 example to see clearly why *both* sets (1) and (2) are necessary.

The format in (7-36) also makes clear the extreme degeneracy inherent in the assignment problem. If we try to use the stepping-stone method and the northwest-corner rule, we see that row and column requirements are *always* met simultaneously, and hence our initial feasible solution contains only the *three* ($= n$) diagonal elements x_{11}, x_{22}, and x_{33}, as in (7-37). More-

Men \ Jobs	1	2	3	Capacities
1	1			1
2		1		1
3			1	1
Demands	1	1	1	

(7-37)

over, calculation of the costs associated with unoccupied cells is not as easily accomplished as in the regular transportation model, since unique closed loops do not exist for those cells. Thus the stepping-stone approach is somewhat unsatisfactory. However, an even simpler solution procedure is available; it takes advantage of the fact that row and column requirements are all 1's *and* any assignment (nonzero x_{ij}) is a 1.

Consider a particular 3×3 problem. The final row and column from (7-36) have been eliminated, since they both contain all 1's, and the objective function coefficients (the k_{ij}) occupy the entire cell; if an assignment is made, it will always be a 1, and this can be designated in some way other than by placing a 1 in the cell. The individual costs are shown in (7-38).

Men \ Jobs	1	2	3
1	10	3	8
2	5	6	2
3	4	7	4

(7-38)

We reason as follows: for each job (column) find (1) the lowest-cost man and (2) the *penalty costs* involved if other than the lowest-cost man did the job. That is, form a first penalty-cost tableau by subtracting from each entry in a column the smallest number in that column. This has been done in (7-39).

Men \ Jobs	1	2	3
1	6	0	6
2	1	3	0
3	0	4	2

(7-39)

When, as in this case, the result is one and only one zero (that is, no penalty costs) in each row and column, then an optimal assignment can be made. Here this assignment is

man 1 to job 2 at a penalty cost of 0 and a real cost of 3,
man 2 to job 3 at a penalty cost of 0 and a real cost of 2,
man 3 to job 1 at a penalty cost of 0 and a real cost of 4,

and total cost is 9.

Suppose, however, that the individual-cost and first penalty-cost tableaux had been as in (7-40) and (7-41), respectively.

Men \ Jobs	1	2	3
1	10	12	9
2	5	7	2
3	4	3	4

(7-40)

Men \ Jobs	1	2	3
1	6	9	7
2	1	4	0
3	0	0	2

(7-41)

Individual Costs   First Penalty Costs

Now man 3 has a comparative advantage on both jobs 1 and 2; yet he can be assigned to only one of them. Clearly, then, an assignment with zero penalty cost is impossible. Man 1 must be given some job, and in this case it is obvious (because the example is so small) that it is relatively less expensive to assign man 1 to job 1, leaving man 3 for job 2 and man 2 for job 3. Total cost is thus $10 + 2 + 3 = 15$. We need a method for carrying out this reasoning in larger problems in which the solution is not completely obvious by inspection.

Consider (7-41). Since *all* men cannot be assigned so that no penalty costs are incurred, we need to examine the "next best" possibilities; we must examine, for each "unwanted" man (each row with no zeros), the *further* penalty costs of forcing an assignment upon him. That is, the smallest figure in each of these *rows* should be subtracted from all other entries in the row. (In this example only row 1 is involved.) This produces (7-42),

Men \ Jobs	1	2	3
1	0	3	1
2	1	4	0
3	0	0	2

(7-42)

which might be labeled "second penalty" costs. The optimal assignment is then:

man 1 to job 1,
man 2 to job 3,
man 3 to job 2,

Although man 3 is a candidate for either job 1 or job 2, he must bypass job 1 to allow man 1 to be assigned to it.

The important characteristic that distinguishes (7-39) and (7-42) from (7-41) can be described in the following way. Each zero represents a desirable combination of a man and a job. For a three-man, three-job assignment problem, it is obvious not only that one needs a penalty-cost tableau that contains at least three zeros, but also that the zeros must be placed so that each man can be assigned and each job filled. If a row or column has at least one zero in it, we can draw a line through it, indicating that an assignment could be made. This can also be visualized as "blotting out" or "covering" a row or column. The notion of covering an assignment matrix provides a method for determining whether or not an optimal assignment can be made and (indirectly) what to do if the assignment cannot be made.[25] Consider the following 3 × 3 examples, where the tableaux show only the positions of zeros; unfilled cells contain nonzero penalty costs.

0		
	0	
		0

(7-43)

0		
0		
		0

(7-44)

0		
0		
0	0	0

(7-45)

0		0
0		
0	0	0

(7-46)

[25] This covering procedure is based on fundamental theorems in combinatorial mathematics—especially on work done by two Hungarian mathematicians, König and Egerváry; hence the procedure has come to be known as the Hungarian method.

For (7-43), three lines are necessary to cover all zeros. If the lines are drawn horizontally, they indicate an assignment of each man to a different job; if drawn vertically, each job is filled by a different man. Or any combination of three vertical and horizontal lines indicates a complete assignment. In (7-44), if a line is drawn through row 1, then a second line through row 2, to cover the zero in that row, is invalid, since it assigns man 2 to job 1, which has already been taken by man 1. This is reflected in the fact that the zeros in cells (1, 1) and (2, 1) can be eliminated by a *single* vertical line in column 1. A second line through row 3 (*or* down column 3) completes the covering. Since only two lines are *necessary*, no complete optimal assignment can be made; either $x_{11} = 1$ *or* $x_{21} = 1$ fills job 1, and then $x_{33} = 1$, so that job 2 is unfilled and either man 2 or man 1 is unassigned. Similarly, the reader should see that (7-45) can be covered in two lines and no complete assignment is possible; jobs 2 and 3 both want only man 3, and men 1 and 2 want only job 1. Finally, three horizontal or three vertical lines *are* a valid cover for (7-46). (As is any combination of vertical and horizontal lines.) The reader should be clear that the optimal assignment is $x_{13} = 1$, $x_{21} = 1$, and $x_{32} = 1$.

To return to the sample problem, in (7-41), we see that it takes three lines to eliminate the zeros if one considers only columns, but only *two* lines are needed if one uses rows (or row 3 and column 3). Since it is *possible* to cover all zeros in (7-41) with less than three lines, no complete assignment can be made and further penalty-cost calculations are required—as in (7-42). On the other hand, in (7-39) and (7-42), it is impossible to cover all zeros with less than three lines; hence complete and optimal assignments can be made.

Jobs / Men	1	2	3
1	10	5	9
2	4	3	2
3	5	3	4

(7-47)

Consider, finally, the problem that arises when there is still no obvious assignment after both the column- and row-oriented calculations described above—that is, in the tableau of "second penalty" costs. For example, let the original-cost tableau be given by (7-47). Tableaux (7-48) and (7-49) show the result of a column calculation of first penalty costs and subsequently the row calculation of second penalty costs. In (7-48) there is no assignment indicated for man 1; in (7-49) there is no possible assignment (zero cells) using each man and filling each job. Although one *can* use three horizontal—or three vertical—lines to cover the zeros in (7-49), it is also *possible* to do it using only two (row 2 and column 2). To repeat: it is the fact that it is possible to eliminate all zero cells (indicating a man-job combination) with *less than* three lines that shows that the tableau does not allow an optimal assignment.

Jobs Men	1	2	3
1	6	2	7
2	0	0	0
3	1	0	2

(7-48)

Jobs Men	1	2	3
1	4	0	5
2	0	0	0
3	1	0	2

(7-49)

First Penalty Costs   Second Penalty Costs

The way out of the dilemma is to *force* a zero to appear in at least one of the uncovered cells. [In (7-49) this means in cells (1, 1), (1, 3), (3, 1), or (3, 3), since row 2 and column 2 are eliminated by the two lines.] The rules are: find the *smallest* uncovered number [here 1, in cell (3, 1)] and *subtract* it from all uncovered cells, including itself—thus automatically producing at least one new zero. Now, although the motivation may be less clear, the solution procedure requires that this same number be *added* to those cells that are crossed by both a vertical and a horizontal line.[26] In terms of the sample arrangements in (7-45) and (7-46), this has the effect of assuring that the most unsatisfactory assignment is disallowed. In the case of (7-45), this is $x_{31} = 1$; if man 3 is given job 1, then there is no job left for either man 1 or man 2 and no man left for either job 2 or job 3. In (7-46), if $x_{31} = 1$, then man 2 cannot be assigned and job 2 cannot be filled.

Thus (7-49) is changed to (7-50). Now the minimum number of lines

---

[26] These two rules actually are shortcuts for the following: (1) subtract the smallest uncovered number (here 1) from *all* entries in the tableau, thus producing a new zero but also eliminating the old zeros by making those cells negative; therefore (2) to restore previous zeros and remove negative entries, add this same number to all covered rows *and* covered columns. The reader should convince himself that the rules in the text, above, do just this.

Jobs / Men	1	2	3
1	3	0	4
2	0	1	0
3	0	0	1

(7-50)

needed to cover all zeros is three, and hence an optimal assignment can be made:

man 1 must be given job 2;
then: man 3 must be given job 1;
this leaves: man 2 for   job 3.

If the tableau generated by the subtracting-adding procedure still does not allow an optimal assignment, the step is repeated (always on the newest tableau) as often as necessary. Minimum cost is then found by adding costs from the original tableau for the optimal assignment. In this example, since $x_{12} = x_{31} = x_{23} = 1$, the total cost [from (7-47)] is $5 + 5 + 2 = 12$.

For problems with unequal numbers of jobs and men, the convenient row and column sum properties of the examples above disappear and the solution procedure requires considerable modification. In a problem for which the objective function is to be maximized,[27] all entries in the initial tableau can be subtracted from the largest, giving a matrix of relative costs for which the minimization procedure above is appropriate.

7.6.   INTEGER PROGRAMMING

In this section we consider the consequences of including in any linear programming problem the added requirement that the solution values of the variables be whole numbers; this makes the problem a *discrete* or *integer* program. In all of the preceding examples of Chapters 6 and 7 we stopped the simplex calculations when the criterion on top-row elements indicated that an optimum had been reached. We accepted—for example,

---

[27] For example, if labor costs are the only variable costs in each of the jobs, and if the jobs in fact produce a salable product, then sales price less labor cost would give a matrix of unit "profits." Or one might have a matrix of "efficiency scores," rating each man's performance on each job; the object could be to find the maximum-efficiency assignment. Dantzig [7, chap. 15] has additional details.

in (6-27)—the result that one or more of the x_i^0 were not whole numbers. Clearly there are situations in which a noninteger result is not disturbing—for example, if x_1^0 and x_2^0 are dimensions of a rectangular field, then to find that $x_1^0 = 2\frac{1}{2}$ feet, $x_2^0 = 3\frac{3}{4}$ feet is completely useful information. If the optimal number of cases of product A that should be produced during the next quarter, x_1^0, turns out to be 1243.3, one is not too uncomfortable (because the relative error is so small) in rounding to 1243, or perhaps even 1240.[28] Suppose, however, that x_1^0 represents the optimal number of dams to build above a certain point on a river for hydroelectric purposes, and that in a particular problem $x_1^0 = 2.6$. Now clearly the *relative* error involved in rounding (either to 3 or to 2) is not small, and one would be far more comfortable if the problem could be *required* to generate a whole-number answer for x_1^0.

Sometimes, then, noninteger answers are acceptable because the units of measurement (feet, dollars) are easily interpreted in fractions, at least up to some point. In other cases, noninteger answers are tolerable because the relative error incurred by rounding is small.[29] Sometimes, however, only whole numbers make sense. This was true of the dam example and is generally true of problems in which optimal solution values are relatively small and represent highly indivisible units. It is also the case for other classes of problems. For example, so-called capital budgeting problems, with upper limits on the total amount of financial outlay, define $x_j = 0$ to mean that project j is not undertaken or financed and $x_j = 1$ to mean that it is. Then if, for all j, x_j has a lower bound of 0 ($x_j \geq 0$) and an upper bound of 1 ($x_j \leq 1$) *and* x_j is required to be integer, only solutions of 0 or 1 can result. In other problems, integer values are required because optimal solutions refer to items on a numbered list. For example, let ten cities in a routing problem be listed and each given a label from 1 to 10. Then a solution to certain kinds of problems would be, for example, $x_t = 7, x_{t+1} = 3$, meaning at time t go to city 7, and then (time $t + 1$) go to city 3. Thus in any such indexing or labeling situation, the optimal solution must consist entirely of integers. Moreover, it turns out that several kinds of nonlinear problems can be solved by addition of integer-valued variables.[30]

[28] The accuracy of one's input data—the a_{ij}'s, r_i's and p_j's—is obviously relevant. Extremely precise solutions are not very meaningful if derived from a problem with relatively inaccurate data and coefficients. The areas of *stochastic* and *parametric* programming deal with the effects of probability distributions of coefficient values on the accuracy or stability of solution values. These techniques are beyond the scope of this book; the interested reader is referred to Dantzig [7, chap. 25] and other references cited there.

[29] Note that in a maximization problem, with "less than or equal to" constraints, the rounding must usually be downward to maintain feasibility. The reverse is generally true in a minimization problem.

[30] The interested reader should consult Baumol [2] and Hadley [11] for further details.

The geometry of integer programs

A simple example will illustrate the particulars of the integer programming problem and will indicate (at least geometrically) what the solution procedure must accomplish. When only whole-number nonnegative solution values of x_1 and x_2 are allowed, the character of the feasible region alters drastically, since, within the bounds set by the constraints, only the integer points or *lattice points* are feasible. Thus the majority of the space enclosed by the constraints becomes infeasible. Figure 7.4 illustrates a feasible region in the noninteger as well as integer cases.

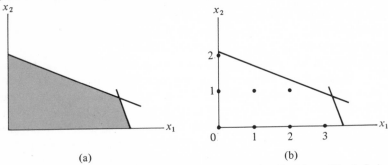

(a)   (b)

Figure 7.4.   (a) Feasible Region, Noninteger Problem (Shaded Area),
(b) Feasible Region, Integer Problem (Black Dots)

We see from Figure 7.4(b) that the fundamental and extremely useful linear programming property that the optimum is always at a corner of the feasible region defined by the linear inequalities now no longer holds. In general the integer optimum will be *interior* to this feasible region. (In some cases, but not in general, the simplex arithmetic of Chapter 6 will lead to an optimal solution that happens also to be all integer.) By adding objective function contours to Figure 7.4(b), we can also see in general why rounding—downward, so as not to violate the constraints—is unsatisfactory. Consider Figure 7.5. The optimal noninteger solution is approximately $x_1^0 = 3\frac{1}{4}$, $x_2^0 = \frac{3}{4}$. Rounding to the next lowest integers would

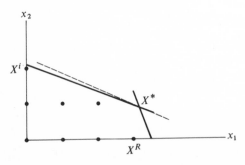

Figure 7.5.   Noninteger versus Integer Optimum

give $x_1^R = 3$, $x_2^R = 0$, which is clearly inferior—from the point of view of objective function value—to $x_1^i = 0$, $x_2^i = 2$. What is needed, therefore, is an algebraic procedure for moving from a noninteger optimum like $x_1^0 = 3\frac{1}{4}$, $x_2^0 = \frac{3}{4}$ to the associated integer-valued optimum (here $x_1^i = 0$, $x_2^i = 2$) when we do not have the luxury of an accurate geometric picture in front of us.

In Figure 7.6 we have reproduced the feasible region from Figure 7.4(b) with the added dotted lines that connect the "outermost" feasible lattice points. The convex region formed by the x_1 and x_2 axes (as lower bounds) and these dotted lines (as upper bounds) has two useful properties: (1) it includes, on its boundaries or in its interior, all of the feasible lattice points from Figure 7.4(b), and (2) each of its extreme points is also a lattice point. Hence (and this is generally true, but we do not prove it) the'optimal integer solution to the problem whose inequality constraints define the

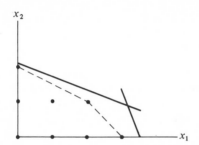

Figure 7.6.   Reduced Feasible Region for Integer Problem

boundaries in Figure 7.6 will occur at an extreme point of the feasible region whose boundaries are the dotted lines in the same figure. Thus, a solution method for integer programs would be one that removed, through the addition of *constraints*, the "excess" feasible region—the area between the solid and the dotted boundaries. This is, in effect, what we do; the procedure was developed by R. Gomory and is known as the Gomory method for integer programming problems.

The algebra of integer programs

The first step in solving a linear program with the added requirement that all solution values be whole numbers is to apply the simplex method of Chapter 6. It is always possible that the solution will happen to be all integers; if so, the problem is solved.[31] If not, one or more new constraints must be added. We now indicate how this is done.

---

[31] We consider here only the *all-integer* programming problem in which all x_j^0 are required to be whole numbers. Variations in the technique handle the *mixed* problem in which only a subset of the x_j^0 is required to be integer while the rest may have fractional values.

Consider a 2×2 maximization problem that has generated the optimal noninteger tableau shown in (7-51). The two basic (and optimal) variables are labeled x_1^0 and x_2^0 for convenience; they represent any combination of original and slack variables—except, presumably, both slacks, which would represent the origin and a rather uninteresting maximum. Similarly, x_1^{nb} and x_2^{nb} represent the two variables excluded from the optimal basis. Clearly either a_{10} or a_{20} (or both) must be noninteger; otherwise the optimum would be integer-valued and the integer programming problem would be solved, since the optimal values are $x_1^0 = a_{10}$ and $x_2^0 = a_{20}$.

	x_1^{nb}	x_2^{nb}
π	a_{00}	a_{01}	a_{02}
x_1^0	a_{10}	a_{11}	a_{12}
x_2^0	a_{20}	a_{21}	a_{22}

(7-51)

For purposes of exposition only, we assume that only a_{10} is fractional. Recall the way in which information is read from a row of any tableau in the simplex calculations. Each line expresses an included (basic) variable as a linear combination of the excluded (nonbasic) ones and a constant. For example, from the x_1 line:

$$x_1^0 = a_{10} + a_{11}x_1^{nb} + a_{12}x_2^{nb}. \qquad (7\text{-}52)$$

Or, rearranging,

$$a_{10} = x_1^0 - a_{11}x_1^{nb} - a_{12}x_2^{nb}. \qquad (7\text{-}53)$$

Since it is the existence of a fractional part in a_{10} that is spoiling the solution, we consider the two aspects of a_{10}: its whole-number, or integer, part, I_{10}, and its nonnegative fractional part, f_{10}.[32] In fact, we break up each of the coefficients a_{1j}, in the x_1 row, into an integer (I_{1j}) and a nonnegative fractional (f_{1j}) part.[33] Thus, (7-53) becomes (where the negative signs are absorbed, where necessary, into the I_{1j})

$$(I_{10} + f_{10}) = x_1^0 + (I_{11} + f_{11})x_1^{nb} + (I_{12} + f_{12})x_2^{nb}. \qquad (7\text{-}54)$$

Or, subtracting I_{10} from both sides and rearranging

$$f_{10} = x_1^0 + (f_{11}x_1^{nb} + f_{12}x_2^{nb}) + (I_{11}x_1^{nb} + I_{12}x_2^{nb}) - I_{10}. \qquad (7\text{-}55)$$

---

[32] Since a_{10} is always nonnegative, so is f_{10}.

[33] If an a_{ij} is negative, say, $-3\frac{3}{4}$, it is thought of as $-4 + \frac{1}{4}$, and its nonnegative fractional part is thus $\frac{1}{4}$.

Let

$$F = f_{11}x_1^{nb} + f_{12}x_2^{nb} \equiv \sum_{i=1}^{2} f_{1i}x_i^{nb};$$

then

$$f_{10} - F = x_1^0 + I_{11}x_1^{nb} + I_{12}x_2^{nb} - I_{10}. \tag{7-56}$$

Since we are concerned with linear programming problems in which all x_j are required to be integer, all slack variables are also integers. The reason is that any of the original constraints in the problem that involved fractional a_{ij}'s or a fractional right-hand side, r_i, can be converted to all-integer a_{ij} and r_i through multiplication of both sides of the inequality by the lowest common denominator for the fractional parts. Thus, whether x_1^0 represents an original (x_j) or slack (s_i) variable, an all-integer solution will make the right-hand side of (7-56) an integer. Then, of course, the left-hand side of (7-56) must also be an integer. But since (1) $1 > f_{10} \geq 0$, and (2) $F \geq 0$ (by definition), the left-hand side of (7-56) can be an integer *only if*

$$F \geq f_{10}. \tag{7-57}$$

[This is a *necessary* condition for the left-hand side of (7-56) to be a whole number; it is clearly not specific enough to also be *sufficient*.] And it is precisely from (7-57) that we form an additional constraint for the problem, to be added to the optimal tableau to generate further pivoting. Replacing F by its definition in terms of x_i^{nb}'s, (7-57) is

$$\sum_{i=1}^{2} f_{1i}x_i^{nb} \geq f_{10}, \tag{7-58}$$

or, attaching a nonnegative slack variable, s_1^G (to denote the slack in the first Gomory constraint),

$$\sum_{i=1}^{2} f_{1i}x_i^{nb} - s_1^G = f_{10}. \tag{7-59}$$

Finally, expressing the slack variable, as is usual for simplex arithmetic, as a function of the nonbasic variables,

$$s_1^G = -f_{10} + \sum_{i=1}^{2} f_{1i}x_i^{nb} = -f_{10} + f_{11}x_1^{nb} + f_{12}x_2^{nb}. \tag{7-60}$$

This becomes an additional constraint that must hold if an integer solution is found; it is in exactly the correct form to add to (7-51), which is done in (7-61).

	x_1^{nb}	x_2^{nb}
π	a_{00}	a_{01}	a_{02}
x_1^0	a_{10}	a_{11}	a_{12}
x_2^0	a_{20}	a_{21}	a_{22}
s_1^G	$-f_{10}$	f_{11}	f_{12}

$$(7\text{-}61)$$

Since $-f_{10}$ is clearly negative, the primal solution in (7-61) is now infeasible; pivoting on a *positive* element in the s_1^G row will remove the infeasibility, since the simplex rules require dividing pivot *row* elements by the *negative* of the pivot element. Thus the pivot *row* selection has been made first. The ordinary simplex decisions of Chapter 6 have been reversed. It appears that (7-61) has been viewed as if turned on its side; it is just that, and the procedure is in fact called the *dual simplex method*. The pivot column is therefore that one, among those with positive elements in the pivot row, for which $|a_{0j}/a_{ij}|$ is minimum.[34] Then pivoting follows exactly the rules of Chapter 6. The new tableau (after pivoting) may still contain noninteger solution values—in the zeroth column. If so, another Gomory constraint is added, with coefficients derived exactly as described above. In general, if there are several noninteger a_{i0}, a good rule seems to be to select from among those associated with x_j variables (and not slacks) that one with the largest fractional part.[35] We now illustrate with an example.

Example

$$
\begin{aligned}
\text{Maximize:} \quad & 2x_1 + 6x_2 \\
\text{subject to:} \quad & 3x_1 + x_2 \le 5, \\
& 4x_1 + 4x_2 \le 9, \\
\text{and} \quad & x_1, x_2 \ge 0 \quad \textit{and integer.}
\end{aligned}
$$

$$(7\text{-}62)$$

The reader should work through the one pivot step necessary to produce the optimal noninteger tableau (7-63).

---

[34] This prevents us from destroying dual feasibility by turning a top-row coefficient positive. (Recall the negative signs attached to the top-row labels when reading the dual solution.) The (primal) simplex method of Chapter 6 maintains *primal* feasibility at all times and pivots until dual feasibility is also achieved (negative top-row elements). The dual simplex method maintains dual feasibility and pivots to achieve primal feasibility also.

[35] Some problems occasionally fail to converge on the optimal integer solution after a "reasonable" number of Gomory constraints have been added. Usually, however, the procedure works well.

		x_1	s_2
π	$13\frac{1}{2}$	-4	$-1\frac{1}{2}$
s_1	$2\frac{3}{4}$	-2	$\frac{1}{4}$
x_2	$2\frac{1}{4}$	-1	$-\frac{1}{4}$

(7-63)

Although the fractional part of s_1—$\frac{3}{4}$—is larger than that of x_2—$\frac{1}{4}$—we begin by concentrating on fractional parts of x variables in the optimal basis. Thus, from the bottom row of (7-63), parallel to (7-52), we have

$$x_2^0 = 2\frac{1}{4} - x_1 - \tfrac{1}{4}s_2, \qquad (7\text{-}52')$$

or, rearranging,

$$2\tfrac{1}{4} = x_2^0 + x_1 + \tfrac{1}{4}s_2. \qquad (7\text{-}53')$$

Extracting nonnegative fractional parts,

$$(2 + \tfrac{1}{4}) = x_2^0 + (1 + 0)x_1 + (0 + \tfrac{1}{4})s_2, \qquad (7\text{-}54')$$

and, rearranging,

$$\tfrac{1}{4} = x_2^0 + (0x_1 + \tfrac{1}{4}s_2) + (1x_1 + 0s_2) - 2. \qquad (7\text{-}55')$$

Therefore the Gomory constraint to be added is

$$0x_1 + \tfrac{1}{4}s_2 \geq \tfrac{1}{4}, \qquad (7\text{-}58')$$

or, with slack variable s_1^G,

$$s_1^G = -\tfrac{1}{4} + 0x_1 + \tfrac{1}{4}s_2. \qquad (7\text{-}60')$$

In (7-60') the new slack variable has been expressed as a linear combination of the two excluded variables in the optimal noninteger tableau (7-63) and a constant. Thus the new constraint can be added directly to that tableau, as in (7-64).

		x_1	s_2
π	$13\frac{1}{2}$	-4	$-1\frac{1}{2}$
s_1	$2\frac{3}{4}$	-2	$\frac{1}{4}$
x_2	$2\frac{1}{4}$	-1	$-\frac{1}{4}$
s_1^G	$-\frac{1}{4}$	0	$\frac{1}{4}^*$

(7-64)

Since all that we need are the *coefficients* relating s_1^G to x_1 and s_2 and a constant term, the entire derivation can be done in simple tabular form, showing only the coefficients. From (7-63),

$$2\tfrac{1}{4} \qquad -1 \qquad -\tfrac{1}{4}. \tag{7-52''}$$

Now change signs of all elements but the leftmost,

$$2\tfrac{1}{4} \qquad 1 \qquad \tfrac{1}{4}, \tag{7-53''}$$

and find the nonnegative fractional parts:

$$\tfrac{1}{4} \qquad 0 \qquad \tfrac{1}{4}. \tag{7-55''}$$

Finally, change the sign of the leftmost element:

$$-\tfrac{1}{4} \qquad 0 \qquad \tfrac{1}{4}. \tag{7-60''}$$

These are exactly the coefficients for the s_1^G row that is added to (7-63).

Pivoting *must* be done in the bottom row. Among positive elements in this row, examine the absolute values of a_{0j}/a_{ij} and select as pivot column that one for which this ratio is smallest. In this case it is the s_2 column; hence the lower right element has been starred and must act as the pivot. Using the rules of Chapter 6, we obtain the optimal integer tableau with only one added constraint.

		x_1	s_1^G
π	12	-4	-6
s_1	3	-2	1
x_2	2	-1	-1
s_2	1	0	4

$$\tag{7-65}$$

$x_1^0 = 0$, $x_2^0 = 2$, and the objective function has a value of 12. Here the optimal integer solution *could* have been obtained by rounding downward; this is very often not the case, as several of the problems at the end of this chapter will demonstrate. Moreover, to repeat: in general it will require more than one new (Gomory) constraint before the final integer result is obtained.

Consider the geometry of this linear program and of the added constraint. The feasible region for the original problem, (7-62), without the integer requirement, would be given by the heavy lines in Figure 7.7. The heavy dashed line gives the location of the optimal noninteger objective function contour, as shown in (7-63). Consider now the inequality form of the added

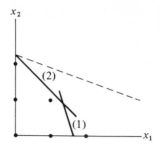

Figure 7.7.   Feasible Region for Problem (7-62)

Gomory constraint (7-58′): $0x_1 + \frac{1}{4}s_2 \geq \frac{1}{4}$. From the original problem, (7-62), we know that $s_2 = 9 - 4x_1 - 4x_2$. Thus, in terms of x_1 and x_2 only—so that we can show it in the x_1x_2 space of the original problem in Figure 7.7—

$$0x_1 + \tfrac{1}{4}(9 - 4x_1 - 4x_2) \geq \tfrac{1}{4},$$

or

$$x_1 + x_2 \leq 2. \tag{7-66}$$

We add this to Figure 7.7 with a dotted line and see that this new constraint connects lattice points (0, 2) and (1, 1) and hence, because of the slope of

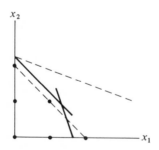

Figure 7.8.   Added Gomory Constraint for Problem (7-62)

the objective function, has "cut away" enough of the feasible region to expose the optimal integer corner. It happens that in this problem exactly the same Gomory constraint is added (in x_1x_2 space) if the coefficients are taken from the s_1 row in (7-63).

As a very brief digression, we note that imposition of an integer require-ment on a primal problem influences the character of the associated dual. Since each primal constraint has an associated dual variable, it is clear that the requirement of an integer solution to the primal will add variables to the dual problem. For example, the noninteger solution to problem (7-62), shown in (7-63), gives $v_1 = 0$, $v_2 = 1\frac{1}{2}$, $t_1 = 4$, $t_2 = 0$. In the integer solution, (7-65), we find $v_1 = 0$, $v_2 = 0$ (because, in the integer solution, neither constraint is binding; see Figure 7.8), $t_1 = 4$, $t_2 = 0$, and $v_1^G = 6$ is the value of the dual variable associated with the new primal constraint. These added dual variables, and the fact that most primal constraints will be met as inequalities in the optimal integer solution and hence have zero-valued dual variables, present fundamental and interesting problems for the interpretation of the dual to an integer programming problem.[36]

7.7.   GAME THEORY AND LINEAR PROGRAMMING

Fundamentals of game theory

In this section we examine briefly a model offering a theory of action in situations involving conflicts of interest between individuals or groups of any kind. Our coverage is intentionally brief;[37] of principal interest is the fact that a particular class of game theory models can be expressed as linear programs. This is important because (1) it therefore provides a straightforward method of solution for the gaming problem (the simplex method) and (2) it means that the primal-dual theorems can be applied, providing interesting insights and conclusions for the game theory formulation.

We concentrate our attention on two-person zero-sum game situations.[38] "Person" should be interpreted to mean either individuals or collections of individuals—political parties, firms, countries, or whatever. The "zero-sum" character of the situations means that the two persons are rivals in the strictest sense; their interests are diametrically opposed, so that one's loss is exactly the other's gain. Assume that the two persons (or "players"), call them A and B, are both facing a decision in which each has several choices—price to charge for a new product, number of men to send into a

[36] For further details on methods and uses of integer programming, the reader is referred to Balinski [1], Beale [3], Dantzig [7, chap. 26], Simonnard [19, chaps. 8 and 9], Hadley [11, chap. 8], Saaty [18], and references therein cited. An alternative computational approach, the so-called "branch-and-bound" method, is discussed in Lawler and Wood [13]. The original Gomory paper, "An Algorithm for Integer Solutions to Linear Programs," is reprinted in Graves and Wolfe [9, pp. 269–302].

[37] The interested reader is referred to any of the game theory books (which are obvious by their titles) in the References at the end of this chapter.

[38] For more advanced discussions of games that involve more than two persons and/or that are not zero-sum, the reader is again referred to game theory texts.

battle, attitude to adopt at a labor-management bargaining session, and the like. Suppose, for each pair of decisions—a choice by A and a *simultaneous* choice by B—that we can evaluate the outcome.[39] For example, if firm A decides to charge 79 cents for a new product and firm B chooses not to change the price of its existing product, the outcome may be that A will capture 60 percent of a given market (in which the two firms are rivals), which represents a 15 percent *gain* for A and a 15 percent *loss* for B from their current 45-55 percent shares. If we measure outcomes (or "payoffs") in terms of A's market share gains (and thus B's losses), this set of choices has a payoff of 15. Had the outcome been just reversed—B's share going up to 70 and A's declining to 30 percent—this payoff would be recorded as -15.

Thus we can form a table with a row for each of A's m possible choices of action or "strategies" A_i ($i = 1, \ldots, m$) and a column for each of B's n alternatives or "strategies" B_j ($j = 1, \ldots, n$). If we enter the payoffs for each pair of decisions, A_i in conjunction with B_j, we have a "payoff matrix." The underlying philosophy of the theory of games is that player A wants to act so that the *least* gain he may expect in the conflict situation with B is as *large* as possible. (Recall that the payoff matrix is written in terms of A's gains.) Similarly, the theory requires that B's objective be to make his *largest* possible loss as *small* as possible, regardless of the alternative that A selects. *Provided* that both players have this kind of goal, then the theory of games specifies how they should act—it provides for both players an optimal selection of strategies, or a "grand strategy" of action.

Consider a small example where both players have two strategies.[40] Suppose the payoff matrix (in dollars) were as shown in (7-67). We see, for

	Player B B_1	B_2
A_1	10	2
A_2	6	4

Player A

(7-67)

example, that if player A chooses his second alternative and at the same

---

[39] In a great many situations of conflict a single, unambiguous measure of the outcome, or payoff, is not easy to find. This problem, which is behind much of the recent work on measurement of utility, takes us beyond the scope of this book.

[40] That is, $m = n = 2$. There is, in general, absolutely no need for a payoff matrix to be square.

time B chooses his first, the outcome is that A gains \$6 (and hence B loses \$6).[41] The game theory philosophy now requires:

Player A must examine the *worst* outcome resulting from each of his possible strategies; that is, he must find the smallest number in each row. He thus forms a column vector of row minima: $\begin{bmatrix} 2 \\ 4 \end{bmatrix}$. Now he chooses the action associated with the largest (here larger) of these minima—4. That is, he selects his second alternative. In general, with m choices for player A and n choices for player B, A's problem is to find $\min_j a_{ij}$ for each i ($i = 1, \ldots, m$)—that is, the smallest entry in each row—and to select $\max_i (\min_j a_{ij})$, the largest of these numbers. His choice, then, is determined by *maximinimization*.

Player B, at the same time, examines the most he can lose for each of his choices (which is, from his point of view, the worst outcome). That is, he finds the largest number in each column. These column maxima can be expressed in a row vector: [10   4]. Player B selects the action associated with the smallest (here smaller) of these maxima, namely 4, or his second strategy.[42] Again, in general terms, B selects $\max_i a_{ij}$ for each j ($j = 1, \ldots, n$)—the largest element in each column—and then finds $\min_j (\max_i a_{ij})$, the smallest of these numbers. His problem, therefore, is described as one of *minimaximization*.

In the example, (7-67), the maximum of the row minima and the minimum of the column maxima were equal, namely 4. When this is true (and we will soon see that it need not be), this common number is termed the "value of the game," and moreover the game is said to have a "saddle point" or equilibrium point at that value.

The term saddle point is descriptive of the characteristics of the payoffs around the equilibrium point. It is easier to visualize in a larger problem, in which each player has many alternatives. Imagine the payoff matrix in three dimensions, with heights above each square representing the payoff for that pair of choices. Viewed from A's perspective, the "valley" in each

---

[41] Clearly this matrix does not represent a "fair" game, since all entries are positive and hence A is certain to win. To make it a fair game, A should pay B

$$\$(10 + 6 + 2 + 4)/4 = \$5\tfrac{1}{2}$$

each time the simultaneous choices are made—that is, each time the game is "played." The \$5$\tfrac{1}{2}$ represents A's expected winnings.

[42] The fact that both players select their second alternative does not mean that there is necessarily anything similar about their resulting actions. Choice 2 for player A may mean "introduce the new product at 79 cents" while choice 2 for B may be "don't lower price."

row is found, and then the choice (row) corresponding to the highest valley is taken. B, on the other hand, views "mountain tops" in each column and selects the column with the lowest of these peaks. A saddle point exists when the highest valley corresponds to the lowest peak; it is not unlike a mountain pass in shape.[43]

Note why this can be characterized as an equilibrium point. If either player knew *in advance* which choice his opponent was going to make, he would not alter his own choice. If A knew that B would choose B_2, A still would want A_2 (he wins 4 rather than 2); if B knew that A_2 would be selected, he still would want B_2 (better to give up 4 than 6). When a payoff matrix has a saddle point, the choices by the two players that lead to this point are called *pure strategies*. These have the characteristic that each player knows the payoff for him will be better if his opponent departs from minimax or maximin reasoning.[44]

Mixed strategies

Consider now the more interesting case in which an equilibrium point does not exist. An example is provided by (7-68). Player A, the maximini-

---

[43] Saddle points will be defined and discussed more fully in Chapter 8, since they appear in nonlinear programming theory. As a prelude to that discussion, we make the following observations. At the saddle point,

$$\max_i \left(\min_j a_{ij} \right) = \min_j \left(\max_i a_{ij} \right);$$

denote this value by a_{i*j*}. By definition,

$$\max_i \left(\min_j a_{ij} \right) \geq \min_j a_{ij} \qquad \text{for any } i;$$

denote the right-hand side by a_{ij*}. Similarly,

$$\min_j \left(\max_i a_{ij} \right) \leq \max_i a_{ij} \qquad \text{for any } j;$$

denote this right-hand side by a_{i*j}. Thus a characteristic feature of the saddle point a_{i*j*} is that

$$a_{i*j} \geq a_{i*j*} \geq a_{ij*}.$$

[44] Reasoning that is, of course, ultraconservative. Each player assumes the worst in each possible case and then tries to make the worst as good as possible (for himself). For example, in (7-67), player A has ignored the fact that he *could* win 10 by selecting A_1. Maximin strategy provides one criterion in situations of decision making under uncertainty (when the probabilities of occurrence of the various "states of nature" are unknown). This "pessimistic criterion," suggested by A. Wald, says that one should act as if he were opposing a rational opponent in a two-person zero-sum game situation. This provides protection against the worst in situations of uncertainty. For an introduction to decision theory, the reader is referred to Baumol [2, chap. 24], Chernoff and Moses [6], Luce and Raiffa [14], or Raiffa [17].

Player B
B_1 B_2

	B_1	B_2
A_1	3	6
A_2	5	4

Player A

(7-68)

mizer, would look at the row minima, 3 and 4, and take A_2, since 4 is the larger. Player B would select B_1, since 5 is smaller than 6; he is minimaximizing. Here the maximum of the row minima, 4, is different from the minimum of the column maxima, 5. This tells us that there is no saddle, or equilibrium, point. Choices A_2, B_1 are unstable in the following sense. Although A would still prefer A_2 if he knew *in advance* that B_1 would be used, the same is not true for player B. Given advance knowledge of A_2, B would switch to B_2, thus giving up only 4 instead of 5. But *then*, A could think this far ahead, too, and realizing that B would be led to B_2, he would actually select A_1, thus getting 6. But B could *also* think this far ahead, and would thus choose B_1; and so on.

Clearly, then, player A should make his choice in such a way that B cannot know in advance which A_i will result; and B should do the same. That is, the players should assign *probabilities* to each of their strategies and then make their selections on the basis of some chance device (such as drawing from a pack of cards) that properly reflects the probabilities to be assigned to the different outcomes. For example, if player A decided that the probabilities on A_1 and A_2 should be $\frac{1}{4}$ and $\frac{3}{4}$, respectively, then he could draw from a regular pack of 52 cards and play A_1 if he drew a heart, A_2 otherwise, since the probability of getting a heart is $\frac{13}{52} = \frac{1}{4}$.[45] In this way neither player A *nor his opponent* can know ahead of time which A_i will be chosen; and B should do likewise. This mode of action has the following rather remarkable result: A assures himself of gaining *at least* 4 and B is assured of losing *at most* 5. That is, both players have the possibility of bettering what they had (individually) expected when examining pure strategies—4 for A, 5 for B.

Each player in this two-person zero-sum game situation wants to protect himself against the uncertainty of what his opponent is going to choose. That is, each wants to be assured that the outcome to him will be the same *no matter which choice his opponent makes.* This is the whole point of using *mixed strategies* (that is, assigning probabilities to each of the pure strat-

---

[45] Clearly, if the game situation with the same payoffs is encountered regularly (say, weekly), then one could use the probabilities to determine the relative frequencies with which the alternatives were chosen (for example, in the next four weeks A would use A_1 once—say in the third week— and A_2 the other three times). If choices represent allocation of budget or promotional effort, for example, the probabilities could be translated into amounts of money or hours of effort, and so on.

egies). Consider, then, the problem for A in (7-68). Since he has only two choices, A_1 and A_2, we can give them probabilities p and $(1-p)$. Thus, if B selects his first alternative, B_1, A's *expected gain* will be $3p + 5(1-p)$; if B_2 is chosen by player B, A's expected gain will be $6p + 4(1-p)$. Since A wants the outcome for him to be the same no matter what choice B actually makes, he wants

$$3p + 5(1-p) = 6p + 4(1-p)$$

—that is, $-2p + 5 = 2p + 4$, or $p = \frac{1}{4}$ (and hence $1 - p = \frac{3}{4}$). Thus A should make his selection in such a way that A_2 has three times as much chance of being selected as A_1 (as in the deck-of-cards example).

B's reasoning is the same. His problem is to find the probabilities for B_1 and B_2, call them q and $(1-q)$, respectively. If A_1 is selected, the outcome for B will be $3q + 6(1-q)$; if A_2, it will be $5q + 4(1-q)$. And B wants

$$3q + 6(1-q) = 5q + 4(1-q),$$

—that is, $-3q + 6 = q + 4$, or $q = \frac{1}{2}$ (and hence $1 - q = \frac{1}{2}$). Thus B should select his alternatives in such a way that B_1 and B_2 are equally likely (for example, by tossing a fair coin, where heads $=$ select B_1). We add these probabilities to the information in (7-68).

			Player B	
	Probabilities		$\frac{1}{2}$	$\frac{1}{2}$
		Choices	B_1	B_2
Player A	$\frac{1}{4}$	A_1	3	6
	$\frac{3}{4}$	A_2	5	4

(7-69)

Consider now A's expected gains. They are $3(\frac{1}{4}) + 5(\frac{3}{4}) = 6(\frac{1}{4}) + 4(\frac{3}{4}) = 4\frac{1}{2}$. Similarly, for B: $3(\frac{1}{2}) + 6(\frac{1}{2}) = 5(\frac{1}{2}) + 4(\frac{1}{2}) = 4\frac{1}{2}$. Thus by randomizing in this way—using mixed strategies—each player has gained (in the expected-value sense) over what he expected from examining only pure strategies (4 for A, 5 for B).

For larger games in which no saddle point exists—games in which either player (or both) has more than two strategy alternatives—the computation of optimal mixed strategies becomes much more complicated. This is largely because the defining characteristic of such strategies was somewhat misrepresented above in the 2 × 2 case (in the interests of simplicity at that point). Stated completely, an optimal mixed strategy for a player has the property that it gives the same expected payoff to that player when used against any of his opponent's pure strategies that are included in the opponent's set of optimal mixed strategies. In the 2×2 case when there was no saddle point, both players would use *both* their strategies; hence both columns and both rows were in the set of optimal mixed strategies for one player or the other. Therefore, for example, in order to write equations for player A of the same sort used to find p in the 2×2 case, one needs to know *which* strategies will be in B's set. But B's good strategies will depend on which ones A has selected, and the problem appears circular.

Three observations help us out of the dilemma. The first, a property of two-person zero-sum games arising from their relationship to linear programming models (a relationship we are about to explore), is that in an $m \times n$ game, where player A has m pure strategies and player B has n, if $m < n$ then player B's optimal mixed strategy will contain at most m of his n alternatives. Similarly, if $m > n$, player A will use at most n strategies in his optimal mix.[46] Thus the optimal mixed strategies for both players in a 2×26 game will come from some particular 2×2 subgame; in a 15×3 game, both players will utilize at most three of their strategies. Of course, in a 3×10 game, there are $C_3^{10} = 120$ 3×3 sub-games that, in principle, must be examined.

Second, the problem of size is sometimes alleviated through use of the concept of dominance. Since we have chosen to express payoffs in terms of the gains of A (the row player), it is clear that any row, i, of a payoff matrix that contained elements that were, column by column, *smaller* than those in some other row, i', would never be chosen by A. He could always do better by selecting i' over i; row i' is said to *dominate* row i. Thus, for computational purposes, the dominat*ed* row, i, can be removed from consideration.[47] By the same sort of reasoning, player B would never select a column j if another, j', had smaller (or, more correctly, no larger) elements, row by row. That is, dominat*ing* columns can be eliminated. In this way game matrices can sometimes be reduced in size.

Third, it is useful to observe that there is a very simple graphical method for solving $2 \times n$ (or $m \times 2$) games. Consider the following 2×4 payoff matrix (remember, a negative number is a *gain* for B):

	B_1	B_2	B_3	B_4
A_1	-6	-1	4	3
A_2	7	-2	-5	7

$$(7\text{-}70)$$

---

[46] The reader must remember that we are concerned here with games that do not have a saddle point. One *always* looks for a saddle point at the outset; this is an extremely simple scanning operation (max of row min, min of column max). If one is found, the work is finished. If not, we proceed as described in the text.

[47] In fact, elements in the dominated row need only be *no larger* than those in the dominating row; if they were equal, player A would be indifferent between them.

It is clear that B_4 is a dominating column (compare with B_2; $3 > -1$, $7 > -2$) and could be eliminated. We retain it, however, for purposes of exposition. We use two vertical axes to represent the outcomes associated with A's two possible strategies, A_1 and A_2. Then the elements in the first column, associated with B_1, can be located on the appropriate axis; -6 on

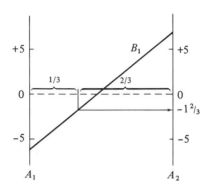

Figure 7.9. Graphics for B_1 from the Game in (7-70)

A_1 and $+7$ on A_2. We then connect the points. Consider any other point on this line, say the one that is one-third of the way from A_1 to A_2. (We can imagine the horizontal separation between A_1 and A_2 to be defined as one unit; this in no way interferes with the scale used on the two axes themselves.) Its value, $-1\frac{2}{3}$ (read off either axis), represents A's expected winnings against B_1 if he assigns probabilities $\frac{2}{3}$ to A_1 and $\frac{1}{3}$ to A_2.[48] Thus the line connecting -6 on the A_1 axis and $+7$ on the A_2 axis represents A's expected gains against B_1 for all possible probabilities p_1 and p_2 (p_1, $p_2 \geq 0$ and $p_1 + p_2 = 1$) with which he can choose A_1 and A_2. On the same pair of axes we can show A's expected gains against *each* of the other strategies available to B (Figure 7.10). Note that we can accommodate as many strategies (lines) as we wish for player B; all that is required is that one of the players (here A) has only two alternatives. The lines represent A's expected gains. Since A is the maximinimizer—that is, considers, for each of his courses of action, the worst possible outcome and then attempts to find the best among these worst—it should be clear that the heavy lower line represents A's worst outcomes for all possible mixed strategies, plus the pure strategies A_1 only (worst payoff: -6) and A_2 only (worst payoff: -5). Player A wants to find the highest point on this lower "envelope," and thus he will select the mix of A_1 and A_2 given by the starred point. Since we chose to call the distance between A_1 and A_2 one unit, p_1 will be

---

[48] In the figure the distance to the *nearer* axis (A_1) gives the probability for the *farther* strategy (A_2). Clearly if player A always chose A_1—that is, if $p_1 = 1$, he would be on the A_1 axis, 0 distance from A_1 ($p_2 = 0$) and 1 unit away from A_2 ($p_1 = 1$).

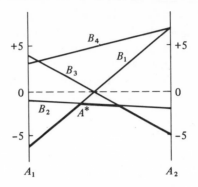

Figure 7.10. Graphics for the Entire Game in (7-70)

given by the length of the line from A^* to A_2 (perpendicular to it, of course), and p_2 will be the distance from A^* to A_1.

The following fact is possibly even more important: the two strategies for B that intersect at the point A^* represent the two that should be contained in B's optimal mix. That is, we could ignore the determination of p_1 and p_2 through measurement of the distances to the axes and instead solve the following 2×2 game by the simple methods discussed earlier.

	B_1	B_2
A_1	-6	-1
A_2	7	-2

Since $p_1 + p_2 = 1$ and $q_1 + q_2 = 1$, we have for A

$$-6p_1 + 7(1 - p_1) = -p_1 - 2(1 - p_1),$$
$$p_1 = \tfrac{9}{14},$$
$$p_2 = \tfrac{5}{14},$$

and for B

$$-6q_1 - (1 - q_1) = 7q_1 - 2(1 - q_1),$$
$$q_1 = \tfrac{1}{14},$$
$$q_2 = \tfrac{13}{14}.$$

Thus, in the original game, (7-70), A's probabilities for A_1 and A_2 are $\tfrac{9}{14}$ and $\tfrac{5}{14}$, respectively; B uses B_1, B_2, B_3, and B_4 with probabilities $\tfrac{1}{14}$, $\tfrac{13}{14}$, 0, and 0, respectively.

To indicate *why* B_1 and B_2 are the only strategies in B's optimal mixed set, we add a horizontal dashed line through A^* in Figure 7.10. We know

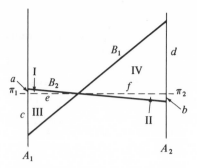

Figure 7.11. Relevant Strategies for B in (7-70)

that the intercept of this line on either axis, which represents the value of the payoff for the point A^*, gives the value of the game to player A. This is $-\frac{19}{14}$. But we know that this is also the value to player B and moreover must be obtained by B *whichever* strategy A actually selects (through the use of his properly weighted random device) in a particular play of the game; if A_1, then the payoff is the point π_1 $(-\frac{19}{14})$, if A_2, the payoff is at π_2 $(-\frac{19}{14})$. Owing to the properties of similar triangles, it is with respect to the endpoints of B_1 and B_2 *only* that π_1 and π_2 can be described by the *same* set of weights.[49] The same convex combination of -1 and -6 used to describe π_1 $(-\frac{19}{14})$ also describes π_2 (again, $-\frac{19}{14}$) in terms of -2 and 7.[50]

[49] Schematically, the relevant triangles are as follows:

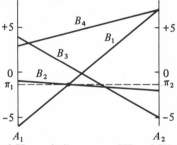

Specifically, triangles I and II are similar, as are III and IV. Therefore $a/b = c/f$ and $c/d = e/f$; thus $a/b = c/d$. Since all sides are of positive length *and* $a + c = 1 = b + d$ (they are weights in two convex combinations), it follows that $a = b$ and $c = d$.

[50] These weights are $\frac{13}{14}$ and $\frac{1}{14}$, respectively, precisely the q_1 and q_2 found above. But in the present case they were found as a solution to the following (consistent) set of three equations in two unknowns:

$$-w_1 - 6w_2 = -\tfrac{19}{14},$$
$$-2w_1 + 7w_2 = -\tfrac{19}{14},$$
$$w_1 + w_2 = 1.$$

For any other pair of B's strategies, say B_1 and B_3, the similarly constructed 3×2 set of equations is *inconsistent* (Chapter 2).

In larger games, say 4×10, it is not generally possible to use any graphical approach that will tell, for player B, which of his (at least) six "extra" strategies to eliminate. The solution to the 4×10 game will definitely be the solution to a 4×4, 3×3, or 2×2 subgame—when there is no saddle point—but this still leaves a great deal of choice.

Tentatively, one might examine each 4×4 subgame under the assumption that all (four) strategies are active. Let one such subgame have the following payoffs.[51]

	B_1	B_2	B_3	B_4	
A_1	1	7	0	3	
A_2	0	0	3	5	(7-71)
A_3	1	2	4	1	
A_4	6	0	2	0	

If B thinks that A will use all four strategies in his optimal mixed set, then B is looking for probabilities $q_1, \ldots, q_4$ such that

$$q_1 + 7q_2 + 3q_4 = 3q_3 + 5q_4 = q_1 + 2q_2 + 4q_3 + q_4 = 6q_1 + 2q_3 \quad (7\text{-}72)$$

and $q_1 + q_2 + q_3 + q_4 = 1$. More usefully, subtracting the right-hand side of each equality in (7-72) from the left, we get

$$
\begin{aligned}
q_1 + 7q_2 - 3q_3 - 2q_4 &= 0, \\
-q_1 - 2q_2 - q_3 + 4q_4 &= 0, \\
-5q_1 + 2q_2 + 2q_3 + q_4 &= 0, \\
q_1 + q_2 + q_3 + q_4 &= 1.
\end{aligned}
\qquad (7\text{-}73)
$$

The first three equations constitute all of the information given in (7-72),[52] and the last is just one of the defining properties of a set of probabilities. Because all but the last are homogeneous equations, Cramer's rule turns out to be easy to apply. For example:

$$
q_1 = \begin{vmatrix} 0 & 7 & -3 & -2 \\ 0 & -2 & -1 & 4 \\ 0 & 2 & 2 & 1 \\ 1 & 1 & 1 & 1 \end{vmatrix} \div \begin{vmatrix} 1 & 7 & -3 & -2 \\ -1 & -2 & -1 & 4 \\ -5 & 2 & 2 & 1 \\ 1 & 1 & 1 & 1 \end{vmatrix}
\qquad (7\text{-}74)
$$

$$
= - \begin{vmatrix} 7 & -3 & -2 \\ -2 & -1 & 4 \\ 2 & 2 & 1 \end{vmatrix} \div 353 = \frac{89}{353} \cong .26
$$

---

[51] The numbers are from Williams [22, p. 136]. They are used here so that the interested reader can compare our result, via Cramer's rule for equation systems whose logic we are about to develop, with the clever but not-so-intuitive discussion in Williams.

[52] Quantities equal to the same quantity are equal to each other.

The reader might observe that in evaluating $|A|$ along the bottom row (all 1's), each of the 3×3 determinants involved is actually also the numerator for a q_j, because of the placement of 0's in the right-hand sides of (7-73).[53] A similar set of equations will give the relationships among the four p_i that constitute A's probabilities; these are [and the reader should be clear how these are developed from the information in the payoff matrix in (7-71)]

$$\begin{aligned}
-6p_1 \quad\quad\quad - \quad p_3 + 6p_4 &= 0, \\
7p_1 - 3p_2 - 2p_3 - 2p_4 &= 0, \\
-3p_1 - 2p_2 + 3p_3 + 2p_4 &= 0, \\
p_1 + \quad p_2 + \quad p_3 + \quad p_4 &= 1
\end{aligned} \qquad (7\text{-}75)$$

with the unique solution $p_1 = \frac{88}{353}$, $p_2 = \frac{86}{353}$, $p_3 = \frac{78}{353}$, $p_4 = \frac{101}{353}$.

If some q_j or p_i turn out to be negative, or if for one of the players the probabilities are all zero, then the assumption of all strategies active was incorrect and a search must be made among the 16 3×3 subgames. If the probabilities are all nonnegative (and not *all* zero), and if the 4×4 matrix was taken from one in which either (or both) players had more strategies, then the q_j are a solution to the larger, original game only if the payoff to B is larger (his losses are less) when the q_j are used against *each* of A's strategies not in A's optimal mixed set. Similarly, if B had more than four strategies, then the p_i found as above must give to A a larger payoff when employed against each of B's nonincluded strategies. If this test is not passed, then some other 4×4 subgame must be examined. Clearly these methods based on the fundamental properties of optimal mixed strategies have a certain element of chance in them, and for this reason they can be computationally very unsatisfactory. Fortunately, there is an alternative approach.

Games and linear programming

It is easy to show that *any* two-person zero-sum game can be written as a linear programming problem. This provides an immediate method of solution, the simplex method, which we recall will generate results for a primal and a dual problem simultaneously. These turn out to be A's and B's optimal mixed strategies, respectively. In addition, the primal-dual relationships of Section 6.4 are then relevant; for this reason we were able to observe, above, that in a nonsquare game both players have optimal mixed strategies involving no more pure strategies than are available to the player who has the fewer number of alternatives.

Consider a general 2×3 game; the extension to games of any size is completely straightforward. Denote the general payoff matrix as

---

[53] The remaining values are: $q_2 = \frac{62}{353}$, $q_3 = \frac{119}{353}$, and $q_4 = \frac{83}{353}$.

Player B

	a_{11}	a_{12}	a_{13}
Player A	a_{21}	a_{22}	a_{23}

(7-76)

Let x_1 and x_2 be A's probabilities, and y_1, y_2, and y_3 be those for B.[54] We consider the problems as viewed by A and by B simultaneously.

Player A's expected gains, g_1, g_2, and g_3, against each of B's pure strategies (three in number) are

$$
\begin{aligned}
a_{11}x_1 + a_{21}x_2 &= g_1, \\
a_{12}x_1 + a_{22}x_2 &= g_2, \\
a_{13}x_1 + a_{23}x_2 &= g_3.
\end{aligned}
$$

(7-77)

Player B's expected losses, l_1 and l_2, against each of A's two possible choices are

$$
\begin{aligned}
a_{11}y_1 + a_{12}y_2 + a_{13}y_3 &= l_1, \\
a_{21}y_1 + a_{22}y_2 + a_{23}y_3 &= l_2.
\end{aligned}
$$

(7-78)

The objective of A is to choose the x_i so as to maximize his minimum gain; he is the maximinimizer. Define u to be his minimum gain—that is,

$$ u = \min_j g_j. $$

Conversely, B's aim is to minimize his maximum loss; he is the minimaximizer. Define

$$ v = \max_i l_i. $$

Then (7-77) and (7-78) can be rewritten:

$$
\begin{array}{lll}
a_{11}x_1 + a_{21}x_2 \geq u, & & -a_{11}x_1 - a_{21}x_2 + u \leq 0, \\
a_{12}x_1 + a_{22}x_2 \geq u, \quad \text{or} & & -a_{12}x_1 - a_{22}x_2 + u \leq 0, \\
a_{13}x_1 + a_{23}x_2 \geq u; & & -a_{13}x_1 - a_{23}x_2 + u \leq 0;
\end{array}
$$

(7-77′)

$$
\begin{array}{lll}
a_{11}y_1 + a_{12}y_2 + a_{13}y_3 \leq v, & & -a_{11}y_1 - a_{12}y_2 - a_{13}y_3 + v \geq 0, \\
a_{21}y_1 + a_{22}y_2 + a_{23}y_3 \leq v; \quad \text{or} & & -a_{21}y_1 - a_{22}y_2 - a_{23}y_3 + v \geq 0.
\end{array}
$$

(7-78′)

Subject to (7-77′), A wants to maximize u; subject to (7-78′), B wants to minimize v. Clearly it is also required that $x_i \geq 0$ $(i = 1, 2)$ and $y_j \geq 0$ $(j = 1, \ldots, 3)$. Moreover the payoff matrix can be altered so that u and v will be nonnegative if they would not have been so originally—as, for

---

[54] We use these instead of the p_i and q_j in order to emphasize the linear programming structure as developed in Chapter 6. We have used y's here for the dual variables that were denoted by v's in the previous chapter; both are widely used in the literature.

example, in a payoff matrix with all negative entries. This is because any constant added to all the entries in a payoff matrix will add that amount to the value of the game but will leave the optimal strategies for both players unaltered.[55] Therefore we may also assume that $u \geq 0$ and $v \geq 0$. Finally, we require that the sums of the probabilities, the x's and the y's, be unity. In fact, since A wants to *maximize u*, and as long as u is nonnegative, A would never use less than the 100 percent that is possible for his probability sum; hence for A we can write $x_1 + x_2 \leq 1$, knowing that at A's optimum the equality will hold. Similarly B, being the minimizer, would prefer to use as little of his 100 percent as possible; since $v \geq 0$ he would in general prefer not to play at all. Thus for him we can write $y_1 + y_2 + y_3 \geq 1$; from B's point of view the equality will hold at optimum.

Thus the problems of the two players are given by (7-79).

$$\text{A's problem}$$

$$\begin{aligned}
\text{Maximize:} \quad & 0x_1 + 0x_2 + u \\
\text{subject to:} \quad & -a_{11}x_1 - a_{21}x_2 + u \leq 0, \\
& -a_{12}x_1 - a_{22}x_2 + u \leq 0, \\
& -a_{13}x_1 - a_{23}x_2 + u \leq 0, \\
& x_1 + x_2 \leq 1, \\
\text{and} \quad & x_1, x_2, u \geq 0.
\end{aligned}$$

$$(7\text{-}79)$$

$$\text{B's problem}$$

$$\begin{aligned}
\text{Minimize:} \quad & 0y_1 + 0y_2 + 0y_3 + v \\
\text{subject to:} \quad & -a_{11}y_1 - a_{12}y_2 - a_{13}y_3 + v \geq 0, \\
& -a_{21}y_1 - a_{22}y_2 - a_{23}y_3 + v \geq 0, \\
& y_1 + y_2 + y_3 \geq 1, \\
\text{and} \quad & y_1, y_2, y_3, v \geq 0.
\end{aligned}$$

This is, clearly, a pair of dual linear programs. We therefore know that in a two-person zero-sum game the optimal strategies for both players will assure $u^0 = v^0$; this number is the value of the game. We know more than this. The constraints for both programs are entirely definitional (the definitions of u and v and the character of probability distributions). Hence both problems *must have* feasible solutions. But then, from Theorem P-D4 of Section 6.4, both problems have optimal solutions. This is the so-called minimax theorem in game theory; in a two-person zero-sum game there *always* exist optimal strategies for players A and B, for which $u = v$. Clearly, any departure by either player from his optimal strategies would offer his

---

[55] Since equations (7-73), from which B's optimal strategy mix was derived, were found, essentially, by *subtracting* elements in adjacent rows of the payoff matrix [see (7-71) and the relations in (7-72)], it is clear that all *differences* will remain unchanged if a constant is added to all elements.

opponent the opportunity of greater gain; neither player can do better for himself, when faced with an optimizing opponent, than to use his optimal mixed strategy.

Consider, finally, the implications of the dual programming formulation from the point of view of Theorem P-D3 of Chapter 6. If, at the optimum, A's first constraint is an inequality (requires a *positive*, rather than zero-valued, slack variable)—$a_{11}x_1 + a_{12}x_2 > u$—then the corresponding dual variable, y_1, will be zero at optimum. Thus in B's problem a zero probability has been assigned to his first strategy, which is an *inferior* one since it would give A more than u, A's *minimum* expected gain. Optimal mixed strategies thus automatically insure a player against the risk of utilizing a pure strategy that would allow his opponent to do better than is necessary.

The beauty of the programming formulation is that it takes care of game situations of any size and shape, and does so via an extremely simple computational procedure. We use it for illustration on the 2×4 game in (7-70), which has already been solved with the help of graphics. To insure the non-negativity of u and v, a quick rule is to add the absolute value of the largest negative number (here 6) to all entries. Hence the converted payoff matrix is

Player B

Player A

0	5	10	9
13	4	1	13

(7-70′)

The strategies will be unaffected; the value of the game is increased by 6. We need consider the maximizing linear program only; the optimal solution to the dual (B's problem) is found in the top row of the final tableau. We use the convention of denoting u by x_{m+1} and v by y_{n+1}; here $u = x_3$ and $v = y_5$. A's problem, in linear programming terms, is thus

$$
\begin{aligned}
\text{maximize:} \quad & 0x_1 + 0x_2 + x_3 \\
\text{subject to:} \quad & - 13x_2 + x_3 \le 0, \\
& -5x_1 - 4x_2 + x_3 \le 0, \\
& -10x_1 - x_2 + x_3 \le 0, \\
& -9x_1 - 13x_2 + x_3 \le 0, \\
& x_1 + x_2 \le 1, \\
\text{and} \quad & x_1, x_2, x_3 \ge 0.
\end{aligned}
$$

(7-80)

The interested reader should work through the simplex tableaux to the optimum; three pivots are required. The top row and leftmost column of the final tableau are

		s_5	s_2	s_1
π	$\frac{65}{14}$	$-\frac{65}{14}$	$-\frac{13}{14}$	$-\frac{1}{14}$
x_3	$\frac{65}{14}$			
x_2	$\frac{5}{14}$			
s_3	$\frac{30}{14}$			
s_4	$\frac{81}{14}$			
x_1	$\frac{9}{14}$			

The optimal mixed strategies are thus $x_1^0 = \frac{9}{14}$, $x_2^0 = \frac{5}{14}$ for player A and $y_1^0 = \frac{1}{14}$, $y_2^0 = \frac{13}{14}$, $y_3^0 = 0$, $y_4^0 = 0$ for player B. The value of this game is $\frac{65}{14}$; hence the value of the original game is $\frac{65}{14} - 6 = -\frac{19}{14}$. These coincide with our earlier results.

SUMMARY

This chapter has extended our investigation of linear programming models. We have considered the effect of peculiarities that could be present in the data of a particular problem (multiple optima, degeneracy, the origin not a feasible basis). We have also investigated the implications of peculiarities in the fundamental structure of a problem (equality constraints, transportation and assignment models, integer requirements on the solution values). We have seen that sometimes simplifications of solution methods are possible; sometimes complications in interpretation, especially of the dual, arise. Finally, we investigated the fundamentals of two-person zero-sum game theory and, in particular, the relationships between these models and linear programs.

There is still a great deal in the linear programming area that has been omitted—for example, the use of these models to solve problems of the network flow variety, and the theory and results for parametric and stochastic programming models. Finally, the more complicated so-called dynamic programming models for multistage optimization have not been covered. These variations are adequately covered in more detailed and specialized books. The interested reader should consult the linear or dynamic programming texts listed in the References that follow.

PROBLEMS

1. Find all solutions to the following linear program:

$$\text{maximize:} \quad 6x_1 + 9x_2$$
$$\text{subject to:} \quad x_1 + 2x_2 \leq 14,$$
$$3x_1 + 2x_2 \leq 28,$$
$$2x_1 + 3x_2 \leq 22,$$
$$\text{and} \qquad x_1,\, x_2 \geq 0.$$

2. Find the optimal solution to the following problem and its dual:

$$\text{maximize:} \quad 8x_1 + 15x_2 + 3x_3$$
$$\text{subject to:} \quad 2x_1 + 6x_2 + 5x_3 \leq 30,$$
$$4x_1 + 5x_2 + 10x_3 \leq 39,$$
$$2x_1 + 4x_2 + 3x_3 \leq 24,$$
$$\text{and} \qquad x_1,\, x_2,\, x_3 \geq 0.$$

If more than one solution exists to either the primal or the dual, find all solutions.

3. Maximize: $\quad 2x_1 + x_2$

subject to: $\quad 15x_1 + 9x_2 \leq 170,$
$$-2x_1 + 4x_2 \geq 16,$$
$$x_1 \qquad\quad \geq 2,$$

and both variables nonnegative.

4. Consider the following transportation problem:

$$\text{minimize:} \quad 10x_{11} + 20x_{12} + 12x_{13} + 15x_{21} + 10x_{22} + 18x_{23}$$

subject to origin capacities of 30 and 50, respectively, and destination demands of 20, 45 and 15, respectively.

(a) Solve the problem by the stepping-stone method.

(b) Since equations as constraints can be handled with the two-phase method, solve the problem this way. [Compare with the amount of work necessary to find the solution using the stepping-stone method, as in (a).]

5. Determine the optimal shipments for a problem with the following data (where cell entries indicate unit transport costs):

	D_1	D_2	D_3	D_4	D_5	D_6	Capacities
O_1	2	1	4	0	1	2	18
O_2	3	2	0	4	2	5	23
O_3	1	3	3	5	3	0	6
Demands	8	6	6	10	7	10	

6. An ice cream distributor has four pushcarts and one man to sell from each of them. One cart will be sent to each of four tourist areas in the city during the summer season. Expected weekly sales (in dollars) are shown below for carts 1, ..., 4 in areas A, ..., D. What should the assignment be to maximize profit? (Assume that costs are the same for all carts and that they do not vary with location.)

	A	B	C	D
1	60	90	40	100
2	120	100	80	110
3	50	70	40	60
4	180	100	110	140

7. Five waitresses ($W_1, \ldots, W_5$) are available to work in five branches of a restaurant chain. The entries in the matrix below indicate the costs associated with each waitress-location assignment. An X indicates that a waitress cannot work at the indicated location (for example, because of travel-time constraints). W_r represents costs of a waitress who is available as a replacement for one of the current waitresses. Find the best combination of waitresses and the optimal assignment of locations to them. What is the cost of this assignment?

	L_1	L_2	L_3	L_4	L_5
W_1	12	4	8	X	5
W_2	3	11	2	7	8
W_3	6	X	10	8	9
W_4	X	5	9	6	4
W_5	5	X	7	12	6
W_r	9	3	5	10	X

8. Maximize: $10x_1 + 7x_2$
   subject to: $4x_1 + 3x_2 \leq 26$,
   $x_1 \leq 6$,
   $2x_1 + 4x_2 \leq 20$,
   and $x_1, x_2 \geq 0$ and integer.
9. Add the requirement that x_1, x_2, and x_3 be integers to Problem 1 in Chapter 6.
10. A company is deciding how to allocate its budget for the coming period. Two proposals have been presented (call them projects A and B), but there is a capital constraint. Project A requires $2000 and project B $3000. The company has $4000 available. Project A gives a net profit of $6000 and project B a net profit of $5000. Set this problem up as an integer program and solve it using Gomory's method. [*Hint:* Include the constraints $x_1 \leq 1$, $x_2 \leq 1$ and the requirement that x_1 and x_2 be integer, where x_1 and x_2 represent the number of units of projects A and B that are adopted.] Note that while this problem can very easily be solved intuitively or graphically, there is need for some formal method such as this when there are many projects and many constraints.
11. Anton's restaurant has just opened in an area where its major competition is from Luigi's. Anton's management has observed that Luigi's promotional effort varies between two alternatives: reduced prices on certain nights and special menus on other nights. Denote these alternatives L_1 and L_2, respectively.

To attract customers, Anton's can also reduce prices (A_1), serve special meals (A_2), or emphasize a takeout service (A_3). Both restaurants use the same advertising media on the same day to promote one special attraction each week. Differences in facilities and experience mean that each restaurant excels in certain specialities. Payoffs, in terms of percentage gain or loss in their share of the market for the week, have been estimated by Anton's management for each outcome as follows:

	L_1	L_2
A_1	-3	6
A_2	2	-6
A_3	-1	5

What strategy should Anton's management follow in scheduling weekly specials if they assume that Luigi's will act so as to minimize their maximum possible market share loss? Solve in two different ways.

REFERENCES

1. Balinski, M., "Integer Programming: Methods, Uses, Computation," *Management Science*, vol. 12 (1965), pp. 253–313.
2. Baumol, W. J., *Economic Theory and Operations Analysis*, 2d ed. Englewood Cliffs, N.J.: Prentice-Hall, Inc., 1965.
3. Beale, E. M. L., "Survey of Integer Programming," *Operational Research Quarterly*, vol. 16 (1965), pp. 219–228.
4. Beckmann, M. J., *Dynamic Programming of Economic Decisions.* Berlin: Springer-Verlag, 1968.
5. Bellman, R., and S. Dreyfus, *Applied Dynamic Programming.* Princeton: Princeton University Press, 1962.
6. Chernoff, H., and L. E. Moses, *Elementary Decision Theory.* New York: John Wiley & Sons, Inc., 1959.
7. Dantzig, G. B., *Linear Programming and Extensions.* Princeton: Princeton University Press, 1963.
8. Glicksman, A. M., *An Introduction to Linear Programming and the Theory of Games.* New York: John Wiley & Sons, Inc., 1963.
9. Graves, R. L., and P. Wolfe, eds. *Recent Advances in Mathematical Programming.* New York: McGraw-Hill, Inc., 1963.
10. Hadley, G., *Linear Programming.* Reading, Mass.: Addison-Wesley Publishing Company, Inc., 1962.
11. ———, *Nonlinear and Dynamic Programming.* Reading, Mass.: Addison-Wesley Publishing Company, Inc., 1964.
12. Howard, R., *Dynamic Programming and Markov Processes.* New York: The Technology Press and John Wiley & Sons, Inc., 1960.

13. Lawler, E. L., and D. E. Wood, "Branch-and-Bound Methods: A Survey," *Operations Research*, vol. 14 (1966), pp. 699–719.

14. Luce, R. D., and H. Raiffa, *Games and Decisions: Introduction and Critical Survey*. New York: John Wiley & Sons, Inc., 1957.

15. Nemhauser, G. L., *Introduction to Dynamic Programming*. New York: John Wiley & Sons, Inc., 1966.

16. Owen, G., *Game Theory*. Philadelphia: W. B. Saunders Company, 1968.

17. Raiffa, H., *Decision Analysis: Introductory Lectures on Choices Under Uncertainty*. Reading, Mass.: Addison Wesley Publishing Company, Inc., 1968.

18. Saaty, T., *Optimization in Integers*. New York: McGraw-Hill, Inc., 1970.

19. Simonnard, M., trans. W. S. Jewell, *Linear Programming*. Englewood Cliffs, N.J.: Prentice-Hall, Inc., 1966.

20. Vajda, S., *An Introduction to Linear Programming and the Theory of Games*. New York: John Wiley & Sons, Inc., 1960.

21. von Neumann, J., and O. Morgenstern, *Theory of Games and Economic Behavior*. New York: John Wiley & Sons, Inc. (Science Editions), 1964.

22. Williams, J. D., *The Compleat Strategyst*. New York: McGraw-Hill, Inc., 1954.

8

NONLINEAR PROGRAMMING MODELS—I: FUNDAMENTALS

The great strength of linear programs lies precisely in their linearity. It is because both the objective function and each of the constraints are linear functions of the decision variables that all of the fundamental results relating linear programs, convex sets, and basic solutions to sets of linear equations hold. These results, in turn, make possible the computational approach of the simplex method, a powerful set of arithmetic rules that efficiently finds the way to an optimum solution. Clearly the linearity requirements are stringent but the rewards are great, as we shall see in this and the following chapter. As soon as one or more of the constraints is a nonlinear function of the x_j and/or the objective function is nonlinear in these same variables, the logical foundations of the simplex calculations are undermined. This, as we shall see, is a great loss. On the other hand, not all constrained optimization problems that arise in the real world can be said to fit—either naturally or after a reasonable amount of simplification—the mold required of the linear programming framework.

Consider, for example, the function that relates profits to output for a producer facing the usual downward-sloping demand curve, which asserts that less of his product is demanded (sold) at higher prices. A general (but linear) case is shown in Figure 8.1; the equation for this line (without

Price (p)

Quantity Sold (x)

Figure 8.1. Downward Sloping Linear Demand Curve

specifying parameters) is $p = a - bx$, where a and b are positive. Thus total revenue for the producer is, logically, the number of units sold times the unit price at which they are sold. That is,

$$TR = x \cdot p = x(a - bx) = ax - bx^2. \tag{8-1}$$

If each unit costs c to produce (where p and c are measured in the same units), then total profit, π, is given by

$$\pi = ax - bx^2 - cx = (a - c)x - bx^2. \tag{8-2}$$

This is a nonlinear function of x, the decision variable.[1] Since π is a function of one variable only, the problem is not a very difficult one, even with constraints on x. But it serves to illustrate how easily nonlinearities may appear in an optimization problem. If the manufacturer were deciding on outputs of, for example, two products, each of which was sold under conditions of downward-sloping demand (as in Figure 8.1), then it is clear that his total profit function would be nonlinear in x_1 and x_2. Even if all the input-use constraints on these two variables were linear, for example as the constraints in problem (6-5) of Chapter 6, the programming problem would be a nonlinear one.[2] And to the extent that there are increasing returns to scale (at least up to some output level, so that resources consumed by $5x$ units of output are less than five times those used in producing x units) the constraints in a problem like (6-5) would also exhibit nonlinearities.

Our interest in this chapter is to understand the implications of such nonlinearities for (1) the nature of the optimal solution and (2) the method of finding an optimal solution. Because of the sharply increased complexity of nonlinear programming problems, one of our aims is to help the reader better understand the tradeoffs in situations in which he must make a choice between the relatively more accurate representation of a nonlinear model (with its generally less tractable solution methods) and the often oversimplified linear model (with its simplex arithmetic). As will become evident in the sections to follow, there are no *universally* valid solution procedures for *general* nonlinear programming models. For this reason, the material of this chapter may appear to the reader to be somewhat more abstract; this seems inherent in the nature of the subject.

---

[1] If there were no constraints of any sort on amounts produced, we know (from Chapter 3) that the profit-maximizing output would be where $d\pi/dx = 0$ and $d^2\pi/dx^2 < 0$. Here $d\pi/dx = (a - c) - 2bx$; thus we have either a maximum or a minimum of π when $x^* = (a - c)/2b$. Since $d^2\pi/dx^2 = -2b$, which is clearly negative for $b > 0$, x^* represents the profit-maximizing output in the no-constraint situation.

[2] Even though the demand function in Figure 8.1 is itself *linear*. The point is that the function relating profits (the objective) to output or outputs (the decision variable or variables) is nonlinear.

We will investigate, initially, the geometry of nonlinearities in the programming problem and see how the simplex arithmetic is thereby invalidated. Then we will examine the implications for the results for the general constrained optimization problem in Chapter 4 of adding the usual programming requirement of nonnegative variables. Next, we prepare the way for an entirely new class of solution procedures—so-called *gradient methods*—by examining more carefully further implications of some results on the geometry of vectors that were first presented in Section 1.4. After these foundations, we turn to gradient methods as such. Finally we see how the Kuhn-Tucker results (Section 4.8), which are necessary and sometimes sufficient conditions for a maximizing or a minimizing point, can be arrived at in a somewhat different way. This alternative route to the same outcome introduces the notion of a *saddle point* of a function—an addition that is relevant because techniques exist for finding saddle points in some cases; thus, it is of computational help.

8.1. THE ALGEBRA AND GEOMETRY OF NONLINEAR PROGRAMMING

Algebra

Parallel to the general linear program statement in (6-4) of Chapter 6, the nonlinear programming maximization problem can be stated as

$$
\begin{aligned}
\text{maximize:} \quad & f(x_1, \ldots, x_n) \\
\text{subject to:} \quad & g_1(x_1, \ldots, x_n) \leq r_1, \\
& \quad \vdots \qquad\qquad\qquad \vdots \\
& g_m(x_1, \ldots, x_n) \leq r_m, \\
\text{and} \quad & x_1 \geq 0, \quad \ldots, \quad x_n \geq 0,
\end{aligned}
\tag{8-3}
$$

or, more compactly—parallel to (6-1) and letting $X = \begin{bmatrix} x_1 \\ \vdots \\ x_n \end{bmatrix}$—

$$
\begin{aligned}
\text{maximize:} \quad & f(X) \\
\text{subject to:} \quad & g_i(X) \leq r_i \quad (i = 1, \ldots, m) \\
\text{and} \quad & X \geq 0.
\end{aligned}
\tag{8-3'}
$$

In fact, (8-3) and (8-3') state the general *mathematical* programming maximization problem; when both the function f and all functions g_i $(i = 1, \ldots, m)$ are linear in the x_j $(j = 1, \ldots, n)$, then the problem is a linear program; otherwise it is a nonlinear one.

It is sometimes convenient (as we saw in Chapter 4) to rewrite the constraints $g_i(X) \leq r_i$ as $h_i(X) \equiv g_i(X) - r_i \leq 0$. Then the problem is

$$\text{maximize:} \quad f(X)$$
$$\text{subject to:} \quad h_i(X) \leq 0 \quad (i = 1, \ldots, m) \qquad (8\text{-}4)$$
$$\text{and} \qquad \qquad X \geq O.$$

Geometry

Consider again the feasible region associated with the three linear constraints in x_1 and x_2 for problem (6-5). This was shown in Figure 6.1(d), repeated here as Figure 8.2.

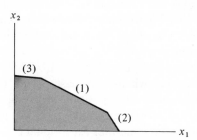

Figure 8.2.   Feasible Region for Problem (6-5)

In the next figure we add (in dashed lines) the contours of two possible nonlinear objective functions. Assume, for the moment, that in both cases higher values of the objective function are associated with contours that are farther from the origin. Then, if the objective function contour is concave to the origin [Figure 8.3(a)] the maximum will still occur at a corner of the feasible region; hence it will be identical with one of the nonnegative *basic* solutions to the constraining equations of the augmented problem. When an objective function contour is convex to the origin, this property

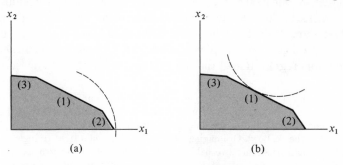

       (a)   (b)

Figure 8.3.   (a) Linear Constraints, Concave Objective Function Contours, (b) Linear Constraints, Convex Objective Function Contours

may be lost, as it is in Figure 8.3(b).[3] The maximum value will generally occur along an edge; in Figure 8.3(b) the optimum will have *four* positive-valued variables—x_1, x_2, s_2, and s_3. Since there are *three* constraints, we know that a *basic* solution to the constraints in augmented form will have (at most) *three* variables positive. The simplex tableaux are constructed in such a way that *only* basic solutions are considered as candidates for the optimum; hence the simplex method would be invalid for a problem such as the one sketched in Figure 8.3(b).

Even further deviations from the linear programming basic optima are possible. If we consider the complete objective function surface, one of whose contours appears in Figure 8.3(a), we see that it could have essentially the shape of (a part of) a bowl—*not* inverted—whose lowest point is at the origin or somewhat southwest of it.[4]

Similarly, the objective surface in Figure 8.3(b) could be an *inverted* bowl whose high point was somewhere northeast of the feasible region.[5] We consider possible variations on the position of the bowl in Figure 8.4, in which several contours plus the high point (dark dot) are shown. The first, Figure 8.4(a), illustrates the somewhat exceptional case mentioned in foot-note 3, in which the optimum would be a basic solution. The second, Figure 8.4(b), is one possibility that could have led to the contour in Figure 8.3(b). The case in Figure 8.4(c), however, illustrates an even further deviation from the linear programming optimum. It shows an objective function sur-face whose maximum is *interior* to the feasible region; hence at optimum in this three-constraint problem all *five* variables will be positive—both x's and all three slacks. Thus not only can it happen that the optimum is not at a *corner* of the feasible region; it may not be on the boundary at all.

With nonlinear constraints the complication is rather different but it leads to the same result—invalidation of the simplex arithmetic as a solu-tion procedure. Imagine a feasible region whose border (except for the axes) consists of one linear and one nonlinear segment. Figure 8.5 illustrates the case with a linear objective function contour for which the optimum *is* on the boundary of the feasible region. The shaded area is clearly a convex region (see Section 4.7 of Chapter 4). Consider, however, the *extreme points* of this feasible region. Recall that an extreme point of a convex set is one

---

[3] The reader can easily change the objective function contour in this figure so that the optimum happens, in fact, to fall at a corner. This will not *generally* be the case, however.

[4] This is something like the picture one would have from a ski lodge (the origin) looking out and up into the ski bowl. Or imagine a sail in the shape of a right triangle, with one corner at the origin, the other two held directly above each of the two axes, and the wind blowing from above, so that the sail billows outward and downward.

[5] Or consider the sail from the preceding footnote with the wind coming from below, so that it billows upward.

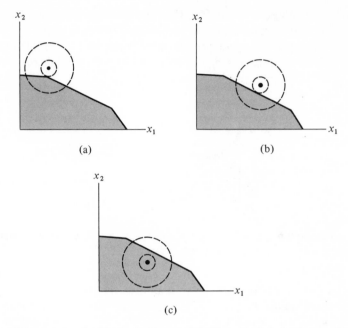

Figure 8.4.   (a) Basic Optimum, (b) "Less Basic" Optimum, (c) "Very Nonbasic" Optimum

that cannot be expressed as a convex combination of any other *pair* of points in the set. In addition to the "obvious" corners—namely the origin, c_1, c_2, and c_3—it should be clear that *all* points on the curve connecting c_1 and c_2 are also extreme points of the shaded region. Thus the optimum *does* occur at an extreme point of the feasible region. However, there is an infinite number of points along this curve; therefore *any* solution method that examined extreme points one by one (and hence whose convergence

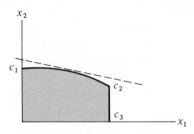

Figure 8.5.   Nonlinear Constraint, Linear Objective Function (Convex Feasible Region)

depended, ultimately, on the fact that there was a finite number of such points) could conceivably take forever to find the optimum.[6]

Nonlinear constraints can present a different sort of problem as well; this is illustrated in Figure 8.6. The boundaries of the feasible region (except

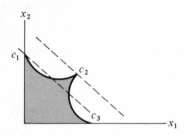

Figure 8.6.   Nonlinear Constraints, Linear Objective Function (Nonconvex Feasible Region)

for the two axes) are formed by two nonlinear segments (c_1c_2 and c_2c_3). But because these nonlinear parts of the boundary are convex, the resulting feasible region—the shaded area in Figure 8.6—is nonconvex. The fundamental importance of the convexity of the feasible region for simplex-like calculations is made clear when we consider the objective function contours. Again, assume that lines further from the origin represent higher values of the objective function, so that the maximum for this problem is at corner c_2. Note also that the value of the objective function is higher at c_1 than at points on the boundary on either side of c_1, and similarly for c_3. Thus if a simplex calculation moved from the origin to either point c_1 or c_3, it would then be unable to move away from that point, since examination of the consequences of a *small* introduction into the basis of x_1 (for c_1) or x_2 (for c_3) would lead to the conclusion that the objective function would *decrease*.[7] This is how nonconvex feasible regions, which are possible in nonlinear programming problems, can lead to a *local* but not a *global* optimum. Clearly, since the feasible region in a linear program is necessarily convex (does not turn in on itself), this problem cannot possibly arise.

When both nonlinear constraints and a nonlinear objective function appear in the same problem, things do not in general become any simpler. Thus, in a nonlinear programming problem the optimum may be:

---

[6] The reader must not be deceived by the inherent simplicity of the two-dimensional picture in Figure 8.5. One (or at least *most* people) cannot rely on intuition alone when n dimensions ($n > 3$) are involved.

[7] This is what Baumol has termed the *myopia* of the simplex method. See Baumol [2, chap. 7].

1. At an extreme point of the feasible region, of which there may be an infinite number; or at one of a finite number of extreme points, which, however, cannot be reached from adjacent corners if one is using marginal (shortsighted) calculations.
2. On the boundary of the feasible region but not at an extreme point.
3. Interior to the feasible region—not on the boundary at all.

The simplex method is thus totally inadequate as a general solution procedure.

8.2. NONLINEAR PROGRAMMING AND THE GENERAL CONSTRAINED OPTIMIZATION PROBLEM

The reader will note the similarity between the nonlinear problem as stated in (8-3) or (8-4) and the problem discussed in Section 4.8, especially pages 175–181, where several inequality constraints were imposed. The so-called Kuhn-Tucker conditions were found by converting each inequality to an equation through the addition of a squared slack variable, s_i^2, imposing the first-order conditions on the first partial derivatives of the Lagrangean function, and simplifying the outcome. These results, (4-45) in Chapter 4, are repeated here as (8-5).[8]

The necessary conditions for a point $X^* = [x_1^*, \ldots, x_n^*]'$ to be a relative maximum of $f(x_1, \ldots, x_n)$ subject to $h_i(x_1, \ldots, x_n) \leq 0$ are that nonnegative λ_i exist such that they and X^* satisfy

$$\text{(a)} \quad f_j - \sum_{i=1}^{m} \lambda_i h_j^i = 0 \quad (j = 1, \ldots, n),$$

$$\text{(b)} \quad \lambda_i[h_i(x_1, \ldots, x_n)] = 0 \quad (i = 1, \ldots, m),$$

$$\text{(c)} \quad h_i(x_1, \ldots, x_n) \leq 0 \quad (i = 1, \ldots, m).$$

$$(8\text{-}5)$$

These were shown also to be sufficient conditions for a maximum when $f(x_1, \ldots, x_n)$ is a *concave* function and all the constraints $h_i(x_1, \ldots, x_n)$, $(i = 1, \ldots, m)$, are *convex* functions. And if f is *strictly* concave, the maximum is an *absolute*, or *global*, one.

The only difference between this most general problem from Chapter 4

---

[8] The statements on Kuhn-Tucker conditions throughout this chapter and the next (as well as in Chapter 4) omit reference to the so-called "constraint qualification" (or regularity assumption) imposed by Kuhn and Tucker in their original work [10]. It is designed to rule out certain exceptionally troublesome behavior on the boundaries of the feasible region, such as outward-pointing "cusps" as at c_2 in Figure 8.6. Various forms that this constraint qualification can take are discussed at some length in Abadie [1, chap. 2].

and the general nonlinear programming problem is that in the latter we have the additional nonnegativity constraints $x_j \geq 0$ $(j = 1, \ldots, n)$, the last set in either (8-3) or (8-4). Clearly these can be treated in the same general way as the $h_i(x_1, \ldots, x_n) \leq 0$ $(i = 1, \ldots, m)$ in the reasoning that led to the Kuhn-Tucker results in (8-5). We can rewrite problem (8-3) as follows:

$$\begin{array}{ll} \text{maximize:} & f(x_1, \ldots, x_n) \\ \text{subject to:} & h_1(x_1, \ldots, x_n) \leq 0, \\ & \quad \vdots \\ & h_m(x_1, \ldots, x_n) \leq 0, \\ \text{and} & -x_1 \leq 0, \quad \ldots, \quad -x_n \leq 0. \end{array} \tag{8-6}$$

That is, the nonnegativity requirements add n more constraints of the same general form as the first m in (8-6), namely

$$h_{m+1}(x_1, \ldots, x_n) \leq 0, \quad \ldots, \quad h_{m+n}(x_1, \ldots, x_n) \leq 0,$$

where, in fact, these n new functions h are extremely simple:

$$h_{m+j}(x_1, \ldots, x_n) \equiv -x_j, \quad \text{for } (j = 1, \ldots, n).$$

We now formulate the Lagrangean function for (8-6) and go through the same kind of reasoning as that which produced the Kuhn-Tucker results in (8-5). A total of $m + n$ slack variables (squared), s_i^2 and s_{m+j}^2, must be added to the $m + n$ constraints $h(x_1, \ldots, x_n) \leq 0$, converting them to equalities. Then we use the approach of Sections 4.6 and 4.8. The Lagrangean function is

$$L = f(X) - \sum_{i=1}^{m} \lambda_i[h_i(X) + s_i^2] - \sum_{j=1}^{n} \lambda_{m+j}[h_{m+j}(X) + s_{m+j}^2].$$

Setting all first partial derivatives equal to zero gives (using the standard notation, employed in Chapter 4, for partial derivatives)

(a) $\dfrac{\partial L}{\partial x_j} \equiv L_j \quad = f_j - \displaystyle\sum_{i=1}^{m} \lambda_i h_j^i - \lambda_{m+j} h_j^{m+j} = 0 \quad (j = 1, \ldots, n),$

(b) $\begin{cases} \dfrac{\partial L}{\partial \lambda_i} \equiv L_{\lambda_i} \quad = -[h_i(X) + s_i^2] = 0 & (i = 1, \ldots, m), \\[3mm] \dfrac{\partial L}{\partial \lambda_{m+j}} \equiv L_{\lambda_{m+j}} = -[h_{m+j}(X) + s_{m+j}^2] = 0 & (j = 1, \ldots, n), \end{cases}$

(c) $\begin{cases} \dfrac{\partial L}{\partial s_i} \equiv L_{s_i} \quad = -2\lambda_i s_i = 0 & (i = 1, \ldots, m), \\[3mm] \dfrac{\partial L}{\partial s_{m+j}} \equiv L_{s_{m+j}} = -2\lambda_{m+j} s_{m+j} = 0 & (j = 1, \ldots, n). \end{cases}$

$$\tag{8-7}$$

For this problem there are thus $2m + 3n$ equations, n for the original variables (x's), $m + n$ for the slack variables (s_i's and s_{m+j}'s), and $m + n$ for the Lagrange multipliers (λ_i's and λ_{m+j}'s). The reasoning now parallels that in Section 4.8. From the equations in (8-7)(c) we know that, for *each* i, either $\lambda_i = 0$ or $s_i = 0$, or both, and for *each* j either $\lambda_{m+j} = 0$ or $s_{m+j} = 0$ or both. If $s_i = 0$ or $s_{m+j} = 0$, then from (8-7)(b), after multiplying through by (-1), $h_i(X) = 0$ or $h_{m+j}(X) = 0$. Thus the slack variables, s_i and s_{m+j}, can be eliminated from the first-order conditions in (8-7) through replacement of (8-7)(b) *and* (8-7)(c) with

$$(d) \quad \begin{cases} \lambda_i[h_i(X)] = 0 & (i = 1, \ldots, m), \\ \lambda_{m+j}[h_{m+j}(X)] = 0 & (j = 1, \ldots, n). \end{cases} \qquad (8\text{-}7)$$

Since the functions $h_{m+j}(X)$ are simply $(-x_j)$, the n relations in the second part of (8-7)(d) require that $-\lambda_{m+j}x_j = 0$.

As before, since the squared slack variables are eliminated, once they have been used to convert the problem to an equality-constrained one, the *direction* of the original inequalities has been lost. Note also that the partial derivative of $h_{m+j}(X)$ with respect to x_j—that is, h_j^{m+j}—is just (-1). The restated first-order conditions, then, in terms of the original x_j and the $m + n$ Lagrange multipliers, with the inequalities reintroduced, are[9]

$$(a) \quad f_j - \sum_{i=1}^{m} \lambda_i h_j^i + \lambda_{m+j} = 0,$$

$$(b) \quad \begin{cases} \lambda_i[h_i(X)] = 0, \\ -\lambda_{m+j}x_j = 0, \end{cases} \qquad (8\text{-}7')$$

$$(c) \quad \begin{cases} h_i(X) \leq 0, \\ X \geq O. \end{cases}$$

In complete form, then, the Kuhn-Tucker statement for the general non-linear programming problem is as follows:

> The necessary conditions for a point $X^* = [x_1^*, \ldots, x_n^*]'$ to be a relative maximum of $f(x_1, \ldots, x_n)$ subject to $h_i(x_1, \ldots, x_n) \leq 0$ and $x_j \geq 0$ are that nonnegative λ_i and λ_{m+j} exist such that they and X^* satisfy (8-7'). $\qquad (8\text{-}8)$

As we saw in Section 4.8, these are also sufficient conditions for a maximum if $f(X)$ is a *concave* function and all of the constraints are *convex* functions. Since the $x_j \geq 0$ are linear in the x's (and hence both concave and convex), the added requirement is still the convexity of the constraints exclusive of the nonnegativity restrictions—that is, that the $h_i(X)$ must be

---

[9] Compare the discussion on pages 172–173, relating the first-order conditions in (4-39) and (4-40).

convex for these conditions to also be sufficient. Finally, if $f(X)$ is *strictly* concave, the maximum is an *absolute* one.

These conditions are often expressed slightly differently in the literature, in a way that eliminates the Lagrange multipliers associated with the nonnegativity requirements on the x_j—the λ_{m+j}—from explicit consideration. We can rewrite (8-7')(a) as

$$f_j - \sum_{i=1}^{m} \lambda_i h_j^i = -\lambda_{m+j}$$

and substitute into the second set of equations in (8-7')(b):

$$x_j \left(f_j - \sum_{i=1}^{m} \lambda_i h_j^i \right) = 0.$$

Recall from Chapter 4 that for the maximum problem in standard form, all λ's must be nonnegative. This requirement for the λ_{m+j} is equivalent to requiring, in (8-7')(a), that

$$f_j - \sum_{i=1}^{m} \lambda_i h_j^i \leq 0.$$

Therefore, finally, we may also write:

> The necessary conditions for a point $X^* = [x_1^*, \ldots, x_n^*]'$ to be a relative maximum of $f(X)$ subject to $h_i(X) \leq 0$ and $X \geq 0$ are that nonnegative λ_i exist such that they and X^* satisfy

(a) $$f_j - \sum_{i=1}^{m} \lambda_i h_j^i \leq 0,$$

(b) $$x_j \left(f_j - \sum_{i=1}^{m} \lambda_i h_j^i \right) = 0,$$ (8-9)

(c) $$h_i(X) \leq 0,$$
(d) $$\lambda_i[h_i(X)] = 0,$$
(e) $$X \geq 0.$$

As before, sufficiency is established by the concavity-convexity requirements stated above, after (8-7'), and the maximum is an absolute one when $f(X)$ is strictly concave.

When stated in the form shown in (8-9), the nature of the approach that must be taken for a solution is clear.[10] We must begin with the implications of conditions (b) and (d).

1.   Consider (8-9)(b).

---

[10] This discussion parallels but is much more involved than that in Section 4.8 on the example with two inequality constraints, pages 178–181.

(a) For *each j*, if $x_j \neq 0$, then the corresponding $f_j - \sum_{i=1}^{m} \lambda_i h_j^i$ *must*
     be zero and the x_j *must* be positive, from (8-9)(e); and

(b) for *each j*, if $\left(f_j - \sum_{i=1}^{m} \lambda_i h_j^i \right) \neq 0$, then the corresponding x_j
     must be zero and the parenthetical term *must* be negative, from
     (8-9)(a).

At the same time:

2. Consider (8-9)(d).
    (a) For *each i*, if $\lambda_i \neq 0$, then $h_i(X)$ must be zero and the λ_i *must*
         be positive [from the conditions in the statement of (8-9)]; and
    (b) for *each i*, if $h_i(X) \neq 0$, then the associated λ_i *must* be zero and
         the resulting $h_i(X)$ must be negative, from (8-9)(c).

The problem here, of course, is that, under item 1 for example, *each x_j*
alone may be zero or nonzero. There are thus two possibilities for each
of n variables and hence a total of 2^n combinations of zero and nonzero
x_j's. This can become immense, for even modest-sized n. Moreover, each
of these possibilities must be paired with each of the 2^m combinations for
zero or nonzero λ_i under item 2.

The reader should note that the conditions in (8-7′)—as well as in (8-9)—
involve more than just an addition to the conditions given in (8-5) of a
nonnegativity requirement on each of the x's. That is, in addition to $X \geq O$
in (8-7′)(c), the structure of (8-7′)(a) and that of the second part of (8-7′)(b)
differ from their counterparts in (8-5), where nonnegativity of the x's is
not a requirement of the problem. Parallel to the discussion from the end
of Section 4.8 on exploration along each of the boundaries set by the inequality constraints, the conditions in (8-9), particularly (8-9)(b), introduce
the lines set by the nonnegativities (the x_j axes) as additional boundaries
along which to explore for local maxima. (This is illustrated, both algebraically and geometrically, for the interested reader in Appendix 8.1.)

Clearly, as in the simpler example of Chapter 4, a great many (in fact,
usually most) possibilities will violate one or more of the inequality requirements, and from among the remainder, that giving the largest objective
function value would be chosen. But it is a difficult and often impossible
task just to enumerate and examine each possibility. For this reason, a
number of special computational methods and algorithms have been (and
are being) developed for particular classes of nonlinear programs. We will
investigate some of these in this and the next chapter.[11]

---

[11] Other discussions can be found in many of the References to this chapter, especially
Hadley [8], Künzi, Krelle, and Oettli [11], Lavi and Vogl [12], Saaty and Bram [15], and
Wilde and Beightler [17].

Because of the extreme complexity of this generalized approach (of Chapter 4) to the general nonlinear program, we examine in the next sections a procedure that "moves toward" the optimum in a (possibly) large number of steps, rather than giving a complete description of the conditions that the optimum must satisfy. Then, in Section 8.5, we examine the nature of the correspondence between constrained maximization (or minimization) problems and so-called saddle-point problems. This relationship, as we shall see, is of both theoretical and practical (that is, computational) interest.

8.3.   MORE ON THE ALGEBRA AND GEOMETRY OF VECTORS

In this section we recall and then extend some results from linear algebra, especially with respect to vectors, that were first presented in Chapter 1. These new observations provide the basis for an approach to the solution of nonlinear programming problems.

Normals

Let V and W be m-element column vectors. Recall that the dot product, or inner product, denoted $V \cdot W$ was defined (Section 1.4) as $\sum_{i=1}^{m} v_i w_i$; that is, it is the sum of the products of corresponding elements in the two vectors. If the angle included between the two vectors is denoted ϕ, then we saw— for the two-element vector case—that the cosine of this angle was given by $\cos \phi = V \cdot W / \|V\| \|W\|$, where $\|V\|$ represents the norm, or length of the vector V, given as $\left(\sum_{i=1}^{m} v_i^2 \right)^{1/2}$, and $\|W\|$ is similarly defined. From this expression we are able to conclude that the two vectors are perpendicular (orthogonal) if and only if $V \cdot W = 0$, since $\cos 90° = 0$.

Consider now any line through the origin in two-dimensional space: $a_1 x_1 + a_2 x_2 = 0$. Letting

$$A = \begin{bmatrix} a_1 \\ a_2 \end{bmatrix} \quad \text{and} \quad X = \begin{bmatrix} x_1 \\ x_2 \end{bmatrix},$$

we can write this equation as $A \cdot X = 0$. When the equation is written in this "inner-product" form, it becomes clear that A is orthogonal to *any* X^* satisfying the equation. That is, for $X^* = \begin{bmatrix} x_1^* \\ x_2^* \end{bmatrix}$, such that $A \cdot X^* = 0$, A is clearly orthogonal to X^*, by definition.[12] Since we choose to let all

---

[12] The cosine of the angle included between them is $A \cdot X^* / \|A\| \|X^*\| = 0 / \|A\| \|X^*\| = 0$.

vectors emanate from the origin, the vector X^* will be collinear with a portion of the line $A \cdot X = 0$, as in Figure 8.7. (Note that one set of axes accommodates both solution space and vector space, since two dimensions are needed in each case.) And since A will be orthogonal to *all* X^* satisfying the equation, it can be described, simply, as orthogonal to the line.

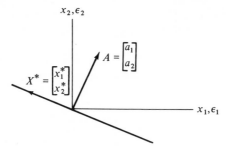

Figure 8.7. $A \cdot X = 0$

Consider next a line in two-dimensional space that does not pass through the origin. This is $a_1 x_1 + a_2 x_2 = b$, where $b \neq 0$; in inner-product form, $A \cdot X = b$. Select two points,

$$X^* = \begin{bmatrix} x_1^* \\ x_2^* \end{bmatrix} \quad \text{and} \quad X^{**} = \begin{bmatrix} x_1^{**} \\ x_2^{**} \end{bmatrix},$$

both of which satisfy $A \cdot X = b$—that is, both of which lie on the line. Their difference, $D = X^{**} - X^*$, is a vector that originates at the origin and is parallel to the line $A \cdot X = b$. Figure 8.8 illustrates.[13] However, since $A \cdot X^{**} = A \cdot X^* = b$,

$$A \cdot D = A \cdot (X^{**} - X^*) = b - b = 0.$$

Hence, A and D are orthogonal. Since *any* pair of X^{**} and X^* on the line

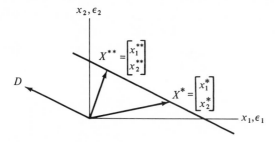

Figure 8.8. $A \cdot X = b$

[13] The reader should recall the "parallelogram" geometry of addition and subtraction of vectors, again from Section 1.4.

can be chosen and their difference D found, it is clear that A is orthogonal to *all* vectors through the origin and parallel to the line $A \cdot X = b$. Hence, A can be described as orthogonal to the line; A is also said to be *normal* to the line.

The notion is easily generalized more than two dimensions. Let

$$A = \begin{bmatrix} a_1 \\ a_2 \\ a_3 \end{bmatrix} \quad \text{and} \quad X = \begin{bmatrix} x_1 \\ x_2 \\ x_3 \end{bmatrix},$$

then a plane through the origin in three-dimensional space can be written as $A \cdot X = 0$. Clearly, A is normal to this plane, since it, by definition, is orthogonal to all vectors

$$X^* = \begin{bmatrix} x_1^* \\ x_2^* \\ x_3^* \end{bmatrix}$$

that satisfy the equation—that is, all points X^* on the plane. An argument exactly parallel to that above for the two-dimensional line not through the origin shows that A is perpendicular to every vector through the origin and parallel to the plane $A \cdot X = b$ and hence is normal to it. Finally, if A and X are n-element column vectors, A can be shown orthogonal to every vector through the origin and parallel to the hyperplane

$$A \cdot X = \sum_{j=1}^{n} a_j x_j = b;$$

hence A is said to be normal to the hyperplane. We will utilize this fact almost immediately.

Gradients

The *gradient* of a function is a vector of the first partial derivatives of the function. (We choose to define it always as a column vector; some texts prefer a row vector.) The usual notation is $\nabla f(x_1, \ldots, x_n)$, or more simply ∇f, if there is no ambiguity about the function involved. Thus, for $f(x_1, \ldots, x_n)$,

$$\nabla f(x_1, \ldots, x_n) \equiv \nabla f = \begin{bmatrix} \dfrac{\partial f}{\partial x_1} \\ \vdots \\ \dfrac{\partial f}{\partial x_n} \end{bmatrix} = \begin{bmatrix} f_1 \\ \vdots \\ f_n \end{bmatrix}. \tag{8-10}$$

If the first partial derivatives are evaluated at a particular point

$$X^* = \begin{bmatrix} x_1^* \\ \vdots \\ x_n^* \end{bmatrix},$$

the gradient at that point is denoted $\nabla f(x_1^*, \ldots, x_n^*)$ or more simply ∇f^*.

For all *linear* functions (lines, planes, hyperplanes) it is clear that the gradient is *normal* to the function. Since for

$$f(x_1, \ldots, x_n) = \sum_{j=1}^{n} a_j x_j = b,$$

or $A \cdot X = b$, the gradient is

$$\nabla f = \begin{bmatrix} a_1 \\ \vdots \\ a_n \end{bmatrix},$$

which is exactly A; and we have just seen that A is normal to the line, plane, or hyperplane represented by $A \cdot X = b$.

Recall, now, from Section 3.2, that the first total differential of a function, evaluated at a point, gives the equation of the tangent line, plane, or hyperplane at that point. For $y = f(x_1, \ldots, x_n)$,

$$df = f_1\, dx_1 + \cdots + f_n\, dx_n.$$

Letting

$$dX = \begin{bmatrix} dx_1 \\ \vdots \\ dx_n \end{bmatrix},$$

and using the notion of the gradient of f, this first total differential for any n-variable function can be written

$$df = [\nabla f] \cdot [dX].$$

Thus, at a particular point X^*, the equation of the tangent hyperplane is $[\nabla f^*] \cdot [dX]$. Hence the gradient at that point, ∇f^*, is normal to the tangent hyperplane at X^*. Figure 8.9 illustrates for a specific two-variable case, $y = f(x_1, x_2) = x_1^2 + x_2^2$. At

$$X^* = \begin{bmatrix} 1 \\ 1 \end{bmatrix}, \qquad \nabla f^* = \begin{bmatrix} 2 \\ 2 \end{bmatrix},$$

which is perpendicular to the straight-line contour of the total differential to y at X^*—that is, to the line tangent (dashed in Figure 8.9) to the circular contour for $y = f(1, 1) = 2$ at X^*.

For purposes of this chapter, our interest in gradients comes from the following interesting fact: the gradient for any function, evaluated at a

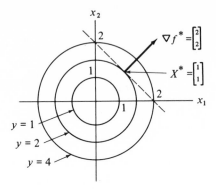

Figure 8.9. ∇f^* for $y = x_1^2 + x_2^2$ at $X^* = \begin{bmatrix} 1 \\ 1 \end{bmatrix}$

particular point, indicates the direction of *maximum increase* of the function from that point. Note that the gradient of an n-variable function, $y = f(x_1, \ldots, x_n)$, is itself an n-element vector. Although y is a surface in $(n + 1)$-dimensional space, its *contours* are represented in n-dimensional space (refer to Figure 8.9). Hence the gradient is normal to the tangent to a *contour* of $f(x_1, \ldots, x_n)$ at a particular point.

It is relatively easy to see why the gradient has the property of indicating the direction of maximum increase. Recall, first, from the fundamental notion of the differential, that the first partial derivatives of a function translate changes in each of the independent variables, x_j, into changes of the dependent variable, y;

$$df = \sum_{j=1}^{n} f_j \, dx_j = [\nabla f] \cdot [dX].$$

At a specific point X^*, $df^* = [\nabla f^*] \cdot [dX]$. For any *given* small changes in $x_1, \ldots, x_n$, dX is a vector in the n-dimensional space of $x_1, \ldots, x_n$; that is, dX indicates a *direction* in that space. Let the small changes in $x_1, \ldots, x_n$, from the point $x_1^*, \ldots, x_n^*$, be $c_1, \ldots, c_n$. That is, we estimate the change in the value of y from $[x_1^*, \ldots, x_n^*]$ to $[x_1^* + c_1, \ldots, x_n^* + c_n]$ via the differential;

$$df^* = f_1^* c_1 + \cdots + f_n^* c_n \equiv [\nabla f^*] \cdot [C], \qquad \text{where } C = \begin{bmatrix} c_1 \\ \vdots \\ c_n \end{bmatrix}.$$

If these small changes, c_j, in the values of the variables had the property that $||C|| = 1$ (that is, $\sqrt{c_1^2 + \cdots + c_n^2} = 1$, the *length* of the vector were unity), then we could think of df^* as showing the (average) rate of change of $y = f(x_1, \ldots, x_n)$ at X^* *in the direction C*.

We can now pose the question: for what direction, C, is this rate of change, df^*, a maximum? That is, we want to maximize $[\nabla f^*] \cdot [C]$, subject to the condition that $||C|| = 1$. This is a straightforward constrained optimization problem—the objective function is linear in the variables c_j but the constraint is not; hence the classical Lagrange multiplier techniques can be applied.[14] The solution can also be found almost by inspection. We want to maximize the inner product of two vectors, the gradient at X^* and C. But the inner product appears in the numerator of the expression for the cosine of the angle between two vectors; here

$$\cos \phi = \frac{[\nabla f^*] \cdot [C]}{||\nabla f^*||\ ||C||} = \frac{[\nabla f^*] \cdot [C]}{||\nabla f^*||},$$

since $||C||$ is required to be unity. That is, we can equally well express the problem as one of maximization of $(\cos \phi)||\nabla f^*||$. But since $||\nabla f^*||$, the norm of the gradient evaluated at a point X^*, is a constant, we want only to maximize $\cos \phi$. Since the cosine function varies between -1 and $+1$, we know its maximum is when $\cos \phi = 1$, which occurs at $\phi = 0°$, $360°$, and so on. In vector geometry ϕ is always the included angle, and hence never exceeds $180°$. Thus the expression is maximized when there is *no* angle between C and the gradient at X^*—that is, when C points in the same direction as ∇f^*, the gradient at the point.[15] And, since

$$\cos \phi = \frac{[\nabla f^*] \cdot [C]}{||\nabla f^*||},$$

it is clear[16] that for $\cos \phi = 1$,

$$C^0 = \frac{[\nabla f^*]}{||\nabla f^*||},$$

since then

---

[14] This is done in Appendix 8.2. The interested reader may wish to test his recollection of these techniques by trying the problem himself before turning to the Appendix. He should be advised, however, that a reexpression of the constraint, obtained by squaring both sides, makes the problem less cumbersome.

[15] This approach to the problem also shows clearly the implication of $\phi = 180°$—that is, $\cos \phi = -1$. Since -1 is the minimum value for $\cos \phi$, the direction of minimum increase (= maximum decrease) in the function at a point is *exactly opposite* to the gradient—that is, the direction of the *negative gradient*.

[16] The unwary reader might be tempted to "divide through" both sides of the equation by $[\nabla f^*]$ and multiply by $||\nabla f^*||$, but $[\nabla f^*]$ is a vector and we have attached no meaning to division by a nonsquare matrix.

$$\cos \phi = \frac{[\nabla f^*] \cdot [\nabla f^*]}{\|\nabla f^*\|^2} = \frac{\sum_{j=1}^{n} (f_j^*)^2}{\|\nabla f^*\|^2} = \frac{\|\nabla f^*\|^2}{\|\nabla f^*\|^2} = 1.$$

Hence the *direction* of maximum increase is given by the gradient; the scalar $1/\|\nabla f^*\|$ in C^0 serves to assure that the norm of the vector C^0 is one.[17]

8.4.   GRADIENT METHODS OF OPTIMIZATION

This property of the gradient vector—that it indicates the direction of maximum increase of a function at a point—provides the cornerstone upon which to build a set of computational methods for maximization and minimization problems, either unconstrained or subject to inequality restrictions. Because of the fundamental role played by gradient vectors in all of these methods, they are known by that name. We examine the unconstrained case first.

Gradient methods for unconstrained maximization or minimization

Consider the problem of maximizing $y = f(x_1, \ldots, x_n)$. We treated this problem in a general way in Section 4.2, developing first- and second-order conditions for (1) isolating stationary points (horizontal tangent hyperplane) and (2) distinguishing the maxima from the minima. In the classical methods of Chapter 4 we required the first partial derivatives and second partials and cross-partials. We now employ gradients for the same problem. We will evaluate the gradient at various points on the function, and hence first partial derivatives are still required. Higher-order derivatives may or may not be needed, as we shall see.

Suppose that we start with any initial point,

$$X^1 = \begin{bmatrix} x_1^1 \\ \vdots \\ x_n^1 \end{bmatrix}$$

and evaluate $y^1 = f(X^1)$ at that point. Next, we want to choose a new point—that is, we want to move away from X^1—such that $y^2 = f(X^2) > y^1 = f(X^1)$. (Note that the numbers as superscripts refer to "steps" in the process, not powers to which variables or functions are raised.) Next, we want to find an X^3 such that $f(X^3) > f(X^2)$, and so on, until it is impossible

---

[17] $\|C^0\| = [(f_1^*)^2/\|\nabla f^*\|^2 + \cdots + (f_n^*)^2/\|\nabla f^*\|^2]^{1/2} = (1/\|\nabla f^*\|)[(f_1^*)^2 + \cdots + (f_n^*)^2]^{1/2}$
$= (1/\|\nabla f^*\|)(\|\nabla f^*\|) = 1.$

to find an X^{n+1} that gives a larger value to y than the "current" point, X^n—that is, until we have found a maximum.[18]

Thus, after the $(k - 1)$st move, we have a point

$$X^k = \begin{bmatrix} x_1^k \\ \vdots \\ x_n^k \end{bmatrix}$$

and a corresponding $y^k = f(X^k)$. The next (kth) move is now to be made; each x_j^k is to be changed by an amount Δx_j^k; that is, $X^{k+1} = X^k + \Delta X^k$. The n-element vector ΔX^k, which distinguishes the "next" vector from the "current" one, has both a magnitude and a direction, as do all vectors. But since the gradient at X^k, $\nabla f(X^k)$, gives the direction of maximum increase in $f(X)$ from the point X^k, it seems clear that the *direction* component in ΔX^k should be $\nabla f(X^k)$.[19] The question of an appropriate *length* for ΔX^k remains.

THE METHOD OF STEEPEST ASCENT (CAUCHY'S METHOD)

Since, except for linear functions, one or more of the partial derivatives in the gradient vector will be functions of X, the gradient vector changes as one moves about on the function $f(X)$. Hence the best direction at X^k (the direction of maximum increase) will not generally remain "best" over a very wide area around X^k. This means that while we want to move from X^k in the direction $\nabla f(X^k)$, we do not necessarily want to move very far. That is, a "step length" must be found:

$$X^{k+1} = X^k + \alpha^k [\nabla f(X^k)]. \tag{8-11}$$

As stated in (8-11), the problem is to find, at each step k, a scalar, α^k, which indicates how far to move along the gradient at that step, away from X^k. There are many procedures for finding an "optimal" α^k; we indicate the logic behind one such method.[20] The quadratic approximation to a function $f(X)$ in a neighborhood of X^0 is given by the second-order Taylor's series expansion

$$f^Q(X) = f(X^0) + [\nabla f(X^0)]'(X - X^0) + \tfrac{1}{2}(X - X^0)'H^0(X - X^0), \tag{8-12}$$

---

[18] A maximum that may unfortunately, however, be only a local and not a global one. This is a common weakness of most optimization methods; as we saw in Section 4.8, it may not be troublesome if the function involved has the proper shape (the concavity and convexity requirements).

[19] For a minimization problem, the direction component would be $-\nabla f(X^k)$, of course, since this is the direction of maximum decrease.

[20] For more details on other methods as well the reader is referred to Crockett and Chernoff [3]; Fiacco and McCormick [5]; Goldfeld, Quandt, and Trotter [6], A. Leon, "A Comparison among Eight Known Optimizing Procedures," in Lavi and Vogl [12]; Saaty and Bram [15]; Wilde [16]; Wilde and Beightler [17]; P. Wolfe, "An Outline of Nonlinear Programming," in Dantzig and Veinott [4, pp. 365–400]; and P. Wolfe, "Methods of Nonlinear Programming," in Graves and Wolfe [7, chap. 10].

where H^0 is the Hessian matrix of second partial derivatives and cross-partials, evaluated at X^0. (Taylor's series approximations were touched upon in Appendix 4.1; the discussion is extended in Appendix 8.3, to which the interested reader should turn at this point.) In terms of a "new" point X^{k+1} and an "original" point X^k, the approximation given by (8-12) becomes

$$f(X^{k+1}) = f(X^k) + [\nabla f(X^k)]'(X^{k+1} - X^k) + \tfrac{1}{2}(X^{k+1} - X^k)'H^k(X^{k+1} - X^k).$$
(8-13)

Since, from (8-11), $X^{k+1} - X^k = \alpha^k[\nabla f(X^k)]$, we can express the *difference* between the value of the function at the new point X^{k+1} (as given by the quadratic approximation) and at the old as

$$D^{k+1} = f(X^{k+1}) - f(X^k) = [\nabla f(X^k)]'\alpha^k[\nabla f(X^k)]$$
$$+ \tfrac{1}{2}\{\alpha^k[\nabla f(X^k)]\}'H^k\{\alpha^k[\nabla f(X^k)]\},$$

which becomes, because of the properties of matrix multiplication by a scalar,

$$D^{k+1} = \alpha^k[\nabla f(X^k)]'[\nabla f(X^k)] + \tfrac{1}{2}(\alpha^k)^2\{[\nabla f(X^k)]'H^k[\nabla f(X^k)]\}. \quad (8\text{-}14)$$

Thus the change in the value of $f(X)$ is a function of α^k, the step size, since the gradient vector and the Hessian matrix, evaluated at any particular X^k, are constants. To maximize this change (which for maximization problems is an increase) we differentiate (8-14) with respect to α^k, the variable, and set the derivative equal to zero.[21]

$$\frac{dD^{k+1}}{d\alpha^k} = [\nabla f(X^k)]'[\nabla f(X^k)] + \alpha^k\{[\nabla f(X^k)]'H^k[\nabla f(X^k)]\} = 0;$$

that is,

$$\alpha^k = -\{[\nabla f(X^k)]'H^k[\nabla f(X^k)]\}^{-1}[\nabla f(X^k)]'[\nabla f(X^k)]. \quad (8\text{-}15)$$

For a maximum,

$$\frac{d^2D^{k+1}}{(d\alpha^k)^2} = \{[\nabla f(X^k)]'H^k[\nabla f(X^k)]\} < 0,$$

which will always be true if the Hessian matrix, H, evaluated at any point, X^k, is negative definite. This will be the case when $f(X)$ is a concave function.[22] Note in (8-15) that the -1 exponent does not denote an inverse matrix but merely the reciprocal of the scalar in curly brackets. In fact the entire expression (8-15) looks much more complicated than it is. The optimal step size is just the product of the gradient vector at X^k with itself

---

[21] Note that in both terms of (8-14) α^k is multiplied by a scalar. If $f(X)$ is a function of n variables, the first term involves a matrix product of dimensions $(1 \times n) \times (n \times 1)$, the second is $(1 \times n) \times (n \times n) \times (n \times 1)$.

[22] This relationship is treated in Appendix 8.3.

(transposed) divided by a scalar involving the gradient and the Hessian at X^k.

When the shape of $f(X)$ does not assure negative definiteness of the Hessian, this particular "optimum" gradient method may be unsuccessful. We do not explore further variations here.[23] The idea has been to indicate the way in which straightforward methods of simple maximization can be utilized to derive a "best" step size to use in conjunction with a "best" direction of movement in the general scheme $X^{k+1} = X^k + \alpha^k[\nabla f(X^k)]$, as given in (8-11).

NEWTON'S METHOD

One can imagine somewhat irregular functions, "bumpy" hills, on which the direction of steepest ascent (the gradient direction) from a point would be optimal for only a very short part of a given step length, whereas some other direction from that point would lead to a greater total increase in the function for the same step length. Thus, in effect, the general scheme in (8-11) might be modified to

$$X^{k+1} = X^k + \alpha^k[A^k][\nabla f(X^k)], \qquad (8\text{-}16)$$

where at each step, k, a "weighting" matrix, A^k, is used to possibly modify the gradient direction.[24] A particular form of (8-16), known as Newton's method, proceeds as follows. Consider again the quadratic approximation given by (8-13), and maximize this function directly with respect to X^{k+1}. That is, find the coordinates of the "new" point, X^{k+1}, for which the value of the function, as given by the approximation, is largest. Again, the first derivative must be set equal to zero.[25]

$$\frac{\partial f(X^{k+1})}{\partial X^{k+1}} = [\nabla f(X^k)] + H^k X^{k+1} - H^k X^k = 0, \qquad (8\text{-}17)$$

from which we find, if H^k has an inverse, that

$$X^{k+1} = X^k - (H^k)^{-1}[\nabla f(X^k)]. \qquad (8\text{-}18)$$

---

[23] The interested reader is again referred to the material noted in footnote 20.

[24] The procedure in (8-11) may be considered as a special case of (8-16) with $A^k = I$, for all steps k.

[25] $f(X^{k+1})$ is obviously a matrix function of X^{k+1}. Hence we are finding derivatives of vectors and matrices. The reader should be able to convince himself that no new principles are involved while the notational convenience of matrices is retained. In particular, note that

if $f(X) = \underset{(1 \times n)}{B} \underset{(n \times 1)}{X}$, then $\dfrac{\partial f(X)}{\partial X} = B$;   if $f(X) = X'AX$, then $\dfrac{\partial f(X)}{\partial X} = 2AX$.

Bear in mind that all products in (8-13) involving only $[\nabla f(X^k)]$, X^k, and/or H^k are constants.

As with the result in (8-15), we require a negative-definite H^k for a maximum; note that this implies n sign conditions on the principal minors of H^k. Thus Newton's method has the form of (8-16) with $\alpha^k = 1$ and $A^k = -(H^k)^{-1}$. Calculations of the inverse of the Hessian at each step can be a time-consuming procedure, although approximations may be adequate. The details of subtle variations are again omitted.

EXAMPLE

The aim of this subsection has been to give the reader a feeling for the underlying logic of gradient methods for unconstrained maximization (and minimization) problems. This is especially important, since these methods also play a role in problems constrained by inequalities—that is, in nonlinear programs. Before we turn to these, however, we conclude with an example that illustrates the gradient method in action (and also points out the importance of the choice of the step size). We use the simple form in (8-11). Consider the problem of maximizing

$$y = 4x_1 + 5x_2 + x_1x_2 - x_1^2 - x_2^2 + 5.$$

Obviously, the results of Chapter 4 could be applied directly; if one does (and the reader is encouraged to work this through), a maximum, $y^* = 25\frac{1}{3}$, is found at $x_1^* = 4\frac{1}{3}$; $x_2^* = 4\frac{2}{3}$. We illustrate the gradient approach to the same problem; here

$$\nabla f(x_1, x_2) = \begin{bmatrix} -2x_1 + x_2 + 4 \\ x_1 - 2x_2 + 5 \end{bmatrix}.$$

For simplicity only, we let the step length be $\frac{1}{2}$ throughout—that is, $\alpha^1 = \alpha^2 = \cdots = \frac{1}{2}$—and we begin at the origin. The moves are summarized in Table 8.1, where, in each case, $X^{k+1} = X^k + \frac{1}{2}\nabla f(X^k)$.

The table illustrates the fact that gradient methods need not (and do not, usually) generate exact answers; how close they come to a true maximum will depend largely on how well the step length, α, is modified as one nears the maximum, for example to avoid an "overshoot." In theory, one can come as close as one likes by taking relatively small steps; on the other hand, this increases the number of steps that must be taken and hence the calculation time. Large step lengths move one quickly around the surface but can easily fail to converge, and, in fact, they can oscillate explosively, getting farther and farther away from the true maximum. For example, if we were (unwisely) to try a step length of *unity* on the problem above, the first few moves would be as shown in Table 8.2.

This serves to illustrate, again, the possible importance of the modification of the gradient in (8-11) or (8-16). The sizes of the elements in the gradient are very much influenced by the location of the trial points— obviously, since the gradient elements are functions of the x_j; the *direction*

Table 8.1.   Gradient Maximization, $\alpha = \frac{1}{2}$

k	X^k	$f(X^k)$	$\nabla f(X^k)$
1	$\begin{bmatrix} 0 \\ 0 \end{bmatrix}$	5	$\begin{bmatrix} 4 \\ 5 \end{bmatrix}$
2	$\begin{bmatrix} 2 \\ \frac{5}{2} \end{bmatrix}$	$20\frac{1}{4}$	$\begin{bmatrix} \frac{5}{2} \\ 2 \end{bmatrix}$
3	$\begin{bmatrix} \frac{13}{4} \\ \frac{7}{2} \end{bmatrix} = \begin{bmatrix} 3\frac{1}{4} \\ 3\frac{1}{2} \end{bmatrix}$	$24\frac{1}{16}$	$\begin{bmatrix} 1 \\ \frac{5}{4} \end{bmatrix}$
4	$\begin{bmatrix} \frac{15}{4} \\ \frac{33}{8} \end{bmatrix} = \begin{bmatrix} 3\frac{3}{4} \\ 4\frac{1}{8} \end{bmatrix}$	25.016	$\begin{bmatrix} \frac{5}{8} \\ \frac{1}{2} \end{bmatrix}$
5	$\begin{bmatrix} \frac{65}{16} \\ \frac{35}{8} \end{bmatrix} = \begin{bmatrix} 4\frac{1}{16} \\ 4\frac{3}{8} \end{bmatrix}$	25.254	$\begin{bmatrix} \frac{1}{4} \\ \frac{5}{16} \end{bmatrix}$
6	$\begin{bmatrix} \frac{67}{16} \\ \frac{145}{32} \end{bmatrix} = \begin{bmatrix} 4.19 \\ 4.53 \end{bmatrix}$	25.313	

is not so sensitive. For example, the direction of optimal movement from steps 2 and 6 in Table 8.2 [as obtained from observing $\nabla f(X^2)$ and $\nabla f(X^6)$] is the same, while the elements in the latter vector are 16 times as large.
In view of the way in which gradient methods tend to move rather

Table 8.2.   Gradient Maximization, $\alpha = 1$

k	X^k	$f(X^k)$	$\nabla f(X^k)$
1	$\begin{bmatrix} 0 \\ 0 \end{bmatrix}$	5	$\begin{bmatrix} 4 \\ 5 \end{bmatrix}$
2	$\begin{bmatrix} 4 \\ 5 \end{bmatrix}$	25	$\begin{bmatrix} 1 \\ -1 \end{bmatrix}$
3	$\begin{bmatrix} 5 \\ 4 \end{bmatrix}$	24	$\begin{bmatrix} -2 \\ 2 \end{bmatrix}$
4	$\begin{bmatrix} 3 \\ 6 \end{bmatrix}$	20	$\begin{bmatrix} 4 \\ -4 \end{bmatrix}$
5	$\begin{bmatrix} 7 \\ 2 \end{bmatrix}$	4	$\begin{bmatrix} -8 \\ 8 \end{bmatrix}$
6	$\begin{bmatrix} -1 \\ 10 \end{bmatrix}$	-60	$\begin{bmatrix} 16 \\ -16 \end{bmatrix}$
7	$\begin{bmatrix} 15 \\ -6 \end{bmatrix}$	-316	

cautiously around the surface, they are sometimes referred to as "creeping" methods. In contrast to creeping (a large number of small steps), the simplex method for *linear* programs has been termed a "hopping" method, since it involves a relatively small number of generally large steps.

Gradient methods for amximization or minimization with inequality constraints

The logic of maximization over a constrained area is extremely simple; the mathematical formulation of the ideas is rather complex.[26] In words [if we are using the approach of (8-11), where $X^{k+1} = X^k + \alpha^k \, \nabla f(X^k)$], we must begin with a feasible X^1—this is not *usually* difficult—and, select an α^k at each step so that X^{k+1} is also feasible *and* $f(X^{k+1}) > f(X^k)$. This means, in fact, that we may have to modify the *direction* of movement given by the gradient in cases where the gradient leads us out of the feasible region. For example, we could *reverse* the direction by multiplying the gradient by -1 (recall that this sends a vector the same distance in the *opposite* direction); this, however, is not likely to be very efficient, since it is the direction of *least* advantageous, although possibly feasible, movement.

Consider, for example, a maximization problem involving a nonlinear objective function and a set of linear constraints; maximize $f(x_1, \ldots, x_n)$ subject to $AX \leq R$ and $X \geq O$. A procedure for finding *feasible directions* of movement, developed by Zoutendijk, has the following general character. Given a "current" feasible point, X^k, the *direction* of movement should be $\nabla f(X^k)$ if that is possible (exactly as in the unconstrained case). However, if X^k was on one or more of the boundaries, it is quite possible that the gradient will point outward from the feasible region. If that is the case, Zoutendijk suggests that we find a direction, D^k, that deviates from $\nabla f(X^k)$ as little as possible (making as small an angle as possible with the gradient at X^k), while assuring that *some* movement along this direction is feasible. We saw in Section 8.3 that maximizing the inner product of two vectors was tantamount to maximizing the cosine of the angle included between them, which in turn was the same as *minimizing* the angle between them. Hence, in this approach we want to find elements d_j^k of the vector D^k such that $D^k \cdot \nabla f(X^k)$ is maximized. Since the elements of $\nabla f(X^k)$ are constants, the objective function is linear.[27] We want to do this subject to (1) some kind of normalization constraint on the sizes of the elements d_j^k (since

---

[26] We concern ourselves with maximization only. For minimization problems one simply moves in the *direction* of the negative gradient, as we have seen. Problems of choice of step length are essentially the same.

[27] This is, in fact, fundamentally the same objective as we had in the previous section when we were determining the direction of maximum increase for a function based on observations on the form of the total differential.

direction is all that we are interested in at the moment) and (2) the requirements of the constraints (feasibility). We consider these in turn:

1.   A simple normalization is $-1 \leq d_j^k \leq 1$, for all j. Note that these are *linear* constraints. Or one could require that $||D^k|| \leq 1$, a *nonlinear* constraint. There are numerous other "normalization" constraints, which it is unnecessary to specify here; we are primarily interested in the fundamental logic of the method.[28]

2.   For feasibility, we need to require that if a constraint was met as an equality, the new direction is not outward from it. In terms of the *gradient of the constraint*, this means that the new direction must make an angle of *at least* 90° with that gradient.[29] Again the representation of the cosine of the included angle between two vectors as the inner product of the vectors divided by the product of their lengths is relevant. In the range from 0 to 90 to 180° (the possible range of an *included* angle), the cosine goes from 1 to 0 to -1; hence requiring the cosine to be nonpositive assures that the angle between the vectors is at least 90°. Since the product of the vector lengths is necessarily positive, the cosine will be nonpositive if, and only if, the inner product of the vectors is nonpositive. Let $_iA$ denote the ith *row* of A in the $AX \leq R$ set—that is, the coefficients from $a_{i1}x_1 + \cdots + a_{in}x_n \leq r_i$. Recall that the gradient of this linear function is just the vector

$$\begin{bmatrix} a_{i1} \\ \vdots \\ a_{in} \end{bmatrix}$$

—that is, $_iA'$. Hence we must require, for all i for which $_iAX^k = r_i$, that $[_iA'] \cdot [D^k] \leq 0$—that is, that $_iAD^k \leq 0$. This assures us that the elements of the direction vector will direct us at least along an edge or face of the feasible region ($_iAD^k = 0$) and possibly back into the interior ($_iAD^k < 0$). Similarly, to assure continued nonnegativity, we require, for those j for which $x_j^k = 0$, that $d_j^k \leq 0$. Notice that both feasibility constraints are *linear* in the d_j^k.

Thus we can find a feasible direction at each step by solving an associated problem that can be constructed as a *linear* program (by using a linear normalization constraint). In doing so, we deviate as little as possible from the direction that would be optimal in an unconstrained maximization problem, namely the direction given by the gradient. When the normalization constraints are nonlinear, the associated problem at each step is nonlinear in the constraints (although smaller than the original problem, and

[28] The reader is referred in particular to Künzi, Krelle, and Oettli [11, chap. 14].

[29] Recall that we are dealing here with problems having linear constraints. Modifications are necessary in the case of non-linearities in the constraints.

with a linear objective). In either case the step length still remains to be determined, as with all gradient methods. However, with inequality constrained problems, the step length (once a feasible direction has been established) is really determined by the nearer of the following two points: (1) where the direction vector leaves the feasible region or (2) where $f(x_1, \ldots, x_n)$ reaches a maximum on the direction ray.

Rosen's *gradient projection* method is also designed to modify the gradient direction when this points out of a feasible region. Consider again the problem with a nonlinear objective function and linear constraints. For ease of exposition, we imagine a function of three variables, so that the boundaries of the feasible region are made up of faces (that is, planes—two-dimensional regions), edges (lines—one-dimensional regions), and vertices (points—zero-dimensional regions). Rosen suggests that when the current point, X^k, is on a boundary and the gradient points outward, one should use as a direction of feasible movement the projection of the gradient onto the boundary of smallest dimension (but no less than one) on which X^k lies. That is, if X^k is on a face but not on an edge, use the projection on the face; if X^k is on an edge, project onto the edge; and if X^k is at a vertex, project onto an edge. No optimization is involved; one simply finds an acceptable (feasible) direction along which the objective function changes in the correct manner. We omit the details of how these gradient projections are found, especially in large, multidimensional problems. Determination of a number of "projection matrices" is required, each of which involves most of the usual matrix operations (such as transposition, subtraction, multiplication, and inversion) on possibly large matrices.

To contrast the two approaches, consider the following figure, in which the gradient from the current X^k, on an edge, points upward and outward from the feasible region (the interior and faces of the distorted cube). Zoutendijk's direction, Z, will be on the upper face; Rosen's, R, will be along the edge. (Note that when X^k is on a face, the directions will be the same.)

It should be clear that gradient methods *could* be used on linear pro-

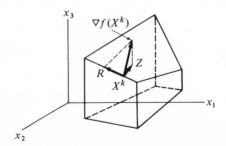

Figure 8.10.   Zoutendijk's and Rosen's Modification of the Gradient

gramming problems; it is generally the case that a simplex method approach is more efficient. We briefly explore the geometry of the two-variable, three-constraint linear programming problem, (6-5), of Chapter 6, repeated here as (8-19).

$$
\begin{aligned}
\text{Maximize:} \quad & \pi = 2x_1 + 5x_2 \\
\text{subject to:} \quad & x_1 + 2x_2 \leq 10, \\
& 3x_1 + 2x_2 \leq 24, \\
& x_1 + 10x_2 \leq 40, \\
\text{and} \quad & x_1,\ x_2 \geq 0.
\end{aligned}
\tag{8-19}
$$

For this problem it was found, in (6-27), that the optimum occurred at $x_1^0 = 2\frac{1}{2}$, $x_2^0 = 3\frac{3}{4}$, and $\pi^0 = 23\frac{3}{4}$. The feasible region is shown in Figure 8.11 [this is the same as Figure 6.1(d)].

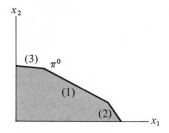

Figure 8.11. Feasible Region for (8-19)

Consider the origin as the initial feasible point for either Zoutendijk's or Rosen's variation of a gradient method. (In a simple two-dimensional problem both paths from the origin to the optimum corner will be the same; the reader should be clear why this is true.) The gradient of the objective function, $\nabla f(X)$, is $\begin{bmatrix} 2 \\ 5 \end{bmatrix}$. We add this vector to Figure 8.11 and use Zoutendijk's method of feasible directions in order to illustrate the associated linear programming problem. In Figure 8.12, we would move in

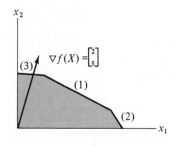

Figure 8.12. Gradient Direction from $\begin{bmatrix} 0 \\ 0 \end{bmatrix}$

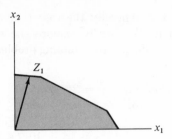

Figure 8.13.   First Feasible Direction Step

the $\nabla f(X)$ direction until a constraint (here the third) is met—point Z_1 in Figure 8.13.[30] Here we must determine a direction vector,

$$D^1 = \begin{bmatrix} d_1^1 \\ d_2^1 \end{bmatrix},$$

from the following linear program:

$$
\begin{aligned}
\text{maximize:} &\quad 2d_1^1 + 5d_2^1 \\
\text{subject to:} &\quad -1 \le d_1^1 \le 1, \\
&\quad -1 \le d_2^1 \le 1, \\
\text{and} &\quad d_1^1 + 10d_2^1 \le 0.
\end{aligned}
\tag{8-20}
$$

Clearly at least one of the variables will be negative, because of the third constraint, and hence the simplex method of Chapter 6, which *automatically* assures nonnegativity of the variables, would have to be modified. However, by studying the geometry of this linear program, we can see immediately what the solution is (Figure 8.14).

The maximum is achieved where the $d_1^1 = 1$ and $d_1^1 + 10d_2^1 = 0$ con-

---

[30] This occurs at $x_1 = \frac{20}{13}$, $x_2 = \frac{50}{13}$, which is not particularly important information in a problem with a linear objective function, since the gradient is a constant. These values are found by solving $x_1 + 10x_2 = 40$ (constraint 3 as an equation) and $5x_1 - 2x_2 = 0$, simultaneously. The latter is one way of expressing the equation of the line, a part of which is given by the gradient $\begin{bmatrix} 2 \\ 5 \end{bmatrix}$ from the origin. We know that this line must itself have a gradient that is *orthogonal* to $\begin{bmatrix} 2 \\ 5 \end{bmatrix}$; and we know that orthogonality requires a zero-valued inner product. Hence by reversing the order of the elements and changing the sign of one of them, we assure an inner product of 0—that is,

$$\begin{bmatrix} 2 \\ 5 \end{bmatrix} \cdot \begin{bmatrix} 5 \\ -2 \end{bmatrix} = 0.$$

But $\begin{bmatrix} 5 \\ -2 \end{bmatrix}$ is clearly the gradient of $5x_1 - 2x_2 = b$; since the equation goes through the origin, its right-hand side must be 0.

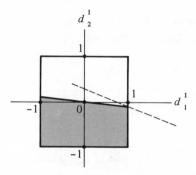

Figure 8.14. Feasible Region and Objective Function Contours for (8-20)

straints intersect—that is, at $d_1^1 = 1$, $d_2^1 = -\frac{1}{10}$. Hence $D^1 = \begin{bmatrix} 1 \\ -\frac{1}{10} \end{bmatrix}$;

we add this to the information in Figure 8.13 (see Figure 8.15). Thus we move along constraint 3—that is, in direction $\begin{bmatrix} 1 \\ -\frac{1}{10} \end{bmatrix}$ from Z_1, until the next constraint is met, at Z_2. This is where $x_1 + 2x_2 = 10$ and $x_1 + 10x_2 = 40$ hold simultaneously—where $x_1 = 2\frac{1}{2}$, $x_2 = 3\frac{3}{4}$ (the reader should use Cramer's rule for review). Now we look for a new direction, $D^2 = \begin{bmatrix} d_1^2 \\ d_2^2 \end{bmatrix}$. This is to be found as a solution to the linear program

$$\begin{aligned} \text{maximize:} \quad & 2d_1^2 + 5d_2^2 \\ \text{subject to:} \quad & -1 \le d_1^2 \le 1, \\ & -1 \le d_2^2 \le 1, \\ \text{and} \quad & d_1^2 + 10d_2^2 \le 0, \\ & d_1^2 + 2d_2^2 \le 0. \end{aligned} \qquad (8\text{-}21)$$

That is, the new point must satisfy the previous constraint [from (8-20)] as well as the new one, in addition to the normalization requirements on the

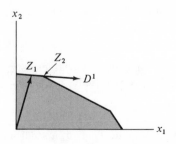

Figure 8.15. Second Feasible Direction

elements of the direction vector. The feasible region and objective function contours are now as shown in Fig. 8.16. The optimum is thus at $d_1^2 = 0$

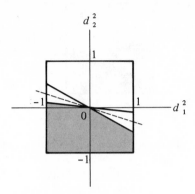

Figure 8.16.   Feasible Region and Objective Function Contours for (8-21)

and $d_2^2 = 0$, which is to say that there is no incentive to move at all from the position Z_2. This is, of course, the same optimum as was found by using the simplex method in Chapter 6.

8.5.   SADDLE-POINT PROBLEMS AND NONLINEAR PROGRAMMING

In this section we examine the characteristics of saddle points of functions. Then we investigate the connections between saddle points and optimal solutions, first, to linear programs and, second, to certain nonlinear programs. These relationships not only provide clues for computational procedures for nonlinear programming problems; they also provide an interpretation of the Lagrange multipliers that were introduced in the inequality-constrained maximization and minimization problems in Section 4.8 and that were used in Section 8.2.

Saddle points

Consider a function, ϕ, of $n + m$ variables; specifically[31] $\phi(x_1, \ldots, x_n; v_1, \ldots, v_m)$. Using X and V, respectively, for the n- and m-element vectors

---

[31] The notation ϕ is used to avoid confusion with functions f, g, and h, which we use for progamming problems. It is quite standard in saddle-point literature and should cause no confusion with the ϕ that was used to designate the included angle between two vectors.

of unknowns, we represent the function as $\phi(X, V)$. This function is said to have a saddle point at (X^0, V^0) if and only if

$$\phi(X^0, V) \geq \phi(X^0, V^0) \geq \phi(X, V^0). \tag{8-22}$$

We examine this statement in two parts. The right-hand inequality says that X^0 maximizes $\phi(X, V^0)$; that is, for $V = V^0$, $\phi(X, V)$ is maximized by the X^0. And the left-hand inequality says that V^0 minimizes $\phi(X^0, V)$; that is, for $X = X^0$, $\phi(X, V)$ is minimized by the V^0. Put somewhat differently, the X^0 are chosen so that they

$$\max_{X} \{\min_{V} \phi(X, V)\};$$

similarly, the V^0 are found so that they

$$\min_{V} \{\max_{X} \phi(X, V)\}.$$

Thus, from the point of view of the X's, saddle points are *maximinimizing* points; from the standpoint of the V's they are *minimaximizing* points.[32]

We now examine in more detail the problem in the nonnegative orthant only—that is, the problem of finding (if it exists) an $X^0 \geq O$ and a $V^0 \geq O$ such that (8-22) holds over all $X, V \geq O$. We might call this the non-negative saddle-point problem.[33] Define the following "partial gradients" of the function $\phi(X, V)$:

$$\nabla \phi_{X^0} = \begin{bmatrix} \dfrac{\partial \phi^0}{\partial x_1} \\ \vdots \\ \dfrac{\partial \phi^0}{\partial x_n} \end{bmatrix}, \qquad \nabla \phi_{V^0} = \begin{bmatrix} \dfrac{\partial \phi^0}{\partial v_1} \\ \vdots \\ \dfrac{\partial \phi^0}{\partial v_m} \end{bmatrix}, \tag{8-23}$$

where the superscripts indicate that the partial derivatives making up the gradients are evaluated at (X^0, V^0). We now present a set of necessary conditions for a nonnegative saddle point [which require, as the reader will see, that $\phi(X, V)$ be differentiable, so that the elements of the partial gradient vectors can be found].

THEOREM SP1.   For (X^0, V^0) to be a saddle point of $\phi(X, V)$ it is necessary that: (a) $\nabla \phi_{X^0} \leq 0$, $[\nabla \phi_{X^0}]' X^0 = 0$, and (b) $\nabla \phi_{V^0} \geq 0$, $[\phi_{V^0}]' V^0 = 0$, for $X^0 \geq O$, $V^0 \geq O$.

---

[32] This was anticipated in the discussion of saddle points in two-person, zero-sum games in Section 7.7.

[33] This is clearly a rather specialized problem, in much the same way that nonnegativity requirements on the solution variables in a pair of dual linear programs made them somewhat specialized optimization problems. We will soon see (in this section) why our concern is exclusively with nonnegative saddle points.

This information is more useful than may appear at first reading. Note what each part says. Recall that the function ϕ, for $V = V^0$, is maximized by X^0. That is, for each x_j^0 (the value of each x_j at the saddle point), $\partial\phi^0/\partial x_j \leq 0$ at the saddle point, since if $\partial\phi^0/\partial x_j > 0$, one should increase the value of that x_j (and hence of ϕ). Presumably, however, if $\partial\phi^0/\partial x_j < 0$, for some j, one would prefer an even lower value of x_j, in order to increase ϕ. Clearly one would stop decreasing x_j only if the lower limit, namely zero, were reached. Thus (a) if $\partial\phi^0/\partial x_j < 0$, then $x_j^0 = 0$, and (b) if $\partial\phi^0/\partial x_j = 0$, then $x_j^0 \geq 0$. This is precisely what part (a) of the theorem says. The partial derivatives of ϕ with regard to the x's, evaluated at the saddle point, can never be positive, and at least one term in each of the products $(\partial\phi^0/\partial x_j)x_j$ must be zero. The interpretation of part (b) is similar, except that the v's minimize $\phi(X, V)$ for $X = X^0$, and hence the $\partial\phi^0/\partial v_i$ can never be negative. Thus (a) and (b) describe the characteristics that a saddle point must *necessarily* have.[34]

Parallel to the development of first- and second-order conditions for maxima and minima in Chapter 4, we now examine a theorem that gives conditions *sufficient* to assure a saddle point.

THEOREM SP2.   For (X^0, V^0) to be a saddle point of $\phi(X, V)$ it is *sufficient* that:

(a)   both conditions of Theorem SP1 hold;
(b) $\phi(X, V^0) \leq \phi(X^0, V^0) + [\nabla\phi_{X^0}]' (X - X^0)$; and
(c) $\phi(X^0, V) \geq \phi(X^0, V^0) + [\nabla\phi_{V^0}]' (V - V^0)$.

As with the previous theorem, these conditions [(b) and (c)] have a logical interpretation.[35] Recall that the first total differential of a function at a point gives the equation of the tangent (line, plane or hyperplane) at that point. Consider (b), and move the first term on the right-hand side of the inequality to the left; rewrite (b) as $\phi(X, V^0) - \phi(X^0, V^0) \leq [\nabla\phi_{X^0}]' (X - X^0)$. Now the right-hand side of the inequality is just the equation of the tangent to $\phi(X, V)$ at (X^0, V^0), in the n-dimensional space of X—that is, with V fixed at V^0. The left-hand side is the difference in the value of $\phi(X, V)$ at some point X and at X^0, with V always fixed at V^0. Hence the inequality requires that for an X different from X^0, the tangent plane (the approximation given by the differential) *overestimates* the actual change in

---

[34] These are first-order conditions, parallel to the $df = 0$ requirement for maxima and minima discussed in Chapter 4. The case where *all* $\partial\phi^0/\partial x_j = 0$ and *all* $\partial\phi^0/\partial v_i = 0$, which would occur at a maximum or minimum—if $\phi(X, V)$ has such stationary points— rules out the *sufficiency* of the conditions in Theorem SP1.

[35] The interested reader may wish to note that these conditions represent applications of the discussion on convexity and concavity in Appendix 8.3, particularly inequality (8-39).

the value of the function ϕ—that is, that $\phi(X, V^0)$ is *below* its tangent plane at (X^0, V^0). Exactly similar reasoning shows that part (c) of Theorem SP2 requires that $\phi(X^0, V)$ be *above* its tangent plane at (X^0, V^0).[36]

These conditions on the tangent planes will *always* be satisfied when $\phi(X, V^0)$ is a *concave* function of X and $\phi(X^0, V)$ is a *convex* function of V. Hence, if these concavity-convexity conditions hold for $\phi(X, V)$, the two conditions in Theorem SP1 are both necessary *and* sufficient for (X^0, V^0) to be a saddle point of $\phi(X, V)$.[37]

Saddle points and linear programming problems

As a prelude to our discussion of the relationship between saddle points and nonlinear programs, we investigate the linear programming case. Using the compact matrix notation of Chapter 6, especially Section 6.4, we recall the pair of dual programs (6-30):

	Primal		*Dual*	
maximize:	$\pi = P'X$	minimize:	$\Delta = R'V$	
subject to:	$AX \leq R$	subject to:	$A'V \geq P$	(8-24)
and	$X \geq 0;$	and	$V \geq 0.$	

We now want to show the connection between an optimal solution to the primal problem in (8-24) and a particular kind of saddle point to an associated Lagrangean function.

THEOREM SP3. X^0 is an optimal solution to the maximizing (primal) problem in (8-24) if and only if a vector $V^0 (\geq 0)$ exists such that (X^0, V^0) is a saddle point of the Lagrangean function $L(X, V) = P'X - V'(AX - R)$ for all nonnegative values of X and V.

In other words, an optimal solution to the linear programming maximization problem is identical to the X vector of a *nonnegative saddle point* to the function $L(X, V)$. (Proof of both the necessity and the sufficiency is

---

[36] Once again we see the intimate connection between geometric and algebraic approaches to a problem. Logically the (geometric) condition on positions of ϕ relative to tangent planes at a saddle point make sense. Consider the algebra of part (b) on Theorem SP2, in the light of the conditions of Theorem SP1. The last term on the right can be written $[\nabla \phi_{X^0}]'X - [\nabla \phi_{X^0}]'X^0$. By (a) of Theorem SP1, the second term is zero, and the first is nonpositive for $X \geq 0$. Hence it follows from (b) of Theorem SP2 that $\phi(X, V^0) \leq \phi(X^0, V^0)$. Similar use of (b) from Theorem SP1 in (c) of Theorem SP2 shows that $\phi(X^0, V) \geq \phi(X^0, V^0)$. Putting these results together, $\phi(X^0, V) \geq \phi(X^0, V^0) \geq \phi(X, V^0)$, precisely the (algebraic) definition of (X^0, V^0) as a saddle point of $\phi(X, V)$.

[37] This is parallel to the situation in Chapter 4 of unconstrained maximization of $f(x_1, \ldots, x_n)$, where, if we know that d^2f is always negative (the second-order condition that is *sufficient* to distinguish maxima, given that the first-order, necessary condition holds), then the (first-order) condition $df = 0$ becomes both necessary and sufficient for a local maximum.

given in Appendix 8.4.) The impact of the theorem is that a maximization problem subject to (possibly many) linear inequality constraints on the variables has been converted to a much less constrained (nonnegativity only) saddle-point problem. Thus to the extent that procedures are available for finding saddle points (and since the constraints in a maximization or minimization problem virtually always complicate the calculations), one *could* be interested in this correspondence between linear programming optimal solutions and saddle points. This is not likely, however, since the simplex method provides such a simple approach for the linear programming problem directly. It is important, however, to see whether a similar relationship holds for nonlinear programming problems.

Saddle points and nonlinear programming problems

We repeat the general nonlinear programming problem in (8-4):

$$\text{maximize:} \quad f(X)$$
$$\text{subject to:} \quad h_i(X) \leq 0 \quad (i = 1, \ldots, m) \tag{8-4}$$
$$\text{and} \quad X \geq O.$$

As in the general Lagrangean approach to inequality constraints (Section 4.8), we formulate an associated function

$$L(X, V) = f(X) - \sum_{i=1}^{m} v_i h_i(X). \tag{8-25}$$

The correspondence between saddle points and *nonlinear* programming problems is given in the following two theorems (which require differentiability of the objective function f and all constraints h_i).

THEOREM SP4.   For X^0 to be a solution to the nonlinear maximization problem in (8-4), it is *necessary* that X^0 and some V^0 satisfy the conditions of Theorem SP1, for $\phi(X, V) \equiv L(X, V)$ as given in (8-25).

Specifically, the theorem requires (from Theorem SP1, and using the notation for partial derivatives from Chapter 4—$\partial f/\partial x_j \equiv f_j$ and $\partial h_i/\partial x_j \equiv h_j^i$):

(a)   (i) $\partial L/\partial x_j \leq 0$—that is, $f_j - \sum_{i=1}^{m} v_i h_j^i \leq 0$, for $j = 1, \ldots, n$, and

(ii) $\left(f_j - \sum_{i=1}^{m} v_i h_j^i \right) x_j = 0;$

(b)   (i) $\partial L/\partial v_i \geq 0$—that is, $-h_i(X) \geq 0$ [or $h_i(X) \leq 0$], for $i = 1, \ldots, m$, and

(ii) $[h_i(X)v_i] = 0,$
for all $X, V \geq O.$

Written out in this way, we see that these requirements are identical to the Kuhn-Tucker conditions developed in Section 8.2 and listed in (8-9), with the λ's represented here as v's. However, in the earlier development, via Lagrange multipliers, the relationship between the optimum to the maximization problem and a saddle point to the associated Lagrangean function was not clear.

Moreover, in view of Theorem SP3 for *linear* programs, we suspect that the v's of Theorem SP4—the Lagrange multipliers of Section 8.2—may be precisely the variables in the program that is dual to the maximization problem in (8-4). We explore this further in the next chapter, where the concept of duality for nonlinear programming problems is treated. Furthermore, if we interpret the nonlinear problem in (8-4) as one of profit (or revenue) maximization subject to resource constraints (as we did for the *linear* programming maximization problem in Chapter 6), then the conditions of Theorem SP4 have interesting and logical interpretations. In this case, $\partial f / \partial x_j \equiv f_j$ represents the marginal profit (or marginal revenue) of product j; $\partial h_i / \partial x_j \equiv h_j^i$ gives the *input* of resource i for a marginal amount of j, and the v_i, since there is one for each resource, may be thought of (as before) as a shadow price or valuation on each resource i. Then conditions (a) require that (i) the net marginal profit (or the net marginal revenue) for each j be zero or negative, and (ii) if negative, no j is produced ($x_j = 0$). Conditions (b) require (i) that resource constraints be met and (ii) that if a particular resource, i, is not fully used,[38] its corresponding valuation is zero ($v_i = 0$).

The reader may note the general similarity to the interpretations given to some of the primal-dual relationships in linear programs, especially Theorem P-D3 of Chapter 6. This again suggests that the v_i here, from the saddle-point problem for $\phi(X, V)$, might be thought of as the variables from the programming problem dual to (8-4).

Parallel to the sufficient conditions for a saddle point, given in Theorem SP2, we have:

THEOREM SP5.   For X^0 to be a solution to the nonlinear maximization problem in (8-4), it is *sufficient* that X^0 and some V^0 satisfy conditions (a) and (b) of Theorem SP2, for $\phi(X, V) \equiv L(X, V)$ as given in (8-25).

Consider part (b) of Theorem SP2; we have seen that this will hold when $\phi(X, V^0)$ is a concave function of X. That is, when $L(X, V^0)$—or, more particularly $f(X) - \sum_{i=1}^{m} v_i^0[h_i(X)]$ [from (8-25)]—is concave in X. Rewrite $L(X, V^0)$ as

$$L(X, V^0) = f(X) + \sum_{i=1}^{m} v_i^0[-h_i(X)]. \qquad (8\text{-}26)$$

---

[38] That is, if $h_i(X) < 0$, which means $g_i(X) - r_i < 0$ or $g_i(X) < r_i$.

Then if $-h_i(X)$ is concave, for all i, the functions $h_i(X)$ will be convex. Since all v_i are nonnegative, $L(X, V^0)$ in (8-26) is a nonnegative linear combination of $f(X)$ and the $[-h_i(X)]$. Thus $L(X, V^0)$ will be a concave function if $f(X)$ and all $[-h_i(X)]$ are concave—that is, if $f(X)$ is a *concave* function of X and the $h_i(X)$ are all *convex* functions of X.

Since $L(X^0, V) = f(X^0) - \displaystyle\sum_{i=1}^{m} v_i[h_i(X^0)]$ is *linear* in the v_i (and hence convex as well as concave), the requirements of part (c) of Theorem SP2, which we saw will always hold when $\phi(X^0, V)$ is a *convex* function of V, will *automatically* be fulfilled. This is why part (c) from Theorem SP2 did not need explicit treatment in Theorem SP5.

Therefore we conclude that when the objective function, $f(X)$, is a *concave* function of X and when each of the constraints, $h_i(X)$, is a *convex* function of X, the conditions of Theorem SP4 are both necessary *and* sufficient for a solution to the general nonlinear programming maximization problem of (8-4). The object of this investigation, once again, is to give a new interpretation to primal and dual variables in a pair of linear programming problems, as maximinimizing and minimaximizing variables in a saddle-point problem. This in turn suggests possible parallels for duals in nonlinear programming problems. It also shows how a constrained optimization problem, such as (8-4), involving (in general) n variables, m nonlinear constraints, *and* the nonnegativity of all the variables, can be converted into an equivalent saddle-point problem in $(n + m)$ variables constrained only by the requirement that all variables be nonnegative. Since gradient methods can be adapted to locate saddle points, this provides a solution procedure for those nonlinear programming problems that satisfy the concavity-convexity requirements—those that seek the maximum of a concave function over a convex set, which is to say over the area defined by the $h_i(X) \leq 0$, where each $h_i(X)$ is convex.

SUMMARY

This chapter has introduced the reader to the nature of the problems caused by nonlinearities in the objective function and/or the constraints of a mathematical programming problem. A brief consideration of the geometry of nonlinearities indicated several reasons why the simplex method approach, concentrating as it does on extreme points of the feasible region (basic solutions), was not generally applicable.

We then examined the underlying principles of gradient methods for finding maxima and minima, with or without constraints. The idea is extremely simple: move in the "best" direction if possible (although we saw that there is clearly more than one way to define the "best" direction and to decide how far along it to move). Otherwise move in a "good" direction that is feasible. If modification is necessary because of boundaries, there are obviously many possible approaches. We looked briefly at two in the case of linear constraints. The reader will appreciate that a wide variety of "boundary rules" is possible and that nonlinear constraints further complicate the issue. We have avoided a detailed examination of methods for trying to determine the optimal "step length," once the direction of movement—the gradient or some modification of it—has been established. These refinements are beyond the level of this text; they are areas in which fundamental work is still being done.

Finally, the chapter introduced the saddle-point problem and connected it to both linear and nonlinear programs. We saw that this provides insights into the Lagrange multipliers of Section 4.8 and suggests properties for nonlinear duality theory. It also indicates one direction for a computational approach to nonlinear problems; we will explore this and several other computational techniques in the next chapter.

In addition, we will examine in some detail the notion of duality for non-linear programming problems. Finally, we will see that special computational techniques can be employed when the nonlinear problem has a quadratic objective function and linear constraints.

APPENDIX 8.1

Nonnegativity Constraints in the Kuhn-Tucker Conditions

A small example will serve to illustrate precisely why it is *not* sufficient simply to add $X \geq O$ to the conditions of (8-5) when nonnegativity of the variables is a requirement of the problem. Consider the problem

$$\text{maximize:} \quad f(X) = -x_1^2 - x_2^2 - 4x_1 + 6x_2$$

$$\text{subject to:} \quad \begin{cases} (1) & x_1 + x_2 \leq 10, \\ (2) & x_1 \leq 4, \end{cases} \tag{8-27}$$

$$\text{and} \quad x_1 \geq 0, \quad x_2 \geq 0 \text{[39]}$$

---

[39] The objective function is similar to that used in the example in Figure 4.12; it has been shifted to the left so that the unconstrained maximum involves a negative x_j, and the constraints have been altered for variety.

The reader can easily find that an unconstrained maximum occurs at $x_1^* = -2$, $x_2^* = 3$, at which point $f(X^*) = 13$. This is point A in Figure 8.17, in which the feasible region is shaded and several contours of the objective function have been shown.

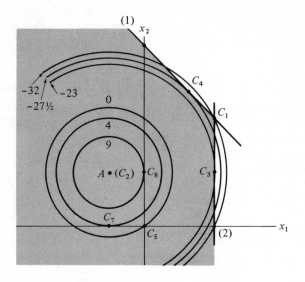

Figure 8.17. Feasible Region and Objective Function Contours for (8-27)

If we were to impose the Kuhn-Tucker conditions from (8-5) and simply add the requirement that $x_1 \geq 0$ and $x_2 \geq 0$, we would have:

$$\text{(a)} \quad \begin{cases} -2x_1 - 4 - \lambda_1 - 2\lambda_2 = 0, \\ -2x_2 + 6 - \lambda_1 = 0, \end{cases}$$

$$\text{(b)} \quad \begin{cases} \lambda_1(x_1 + x_2 - 10) = 0, \\ \lambda_2(x_1 - 4) = 0, \end{cases} \qquad (8\text{-}28)$$

$$\text{(c)} \quad \begin{cases} x_1 + x_2 \leq 10, \\ x_1 \leq 4, \end{cases}$$

where, in addition, $x_1 \geq 0$ and $x_2 \geq 0$.

Working, as usual, with the implications of the second set of relations—those in (8-28)(b)—we would have the following cases.

CASE 1. $\lambda_1 \neq 0$, $\lambda_2 \neq 0$. Then $x_1^* = 4$, $x_2^* = 6$; this is point C_1 in the figure, where the constraints intersect. The fact that both λ's are nonzero means that we are imposing both constraints as equations. Since $\lambda_1^* = -6 < 0$, this point does not qualify as a local maximum; $f(X^*) = -32$.

CASE 2. $\lambda_1 = 0$, $\lambda_2 = 0$.   This is the case in which constraints (1) and (2) are completely ignored. It leads, as we saw above, to point A (also labeled C_2) which is unacceptable because it violates one of the added conditions, namely that x_2 be nonnegative; $f(X^*) = 13$.

CASE 3. $\lambda_1 = 0$, $\lambda_2 \neq 0$.   Under these conditions we are ignoring the first constraint and finding the maximum when the second constraint is imposed as an equation; that is, we are exploring along the boundary imposed by the second constraint. We find (and the reader should work this through for practice) $x_1^* = 4$, $x_2^* = 3$, but $\lambda_2^* = -12 < 0$, which disqualifies the point as a local maximum. [This is point C_3 in Figure 8.17, where $f(X^*) = -23$.]

CASE 4. $\lambda_1 \neq 0$, $\lambda_2 = 0$.   Now constraint (2) is ignored and constraint (1) is an equation; we explore along the boundary set by constraint (1). This results in point C_4 in the figure, where $x_1^* = 2\frac{1}{2}$ and $x_2^* = 7\frac{1}{2}$ but $\lambda_1^* = -9 < 0$, so, once more, this cannot be a local maximum. At this point $f(X^*) = -27\frac{1}{2}$.

Thus the explorations along constraints (1) and (2) have not turned up an acceptable local maximum, and the unconstrained maximum violates one of the nonnegativity requirements. The reason that (8-5), plus the non-negativity requirement $X \geq O$, is inadequate is that the additional boundaries given by the x_1 and x_2 axes are not explicitly considered as possible locations for local maxima. Utilizing the full set of Kuhn-Tucker conditions as given in (8-7') or (8-9) allows precisely for exploration along these added sides of the feasible region.

Specifically, the requirements are as follows—using (8-9):

$$\text{(a)} \quad \begin{cases} -2x_1 - 4 - \lambda_1 - 2\lambda_2 \leq 0, \\ -2x_2 + 6 - \lambda_1 \qquad\quad \leq 0 \end{cases}$$

$$\text{(b)} \quad \begin{cases} x_1(-2x_1 - 4 - \lambda_1 - 2\lambda_2) = 0, \\ x_2(-2x_2 + 6 - \lambda_1) \qquad\quad = 0, \end{cases}$$

$$\text{(c)} \quad \begin{cases} x_1 + x_2 - 10 \leq 0, \\ x_1 - 4 \qquad\quad \leq 0, \end{cases} \qquad (8\text{-}29)$$

$$\text{(d)} \quad \begin{cases} \lambda_1(x_1 + x_2 - 10) = 0, \\ \lambda_2(x_1 - 4) \qquad\quad = 0, \end{cases}$$

$$\text{(e)} \quad x_1 \geq 0, \quad x_2 \geq 0,$$

and also λ_1 and $\lambda_2 \geq 0$.

Working with the relations in (8-29)(b) leads to four cases, which we designate as Cases 5 through 8. (The reader may wish to work through some of these for review.)

CASE 5. $-2x_1 - 4 - \lambda_1 - 2\lambda_2 \neq 0$, $-2x_2 + 6 - \lambda_1 \neq 0$.   From this it follows that x_1^* and x_2^* must be zero. This, via (8-29)(d), causes $\lambda_1 = \lambda_2 = 0$, and the second inequality in (8-29)(a) is violated; $f(X^*) = 0$. This point, the origin, is labeled C_5 in Figure 8.17. Although it does not meet all necessary requirements for a local maximum, note that it generates a larger value of the objective function than points C_1, C_3, and C_4, isolated previously, each of which produced a negative $f(X)$.

CASE 6. $x_1 \neq 0$, $x_2 \neq 0$. Then $-2x_1 - 4 - \lambda_1 - 2\lambda_2 = 0$ and $-2x_2 + 6 - \lambda_1 = 0$. In this case, requirements (8-29)(a) are met as equalities and we have precisely the set of conditions used above to generate Cases 1 through 4 and the corresponding points on Figure 8.17.

CASE 7. $x_1 \neq 0$, $-2x_2 + 6 - \lambda_1 \neq 0$. Then $x_2 = 0$ and $-2x_1 = \lambda_1 + 2\lambda_2 + 4$. Geometrically, since $x_2 = 0$ in this case, we are exploring along the x_1 axis. Now the four possibilities implied by (8-29)(d) must be considered in turn.

(a) $\lambda_1 \neq 0$, $\lambda_2 \neq 0$; that is, both constraints are imposed as equalities. This leads to the impossible requirements that $x_1^* = 10$ and $x_1^* = 4$. This simply reflects the fact that the x_1 axis intersects constraints (1) and (2) at different points (specifically, at 10 and 4, respectively).

(b) $x_1 + x_2 - 10 \neq 0$, $x_1 - 4 \neq 0$. This means $\lambda_1^* = \lambda_2^* = 0$ and as a result $x_1^* = -2$, which violates (8-29)(e). Otherwise, however, all requirements are met. This is point C_7 in the figure, where $f(X^*) = 4$.

(c) $\lambda_1 \neq 0$, $x_1 - 4 \neq 0$. This results in $x_1^* = 10$ but $\lambda_1^* = -24 < 0$; hence this point is unacceptable as a local maximum.

(d) $x_1 + x_2 - 10 \neq 0$, $\lambda_2 \neq 0$. Now $x_1^* = 4$ but $\lambda_2^* = -6 < 0$; this point is also unacceptable.

The reader should note what Case 7 has done. It has provided a mechanism for examining the acceptability of four particular points along the x_1 axis (that is, along one of the *new* boundaries generated when $x_1 \geq 0$, $x_2 \geq 0$ are added to the problem). These were, in turn:

(a) the point where both constraints are equalities (an impossibility in this problem);
(b) the maximum along the x_1 axis when both of the two original constraints are ignored;
(c) the point where constraint (1) intersects the x_1 axis; and
(d) the point where constraint (2) intersects the x_1 axis.

It happens that none of these is acceptable as a local maximum. We now turn to the final case implied by conditions (8-29)(b).

CASE 8. $x_1 + x_2 - 10 \neq 0$, $x_2 \neq 0$. Since $x_1 = 0$, this corresponds to exploration along the x_2 axis. The possibilities parallel those under Case 7.

(a) $\lambda_1 \neq 0$, $\lambda_2 \neq 0$. This means that both constraints are equalities. In particular, it requires $x_1^* = 4$, which is impossible in Case 8, which is the $x_1 = 0$ case.

(b) $x_1 + x_2 - 10 \neq 0$, $x_1 - 4 \neq 0$. That is, both original constraints are ignored. From this it follows that $\lambda_1^* = \lambda_2^* = 0$ and $x_2^* = 3$. In this case, all other constraints are met. Hence the point $x_1^* = 0$, $x_2^* = 3$ meets all the necessary requirements for a local maximum subject to the two original constraints plus nonnegativity. Here $f(X^*) = 9$; this is point C_8 in Figure 8.17.

(c) $\lambda_1 \neq 0$, $x_1 - 4 \neq 0$. This examines the point where the first constraint cuts the x_2 axis. Here $\lambda_1^* = -14 < 0$, so the point is not acceptable.

(d) $x_1 + x_2 - 10 \neq 0$, $\lambda_2 \neq 0$. As in Case 8(a), this is impossible, since x_1 cannot be both 0 and 4 at the same time.

Thus we have explored relevant points along the second new boundary (given when $x_2 \geq 0$ is added to the problem) and, in so doing, we have found the solution to the constrained maximization problem. The ramifications of the nonnegativity requirements are (1) possibly to eliminate some points that otherwise would be allowed by the simpler Kuhn-Tucker conditions in (8-5) and (2) to add more boundary lines (which actually are axes) along which to explore.

APPENDIX 8.2

Proof of the "Direction of Maximum Increase" Property of Gradients

The problem is to find the elements of the vector C so that they

maximize: $[\nabla f^*] \cdot C \equiv f_1^* c_1 + \cdots + f_n^* c_n$
subject to: $\|C\| = 1$ —that is, to $(c_1^2 + \cdots + c_n^2)^{\frac{1}{2}} = 1$.

The constraint is essentially unaltered if we square both sides. Then it becomes

$$\sum_{j=1}^{n} c_j^2 - 1 = 0.$$

Forming the Lagrangean function

$$L = \sum_{j=1}^{n} f_j^* c_j - \lambda \left[\sum_{j=1}^{n} c_j^2 - 1 \right] \tag{8-30}$$

and differentiating in the usual way:

$$\frac{\partial L}{\partial c_j} = f_j^* - 2\lambda c_j = 0 \qquad (j = 1, \ldots, n),$$

$$\frac{\partial L}{\partial \lambda} = - \left[\sum_{j=1}^{n} c_j^2 - 1 \right] = 0. \tag{8-31}$$

From the first n equations in (8-31) find that $c_j^0 = f_j^*/2\lambda$ and hence that $C^0 = \left(\dfrac{1}{2\lambda} \right) [\nabla f^*]$; that is, the optimal direction from X^* is given by the gradient at X^* multiplied by a scalar, $\dfrac{1}{2\lambda}$. The only question, then, concerns the sign of λ.

From the last of the first-order conditions in (8-31) it is necessary that

$$\sum_{j=1}^{n} c_j^2 = 1.$$

But from the results of the other first-order conditions, this means

$$\sum_{j=1}^{n} \left(\frac{f_j^*}{2\lambda} \right)^2 = 1.$$

A little algebra, and the definition of $\|\nabla f^*\|$, shows that

$$\lambda^2 = \tfrac{1}{4} \|\nabla f^*\|^2 \quad \text{and hence} \quad \lambda^0 = \pm \tfrac{1}{2} \|\nabla f^*\|.$$

Thus

$$C^0 = \frac{\nabla f^*}{\pm \|\nabla f^*\|}.$$

Examination of the original function $[\nabla f^*] \cdot C$, which is now known to be

$$[\nabla f^*] \cdot \frac{[\nabla f^*]}{\pm \|\nabla f^*\|},$$

shows that the *positive* denominator gives the maximum, since each element of ∇f^* is multiplied by itself and hence has a positive sign in the product (the numerator). Hence the direction of maximum increase from X^* is given by $\nabla f^*/\|\nabla f^*\|$, the gradient elements divided by a "normalizing" scalar, the length of the gradient.[40] This simply assures that the norm of the vector C^0 is one, as was required.

APPENDIX 8.3

Taylor's Series, Concavity, and Convexity Once Again

We review the fundamental idea of Taylor's series, which was originally presented in Appendix 4.1, using vector notation.[41] Recall that an approximation to the value of a function $f(X)$ for values of X in the neighborhood[42] of a specific point X^0 is given by a function involving $f(X^0)$ and its derivatives evaluated at X^0. In particular

$$f(X) = f(X^0) + [\nabla f(X^0)]'(X - X^0) \\ + \tfrac{1}{2}(X - X^0)'H^0(X - X^0) + \cdots, \quad (8\text{-}32)$$

where H^0 is the Hessian matrix evaluated at X^0 and terms involving third- and higher-order partials and cross-partials have been omitted and are covered by the "$+ \cdots$." The so-called second-order Taylor's series expansion ignores these terms and is written

$$f(X) \cong f(X^0) + [\nabla f(X^0)]'(X - X^0) + \tfrac{1}{2}(X - X^0)'H^0(X - X^0). \quad (8\text{-}33)$$

[These correspond to (4-54) and (4-55), using the vector and gradient notation of the present chapter.] We extend the discussion of convexity and

---

[40] And clearly the other value of λ that satisfies these first-order conditions, (8-31), namely $-\|\nabla f^*\|$, represents the minimum of the function. That is, the negative gradient indicates the direction of minimum increase (= maximum decrease) of the function. The distinction between the maximum and the minimum can also be made using the bordered Hessian rules of Section 4.5. When $\lambda^0 = +\tfrac{1}{2}\|\nabla f^*\|$, v_{jj}^0 and c_j^0 are always of the same sign; when $\lambda^0 = -\tfrac{1}{2}\|\nabla f^*\|$, they are always of opposite sign. In all cases, $v_{jk}^0 = 0$.

[41] Further details can be found among the references, in particular in Hadley [8, chap. 3, sec. 10] and Karlin [9, app. B, sec. 4].

[42] These "nearby" values of X are often designated $(X^0 + dX)$, in which case, in the expressions following, $(X - X^0)$ is just (dX).

concavity from that in Appendix 4.1, since these concepts are central to many nonlinear programming techniques.

The right-hand side of (8-33) consists of a constant, $f(X^0)$, a linear function of X, $[\nabla f(X^0)]'(X - X^0)$, and a quadratic function of X, $\frac{1}{2}(X - X^0)'H^0(X - X^0)$. We therefore say that all of (8-33), the second-order Taylor's series expansion, provides a *quadratic approximation* to $f(X)$ in the neighborhood of X^0. That is,

$$f(X) \cong f^Q(X) = f(X^0) + [\nabla f(X^0)]'(X - X^0)$$
$$+ \tfrac{1}{2}(X - X^0)'H^0(X - X^0). \quad (8\text{-}34)$$

On the other hand, we have a *linear approximation* to $f(X)$ in the neighborhood of X^0 if the quadratic term in (8-33) is ignored. (This is the first-order Taylor's series expansion.)

$$f(X) \cong f^L(X) = f(X^0) + [\nabla f(X^0)]'(X - X^0). \quad (8\text{-}35)$$

Recall from Section 4.7 that a function of n variables, $f(X)$, over a convex set of points was defined as convex if

$$f[\alpha X' + (1 - \alpha)X''] \leq \alpha f(X') + (1 - \alpha)f(X'') \quad (8\text{-}36)$$

for any pair of points, X' and X'', in the set and for any α in the range $0 \leq \alpha \leq 1$. When the inequality is a strict one (for distinct points X' and X'' and $0 < \alpha < 1$), the function is termed *strictly* convex. When the inequality in (8-36) is reversed, the function is concave or strictly concave. We now examine two additional characteristics relating to convexity (and concavity). The first requires the existence of first partial derivatives everywhere; the second requires also second partials and cross-partials.

Let $f(X)$ be convex, so that (8-36) holds. Restrict the range of α to $0 < \alpha \leq 1$ and rewrite (8-36) as

$$\alpha f(X'') + f[\alpha X' + (1 - \alpha)X''] - f(X'') \leq \alpha f(X'). \quad (8\text{-}37)$$

Divide both sides by α (which is greater than zero) and write $\alpha X' + (1 - \alpha)X''$ as $X'' + \alpha(X' - X'')$

$$f(X'') + \frac{f[X'' + \alpha(X' - X'')] - f(X'')}{\alpha} \leq f(X'). \quad (8\text{-}38)$$

Consider, from (8-35), the first-order Taylor's series expansion of $f[X'' + \alpha(X' - X'')]$ about the point X'' [which requires differentiability of $f(X)$ at the point X'']

$$f[X'' + \alpha(X' - X'')] = f(X'') + [\nabla f(X'')]'[\alpha(X' - X'')].$$

Thus (8-38) becomes

$$f(X'') + [\nabla f(X'')]'(X' - X'') \leq f(X'),$$

or
$$[\nabla f(X'')]'(X' - X'') \leq f(X') - f(X''), \quad (8\text{-}39)$$

which is another characteristic of a convex function $f(X)$. Formally, $f(X)$ is convex if and only if for two points X' and X'' in the convex set over which $f(X)$ is defined, (8-39) holds. Geometrically this condition simply says that a convex function lies nowhere below its tangent. Figure 8.18 illustrates

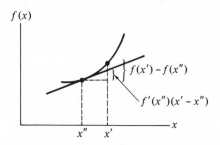

Figure 8.18.   Geometry of (8-39) for $f(x)$

for a function of one variable. *Strict* convexity is associated with strict inequality in (8-39); hence a strictly convex function lies everywhere above its tangent. For concavity and strict concavity the inequality is reversed. A concave (strictly concave) function therefore lies nowhere above (everywhere below) its tangent. In several dimensions, of course, the function represents a hypersurface and the tangents are hyperplanes.

Consider now the second-order Taylor's series expansion (8-34), using points X' and X'' for X and X^0, respectively:

$$f(X') - f(X'') - [\nabla f(X'')]'(X' - X'')$$
$$= \tfrac{1}{2}(X' - X'')'H(X'')(X' - X''). \quad (8\text{-}40)$$

If the left-hand side is always nonnegative, the right-hand side must be also. But nonnegativity of the left-hand side is, from (8-39), both necessary and sufficient for convexity of $f(X)$, for all X', X'' in the convex set over which X is defined. Hence nonnegativity of the right-hand side of (8-40) is also necessary and sufficient for convexity of $f(X)$. But this is equivalent to the requirement that $H(X'')$, the Hessian of $f(X)$, evaluated at X'', be positive semidefinite for all X'' in the convex set over which $f(X)$ is defined. If the Hessian is positive definite, the function is strictly convex; and for concavity (and strict concavity), negative semidefiniteness (and negative definiteness) are required. This extends the fundamental concepts of Appendix 4.1 to the Taylor series expansion of a function around *any* point; in that appendix we were concerned with behavior around a stationary point, where $f'(x)$—or $\nabla f(X)$, for functions of many variables—was equal to zero.

APPENDIX 8.4

Proof of Theorem SP3

Primal	*Dual*	
Maximize: $\pi = P'X$	Minimize: $\Delta = R'V$	
subject to: $AX \leq R$	subject to: $A'V \geq P$	(8-24)
and $X \geq O.$	and $V \geq O.$	

THEOREM SP3. X^0 is an optimal solution to the maximizing (primal) problem in (8-24) if and only if a vector $V^0(\geq O)$ exists such that (X^0, V^0) is a saddle point of $L(X, V) = P'X - V'(AX - R)$ for all $X, V \geq O.$

The proof is in two parts. Consider first the "if" part of the theorem—a nonnegative saddle point at (X^0, V^0) means that X^0 is optimal for the linear program.

A saddle point of $L(X, V)$ at (X^0, V^0) means

$$L(X^0, V) \geq L(X^0, V^0) \geq L(X, V^0)$$

—that is,

$$P'X^0 - V'(AX^0 - R) \geq P'X^0 - V'^0(AX^0 - R) \geq P'X - V'^0(AX - R). \tag{8-41}$$

Consider the left-hand inequality in (8-41). Since this must hold for all $V' \geq O$, it must follow that $(AX^0 - R) \leq O$; otherwise [if $(AX^0 - R)$ were positive] for any given $V'^0 (\geq O)$ a larger set of elements could be chosen for V' ($> V'^0$), and the inequality would be violated.[43] In particular, the left-hand inequality in (8-41) must hold when $V' = O$. Then it must follow that $V'^0(AX^0 - R) = 0$. But then the right-hand inequality in (8-41) reads $P'X^0 \geq P'X - V'^0(AX - R)$. Since this is required to hold for *all* $X \geq O$, it must hold in particular for all X for which $(AX - R) \leq O$ [all X that are feasible for the primal in (8-24)]. But then, since $V'^0 \geq O$, $P'X^0 \geq P'X$. Hence X^0 is an optimal solution for the primal. It gives a value to the objective function that is no less than[44] that given by any other X.

---

[43] Since $(AX^0 - R) \leq O$, or $AX^0 \leq R$, it follows that X^0 must be a *feasible* solution for the primal problem in (8-24).

[44] Except in the case of primal multiple optima, the value will be strictly greater for $P'X^0$.

Now we treat the "only if" part of the theorem—that the optimality of X^0 in the primal of (8-24) implies the existence of a $V^0 \geq O$ such that (X, V^0) constitute a saddle point of $L(X, V)$.

In Section 6.4 on duality in linear programs we saw that $P'X \leq V'AX \leq R'V$ for all feasible X and V for the primal and dual problems, respectively. And at optimum $P'X^0 = R'V^0 = V'^0AX^0$. Therefore $P'X \leq V'^0AX$, and hence $P'X - V'^0AX \leq P'X^0 - V'^0AX^0$. But[45]

$$L(X^0, V^0) = P'X^0 - V'^0AX^0 + R'V^0$$
$$\text{and} \quad L(X, V^0) = P'X - V'^0AX + R'V^0.$$

Therefore we conclude that

$$L(X^0, V^0) \geq L(X, V^0).$$

Similarly $V'AX^0 \leq R'V$ and $V'^0AX^0 = R'V^0$. Thus $R'V \geq V'AX^0$, and so

$$R'V - V'AX^0 \geq R'V^0 - V'^0AX^0.$$

But $L(X^0, V) = P'X^0 - V'AX^0 + R'V$ and $L(X^0, V^0)$ was just examined. Thus

$$L(X^0, V) \geq L(X^0, V^0)$$

and hence

$$L(X^0, V) \geq L(X^0, V^0) \geq L(X, V^0)$$

—that is, (X^0, V^0) is a saddle point to the function $L(X, V)$.

PROBLEMS

1. Find the maximum of $f(X) = -x_1^2 - x_2^2 - x_3^2 + 4x_1 + 6x_2$ subject to the constraints $x_1 + x_2 \leq 2$ and $2x_1 + 3x_2 \leq 12$ and the requirement that all three variables be nonnegative, using the Kuhn-Tucker results in (8-9). Establish the sufficiency of conditions (8-9) by testing the function for concavity or convexity.
2. Minimize $6x_1^2 + 5x_2^2$ subject to the constraint that $x_1 + 5x_2 \geq 3$ and the requirement that both variables be nonnegative. Use the Kuhn-Tucker approach, as in Problem 1.
3. Minimize the same function as in Problem 2, subject to the requirement that both variables be nonnegative and also that $x_1 + 5x_2 \leq 3$, again using the Kuhn-Tucker approach as in Problem 1.
4. Find the gradient vector for each of the following functions at the point indicated:
   (a) $x_1^2 + x_1x_2 + x_2^2 - x_2$ at $x_1 = -1$, $x_2 = 2$.

---

[45] Recall that for any m-element column vectors A and B, $A'B \equiv B'A$ (and both equal the inner product $A \cdot B$).

   (b) $x_1^2 + x_2^2 + (3x_1 + 4x_2 - 26)^2$ at $x_1 = 1$, $x_2 = 6$.

   (c) $9x_1^2 - 18x_1 - 16x_2^2 - 64x_2 - 55$ at $x_1 = 0$, $x_2 = 0$.

   (d) $16 - 2(x_1 - 3)^2 - (x_2 - 7)^2$ at $x_1 = 3$, $x_2 = 7$.

   (e) $12x_1 + 10x_2$ at $x_1 = 56$, $x_2 = 37$.

5. Using the simple gradient method approach of (8-11), with $\alpha^k = \frac{1}{4}$ for all k, find an approximation to the maximum of $f(X) = 16 - 2(x_1 - 3)^2 - (x_2 - 7)^2$, the function in Problem 4(d), above. Let $X^1 = \begin{bmatrix} 0 \\ 0 \end{bmatrix}$. Check your result by finding the maximum exactly, using the methods of Chapter 3. [This was Problem 6(d) of Chapter 3.]

6. Using the same gradient approach as in Problem 5, find the minimum of:

   (a) $f(X) = x_1^2 + x_1 x_2 - x_2^2 - x_2$, from Problem 4(a), above, using $\alpha^k = \frac{1}{2}$ for all k.

   (b) $f(X) = x_1^2 + x_2^2 + (3x_1 + 4x_2 - 26)^2$, from Problem 4(b), above, using $\alpha^k = \frac{1}{100}$ for all k.

In both cases, compare your result with the exact answer. [These were Problems 6(a) and (b), respectively, of Chapter 3.]

7. For each of the following problems, formulate the Lagrangean function as in (8-25) and find its saddle point. (Note that if you have solved Problems 1 through 3, above, already, the work is essentially completed.) Maximize:

   (a) $f(X) = -x_1^2 - x_2^2 - x_3^2 + 4x_1 + 6x_2$ subject to $x_1 + x_2 \leq 2$ and $2x_1 + 3x_2 \leq 12$ and x_1, x_2, and $x_3 \geq 0$.

   (b) $f(X) = -6x_1^2 - 5x_2^2$ subject to $-x_1 - 5x_2 \leq -3$ and nonnegative x_1 and x_2.

   (c) $f(X) = -6x_1^2 - 5x_2^2$ subject to $x_1 + 5x_2 \leq 3$ and nonnegativity of x_1 and x_2.

REFERENCES

1. Abadie, J., ed., *Nonlinear Programming.* New York: Interscience Publishers, 1967.

2. Baumol, W. J., *Economic Theory and Operations Analysis*, 2d ed. Englewood Cliffs, N.J.: Prentice-Hall, Inc., 1965.

3. Crockett, J. B., and H. Chernoff, "Gradient Methods of Maximization," *Pacific Journal of Mathematics*, vol. 5 (1955), pp. 33–50.

4. Dantzig, G. B., and A. F. Veinott, Jr., eds., *Mathematics of the Decision Sciences*, vol. I (Lectures in Applied Mathematics, vol. 11). Providence, R.I.: American Mathematical Society, 1968.

5. Fiacco, A. V., and G. P. McCormick, *Nonlinear Programming: Sequential Unconstrained Minimization Techniques.* New York: John Wiley & Sons, Inc., 1968.

6. Goldfeld, S. M., R. E. Quandt, and H. F. Trotter, "Maximization by Quadratic Hill-Climbing," *Econometrica*, vol. 34 (1966), pp. 541–551.

7. Graves, R. L., and P. Wolfe, eds., *Recent Advances in Mathematical Programming.* New York: McGraw-Hill, Inc., 1963.

8. Hadley, G., *Nonlinear and Dynamic Programming.* Reading, Mass.: Addison-Wesley Publishing Company, Inc., 1964.

9. Karlin, S., *Mathematical Methods and Theory in Games, Programming and Economics*, vol. I. Reading, Mass.: Addison-Wesley Publishing Company, Inc., 1959.

10. Kuhn, H. W., and A. W. Tucker, "Nonlinear Programming," in J. Neyman, ed., *Second Berkeley Symposium on Mathematical Statistics and Probability*. Berkeley: University of California Press, 1951. (Reprinted in P. Newman, ed., *Readings in Mathematical Economics*, vol. I. Baltimore: The Johns Hopkins Press, 1968.)

11. Künzi, H. P., W. Krelle, and W. Oettli, *Nonlinear Programming*. Waltham, Mass.: Blaisdell Publishing Company, 1966.

12. Lavi, A., and T. P. Vogl, eds., *Recent Advances in Optimization Techniques*. New York: John Wiley & Sons, Inc., 1966.

13. Mangasarian, O. L., *Nonlinear Programming*. New York: McGraw-Hill, Inc., 1969.

14. Pierre, D. A., *Optimization Theory with Applications*. New York: John Wiley & Sons, Inc., 1969.

15. Saaty, T. L., and J. Bram, *Nonlinear Mathematics*. New York: McGraw-Hill, Inc., 1964.

16. Wilde, D. J., *Optimum Seeking Methods*. Englewood Cliffs, N.J.: Prentice-Hall, Inc., 1964.

17. Wilde, D. J., and C. S. Beightler, *Foundations of Optimization*. Englewood Cliffs, N.J.: Prentice-Hall, Inc., 1967.

18. Zangwill, W. I., *Nonlinear Programming: A Unified Approach*. Englewood Cliffs, N.J.: Prentice-Hall, Inc., 1969.

9

NONLINEAR PROGRAMMING MODELS—II: DUALITY AND FURTHER COMPUTATIONAL METHODS

It is clear from Chapter 8 that nonlinearities in a programming problem largely vitiate any *generally* applicable solution procedures. There are a number of special approaches, most of which depend on the concavity-convexity properties of the nonlinear programming problem. Usually, the objective function must be concave for a maximization problem, convex for a minimization one, and the constraints must be such that their inter-section is a convex set. In this chapter we present some of the most widely used computational techniques. Initially, we also explore the concept of duality for the nonlinear case. Though it is not as well developed as in the linear case, the reader will note many parallels. Finally, we examine the details of quadratic programming problems. In a sense these are the "most linear" of the nonlinear programming models; they have a quadratic objective function (variables may be squared or multiplied together in pairs) and linear constraints. Computational procedures take advantage of this structure, as we shall see.

These topics—computational methods for nonlinear programming problems and the formulation and interpretation of dual programs—are the "frontier" of the mathematical programming field. Even though the computational details will change and the solution algorithms will be refined, the fundamental logic of the various methods will remain valid, and this continues to be our primary interest in solution techniques.

9.1. DUALITY IN NONLINEAR PROGRAMMING

We repeat the general nonlinear programming maximization problem, (8-4):

$$\text{maximize:} \quad f(X)$$
$$\text{subject to:} \quad h_i(X) \leq 0 \quad (i = 1, \ldots, m) \tag{9-1}$$
$$\text{and} \quad X \geq O.$$

Letting

$$[h(X)] = \begin{bmatrix} h_1(X) \\ \vdots \\ h_m(X) \end{bmatrix},$$

the most compact formulation is

$$\text{maximize:} \quad f(X)$$
$$\text{subject to:} \quad [h(X)] \leq O \tag{9-1'}$$
$$\text{and} \quad X \geq O.$$

The associated Lagrangean function, used primarily in development of the Kuhn-Tucker conditions and in the discussion of saddle points, was given in (8-25) and is repeated here in condensed, matrix form:

$$L(X, V) = f(X) - V'[h(X)] \quad \left(\text{where } V = \begin{bmatrix} v_1 \\ \vdots \\ v_m \end{bmatrix} \right). \tag{9-2}$$

The "partial" gradient of (9-2) with respect to the variables v_i, which we denote ∇L_V, is just $\nabla L_V = -[h(X)]$. Thus $f(X)$, the objective function in (9-1'), is exactly the same as $L(X, V) - V' \nabla L_V$; that is,

$$f(X) - V'[h(X)] + V'[h(X)] \equiv f(X).$$

Moreover, $[h(X)] \leq O$ is also expressed by requiring $\nabla L_V \geq O$. Hence the general nonlinear programming maximization problem (9-1') could also be written

$$\text{maximize:} \quad L(X, V) - V' \nabla L_V$$
$$\text{subject to:} \quad -\nabla L_V \leq O \tag{9-3}$$
$$\text{and} \quad X \geq O.$$

A "symmetric" problem related to (9-3) could then be defined as follows:[1]

---

[1] There are other possibilities, and some of the more general developments in nonlinear duality have been accomplished via conjugate function theory, which goes beyond the level of this book. The interested reader might first consult Balinski and Baumol [3] and Dorn [6]. Further discussions, at a higher level of difficulty, can be found in Abadie [1, esp. chaps. 1 (by S. Vajda), 3 (by H. W. Kuhn) and 5 (by A. Whinston)] and many of the references cited there, in particular the work of Rockafellar, which is presented most completely in [15].

$$\begin{aligned} \text{minimize:} \quad & L(X, V) - X' \,\nabla L_X \\ \text{subject to:} \quad & -\nabla L_X \geq 0 \\ \text{and} \quad & V \geq 0. \end{aligned} \tag{9-4}$$

Since, for the Lagrangean function (9-2),

$$\nabla L_X = \left[\frac{\partial L}{\partial x_j} \right] = \left[\frac{\partial f}{\partial x_j} - \sum_i v_i \frac{\partial h_i}{\partial x_j} \right],$$

this "symmetric" problem can be written more explicitly as

$$\text{minimize:} \quad f(X) - \sum_i v_i h_i(X) - \sum_j x_j \left(\frac{\partial f}{\partial x_j} - \sum_i v_i \frac{\partial h_i}{\partial x_j} \right)$$

$$\text{subject to:} \quad \sum_i v_i \frac{\partial h_i}{\partial x_j} - \frac{\partial f}{\partial x_j} \geq 0 \qquad (j = 1, \ldots, n) \tag{9-5}$$

$$\text{and} \qquad\qquad\qquad v_i \geq 0 \qquad (i = 1, \ldots, m),$$

or, using the previous notation for partial derivatives (letting $\partial f/\partial x_j \equiv f_j$ and $\partial h_i/\partial x_j \equiv h_j^i$,

$$\text{minimize:} \quad f(X) - \sum_i v_i h_i(X) - \sum_j x_j \left(f_j - \sum_i v_i h_j^i \right)$$

$$\text{subject to:} \quad \sum_i v_i h_j^i - f_j \geq 0 \qquad (j = 1, \ldots, n) \tag{9-5'}$$

$$\text{and} \qquad\qquad\qquad v_i \geq 0 \qquad (i = 1, \ldots, m).$$

When $f(X)$ in the maximization problem is concave and each constraint, $h_i(X)$, is convex,[2] so that the conditions of Theorem SP4 of Chapter 8 constitute both necessary and sufficient conditions for an optimum to the nonlinear programming problem, then (9-5) [or (9-4)] is taken to be the dual to (9-1) [or (9-3)]. This is primarily because (1) a pair of dual *linear* programs corresponds precisely to (9-3) and (9-4) and (2) a set of theorems parallel to those in duality theory for linear programming can be proved.

Consider a primal linear program [(6-1) in Chapter 6]: maximize $P'X$ subject to $AX \leq R$, or $AX - R \leq 0$, and $X \geq 0$. Then the general Lagrangean function, (9-2), would be

$$L(X, V) = P'X - V'[AX - R], \tag{9-6}$$

from which we see that $\nabla L_V = -[AX - R]$, $\nabla L_X = [P' - V'A]'$. (Note that the latter partial gradient has been transposed to become a column

---

[2] And when the Kuhn-Tucker constraint qualification, which rules out very irregular shapes, holds. The reason for these concavity-convexity requirements here will become obvious in the proofs of the following theorems; the theorems establish a "reasonable" primal-dual connection. This material follows rather closely the discussion in Balinski and Baumol [3].

vector, since we adopted the convention in Chapter 8 of defining gradients as column vectors.) Thus the primal can be written, following the form in (9-3),

$$\text{maximize:} \quad P'X - V'[AX - R] + V'[AX - R] \equiv P'X$$
$$\text{subject to:} \quad AX - R \leq O \quad \text{or} \quad AX \leq R \qquad (9\text{-}7)$$
$$\text{and} \qquad X \geq O.$$

Corresponding to the "symmetric" problem (9-4) we have, in the linear programming case,

$$\text{minimize:} \quad P'X - V'[AX - R] - X'[P' - V'A]'$$

or[3]

$$\text{minimize:} \quad P'X - V'AX + V'R - P'X + V'AX \equiv R'V$$
$$\text{subject to:} \quad -[P' - V'A]' \geq O \quad \text{or} \quad A'V \geq P \qquad (9\text{-}8)$$
$$\text{and} \qquad V \geq O.$$

Clearly (9-7) and (9-8) constitute exactly a pair of dual linear programs.

Next, a set of primal-dual theorems can be developed for problems (9-1) and (9-5). We append an (N) to these theorems to indicate that they are valid for the nonlinear case; there is obvious parallel to the results for linear programs given in Chapter 6. Let $\pi(X)$ and $\Delta(X, V)$ denote the primal and dual objective functions.

THEOREM P-D1(N). For any feasible solutions to the primal and dual problems [(9-1) and (9-5), respectively], $\Delta(X, V) \geq \pi(X)$.

The proof is similar to that for Theorem P-D1 in Chapter 6; it shows that $\Delta(X, V) - \pi(X) \geq 0$ for any pair of feasible solutions. It is somewhat more involved and for that reason has been left for Appendix 9.1. Note, however, that the proof requires concavity of $f(X)$ and convexity of each of the constraints $h_i(X)$ in the primal. This theorem is of great importance in nonlinear programming theory in providing an upper bound to the value of the objective function in the maximization problem and a lower bound to the minimization objective function.[4]

THEOREM P-D2(N). Given a pair of feasible solutions (X^p) and (X^d, V^d) with objective function values $\pi(X^p)$ and $\Delta(X^d, V^d)$; these solutions are optimal if and only if $\pi(X^p) = \Delta(X^d, V^d)$.

Clearly *if* $\pi = \Delta$, then both objective functions have reached their limits [from Theorem P-D1(N)]; hence the solutions are optimal. The *only if* part

---

[3] Recall that, for the operation of transposition, $(A \pm B)' = A' \pm B'$, $(AB)' = B'A'$, $(A')' = A$, and the transpose of a scalar is just the scalar itself.

[4] We will see in Section 9.2 how this information is used in a nonlinear programming solution technique.

of the theorem relies in part on the properties given in Theorem SP4; it is proved in Appendix 9.1. An important outcome of the proof is that, given an optimal X^p for the primal, a vector V^0 can be found such that (X^p, V^0) is an optimal solution to the dual.

THEOREM P-D3(N).   A pair of feasible solutions has $\pi(X^p) = \Delta(X^d, V^d)$ if and only if (1) $v_i^d[-h_i(X^p)] = 0$ for all i, and (2)

$$x_j^p \left[\sum_i v_i^d \, \partial h_i/\partial x_j - \partial f/\partial x_j \right] = 0 \qquad \text{for all } j.$$

The proofs are in Appendix 9.1. Note that the bracketed expression in (1) is the slack variable for the ith primal constraint in (9-1) and the bracketed expression in (2) is likewise the slack variable in the jth dual constraint in (9-5). Thus Theorem P-D3(N) describes a type of "complementary slackness" relationship exactly parallel to that in the linear programming case. This property of the optimal solutions to the pair of dual nonlinear programs given in (9-1) and (9-5) shows the equivalence of these dual variables and the Lagrange multipliers used in Chapter 8 in the development of Kuhn-Tucker conditions and the saddle-point problem connection. Denote the optima by (X^0) and (X^0, V^0).

THEOREM P-D4(N).   Under certain conditions $\partial \pi(X^0)/\partial r_i = v_i^0$.

This marginal valuation property of the dual variables at optimum held for linear programming problems, subject to the qualification that the appropriate derivatives existed. The same sort of requirement is necessary here. Given continuity in the objective function for small changes of r_i around the optimum, we may reason as follows. At optimum [from Theorem P-D2(N)]

$$\pi(X^0) = \Delta(X^0, V^0) = f(X^0) - \sum_i v_i^0 [g_i(X^0) - r_i] - \sum_j x_j^0 \left(f_j - \sum_i v_i^0 h_j^i \right).$$

$$(9-9)$$

We have rewritten $h_i(X^0)$ as $g_i(X^0) - r_i$ in the one place where this is needed.[5] Therefore

$$\frac{\partial \pi(X^0)}{\partial r_i} = v_i^0.$$

The optimal value of a dual variable measures the impact on the optimum of the primal objective function of a marginal change in the (original) right-hand side of the ith primal constraint.

---

[5] Recall that the constraints were originally $g_i(X) \leq r_i$ and were rewritten as $h_i(X) = g_i(X) - r_i \leq 0$.

Because these theorems hold, problem (9-5) seems logically termed the dual to (9-1). Then the connection with the Kuhn-Tucker theory and saddle-point problems is established, since a pair of *feasible* solutions to (9-1) and (9-5) satisfies parts (a)(i) and (b)(i) of Theorem SP4, and a pair of *optimal* solutions also satisfies (a)(ii) and (b)(ii). Thus the economic interpretation of the conditions of Theorem SP4 transfers to the constraints and variables in a pair of dual nonlinear programming problems and parallels the interpretation for the linear case in Chapter 6.

The dual objective function is not quite as straightforward as in the linear case. A possible interpretation is as follows.[6] Rewrite the dual objective function [from (9-9), and omitting the superscripts denoting optimality] as

$$\Delta(X, V) = \left[\sum_i v_i r_i\right] + \left[f(X) - \sum_i v_i g_i(X)\right] - \left[\sum_j x_j \left(f_j - \sum_i v_i h_j^i\right)\right].$$
(9-10)

The first term in brackets corresponds to what we found in linear programming duals: a valuation of the total supply of scarce resources. In the second bracketed term, an amount equal to the total costs to the firm of all scarce inputs used (when valued at their marginal contributions) is subtracted from $f(X)$, total revenue or some other measure of return to the firm. This can be described as economic "rent," an amount that could be demanded by a person who could prevent production by withholding *his* scarce resource—for example, the owner of an essential patent. The third term in brackets is less easily interpreted, but since it is zero at the optimum it is possibly less important. The part in parentheses is nonpositive (from the dual constraints) and is a kind of loss incurred by a marginal increase in the amount of output of j. The entire term is then a weighted sum of these opportunity losses, where the weights are the actual outputs—the "marginal opportunity cost of all outputs."[7] Optimal production will keep this term zero. The dual objective function, then, seeks the minimum of the total value of scarce resources plus payments to rent plus losses due to unprofitable outputs.

9.2. COMPUTATIONAL METHODS FOR NONLINEAR PROGRAMS

We saw in Section 8.2 that the first-order conditions for maxima and minima, when applied to the general nonlinear programming problem, generated a complex set of Kuhn-Tucker conditions—(8-8) or (8-9)—

---

[6] Again, see Balinski and Baumol [3, esp. sec. 4].
[7] Balinski and Baumol [3, p. 246].

involving inequalities and nonlinear equations. Utilizing these conditions directly for optimal solutions would generally be an extremely difficult and involved procedure. We also saw (Sections 8.3 and 8.4) that the properties of the gradient to a function suggested a rather broad class of techniques for unconstrained or constrained maximization and minimization problems. The underlying logic of these methods was quite simple: move toward the optimum along the "best" route possible. Gradient methods differ from one another principally in (1) whether or not they modify the gradient in defining the "best" direction, (2) the manner in which they deal with constraints (if they exist in the problem), and (3) the length of step they take along a currently chosen direction before reevaluating the gradient and hence establishing a new direction of movement.

We now consider several rather different approaches: separable programming, the cutting-plane method, sequential unconstrained techniques, and (briefly) a formulation using differential equations.[8]

Separable programming

One rather obvious idea for nonlinear programming problems is to approximate the nonlinear functions involved—objective function and/or constraints—with straight-line segments. In a completely general nonlinear programming problem in which the nonlinear functions involve powers of variables as well as products of two or more variables or trigonometric, logarithmic, or exponential expressions (such as $3x_1^2 - 2x_1x_2 + x_3 \leq 10$ or $e^{x_1^2} + 5 \log x_1x_2 + x_3 \leq 4$), linear approximations are not generally easy to specify algebraically, even though the basic idea can still be appreciated. However, when the functions involved are what is known as separable, the specification is more easily done. One then uses the simplex method (with slight modification) on a linear program that approximates the original nonlinear one. While the simplex method is exact, the solution only approximates that of the original problem; the accuracy of the solution obviously depends on how well the approximating linear program represents the original problem.

If a function $f(X)$ can be represented as $\sum_{j=1}^{n} f_j(x_j)$, it is termed separable. That is, a separable function can be represented as the sum of several functions (generally nonlinear) of a single variable each. The following is such a function:

---

[8] The discussion will require *no* prior exposure to differential equations.

$$f(X) = 3x_1^2 + 5x_2^2 + x_1 - 6x_2, \tag{9-11}$$

since, by letting $f_1(x_1) = 3x_1^2 + x_1$ and $f_2(x_2) = 5x_2^2 - 6x_2$, we can write

$$f(X) = f_1(x_1) + f_2(x_2) = \sum_{j=1}^{2} f_j(x_j).^9$$

Consider a programming problem in which the objective function *and* each of the constraints[10] can be expressed as separable functions:

$$\text{maximize:} \quad f(X) = \sum_{j=1}^{n} f_j(x_j)$$

$$\text{subject to:} \quad \sum_{j=1}^{n} g_{ij}(x_j) \le r_i \quad (i = 1, \ldots, m) \tag{9-12}$$

$$\text{and} \quad x_j \ge 0 \quad (j = 1, \ldots, n).$$

The methods of this subsection are designed to find an approximate solution to this problem using approximating *linear* programs for which the simplex method (Chapter 6) can be utilized. For example, the constraints in such a problem might be

$$x_1^2 + 6x_2 \le 10,$$
$$x_1 + 4x_2^2 \le 30. \tag{9-13}$$

Letting $g_{11}(x_1) = x_1^2$, $g_{12}(x_2) = 6x_2$, we have

$$g_{11}(x_1) + g_{12}(x_2) \le 10 \quad \text{or} \quad \sum_{j=1}^{2} g_{1j}(x_j) \le 10;$$

similarly, the second constraint can be expressed as

$$\sum_{j=1}^{2} g_{2j}(x_j) \le 30, \quad \text{where } g_{21}(x_1) = x_1 \quad \text{and} \quad g_{22}(x_2) = 4x_2^2.$$

This corresponds to the constraint form in (9-12).

Consider the problem of specifying a piecewise linear approximation to any one of the $f_j(x_j)$ in (9-12)—that is, of approximating a nonlinear function of one variable. Figure 9.1 illustrates the problem for a given

---

[9] Theoretically, a product term such as $x_1 x_2$ can be eliminated as follows: let $y_1 = \frac{1}{2}(x_1 + x_2)$, $y_2 = \frac{1}{2}(x_1 - x_2)$. Thus $x_1 x_2 = y_1^2 - y_2^2$, which *is* separable. In the mathematical programming context, however, this is not always useful; y_2 has become unrestricted in sign, since it is the *difference* between two nonnegative variables.

[10] Obviously, the nonnegativity constraints $x_j \ge 0$ can also be looked upon as extremely simple separable functions. Since this is always the case, the requirement of separability concerns constraints other than the nonnegativity conditions.

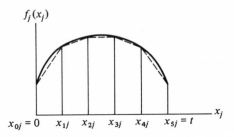

Figure 9.1. Approximating $f_j(x_j)$ over $0 \leq x_j \leq t$

interval $0 \leq x_j \leq t$. Select a number of points x_{kj} in the interval; let $x_{0j} = 0$, $x_{0j} < x_{1j} < \cdots < x_{mj} = t$. For each point x_{kj}, calculate $f_j(x_{kj})$, the vertical heights in Figure 9.1. Connect adjacent points $[x_{kj}, f_j(x_{kj})]$ and $[x_{k+1,j}, f_j(x_{k+1,j})]$ by a straight line—the dashed lines in the figure—and denote this piecewise linear approximation to $f_j(x_j)$ by $\hat{f}_j(x_j)$. Obviously, the smaller the distances between adjacent x_{kj}'s, the better $\hat{f}_j(x_j)$ approximates $f_j(x_j)$. Imagine that we have found an approximation of this kind for each $f_j(x_j)$ and $g_{ij}(x_j)$ in (9-12) by selecting *mesh points* x_{kj} for each variable x_j. Then reexpress (9-12) as

$$\text{maximize:} \quad \hat{f}(X) = \sum_{j=1}^{n} \hat{f}_j(x_j)$$

$$\text{subject to:} \quad \sum_{j=1}^{n} \hat{g}_{ij}(x_j) \leq r_i \quad (i = 1, \ldots, m) \tag{9-14}$$

$$\text{and} \qquad\qquad\qquad x_j \geq 0 \quad (j = 1, \ldots, n).$$

The object is now to find an optimal solution to this approximating problem. To do so, we must be precise about how we write the approximating functions $\hat{f}_j$ and $\hat{g}_{ij}$. Figure 9.2 represents a typical section from Figure 9.1 (with two added lines and some shading). The shaded triangle is

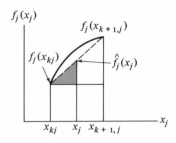

Figure 9.2. Detail from Figure 9.1

similar to the large one of which it is a part; hence corresponding sides are proportional. In particular,

$$\frac{f_j(x_{k+1,j}) - f_j(x_{kj})}{x_{k+1,j} - x_{kj}} = \frac{\hat{f}_j(x_j) - f_j(x_{kj})}{x_j - x_{kj}}, \tag{9-15}$$

from which, with a little algebra,[11] we find

$$\hat{f}_j(x_j) = f_j(x_{kj}) + \frac{f_j(x_{k+1,j}) - f_j(x_{kj})}{x_{k+1,j} - x_{kj}} (x_j - x_{kj}). \tag{9-16}$$

We know that any x_j in the interval $x_{kj} \leq x_j \leq x_{k+1,j}$ can be expressed as a convex combination of the endpoints of the interval (Section 4.7). Thus

$$x_j = \alpha x_{k+1,j} + (1 - \alpha)x_{kj} \tag{9-17}$$

for $0 \leq \alpha \leq 1$; or $(x_j - x_{kj}) = \alpha(x_{k+1,j} - x_{kj})$. Substitution into (9-16) gives

$$\hat{f}_j(x_j) = \alpha f_j(x_{k+1,j}) + (1 - \alpha)f_j(x_{kj}). \tag{9-18}$$

In words, the same convex combination that defines a point x_j relative to x_{kj} and $x_{k+1,j}$ defines the value of the approximating function at that x_j relative to the true values of the original function at x_{kj} and $x_{k+1,j}$. Since this will hold for x_j between any x_{kj} and $x_{k+1,j}$, we let α in (9-17) and (9-18) be denoted by $\alpha_{k+1,j}$ and $(1 - \alpha)$ be α_{kj}. Then

$$x_j = \alpha_{k+1,j}x_{k+1,j} + \alpha_{kj}x_{kj}; \tag{9-17'}$$

also,

$$\hat{f}_j(x_j) = \alpha_{k+1,j}f_j(x_{k+1,j}) + \alpha_{kj}f_j(x_{kj}). \tag{9-18'}$$

Therefore, (9-17') and (9-18'), with the additional requirements that $\alpha_{kj} + \alpha_{k+1,j} = 1$ and $\alpha_{kj}, \alpha_{k+1,j} \geq 0$, serve to describe the approximating function $\hat{f}_j(x_j)$ anywhere in the interval $x_{kj} \leq x_j \leq x_{k+1,j}$ in terms of the *known* values $f_j(x_{k+1,j})$ and $f_j(x_{kj})$. All that need to be specified are α_{kj} and $\alpha_{k+1,j}$—that is, the exact location of x_j in the interval.

It is possible to be even more general. For any x_j in the interval $0 \leq x_j \leq t$ (Figure 9.1) we can write, parallel to (9-17'):

$$x_j = \sum_{k=0}^{m} \alpha_{kj}x_{kj}, \tag{9-19}$$

and, in place of (9-18'),

---

[11] This is simply a variant on the definition of the slope of a line as vertical displacement divided by horizontal displacement. Here the slope of the line connecting $f_j(x_{kj})$ and $f_j(x_{k+1,j})$—and on which $\hat{f}_j(x_j)$ lies—is just $[f_j(x_{k+1,j}) - f_j(x_{kj})]/(x_{k+1,j} - x_{kj})$. Therefore $[\hat{f}_j(x_j) - f_j(x_{kj})]/(x_j - x_{kj})$ equals this same slope, from which (9-15) also results.

$$\hat{f}_j(x_j) = \sum_{k=0}^{m} \alpha_{kj} f_j(x_{kj}), \tag{9-20}$$

where, in addition,

$$\sum_{k=0}^{m} \alpha_{kj} = 1 \quad \text{and} \quad \alpha_{kj} \geq 0 \qquad (k = 0, \ldots, m), \tag{9-21}$$

provided that

$$
\begin{aligned}
&(1) \quad \text{no more than two } \alpha_{kj} \text{ are positive } and \\
&(2) \quad if \text{ two } \alpha_{kj} \text{ are positive, they must be } adjacent.
\end{aligned}
\tag{9-22}
$$

Recall that the approximating problem (9-14) was composed of linear approximating functions $\hat{f}_j(x_j)$ and $\hat{g}_{ij}(x_j)$. Note that in (9-20) we have an expression for any such function. The final step, then, is to incorporate (9-19) through (9-21), with the added conditions (9-22), into (9-14). Suppose that we are given or can find a finite maximum value for each x_j in the problem (this is often possible from the particular context of a problem); call it t_j. Then subdivide the range from 0 to t_j by mesh points x_{kj} so that $x_{0j} = 0 < x_{1j} < \cdots < x_{m_j j} = t_j$. This simply makes a division similar to that in Figure 9.1 for *each* specific variable x_j. Assume that the same mesh points (the same intervals) are chosen for f and all constraints g_i for any particular x_j. Then, following (9-19) through (9-22), we have

$$x_j = \sum_{k=0}^{m_j} \alpha_{kj} x_{kj}, \tag{9-19'}$$

$$
\left\{
\begin{aligned}
\hat{f}_j(x_j) &= \sum_{k=0}^{m_j} \alpha_{kj} f_j(x_{kj}), \\
\hat{g}_{ij}(x_j) &= \sum_{k=0}^{m_j} \alpha_{kj} g_{ij}(x_{kj}),
\end{aligned}
\right.
\tag{9-20'}
$$

$$\sum_{k=0}^{m_j} \alpha_{kj} = 1 \quad \text{and} \quad \alpha_{kj} \geq 0 \qquad (j = 1, \ldots, n; k = 0, \ldots, m_j), \tag{9-21'}$$

and

$$
\begin{aligned}
&(1) \quad \text{for each } j, \text{ no more than two } \alpha_{kj} \text{ are positive } and \\
&(2) \quad if \text{ two are positive, they must be adjacent.}
\end{aligned}
\tag{9-22'}
$$

Thus, the approximating problem (9-14) becomes

$$\text{maximize:} \quad \hat{f}(X) = \sum_{j=1}^{n} \sum_{k=0}^{m_j} f_j(x_{kj})\alpha_{kj}$$

$$\text{subject to:} \quad \sum_{j=1}^{n} \sum_{k=0}^{m_j} g_{ij}(x_{kj})\alpha_{kj} \leq r_i \quad (i = 1, \ldots, m), \tag{9-23}$$

$$\sum_{k=0}^{m_j} \alpha_{kj} = 1 \quad (j = 1, \ldots, n),$$

$$\text{and} \quad \alpha_{kj} \geq 0 \quad (k = 0, \ldots, m),$$

with the added requirement (9-22′). Except for (9-22′), this is a straight-forward[12] *linear* programming problem in the variables α_{kj}. Therefore, a variant of the powerful and simple simplex method that satisfies (9-22′) can be utilized. Once the optimal α_{kj} are obtained, the associated x_j in the original problem (9-12) are found from (9-19′). The reader may note that the size of the problem has increased substantially. Whereas (9-12) had (with slack variables) m constraints (excluding nonnegativity requirements) and $n + m$ variables, the associated linear program, (9-23), has $m + n$ con-straints and $\sum_{j=1}^{n} (m_j + 1) + m = \sum_{j=1}^{n} m_j + n + m$ variables (including slacks). A separable nonlinear problem, with, say, ten variables and five constraints, in which the range of each variable was divided into nine intervals (hence ten x_{kj} for each x_j),[13] would be converted to an approximating linear programming problem with 105 variables subject to 15 constraints.

We conclude with an example:[14]

$$\text{maximize:} \quad f(X) = 3x_1 + 2x_2$$
$$\text{subject to:} \quad g_1(X) = 4x_1^2 + x_2^2 \leq 16 \tag{9-24}$$
$$\text{and} \quad x_1, x_2 \geq 0.$$

We note from the constraints that $x_1 \leq 2$, $x_2 \leq 4$; suppose we let $t_1 = 4$ and $t_2 = 4$, the upper limits for variables x_1 and x_2, respectively. (Again, it is unnecessary that the t_j be equal.) Further, we divide the closed interval $[0, 4]$ into four equally sized subintervals for both x_1 and x_2.[15] Letting

---

[12] The fact that it contains both equality and inequality constraints is not troublesome, as we saw in Chapter 7.

[13] There is no need for the same number of intervals for each variable; this only serves to simplify the example.

[14] For proofs of convergence, extensions, and refinements of the technique of separable programming, the interested reader is referred to Hadley [11] and C. E. Miller, "The Simplex Method for Local Separable Programming," in Graves and Wolfe [10, chap. 12].

[15] The number of subintervals for x_1 and x_2 need not be the same, nor need any set of them be of equal size.

$f_1(x_1) = 3x_1$, $f_2(x_2) = 2x_2$, $g_{11}(x_1) = 4x_1^2$, and $g_{12}(x_2) = x_2^2$, the problem can be expressed in the form of (9-12):

$$\text{maximize:} \quad \sum_{j=1}^{2} f_j(x_j)$$

$$\text{subject to:} \quad \sum_{j=1}^{2} g_{1j}(x_j) \leq 16 \tag{9-25}$$

$$\text{and} \quad x_1, x_2 \geq 0.$$

To operate with the approximating linear program, as in (9-23), we need the values of the f_j and g_{1j} for the chosen mesh points. This information is shown in Table 9.1.

Table 9.1.   Data for Approximating Linear Program
to (9-24)

$x_j \ (j = 1, 2)$	$f_1(x_1)$	$g_{11}(x_1)$	$f_2(x_2)$	$g_{12}(x_2)$
x_{0j}	0	0	0	0	0
x_{1j}	1	3	4	2	1
x_{2j}	2	6	16	4	4
x_{3j}	3	9	36	6	9
x_{4j}	4	12	64	8	16

Therefore, written out completely, the approximating linear program is

maximize: $f(X) = 0\alpha_{01} + 3\alpha_{11} + 6\alpha_{21} + 9\alpha_{31} + 12\alpha_{41}$
$\qquad\qquad\qquad + 0\alpha_{02} + 2\alpha_{12} + 4\alpha_{22} + 6\alpha_{32} + 8\alpha_{42}$

subject to:
$\quad$ (1) $\quad 0\alpha_{01} + 4\alpha_{11} + 16\alpha_{21} + 36\alpha_{31} + 64\alpha_{41}$
$\qquad\qquad + 0\alpha_{02} + 1\alpha_{12} + 4\alpha_{22} + 9\alpha_{32} + 16\alpha_{42} \leq 16$, $\quad$ (9-26)
$\quad$ (2) $\quad \alpha_{01} + \alpha_{11} + \alpha_{21} + \alpha_{31} + \alpha_{41} = 1$,
$\qquad\qquad \alpha_{02} + \alpha_{12} + \alpha_{22} + \alpha_{32} + \alpha_{42} = 1$,

and   all $\alpha_{kj} \geq 0$ $\quad (j = 1, 2; k = 0, \ldots, 4)$.

Because of the equations, (2), among the constraints of (9-26), we could reexpress them as two inequalities each and employ some sort of artificial-variable technique (Section 7.2); here we use a two-phase technique on the equations directly (Section 7.3).[16] In this example α_{01} and α_{02} can play precisely the roles of slack variables for the two equations in (2): they are absent from the other constraints (that is, have a coefficient of zero) and

---

[16] In fact, we essentially combine the two phases by pivoting in order to maximize the objective function in (9-26)—which is formally the Phase II objective—and noting that in the process $\alpha_{01} + \alpha_{02} = 0$—which is really the Phase I objective.

from the objective function; each enters its own constraint with a coefficient of one. Therefore, letting s_1 be the slack variable for constraint (1), the initial simplex tableau will be as shown in Table 9.2. We now use the ordinary simplex method rules for transformation of basic solutions, with the added requirement (9-22′)—that is, with so-called "restricted basis entry."

Table 9.2.   Initial Simplex Tableau for Problem (9-26)

		α_{11}	α_{21}	α_{31}	α_{41}	α_{12}	α_{22}	α_{32}	α_{42}
π	0	3	6	9	12	2	4	6	8
s_1	16	-4	-16	-36	-64	-1	-4	-9	-16
α_{01}	1	-1	-1	-1	-1	0	0	0	0
α_{02}	1	0	0	0	0	-1	-1	-1	-1

The initial basic feasible solution is: $s_1 = 16$, $\alpha_{01} = 1$, $\alpha_{02} = 1$; the objective function value is zero. Examination of positive top-row elements indicates α_{41} as the relatively most attractive among the currently excluded variables. However α_{41} can only be brought into the basis if it *replaces* α_{01}, since otherwise two nonadjacent α_{k1} would be positive, in violation of (9-22′). Examination of the column under α_{41} shows that s_1 would be forced out of the basis before α_{01}; hence α_{41} cannot enter the basis at this time. The next most attractive excluded variable is α_{31}, for which the same observations apply; α_{31} cannot be brought in at this iteration. Consider next α_{42}, the third most attractive excluded variable. Since the criterion for the variable to leave the current simplex tableau shows that *either* s_1 or α_{02} can be replaced by α_{42}, we choose to remove α_{02} from the basis, to meet the requirements of (9-22′). The ordinary simplex method rules then give the next tableau, from which we see that $s_1 = 0$, $\alpha_{01} = 1$, $\alpha_{42} = 1$, and the objective function has increased to eight.

At this point, α_{41} is still the excluded variable with the largest objective function coefficient. In principle, however, it ought not be considered for the next basis, since α_{01} (not adjacent) is in the current basis at positive value and will not be removed if α_{41} comes in; α_{41} replaces s_1. However, we observe that α_{41} would have a value of *zero* in the next basis, and a solution with $\alpha_{01} > 0$ and $\alpha_{41} = 0$ does not violate (9-22′). Thus there are two alternatives at this point. The more rigid (and more easily programmed) is to consider for possible basis entrance only those currently excluded variables that are adjacent to currently included ones—that is, to consider

Table 9.3. Second Simplex Tableau for Problem (9-26)

		α_{11}	α_{21}	α_{31}	α_{41}	α_{12}	α_{22}	α_{32}	α_{02}
π	8	3	6	9	12	-6	-4	-2	-8
s_1	0	-4	-16	-36	-64	15	12	7	16
α_{01}	1	-1	-1	-1	-1	0	0	0	0
α_{42}	1	0	0	0	0	-1	-1	-1	-1

only α_{11} and α_{32}. In that case, α_{11} enters the basis and, after one additional pivot operation (using the same rule for variables to be considered), the optimum is reached. The second alternative is to introduce α_{41}, which will be zero in the next basis (owing to the degeneracy of the basis in Table 9.3). Continuing in this fashion, three further iterations are required before optimum. In either case (and the reader is encouraged to work through at least one of the approaches), both α_{01} and α_{02} are absent from the final optimal basis; the solution is $\alpha_{11}^0 = 1$, $\alpha_{32}^0 = \frac{4}{7}$, and $\alpha_{42}^0 = \frac{3}{7}$. Therefore, from (9-19′) and the information on mesh points in Table 9.1,

$$x_1^0 = \sum_{k=0}^{4} \alpha_{k1}^0 x_{k1} = (0)(0) + (1)(1) + (0)(2) + (0)(3) + (0)(4) = 1,$$

$$x_2^0 = \sum_{k=0}^{4} \alpha_{k2}^0 x_{k2} = (0)(0) + (0)(1) + (0)(2) + (\tfrac{4}{7})(3) + (\tfrac{3}{7})(4)$$

$$= \tfrac{24}{7} = 3\tfrac{3}{7},$$

and

$$\hat{f}(X^0) = (3)(1) + (6)(\tfrac{4}{7}) + 8(\tfrac{3}{7}) = 9\tfrac{6}{7}.$$

In this case it is not difficult to find the exact answer using the methods of Chapter 4. We form the Lagrangean function on the assumption that the constraint will be met as an equality at optimum and that both variables will be strictly positive. (This is *not* generally good policy, but the answer given by the linear approximating problem just solved suggests that it is legitimate in the present case.) That is,

$$L = 3x_1 + 2x_2 - \lambda(4x_1^2 + x_2^2 - 16),$$

which, from first-order conditions, gives $x_1^* = 1\tfrac{1}{5}$, $x_2^* = 3\tfrac{1}{5}$, at which point $f(X^*) = 10$. The second-order conditions indicate that $|\bar{V}^*| > 0$, and hence X^* represents a maximum;[17] clearly $x_1^* > 0$, $x_2^* > 0$ and $\lambda^* = \tfrac{5}{16} > 0$. This

---

[17] Again, the reader is encouraged to solve the problem this way himself, for review.

means that it was correct to treat the constraint as a strict equality in finding a maximum. Thus, the approximating problem has underestimated the optimal value of x_1 by $\frac{1}{5}$ and overestimated that of x_2 by $\frac{8}{35}$, leading to an objective function value $\frac{1}{7}$ below the true maximum. Finer division of the ranges for x_1 and x_2 (more mesh points) would increase the accuracy of the approximation—but also the number of variables in the linear programming problem. If we let $t_1 = 2$, $t_2 = 4$, and divide both intervals into half-unit subintervals (so that the ranges on the α's, and also the x's, are $\alpha_{01}, \ldots, \alpha_{41}; \alpha_{02}, \ldots, \alpha_{82}$), the solution yields $x_1^0 = 1$, $x_2^0 = 3\frac{6}{13}$ and $f(X^0) = 9\frac{12}{13}$. This is somewhat closer to the known true optimum (only $\frac{1}{13}$ too small), although x_1 is still $\frac{1}{5}$ below its actual optimum and x_2 is further from $3\frac{1}{5}$ than previously.

Cutting-plane methods

Separable programming techniques rely on linear approximations to the nonlinearities in a programming problem, both in the objective function and in the constraints (if necessary). Cutting-plane methods also use linear approximations; here the idea is to represent the feasible region as the intersection of (that is, points common to) a number of *linear* inequalities (half-spaces) that contain it. Figure 9.3 illustrates for a two-variable

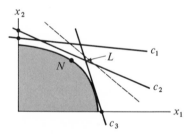

Figure 9.3.   Linear Inequalities Containing a Nonlinear Feasible Region

problem with a linear objective function and one nonlinear constraint (in addition to nonnegativity). The dashed line represents the slope of the linear objective function. Let c_1, c_2, and c_3 represent three artificially constructed linear boundaries; the area defined by (below) them completely encloses the true feasible region (shaded). Point N represents the true optimum; L is the optimum to the linear program with the same objective function and the linear constraints given by c_1, c_2, and c_3.

The object, therefore, is to add linear constraints ("cutting planes"), one at a time, so that L approaches N. Note that the solutions to the linear approximating problems will be infeasible from the point of view of the original nonlinear program; note also that in general they will always be only approximations. Hence a rule for stopping is usually formulated in terms of the amount by which the nonlinear constraints (here there is only one) are violated. When L lies outside of the original feasible region by no more than some prespecified small number in a particular solution, that solution is accepted as the approximation to the optimum of the original problem. We make this procedure specific in what follows.

Note that only nonlinear *constraints* have been discussed. There is an extremely simple way by which any programming problem with a nonlinear objective function *and* nonlinear constraints can be converted to one with a linear objective function and nonlinear constraints. Let the original problem be [as in (8-4)]

$$
\begin{aligned}
\text{maximize:} \quad & f(X) \\
\text{subject to:} \quad & h_i(X) \leq 0 \qquad (i = 1, \ldots, m) \\
\text{and} \quad & X \geq O.
\end{aligned}
\tag{9-27}
$$

Let there be a new variable x_0 with the property that $x_0 \leq f(X)$—that is, $-f(X) + x_0 \leq 0$. Add this new constraint to (9-27) and replace the objective function with x_0. Thus

$$
\begin{aligned}
\text{maximize:} \quad & x_0 \\
\text{subject to:} \quad & h_i(X) \leq 0 \qquad (i = 1, \ldots, m) \\
& -f(X) + x_0 \leq 0, \\
\text{and} \quad & X \geq O
\end{aligned}
\tag{9-28}
$$

poses the same problem as (9-27) with a (very simple) linear objective function and one more nonlinear constraint. Thus it is adequate for a computational method to concern itself exclusively with nonlinearities among the constraints. If the objective function was originally linear, the conversion from (9-27) to (9-28) is unnecessary; if it was not, we may assume that (9-27) represents the converted form. That is, we may think of $f(X)$ in (9-27) as either x_0 or else a linear function of the x_j; if x_0, then we may assume that $-f(X) + x_0 \leq 0$ is included in the constraints of (9-27).

The cutting-plane method then proceeds as follows:
1. Find *some* initial point X^0; it need not even be feasible.
2. Solve the following *linear* program:

$$
\begin{aligned}
\text{maximize:} \quad & f(X) \\
\text{subject to:} \quad & h_i(X^0) + [\nabla h_i(X^0)]'(X - X^0) \leq 0 \qquad (i = 1, \ldots, m) \\
\text{and} \quad & X \geq O.
\end{aligned}
$$

The constraints simply have been linearized by using their first-order Taylor's series expansions about the initial point X^0 [see Appendix 8.3, particularly equation (8-35)]. Given X^0, these expansions are linear functions of X. Call the optimal solution to this problem X^1.

3. Suppose a sequence of solutions X^0, X^1, ..., X^k has been found. If $h_i(X^k) \leq \epsilon$ for all i, where ϵ is some predetermined (small) number, then one should stop. If not, find among the i that constraint which is most violated, linearize it around the point X^k, add that converted constraint to the linear program whose solution gave X^k, and find the optimum, X^{k+1}, to this new linear programming problem.

4. Continue until the solution values of the variables are "sufficiently close" to the feasible region of the original problem, as given by the ϵ criterion in step 3.

This is a satisfactory procedure only when, for the original maximum problem (9-27), $f(X)$ is concave and all $g_i(X)$ are convex functions[18] of X. Only then are we assured that the Taylor's series approximations of the constraints never remove any of the feasible region. (Again, see Appendix 8.3.) We utilize problem (9-24) once again to illustrate the procedure.[19] Recall that this was

$$\begin{aligned} \text{maximize:} \quad & 3x_1 + 2x_2 \\ \text{subject to:} \quad & 4x_1^2 + x_2^2 \leq 16 \qquad\qquad (9\text{-}24)\\ \text{and} \quad & x_1, x_2 \geq 0. \end{aligned}$$

The convexity test for the single constraint is easily carried out. Its Hessian matrix is

$$H = \begin{bmatrix} 8 & 0 \\ 0 & 2 \end{bmatrix},$$

for which $|H_1| = 8$, $|H_2| = 16$; hence it is positive definite (all principal minors positive) and the constraint is convex. Figure 9.4 illustrates the programming problem. The steps are as follows:

1. Let $X^0 = \begin{bmatrix} 1 \\ 1 \end{bmatrix}$. This is a feasible solution to (9-24), but the X^0 selected need not be. (Note that X^0 here does *not* denote the optimum.)

2. For the first linear program (step 2 above) we need $h(X^0)$ and $\nabla h(X^0)$. Since

$$\nabla h(X) = \begin{bmatrix} 8x_1 \\ 2x_2 \end{bmatrix}, \quad \nabla h(X^0) = \begin{bmatrix} 8 \\ 2 \end{bmatrix};$$

$$h(X^0) = 4(1) + 1(1) - 16 = -11.$$

[18] That is, before the observations that led to formulation (9-28) and the subsequent reinterpretation of (9-27). Under the later interpretation, the *new* $f(X)$ is linear and hence concave, but the *old* $f(X)$ appears with a negative sign among the constraints [recall (9-28)]; hence for that constraint to be convex, $-f(X)$ must be convex—that is, $f(X)$ concave.

[19] Further details of the cutting-plane method can be found in P. Wolfe, "An Outline of Nonlinear Programming," in Dantzig and Veinott [5, pp. 365–400]; P. Wolfe, "Methods of Nonlinear Programming," in Graves and Wolfe [10, chap. 10]; and Zoutendijk [16].

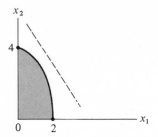

Figure 9.4.   Feasible Region and Objective Function Contour for Problem (9-24)

Therefore we want to find the x_1 and x_2 that

maximize: $3x_1 + 2x_2$

subject to: $-11 + \begin{bmatrix} 8 & 2 \end{bmatrix} \begin{bmatrix} x_1 - 1 \\ x_2 - 1 \end{bmatrix} \leq 0$ (9-29)

—that is, $8x_1 + 2x_2 \leq 21$

and $x_1, x_2 \geq 0.$

We add the cutting plane (here a line, since it involves only two variables) to the original problem as it appeared in Figure 9.4. It is labeled c_1. Figure 9.5 makes clear that the optimal solution will be at the point where c_1 cuts the x_2 axis—that is, at $x_1 = 0$, $x_2 = \frac{21}{2}$. (The simplex method would produce this answer in two iterations, since the larger coefficient on x_1 in

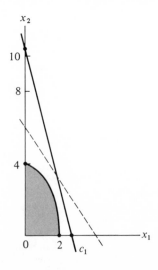

Figure 9.5.   First Cutting-Plane Linear Program

the objective function would lead one to introduce it first; it is not needed here since we have the geometry in front of us.) Thus

$$X^1 = \begin{bmatrix} 0 \\ \frac{21}{2} \end{bmatrix}.$$

3. Let $\epsilon = 0.5$. Since $h(X^1) = \frac{377}{4}$ ($= 94.25$) $> \epsilon$, we proceed to add another constraint.[20]

$$\nabla h(X^1) = \begin{bmatrix} 0 \\ 21 \end{bmatrix},$$

and the constraint to be added is thus

$$\frac{377}{4} + [0 \quad 21] \begin{bmatrix} x_1 - 0 \\ x_2 - \frac{21}{2} \end{bmatrix} \leq 0$$

—that is,

$$21x_2 \leq \frac{505}{4} \ (= 126.25)$$

or

$$x_2 \leq 6.012.$$

In what follows we will work with decimals to three significant figures. The next linear program to be solved is then

$$
\begin{aligned}
&\text{maximize:} && 3x_1 + 2x_2 \\
&\text{subject to:} \begin{cases} (c_1) & 8x_1 + 2x_2 \leq 21, \\ (c_2) & x_2 \leq 6.012, \end{cases} && \quad\quad\quad (9\text{-}30) \\
&\text{and} && x_1, x_2 \geq 0.
\end{aligned}
$$

Figure 9.6 adds this constraint, c_2, to the previous problem (and retains, as before, the original nonlinear feasible region).

Again, the solution is clear from the picture; it will now be at the corner defined by the intersection of c_1 and c_2—that is, where $x_2 = 6.012$ and therefore $x_1 = 1.030$. Thus

$$X^2 = \begin{bmatrix} 1.030 \\ 6.012 \end{bmatrix};$$

since $h(X^2) = 24.388 > \epsilon$, we continue. The relevant information from subsequent calculations is contained in Table 9.4. Each new linear program contains all previous constraints plus one added one. These are all shown in Figure 9.7; the reader should bear in mind that they have been added

---

[20] If there were several constraints in the original problem, the new constraint to be added would be based on that h_i for which $h_i(X^1)$ deviated the most from ϵ. This is the currently most violated constraint.

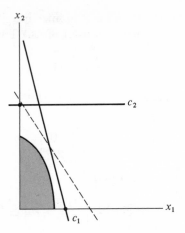

Figure 9.6. Second Cutting-Plane Linear Program

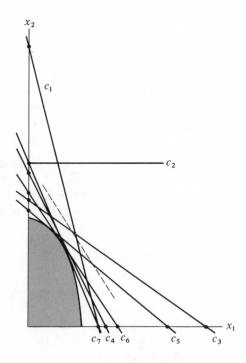

Figure 9.7. Progressive Approximation of Nonlinear Feasible Region for Problem (9-24)

one at a time to generate a series of linear programs of increasing size. The solution accepted as approximating that of the nonlinear program is $x_1 = 1.351$, $x_2 = 2.984$, for which the (single) constraint in the problem is violated by less than .5, the figure arbitrarily set at the outset as the upper limit on the "inaccuracy" of the approximating linear program. For these values, the objective function of the original problem, $3x_1 + 2x_2$, is equal to 10.021. We have already seen that the precise maximum for problem (9-24) occurs at $x_1 = 1.2$, $x_2 = 3.2$, at which point the objective function is equal to ten. The approximation would have been more accurate had a smaller value of ϵ (below 0.210) been specified at the outset; a smaller ϵ would mean additional linear programs to be solved.

Sequential unconstrained techniques

Both the cutting-plane method and the approach of separable programming involve construction of one or more approximating linear programming problems whose solutions can then be found by the simplex method. The technique to be discussed now uses an entirely different kind of approximating problem; rather than formulating linear programs, it employs a series of *unconstrained* maximization or minimization problems. In order to parallel the most important references, we will here discuss a nonlinear *minimization* program. Hence the full title: sequential unconstrained minimization technique or, as it is often denoted, SUMT (an accurate but unattractive acronym).[21] Thus the focus of the *computational* aspects of the technique is on general methods of maximization and minimization; the approach of Chapter 4 will often be useful, otherwise variants of gradient techniques (Section 8.4), particularly Newton's method, are usually employed. Our interest, then, is in how the unconstrained problem is formulated.

Consider the general nonlinear programming minimization problem in which the requirements for nonnegativity of the variables have been incorporated in the constraint set.

minimize: $f(x_1, \ldots, x_n)$
subject to: $h_i(x_1, \ldots, x_n) \geq 0$ $(i = 1, \ldots, m; m + 1, \ldots, m + n)$.

$$(9\text{-}31)$$

Recall from Section 4.8 that the Kuhn-Tucker conditions necessary for a

[21] Sequential unconstrained *maximization* techniques would also be SUMT, but we switch to minimization problems to parallel the work of Fiacco and McCormick who are chiefly responsible for development of the method. This work is presented fully in Fiacco and McCormick [8], although there were numerous earlier articles, such as Fiacco and McCormick [7], [9]. The interested reader is referred to all of these and to Zoutendijk [16] for additional details.

Table 9.4.   Further Cutting-Plane Linear Programs Approximating Problem (9-24)

k	X^k	$\nabla h(X^k)$	$h(X^k)$ (recall that $\epsilon = .5$)	Final Form of Added Constraint (c_{k+1}) $h(X^k) + [\nabla h(X^k)]'(X - X^k) \leq 0$	Pair of Constraints Met as Equalities in Linear Program Solution	Linear Program Optimal Solution $(= X^{k+1})$
2	$\begin{bmatrix} 1.030 \\ 6.012 \end{bmatrix}$	$\begin{bmatrix} 8.240 \\ 12.024 \end{bmatrix}$	24.388	$8.240x_1 + 12.024x_2 \leq 56.387$	c_1 and c_3	$\begin{bmatrix} 1.753 \\ 3.488 \end{bmatrix}$
3	$\begin{bmatrix} 1.753 \\ 3.488 \end{bmatrix}$	$\begin{bmatrix} 14.032 \\ 6.976 \end{bmatrix}$	8.474	$14.032x_1 + 6.976x_2 \leq 40.470$	c_3 and c_4	$\begin{bmatrix} .838 \\ 4.106 \end{bmatrix}$
4	$\begin{bmatrix} .838 \\ 4.106 \end{bmatrix}$	$\begin{bmatrix} 6.704 \\ 8.212 \end{bmatrix}$	3.667	$6.704x_1 + 8.212x_2 \leq 35.669$	c_4 and c_5	$\begin{bmatrix} 1.220 \\ 3.348 \end{bmatrix}$
5	$\begin{bmatrix} 1.220 \\ 3.348 \end{bmatrix}$	$\begin{bmatrix} 9.760 \\ 6.696 \end{bmatrix}$	1.161	$9.760x_1 + 6.696x_2 \leq 33.164$	c_4 and c_6	$\begin{bmatrix} 1.532 \\ 2.720 \end{bmatrix}$
6	$\begin{bmatrix} 1.532 \\ 2.720 \end{bmatrix}$	$\begin{bmatrix} 12.256 \\ 5.440 \end{bmatrix}$	.786	$12.256x_1 + 5.440x_2 \leq 32.787$	c_6 and c_7	$\begin{bmatrix} 1.351 \\ 2.984 \end{bmatrix}$
7	$\begin{bmatrix} 1.351 \\ 2.984 \end{bmatrix}$	$\begin{bmatrix} 10.808 \\ 5.968 \end{bmatrix}$	.210	None added; $h(X^7) < \epsilon$, so X^7 is accepted as optimal.		

minimum of $f(X)$ subject to the constraints in (9-31) are that a set of x_j^*'s $(j = 1, \ldots, n)$ and λ_i^*'s $(i = 1, \ldots, m + n)$ be found to satisfy:[22]

$$\text{(a)} \quad f_j - \sum_i \lambda_i h_j^i = 0,$$

$$\text{(b)} \quad \lambda_i[h_i(X)] = 0,$$
$$\text{(c)} \quad h_i(X) \geq 0, \qquad\qquad (9\text{-}32)$$
$$\text{(d)} \quad \lambda_i \geq 0.$$

Let the vectors of solution values be denoted as usual by corresponding capital letters, X^*, Λ^*. Suppose that there is a point near X^*, Λ^*—call it $[X(r), \Lambda(r)]$, since it will depend on a parameter r—for which the following perturbation of (9-32) holds:

$$\text{(a)} \quad \text{no change,}$$
$$\text{(b)} \quad \lambda_i[h_i(X)] = r > 0,$$
$$\text{(c)} \quad h_i(X) > 0, \qquad\qquad (9\text{-}32')$$
$$\text{(d)} \quad \text{no change.}$$

That is, (c) indicates that the point $[X(r), \Lambda(r)]$ is *strictly inside* the feasible region for problem (9-31).

In addition, imposition of the new requirement (b) in (9-32′) in fact means that, in (d), $\lambda_i > 0$, since, from (9-32′)(b), $\lambda_i = r/h_i(X)$, where both numerator and denominator are strictly positive. Putting this result into (a), and using gradient notation,

$$\nabla f[X(r)] - \sum_i \frac{r}{h_i[X(r)]} \nabla h_i[X(r)] = 0. \qquad (9\text{-}33)$$

But note that (9-33) is just the gradient of the function $L(X; r)$, where[23]

$$L(X; r) = f(X) - r \sum_i \ln h_i(X). \qquad (9\text{-}34)$$

Thus, at $X(r)$, $\nabla L(X; r) = 0$, by (9-33). But we saw in Section 8.3 that the first total differential for any function of several variables can be written as the inner product of the gradient vector of the function and the vector of the small changes in the independent variables; that is, for $f(X)$, $df = [\nabla f] \cdot [dX] = [\nabla f]'[dX]$. But a vanishing first total differential was the necessary condition for maxima or minima (Chapters 3 and 4), and,

---

[22] This is the many-constraint extension of (4-50), parallel to (4-45) for maximization problems.

[23] Recall that "ln" denotes natural logarithm and that, where $u = f(x)$ and $y = \ln u$, $dy/dx \equiv f'(x) = (1/u) \, du/dx$. Note also that by using a semicolon in $L(X; r)$ we wish to indicate that r is a parameter whose value we select. For any given value of r, the function L will depend on X alone.

for $dX \neq O$ (that is, for arbitrary small changes in the independent variables), $df = O$ if and only if $\nabla f = O$. Therefore (9-33) tells us that $X(r)$ satisfies the first-order conditions for a local (unconstrained) minimum of $L(X; r)$; we denote it $X^*(r)$ to indicate that it is a point satisfying these conditions.

We consider a second possible perturbation of conditions (9-32). Remove (d), $\lambda_i \geq 0$, by defining $l_i^2 = \lambda_i$. Then (b) is equivalent to $l_i[h_i(X)] = 0$; and if we now perturb (b) and (c) as before, we have

$$
\begin{array}{lll}
\text{(a)} & \text{no change,} & \\
\text{(b)} & l_i[h_i(X)] = r > 0, & \text{(9-32$''$)} \\
\text{(c)} & h_i(X) > 0. &
\end{array}
$$

From these conditions, $l_i = r/h_i(X)$, and again both numerator and denominator are strictly positive. Then $\lambda_i = r^2/[h_i(X)]^2$, and this, substituted into (a), gives

$$
\nabla f[X(r)] - \sum_i \frac{r^2}{\{h_i[X(r)]\}^2} \, \nabla h_i[X(r)] = 0, \tag{9-35}
$$

which is just the gradient of $\mathcal{L}(X; r)$, where

$$
\mathcal{L}(X; r) = f(X) + r^2 \sum_i \frac{1}{h_i(X)}. \tag{9-36}
$$

And, as with the discussion above on (9-34), since $\nabla \mathcal{L}(X; r) = 0$ at $X(r)$, by (9-35), $X(r)$ satisfies the first-order conditions for an unconstrained local minimum[24] of $\mathcal{L}(X; r)$. Again, then, the notation $X^*(r)$ is appropriate.

The implications of these results are as follows. Find an unconstrained minimum of the function $L(X; r)$ or $\mathcal{L}(X; r)$. These are termed "penalty functions," since they encourage the avoidance of boundaries and penalize the objective $f(X)$ by adding to (in a maximization problem they subtract from) its value as boundaries are approached.[25] The amount of the penalty is determined by r. We know from (9-32$'$)(c) or (9-32$''$)(c) that all of the constraints of the original nonlinear programming problem are strictly satisfied at this minimum point. When r is very small, the weight given to avoiding the boundary is very small and the local unconstrained

[24] Questions of the existence of an $X(r)$ satisfying the perturbed conditions (9-32$'$) or (9-32$''$), as well as conditions for positive definiteness of the Hessians of $L(X; r)$ and $\mathcal{L}(X; r)$, to assure that the second total differential is positive (for a minimum point), are covered in detail in Fiacco and McCormick [8].

[25] These are so-called "interior point" methods, since the solutions they provide are always inside the feasible region. Fiacco and McCormick [8] also present "exterior-point" methods, in which the true minimum [to (9-31)] is approached from outside of the feasible region.

minimum will be close to the constrained minimum of (9-31), since the perturbation in (9-32′) or (9-32″) will be small.

The steps proceed as follows:[26]

1. Find an initial point X^0 for which $h_i(X^0) > 0$ for all i—that is, a point strictly inside the feasible region. This is used primarily in determining an optimum size for r, the initial penalty weight, which is an aspect of the calculations that will not be examined here.

2. Choose a value for r_1 and move from X^0 to $X^*(r_1)$, the local minimum of $L(X; r_1)$ or $\mathcal{L}(X; r_1)$ (depending on which form of penalty function has been chosen), for $r = r_1 > 0$. Note that $X^*(r_1)$ will be interior to the feasible region; if it were not, then $h_i[X(r_1)] = 0$ and, since $\ln 0 = -\infty$ and $1/h_i[X(r_1)] \to \infty$ as $h_i[X(r_1)] \to 0$, both $L(X; r)$ in (9-34) and $\mathcal{L}(X; r)$ in (9-36) would be infinitely large, which contradicts the assumption that $X^*(r_1)$ is a local minimum.

3. Move from $X^*(r_1)$ to the local minimum of $L(X; r_2)$ [or $\mathcal{L}(X; r_2)$], where $r_1 > r_2 > 0$.

4. Continue moving from $X^*(r_{k-1})$ to the local minimum of $L(X; r_k)$ [or $\mathcal{L}(X; r_k)$], where $r_1 > r_2 > \cdots > r_{k-1} > r_k > \cdots > 0$. Stop when some termination criterion is satisfied. For example, one might decide to stop when the value of the objective function, $f(X)$ in (9-31), given by $X^*(r_k)$, the minimum of $L(X; r_k)$ [or $\mathcal{L}(X; r_k)$], deviates by less than some preselected small amount, ϵ, from the theoretical true minimum of $f(X)$.

The duality theory of the previous section provides a criterion in this case. Since (9-31) is a minimization problem, its objective function is what was denoted by Δ in Section 9.1. Let the optimal value of Δ be given by $f(X^0)$. The dual to (9-31) will be a maximization problem in which the constraints appear as *equalities*, since nonnegativity is not specified explicitly in (9-31). Thus, following Section 9.1, the dual is

$$\text{maximize:} \quad \pi(X, V) = f(X) - \sum_i v_i h_i(X)$$

$$\text{subject to:} \quad \sum_i v_i h_j^i - f_j = 0 \tag{9-37}$$

$$\text{and} \quad v_i \geq 0.$$

The final term from the dual objective function (9-5′) is absent here because the dual constraints assure that it is zero. We know that $f(X) \geq \pi(X, V)$ for any feasible solutions X and V to the two problems and, at optimum, $f(X^0) = \pi(X^0, V^0)$. Thus $f(X) \geq f(X^0) \geq \pi(X, V)$; for the particular

---

[26] For detailed aspects of each of these steps, criteria on initial and subsequent sizes of r, and stopping rules, Fiacco and McCormick [7] is recommended as initial reading.

feasible solution involving $X(r_k)$ and corresponding additional dual variables $V(r_k)$,

$$f[X(r_k)] \geq f(X^0) \geq \pi[X(r_k),\ V(r_k)]. \tag{9-38}$$

We want to stop calculations when

$$f[X(r_k)] - f(X^0) < \epsilon, \tag{9-39}$$

since the left-hand side of (9-39) measures exactly the deviation of $f(X)$
evaluated at $X(r_k)$, from the true minimum, $f(X^0)$. But clearly, from (9-38),
if

$$f[X(r_k)] - \pi[X(r_k),\ V(r_k)] < \epsilon, \tag{9-40}$$

then (9-39) will hold. And the difference between primal and dual objective
function values for "current" solutions $X(r_k)$ and $[X(r_k),\ V(r_k)]$ is just

$$\sum_i v_i(r_k)\{h_i[X(r_k)]\}. \tag{9-41}$$

All that remains is to establish the feasibility of the $V(r_k)$. We know that
the $X(r_k)$ are feasible for the primal because of the way in which they were
obtained. Feasibility in the dual requires that the constraints of (9-37) be
met; using gradient notation, these constraints are

$$\sum_i v_i\ \nabla h_i(X) - \nabla f(X) = 0. \tag{9-42}$$

Now observe (9-35), which is always true for feasible $X(r_k)$. If we set

$$v_i(r_k) = \frac{r_k^2}{\{h_i[X(r_k)]\}^2}$$

—that is, equal to the term multiplying $\nabla h_i[X(r_k)]$ in (9-35)—we are assured
of the feasibility of the $v_i(r_k)$ in the dual programming problem (9-37).
(Note that nonnegativity is assured, since both numerator and denominator
are squared.) Thus, finally, the stopping criterion (9-40) can be made explicit. From (9-40), (9-41), and the argument above, we are satisfied with
the solution to the kth unconstrained minimization problem as soon as we
have

$$r_k^2 \sum_i \frac{1}{h_i[X(r_k)]} < \epsilon. \tag{9-43}$$

We conclude with yet another approach to our same example, problem
(9-24), although we introduce two modifications. The first is to multiply
$f(X)$ and $g_1(X)$ by -1 and hence work with the equivalent minimization
problem:

$$\text{minimize:} \quad -f(X) = -3x_1 - 2x_2$$
$$\text{subject to:} \quad -4x_1^2 - x_2^2 + 16 \geq 0, \quad\quad\quad (9\text{-}44)$$
$$x_1, x_2 \geq 0.$$

Secondly, we ignore the nonnegativity requirements in (9-44). This is done only to make the algebra of the illustrative example manageable; it is by no means a general procedure. (Again, since we happen to know the exact answer, in which both $x_1^* > 0$ and $x_2^* > 0$, we know that any fairly accurate approximation will also involve strictly positive x_1 and x_2.) Using the logarithmic penalty function, $L(X; r)$ in (9-34), we have

$$L(X; r) = -3x_1 - 2x_2 - r \ln{(-4x_1^2 - x_2^2 + 16)}. \quad\quad (9\text{-}45)$$

The sequential unconstrained minimization technique would now proceed by selecting an initial X^0 and from that an initial r_1. We avoid the details of this calculation and simply illustrate for various values of r, starting with $r = 1$. It is for this series of minimization problems that gradient methods or other approximating techniques are often needed. For the present example, the direct techniques of Chapter 3 can be applied. Taking first partial derivatives (that is, finding the elements of the gradient vector), we have

$$\frac{\partial L}{\partial x_1} = -3 + \frac{8rx_1}{-4x_1^2 - x_2^2 + 16},$$
$$\frac{\partial L}{\partial x_2} = -2 + \frac{2rx_2}{-4x_1^2 - x_2^2 + 16}.$$

Setting these equal to zero and solving simultaneously gives

$$x_1 = \frac{-6r \pm \sqrt{36r^2 + 3600}}{50}$$

and $\quad\quad\quad\quad\quad\quad\quad\quad\quad\quad\quad\quad\quad\quad\quad\quad\quad\quad\quad\quad\quad (9\text{-}46)$

$$x_2 = \frac{-16r \pm \sqrt{256r^2 + 25,600}}{50}.$$

It is easy to show that the Hessian matrix for (9-45) is positive definite (thus assuring a minimum) as long as x_1 and x_2 have the same sign (and $r > 0$). We can thus compensate for the omission of the nonnegativity constraints by using the positive square roots in (9-46). Table 9.5 shows x_1 and x_2 for a series of values for r, and the corresponding value of the objective function, $-f(X)$, in (9-44) (all to three-decimal accuracy). Owing to rounding, we reach the exact answer when $r = 0.001$. Of course, in the limit, as $r \to 0$, the solutions for x_1 and x_2 given in (9-46) also approach $1\frac{1}{5}$ and $3\frac{1}{5}$, respectively.[27]

---

[27] The maximum value of the objective function for the original problem will be the negative of the minimum in (9-44); that is, the maximum will be $-[-f(X)]$.

Table 9.5. Values of x_1, x_2, and $-f(X)$ for Selected r

r	x_1	x_2	$-f(X)$
1.000	1.086	2.896	−9.040
.500	1.141	3.043	−9.509
.250	1.170	3.121	−9.752
.100	1.188	3.168	−9.900
.010	1.199	3.197	−9.991
.001	1.200	3.200	−10.000

Differential gradient methods

We mention here an entirely different approach to solving a nonlinear programming problem. The gradient methods of Chapter 8 and the minimization procedure generally used for the unconstrained problems in SUMT involve, in effect, making a series of discrete steps along gradient (or modified gradient) directions. The differential gradient approach, by contrast, considers continuous movement from a starting point toward the optimum —that is, infinitesimally small steps—in the sense that one looks for the solution to a set of differential equations that describe the time paths of the variables.

Consider again the general Lagrangean function (8-25), repeated here:

$$L(X, V) = f(X) - \sum_i v_i h_i(X) \tag{9-47}$$

From Theorems SP4 and SP5 and the discussion of duality in Section 9.1, we know that the X^0 and V^0 that make up the optimal solutions to the general nonlinear programming problems (9-1) and (9-5) also constitute a saddle point of $L(X, V)$. This suggests that to reach a solution [a saddle point of $L(X, V)$] one wants to move generally "uphill" with respect to the variables X and "downhill" with respect to the variables V.[28] This suggestion is made explicit in the following set of differential equations, where the derivative of a variable with respect to t (time) denotes the velocity of movement (toward the saddle point and hence the nonlinear program solution) prescribed for that variable.

---

[28] The reader may wish to review the discussion of saddle points in Section 8.5. Additional discussion of differential gradient procedures can be found in Hadley [11, sec. 9.15]; Karlin [12, sec. 7.3]; P. Wolfe, "An Outline of Nonlinear Programming," in Dantzig and Veinott [5, pp. 365–400]; P. Wolfe, "Methods of Nonlinear Programming," in Graves and Wolfe [10, chap. 10]; and in the original publication, Arrow, Hurwicz, and Uzawa [2].

(a) $\dfrac{dx_j}{dt} = 0$ if $\dfrac{\partial L}{\partial x_j} < 0$ and $x_j = 0$;

(b) $\dfrac{dx_j}{dt} = \dfrac{\partial L}{\partial x_j}$ otherwise;

(c) $\dfrac{dv_i}{dt} = 0$ if $\dfrac{\partial L}{\partial v_i} > 0$ and $v_i = 0$;

(d) $\dfrac{dv_i}{dt} = -\dfrac{\partial L}{\partial v_i}$ otherwise.

$$(9\text{-}48)$$

Consider (a) and (b) jointly. They say that each x_j should move along the direction given by its component in the gradient of the Lagrangean function $L(X, V)$ *unless* that direction indicates a decrease in x_j *and* x_j is already at its lower limit, namely zero. Similarly (c) and (d) specify that each v_i should move in a direction opposite to its component in the gradient of $L(X, V)$ *unless* that direction indicates a decrease in v_i (that is, when $\partial L/\partial v_i > 0$, since the direction of movement is given by $-\partial L/\partial v_i$) *and* v_i is already at zero, its lower limit.

These conditions parallel exactly those in Theorem SP1 of Chapter 8, which describe the characteristics necessary for a saddle point. Recall from Theorem SP2 that sufficiency hinged on the concavity and convexity of the function with respect to X and V, respectively. Precisely the same conditions are required here: the differential gradient method is appropriate only when $f(X)$ in (9-47) is a concave function and each of the $h_i(X)$ are convex.

Note that

$$\frac{\partial L}{\partial x_j} = f_j - \sum_i v_i h_j^i \quad \text{and} \quad -\frac{\partial L}{\partial v_i} = h_i(X).$$

Thus the conditions set out in (9-48) have a logic that is independent of the saddle point connection via the Lagrangean in (9-47). From the point of view of the primal nonlinear program (9-1) only, part (b) says that we want to increase each x_j according to its contribution to the gradient of $f(X)$, the function to be maximized, subject to a modification in direction [parts (b), (c), and (d)]. That is, if a constraint $h_i(X) \le 0$ is violated ($\partial L/\partial v_i < 0$), then x_j should be pulled back into the feasible region. This is accomplished by movement along $-h_j^i$, the jth component in $-\nabla h_i$, the negative gradient of constraint h_i. (Recall from Section 8.3 that this "inward normal" is perpendicular to the tangent to the constraint contour and points *into* the feasible region.) The amount of movement along the inward normal is given by v_i, which is necessarily positive and is larger, the more the constraint is violated [part (d)]. Part (a) simply says that if x_j has a negative component in ∇f, namely f_j, *and* if x_j cannot be decreased (is at zero), it should not change at all.

Proofs of convergence and descriptions of some computational experience (the most promising of which has been on analog computers) are contained in the literature cited in footnote 28. The logic of the approach is completely straightforward, but it does not appear that the differential gradient method has been very successful for computational purposes, when compared with the other techniques presented in this and the preceding chapter.

9.3.   QUADRATIC PROGRAMMING

We conclude this chapter with an investigation of the features of so-called quadratic programming problems, seeing how an extension of the powerful and simple simplex method can be used to arrive at an exact solution. This is an advantage that quadratic programs have over more general nonlinear problems. Thus it is often useful, in cases where non-linearities are clearly present and the restrictions of a linear programming framework would be too severe to attempt to approximate an inherently nonlinear program with a quadratic one.

Structure

As mentioned earlier, a quadratic program is defined as one in which all constraints remain linear and the objective function is quadratic. In ordinary algebraic terms this means variables may be squared and pairs of variables may appear multiplied together. In matrix algebraic terms, the objective function consists of a quadratic form and possibly also a linear term.[29] These are shown below.

$$\text{Maximize:} \quad f(X) = \sum_{j=1}^{n} p_j x_j + \frac{1}{2} \sum_{j=1}^{n} \sum_{k=1}^{n} p_{jk} x_j x_k$$

$$\text{subject to:} \quad \sum_{j=1}^{n} a_{ij} x_j \leq r_i \quad (i = 1, \ldots, m) \tag{9-49}$$

$$\text{and} \quad x_j \geq 0 \quad (j = 1, \ldots, n),$$

or

$$\text{maximize:} \quad f(X) = P'X + \tfrac{1}{2} X'QX$$
$$\text{subject to:} \quad AX \leq R \tag{9-50}$$
$$\text{and} \quad X \geq O.$$

In (9-50), Q is a symmetric matrix; this is always possible for quadratic

---

[29] The reader may wish to review the discussion of quadratic forms in Section 4.1.

forms but may involve some rewriting of the original coefficients, hence we distinguish it from the original p_{jk} by using Q. The $\frac{1}{2}$ is for mathematical convenience; any set of coefficients p_{jk} or elements of Q can always be doubled and then preceded by $\frac{1}{2}$.

Since the linear inequalities in (9-49) or (9-50) form a convex set, we need to require only concavity of the objective function to be assured that a local maximum is also the global one. The linear term in the objective function of (9-49) or (9-50) does not alter the basic concavity; hence $f(X)$ is concave if its quadratic part is concave.[30] Geometrically, for the case of two variables, we are looking for the top of an inverted bowl-like surface above a convex feasible region with straight sides. Figures 8.4(a) through (c) illustrate the essentials, where the contours are those of an inverted bowl. A negative semidefinite (negative definite) quadratic form $X'QX$ is a concave (strictly concave) function of X.[31] Thus if Q is negative definite or semidefinite, the objective function, $f(X)$, in (9-50) will be strictly concave or concave.

In the Kuhn-Tucker conditions (8-7') and (8-8) we have the necessary conditions for X to be a relative maximum of the general nonlinear programming problem (9-1) [or (8-4)]. If the objective function is concave and the constraints are each convex, these become sufficient as well. They are repeated here:

$$\text{(a)} \quad f_j - \sum_{i=1}^{m} \lambda_i h_j^i + \lambda_{m+j} = 0,$$

$$\text{(b)} \quad \begin{cases} \text{(i)} & \lambda_i[h_i(X)] = 0, \\ \text{(ii)} & -\lambda_{m+j}x_j = 0, \end{cases} \qquad (9\text{-}51)$$

$$\text{(c)} \quad \begin{cases} \text{(i)} & h_i(X) \leq 0, \\ \text{(ii)} & \lambda_i, \lambda_{m+j}, x_j \geq 0. \end{cases}$$

Thus, if $f(X)$ is concave in (9-49) or (9-50)—if Q is negative definite or semidefinite in (9-50)—these will be necessary and sufficient conditions for the maximum of the general quadratic programming problem. In terms of the quadratic program in (9-49) these requirements are (inserting slack variables explicitly)

---

[30] Various authors differ in the way that the objective function is formulated. For example, if in (9-50) we had $f(X) = P'X - \frac{1}{2}X'QX$, then we would want *convexity* of the quadratic form in order to assure concavity of $f(X)$, since $-X'QX$ would then be concave. If the problem is one of minimization, then we want convexity of the objective function.

[31] This follows directly from the result on Hessians in Appendix 8.3. For $F(X) = X'QX$, $\nabla F(X) = 2QX$, and $H = 2Q$; if $F(X) = \frac{1}{2}X'QX$, $H = Q$. In the latter case, the (symmetric) matrix Q from $F(X) = \frac{1}{2}X'QX$ is precisely the Hessian matrix of $F(X)$; hence if Q is negative definite or semidefinite, the function is strictly concave or concave.

(a) $\quad p_j + \displaystyle\sum_{k=1}^{n} p_{jk}x_k - \sum_{i=1}^{m} \lambda_i a_{ij} + \lambda_{m+j} = 0 \qquad (j = 1, \ldots, n),$

(b) $\begin{cases} \text{(i)} \\ \text{(ii)} \end{cases} \qquad\qquad \begin{aligned} \lambda_i(-s_i) &= 0 \qquad (i = 1, \ldots, m), \\ -\lambda_{m+j}x_j &= 0 \qquad (j = 1, \ldots, n), \end{aligned}$

$(9\text{-}52)$

(c) $\begin{cases} \text{(i)} \\ \text{(ii)} \end{cases} \qquad\qquad \begin{aligned} s_i &\geq 0, \\ \lambda_i, \lambda_{m+j}, x_j &\geq 0, \end{aligned}$

(d) $\qquad\qquad\qquad\qquad\qquad s_i = r_i - \displaystyle\sum_{j=1}^{n} a_{ij}x_j \qquad (i = 1, \ldots, m).$

The important characteristic of these requirements is the following. Conditions (a) and (d) constitute a set of $n + m$ *linear* equations in the variables x_j, λ_i, λ_{m+j}, s_i—that is, in $2n + 2m$ variables. All variables must be nonnegative from (c). But (b) requires that at least $m + n$ of the variables be zero. Hence (9-52) asks for nonnegative *basic* solutions to the linear equations in (a) and (d). This suggests that a kind of simplex method should be appropriate, since generation of nonnegative basic solutions to a set of linear equations was precisely the heart of the simplex technique. We now explore this possibility.[32]

Computational methods

We examine Wolfe's procedure for making use of the simplex method on conditions similar to (9-52). This illustrates well the logic involved, but the reader is advised that there are numerous other variants and also completely different techniques for quadratic programming; Wolfe's method works well and is easily employed in high-speed computers, however.[33]

We assume that the objective function is *strictly* concave; if $X'QX$ is only negative *semi*definite, it is still possible to use a simplexlike technique, but the details become more cumbersome. Moreover, to maintain consistency with most other discussions of Wolfe's method, we assume that the constraints have been converted to equalities through the addition

---

[32] Note that we are *not* using the simplex method to move to adjacent corners of the original feasible region; this would generally not lead to an optimum (recall Figures 8.4). We have enlarged the equation set by the addition of (9-52)(a), obtained through Kuhn-Tucker reasoning.

[33] Many of the references at the end of this and the previous chapter treat quadratic programming problems; in particular, see Boot [4]. Comparisons among computational techniques are studied in detail in Künzi, Krelle, and Oettli [14].

of nonnegative slack variables where necessary. We replace the inequalities by

$$\sum_{j=1}^{n+m} a_{ij}x_j = r_i$$

in (9-49) and $AX = R$ in (9-50); in the latter case we simply understand that the X vector has been increased to include the nonnegative slack variables. This simplifies conditions (9-51) somewhat.

The modified problem, then, in matrix form is

$$\begin{aligned}
\text{maximize:} \quad & P'X + \tfrac{1}{2}X'QX \\
\text{subject to:} \quad & AX = R \\
\text{and} \quad & X \geq 0.
\end{aligned} \tag{9-50'}$$

For the equality-constrained case the Lagrangean is

$$L = f(X) - \sum_i \lambda_i h_i(X) - \sum_j \lambda_{m+j}[-x_j + s_j^2];$$

thus we have

$$\text{(a)} \quad f_j - \sum_i \lambda_i h_j^i + \lambda_{m+j} = 0,$$

$$\text{(b)} \quad -\lambda_{m+j}x_j = 0, \tag{9-51'}$$

$$\text{(c)} \quad \begin{cases} h_i(X) = 0, \\ \lambda_{m+j}, \, x_j \geq 0. \end{cases}$$

(Note that the λ_i are now unrestricted, since they multiply constraints that are always met as strict equalities.) Hence, for the quadratic programming problem in (9-50') we have, parallel to (9-52),

$$\text{(a)} \quad p_j + \sum_k p_{jk}x_k - \sum_i \lambda_i a_{ij} + \lambda_{m+j} = 0,$$

$$\text{(b)} \quad -\lambda_{m+j}x_j = 0,$$

$$\text{(c)} \quad \lambda_{m+j}, \, x_j \geq 0, \tag{9-52'}$$

$$\text{(d)} \quad \sum_j a_{ij}x_j = r_i.$$

The simplex arithmetic proceeds in two phases; both are basically artificial-variable kinds of techniques to cope with equalities (recall Sections 7.2 and 7.3). Add a variable w_i to each of the equations in (9-52')(d) and add a set $(z_{j1} - z_{j2})$ to each equation in (9-52')(a), where w_i, z_{j1}, and $z_{j2} \geq 0$ for all i and j. Assume $r_i \geq 0$ [this can always be accomplished by appropriate multiplication, since the only equations are involved in (9-52')(d)]. Then the Phase I problem is to minimize: $f(w) = \sum_i w_i$

subject to:
$$\begin{cases}
\text{(a)} & p_j + \sum_k p_{jk}x_k - \sum_i \lambda_i a_{ij} + \lambda_{m+j} + z_{j1} - z_{j2} = 0, \\
& \hspace{6cm} (9\text{-}53) \\
\text{(b)} & \sum_j a_{ij}x_j + w_i = r_i, \\
\text{(c)} & \lambda_{m+j},\, x_j,\, w_i,\, z_{j1},\, \text{and } z_{j2} \geq 0; \quad \lambda_i \gtrless 0.
\end{cases}$$

This is a *linear* program with $n + m$ equations and $4n + 2m$ variables. An obvious initial basic solution is: let $x_j = 0$, $\lambda_i = 0$, and $\lambda_{m+j} = 0$; then $w_i = r_i$ (nonnegative by assumption), and $z_{j1} = -p_j$ if p_j is negative (in which case $z_{j2} = 0$) or $z_{j2} = p_j$ if p_j is positive (and then $z_{j1} = 0$). Thus at least $3n + m$ variables are zero and at most $n + m$ are positive; this therefore gives an initial *basic* solution for the linear program. In fact, in Phase I we maintain $\lambda_i = 0$ and $\lambda_{m+j} = 0$ throughout (thus avoiding the sign-unrestrictedness problem of λ_i). The actual program is

minimize: $f(w) = \sum_i w_i$

subject to:
$$\begin{cases}
\text{(a)} & \sum_k p_{jk}x_k + z_{j1} - z_{j2} = -p_j, \\
& \hspace{5cm} (9\text{-}53') \\
\text{(b)} & \sum_j a_{ij}x_j + w_i = r_i,
\end{cases}$$

and $x_j,\, w_i,\, z_{j1},\, z_{j2} \geq 0.$

It has been shown by Wolfe and others that this objective function has a minimum value of zero—that is, a minimum at $w_i = 0$, for all i. This being so, the minimum of $(9\text{-}53')$ will be a *basic feasible* solution to the constraint set:

(a) $p_j + \sum_k p_{jk}x_k - \sum_i \lambda_i a_{ij} + \lambda_{m+j} + z_{j1} - z_{j2} = 0,$

(b) $\sum_i a_{ij}x_j = r_i,$ (9-54)

(c) $x_j,\, \lambda_{m+j},\, z_{j1} \text{ and } z_{j2} \geq 0; \quad \lambda_i \gtrless 0.$

A technique for dealing with variables that are unrestricted in sign is to replace them by the difference of two nonnegative variables. Thus let $\lambda_i = \lambda_{i1} - \lambda_{i2}$; $\lambda_{i1}, \lambda_{i2} \geq 0$. (Of course, this adds m more variables to the problem.) Subject to the *linear* constraints (9-54), Phase II of the quadratic programming technique seeks the minimum of the linear function

$$f(z) = \sum_j z_{j1} + \sum_j z_{j2}, \qquad (9\text{-}55)$$

using as an initial *basic feasible* solution the optimum of (9-53') *and* maintaining throughout the calculations the added requirement that $\lambda_{m+j}x_j = 0$. Note that constraints (9-54) plus the $\lambda_{m+j}x_j = 0$ condition reproduce all of the Kuhn-Tucker requirements (9-52') when $z_{j1} = z_{j2} = 0$ for all j. Again, it can be shown that the minimum of $f(z)$ in (9-55) is zero—that is, that all z_{j1} and z_{j2} are zero at the optimum to the Phase II program.

Thus in Phase II we must incorporate into the simplex technique a restricted basis entry modification similar in concept to that used in the separable programming calculations. Where the minimum is reached, we will have a point satisfying conditions (9-52') that, if the concavity and convexity assumptions hold, will be both necessary and sufficient for a maximum to (9-51'). (A matrix expression of the Phase I and Phase II problems is given in Appendix 9.2 for the interested reader; in many of the references dealing with quadratic programming the discussion is entirely in matrix terms.) We conclude with an example.

Example

$$\begin{aligned}
\text{maximize:} \quad & 2x_1 + x_2 - x_1^2 \\
\text{subject to:} \quad & 2x_1 + 3x_2 \le 6, \\
& 2x_1 + x_2 \le 4, \\
& x_1, x_2 \ge 0.
\end{aligned} \tag{9-56}$$

With slack variables $s_1 = x_3$ and $s_2 = x_4$, the relevant matrices corresponding to the form of (9-50') are

$$P = \begin{bmatrix} 2 \\ 1 \\ 0 \\ 0 \end{bmatrix}, \quad R = \begin{bmatrix} 6 \\ 4 \end{bmatrix}, \quad Q = \begin{bmatrix} -2 & 0 & 0 & 0 \\ 0 & 0 & 0 & 0 \\ 0 & 0 & 0 & 0 \\ 0 & 0 & 0 & 0 \end{bmatrix},$$

$$A = \begin{bmatrix} 2 & 3 & 1 & 0 \\ 2 & 1 & 0 & 1 \end{bmatrix}, \quad X = \begin{bmatrix} x_1 \\ x_2 \\ x_3 \\ x_4 \end{bmatrix}.$$

The Phase I problem, (9-53'), is

minimize: $w_1 + w_2$
subject to:

(a) $-2x_1$		$+ z_{11} - z_{12}$					$= -2,$
	$0x_2$		$+ z_{21} - z_{22}$				$= -1,$
		$0x_3$		$+ z_{31} - z_{32}$			$= 0,$
			$0x_4$		$+ z_{41} - z_{42}$		$= 0,$
(b) $2x_1 + 3x_2 + x_3$						$+ w_1$	$= 6,$
$2x_1 + x_2$	$+ x_4$					$+ w_2$	$= 4,$

and all x_j, z_{j1}, z_{j2}, and $w_i \ge 0$ ($i = 1, 2; j = 1, \ldots, 4$).

$$\tag{9-57}$$

An obvious initial basic feasible solution sets $w_1 = 6$, $w_2 = 4$, $z_{12} = 2$, $z_{22} = 1$, and, since we need six variables in the basis, we let $z_{31} = z_{41} = 0$. Since

$$w_1 = 6 - 2x_1 - 3x_2 - x_3 \quad \text{and} \quad w_2 = 4 - 2x_1 - x_2 - x_4,$$

from (9-57)(b), we reexpress the objective function in (9-57) in terms of initially excluded variables as

$$\text{minimize:} \quad -4x_1 - 4x_2 - x_3 - x_4 + 10. \tag{9-58}$$

The constant, $+10$, obviously plays no role in the simplex calculations. The initial simplex tableau is shown in Table 9.6.

Table 9.6.   Initial Simplex Tableau for Problem (9-57)

		x_1	x_2	x_3	x_4	z_{11}	z_{21}	z_{32}	z_{42}
π_{I}	0	-4	-4	-1	-1	0	0	0	0
w_1	6	-2	-3	-1	0	0	0	0	0
w_2	4	-2	-1	0	-1	0	0	0	0
z_{12}	2	-2	0	0	0	1	0	0	0
z_{22}	1	0	0	0	0	0	1	0	0
z_{31}	0	0	0	0	0	0	0	1	0
z_{41}	0	0	0	0	0	0	0	0	1

In fact, however, it will be useful at the conclusion of Phase I to have the coefficients that express the additional excluded variables, the λ_i's and the λ_{m+j}'s from problem (9-53), in terms of those variables included in the optimal basis. Hence we carry along these variables also, separated from the rest of the tableau by a small space to remind us that they are not ever to enter the basis.[34] To the right-hand side of the tableau in Table 9.6 we therefore add Table 9.7.[35] The problem is a minimization one, of course. We could work with the dual variables—a maximization problem (not advised, since it would involve variables unrestricted in sign and hence a large number of added columns); we could also change the signs of all ob-

---

[34] This, of course, greatly increases the size of the problem, especially when worked by hand. For a modern computer it is much less important.

[35] Note that we have replaced λ_1 and λ_2 by the *pairs* of variables λ_{11}, λ_{12} and λ_{21}, λ_{22}, all four of which can now be required to remain nonnegative.

Table 9.7. Added Section for Initial Tableau for
Problem (9-57)

λ_{11}	λ_{12}	λ_{21}	λ_{22}	λ_3	λ_4	λ_5	λ_6
0	0	0	0	0	0	0	0
0	0	0	0	0	0	0	0
0	0	0	0	0	0	0	0
-2	2	-2	2	1	0	0	0
-3	3	-1	1	0	1	0	0
1	-1	0	0	0	0	-1	0
0	0	1	-1	0	0	0	-1

jective function coefficients and then maximize. But it is equally easy to simply reverse the simplex method logic for the variable to enter the basis (that is, to select at each iteration the one with the largest *negative* coefficient, stop when all are nonnegative) and then proceed exactly as in Chapter 6. If this is done, either x_1 or x_2 should first enter the basis, and the calculations can begin. A solution is obtained after three or four iterations, depending on which one of several equally attractive variables is chosen to enter at each pivot. The optimum is both degenerate and nonunique; it is summarized in Table 9.8 (all excluded variables have a value of zero at optimum). The objective function value shown in the optimal final simplex tableau is -10. This is precisely balanced by the $+10$ in (9-58); therefore, at optimum, the function has a value of zero.

Table 9.8. Optimal Values, Phase I Variables

$x_1 = \frac{3}{2}$	$z_{11} = 1$	$z_{31} = 0$
$x_2 = 1$	$z_{22} = 1$	$z_{41} = 0$

For the Phase II problem, (9-54) and (9-55), we use the optimum from Phase I as the initial basic feasible solution. Columns for the w_i and z_{j1} or z_{j2} that are excluded from the optimal basis are thus eliminated, since they play no role in the Phase II problem. However, to establish the initial Phase II tableau we need coefficients to express the variables from problem (9-54) and (9-55) that are excluded from the initial basis in terms of the included variables. It is for precisely this reason that we attached

Table 9.9. Full Final Tableau, Phase I

		X	X	X	X	X	X	X	X								
		z_{12}	w_1	x_3	w_2	x_4	z_{21}	z_{32}	z_{42}	λ_{11}	λ_{12}	λ_{21}	λ_{22}	λ_3	λ_4	λ_5	λ_6
π_I	-10	0	1	0	1	0	0	0	0	0	0	0	0	0	0	0	0
x_2	1	0	$-\frac{1}{2}$	$-\frac{1}{2}$	$\frac{1}{2}$	$\frac{1}{2}$	0	0	0	0	0	0	0	0	0	0	0
z_{11}	1	1	$\frac{1}{2}$	$\frac{1}{2}$	$-\frac{3}{2}$	$-\frac{3}{2}$	0	0	0	2	-2	2	-2	-1	0	0	0
x_1	$\frac{3}{2}$	$\frac{1}{2}$	$\frac{1}{4}$	$\frac{1}{4}$	$-\frac{3}{4}$	$-\frac{3}{4}$	0	0	0	0	0	0	0	0	0	0	0
x_{22}	1	0	0	0	0	0	1	0	0	-3	3	-1	1	0	1	0	0
z_{31}	0	0	0	0	0	0	0	1	0	1	-1	0	0	0	0	-1	0
z_{41}	0	0	0	0	0	0	0	0	1	0	0	1	-1	0	0	0	-1

Table 9.7 to the initial Phase I tableau and carried it along during the simplex calculations. The full final tableau for Phase I is shown in Table 9.9. (An X denotes a column that is irrelevant for Phase II.)

To obtain an expression for the objective function [in (9-55)]—that is, to find the coefficients for the currently excluded variables (which are the zeroth-row entries for the initial simplex tableau for Phase II)—we need only sum the elements in each remaining column of Table 9.9 for the z rows (here these are the rows for z_{11}, z_{22}, z_{31} and z_{41}). That is, from Table 9.9, since x_3 is excluded from the initial basis for Phase II, we observe that only z_{11} is affected by the value of x_3. Specifically, row 2 of the final tableau in Table 9.9 says (in terms of the variables in the linear program that constitutes Phase II)

$$z_{11} = 1 + \tfrac{1}{2}x_3 - \tfrac{3}{2}x_4 + 2\lambda_{11} - 2\lambda_{12} + 2\lambda_{21} - 2\lambda_{22} - \lambda_3. \qquad (9\text{-}59)$$

Since there is no nonzero coefficient for x_3 in any other z row, we conclude that each unit of x_3 currently contributes $\tfrac{1}{2}$ unit to $(z_{11} + z_{22} + z_{31} + z_{41})$ and hence to the current value of the objective function. The z-row sums for x_3 and all other Phase II variables are shown in Table 9.10; they are obtained directly from Table 9.9.

Table 9.10.   Objective Function Coefficients, Phase II, Initial Tableau

$x_3 = \tfrac{1}{2}$	$\lambda_{11} = 0$	$\lambda_{21} = 2$	$\lambda_3 = -1$	$\lambda_5 = -1$
$x_4 = -\tfrac{3}{2}$	$\lambda_{12} = 0$	$\lambda_{22} = -2$	$\lambda_4 = 1$	$\lambda_6 = -1$

This completes the information necessary to formulate the initial tableau for Phase II, utilizing as the first basic feasible solution the optimum from the Phase I program. Table 9.11 contains this tableau. (Recall that the elements z_j are now either z_{j1} or z_{j2}; hence the new labels on the z-rows.) Again, dealing with the minimization problem directly, λ_{22} is the most attractive variable to enter the basis. Recall that in Phase II we must maintain in all basic solutions the additional condition $\lambda_{m+j}x_j = 0$, which in the current problem means[36]

$$\lambda_{2+1}x_1 = \lambda_{2+2}x_2 = \lambda_{2+3}x_3 = \lambda_{2+4}x_4 = 0. \qquad (9\text{-}60)$$

[36] It would be neater looking if (9-60) read $\lambda_1 x_1 = \lambda_2 x_2 = \lambda_3 x_3 = \lambda_4 x_4 = 0$. But recall from fundamental Kuhn-Tucker reasoning that the initial set of λ_i's were associated with the m inequality constraints in a problem where nonnegativity of the x_j's (n in number) was not required (Section 4.8). Thus the first "unassigned" λ, to use when nonnegativity constraints are added, is λ_{m+1}, and this is associated with x_1; in the present example, $m = 2$.

Table 9.11. Initial Tableau, Phase II

		x_3	x_4	λ_{11}	λ_{12}	λ_{21}	λ_{22}	λ_3	λ_4	λ_5	λ_6
π_{II}	2	$\frac{1}{2}$	$-\frac{3}{2}$	0	0	2	-2	-1	1	-1	-1
x_2	1	$-\frac{1}{2}$	$\frac{1}{2}$	0	0	0	0	0	0	0	0
z_1	1	$\frac{1}{2}$	$-\frac{3}{2}$	2	-2	2	-2	-1	0	0	0
x_1	$\frac{3}{2}$	$\frac{1}{4}$	$-\frac{3}{4}$	0	0	0	0	0	0	0	0
z_2	1	0	0	-3	3	-1	1	0	1	0	0
z_3	0	0	0	1	-1	0	0	0	0	-1	0
z_4	0	0	0	0	0	1	-1	0	0	0	-1

Clearly there is no problem with the introduction of λ_{22}; after three additional iterations an optimum (again, both degenerate and nonunique) is reached. Optimal values are summarized in Table 9.12 (excluded variables have a value of zero at optimum). The objective function has a value of zero at this point. Thus the optimum for the original quadratic programming problem (9-56) is $x_1^0 = \frac{2}{3}$, $x_2^0 = \frac{14}{9}$, $s_1^0 (= x_3^0) = 0$, $s_2^0 (= x_4^0) = \frac{10}{9}$, at which point the quadratic objective function has a value of $\frac{22}{9} = 2.44$.

Table 9.12. Optimal Values, Phase II Variables

$x_1 = \frac{2}{3}$	$x_4 = \frac{10}{9}$	$\lambda_{22} = 0$
$x_2 = \frac{14}{9}$	$\lambda_{11} = \frac{1}{3}$	$\lambda_5 = \frac{1}{3}$

Again it happens that because of the relative simplicity of this example, the methods of Chapter 4 (specifically Section 4.8) could be used—with slight modification, as before. That is, if we again ignore the nonnegativity requirements of (9-56)—which is not generally a good approach—and treat the problem via Lagrange multiplier analysis *as if* both constraints were equations, we find that the first (partial) derivative conditions require $\lambda_2 < 0$. [These λ's refer to the new unknowns in Lagrange multiplier analysis, as in Chapter 4; they are not (directly) comparable with the λ's in the two-phase Wolfe approach to quadratic programs.] Hence the second constraint should be ignored—that is, will be met as a strict inequality at optimum—and the problem should be redone, via a new Lagrangean function, considering only the first constraint as an equality. When this is carried out, the results shown in Table 9.12 for x_1 and x_2 (and hence, by implication, for $s_2 = x_4$ and for $s_1 = x_3$, which is zero by its absence from the optimal basis) are obtained. Because, fortunately, all $x_i \geq 0$, we have satisfied *all* the constraints of (9-56) and hence found the true solution. In general, to repeat, the nonnegativity requirements cannot be treated in so cavalier a fashion; this is one of the reasons for the more elaborate treatment that begins in Section 8.2 and continues through all that follows.

Duality in quadratic programming

Following the general discussion on duality in Section 9.1, we can easily construct the dual to the quadratic maximization program in (9-49) or (9-50). Since, for this problem, $\partial f/\partial x_j = p_j + \sum_k p_{jk}x_k$ and $\partial h_i/\partial x_j = a_{ij}$,

the objective function for the dual programming problem, (9-5), can be written explicitly as

$$\text{minimize:} \quad \Delta(X, V) = \sum_j p_j x_j + \frac{1}{2}\sum_j \sum_k p_{jk}x_j x_k - \sum_i v_i\left(\sum_j a_{ij}x_j - r_i\right)$$
$$- \sum_j x_j\left(p_j + \sum_k p_{jk}x_k - \sum_i v_i a_{ij}\right),$$

which, after a little algebra, becomes

$$\text{minimize:} \quad \Delta(X, V) = \sum_i r_i v_i - \frac{1}{2}\sum_j \sum_k p_{jk}x_j x_k. \tag{9-61}$$

Similarly, the constraints in (9-5) are

$$\sum_i v_i a_{ij} - p_j - \sum_k p_{jk}x_k \geq 0$$

or

$$\sum_i a_{ij}v_i - \sum_k p_{jk}x_k \geq p_j \quad \text{and} \quad v_i \geq 0. \tag{9-62}$$

In matrix terms, the dual quadratic programming minimization problem is

$$\begin{aligned} \text{minimize:} \quad & R'V - \tfrac{1}{2}X'QX \\ \text{subject to:} \quad & A'V - QX \geq P \\ \text{and} \quad & V \geq O. \end{aligned} \tag{9-63}$$

From the primal-dual results in Section 9.1, we know that if X^0 is a solution to (9-50), then X^0 and some V^0 will be a solution to (9-63). But with X given, (9-63) is a *linear* program in the variables V. Hence, once the primal quadratic programming problem is solved, the dual becomes a simple linear problem. We illustrate with the previous example, (9-56), whose solution was given in Table 9.12.

From (9-61), the dual objective function is $6v_1 + 4v_2 + \frac{4}{9}$, where, again, the constant will not affect the computations at all. From (9-62), the constraints are $2v_1 + 2v_2 \geq \frac{2}{3}$ and $3v_1 + v_2 \geq 1$, and v_1, $v_2 \geq 0$. Thus, we want to

$$
\begin{aligned}
\text{minimize:} \quad & 6v_1 + 4v_2 + \tfrac{4}{9} \\
\text{subject to:} \quad & 2v_1 + 2v_2 \geq \tfrac{2}{3}, \\
& 3v_1 + v_2 \geq 1, \\
\text{and} \quad & v_1, v_2 \geq 0.
\end{aligned}
\tag{9-64}
$$

Using the regular simplex method for *maximization* problems on the *dual* linear programming problem to (9-64), we obtain, after two iterations, the optimum for (9-64): $v_1^0 = \frac{1}{3}$, $v_2^0 = 0$, and both dual slack variables equal zero by virtue of their absence from the optimal basis. Note that the minimum value of the dual objective function in (9-64) is $\frac{22}{9}$, the same as the maximum to (9-56), in agreement with the second primal-dual theorem in Section 9.1. The reader may also note that the "complementary slackness" conditions of the third theorem hold as well.

SUMMARY

This chapter has extended the investigation of nonlinear programming problems in two directions. The first was via a presentation of some of the theoretical results on duality in the nonlinear case. As with linear programming, the dual program itself may not always be relevant in a particular problem, yet because of the primal-dual relations [Theorems P-D1(N) through P-D4(N)], the optimal values of the dual variables themselves may be useful. Not all relationships carry over from the linear case; for example, the dual of the dual (9-5) is not the primal problem (9-1). In the process, we saw that the saddle-point conditions of Chapter 8 developed exactly the characteristics that we want to find in a pair of mutually dual nonlinear programs.

Second, we examined a collection of solution methods for nonlinear programs that formulate various kinds of approximating problems (often linear) and then concentrate on procedures for solving these, in contrast to the gradient methods of Chapter 8, which attack the full nonlinear programming problem directly. We also saw how a continuous version of a gradient approach—the so-called differential gradient method—could be derived either from the saddle-point connection or directly from the statement of the nonlinear maximization program using only the fundamental properties of gradient vectors.

Finally, we examined quadratic programs, usually the computationally most tractable nonlinear problems. Because of the simplexlike solution procedure, a problem with a quadratic objective function coupled with linear constraints is usually easily solved, either by hand or by high-speed computer. In this particular case the simplex method is saved, contrary to the general discussion at the outset of Chapter 8, thanks to Kuhn-Tucker theory *and* the fact that the first partial derivatives of a quadratic function are themselves linear functions.

APPENDIX 9.1

Proofs of Primal-Dual Theorems in Nonlinear Programming

THEOREM P-D1(N).   For any feasible solutions to the primal and dual problems, $\Delta(X, V) \geq \pi(X)$.

Recall that $\pi(X) = f(X)$ and

$$\Delta(X, V) = f(X) - \sum_i v_i h_i(X) - \sum_j x_j \left(f_j - \sum_i v_i h_j^i \right).$$

Let (X^p) and (X^d, V^d) be feasible for the primal and dual, respectively. Then,

$$\Delta(X^d, V^d) - \pi(X^p) = f(X^d) - \sum_i v_i^d h_i(X^d) - \sum_j x_j^d f_j \\ + \sum_j x_j^d \sum_i v_i^d h_j^i - f(X^p). \tag{9-65}$$

If a function f is convex, recall (Appendix 8.3) that

$$[\nabla f(X'')]'(X' - X'') \leq f(X') - f(X'')$$

for any pair of points, X' and X'', in the convex set over which f is defined. For concave functions the inequality is reversed. Hence, if the primal objective function is concave,

$$\sum_j (x_j^p - x_j^d) f_j - f(X^p) + f(X^d) \geq 0. \tag{9-66}$$

If the primal constraints are each convex,

$$- \sum_j (x_j^p - x_j^d) h_j^i + h_i(X^p) - h_i(X^d) \geq 0. \tag{9-67}$$

Finally, if $V^d \geq O$ (which is necessary for dual feasibility), then from (9-67)

$$\sum_i v_i^d \left[-\sum_j (x_j^p - x_j^d)h_j^i + h_i(X^p) - h_i(X^d) \right] \geq 0. \qquad (9\text{-}68)$$

Thus the sum of the terms in (9-66) and (9-68) is unambiguously non-negative. This sum differs from the expression in (9-65) in several respects; terms were added in order that conclusions about nonnegativity could be drawn by appeal to the properties of concave and convex functions. The excess terms in (9-66) and (9-68) are

$$\sum_j x_j^p f_j - \sum_i v_i^d \sum_j x_j^p h_j^i + \sum_i v_i^d h_i(X^p). \qquad (9\text{-}69)$$

Hence these must be subtracted from (9-66) and (9-68) to give an exact statement of $\Delta - \pi$. Thus to an already nonnegative expression we append (rearranging (9-69) and preceding by a minus sign)

$$+ \sum_j x_j^p \left(\sum_i v_i^d h_j^i - f_j \right) + \sum_i v_i^d [-h_i(X^p)]. \qquad (9\text{-}70)$$

In the first term $\sum_j x_j^p \geq 0$ by primal feasibility, and the expression in parentheses is nonnegative by dual feasibility [recall the dual constraints in (9-5)]. Similarly $\sum_i v_i^d \geq 0$ from dual feasibility, and, since primal feasibility requires $h_i(X^p) \leq 0$, the bracketed expression is nonnegative. Thus

$$\left\{ \sum_j (x_j^p - x_j^d)f_j - f(X^p) + f(X^d) \right\}$$
$$+ \left\{ \sum_i v_i^d \left[-\sum_j (x_j^p - x_j^d)h_j^i + h_i(X^p) - h_i(X^d) \right] \right\} \qquad (9\text{-}71)$$
$$+ \left\{ \sum_j x_j^p \left(\sum_i v_i^d h_j^i - f_j \right) + \sum_i v_i^d [-h_i(X^p)] \right\} \geq 0$$

and expresses exactly $\Delta(X^d, V^d) - \pi(X^p)$; hence we have

$$\Delta(X^d, V^d) - \pi(X^p) \geq 0, \qquad (9\text{-}72)$$

which is Theorem P-D1(N).

THEOREM P-D2(N).   Given a pair of feasible solutions (X^p) and (X^d, V^d) with objective function values $\pi(X^p)$ and $\Delta(X^d, V^d)$; these solutions are optimal if and only if $\pi(X^p) = \Delta(X^d, V^d)$.

The "if" part of the proof follows directly from the preceding theorem. For the "only if" part, suppose that (1) X^p is an optimal solution to the primal and (2) $\Delta(X^d, V^d) > \pi(X^p)$. Then because of (1) we know from Theorem SP4 in Chapter 8 that a $V \geq O$ can be found for which

$$(a) \begin{cases} \text{(i)} \quad f_j - \sum_i v_i h_j^i \quad \leq 0 \text{ and} \\ \\ \text{(ii)} \quad (f_j - \sum_i v_i h_j^i)x_j^p = 0 \qquad \text{(for all } j) \end{cases}$$

and

$$(b) \begin{cases} \text{(i)} \quad h_i(X^p) \quad \leq 0 \text{ and} \\ \text{(ii)} \quad v_i[h_i(X^p)] = 0 \qquad \text{(for all } i). \end{cases}$$

But then, from (9-5'), (X^p, V) would constitute a solution to the dual and from (9-65) we would have $\Delta(X^p, V) - \pi(X^p) = 0$, or $\Delta(X^p, V) = \pi(X^p)$. But since, from (2), $\Delta(X^d, V^d) > \Delta(X^p, V)$, (X^d, V^d) cannot be an optimal solution for the dual.

THEOREM P-D3(N). A pair of feasible solutions has $\pi(X^p) = \Delta(X^d, V^d)$ if and only if (1) $v_i^d[-h_i(X^p)] = 0$ for all i and (2) $x_j^p \left(\sum_i v_i^d h_j^i - f_j \right) = 0$ for all j.

The "only if" part follows from (9-71), which expresses $\Delta(X^d, V^d) - \pi(X^p)$. Since all three $\{ \, \cdot \, \}$ terms are nonnegative, each must equal zero if $\Delta(X^d, V^d) - \pi(X^p) = 0$. Because of feasibility, every term in each sum is the product of two nonnegative numbers; since each sum must be zero, conditions (1) and (2) of the theorem follow.

The "if" part requires reasoning similar to that used above for Theorem P-D2(N). If (1) and (2) hold, then from Theorem SP4 we see that (X^p) and (X^p, V^d) would constitute a pair of feasible solutions to the primal and dual problems and, as we saw above, $\Delta(X^p, V^d)$ would equal $\pi(X^p)$.

APPENDIX 9.2

Wolfe's Quadratic Programming Technique: Matrix Formulation

The quadratic programming problem is to

$$\begin{aligned} \text{maximize:} \quad & P'X + \tfrac{1}{2}X'QX \\ \text{subject to:} \quad & AX = R \\ \text{and} \quad & X \geq 0. \end{aligned} \qquad (9\text{-}73)$$

The Kuhn-Tucker conditions for this problem are as follows. We use U for the λ_i and V for the λ_{j+m}, since this appears often in the literature.

$$
\begin{aligned}
(1) \quad & P + QX - A'U + V = 0, \\
(2) \quad & V'X = 0, \\
(3) \quad & X, V \geq 0, \quad U \gtrless 0, \\
(4) \quad & AX = R.
\end{aligned}
\qquad (9\text{-}74)
$$

These are the same as (9-52′) in the text. They constitute both necessary and sufficient conditions for an optimum to (9-73) provided Q is negative definite or semidefinite. The Wolfe method as explained here, however, requires negative definiteness.[37]

Phase I.   Define

$$
Z_1 = \begin{bmatrix} z_{11} \\ \vdots \\ z_{n1} \end{bmatrix}, \qquad
Z_2 = \begin{bmatrix} z_{12} \\ \vdots \\ z_{n2} \end{bmatrix}, \quad \text{and} \quad
W = \begin{bmatrix} w_1 \\ \vdots \\ w_m \end{bmatrix}
$$

and find the optimum to

$$
\begin{aligned}
\text{minimize:} \quad & [\,1,\ \cdots,\ 1\,]W \\
\text{subject to:} \quad & \begin{cases} (1) \quad QX + Z_1 - Z_2 = -P, \\ (2) \qquad\quad AX + W = R, \end{cases} \\
\text{and} \quad & X, W, Z_1, Z_2 \geq 0.
\end{aligned}
$$

At optimum, $W^0 = 0$.

Phase II.   Form

$$
Z_3 = \begin{bmatrix} z_1 \\ \vdots \\ z_n \end{bmatrix}
$$

by selecting for z_j either z_{j1} or z_{j2}, whichever was nonzero in the optimal solution to Phase I.[38] Define D as a diagonal matrix with elements $+1$ or -1, depending on whether $z_j = z_{j1}$ or z_{j2}, respectively. Replace U by $U_1 - U_2$. Then find the optimum to

$$
\begin{aligned}
\text{minimize:} \quad & [1,\ \cdots,\ 1]Z_3 \\
\text{subject to:} \quad & (1) \quad QX - A'(U_1 - U_2) + V + DZ_3 = -P, \\
& (2) \qquad\qquad\qquad\qquad\qquad\qquad AX = R, \\
& (3) \qquad\qquad\qquad\quad X, U_1, U_2, V, Z_3 \geq 0, \\
\text{and} \quad & (4) \qquad\qquad\qquad\qquad\qquad\qquad V'X = 0.
\end{aligned}
$$

At optimum, $Z_3^0 = 0$.

---

[37] Negative semidefiniteness *can* be associated with an unbounded objective function. Moreover, it is not possible to prove conclusively that when Phase II is completed the true optimum has been found, although there are techniques for overcoming the difficulties. See Hadley [11, chap. 7, esp. secs. 7.3–7.5].

[38] If the Phase I optimum was degenerate, it may be that both z_{j1} and z_{j2} are zero for one or more j. Then $z_j = 0$ in the new vector Z_3.

PROBLEMS

1. Following the presentation in (9-5) or (9-5′), write the dual to each of the following nonlinear programming primal problems:
   (a) Problem 1 in Chapter 8.
   (b) Problem 2 in Chapter 8.
   (c) Problem 3 in Chapter 8.
2. Consider the problem of finding the maximum to $f(X) = 16 - 2(x_1 - 3)^2 - (x_2 - 7)^2$ subject to $x_1^2 + x_2 \leq 16$ and $x_1, x_2 \geq 0$.
   (a) Use the separable programming approach, with mesh points of 0, 1, 2, 3, and 4 for x_1 and 0, 2, 4, 6, and 8 for x_2. [*Hint:* Define $f_1(x_1)$ as $8 - 2(x_1 - 3)^2$ and $f_2(x_2)$ as $8 - (x_2 - 7)^2$.]
   (b) Ignore the nonnegativity requirements and find the maximum directly [see Problem 6(d) of Chapter 3 and Problem 5 of Chapter 8].
3. Given the problem

$$\begin{aligned} \text{maximize:} \quad & 6x_1 + 8x_2 \\ \text{subject to:} \quad & x_1^2 + x_2^2 \leq 16 \\ \text{and} \quad & x_1, x_2 \geq 0. \end{aligned}$$

   (a) Use the cutting-plane method, with $\epsilon = 1.0$ (that is, stop when the constraint is exceeded by less than one unit) and let $X^0 = \begin{bmatrix} 2 \\ 2 \end{bmatrix}$. [*Hint:* Draw a fairly accurate solution-space picture so that it will be clear which constraints will be met as equalities in each of the linear programming problems.]
   (b) Find the solution exactly using the Lagrange multiplier approach for inequality-constrained problems and ignoring, in the formulation, the nonnegativity requirements.
4. Approximate a solution to the nonlinear program of Problem 3, using the sequential unconstrained minimization technique on $-f(X)$ and a logarithmic penalty function.
   (a) Evaluate at $r = 1.0$, 0.1, and 0.01 only.
   (b) Find the answer exactly. [If you did Problem 3(b), you already have this answer.] Observe that as $r \to 0$, the solution values for x_1 and x_2 approach the exact answer. (Remember that SUMT and indeed all nonlinear programming techniques are designed primarily for problems for which an exact solution cannot be found.)
5. Maximize $16 - 2(x_1 - 3)^2 - (x_2 - 7)^2$ subject to $x_1 + x_2 \leq 10$ and $x_1, x_2 \geq 0$.
   (a) Since this is a quadratic programming problem, use Wolfe's approach to the solution.
   (b) Since the objective function and constraint are also separable, find the solution via separable programming. (Note that this is very close to the work involved in Problem 2.)
   (c) Solve exactly as a check on (a). [Again, this is very close to part (b) of Problem 2.]
6. Write down and solve the dual to the quadratic program in Problem 5. Check that the optimal primal and dual values satisfy the "complementary slackness" properties of Theorem P-D3(N) in Section 9.1 as well as Theorem P-D2(N)—that is, that optimal values of objective functions are equal.

REFERENCES

1. Abadie, J., ed., *Nonlinear Programming*. New York: Interscience Publishers, 1967.
2. Arrow, K. J., L. Hurwicz, and H. Uzawa, *Studies in Linear and Nonlinear Programming*. Stanford: Stanford University Press, 1958.
3. Balinski, M. L., and W. J. Baumol, "The Dual in Nonlinear Programming and Its Economic Interpretation," *Review of Economic Studies*, vol. 35 (1968), pp. 237–256.
4. Boot, J. C. G., *Quadratic Programming*. Skokie, Ill.: Rand McNally & Company, 1964.
5. Dantzig, G. B., and A. F. Veinott, Jr., eds., *Mathematics of the Decision Sciences*, vol. I (Lectures in Applied Mathematics, vol. 11). Providence, R.I.: American Mathematical Society, 1968.
6. Dorn, W. S., "Nonlinear Programming—A Survey," *Management Science*, vol. 9 (1963), pp. 171–208.
7. Fiacco, A. V., and G. P. McCormick, "Computational Algorithm for the Sequential Unconstrained Minimization Technique for Nonlinear Programming," *Management Science*, vol. 10 (1964), pp. 601–617.
8. ———, *Nonlinear Programming: Sequential Unconstrained Minimization Techniques*. New York: John Wiley & Sons, Inc., 1968.
9. ———, "The Sequential Unconstrained Minimization Technique for Nonlinear Programming, A Primal-Dual Method," *Management Science*, vol. 10 (1964), pp. 360–366.
10. Graves, R. L., and P. Wolfe, eds., *Recent Advances in Mathematical Programming*. New York: McGraw-Hill, Inc., 1963.
11. Hadley, G., *Nonlinear and Dynamic Programming*. Reading, Mass.: Addison-Wesley Publishing Company, Inc., 1964.
12. Horowitz, I., *Decision Making and the Theory of the Firm*. New York: Holt, Rinehart and Winston, Inc., 1970.
13. Karlin, S., *Mathematical Methods and Theory in Games, Programming, and Economics*, vol. I. Reading, Mass.: Addison-Wesley Publishing Company, Inc., 1959.
14. Künzi, H. P., W. Krelle, and W. Oettli, *Nonlinear Programming*. Waltham, Mass.: Blaisdell Publishing Company, 1966.
15. Rockafellar, R. T., *Convex Analysis* (Princeton Mathematical Series, no. 28). Princeton: Princeton University Press, 1970.
16. Zoutendijk, G., "Nonlinear Programming: A Numerical Survey," *Society of Industrial and Applied Mathematics Journal (Control)*, vol. 4 (1966), pp. 194–210.

Answers to Odd-numbered Problems

CHAPTER 1

1. $A = \begin{bmatrix} 11 & -1 \\ 0 & 0 \\ -3 & 5 \end{bmatrix}$.

3. $(A + B) - C = \begin{bmatrix} 24 & -5 \\ 7 & 4 \\ 2 & 7 \end{bmatrix}$.

5. (a) AB cannot be performed, BA can be performed. (b) Both are possible. (c) Neither. (d) Both. (e) Neither.

7. $BC = \begin{bmatrix} 100 \\ 200 \end{bmatrix}$, $A(BC) = [-700]$; $AB = [-26, \ -22]$, $(AB)C = [-700]$.

9. (a) -2. (b) Using the diagonals method, $+1$; evaluating across row 2: $-11 + 14 - 2 = +1$. (c) $(-3)(1) + (-1)(1) = -4$.

11. (a) Unique. (b) Unique. (c) Multiple. (d) None.

13. (a) $A^{-1} = \begin{bmatrix} \frac{4}{11} & \frac{1}{11} \\ -\frac{3}{44} & \frac{1}{22} \end{bmatrix}$. (b) B^{-1} does not exist. (c) $C^{-1} = \begin{bmatrix} 1 & 0 & 0 \\ 0 & 1 & 0 \\ 0 & 0 & \frac{1}{2} \end{bmatrix}$.

This illustrates a general rule for inverses of *diagonal* matrices, namely that the inverse contains the reciprocals of the original elements. (The reader should illustrate this for the general 3×3 diagonal matrix; that is, he should find the inverse of

$$\begin{bmatrix} a_{11} & 0 & 0 \\ 0 & a_{22} & 0 \\ 0 & 0 & a_{33} \end{bmatrix}.)$$

(d) $D^{-1} = \begin{bmatrix} \frac{1}{2} & \frac{1}{4} & -1 \\ 0 & -\frac{1}{2} & 1 \\ -\frac{1}{2} & -\frac{1}{4} & 2 \end{bmatrix}$.

CHAPTER 2

1. (a) Yes. (b) Yes. (c) Yes, but $\begin{bmatrix} 6 \\ 4 \end{bmatrix}$ and $\begin{bmatrix} 1 \\ 2 \end{bmatrix}$ are all that are necessary; $\begin{bmatrix} 0 \\ 0 \end{bmatrix}$ contributes nothing. (d) No, one needs *three* linearly independent vectors for three-dimensional vector space. (e) No.

3. (a) There will be at most $C_2^3 = 3$ basic solutions.

(i) Set $x_1 = 0$; then the solution to the remaining system is

$$\begin{bmatrix} x_2 \\ x_3 \end{bmatrix} = \begin{bmatrix} -10 \\ 5 \end{bmatrix}.$$

(ii) Set $x_2 = 0$; then the remaining system has a singular coefficient matrix and the equations are inconsistent.

(iii) Set $x_3 = 0$; then the solution to the remaining system is

$$\begin{bmatrix} x_1 \\ x_2 \end{bmatrix} = \begin{bmatrix} 20 \\ -10 \end{bmatrix}.$$

(b) Any one equation can be dropped; assume the third equation is ignored. Then the remaining system has at most $C_2^3 = 3$ basic solutions.

(i) Set $x_1 = 0$; then the solution to the remaining system is

$$\begin{bmatrix} x_2 \\ x_3 \end{bmatrix} = \begin{bmatrix} \frac{1}{2} \\ 1 \end{bmatrix}.$$

(ii) Set $x_2 = 0$; then the solution to the remaining system is

$$\begin{bmatrix} x_1 \\ x_3 \end{bmatrix} = \begin{bmatrix} -1 \\ 2 \end{bmatrix}.$$

(iii) Set $x_3 = 0$; then the solution to the remaining system is

$$\begin{bmatrix} x_1 \\ x_2 \end{bmatrix} = \begin{bmatrix} 1 \\ 1 \end{bmatrix}.$$

(c) The maximum possible number of basic solutions is $C_2^4 = 6$; we examine these in turn.

(i) Let $x_1 = x_2 = 0$; then the solution to the remaining system is

$$\begin{bmatrix} x_3 \\ x_4 \end{bmatrix} = \begin{bmatrix} -10 \\ 10 \end{bmatrix}.$$

(ii) Let $x_1 = x_3 = 0$; then the solution to the remaining system is

$$\begin{bmatrix} x_2 \\ x_4 \end{bmatrix} = \begin{bmatrix} 5 \\ 0 \end{bmatrix}.$$

(iii) Let $x_1 = x_4 = 0$; then the solution to the remaining system is

$$\begin{bmatrix} x_2 \\ x_3 \end{bmatrix} = \begin{bmatrix} 5 \\ 0 \end{bmatrix}.$$

(iv) Let $x_2 = x_3 = 0$; then the solution to the remaining system is

$$\begin{bmatrix} x_1 \\ x_4 \end{bmatrix} = \begin{bmatrix} 10 \\ 0 \end{bmatrix}.$$

(v) Let $x_2 = x_4 = 0$; then the solution to the remaining system is

$$\begin{bmatrix} x_1 \\ x_3 \end{bmatrix} = \begin{bmatrix} 10 \\ 0 \end{bmatrix}.$$

(vi) Let $x_3 = x_4 = 0$; then the remaining system has a singular coefficient matrix, and the system has multiple solutions.

5. (a) No, $|A| = 0$. (b) Yes, $|A| \neq 0$. (c) Yes, $|A| \neq 0$.
7. (a) For the homogeneous case, when $c = 0$, there will be multiple solutions if and only if $ab = 10$. (b) For the nonhomogeneous case, when $c \neq 0$, x_2 will be equal to zero if and only if $a = 0$.

CHAPTER 3

1. (a) $dy/dx = 8x + 2$. (b) $dy/dx = 12$. (c) $dy/dx = -2/x^3$.
3. (a) $72x - y = 290$. (b) $y = -2$. (c) $12x + y = 58$.
5. (a) $\frac{1}{2}$. (b) 20 and 20.

7. Since $\partial z/\partial x = y^2/(x + y)^2$ and $\partial z/\partial y = x^2/(x + y)^2$, the demonstration is straightforward.
9. $x_1^* = 26.67$, $x_2^* = 6.67$.
11. With upper limit of 50, produce 50; with upper limit of 40, produce 0.

CHAPTER 4

1. (a) Negative definite. (b) Positive definite. (c) Neither.
3. Maximum at $x_1^* = \frac{10}{7}$, $x_2^* = \frac{15}{7}$, and $x_3^* = \frac{5}{7}$.
5. Minimum at $x_1^* = \frac{11}{3}$, $x_2^* = \frac{10}{3}$, and $x_3^* = 8$.
7. (a) $x_1^* = 0$, $x_2^* = 0$. (b) $x_1^* = \frac{3}{31}$, $x_2^* = \frac{18}{31}$.
9. Answer is the same as for Problem 3.

CHAPTER 5

1. Produce eight runs of 600 seats each per year.
3. Yes. Produce 496 for inventory and 124 for back demand each time.
5. (a) Using the total differential, costs increase $21\frac{7}{8}$ percent. (b) The actual increase is 21 percent. (c) The differential estimate is a cost increase of $43\frac{3}{4}$ percent; the actual increase is 35 percent. The differential becomes less accurate for estimation as the changes involved become larger.
7. (a) Four. (b) From $1.11 to $4.29.
9. At present the average waits of current day and advance-sales customers are 16 minutes and 6 minutes, respectively. Under the changeover the average wait for both would be 3.8 minutes.
11. The second channel should be opened if the arrival rate reaches 4.38 customers per hour.

CHAPTER 6

1. $x_1^0 = 0$, $x_2^0 = 0$, $x_3^0 = 3\frac{3}{8}$; $s_1^0 = 8\frac{2}{5}$, $s_2^0 = 0$; $f(X^0) = 54$.
3. $x_1^0 = 0$, $x_2^0 = \frac{3}{2}$; $s_1^0 = 4$, $s_2^0 = 0$; $f(X^0) = \frac{27}{2}$.
5. The feasible region is unbounded; there is no finite maximum.
7. In the problem whose ith constraint is k times the ith constraint of the other, the dual variable will be $(1/k)$th as large at optimum (unless it was zero in the optimal solution, in which case it will remain zero).
9. Adding variables (slack) to the primal adds constraints to the dual; these constraints require the nonnegativity of the dual variables.
11. 140 Clippers, 150 Cruisers, for a profit of $43,000.

13. (a) 15 Regular, 30 Extra Smooth Draft; $f(X^0) = \$120$. (b) At \$3 per case for Regular. (c) No change; the optimal solution satisfies the added constraint. (d) (1) \$20 per hour ($\$\frac{4}{9}$ per minute during a 45-minute hour), (2) nothing.

CHAPTER 7

1. $x_1^0 = 2$, $x_2^0 = 6$; also $x_1^0 = 8$, $x_2^0 = 2$; and all convex combinations of these two points.
3. $x_1^0 = 6\frac{34}{39}$, $x_2^0 = 7\frac{17}{39}$; $f(X^0) = 21\frac{7}{39}$.
5. There are alternative optima. One optimal solution is: $x_{14}^0 = 10$, $x_{15}^0 = 4$, $x_{16}^0 = 4$, $x_{21}^0 = 8$, $x_{22}^0 = 6$, $x_{23}^0 = 6$, $x_{25}^0 = 3$, $x_{36}^0 = 6$; total costs are 54.
7. Assign W_5 to L_1, W_r to L_2, W_2 to L_3, W_4 to L_4, and W_1 to L_5; thus waitress W_r replaces W_3 and the total cost is 21.
9. $x_1^0 = 0$, $x_2^0 = 3$, $x_3^0 = 3$; $f(X^0) = 51$.
11. Adopt A_2 with probability $\frac{3}{7}$ and A_3 with probability $\frac{4}{7}$; never use A_1.

CHAPTER 8

1. $x_1^0 = \frac{1}{2}$, $x_2^0 = \frac{3}{2}$, $x_3^0 = 0$.
3. $x_1^0 = 0$, $x_2^0 = 0$.
5. Exact solution: $x_1^* = 3$, $x_2^* = 7$; $f(X^*) = 16$. Using the gradient method of (8-11), $X^5 = \begin{bmatrix} 3 \\ 6.56 \end{bmatrix}$, and $f(X^5) = 15.81$.
7. (a) $L(X, V) = -x_1^2 - x_2^2 - x_3^2 + 4x_1 + 6x_2 - v_1(x_1 + x_2 - 2) - v_2(2x_1 + 3x_2 - 12)$; $x_1^0 = \frac{1}{2}$, $x_2^0 = \frac{3}{2}$, $x_3^0 = 0$; $v_1^0 = 3$, $v_2^0 = 0$.
   (b) $L(X, V) = -6x_1^2 - 5x_2^2 - v(-x_1 - 5x_2 + 3)$; $x_1^0 = \frac{3}{31}$, $x_2^0 = \frac{18}{31}$; $v^0 = \frac{36}{31}$.
   (c) $L(X, V) = -6x_1^2 - 5x_2^2 - v(x_1 + 5x_2 - 3)$; $x_1^0 = 0$, $x_2^0 = 0$; $v^0 = 0$.

CHAPTER 9

1. (a) Minimize: $-x_1^2 - x_2^2 - x_3^2 + 4x_1 + 6x_2 - v_1(x_1 + x_2 - 2) - v_2(2x_1 + 3x_2 - 12) - x_1(-2x_1 + 4 - v_1 - 2v_2) - x_2(-2x_2 + 6 - v_1 - 3v_2) - x_3(-2x_3)$

   subject to: $v_1 + 2v_2 + 2x_1 - 4 \geq 0$,
   $v_1 + 3v_2 + 2x_2 - 6 \geq 0$,
   $2x_3 \geq 0$,

   and $v_1, v_2 \geq 0$.

   (b) Minimize: $-6x_1^2 - 5x_2^2 - v(-x_1 - 5x_2 + 3) - x_1(-12x_1 + v) - x_2(-10x_2 + 5v)$

   subject to: $-v + 12x_1 \geq 0$,
   $-5v + 10x_2 \geq 0$,

   and $v \geq 0$.

(c) Minimize: $-6x_1^2 - 5x_2^2 - v(x_1 + 5x_2 - 3) - x_1(-12x_1 - v) -$
$x_2(-10x_2 - 5v)$

subject to: $v + 12x_1 \geq 0,$
$5v + 10x_2 \geq 0,$

and $v \geq 0.$

3. After adding the fourth cutting plane,

$$X^4 = \begin{bmatrix} \frac{7}{3} \\ \frac{10}{3} \end{bmatrix} = \begin{bmatrix} 2.33 \\ 3.33 \end{bmatrix} \quad \text{and} \quad h(X^4) = \tfrac{5}{9} < 1;$$

at this point $f(X^4) = 40.67$. The exact answer is

$$X^* = \begin{bmatrix} \frac{12}{5} \\ \frac{16}{5} \end{bmatrix} = \begin{bmatrix} 2.4 \\ 3.2 \end{bmatrix} \quad \text{and} \quad f(X^*) = 40.$$

5. $x_1^0 = 3$ and $x_2^0 = 7$.

INDEX